The *Sams Teach Yourself in 24 Hours* Series

Sams Teach Yourself in 24 Hours books provide quick and easy answers in a proven step-by-step approach that works for you. In just 24 sessions of one hour or less, you will tackle every task you need to get the results you want. Let our experienced authors present the most accurate information to get you reliable answers—fast!

W9-BIE-077

Instant HTML Reference Sheets

Instant HTML

Callout reference
1 Page title
2 Image
3 Headings
4 Hard rule
5 Text and Image alignment
6 Link

1

```
<HTML><HEAD><TITLE>Title of the Page</TITLE></HEAD>
<BODY BACKGROUND="paper.jpg" BGCOLOR=WHITE
    TEXT=BLACK LINK=BLUE VLINK=PURPLE ALINK=RED>
<!-- Comments won't show up on the page. -->
<IMG SRC="instant.gif" ALT="Text about the image"
ALIGN=RIGHT WIDTH=143 HEIGHT=275 VSPACE=5 HSPACE=20>
<H1>Big Papa Heading</H1><H2>Middle-Sized Mama Heading</H2>
<H3>Tiny Little Baby Heading</H3>
Web browsers automatically wrap text to fit in the space
available, unless you force a line break:<BR>
or force a paragraph break:<P>
You can also insert horizontal rules.<HR>
Text can be plain, <B>boldface</B> <I>or italicized.</I>
<TT>You can also use a typewriter font or</TT>
<FONT FACE="Arial" SIZE=1 COLOR=BLUE>
 the font face, size, and color of your choice.</FONT>
<P>This text is left-justified and
<IMG SRC="thisimg.gif"> is bottom-aligned.
<P ALIGN=CENTER>This text is centered and
<IMG SRC="thisimg.gif" ALIGN=MIDDLE> is middle-aligned.
<P ALIGN=RIGHT>This text is right-justified and
<IMG SRC="thisimg.gif" ALIGN=TOP> is top-aligned. <P>
<A HREF="nextpage.htm">
   <IMG SRC="rtarrow.gif" ALIGN=LEFT BORDER=0>
   Click here to go to another page.</A>
</BODY></HTML>
```

1 — Page title
2 — Image
3 — Headings
4 — Hard rule
5 — Text and Image alignment
6 — Link

This is what you type in Notepad or your favorite text editor. Save it as plain text, and give it a file name ending in .htm *or* .html.

This is what you see when you open the text file in a Web browser, assuming that you have created the four images with a graphics program and saved them as paper.jpg, instant.gif, thisimg.gif, *and* rtarrow.gif.

Title of the Page - Netscape
File Edit View Go Communicator Help

Big Papa Heading

Middle-Sized Mama Heading

Tiny Little Baby Heading

Web browsers automatically wrap text to fit in the space available, unless you force a line break:
or force a paragraph break:

You can also insert horizontal rules:

Text can be plain, **boldface,** *or italicized.* You can also use a typewriter font `or the font face, size, and color of your choice.`

This text is left-justified and [This Image] is bottom-aligned.

   This text is centered and [This Image] is middle-aligned.

      This text is right-justified and [This Image] is top-aligned.

➡ Click here to go to another page.

Document Done

Callout reference
1 Page title
2 Image
3 Headings
4 Hard rule
5 Text and image alignment
6 Link

Teach Yourself HTML 4 in 24 Hours

Instant Lists and Tables

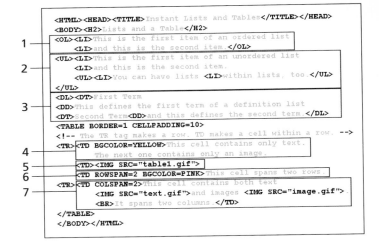

1
2
3
4
5
6
7

This is what you type in Notepad or your favorite text editor.

```
<HTML><HEAD><TITLE>Instant Lists and Tables</TITLE></HEAD>
<BODY><H2>Lists and a Table</H2>
<OL><LI>This is the first item of an ordered list
    <LI>and this is the second item.</OL>
<UL><LI>This is the first item of an unordered list
    <LI>and this is the second item.
    <UL><LI>You can have lists <LI>within lists, too.</UL>
</UL>
<DL><DT>First Term
<DD>This defines the first term of a definition list
<DT>Second Term<DD>and this defines the second term.</DL>
<TABLE BORDER=1 CELLPADDING=10>
<!-- The TR tag makes a row. TD makes a cell within a row. -->
<TR><TD BGCOLOR=YELLOW>This cell contains only text.
    The next one contains only an image.
    <TD><IMG SRC="table1.gif">
    <TD ROWSPAN=2 BGCOLOR=PINK>This cell spans two rows.
<TR><TD COLSPAN=2>This cell contains both text
    <IMG SRC="text.gif">and images <IMG SRC="image.gif">.
    <BR>It spans two columns.</TD>
</TABLE>
</BODY></HTML>
```

This is what you see in a Web browser, assuming that you have three graphics named table1.gif, text.gif, *and* image.gif.

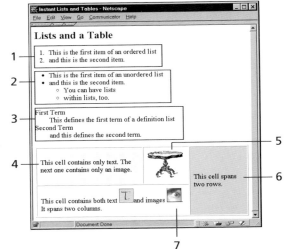

1
2
3
4
5
6
7

Callout reference for both figures
1 Ordered list
2 Unordered list
3 Definition list
4 Table cell with text
5 Table cell with an image
6 Table cell spanning 2 rows
7 Table cell spanning 2 columns

What's New in This Edition

Sams Teach Yourself HTML 4 in 24 Hours has been extensively revised and updated for the third edition!

- Every example Web page illustrated in this edition is new, and the accompanying Web site (`http://24hourHTMLcafe.com/`) now contains over 250 online example pages for you to explore, modify, and reuse.

- All examples have been thoroughly tested with both Netscape Navigator 4.0 and Microsoft Internet Explorer 4.0. For maximum compatibility, every example was also tested with earlier versions of Navigator and Internet Explorer, as well as Opera 3.21 and the preview release of Internet Explorer 5.0. The examples were also checked against the official HTML 4.0 standard and Netscape's stated goals for Navigator 5.0. The HTML in this book is fully compatible with Windows 95 & 98, the Macintosh, and UNIX/X-Windows systems.

- Tips, notes, quiz questions, and exercises now incorporate feedback from more than 1,200 readers who sent in email suggestions and questions. Reader feedback has also influenced every aspect of the new edition, from the enhanced step-by-step instructions on creating your first Web page to the expanded coverage of advanced topics later in the book. You'll find answers to the most frequently asked reader questions in the new Appendix A, "Readers' Most Frequently Asked Questions."

- This edition includes completely new coverage of cutting-edge topics like Multimedia (Hour 17, "Embedding Multimedia in Web Pages"), Dynamic HTML (Hour 20, "Setting Pages in Motion with Dynamic HTML"), using JavaScript to add up forms and create interactive animation (Hour 19, "Web Page Scripting for Non-Programmers"), and making your pages appear most prominently on all the major Internet search sites (Hour 23, "Helping People Find Your Web Pages"). These advanced topics are covered in the same plain-English, beginner-friendly style that have made every edition of this book a nonstop bestseller.

- The complete HTML 4 quick reference (Appendix C, "Complete HTML 4.0 Quick Reference") has been expanded and updated to include the entire HTML 4.0 standard, including scripting events for each tag. A new Appendix D, "HTML Character Entities," covers all the special characters and accented letters you can put on your HTML pages.

Praise from Readers

"I knew nothing about HTML before I purchased your book. Within hours of opening the cover, I had a Web page! Many told me you can't possibly design a page without a special program—HTML was too hard and confusing. Frankly, this has been a piece of cake thanks to you!" —Julie Conroy

"…possibly the best learning book I have ever had…Love your graphics, love your books, love your Web site and love your sense of humour." —Lori Coon

"…much easier to understand and use than others I have used. I am encouraging my students at Central Maine Technical College to buy a copy as a handy reference…" —John R. Clark, M.Ed., MLIS

"You have a wonderful sense of humour that made reading and learning from your book a real pleasure! I do not think I could trust myself to another author now that I have found you!" —Ian Hambelton

"I was really amazed how easy it was for me to create Web Pages using your book. It didn't take very long to learn all the tricks that Web masters are using on the Internet. Your book was so easy to use and understand; that makes HTML fun! I browsed some other books and no one can even come close to you." —Rey Rios

"My Web site has already gone through a dramatic metamorphosis and I'm only a third of the way through the book." —Kevin Wiesner

"Since I bought *Sams Teach Yourself HTML in 24 Hours* I have been a crazy man. We started our family Web site with 2 pages and because of my reading your book it has expanded to about 24 pages. I am still learning and using your book… You have made it fun." —John Ingalls

"Thanks a bunch for writing it in a way I could understand (and enjoy). Everything else makes my brain hurt!" —Mykayl Guerin

"I had been 'stalling' on learning HTML because it looked so hard, but your book made it easy! …I especially like the clear examples you gave. It was a very short step from copying your examples to learning to use my own data! I also liked having this coordinating Web site and looking at the pages done by other 'newbies.' Thanks!" —Sue Powell

More Praise from Readers

"I already knew basic HTML, but your book is a lucid, thorough reference. I borrowed it from a library but will buy it." —Ken Sternberg

"…your book was an extraordinary resource. It had answers to just about all my questions in it, and if I couldn't find the answer in your book then your Appendix enabled me to find it on the Web. It was easy to follow and hard to put down. My copy is incredibly dog-eared!" —Jim Kiley-Zufelt

"Add my name to the very long list of very satisfied readers… I will soon be completing my own Web site thanks to the invaluable information contained in your book… I found your writing style exceptional." — David E. Braund

"I really like your book. I can't put the crazy thing down." —Michael Odendahl

"…the most valuable computer book I have." —Jack Rumple

"I knew nothing about HTML before your book. Now I have a Web page up and running and am thrilled to death about how much I've learned in such a short amount of time… You have a wonderful way of explaining things." —Angie Sagan

"Simple and easy to comprehend for anyone. I enjoyed actually being able to sit down and understand something to do with computers for once." —Tony Yamada

"...very helpful and very well written. I was able to literally build a Web site for my company from scratch." —Sean McVay

"I loved the way you explained how to do everything and then showed what it should look like when it's typed in Notepad and then how it would look in a browser… I have recommended the book to all my friends on the Internet who want to create their own Web page but don't know the first thing about it." —Laurie Jersey

"I loved your book. It was so easy to follow. I got through Hour 10, then I just TOOK OFF and started doing all kinds of things on my own!! My site isn't completely finished yet, but I had a BLAST building it!" —Bonnie Richmond

"I had to learn fast, and your book did it for me! This old dog had to learn new tricks; the layout and step by step lessons were perfect for my needs." —David Cowlishaw

"Not only is your book an excellent resource, it is written with NON-programmers in mind! I really appreciate that. While I am interested in programming, I am not intrigued by lengthy lists of command definitions that have no context or examples as other books do. Your style is right on target." —Richard Rivette

"I could not believe how effective your method was until I gave it a try. Unlike other books that have currently flooded the market, yours cuts straight to the chase in a precise, easily understood text, with logical graphic illustrations, that is also an entertaining read." —Clark Thompson

"It was so effortless. After a couple of chapters I had created a page and could say, 'I wrote that.' There was a tremendous sense of achievement that really encouraged me to continue with the book. At the end of every chapter I could incorporate the new bit of knowledge into my Web page and see it change and grow." —Aidan Whitehall

"Today… I bought your book on a whim and am gleeful I did. It's dizzying to be able to boast already that I have created a Web page." —Paul Maglic

"I love this book. I am half way through it now and am making more progress than I ever thought possible." —Robert Doherty

"You write one mean book. I've purchased a bunch of them, and your book is the only one written from a practical point of view. It's so good that I told my local library I lost it and gave them full payment." —Al Jarvis

"I bought your book a few months ago and I wanted to tell you that it changed my life! I'm now a professional Web developer in Phoenix and have made more money in 40 hours of work so far than I've ever made in my life!" —Scott Ritshie

Dick Oliver

SAMS
Teach Yourself
HTML 4
in 24 Hours
Third Edition

SAMS

A Division of Macmillan Computer Publishing
201 West 103rd St., Indianapolis, Indiana, 46290 USA

Sams Teach Yourself HTML 4 in 24 Hours, Third Edition

Copyright © 1998 by Sams Publishing

International Standard Book Number: 0-672-31369-3

Library of Congress Catalog Card Number: 98-85560

Printed in the United States of America

First Printing: September, 1998

00   99   98   4   3   2

Trademarks

Warning and Disclaimer

EXECUTIVE EDITOR
Mark Taber

ACQUISITIONS EDITOR
Bob Correll

DEVELOPMENT EDITOR
Bob Correll

MANAGING EDITOR
Patrick Kanouse

SENIOR EDITOR
Elizabeth A. Bruns

COPY EDITOR
Patricia Kinyon

INDEXER
Becky Hornyak

TECHNICAL EDITOR
Sunil Hazari

INTERIOR DESIGN
Gary Adair

COVER DESIGN
Aren Howell

PRODUCTION
Mike Henry
Linda Knose
Tim Osborn
Staci Somers
Mark Walchle

Contents at a Glance

Contents

About the Author

Dick Oliver (dicko@netletter.com) is the tall, dark, handsome author of lots of great books and software, including *Web Page Wizardry*, *Netscape Unleashed*, *Create Your Own Web Page Graphics*, and *Tricks of the Graphics Gurus*. He is also the president of Cedar Software and the warped mind behind the Nonlinear Nonsense Netletter at http://netletter.com (and many other Web sites). When he isn't banging on a keyboard, he's usually snowboarding, sledding, skiing, or warming up by the woodstove in his cozy Northern Vermont home (where they celebrate a day of summer each year, too). He likes writing HTML, eating killer-spicy Indian food, and waltzing wildly around the office with his daughters—not necessarily in that order. He also thinks it's pretty cool that authors get to write their own "About the Author" sections.

Tell Us What You Think!

As the reader of this book, *you* are our most important critic and commentator. We value your opinion and want to know what we're doing right, what we could do better, what areas you'd like to see us publish in, and any other words of wisdom you're willing to pass our way.

As the Executive Editor for the HTML team at Macmillan Computer Publishing, I welcome your comments. You can fax, email, or write me directly to let me know what you did or didn't like about this book—as well as what we can do to make our books stronger.

Please note that I cannot help you with technical problems related to the topic of this book, and that due to the high volume of mail I receive, I might not be able to reply to every message.

When you write, please be sure to include this book's title and author as well as your name and phone or fax number. I will carefully review your comments and share them with the author and editors who worked on the book.

Fax:	317-817-7070
E-mail:	html@mcp.com
Mail:	Mark Taber
	Executive Editor, Web Publishing
	Macmillan Computer Publishing
	201 West 103rd Street
	Indianapolis, IN 46290 USA

Dedication

This book is dedicated to my mother, Darlene Hewins, who had to teach herself HTML before the book was written, and told me in no uncertain terms that I'd better do a lot better job than those other books.

Acknowledgments

This book would certainly not exist today were it not for the author's loving family, who brought enough fresh carrot juice, tender popcorn, and buttery kisses to sustain him through the long hours of its creation.

Special thanks must also go to the folks at the Buffalo Mountain Food Cooperative in Hardwick, Vermont, for providing the carrots, popcorn, and butter.

Introduction

I didn't write this book. Well, not all of it, at least. The most important parts came from readers like you. More than 1,200 of the many tens of thousands of people who bought the first and second editions of this book sent me email with questions, praise, and criticism. Mostly praise, I humbly confess. But also hundreds of helpful suggestions as to where you needed that little extra hint, what went wrong when you thought you'd done it right, and which topics you wanted me to cover in more depth.

Only through the Internet could an author ever get so much invaluable, detailed feedback. I've tried to make every bit of it count. You'll find answers to the top 24 reader questions in Appendix A, and an updated version of the appendix online at the 24-Hour HTML Café, (`http://24hourHTMLcafe./com`), the online companion to this book.

Reader feedback has also influenced all the changes I made for this edition. Every sample Web page in this edition is new, and the accompanying Web site now contains more than 250 online examples for you to explore, modify, and reuse. The Q&A sections in each hour answer real questions from real readers, and the Quiz and Exercise sections reinforce exactly those points with which readers needed the most help. I've reorganized and rewritten many of the lessons to make them even easier to follow, and presented the information you most urgently need earlier in the book. The easy lessons now move faster, and the difficult ones give you more step-by-step guidance.

Best of all, this edition includes completely new coverage of cutting-edge topics like Dynamic HTML, using JavaScript to add up forms and create interactive animation, and making your pages appear most prominently on all the major Internet search sites. And these more advanced topics are presented in the same plain-English, good-humored style that made earlier editions of this book nonstop bestsellers.

Put Your HTML Page Online Today

In the next 24 hours, approximately 100,000 new Web pages will be posted in publicly accessible areas of the Internet. At least as many pages will be placed on private intranets to be seen by businesspeople connected to local networks. Every one of those pages—like more than 100 million pages already online—will use the Hypertext Markup Language, or HTML.

If you read on, your Web pages will be among those that appear on the Internet in the next 24 hours. And this will be the day that you gained one of the most valuable skills in the world today: mastery of HTML.

Can you really learn to create top-quality Web pages yourself, without any specialized software, in less time than it takes to schedule and wait for an appointment with a highly paid HTML wizard? Can this thin, easy-to-read book really enable you to teach yourself state-of-the-art Web page publishing?

Yes. In fact, within two hours of starting this book, someone with no previous HTML experience at all can have a Web page ready to place on the Internet's World Wide Web.

How can you learn the language of the Web so fast? By example. This book breaks HTML down into simple steps that anyone can learn quickly, and shows you exactly how to take each step. Every HTML example is pictured right above the Web page it will produce. You see it done, you read a brief plain-English explanation of how it works, and you immediately do the same thing with your own page. Ten minutes later, you're on to the next step.

The next day, you're marveling at your own impressive pages on the Internet.

Before you go any further, there's something you should know from the outset. Professional Web page authors talk about three kinds of HTML pages:

- *First-generation* pages use old-fashioned HTML 1.0, and are mostly text with a hokey picture or two stuck in the middle. They were the best you could do in 1989, but having a first-generation page today marks you as more technologically backward than having no Web page at all.
- *Second- and third-generation* pages use a few HTML 2.0 and 3.2 tricks, such as putting a pretty (or garish) background behind a page, arranging text in tables, and offering an online order form. They can look nice, but rarely match the quality that people have come to expect from paper documents.
- *Fourth-generation* pages are what the world is talking about now that HTML 4.0 is the standard. They use creative layout, custom color, fast graphics, fonts, and interactive feedback to make your Web site more engaging than anything on paper.

The goal of this book is to help you skip straight to the exciting world of fourth-generation Web pages. So don't expect to learn obsolete HTML or create boring pages with no visual interest. Fortunately, if you start with a "fourth-generation mindset," learning HTML can be faster, easier, and more rewarding than ever.

How to Use This Book

There are several ways to go through this book, and the best way for you depends on your situation. Here are five recommended options. Pick the one that matches your needs.

1. *"I need to get some text on the Internet today. Then I can worry about making it look pretty later."*

   - Read Hour 1, "Understanding HTML and the Web."
   - Read Hour 2, "Create a Web Page Right Now."
   - Read Hour 4, "Publishing Your HTML Pages."
   - Put your first page on the Internet!

     (Total work time: 2–4 hours.)

   - Read the rest of the book, and update your pages as you learn more HTML.

2. *"I need a basic Web page with text and graphics on the Internet as soon as possible. Then I can work on improving it and adding more pages."*

   - Read Hour 1, "Understanding HTML and the Web."
   - Read Hour 2, "Create a Web Page Right Now."
   - Read Hour 9, "Creating Your Own Web Page Graphics."
   - Read Hour 10, "Putting Graphics on a Web Page."
   - Read Hour 4, "Publishing Your HTML Pages."
   - Put your first page on the Internet!

     (Total work time: 4–8 hours.)

   - Read the rest of the book, and update your pages as you learn more HTML.

3. *"I need a professional-looking business Web site with an order form right away. Then I can continue to improve and develop my site over time."*

   - Read all four hours in Part I, "Your First Web Page."
   - Read Hour 8, "Creating HTML Forms."
   - Read Hour 9, "Creating Your Own Web Page Graphics."
   - Read Hour 10, "Putting Graphics on a Web Page."
   - Read Hour 11, "Custom Backgrounds and Colors."
   - Put your pages and order form on the Internet!

     (Total work time: 6–12 hours.)

   - Read the rest of the book, and update your pages as you learn more HTML.

4. *"I need to develop a creative and attractive 'identity' Web site on a tight schedule. Then I will need to develop many pages for our corporate intranet as well."*

   - Read all four hours in Part I, "Your First Web Page."
   - Read all four hours in Part II, "Web Page Text."
   - Read all four hours in Part III, "Web Page Graphics."
   - Read all four hours in Part IV, "Web Page Design."
   - Put your pages on the Internet and/or your intranet!
     (Total work time: 8–16 hours.)
   - Read the rest of the book, and update your pages as you learn more HTML.

5. *"I need to build a cutting-edge interactive Web site or HTML–based multimedia presentation—fast!"*

   - Read this whole book.
   - Put your pages on the Internet and/or CD-ROM!
     (Total work time: 12–24 hours.)
   - Review and use the techniques you've learned to continue improving and developing your site.

It may take a day or two for an Internet service provider to set up a host computer for your pages, as discussed in Hour 4, "Publishing Your HTML Pages." If you want to get your pages online immediately, read Hour 4 now so you can have a place on the Internet all ready for your first page.

No matter which of these approaches you take, you'll benefit from the unique presentation elements that make this book the fastest possible way to learn HTML.

Visual Examples

Like the "Instant HTML" reference card in the front of this book, every example is illustrated in two parts. The text you type in to make an HTML page is shown first, with all HTML commands highlighted. The resulting Web page is shown as it will appear to people who view it with the world's most popular Web browser, Netscape Navigator. You'll often be able to adapt the example to your own pages without reading any of the accompanying text at all.

(Though the figures use Netscape Navigator 4.0, I always tell you if the page will look different in other browsers or older versions. Everything in this book works with both Netscape Navigator and Microsoft Internet Explorer.)

Special Highlighted Elements

 As you go through each hour, sections marked "To Do" guide you in applying what you just learned to your own Web pages at once.

NEW TERM Whenever a new term is used, it will be highlighted with a special icon like this one. No flipping back and forth to the Glossary!

 Tips and tricks to save you precious time are set aside so you can spot them quickly.

 Crucial information you should be sure not to miss is also highlighted.

 "Coffee Break" sections give you a chance to take a quick break and have some fun exploring online examples.

 When there's something you need to watch out for, you'll be warned about it in these sections.

Q&A, Quiz, and Exercises

Every hour ends with a short question-and-answer session that addresses the kind of "dumb questions" everyone wishes they dared to ask. A brief but complete quiz lets you test yourself to be sure you understand everything presented in the hour. Finally, one or two optional exercises give you a chance to practice your new skills before you move on.

The 24-Hour HTML Café

Every example page illustrated in this book, plus more than 150 additional complete Web pages designed to reinforce and expand your knowledge of HTML, can be found at an Internet site called the 24-Hour HTML Café (`http://24hourHTMLcafe.com/`). I built and opened the café especially to provide readers of this book with oodles more examples and reusable HTML pages than I could ever picture in a short book.

You'll also get to have some fun with whimsical "edutainment" pages and break-time surprises, plus an extensive hotlist of links to a wide variety of Internet resources to help you produce your own Web pages even faster. See you there!

PART I
Your First Web Page

Hour

HOUR 1

Understanding HTML and the Web

Before you begin creating your own Web pages with HTML, you need a little background knowledge about what Web pages are, how to view and edit them, and what you can expect to achieve with them. This hour provides a quick summary of those basics, and some practical tips to make the most of your time as a Web page author and publisher.

To Do

Here's a review of what you need to do before you're ready to use the rest of this book.

1. Get a computer. I used a Windows 95 computer to create the figures in this book, but you can use any Windows, Macintosh, or UNIX machine to create your Web pages. The speed of the computer itself doesn't matter much for accessing Web pages, but the speed of the computer's modem or network interface card (NIC) should be at least 28.8Kbps, and faster is better. If you are buying a new modem, be sure it's compatible with the V.90 56Kbps standard.

▼   2. Get a connection to the Internet. You can either dial up an Internet service provider
        (ISP) by using the modem in your computer, or connect through the local network
        of your school or business. An old UNIX "shell" account won't do the trick; it has
        to be a modern PPP (Point-to-Point Protocol) connection, which most ISP compa-
        nies now offer for about $20 per month. The ISP, school, or business that provides
        your connection can help you with the details of setting it up properly.

     3. Get a Web browser program. This is the software your computer needs to retrieve
        and display HTML Web pages. The most popular browser programs are currently
        Netscape Navigator 4.0 (part of the Netscape Communicator suite) and Microsoft
        Internet Explorer 4.0. One or the other of these two Web browser programs is used
        by more than 90 percent of the people who look at Web pages, so it's a good idea
        to get them both. You can buy them in software stores, or get them free through the
        Internet at `http://home.netscape.com` and `http://www.microsoft.com`.

     4. Explore! Use Netscape Navigator or Microsoft Internet Explorer to look around the
        Internet for Web pages that are similar in content or appearance to those you'd like
        to create. Note what frustrates you about some pages, what attracts you and keeps
▲   you reading, and what makes you come back to some pages over and over again.

> If you plan to put your HTML pages on the Internet (as opposed to publish-
> ing them on CD-ROM or a local intranet), you'll need to transfer them to a
> computer that is connected to the Internet 24 hours a day. The same compa-
> ny or school that provides you with Internet access may also let you put Web
> pages on its computer; if not, you may need to pay another company to
> "host" your pages.
>
> You can start learning HTML with this book right away and wait to find an
> Internet host for your pages when they're done. However, if you want to
> have a place on the Internet ready for your very first page as soon as it is
> finished, you might want to read Hour 4, "Publishing Your HTML Pages,"
> before you continue.

What Is a Web Page?

Once upon a time, back when there weren't any footprints on the moon, some far-sighted
folks decided to see whether they could connect several major computer networks
together. I'll spare you the names and stories (there are plenty of both), but the eventual
result was the "mother of all networks," which we call the Internet.

Until 1990, accessing information through the Internet was a rather technical affair. It
was so hard, in fact, that even Ph.D.-holding physicists were often frustrated when trying

to swap data. One such physicist, the now famous Tim Berners Lee, cooked up a way to easily cross-reference text on the Internet through "hypertext" links. This wasn't a new idea, but his simple *Hypertext Markup Language* (HTML) managed to thrive while more ambitious hypertext projects floundered.

New Term *Hypertext* means text stored in electronic form with cross-reference links between pages.

New Term *Hypertext Markup Language (HTML)* is a language for describing how pages of text, graphics, and other information are organized, formatted, and linked together.

By 1993, almost 100 computers throughout the world were equipped to serve up HTML pages. Those interlinked pages were dubbed the *World Wide Web* (WWW), and several Web browser programs had been written to allow people to view Web pages. Because of the popularity of "the Web," a few programmers soon wrote Web browsers that could view graphics images along with the text on a Web page. One of these programmers was Marc Andressen; he went on to become rich and famous selling the world's most popular Web browser, Netscape Navigator.

Today, HTML pages are the standard interface to the Internet. They can include animated graphics, sound and video, complete interactive programs, and good old-fashioned text. Millions of Web pages are retrieved each day from thousands of Web server computers around the world.

The Web is on the verge of becoming a mass-market medium, as high-speed Internet connections through TV cables, modernized phone lines, and direct satellite feeds become commonplace. You can already browse the Web using a $300 box attached to your television instead of using your computer, and the cost of such devices is likely to fall sharply over the next few years.

Yet the Internet is no longer the only place you'll find HTML. Most private corporate networks now use HTML to provide business information to employees and clients. HTML is now the interface of choice for publishing presentations on CD-ROM and the new high-capacity digital versatile disk (DVD) format. Microsoft is even integrating HTML directly into the Windows operating system, allowing every storage folder in your computer to be associated with an HTML page and hypertext links to other folders and pages.

In short, HTML is everywhere. Fortunately, you're in the right place to find out how HTML Web pages work and how to create them.

How Web Pages Work

When you are viewing Web pages, they look a lot like paper pages. At first glance, the process of displaying a Web page is simple: You tell your computer which page you want to see, and the page appears on your screen. If the page is stored on a disk inside your computer, it appears almost instantly. If it is located on some other computer, you might have to wait for it to be retrieved.

Of course, Web pages can do some very convenient things that paper pages can't. For example, you can't point to the words "continued on page 57" in a paper magazine and expect page 57 to automatically appear before your eyes. Nor can you tap your finger on the bottom of a paper order form and expect it to reach the company's order fulfillment department five seconds later. You're not likely to see animated pictures or hear voices talk to you from most paper pages either (newfangled greeting cards aside). All these things are commonplace on Web pages.

But there are some deeper differences between Web pages and paper pages that you'll need to be aware of as a Web page author. For one thing, what appears as a single "page" on your screen may actually be an assembly of elements located in many different computer files. In fact, it's possible (though uncommon) to create a page that combines text from a computer in Australia with pictures from a computer in Russia and sounds from a computer in Canada.

Figure 1.1 shows a typical page as seen by Netscape Navigator, the world's most popular software for viewing Web pages. A Web browser such as Netscape Navigator does much more than just retrieve a file and put it on the screen. It actually assembles the component parts of a page and arranges those parts according to commands hidden in the text by the author. Those commands are written in a standard language called Hypertext Markup Language, or HTML.

NEW TERM   A *Web browser* is a computer program that interprets (HTML) commands to collect, arrange, and display the parts of a Web page.

Figure 1.2 shows the text, including the HTML commands, I typed to create the page in Figure 1.1. This text file can be read and edited with any word processor or text editor. It looks a bit strange with all those odd symbols and code words, but the text file itself doesn't include any embedded images, boldface text, or other special formatting.

Netscape Navigator adds all the images and formatting you see in Figure 1.1. It reads the coded HTML commands in the text, which tell it to look for separate image files and display them along with the text itself. Other commands tell it which text to display in boldface and how to break up the lines of text on the page.

FIGURE 1.1.

A Web browser assembles separate text and image files to display them as an integrated page.

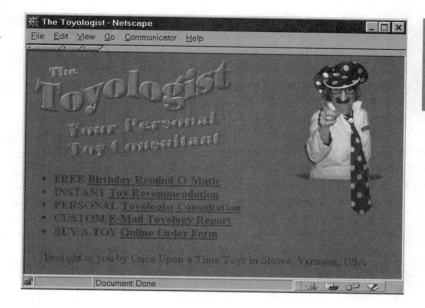

To see the HTML commands for any page on the Web, click with the right mouse button (or hold down the mouse button if you're using a Macintosh computer), and then select View, Source from the pop-up menu. This is a great way to get an intuitive idea how HTML works and learn by others' examples.

Some Web pages use an advanced featured called frames to display more than one HTML page at the same time. In Netscape Navigator 4.0 and Microsoft Internet Explorer 4.0, you can view the HTML commands for any frame by right-clicking it and selecting View, Frame Source.

Other Web browsers have slightly different menu commands for viewing the HTML "source code."

How to Edit Web Pages

You'll learn how to understand and write HTML commands soon. The important point to note right now is that creating a Web page is just a matter of typing some text. You can type and save that text with any word processor or text editor you have on hand. You then open the text file with Netscape Navigator or Microsoft Internet Explorer to see it as a Web page.

FIGURE 1.2.

This is the text I typed to create the page in Figure 1.1. The words between < and > are HTML tags.

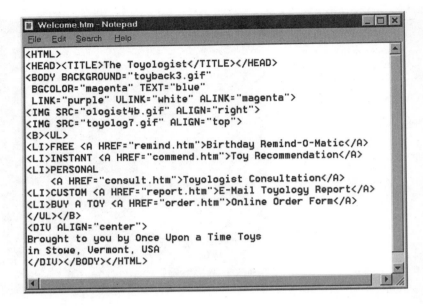

```
Welcome.htm - Notepad
File  Edit  Search  Help
<HTML>
<HEAD><TITLE>The Toyologist</TITLE></HEAD>
<BODY BACKGROUND="toyback3.gif"
 BGCOLOR="magenta" TEXT="blue"
 LINK="purple" ULINK="white" ALINK="magenta">
<IMG SRC="ologist4b.gif" ALIGN="right">
<IMG SRC="toyolog7.gif" ALIGN="top">
<B><UL>
<LI>FREE <A HREF="remind.htm">Birthday Remind-O-Matic</A>
<LI>INSTANT <A HREF="commend.htm">Toy Recommendation</A>
<LI>PERSONAL
    <A HREF="consult.htm">Toyologist Consultation</A>
<LI>CUSTOM <A HREF="report.htm">E-Mail Toyology Report</A>
<LI>BUY A TOY <A HREF="order.htm">Online Order Form</A>
</UL></B>
<DIV ALIGN="center">
Brought to you by Once Upon a Time Toys
in Stowe, Vermont, USA
</DIV></BODY></HTML>
```

When you want graphics, sound, animations, video, or interactive programming to appear on a Web page, you don't insert them into the text file directly, as you would if you were creating a document in most paper-oriented page layout programs. Instead, you type HTML text commands telling the Web browser where to find the media files. The media files themselves remain separate, even though the Web browser will make them *look* as if they're part of the same document when it displays the page.

For example, the HTML document in Figure 1.2 refers to three separate graphics images. Figure 1.3 shows these three image files being edited in the popular graphics program Paint Shop Pro.

You could use any graphics program you like to modify or replace these images at any time. Changing the graphics might make a big difference in how the page looks, even if you don't make any changes to the HTML text file. You can also use the same image on any number of pages while storing only one copy of the graphics file. You'll learn much more about incorporating graphics files into Web pages in Part III, "Web Page Graphics."

FIGURE 1.3.

Though text and graphics appear integrated in Figure 1.1, the graphics files are actually stored, and can be edited, separately.

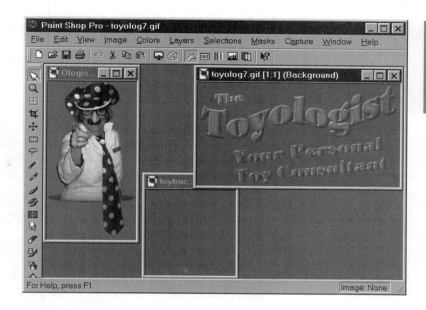

There are two basic approaches to making an HTML page: You can type out the text and HTML commands yourself with a text editor, or you can use graphical software that generates the HTML commands for you.

For now, I strongly recommend that you *do not* use a graphical, "What-You-See-Is-What-You-Get" Web page editor, such as Microsoft FrontPage, Netscape Navigator Gold (which is a different program than Netscape Navigator), or the HTML editor built into Microsoft Office. All graphical Web page editors currently suffer from at least two major problems: They often display pages incorrectly, and they generate very messy HTML that is difficult to read and maintain.

You will be able to follow along with this book and learn HTML much more easily if you work with an editor that shows the actual HTML text. Any word processor or text editor you already have—even the Windows Notepad or Macintosh SimpleText editor—will do nicely.

The Many Faces of HTML

You'll find detailed, step-by-step instructions for creating, saving, and viewing your first Web page in the next hour.

You should be aware from the outset, however, that a single Web page can take on many different appearances, depending on who views it and with what browser they view it. Figure 1.4 is the same Web page pictured earlier in Figure 1.1, as seen with the text-based Lynx Web browser. Lynx users can only see the images if they click the [IMAGE] links at the top of the page.

FIGURE 1.4.

The page from Figure 1.1 looks very different in the DOS Lynx browser.

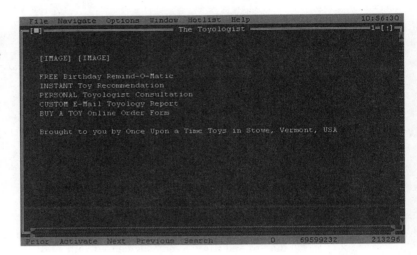

Not many people use text-based Web browsers like DOS Lynx these days. That's good news for Web page authors who want control over the appearance of their pages. And there's more good news to go with it: Most Web pages will look almost exactly the same in Netscape Navigator as they do in Microsoft Internet Explorer, and they will also look the same on PCs, Macintoshes, and UNIX machines. The page in Figure 1.1, for example, would look the same on any of these machines as long as the size of the viewing window, fonts, and program settings were the same on each machine.

Now for the bad news. Even users of the same version of the same Web browser can alter how a page appears by choosing different display options and/or changing the size of the viewing window. Both Netscape Navigator and Microsoft Internet Explorer allow users to override the background and fonts specified by the Web page author with those of their own choosing. Screen resolution, window size, and optional toolbars can also change how much of a page someone sees when it first appears.

The page in Figure 1.1 is shown in a 640×480 window, with the normal font settings. Figure 1.5 shows the same page at 800×600 resolution, with the Arial font at a large size. These are settings that you as a Web page author have no direct control over; each individual who looks at your pages can always choose whatever settings he or she prefers by selecting Edit, Preferences in Netscape Navigator or Microsoft Internet Explorer.

FIGURE 1.5.

The page from Figure 1.1, displayed by Microsoft Internet Explorer 4.0 at a higher resolution with larger fonts.

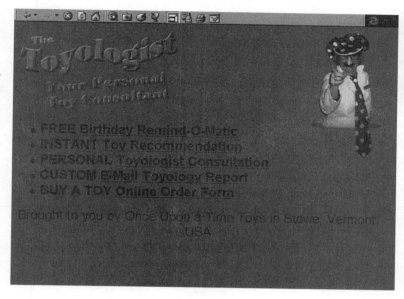

You can't even assume that people will be viewing your Web pages on a computer screen. The page in Figures 1.1, 1.4, and 1.5 might also be read on a low-resolution television screen (see Figure 1.6) or a high-resolution paper printout (see Figure 1.7).

FIGURE 1.6.

Television screens may blur images, and TV Web browsers usually use a larger font to make text readable from a distance.

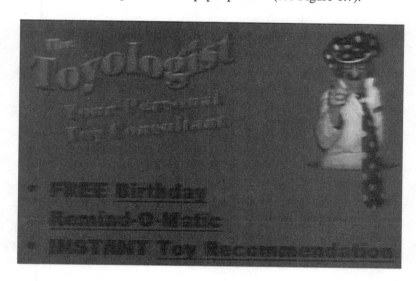

FIGURE 1.7.

Web browsers usually change the background to white when sending pages to a printer.

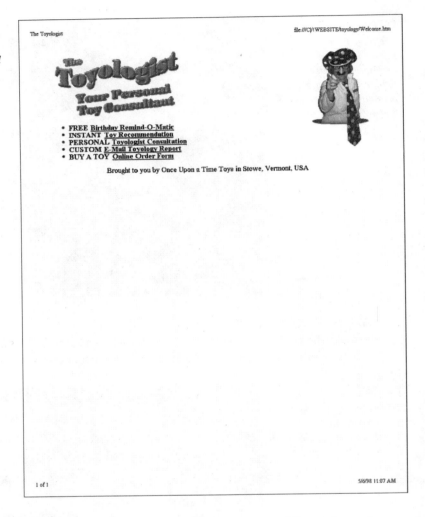

As you learn to make your own Web pages, remember how many different forms they can take when people view them. Some Web page authors fall into the trap of trying to make pages appear "perfect" on their computer and are sorely disappointed the first time they discover that it looks different on someone else's screen. (Even worse, some authors put silly messages on their pages demanding that everyone change the size of their viewing window and font settings to match the author's computer, or proclaiming "This page is best viewed by such-and-such." If you've ever encountered such messages, I'm sure you ignored them just like everyone else does.)

In Part IV, "Web Page Design," you'll find many tips and tricks for ensuring that your pages look great in the widest variety of situations.

> In this book, you'll encounter many example Web pages. At the accompanying *24-Hour HTML Café* Web site, (http://24hourHTMLcafe.com) you'll find all those examples in living color, along with many more sample pages to explore.
>
> To get to the online examples for each hour in the book, click that hour number on the clock marked "Hour by Hour Examples from the Book" at:
>
> http://24hourHTMLcafe.com
>
> Or you can go directly to a specific hour by entering an address like the following into your Web browser.
>
> http://24hourHTMLcafe.com/hour1/

Summary

This hour introduced the basics of what Web pages are and how they work. You learned that coded HTML commands are included in the text of a Web page, but images and other media are stored in separate files. You also learned why typing HTML text yourself is often better than using a graphical editor to create HTML commands for you. Finally, you saw that a single Web page can look very different, depending on what software and hardware are used to display it.

Q&A

Q **I'm still not quite sure what the difference between a "Web page" and an "HTML page" is. And how are these different from a "home page" or a "Web site"?**

A If you want to get technical, I suppose a "Web page" would have to be from the Internet instead of a disk on your own computer. But in practice, the terms "Web page" and "HTML page" are used interchangeably. A "Web site" is one or more pages that are created together and related in content, like the pages of a book. "Home page" usually means the first page people visit when they look at a Web site, though some people use home page to mean any Web page. Others use home page to mean a personal page, as opposed to a corporate Web site.

Q **I've looked at the HTML "source" of some Web pages on the Internet, and it looks frighteningly difficult to learn. Do I have to think like a computer programmer to learn this stuff?**

A Though complex HTML pages can indeed look daunting, learning HTML is several orders of magnitude easier than other computer languages like BASIC, C, or Java. You don't need any experience or skill as a computer programmer to be a very successful HTML author.

Q **Do you need to be connected to the Internet constantly while you create HTML pages?**

A No. In fact, you don't need any Internet connection at all if you only want to produce Web pages for publication on a CD-ROM, zip or floppy disk, or local network. Hour 2, "Create a Web Page Right Now," gives more detailed instructions for working with Web pages offline.

Workshop

Quiz

1. Define the terms Internet, Web page, and World Wide Web.

2. How many files would you need to store on your computer to make a Web page with some text and two images on it?

3. Can you create Web pages with Microsoft Word or WordPerfect?

Answers

1. The Internet is the "network of networks" that connects millions of computers around the globe.

   A Web page is a text document that uses commands in a special language called HTML to add formatting, graphics and other media, and links to other pages.

   The World Wide Web is a collective name for all the Web pages on the Internet.

2. At least three files: one for the text (which includes the HTML commands), and one for each graphics image. In some cases, you might need more files to add a background pattern, sound, or interactive features to the page.

3. Yes, or with any other word processor on any computer (as long as the word processor will save plain text or ASCII files).

Exercise

At the end of each hour in this book, you'll find some suggestions for optional exercises to reinforce and expand what you learned in the hour. However, because you're undoubtedly eager to get started learning HTML, let's skip the warm-up calisthenics and dive right in to Hour 2, "Create a Web Page Right Now."

1

Hour 2

Create a Web Page Right Now

This hour will guide you through the creation of your first Web page. The best way to follow along with this hour is to actually create a Web page as you read, modeled after the example page developed here in the book. If you're a little nervous about jumping right in, you might want to read this hour once to get the general idea, and then go through it again at your computer while you work on your own page.

As mentioned in Hour 1, "Understanding HTML and the Web," you can use any text editor or word processor to create HTML Web pages. Though you may eventually want to use an editor especially designed for HTML, for this hour I recommend you use the editor or word processor with which you're most familiar. That way you won't have to learn a new software program at the same time you're starting to learn HTML. Even a simple text editor like Windows Notepad will work just fine.

To Do

Before you begin working with this hour, you should start with some text that you want to put on a Web page.

1. Find (or write) a few paragraphs of text about yourself, your company, or the intended subject of your Web pages.

2. Be sure to save it as plain, standard ASCII text. Notepad and most simple text editors always save files as plain text, but you may need to choose it as an option if you're using a word processor. For most word processors, you'll see a check box labeled "text," "plain text," or "ASCII text" when you select File, Save As.

3. As you go through this hour, you will add HTML commands (called *tags*) to the text file, making it into a Web page. You can do this with the same text editor or word processor you used to type the text in the first place.

4. Always give files containing HTML tags a name ending in .htm or .html (your choice) when you save them. (This is important, because if you forget to type the .htm or .html at the end of the file name when you save the file, most text editors will give it some other extension like .txt or .doc. If that happens, you won't be able to find it when you go to look at it with a Web browser.)

A Simple Sample Page

Figure 2.1 shows the text you would type and save to create a simple HTML page. If you opened this file with a Web browser such as Netscape Navigator, you would see the page in Figure 2.2.

In Figure 2.1, as in every HTML page, the words starting with < and ending with > are actually coded commands. These coded commands are called HTML *tags* because they "tag" pieces of text and tell the Web browser what kind of text it is. This allows the Web browser to display the text appropriately.

 An HTML *tag* is a coded command used to indicate how part of a Web page should be displayed.

 In Figure 2.1, and most other figures in this book, HTML tags are printed darker than the rest of the text so you can easily spot them. When you type your own HTML files, all the text will be the same color (unless you are using a special HTML editing program that uses color to highlight tags, such as HTMLED).

FIGURE 2.1.

Every Web page you create must include the <HTML>, <HEAD>, <TITLE>, *and* <BODY> *tags.*

```
<HTML>
<HEAD>
<TITLE>The First Web Page</TITLE>
</HEAD>
<BODY>
In the beginning, Tim created the HyperText Markup Language.
The Internet was without form and void, and text was upon
the face of the monitor and the Hands of Tim were moving over
the face of the keyboard. And Tim said, Let there be links;
and there were links. And Tim saw that the links were good;
and Tim separated the links from the text. Tim called the
links Anchors, and the text He called Other Stuff. And the
whole thing together was the first Web Page.
</BODY>
</HTML>
```

FIGURE 2.2.

When you view the Web page in Figure 2.1 with a Web browser, only the actual title and body text are displayed.

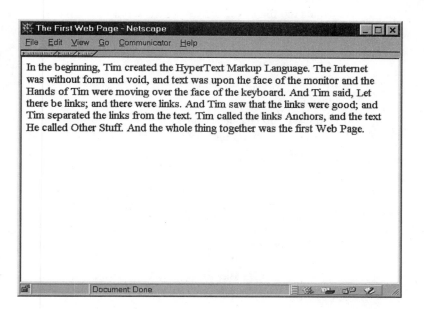

In the beginning, Tim created the HyperText Markup Language. The Internet was without form and void, and text was upon the face of the monitor and the Hands of Tim were moving over the face of the keyboard. And Tim said, Let there be links; and there were links. And Tim saw that the links were good; and Tim separated the links from the text. Tim called the links Anchors, and the text He called Other Stuff. And the whole thing together was the first Web Page.

Figure 2.2 may look a little bit different than your Web browser does (even if you are using the same version of Netscape Navigator), because I have hidden all the button bars. All the figures in this book have the button bars hidden to leave more room for the Web pages themselves.

Before you learn what the HTML tags in Figure 2.1 mean, you might want to see exactly how I went about creating and viewing the document itself.

1. In Windows Notepad or any other word processor, type all the text in Figure 1.1, including the HTML tags.

2. Select File, Save As. (DO NOT choose File, Save As HTML if you are using Microsoft Word or another program that supports automatic HTML generation. This would tell the program to add the HTML commands for you automatically, but you want to take charge and make your HTML all by yourself. So you just tell Mr. Big-Shot Word Processor you don't need no stinking automatic HTML, okay?)

3. Be sure to select Text Documents as the file type if you are using Notepad. In Microsoft Word, you would select Text Only. Other word processors have similar choices for saving plain text. DO NOT choose a word processing format such as Microsoft Word Document or Word Perfect Document.

4. Name the file `myfirst.html`. (If you're using a Windows 3.1 or DOS program, you'll need to name it `myfirst.htm` instead because those old operating systems are too prudish to handle file names ending in four-letter words.)

5. Choose the directory folder on your hard drive where you would like to keep your Web pages—and remember which one you choose! Click the Save or OK button to save the file.

6. Now start up Netscape Navigator or Microsoft Internet Explorer. (Leave the word processor running, too. That way you can easily switch back and forth between viewing your page and editing it.)

> You don't need to be connected to the Internet to view a Web page stored on your own computer. If your Web browser program tries to connect to the Internet every time you start it, it is being a bad browser and you must discipline it severely. The appropriate disciplinary action will depend on your breed of browser:
>
> - In Microsoft Internet Explorer 4.0, select View, Internet Options, click the General tab, and click Use Blank under Home page.
> - In Netscape Navigator 4.0, select Edit, Preferences, choose the Navigator category, and select Blank page under Navigator Starts With.
>
> This will teach your browser not to run off and fetch a page from the Internet every time it starts.

7. In Netscape Navigator 4.0, select File, Open Page and click the Choose File button. If you're using Microsoft Internet Explorer 4.0, select File, Open and click Browse. Then navigate to the appropriate folder and select the `myfirst.html` file.

Voilá! You should see the page in Figure 2.2.

Tags that Every HTML Page Must Have

The time has come for the secret language of HTML tags to be revealed to you. When you understand this language, you will have creative powers far beyond other humans. Don't tell the other humans, but it's really pretty easy.

Most HTML tags have two parts: an *opening tag*, to indicate where a piece of text begins, and a *closing tag*, to show where the piece of text ends. Closing tags start with a / (forward slash) just after the < symbol.

For example, the <BODY> tag in Figure 2.1 tells the Web browser where the actual body text of the page begins, and </BODY> indicates where it ends. Everything between the <BODY> and </BODY> tags will appear in the main display area of the Web browser window, as you can see in Figure 2.2.

Netscape Navigator displays any text between <TITLE> and </TITLE> at the very top of the Netscape window, as you can also see in Figure 2.2. (Some older Web browsers display the title in its own special little box instead.) The title text will also be used to identify the page on the Netscape Navigator Bookmarks menu or Microsoft Internet Explorer Favorites list.

You will use the <BODY> and <TITLE> tags in every HTML page you create because every Web page needs a title and some body text. You will also use the other two tags shown in Figure 2.1, <HTML> and <HEAD>. Putting <HTML> at the very beginning of a document simply indicates that this is a Web page. The </HTML> at the end indicates that the Web page is over.

Don't ask me to explain why you have to put <HEAD> in front of the <TITLE> tag and </HEAD> after the </TITLE> tag. You just do. (Hour 22, "Organizing and Managing a Web Site," reveals some other advanced header information that can go between <HEAD> and </HEAD>, but none of it is necessary for most Web pages.)

> You may find it convenient to create and save a "bare-bones" page with just the opening and closing <HTML>, <HEAD>, <TITLE>, and <BODY> tags, similar to the document in Figure 2.1. You can then open that document as a starting point whenever you want to make a new Web page and save yourself from typing out all those "obligatory" tags every time.
>
> (This won't be necessary if you use a dedicated HTML editing program, which will usually put these tags in automatically when you begin a new page.)

Paragraphs and Line Breaks

When a Web browser displays HTML pages, it pays no attention to line endings or the number of spaces between words. For example, the top poem in Figure 2.3 appears with a single space between all words in Figure 2.4. When the text reaches the edge of the Netscape window, it automatically wraps down to the next line, no matter where the line breaks were in the original HTML file.

To control where line and paragraph breaks actually appear you must use HTML tags. The <BR> tag forces a line break, and the <P> tag creates a paragraph break. The only practical difference between these two tags is that <P> inserts an extra blank line between paragraphs, and <BR> does not.

The second poem in Figures 2.3 and 2.4 shows the <BR> and <P> tags being used to separate the lines and verses of a nursery rhyme and to separate two paragraphs of text commenting on the rhyme.

FIGURE 2.3.

In HTML, extra spaces and line breaks (like those in the top poem here) are ignored.

```
<HTML>
<HEAD><TITLE>The Advertising Agency Song</TITLE></HEAD>
<BODY>
When your client's    hopping mad,
put his picture in the ad.

If he still should    prove refractory,
add a picture of his factory.

<HR>

When your client's hopping mad,<BR>
put his picture in the ad.<P>
If he still should prove refractory,<BR>
add a picture of his factory.
</BODY></HTML>
```

You might have also noticed the <HR> tag in Figure 2.3, which causes a horizontal "rule" line to appear in Figure 2.4. Inserting a horizontal rule with the <HR> tag also causes a line break, even if you don't include a <BR> tag along with it. For a little extra blank space above or below a horizontal rule, you can put a <P> tag before or after the <HR> tag.

Neither the <BR> line break tag nor the <HR> horizontal rule tag needs a closing </BR> or </HR> tag.

2

FIGURE 2.4.

When the HTML in Figure 2.3 is viewed as a Web page, line breaks and paragraph breaks only appear where there are <BR> and <P> tags.

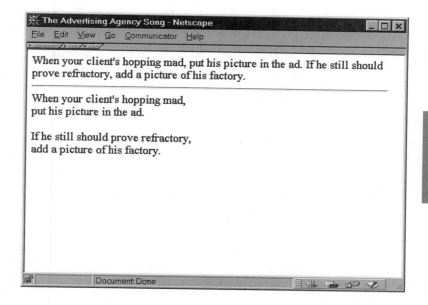

> When your client's hopping mad, put his picture in the ad. If he still should prove refractory, add a picture of his factory.
>
> ―――――――――――――――――――
>
> When your client's hopping mad,
> put his picture in the ad.
>
> If he still should prove refractory,
> add a picture of his factory.

The <P> paragraph tag doesn't require a closing </P> tag at the end of the paragraph because a paragraph obviously ends whenever the next one begins.

You may occasionally see Web pages that do use the </P> tag to close paragraphs, but this is never necessary.

To Do

Take a passage of text you have on hand and try your hand at formatting it as proper HTML.

1. Add <HTML><HEAD><TITLE>*My Title*</TITLE></HEAD><BODY> to the beginning of the text (using your own title for your page Instead of *My Title*).

2. Add </BODY></HTML> to the very end of the text.

3. Add <P> tags between paragraphs, and <BR> tags anywhere you want single-spaced line breaks.

4. Use <HR> to draw horizontal rules separating major sections of text, or wherever you'd like to see a line across the page.

5. Save the file as *mypage.htm* (using your own file name instead of *mypage*). If you are using a word processor, always be sure to save HTML files in plain text or ASCII format.

▼ 6. Open the file with Netscape Navigator or Microsoft Internet Explorer to see your Web page.

7. If something doesn't look right, go back to the text editor or word processor to make corrections and save the file again. You will then need to click `Reload` (in Netscape Navigator) or `Refresh` (in Microsoft Internet Explorer) to see the changes

▲ you made to the Web page.

Headings

When you browse through Web pages on the Internet, you can't help but notice that most of them have a heading at the top that appears larger and bolder than the rest of the text. Figure 2.6 is a simple Web page, containing examples of the three largest heading sizes you can make with HTML.

As you can see in Figure 2.5, the HTML to create headings couldn't be simpler. For a big level 1 heading, put a `<H1>` tag at the beginning and a `</H1>` tag at the end. For a slightly smaller level 2 heading, use `<H2>` and `</H2>` instead, and for a little level 3 heading, use `<H3>` and `</H3>`.

Theoretically, you can also use `<H4>`, `<H5>`, and `<H6>` to make progressively less important headings, but nobody uses these very much—after all, what's the point of a heading if it's not big and bold? Besides, most Web browsers don't show a noticeable difference between these and the already-small `<H3>` headings anyway.

On many Web pages nowadays, graphical images of ornately rendered letters and logos are often used in place of the ordinary text headings discussed in this hour. You'll discover how to create graphics and put them on your pages in Part III, "Web Page Graphics." However, old-fashioned text headings are still widely used, and have two major advantages over graphics headings:

- Text headings transfer and display almost instantly, no matter how fast or slow the reader's connection to the Internet is.
- Text headings can be seen in *all* Web browsers and HTML-compatible software, even old DOS and UNIX programs that don't show graphics.

FIGURE 2.5.

*Any text between <H1>
and </H1> tags will
appear as a large
heading. <H2> and
<H3> make smaller
headings.*

```
<HTML>
<HEAD><TITLE>Teach Yourself</TITLE></HEAD>
<BODY>
<H1>Teach Yourself Clock Programming in 13 Hours</H1>
Tired of blinking VCRs and Microwaves? Embarrassed that
every fax from your office says it was sent from the year
1907? Wondering whether you're ten, sixteen, or
twenty-two minutes late for work when all your LEDs
and LCDs disagree?
<H2>Take charge of your time.</H2>
Pick up a copy of Teach Yourself Clock Programming in
13 Hours, and you'll never have to ignore
another flashing 12:00AM again. In just 13 easy one-hour
lessons, you'll learn to set the time and date you want
on any digital device, from your bedside radio to the
office copier.
<H3>Complete, comprehensive, and FAST.</H3>
Popular makes and models from every major
appliance manufacturer are covered, from convection ovens
to car stereos. PLUS special appendixes on VCR and fax
programming will take you beyond time, into the
hallowed realms of prescheduled recording and late-night
"paper Spam".<P>
Never ask your spouse how to reset the nuker again.
Get Teach Yourself Clock Programming in 13 Hours today.
</BODY></HTML>
```

2

It's important to remember the difference between a *title* and a *heading*. These two words
are often interchangeable in day-to-day English, but when you're talking HTML, <TITLE>
gives the entire page an identifying name that isn't displayed on the page itself, but only
on the window title bar. The heading tags, on the other hand, cause some text on the
page to be displayed with visual emphasis. There can only be one <TITLE> per page, but
you can have as many <H1>, <H2>, and <H3> headings as you want, in any order that suits
your fancy.

You'll learn to take complete control over the appearance of text on your Web pages in
Part II, "Web Page Text." Yet headings provide the easiest and most popular way to draw
extra attention to some important text.

Peeking at Other People's Pages

If you've even taken a quick peek at the World Wide Web, you know that the simple text
pages described in this hour are only the tip of the HTML iceberg. Now that you know
the basics, you may surprise yourself with how much of the rest you can pick up just by
looking at other people's pages on the Internet. As mentioned in Hour 1, you can see the
HTML for any page by right-clicking and selecting View, Source (or View, Frame
Source) in Netscape Navigator or Microsoft Internet Explorer.

FIGURE 2.6.

The <H1>, <H2>, and <H3> tags in Figure 2.5 make the three progressively smaller headings shown here.

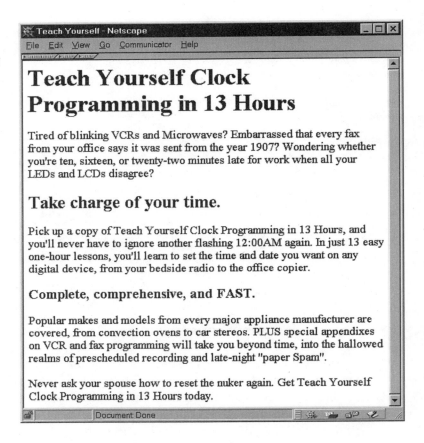

Don't worry if you aren't yet able to decipher what some HTML tags do, or exactly how to use them yourself. You'll find out about all that in the next few hours. However, sneaking a preview now will show you the tags you do know in action and will give you a taste of what you'll be able to do soon with your Web pages.

The HTML goodies at my *24-Hour HTML Café* are especially designed to be intuitive and easy to understand.

The HTML used in the main entrance page at http://24houHTMLcafe.com may look a bit intimidating now, but you'll soon learn how to develop sophisticated sites like this yourself.

For some less intimidating example pages, go to:

`http://24hourHTMLcafe.com/hour2/`

Click the link to each example page, and then use View, Page Source in Netscape Navigator (View, Source in Microsoft Internet Explorer) to look at the HTML I wrote to create that page.

2

Summary

In this hour, you've been introduced to the most basic and important HTML tags. By adding these coded commands to any plain text document, you can quickly transform it into a bona fide Web page.

The first step in creating a Web page is to put a few obligatory HTML tags at the beginning and end, including a title for the page. You then mark where paragraphs and lines end, and add horizontal rules and headings if you want them. Table 2.1 summarizes all the tags introduced in this hour.

TABLE 2.1. HTML TAGS COVERED IN HOUR 2.

Tag	Function
`<HTML>...</HTML>`	Encloses the entire HTML document.
`<HEAD>...</HEAD>`	Encloses the head of the HTML document.
`<TITLE>...</TITLE>`	Indicates the title of the document. Used within `<HEAD>`.
`<BODY>...</BODY>`	Encloses the body of the HTML document.
`<P>...</P>`	A paragraph. The closing tag (`</P>`) is optional.
` `	A line break.
`<HR>`	A horizontal rule line.
`<H1>...</H1>`	A first-level heading.
`<H2>...</H2>`	A second-level heading.
`<H3>...</H3>`	A third-level heading.
`<H4>...</H4>`	A fourth-level heading (seldom used).
`<H5>...</H5>`	A fifth-level heading (seldom used).
`<H6>...</H6>`	A sixth-level heading (seldom used).

Q&A

Q When I open the file in my Web browser, I see all the text including the HTML tags. Sometimes I even see weird looking gobbly-gook characters at the top of the page! What did I do wrong?

A You didn't save the file as plain text. Try saving the file again, being careful to save it as "Text Only" or "ASCII Text." If you can't quite figure out how to get your word processor to do that, don't stress. Just type your HTML files in Notepad or SimpleText instead and everything should work just fine. (Also, always make sure the file name of your Web page ends in .htm or .html.)

Q Okay, so I've got this HTML Web page on my computer now. How do I get it on the Internet so everyone else can see it?

A Hour 4, "Publishing Your HTML Pages," explains how to put your pages on the Internet as well as how to get them ready for publishing on a local network or CD-ROM.

Q I want "Fred's Fresh Fish" to appear both at the top of my page *and* on people's bookmark (or favorites) lists when they bookmark my page. How can I get it to appear both places?

A Make a heading at the top of your page with the same text as the title, like this:

```
<HTML><HEAD><TITLE>Fred's Fresh Fish</TITLE></HEAD>
<BODY><H1>Fred's Fresh Fish</H1>
...the rest of the page goes here...
</BODY></HTML>
```

Q I've seen Web pages on the Internet that don't have `<HTML>` tags at the beginning. I've also seen pages with some other weird tags in front of the `<HTML>` tag. You said pages always have to start with `<HTML>`. What's the deal?

A Many Web browsers will forgive you if you forget to put in the `<HTML>` tag and will display the page correctly anyway. Yet it's a very good idea to include it because some software does need it to identify the page as valid HTML.

In fact, the official standard goes one step further and recommends that you put a tag at the beginning that looks like this: `<!DOCTYPE HTML PUBLIC "-//IETF//DTD HTML//EN//4.0">` to indicate that your document conforms to the HTML 4.0 standard. No software that I've ever heard of pays any attention to this tag, however. Nor is it likely to be required in the near future, since so few of the millions of Web pages in the world include it.

Workshop

Quiz

1. What four tags are required in every HTML page?

2. Insert the appropriate line break and paragraph break tags to format the following poems with a blank line between them:

Good night, God bless you,
Go to bed and undress you.

Good night, sweet respose,
Half the bed and all the clothes.

3. Write the HTML for the following to appear one after the other:

   - A small heading with the words, "We are Proud to Present"
   - A horizontal rule across the page
   - A large heading with the one word "Orbit"
   - A medium-sized heading with the words, "The Geometric Juggler"
   - Another horizontal rule

4. Write a complete HTML Web page with the title "Foo Bar" and a heading at the top which reads "Happy Hour at the Foo Bar," followed by the words "Come on down!" in regular type.

Answers

1. `<HTML>`, `<HEAD>`, `<TITLE>`, and `<BODY>` (along with their closing tags, `</HTML>`, `</HEAD>`, `</TITLE>`, and `</BODY>`).

2.
```
Good night, God bless you,<BR>
Go to bed and undress you.
<P>
Good night, sweet respose,<BR>
Half the bed and all the clothes.
```

3.
```
<H3>We are Proud to Present</H3>
<HR>
<H1>Orbit</H1>
<H2>The Geometric Juggler</H2>
<HR>
```

4.
```
<HTML>
<HEAD><TITLE>Foo Bar</TITLE></HEAD>
<BODY>
```

```
<H1>Happy Hour at the Foo Bar</H1>
Come on Down!
</BODY></HTML>
```

Exercises

- Even if your main goal in reading this book is to create Web pages for your business, you might want to make a personal Web page just for practice. Type a few paragraphs to introduce yourself to the world, and use the HTML tags you've learned in this hour to make them into a Web page.

- You'll be using the HTML tags covered in this hour so often that you'll want to commit them to memory. The best way to do that is to take some time now and create several Web pages before you go on. You can try creating some basic pages with serious information you want to post on the Internet, or just use your imagination and make some fun "joke" pages.

HOUR 3

Linking to Other Web Pages

In the previous two hours, you learned how to create an HTML page with some text on it. However, to make it a "real" Web page you need to connect it to the rest of the World Wide Web—or at least to your own personal or corporate "web" of pages.

This hour will show you how to create *hypertext links*—those underlined words that take you from one Web page to another when you click them with your mouse. You'll learn how to create links that go to another part of the same page in Hour 7, "Email Links and Links within a Page."

Though the same HTML tag you'll learn in this hour is also used to make graphics images into clickable links, graphical links aren't explicitly discussed here. You'll find out about those in Hour 10, "Putting Graphics on a Web Page."

Linking to Another Web Page

The tag to create a link is called <A>, which stands for "anchor." (Don't even try to imagine the thought process of the person who came up with this strange name for a link between pages. As Thomas Carlyle once said, "The coldest word was once a glowing new metaphor.") You put the address of the page to link to in quotes after HREF=, like the following:

```
<A HREF="http://netletter.com/dicko/welcome.htm">Click here!</A>
```

This link would display the words Click here! in blue with an underline. When someone clicks it, he or she would see the Web page named welcome.htm, which is located in the dicko folder on the Web server computer whose address is netletter.com—just as if he or she had typed the address into the Web browser by hand. (Internet addresses are also called *Uniform Resource Locators*, or *URLs*, by techie types, by the way.)

HREF stands for Hypertext Reference, and is called an *attribute* of the <A> tag. You'll learn more about attributes in Hour 5, "Text Alignment and Lists."

As you might know, you can leave out the http:// or http://www. at the front of any address when typing it into most Web browsers. You *cannot* leave that part out when you type an address into an <A HREF> link on a Web page, however.

One thing you *can* often leave out of an address is the actual name of the HTML page, because most computers on the Internet will automatically pull up the home page for a particular address or directory folder. For example, you can use http://netletter.com to refer to the page located at http://netletter.com/welcome.htm because my server computer knows welcome.htm is the page you should see first. (See Hour 4, "Publishing Your HTML Pages.")

Figure 3.1 includes a number of <A> tags, which show up as underlined links in Figure 3.2. For example, clicking the words Alloway, New Jersey in Figure 3.2 will take you to the page located at http://www.accsyst.com/cow.html as shown in Figure 3.3.

FIGURE 3.1.

Words between <A> and </A> tags will become links to the addresses given in the HREF attributes.

```
<HTML>
<HEAD><TITLE>You Aren't There</TITLE></HEAD>
<BODY>
<H1>Wonders of the World</H1>
Vacations aren't cheap. But who needs them anymore,
with so many live cameras connected to the World
Wide Web? Pack a picnic, and you can visit spacious
pastures (complete with scenic cows) in
<A HREF="http://www.accsyst.com/cow.html">
Alloway, New Jersey</A> or, for the more
scientifically minded, at <A HREF=
"http://www.almaden.ibm.com/almaden/cattle/home_cow.htm">
IBM's Almaden Research Center</A>.
<P>
If you're into excercise, why not hike your
eyeballs up the slopes of <A HREF=
"http://www-nmr.banffcentre.ab.ca/banffcam.html">
an uninhabited mountain in Banff, Alberta?</A>
Or if it's scenery you're after, adventure
to <A HREF="http://www.inwap.com/backyard/">
a half-paved backyard in Fremont, California.</A>
<P>
Not the outdoorsy type? Take in the sights of
<A HREF="http://naomi.espy.net/naomi/closetcam.html">
Naomi's (usually dark) closet in Memphis, Tennessee</A>
or a lovely plate-glass <A HREF=
"http://members.iquest.net/~jknapp/windowcam.html">
window with a tree in front of it, Somewhere</A>.
Bon voyage!
</BODY></HTML>
```

3

FIGURE 3.2.

The HTML in Figure 3.1 produces this page, with links appearing as blue or purple underlined text.

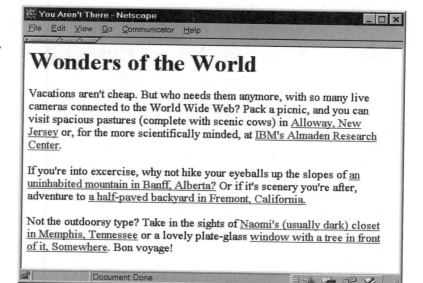

FIGURE 3.3.

Clicking on Alloway, New Jersey *in Figure 3.2 retrieves this page from the Internet.*

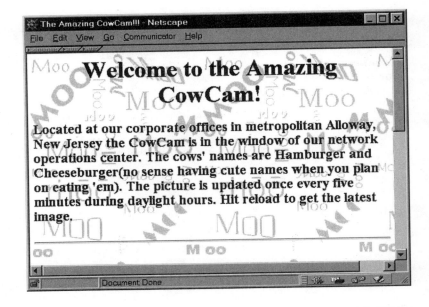

You can easily transfer the address of a page from your Web browser to your own HTML page by using the Windows or Macintosh clipboard. Just highlight the address in the Location, Address, Bookmark Properties or Edit Favorites box in your Web browser, and select Edit, Copy (or press Ctrl+C). Then type <A HREF=" and select Edit, Paste (Ctrl+V) in your HTML editor.

Linking Between Your Own Pages

When you create a link from one page to another page on the same computer, it isn't necessary to specify a complete Internet address. If the two pages are in the same directory folder, you can simply use the name of the HTML file, like this:

```
<A HREF="pagetwo.htm">Click here to go to page 2.</A>
```

As an example, Figures 3.4 and 3.6 show a quiz page with a link to the answer pages in Figures 3.5 and 3.7. The answers page contains a link back to the quiz page.

Using just filenames instead of a complete Internet addresses saves you a lot of typing. And more importantly, the links between your pages will work properly no matter where the pages are located. You can test the links while the files are still right on your computer's hard drive. Then you can move them to a computer on the Internet, or to a CD-ROM or DVD disk, and all the links will still work correctly.

FIGURE 3.4.

Because this page links to another page in the same directory, the filename can be used in place of a complete address.

```
<HTML>
<HEAD><TITLE>History Quiz</TITLE></HEAD>
<BODY>
<H1>History Quiz</H1>
Complete the following rhymes. (Example:
William the Conquerer played cruel tricks
on the Saxons in... ten sixty-six.)<P>
1. Columbus sailed the ocean blue in...<BR>
2. The Spanish Armada met its fate in...<BR>
3. London burnt like rotten sticks in...<BR>
4. Tricky Dickie served his time in...<BR>
5. Billy C. went on a spree in...<P>
<A HREF="answers.htm">Click here for answers.</A>
</BODY></HTML>
```

FIGURE 3.5.

This is the answers.htm *file, and Figure 3.4 is* quizzer.htm, *to which this page links back.*

```
<HTML>
<HEAD><TITLE>History Quiz</TITLE></HEAD>
<BODY>
<H1>History Quiz Answers</H1><P>
1. ...fourteen hundred and ninety-two.<BR>
2. ...fifteen hundred and eighty eight.<BR>
3. ...sixteen hundred and sixty-six.<BR>
4. ...nineteen hundred and sixty-nine.<BR>
5. ...nineteen hundred and ninety-three.<P>
<A HREF="quizzer.htm">Click here for the questions.</A>
</BODY></HTML>
```

3

FIGURE 3.6.

This is the quizzer.htm *file listed in Figure 3.4 and referred to by the link in Figure 3.5.*

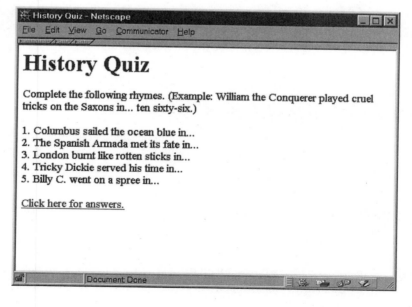

FIGURE 3.7.

Click here for
answers *in Figure 3.6
takes you here.* Click
here for the ques-
tions *takes you back
to Figure 3.6.*

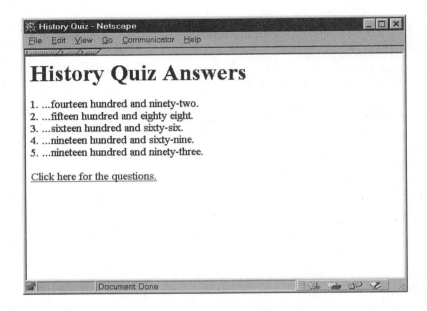

At the *24-Hour HTML Café*, you'll find some fun example pages demonstrat-
ing hypertext links, including a tour of "Indigestible Ingestibles Research"
sites on the Internet and a light-hearted literary history quiz. These intriguing pages can be found, along with the other examples from this hour, at:

`http://24hourHTMLcafe.com/hour3/`

Relative Addresses

If you have many pages, you'll want to put them in more than one directory folder. In
that case, you still shouldn't use the full Internet address to link between them. You can
use relative addresses, which include only enough information to find one page from
another.

NEW TERM A *relative address* describes the path from one Web page to another, instead of a
full (or "absolute") Internet address.

For instance, suppose you are creating a page named `zoo.htm` in a directory folder
named `webpages` on your hard drive. You want to include a link to a page named
`african.htm`, which is in a sub-folder named `elephants` within `webpages`. The link
would look like the following:

```
<A HREF="elephants/african.htm">Learn about African elephants.</A>
```

> The / forward-slash is always used to separate directory folders in HTML.
> Don't use the \ backslash normally used in Windows and DOS!

The `african.htm` page might contain a link back to the main `zoo.htm` page:

```
<A HREF="../zoo.htm">Return to the zoo.</A>
```

The double-dot `..` is a special code that means "the folder containing the current folder." (The `..` means the same thing in DOS, Windows, MacOS, and UNIX.)

You can then move these pages to another directory folder, disk drive or Web server without changing the links, as long as you always put `african.htm` inside a sub-folder named `elephants`.

Relative addresses can span quite complex directory structures if necessary; Hour 22, "Organizing and Managing a Web Site," offers more detailed advice for organizing and linking among large numbers of Web pages.

To Do

You probably created a page or two of your own while working through Hour 2, "Create a Web Page Right Now." Now is a great time to add a few more pages and link them together.

- Use a home page as a main entrance and central "hub" to which all your other pages are connected. If you created a page about yourself or your business in Hour 2, use that as your home page. You also might like to make a new page now for this purpose.

- On the home page, put a list of `<A HREF>` links to the other HTML files you've created (or plan to create soon). Be sure that the exact spelling of the filename, including any capitalization, is correct in every link.

- On every other page, include a link at the bottom (or top) leading back to your home page. That makes it simple and easy to navigate around your "site."

- You may also want to include a list of links to sites on the Internet, either on your home page or a separate "hotlist" page. People often include a list of their friends' personal pages on their own home page. (Businesses, however, should be careful not to lead potential customers away to other sites too quickly—there's no guarantee they'll come back!)

Remember to only use filenames (or relative addressing) for links between your own pages, but full Internet addresses for links to other sites.

There is one good reason to sometimes use the complete address of your own pages in links. If someone saves one of your pages on his or her own hard drive, none of the links to your other pages from that page will work unless they include full Internet addresses.

I like to include a link with the full address of my main home page at the bottom of every page, and use simple filenames or relative addresses in all the rest of the links.

Summary

The <A> tag is what makes Hypertext "hyper." With it, you can create clickable links between pages, as well as links to specific anchor points on any page.

When creating links to other people's pages, include the full Internet address of each page in an <A HREF> tag. For links between your own pages, include just the filenames and enough directory information to get from one page to another.

Table 3.1 summarizes the <A> tag discussed in this hour.

TABLE 3.1.   HTML TAGS AND ATTRIBUTES COVERED IN HOUR 3.

Tag/Attribute	Function
<A>...</A>	With the HREF attribute, creates a link to another document or anchor.
	Attributes:
HREF="..."	The address of the document and/or anchor point to link to.

Q&A

Q When I make links, some of them are blue and some of them are purple. Why? And how come most of the links I see on the Internet aren't blue and purple?

A A link will appear blue to anyone who hasn't recently visited the page to which it points. Once you visit a page, any links to it will turn purple. These colors can be (and often are) changed to match any color scheme a Web page author wants, so many links you see on the Web won't be blue and purple. (Hour 11, "Custom Backgrounds and Colors," tells how to change the colors of text and links on your Web pages.)

Q **What happens if I link to a page on the Internet and then the person who owns that page deletes or moves it?**

A That depends on how that person has set up his or her server computer. Usually, people will see a message when they click the link saying `Page not found` or something to that effect. They can still click the Back button to go back to your page.

Q **One of my links works fine on my computer, but when I put the pages on the Internet the link doesn't work anymore. What's up?**

A The most likely culprit is capitalization. On Windows computers, linking to a file named `Freddy.HTM` with `<A HREF="freddy.htm">` will work. But on most Web servers (which are usually UNIX machines), the link must be `<A HREF="Freddy.HTM">` (or you must change the name of the file to `freddy.htm`). To make matters worse, some text editors and file transfer programs actually change the capitalization without telling you! The next hour explains how to upload files to a Web site, and how to rename files once they're online so that you can make sure the spelling and capitalization are perfect.

Workshop

Quiz

1. Your best friend from elementary school finds you on the Internet and says he wants to trade home page links. How do you put a link to his page at `www.cheap-suits.com/~billybob/` on your page?

2. Your home page will be at `http://www.mysite.com/home.htm` when you put it on the Internet. Write the HTML code to go on that page so that when someone clicks the words `All about me`, they see the page located at `http://www.mysite.com/mylife.htm`.

3. You plan to publish a CD-ROM disk containing HTML pages. How do you create a link from a page in the `\guide` directory folder to the `\guide\maine\katahdin.htm` page?

4. How about a link from `\guide\maine\katahdin.htm` to the `\guide\arizona\superstitions.htm` page?

Answers

1. On your page, put:
```
<A HREF="http://www.cheapsuits.com/~billybob/">
My Buddy Billy Bob's Page of Inexpensive Businesswear</A>
```

2. `<A HREF="mylife.htm">All about me</A>`

   The following would work equally well (though it would be harder to test on your hard drive):

   `<A HREF="http://www.mysite.com/mylife.htm">All about me</A>`

3. `<A HREF="maine/katahdin.htm">Mount Katahdin</A>`

4. `<A HREF="../arizona/superstitions.htm">`

   `The Superstition Range</A>`

Exercise

To make a formatted list of your favorite sites, click the Bookmarks button in Netscape Navigator 4.0, click Edit Bookmarks, and then select File, Save As. You can then open that bookmark page in any text editor and add other text and HTML formatting as you want. (Alas, there's no easy way to export your Microsoft Internet Explorer favorites list as a single Web page.)

HOUR 4

Publishing Your HTML Pages

Here it is, the hour you've been waiting for! Your Web pages are ready for the world to see, and this hour explains how to get them to appear before the eyes of your intended audience.

The most obvious avenue for publishing Web pages is, of course, the Internet. But you may want to limit the distribution of your pages to a local *intranet* within your organization, instead of making them available to the general public. You may also choose to distribute your Web pages on CD-ROMs, floppy disks, Zip disks, or the new DVD-ROM disks.

This hour covers all of these options, and offers advice on designing your pages to work best with the distribution method you choose.

NEW TERM An *intranet* is a private network with access restricted to one organization, but which uses the same standards and protocols as the global public Internet.

To Do

Before you read about publishing your pages, you should give some thought to which methods of distribution you will be using. You probably already know if you're going to be publishing on a corporate intranet, but the decision of whether to publish on the Internet or on disk can be harder to make.

- If you want your pages to be visible to as many people as possible all over the world, Internet publishing is a must. But don't rule out other distribution methods; you can easily adapt Internet-based pages for distribution on disks and/or local networks.

- If you want to reach a specific group of people who have computers but may not be on the Internet yet, publish your pages on floppy disk (if there aren't very many of them) or CD-ROM (if you have an extensive site). But first, consider seriously whether you can present the same information on good old-fashioned paper.

- If you want to provide very large graphics, multimedia, or other content that would be too slow to transfer over today's modems, consider publishing on a CD-ROM. You can easily link the CD-ROM to an Internet Web site, and offer the CD-ROM to people who find you through the Internet, but want the "full experience."

- If you plan to make a presentation at a meeting, and would also like to publish related material on the Internet or an intranet, why not use HTML instead of old-fashioned Powerpoint slides as a visual aid? I often give out floppy disks containing my HTML presentations to conference participants as well, with additional pages linked in for them to explore on their own.

▲

Setting Up an Internet Web Site

To make an HTML page part of the publicly accessibly World Wide Web, you need to put it on a *Web server* (a computer permanently connected to the Internet and equipped to send out Web pages on request). If you run your own Web server, this procedure is simply a matter of copying the file to the right directory folder. But most people use a Web server run by an Internet Service Provider (ISP) to host their pages.

Almost all service providers that offer Internet access also now offer space to place your own personal Web pages for little or no additional cost. But if you plan (or even hope) to attract large numbers of people, you should pay a little more to get a fully supported business site with a major Internet Service Provider company.

Don't think that you have to use the same local company that provides you with Internet access to host your pages. If you run a busy business Web site, you may save a lot of money and get more reliable service from a company in another city. For example, I use a company in Vermont to access the Internet, but a different company in Boston hosts my Web site.

To comparison shop the hosting services offered by various Internet service providers, go to the list of ISPs at http://thelist.internet.com/.

Prices for a business site start well under $100 per month, but you usually pay more when lots of people start viewing your pages. For a site with about a hundred different Web pages, I have paid as little as $40 per month when a few thousand people looked at my pages, and as much as $2,000 per month when hundreds of thousands of people looked at my pages.

Free Web hosting services such as Geocities (www.geocities.com), Tripod (www.tripod.com), and Angelfire (www.angelfire.com) are very popular with Web page authors—and yes, they really are free—though most such services do require that you include advertisements of their choosing on your pages.

One of the most important choices you'll need to make when you set up a Web site is the name you want to use as the address of the site.

If you aren't willing to pay $100 up front and $50 a year to maintain your own domain name, the address of your site will include the name of your Internet Service Provider (example: http://www.shore.net/~smith/). If you're willing to pay for it, you can pick any name that isn't already in use by another company (example: http://mister-smith.com/).

You can check to see if the name you want is already in use at http://domain-registration.com/. (Or you can just enter the name in your Web browser to see if you get a page.) Once you find a name that isn't already taken, ask your Internet Service Provider to help you apply for that name as soon as possible.

Transferring Pages to a Web Server

When a Web server computer sends Web pages to people through the Internet, it uses an information exchange standard called Hypertext Transfer Protocol (HTTP). To upload a page to your Web site, however, you need software that uses an older communications standard called File Transfer Protocol (FTP).

NEW TERM   *File Transfer Protocol* is the standard that your file transfer software must adhere to when sending files to a Web server. The server then sends those files out to anyone who asks for them using the Hypertext Transfer Protocol.

Netscape Navigator can receive files by using both the HTTP and FTP standards. It can also send files by using FTP, so you can use it to upload your pages to a Web server. Follow these steps:

1. Enter the address of your Web directory in Netscape Navigator's Location box, as in the following example:

   `ftp://myname:mypassword@myisp.net/home/web/wherever/`

   Put your username and password for accessing the site instead of *myname* and *mypassword*, your Internet Service Provider's address instead of *myisp.net*, and the top-level directory where your Web pages reside instead of */home/web/wherever/*.

2. Select File, Upload File, as shown in Figure 4.1. (If you are using Netscape Navigator version 2.0 or 3.0, you must drag the file into the Netscape window from Windows Explorer or another file management program, because the Upload File menu choice is new in Navigator version 4.0).

3. Choose the file you want to upload, and click Open. Wait while the files are transferred.

4. Test your page by clicking the HTML file you just uploaded in the FTP directory listing (in the Netscape window). You're on the Web!

FIGURE 4.1.

You can connect to your Web hosting service and publish your HTML pages using the Upload File feature of Netscape Navigator 4.0.

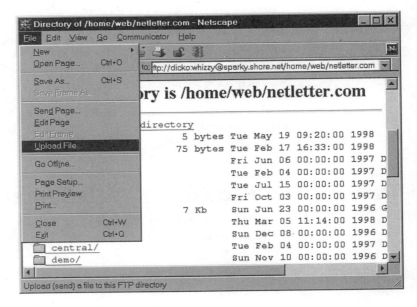

Even though Netscape Navigator can send files to any Web server on the Internet, specialized FTP programs such as WS_FTP or CuteFTP offer much more control for managing your Web pages. For example, Navigator doesn't give you any way to delete an old Web page you want to get rid of, or change the name of a Web page on the server computer. You'll definitely want a specialized FTP program to maintain your Web site.

As you may be aware, Netscape Composer and Microsoft FrontPage are Web page publishing solutions that are designed to be tightly integrated with their respective companys' Web browsers. I don't recommend that you use these programs when learning HTML, since the current versions of both programs hide the actual HTML behind a complex graphical interface and often make serious errors when creating HTML for you.

Once you finish this book, you will be savvy enough to correct the HTML errors these programs make, and you may find them useful. Meanwhile, you will probably find it much less frustrating to publish your Web pages with a good old-fashioned text editor and one of the simple file transfer programs discussed in this hour.

Figure 4.2 shows one of the most popular FTP programs, CuteFTP for Windows. You can download a free copy of CuteFTP (see the following To Do section), although CuteFTP does require a modest registration fee for business users. (See the documentation that comes with the program for details.)

Similar programs are available for Macintosh computers (Fetch is a popular favorite), and FTP utilities come pre-installed on most UNIX computers. You can find these and other FTP programs at http://www.shareware.com.

To Do

I recommend that you download CuteFTP now and use it to send some files to your own Web site as you read on (if you have a Web site set up, that is).

- Go to the CuteFTP home page at http://www.cuteftp.com/ and follow the Download CuteFTP links.

- Once the download is complete, run the self-extracting .exe program, which will install the CuteFTP program.

No matter which FTP program you choose, transferring your Web pages to a Web server involves the following steps. (The steps are illustrated here with CuteFTP, but other FTP programs work similarly.)

FIGURE 4.2.

*CuteFTP is a powerful
and user-friendly
FTP program that
individuals can
use for free.*

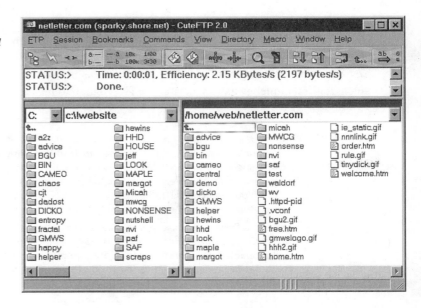

1. Before you can access the Web server, you must tell your FTP program its address,
   as well as your account name and password. In CuteFTP, select a category for your
   site in the FTP Site Manager window (Personal Web Sites in Figure 4.3), and click
   Add Site to access the FTP Site Edit dialog box in Figure 4.4.

FIGURE 4.3.

*CuteFTP includes an
intuitive FTP Site
Manager, although
most Web page authors
only need a single FTP
site entry.*

FIGURE 4.4.

Clicking Add Site or Edit Site in Figure 4.3 brings up this dialog box.

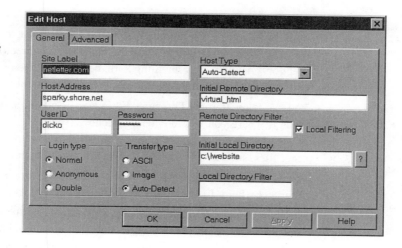

2. Here's how to fill in each of the items in Figure 4.4.

   - Site Label is the name you'll use to refer to your own site. Nobody else will see this name, so enter whatever you want.

   - Host Address is the FTP address of the Web server to whom you need to send your Web pages. This usually (but not always) starts with `ftp`. Notice that it may or may not resemble the address that other people will use to view your Web pages. The Internet Service Provider company that runs your Web server will be able to tell you the correct address to enter here.

   - The company that runs the Web server also issues UserID and Password. Be aware that CuteFTP (and most other FTP programs) will remember your password automatically, which means that anyone who has physical access to your computer will be able to modify your Web site.

   - You should set the Login Type to Normal unless somebody important tells you otherwise. (The Anonymous setting is for downloading files from public FTP services that don't require userIDs or passwords.)

   - Set the Transfer Type to Auto-Detect. (This will automatically send HTML and other text files using a slightly different protocol than images and other non-text files, to ensure complete compatibility with all types of computers.)

   - The Host Type should also be set to Auto-Detect, unless you have trouble connecting. In that case, you would need to find out what type of computer you're connecting to and pick the corresponding Host Type.

4

- For the Initial Remote Directory, fill in the name of the main directory folder on the Web server where your Web pages will be located. The people who run your Web server will tell you the name of that directory. (In some cases, you don't need to enter anything here, because the Web server computer will automatically put you in the directory when you connect to it.)

- You can leave Remote Directory Filter and Local Directory Filter both blank. (This is where you would enter "wildcards" such as `*.htm*` if you only wanted to see files ending in `.htm` or `.html` when you connect to this site. All other files, such as `.gif` and `.jpg` images, would then be ignored.)

- For the Initial Local Directory, enter the drive and directory folder on your computer's hard drive where you keep your Web pages.

- Normally, you won't need to change any settings on the Advanced tab unless you experience problems with your connection. If that happens, have your service provider help you figure out the best settings.

3. When you click OK, you'll go back to the window shown in Figure 4.3. Make sure you are connected to the Internet, and click Connect to establish a connection with the Web server computer.

   Most server computers issue a short message to everyone who connects to them. Many FTP programs ignore this message, but CuteFTP presents it to you as shown in Figure 4.5. It seldom says anything important, so just click OK.

FIGURE 4.5.

CuteFTP displays the "boilerplate" message that some server computers send whenever you connect to them.

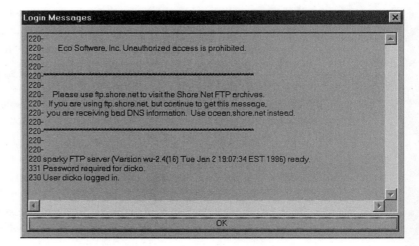

4. Once you're connected to the server, you'll see two lists of files, as shown earlier in Figure 4.2. The left window pane lists the files on your computer, while the right pane lists the files on the server computer.

To transfer a Web page to the server, select the HTML file and any accompanying image files in the left window. (Remember that you can hold down the Ctrl key and click with the mouse to select multiple files in any Windows program.) Then select Commands, Upload (see Figure 4.6), or click the upload button on the toolbar.

As you can see, the same menu contains commands to delete or rename files (on either your computer or the server), as well as commands to make and change directory folders.

Most Web servers have a special name for the file that should be sent if someone doesn't include a specific filename when he or she requests a page. For example, if you go to http://netletter.com/, my Web server will automatically give you the welcome.htm file. Other Web servers use different names for the default file, such as index.html.

Be sure to ask your service provider the default file name so you can give your home page that name.

4

FIGURE 4.6.

To send files to the server, select Commands, Upload in CuteFTP.

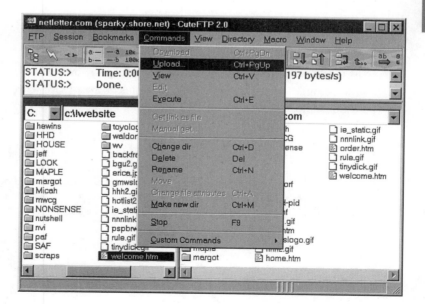

5. That's all there is to it! In most cases, you can immediately view the page you just put on the Web server by using Netscape Navigator (see Figure 4.7) or Microsoft Internet Explorer.

FIGURE 4.7.

Most Web servers make pages immediately available on the Internet seconds after you upload them.

6. When you're done sending and modifying files on the Web server, select FTP, Disconnect to close the connection.

The next time you need to upload some Web pages, you won't need to fill in all the information in step 2. You can just click Connect, select the pages you want to send, and click the upload button.

Most Web servers are set up so that any documents placed onto them are immediately made available to the entire World Wide Web. However, some require that users manually change file permission settings, which control who is allowed to access individual files. Your Internet Service Provider company can tell you exactly how to change permission settings on their server and whether it's necessary to do so.

Making a File Available for Downloading

May Web authors want to know how to make a file that isn't a Web page (say, a zip archive or an exe program) available for downloading from a Web site.

Just upload the file to your Web site, following the instructions in this hour for uploading. Then create a link to the file on one of your Web pages, as explained in Hour 3. For example, if the file was called neatgame.zip the link would look like this:

```
<A HREF="neatgame.zip">Click here to download a neat game I wrote.</A>
```

You might want to put a reminder somewhere near the link telling people that the easiest way to download the file is to right-click (or, if you're a Mac user, hold down the mouse button) on the link and select Save Link as from the pop-up menu. (It will also work fine if people just click on the link normally.)

Just remember that some Web host services charge by the number of bytes sent out, so if 10,000 people a day download a 2,000,000 byte file from your site, it might start costing you some serious money and/or overburden your Web server.

Putting Web Pages on an Intranet

4

The outlined procedure for sending pages to a public Internet server is fairly standard. But the internal workings of private corporate intranets vary considerably from company to company. In some cases, you may need to use an FTP program to send files to an intranet server. In others, you may be able to transfer files by using the same file management program you use on your own computer. You may also need to adjust permission settings, or make special allowances for the firewall that insulates a private intranet from the public Internet.

About all I can tell you here in this book about putting files on your company's intranet is to consult with your systems administrator. He or she can help you put your Web pages on the company server in the way that best ensures their accessibility and security.

Publishing Web Pages on Disk

Unless you were hired to create documents for a company intranet, you have probably assumed that the Internet is the best way to get your pages in front of the eyes of the world. But there are three major incentives for considering distribution on some form of disk instead:

- Currently, more people have disk drives than Internet connections.

- Disks can deliver information to the computer screen much faster than people can download it from the Internet.
- You can distribute disks to a select audience, whether or not they are connected to the Internet or any particular intranet.

In the not-too-distant future, as Web-enabled televisions and high speed networks become more commonplace, these advantages may disappear. But for now, publishing on disk can be an excellent way to provide a bigger, faster, more tightly targeted Web presentation than you could on today's Internet.

Publishing on 1.44MB floppy disks or 100MB Zip disks is simply a matter of copying files from your hard disk with any file management program. You just need to keep in mind that any links starting with `http://` will only work if and when someone reading your pages is also connected to the Internet. The cost is currently about $0.50 per floppy disk, or $10 per Zip disk, plus any delivery or mailing costs.

> Never use drive letters (such as C:) in `<A HREF>` link tags on your Web pages or they won't work when you copy the files to a different disk. Refer back to Hour 3, "Linking to Other Web Pages," for more details on how to make links that will work both on disk and on the Internet.

Publishing on CD-ROM or the new DVD-ROM disks isn't much more complicated; you either need a drive (and accompanying software) capable of creating the disks, or you can send the files to a disk mastering and duplication company. Costs for CD-ROM duplication vary a lot depending on how many disks you need. For less than a hundred CD-ROMs, it may cost more than $10 per disk. But for thousands of copies, expect to pay less than $1 each plus delivery or mailing costs. DVD-ROM pricing hasn't settled down yet, but it will eventually be similar to CD-ROM.

> Web browser software is always necessary for reading HTML pages. However, these days almost everyone already has a Web browser, so you may not need to supply one along with your Web pages. If you do wish to include a browser, you might consider Opera, which includes most of the features of Netscape Navigator and Microsoft Internet Explorer but is small enough to fit on a single 1.44MB floppy disk and can be freely distributed in the form of a 30-day evaluation version. (You can download Opera at `www.operasoftware.com`.)

Microsoft and Netscape are also often willing to allow their browsers to be included on CD-ROMs if you ask nicely in writing and/or pay them a licensing fee. Never give out copies of Microsoft or Netscape software without written permission, since these companies have Big Scary Lawyers who just love that sort of thing.

Testing Your Pages

Whenever you transfer Web pages to a disk, Internet site, or intranet server, you should immediately test every page thoroughly.

The following checklist will help you make sure everything on your pages behaves the way you expected.

1. Before you transfer the pages, follow all of these steps to test the pages while they're on your hard drive. After you transfer the pages to the master disk or Web server, test them again—preferably through a 28.8Kbps modem connection, if your pages are on the Internet.

2. Do each of the following steps with the latest version of Netscape Navigator, the latest Microsoft Internet Explorer, and at least one other browser such as DOS Lynx and/or Opera. Testing with an older version of Navigator or Internet Explorer isn't such a bad idea, since many people still use outdated versions and some pages will appear differently.

3. Make sure the computer you're testing with is set to a 16-color video mode, or at most a 256-color mode. (Pages look better in higher color modes, but you want to see the "bad news" of how they'll look to most people.)

4. If possible, use a computer with 800×600 resolution for testing purposes, but adjust the size of the browser window to exactly 640×480 pixels. On each page, use the maximize button on the corner of the window to switch back and forth between full 800×600 resolution and 640×480 resolution. If pages look good at these two resolutions, they'll probably look fine at larger resolutions, too. (Additional testing at 1024×768 or 1600×1200 resolution can't hurt, though.)

5. Turn off auto image loading in Netscape Navigator before you start testing, so you can see what each page looks like without the graphics. Check your ALT tag messages, and then click the Load Images button on the toolbar to load the graphics and review the page carefully again.

6. Use your browser's font size settings to look at each page at a variety of font sizes, to ensure that your careful layout doesn't fall to pieces.

4

7. Start at the home page and systematically follow every link. (Use the Back button to return after each link, and then click the next link on the page.)

8. Wait for each page to completely finish loading, and scroll down all the way to make sure all images appear where they should.

9. If you have a complex site, it may help to make a checklist of all the pages on your site to make sure they all get tested.

10. Time how long it takes each page to load through a 28.8Kbps modem, preferably when connected through a different Internet Service Provider than the one who runs the Web server. Then multiply that time by 2 to find out how long 14.4Kbps modem users will need to wait to see the page. Is the information on that page valuable enough to keep them from going elsewhere before the page finishes loading?

If your pages pass all those tests, you can be pretty certain that they'll look great to every Internet surfer in the world.

Summary

This hour gave you the basic knowledge you need to choose between the most common distribution methods for Web pages. It also stepped you through the process of placing Web pages on a Web server computer by using freely available file transfer software. Finally, it offered a checklist to help you thoroughly test your Web pages once they are in place.

Q&A

Q When I try to send pages to my Web site from home, it works fine. But when I try it from the computer at work, I get error messages. Any idea what the problem might be?

A The company where you work probably has a *firewall*, which is a layer of security protecting their local network from tampering via the Internet. You will need to set some special configuration options in your FTP program to help it get through the firewall when you send files. Your company's network administrator can help you with the details.

Q I don't know which Internet Service Provider to pick to host my pages—there are so many! How do I choose?

A Obviously, you should compare prices of the companies listed at `http://thelist.internet.com` that provide hosting services. You should also ask for the names of some customers with sites of about the same size as you plan yours to be, and ask them (via email) how happy they are with the company's service and support. Also, make sure that your provider has at least two major (T3 or bigger) links to the Internet, preferably provided to them by two different network companies.

Q All the tests you recommend would take longer than creating my pages! Can't I get away with less testing?

A If your pages aren't intended to make money or provide an important service, it's probably not a big deal if they look funny to some people or produce errors once in a while. In that case, just test each page with a couple of different window and font sizes and call it good. However, if you need to project a professional image, there is no substitute for rigorous testing.

Q I wanted to name my site `jockitch.com` but Proctor and Gamble beat me to it. Is there anything I can do?

A Well, if your company was named Jockitch Inc. before Proctor and Gamble registered the domain name, you could always try suing them. (Good luck.) But even if you don't have the budget to take on their lawyer army, there may be hope. Many new three-letter extensions for site names will probably soon be approved for use, so you may be able to get `jockitch.inc` or `jockitch.biz` (if P&G doesn't scoop you again).

4

Workshop

Quiz

1. How do you put a few Web pages on a floppy disk?

2. Suppose your Internet Service Provider tells you to put your pages in the `/top/user/~elroy` directory at `ftp.bigisp.net`, your username is `rastro`, and your password is `rorry_relroy`. You have the Web pages all ready to go in the `\webpages` folder on your C drive. Where do you put all that information in CuteFTP so you can get the files on the Internet?

3. What address would you enter in Netscape Navigator to view the Web pages you uploaded in question 2?

4. If the following Web page is named `mypage.htm`, which files would you need to transfer to the Web server to put it on the Internet?

```
<HTML><HEAD><TITLE>My Page</TITLE></HEAD>
<BODY BACKGROUND="joy.gif">
<IMG SRC="me.jpg" ALIGN="right">
<H1>My Web Page</H1> Oh happy joy I have a page on the Web!<P>
<A HREF="otherpage.htm">Click here for my other page.</A>
</BODY></HTML>
```

Answers

1. Just copy the HTML files and image files from your hard drive to the disk. Anyone can then insert the disk in his or her computer, start his or her Web browser, and open the pages right from the floppy.

2. Click Add Site in the FTP Site Manager window, and then enter the following information:

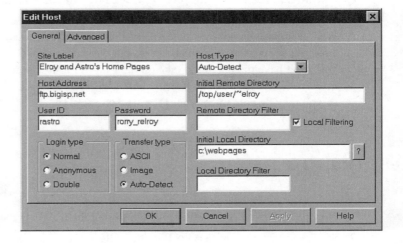

3. You can't tell from the information given in question 2. A good guess would be `http://www.bigisp.net/~elroy/` but you might choose a completely different domain name like `http://elroy-and-astro.com/`.

4. You would need to transfer all three of the following files into the same directory on the Web server:
```
mypage.htm
joy.jpg
me.gif
```

If you want the link on that page to work, you must also transfer

`otherpage.htm`

(and any image files that are referred to in that HTML file).

Exercise

So put your pages on the Internet already!

4

PART II
Web Page Text

Hour

HOUR 5

Text Alignment and Lists

When you present information on paper (or with a good old-fashioned over-head projector) you probably often include lists of numbered steps or "bullet points." You've also undoubtedly written many indented lists to organize information such as terms and their definitions or the outline of a business plan. Because lists are so common, HTML provides tags that automatically indent text and add numbers or bullets in front of each listed item.

In this hour, you'll find out how to center text or align it to the right side of the page. You will also see how to format numbered and bulleted lists, and how the HTML tags for creating "definition" lists can also be used for almost any other type of indentation you want on your Web pages.

To do these things, you'll need a few more HTML tags. You'll also need to learn how to control optional settings (called attributes) for some of the tags you already know.

To Do

▼ To Do

You can make the most of this hour if you have some text that needs to be indented or centered to be presentable.

- Any type of outline, "bullet points" from a presentation, numbered steps, glossary, or list of textual information from a database will serve as good material with which to work.

- If the text you'll be using is from a word processor or database program, be sure to save it to a new file in plain text or ASCII format. You can then add the appropriate HTML tags to format it as you go through this chapter.

▲

Text Alignment

Some HTML tags allow you to specify a variety of options, or attributes, along with the basic tag itself. For example, when you begin a paragraph with the <P> tag you can specify whether the text in that paragraph should be aligned to the left margin, right margin, or center of the page.

To align a paragraph to the right margin, you can put ALIGN="right" inside the <P> tag at the beginning of the paragraph. To center a paragraph, use <P ALIGN="center">. Similarly, the tag to align a paragraph to the left is <P ALIGN="left"> (though this is seldom used, since paragraphs are always aligned to the left when you use plain old <P>).

The word ALIGN is called an attribute of the <P> tag. You can use the ALIGN attribute with just about any HTML tag that contains text, including <H1>, <H2>, the other heading tags, and some tags you will meet later. There are many other attributes besides ALIGN. You will find out how to use them as you learn more HTML tags.

NEW TERM *Attributes* are special code words used inside an HTML tag to control exactly what the tag does.

As with tags, it generally makes no difference whether attributes are in lowercase or uppercase. It also usually doesn't matter if you include the quotation marks around attribute values like "center". In other words all three of the following are equally correct:

```
<DIV ALIGN="center">
<DIV ALIGN=CENTER>
<div align=center>
```

The only time you really do need the quotes is when the value contains a blank space or a character that has special meaning in HTML. In this book, I always include the quotes so that neither you nor I need to worry about when they're needed and when they're not.

Keep in mind that sometimes the same attribute word can have different
meanings when used with different tags. For instance, you will discover in
Hour 10, "Putting Graphics on a Web Page," that ALIGN="left" does something quite different when used with the <IMG> image tag than it does with
the text tags discussed in this chapter.

When you want to set the alignment of more than one paragraph or heading at a time,
you can use the ALIGN attribute with the <DIV>, or *division,* tag. By itself, <DIV> and its
corresponding closing tag </DIV> actually don't do anything at all—which would seem
to make it a peculiarly useless tag!

Yet if you include an ALIGN attribute, <DIV> becomes quite useful indeed. Everything you
put between <DIV ALIGN="center"> and </DIV>, for example, will be centered. This
may include lines of text, paragraphs, headings, images, and all the other things you'll
learn how to put on Web pages in upcoming chapters. Likewise, <DIV ALIGN="right">
will right-align everything down to the next </DIV> tag.

Figure 5.1 demonstrates the ALIGN attribute with both the <P> and <DIV> tags. The results
are shown in Figure 5.2. You'll learn many more advanced uses of the <DIV> tag in Hour
16, "Using Style Sheets," and Hour 20, "Setting Pages in Motion with Dynamic HTML."

FIGURE 5.1.

The ALIGN *attribute
allows you to left-
justify, right-justify,
or center text.*

5

```
<HTML><HEAD><TITLE>Bohemia</TITLE></HEAD>
<BODY>
<DIV ALIGN="center">
<H2>Bohemia</H2>
<B>by Dorothy Parker</B>
</DIV>
<P ALIGN="left">
Authors and actors and artists and such<BR>
Never know nothing, and never know much.<BR>
Sculptors and singers and those of their kidney<BR>
Tell their affairs from Seattle to Sydney.
<P ALIGN="center">
Playwrights and poets and such horses' necks<BR>
Start off from anywhere, end up at sex.<BR>
Diarists, critics, and similar roe<BR>
Never say nothing, and never say no.
<P ALIGN="right">
People Who Do Things exceed my endurance;<BR>
God, for a man that solicits insurance!
</BODY></HTML>
```

FIGURE 5.2.

The alignment settings in Figure 5.1, as they appear in a Web browser.

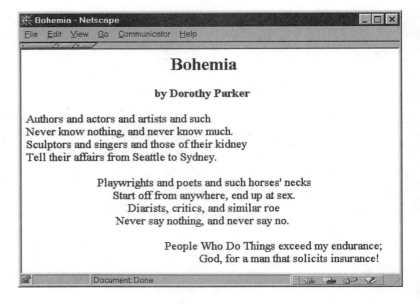

The Three Types of HTML Lists

There are three basic types of HTML lists. All three are shown in Figure 5.3, and Figure 5.4 reveals the HTML to construct them:

- The numbered list at the top is called an *ordered list*. It begins with the <OL> tag and ends with a closing </OL> tag. Numbers and line breaks appear automatically at each <LI> tag, and the entire list is indented.
- The bulleted list is called an *unordered list*. It opens with the <UL> tag and closes with </UL>. It looks just like an ordered list, except that bullets appear at each <LI> tag instead of numbers.
- The list of terms and their meanings is called a *definition list*. It starts with the <DL> and ends with </DL>. The <DT> tag goes in front of each term to be defined, with a <DD> tag in front of each definition. Line breaks and indentations appear automatically.

NEW TERMS   *Ordered lists* are indented lists that have numbers or letters in front of each item. *Unordered lists* are indented lists with a special bullet symbol in front of each item. *Definition lists* are indented lists without any number or symbol in front of each item.

FIGURE 5.3.

The three types of HTML lists, as they appear in Netscape Navigator.

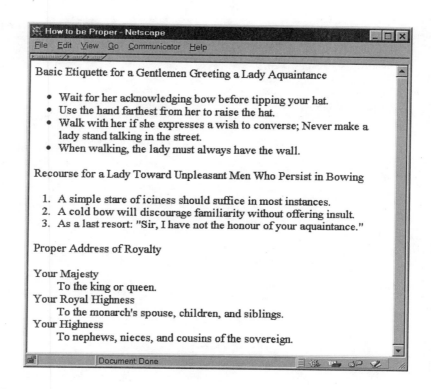

Basic Etiquette for a Gentlemen Greeting a Lady Aquaintance

- Wait for her acknowledging bow before tipping your hat.
- Use the hand farthest from her to raise the hat.
- Walk with her if she expresses a wish to converse; Never make a lady stand talking in the street.
- When walking, the lady must always have the wall.

Recourse for a Lady Toward Unpleasant Men Who Persist in Bowing

1. A simple stare of iciness should suffice in most instances.
2. A cold bow will discourage familiarity without offering insult.
3. As a last resort: "Sir, I have not the honour of your aquaintance."

Proper Address of Royalty

Your Majesty
     To the king or queen.
Your Royal Highness
     To the monarch's spouse, children, and siblings.
Your Highness
     To nephews, nieces, and cousins of the sovereign.

Remember that different Web browsers can display Web pages quite differently. The HTML standard doesn't specify exactly how Web browsers should format lists, so people using older Web browsers may not see the same indentation that you see.

Software of the future may also format HTML lists differently, though all current Web browsers now display lists in almost exactly the same way.

5

Lists Within Lists

Although definition lists are officially supposed to be used for defining terms, many Web page authors use them anywhere they'd like to see some indentation. In practice, you can indent any text simply by putting `<DL><DD>` at the beginning of it and `</DL>` at the end.

You can indent items further by *nesting* one list inside another, like the following:

```
<DL><DD>This item will be indented
<DL><DD>This will be indented further
<DL><DL><DD>And this will be indented very far indeed
</DL></DL></DL></DL>
```

FIGURE 5.4.

Use <OL> and <LI> for ordered lists, <UL> and <LI> for unordered lists, and <DL>, <DT>, and <DD> for definition lists.

```
<HTML><HEAD><TITLE>How to be Proper</TITLE></HEAD>
<BODY>
Basic Etiquette for a Gentlemen Greeting a Lady Aquaintance
<UL>
<LI>Wait for her acknowledging bow before tipping your hat.
<LI>Use the hand farthest from her to raise the hat.
<LI>Walk with her if she expresses a wish to converse;
Never make a lady stand talking in the street.
<LI>When walking, the lady must always have the wall.
</UL>
Recourse for a Lady Toward Unpleasant Men Who Persist in Bowing
<OL>
<LI>A simple stare of iciness should suffice in most instances.
<LI>A cold bow discourages familiarity without offering insult.
<LI>As a last resort: "Sir, I have not the honour of your
aquaintance."
</OL>
Proper Address of Royalty
<DL>
<DT>Your Majesty
<DD>To the king or queen.
<DT>Your Royal Highness
<DD>To the monarch's spouse, children, and siblings.
<DT>Your Highness
<DD>To nephews, nieces, and cousins of the sovereign.
</DL>
</BODY></HTML>
```

Just make sure you always have the same number of closing </DL> tags as opening <DL> tags.

Ordered and unordered lists can also be nested inside one another, down to as many levels as you wish. In Figure 5.5, a complex indented outline is constructed from several unordered lists. You'll notice in Figure 5.6 that Netscape Navigator automatically uses a different type of bullet for each of the first three levels of indentation, making the list very easy to read.

As shown in Figure 5.6, Netscape Navigator (and Microsoft Internet Explorer) will normally use a solid disc for the first-level bullet, a hollow circle for the second-level bullet, and a solid square for all deeper levels. However, you can explicitly choose which type of bullet to use for any level by using <UL TYPE="disc">, <UL TYPE="circle">, or <UL TYPE="square"> instead of <UL>.

FIGURE 5.5.

You can build elaborate outlines by placing lists within lists.

```
<HTML><HEAD><TITLE>Gloves</TITLE></HEAD>
<BODY>
<H2>Gloves</H2>
<UL>
    <LI>Power
    <UL>
        <LI>Sega VR
        <LI>Surgical
        <LI>Elbow length, white
    </UL>
    <LI>Rec
    <UL>
        <LI>Sporting
        <UL>
            <LI>Boxing
            <LI>Driving
            <LI>Biking
        </UL>
        <LI>Evening
        <UL>
            <LI>Elbow length, black
            <LI>Latex
        </UL>
    </UL>
    <LI>Cute
    <UL>
        <LI>Swedish, fake fur
        <LI>Kid
        <LI>Golf
    </UL>
</UL>
</BODY></HTML>
```

5

You can even change the bullet for any single point in an unordered list by using the TYPE attribute in the <LI> tag. For example, the following would display a hollow circle in front of the words Extra and Super, but a solid square in front of the word Special.

```
<UL TYPE="circle">
<LI>Extra
<LI>Super
<LI TYPE="square">Special
</UL>
```

The TYPE attribute also works with ordered lists, but, instead of choosing a type of bullet, you choose the type of numbers or letters to place in front of each item. Figure 5.7 shows how to use roman numerals (TYPE="I"), capital letters (TYPE="A"), and lowercase letters (TYPE="a") along with ordinary numbers in a multi-level list. In Figure 5.8, you can see the resulting nicely formatted outline.

FIGURE 5.6.

*Multi-level unordered
lists are neatly
indented and bulleted
for readability.*

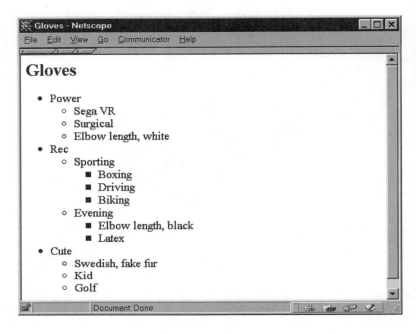

Although Figure 5.7 only uses the TYPE attribute with the <OL> tag, you can also use it for specific <LI> tags within a list (though it's hard to imagine a situation where you would want to). You can also explicitly specify ordinary numbering with TYPE="1", and you can make lowercase roman numerals with TYPE="i".

And here's one more seldom-used but handy-when-you-need-it trick: You can start an ordered list with any number (or letter) with the START attribute. <OL START="3">, for example, starts a numbered list at 3 instead of 1. Individual points can be renumbered with the VALUE attribute (<LI VALUE="12"> for example).

Note that you must always use numbers with the START and VALUE attributes. To make a list that starts with the letter C, for example, you need to type <OL TYPE="A" START="3">.

FIGURE 5.7.

The TYPE attribute lets you make multi-tiered lists with both numbered and lettered points.

```
<HTML><HEAD><TITLE>Document Title</TITLE></HEAD>
<BODY>
<H2>How to Win at Golf</H2>
<OL TYPE="I"><LI>Training
   <OL><LI>Mental prep
      <OL TYPE="A"><LI>Watch PGA on TV religiously
      <LI>Get that computer game with Jack whatsisname
      <LI>Rent "personal victory" subliminal tapes
      </OL>
   <LI>Equipage
      <OL TYPE="A">
      <LI>Make sure your putter has a pro autograph on it
      <LI>Pick up a bargain bag of tees-n-balls at Costco
      </OL>
   <LI>Diet
      <OL TYPE="A"><LI>Avoid baseball or football food
         <OL TYPE="a"><LI>No hotdogs
            <LI>No pretzels
            <LI>No peanuts and Crackerjacks
            </OL>
         <LI>Drink cheap white wine only, no beer
   </OL></OL>
<LI>Pre-game
   <OL><LI>Dress
      <OL TYPE="A">
      <LI>Put on shorts, even if it's freezing
      <LI>Buy a new hat if you lost last time
      </OL>
   <LI>Location and Scheduling
      <OL TYPE="A">
      <LI>Select a course where your spouse won't find you
      <LI>To save on fees, play where your buddy works
      </OL>
   <LI>Opponent
      <OL TYPE="A"><LI>Look for: obesity, femininity,
                              alzheimers, inexperience
      <LI>Shun: suntan, stethescope,
                 strident walk, florida accent
      <LI>Buy opponent as many pre-game drinks as possible
   </OL></OL>
<LI>On the Course
   <OL><LI>Tee first, then develop severe hayfever
   <LI>Drive cart over opponent's ball to degrade aerodynamics
   <LI>Say "fore" just before ball makes contact with opponent
   <LI>Always replace divots when putting
   <LI>Water cooler holes are a good time to correct
      any errors in ball placement
   <LI>Never record strokes taken when opponent is urinating
   </OL></OL>
</BODY></HTML>
```

5

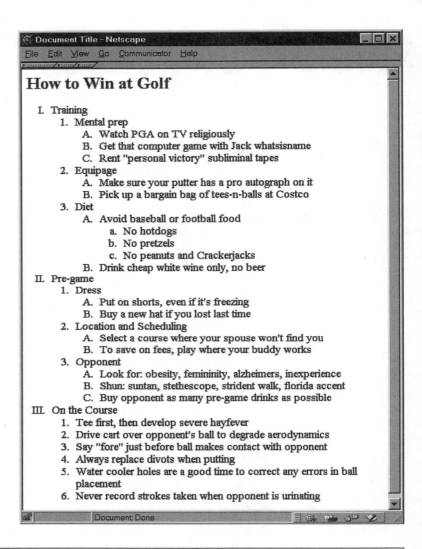

Click the List-O-Mania link, and have some fun trying to figure out what the real titles of the example lists might be, based on the information they contain. Answers are given—as a nested HTML list, of course—at the end of the page.

To Do

Take a list or two of your own, and try to find the best way to present the information so it can be easily understood.

1. Which type of list or combination of list types best suits your list? Use ordered lists only for lists that do actually have a natural order to them. Try to avoid more than seven bullet points in a row in any unordered list, or the list will be hard to read. Use definition lists whenever indenting is sufficient to convey the structure of your information.

2. Start each list (or new level within a multi-tiered list) with an <OL>, <UL>, or <DL>. Start each point within the list with <LI>. Use the TYPE attribute if you want non-standard bullets or letters instead of numbers.

3. If you want a blank line between list items, put a <P> tag next to each <LI> tag.

4. Be very careful to close every <OL> list with </OL>, and make sure that each <UL> or <DL> has a corresponding </UL> or </DL>. Unclosed lists can make pages look very strange, and can even cause some Web browsers not to display the list at all.

Summary

In this hour, you learned that attributes are used to specify options and special behavior of many HTML tags, and you also learned to use the ALIGN attribute to center or right-justify text.

You also found out how to create and combine three basic types of HTML list: ordered lists, unordered lists, and definition lists. Lists can be placed within other lists to create outlines and other complex arrangements of text.

Table 5.1 lists all the tags and attributes covered in this chapter.

TABLE 5.1. HTML TAGS AND ATTRIBUTES COVERED IN HOUR 5.

Tag/Attribute	Function
`<DIV>...</DIV>`	A region of text to be formatted.
`ALIGN="..."`	Align text to CENTER, LEFT, or RIGHT. (Can also be used with `<P>`, `<H1>`, `<H2>`, `<H3>`, and so on.)
`<OL>...</OL>`	An ordered (numbered) list.
Attributes	
`TYPE="..."`	The type of numerals used to label the list. Possible values are A, a, I, i, 1.
`START="..."`	The value with which to start this list.
`<UL>...</UL>`	An unordered (bulleted) list.
Attributes	
`TYPE="..."`	The bullet dingbat used to mark list items. Possible values are DISC, CIRCLE, and SQUARE.
`<LI>`	A list item for use with `<OL>` or `<UL>`.
`TYPE="..."`	The type of bullet or number used to label this item. Possible values are DISC, CIRCLE, SQUARE, A, a, I, i, 1.
`VALUE="..."`	The numeric value this list item should have (affects this item and all below it in `<OL>` lists).
`<DL>...</DL>`	A definition list.
`<DT>`	A definition term, as part of a definition list.
`<DD>`	The corresponding definition to a definition term, as part of a definition list.

Q&A

Q **Most Web pages I've seen on the Internet use `<CENTER>` instead of `<DIV ALIGN="center">`. Should I be using `<CENTER>` to make sure my pages are compatible with older Web browsers?**

A For maximum compatibility, you might prefer to use both the obsolete `<CENTER>` tag and the new `<DIV ALIGN="center">` tag, like this: `<DIV ALIGN="center"><CENTER>This text will be centered in both old and new browsers.</CENTER></DIV>`.

Q I used <UL TYPE="square">, but the bullets still came out round, not square.

A Are you using Netscape Navigator version 2.0 or higher or Microsoft Internet Explorer version 4.0 or higher? Alternate bullet types don't show up in any other Web browsers yet.

Q I've seen pages on the Internet that use three-dimensional looking little balls or other special graphics for bullets. How do they do that?

A That trick is a little bit beyond what this chapter covers. You'll find out how to do it yourself at the end of Chapter 10, "Putting Graphics on a Web Page."

Q How do I "full justify" text, so that both the left and right margins are flush?

A You don't. HTML 4.0 does not support full-justified text. You will be able to full-justify text in the future using style sheets (see Hour 16), although that feature of the style sheet standard isn't supported by any current Web browser.

Workshop

Quiz

1. How would you center everything on an entire page?

2. Write the HTML to create the following ordered list:

   Xylophone

   Y. Yak

   Z. Zebra

3. How would you indent a single word and put a square bullet in front of it?

4. Use a definition list to show that the word "glunch" means "a look of disdain, anger, or displeasure" and that the word "glumpy" means "sullen, morose, or sulky."

5. Write the HTML to create the following indentation effect:

   Apple pie,

   pudding,

   and pancake,

   All begin with an A.

5

Answers

1. Put `<DIV ALIGN="center">` immediately after the `<BODY>` tag at the top of the page, and `</DIV>` just before the `</BODY>` tag at the end of the page.

2. `<OL TYPE="A" START="24"><LI>Xylophone<LI>Yak<LI>Zebra</OL>`

    The following alternative will also do the same thing:

    `<OL TYPE="A"><LI VALUE="24">Xylophone<LI>Yak<LI>Zebra</OL>`

3. `<UL TYPE="square"><LI>Supercalifragilisticexpealidocious</UL>`

    (Putting the `TYPE="square"` in the `<LI>` tag would give the same result because there's only one item in this list.)

4. `<DL>`
    ```
    <DT>glunch<DD>a look of disdain, anger, or displeasure
    <DT>glumpy<DD>sullen, morose, or sulky
    </DL>
    ```

5. `<DL><DT>Apple pie,<DD>pudding,<DL><DD>and pancake</DL>`
    `All begin with an A.</DL>`

    Note that blank lines will appear above and below "and pancake" in Microsoft Internet Explorer 3.0, but not in version 4.0 or any Netscape browser.

Exercise

Try producing an ordered list outlining the information you'd like to put on your Web pages. This will give you practice formatting HTML lists, and also give you a head start on thinking about the issues covered in Part VI, "Building a Web Site."

HOUR 6

Text Formatting and Font Control

In this hour you will learn to control the appearance of the text on your pages. You'll learn to incorporate boldface, italics, superscripts, subscripts, underlining, and "crossed-out" text into your pages, as well as how to choose typefaces and font sizes.

This chapter also shows you how to create special symbols, such as the copyright mark and European language characters such as the *é* in *café*.

There are two completely different approaches to controlling text formatting and alignment in HTML 4.0. The tags you'll learn in this chapter (and the ALIGN attribute from Hour 5, "Text Alignment and Lists") are the "old way," which is actually officially discouraged now. The "new way" is introduced in Hour 16, "Using Style Sheets."

So why learn something that's already out of date? Because in 1998 a large number of people still use Web browsers that don't support style sheets. If you want your pages to look right to everyone, and not just those who use the very latest software technology, you'll need to know everything in this chapter.

All the tricks introduced in this chapter (and the previous one) will work with nearly any Web browser, old or new.

To Do

Before you proceed, you should get some text to work with so you can practice formatting it as you read this chapter.

- Any text will do, but try to find (or type) some text that you want to put onto a Web page. The text from a company brochure or your personal résumé might be a good choice.
- If the text is from a word processor file, be sure to save it as plain text or ASCII text before you add any HTML tags.
- Add the <HTML>, <HEAD>, <TITLE>, and <BODY> tags (discussed in Hour 2, "Create a Web Page Right Now") before you use the tags introduced in this chapter to format the body text.

Boldface, Italics, and Special Formatting

Way back in the age of the typewriter, we were content with plain text and an occasional underline for emphasis. But today, boldface and italicized text have become *de rigueur* in all paper communication. Naturally, you can add bold and italic text to your Web pages too.

For boldface text, put the <B> tag at the beginning of the text and </B> at the end. Similarly, you can make any text italic by enclosing it between <I> and </I>. If you want bold italics, put <B><I> in front of it and </I></B> after it. You can also use italics within headings, but boldface usually won't show in headings because they are already bold.

There are actually two ways to make text display as boldface; the <B> tag and the <STRONG> tag do the same thing in most Web browsers. Likewise, all popular browsers today interpret both <I> and <EM> as italics.

Many purists prefer the <STRONG> and <EM> tags because they imply only that the text should receive special emphasis, rather than dictating exactly how that effect should be achieved. Meanwhile, the vast majority of Web authors use the shorter and easier-to-remember <B> and <I> tags. I'll use <B> and <I> throughout this book, but if you like to be philosophically pure, by all means use <STRONG> and <EM> instead.

In addition to <B>, <I>, <EM>, and <STRONG>, there are several other HTML tags for adding special formatting to text. Table 6.1 summarizes all of them (including the bold-face and italic tags), and Figures 6.1 and 6.2 demonstrate each of them in action.

TABLE 6.1. HTML TAGS THAT ADD SPECIAL FORMATTING TO TEXT.

Tag	Function
<SMALL>	Small text
<BIG>	Big text
<SUP>	Superscript
<SUB>	Subscript
<STRIKE>	Strikeout (draws a line through text)
<U>	Underline
<EM> or <I>	Emphasized (italic) text
<STRONG> or <B>	Strong (boldface) text
<TT>	Monospaced "typewriter" font
<PRE>	Monospaced font, preserving spaces and line breaks

Use the <U> tag sparingly, if at all. People expect underlined text to be a link, and may get confused if you underline text that isn't a link.

6

FIGURE 6.1.

Each of the tags in Table 6.1 is used in this mock advertisement.

```
<HTML><HEAD><TITLE>The Miracle Product</TITLE></HEAD>
<BODY>
<U>New</U>  <SUP>Super</SUP><STRONG>Strength</STRONG>
H<SUB>2</SUB>O  <EM>plus</EM> will
<STRIKE>strike out</STRIKE> any stain, <BIG>big</BIG>
or <SMALL>small</SMALL>.<BR>
Look for new <SUP>Super</SUP><B>Strength</B>
H<SUB>2</SUB>O <I>plus</I> in a stream near you.
<P>
<TT>NUTRITION INFORMATION</TT> (void where prohibited)
<PRE>
                    Calories    Grams     USRDA
                    /Serving    of Fat    Moisture
Regular                3          4        100%
Unleaded               3          2        100%
Organic                2          3         99%
Sugar Free             0          1        110%
</PRE>
</BODY></HTML>
```

FIGURE 6.2.

Here's what all character formatting from Table 6.1 and Figure 6.3 looks like.

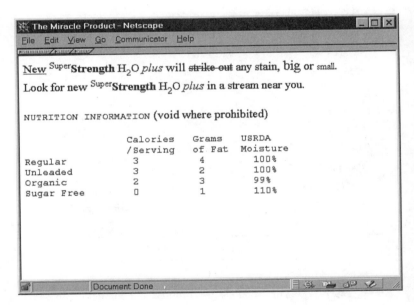

The `<TT>` tag usually changes the typeface to Courier New, a monospaced font. (*Monospaced* means that all the letters are the same width.) However, Web browsers let users change the monospaced `<TT>` font to the typeface of their choice (under Options, General Preferences, Fonts in Netscape Navigator 3.0 and View, Options, General, Font Settings in Microsoft Internet Explorer 3.0). The monospaced font may not even be monospaced for some users, though the vast majority of people just stick with the standard fonts that their browsers come set up with.

The `<PRE>` tag also causes text to appear in the monospaced font, but it also does something more unique and useful. As you learned in Hour 2, multiple spaces and line breaks are normally ignored in HTML files. But `<PRE>` causes exact spacing and line breaks to be preserved. For example, without `<PRE>`, the text at the end of Figure 6.3 would look like the following:

```
Calories Grams USRDA /Serving of Fat Moisture Regular
3 4 100% Unleaded 3 2 100% Organic 2 3 99% Sugar Free 0 1 110%
```

Even if you added `<BR>` tags at the end of every line, the columns wouldn't line up properly. However, when you put `<PRE>` at the beginning and `</PRE>` at the end, the columns line up properly and no `<BR>` tags are needed.

There are fancier ways to make columns of text line up, and you'll learn all about them in Hour 15, "Advanced Layout with Tables." The `<PRE>` tag gives you a quick and easy way to preserve the alignment of any monospaced text files you might want to transfer to a Web page with a minimum of effort.

> You can use the `<PRE>` tag as a quick way to insert extra vertical space between paragraphs. For example, to put several blank lines between the words Up and Down, you could type:
>
> ```
> Up<PRE>
> </PRE>Down
> ```

Font Size and Color

The `<BIG>`, `<SMALL>`, and `<TT>` tags give you some rudimentary control over the size and appearance of the text on your pages. Generally, you should try sticking to those tags until you are ready for the advanced font formatting controls discussed in Hour 16.

However, there are times when you'd just like a bit more control over the size and appearance of your text while maintaining as much compatibility with older Web browsers as possible. For those times, you can use the officially discouraged but widely used `<FONT>` tag.

For example, the following HTML will change the size and color of some text on a page:

```
<FONT SIZE=5 COLOR="purple">This text will be big and purple.</FONT>
```

6

The SIZE attribute can take any value from 1 (tiny) to 7 (fairly big), with 3 being the default size.

The COLOR attribute can take any of the following standard color names: black, white, red, green, blue, yellow, aqua, fuchsia, gray, lime, maroon, purple, navy, olive, silver, or teal.

The actual size and exact color of the fonts will depend on each reader's screen resolution and preference settings, but you can be assured that SIZE=6 will be a lot bigger than SIZE=2, and that COLOR="red" will certainly show its fire.

You'll learn more about controlling the color of the text on your pages in Hour 11, "Custom Backgrounds and Colors." That hour also shows you how to create your own custom colors and control the color of text links.

> Here's a time-saving tag for setting the overall size of all text in a document. Body text is usually size 3, but you can put <BASEFONT SIZE=4> or <BASEFONT SIZE=2> just after the <BODY> tag to make it a bit bigger or smaller. The size of all headings will also be relative to the <BASEFONT SIZE>. This tag can't take any attributes other than SIZE, and doesn't require a closing </BASEFONT> tag.

Choosing a Typeface

With the 3.0 and 4.0 versions of both Navigator and Internet Explorer, Netscape and Microsoft have added another extremely powerful form of font control: the <FONT FACE> attribute. This allows you to specify the actual typeface that should be used to display text—and has been the source of much rejoicing among Webmasters who are *awfully* sick of Times and Courier!

The page in Figures 6.3 and 6.4 uses these font controls to present a quick but colorful history lesson. Notice how <FONT> tags can be nested inside one another, changing some aspects of the font's appearance while leaving others the same; for example, even when <FONT> tags change the size and color of the letters in *A HISTORY OF EVERYTHING*. the typeface specified in the first <FONT> tag still applies. Likewise, the <FONT> tags that make small capitals do not change the color so the entire line ends up maroon.

The following is the code to set the typeface used for most of the text in Figure 6.3:

```
<FONT FACE="Lucida Sans Unicode, Arial, Helvetica">
```

FIGURE 6.3.

*The <FONT> tags give
you control over
the size, color, and
typeface of any text.*

```
<HTML><HEAD><TITLE>A History</TITLE></HEAD>
<BODY>
<FONT FACE="Lucida Sans Unicode, Arial, Helvetica">
<FONT SIZE=5 COLOR="green">
A H<FONT SIZE=4><B>ISTORY OF</B></FONT>
E<FONT SIZE=4><B>VERYTHING</B></FONT>
</FONT><BR>
<FONT FACE="Lucida Sans">
It starts with a <B>bang</B>.</FONT> Then everything
<B>inflates</B> like a super-balloon tied up with
<B>super-strings</B>, until the whole mess curdles into
millions of <B>milky ways</B>. <B>Starlight</B> hits the
<B>volcanic rocks</B>, and cooks up some tasty
<B>double-helix</B> treats. They get eaten by each other,
the <B>fittest</B> (and least tasty) <B>survive</B>, a
<B>meteor</B> kills the <B>big</B> ones, and when it all
<B>freezes over</B> the <B>smart</B> ones move into
<B>caves</B> and start a <B>fire</B>. Growing <B>grass</B>
turns out to be more fun than chasing <B>woolly mammoths</B>,
so the <B>agriculturalists</B> start a <B>revolution</B>.
The <B>pharoahs, ceasars, kings,</B> and <B>fuhrers</B>
mostly win but eventually lose, so the <B>scientists</B>
and <B>industrialists</B> revolt this time. <B>Japan</B>
gets <B>nuked</B> and takes over the <B>world economy,</B>
the <B>Berlin wall</B> and <B>Soviets</B> fall, and the
<B>United States</B> all sue <B>Microsoft</B> over the
<B>Internet</B>.</FONT>
<FONT FACE="Lucida Sans"><I>The end.</I></FONT>
</BODY></HTML>
```

If Netscape Navigator or Microsoft Internet Explorer can find a font named Lucida Sans Unicode on a user's system, that font is used. Otherwise, the browser will look for Arial or Helvetica. Figure 6.5 shows how the page would look on a computer that didn't have Lucida Sans Unicode or Lucida Sans installed, but did have the Arial font.

If none of those fonts could be found, the browser would display the text using the default font (usually Times New Roman). Browsers other than Navigator and Internet Explorer will ignore the <FONT FACE> attribute and display the fonts they always use.

Since only fonts that each user happens to have on his or her system will show up, you have no real control over which fonts appear on your pages. Furthermore, the exact spelling of the font names is important, and many common fonts go by several slightly different names. This means that about the only truly reliable choices are Arial (on Windows machines) and Helvetica (on Macintoshes). Don't be afraid to specify other fonts, but make sure your pages still look acceptable in Times New Roman as well.

You'll find many additional tips on using typefaces in Hour 16.

6

FIGURE 6.4.

If you have the Lucida Sans Unicode and Lucida Sans fonts installed on your computer, they will be used to display the page in Figure 6.5.

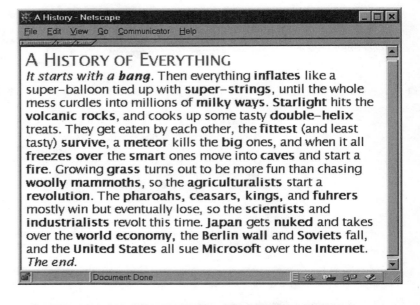

FIGURE 6.5.

If you didn't have Lucida Sans Unicode and Lucida Sans fonts installed, the text from Figure 6.3 would appear in Arial and Times New Roman.

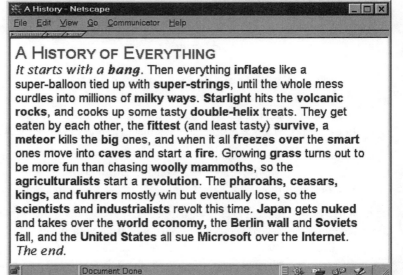

There are currently two competing ways to "embed" fonts into a Web page, so that fonts for a page will automatically be sent along with the page itself.

Bitstream's TrueDoc font-embedding works with both Netscape Navigator 4.0 and Microsoft Internet Explorer 4.0, supports all TrueType and PostScript fonts, and is both secure and reliable. Several commercial programs are available that allow you to create TrueDoc font files for your Web pages, and Bitstream also offers several free fonts for you to use online. You can find out more about TrueDoc at www.truedoc.com.

Microsoft also offers its own proprietary font-embedding technology, which unfortunately only works with their own Web browser. Even more unfortunately, their technology makes it very easy for people to illegally pirate your fonts and use them for non-Web related applications. For these reasons, industry acceptance of Microsoft's font-embedding solution has been lukewarm at best. If you'd like to know more about it anyway, visit www.microsoft.com/truetype for details.

To see a list of the most common TrueType fonts and to find out which of them are installed on your computer, visit the 24-Hour HTML Café at

http://24hourHTMLcafe.com/hour6/

You'll also find some whimsical examples of how text formatting can liven up a page.

Special Characters

Most fonts now include special characters for European languages, such as the accented *é* in *café*. There are also a few mathematical symbols and special punctuation marks such as the circular bullet (•).

You can insert these special characters at any point in an HTML document by looking up the appropriate codes in Table 6.1, or in the complete list of character entities in Appendix D, "HTML Character Entities." You'll find an even more extensive list of codes for multiple character sets online at

http://www.w3.org/TR/REC-html40/sgml/entities.html

For example, the word *café* would look like the following:

Café

6

Each symbol also has a mnemonic name that might be easier to remember than the number. The following is another way to write *café*:

Café

Notice that there are also codes for the < > (angle brackets), " (quotation), and & (ampersand) in Table 6.1. You need to use the codes if you want these symbols to appear on your pages, because the Web browser will otherwise interpret them as HTML commands.

In Figures 6.6 and 6.7, several more of the symbols from Table 6.1 and Appendix D are shown in use.

FIGURE 6.6.

Special character codes begin with & and end with ;.

```
<HTML><HEAD><TITLE>Punchuation Lines</TITLE></HEAD>
<BODY>
Q: What should you do when a British banker picks a
fight with you?<BR>
A: &pound; some &cent;&cent; into him.
<HR>
Q: What do you call it when a judge takes part of a law
off the books?<BR>
A: &sect; violence.
<HR>
Q: What did the football coach get from the locker room
vending machine in the middle of the game?<BR>
A: A &frac14; back at &frac12; time.
<HR>
Q: How hot did it get when the police detective
interrogated the mathematician?<BR>
A: x&sup3;&deg;
<HR>
Q: What does a punctilious plagarist do?<BR>
A: &copy;
<HR>
</BODY></HTML>
```

Looking for the copyright © or registered trademark ® symbols? The codes you need are © and ® respectively.

To create an unregistered trademark ™ symbol, use ^{TM} or <SMALL>^{TM}</SMALL> for a smaller version.

FIGURE 6.7.

This is how the HTML page in Figure 6.6 will look in most (not all) Web browsers.

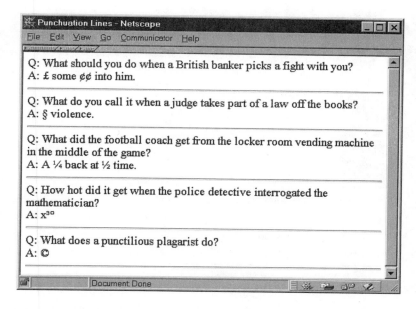

TABLE 6.2. IMPORTANT ENGLISH-LANGUAGE SPECIAL CHARACTERS (SEE APPENDIX D FOR A COMPLETE LIST).

Character	Numeric Code	Code Name	Description
"	&#34;	&quot;	Quotation mark
&	&#38;	&amp;	Ampersand
<	&#60;	&lt;	Less than
>	&#62;	&gt;	Greater than
¢	&#162;	&cent;	Cent sign
£	&#163;	&pound;	Pound sterling
¦	&#166;	¦ or brkbar;	Broken vertical bar
§	&#167;	&sect;	Section sign
©	&#169;	&copy;	Copyright
®	&#174;	&reg;	Registered trademark
°	&#176;	&deg;	Degree sign
±	&#177;	&plusmn;	Plus or minus
^{2}	&#178;	&sup2;	Superscript two
^{3}	&#179;	&sup3;	Superscript three

continues

6

TABLE 6.2. CONTINUED

Character	Numeric Code	Code Name	Description
·	·	·	Middle dot
¹	¹	¹	Superscript one
¼	¼	¼	Fraction one-fourth
½	½	½	Fraction one-half
¾	¾	¾	Fraction three-fourths
Æ	Æ	Æ	Capital AE ligature
æ	æ	æ	Small ae ligature
É	É	É	Accented capital E
é	é	é	Accented small e
×	×		Multiplication sign
÷	÷		Division sign

Some older Web browsers will not display many of the special characters in Table 6.1. Some fonts also may not include all of these characters.

Summary

This hour showed you how to make text appear as boldface, italic, or with superscripts, subscripts, underlines, crossed-out text, special symbols, and accented letters. You saw how to make everything line up properly in preformatted passages of monospaced text and how to control the size, color, and typeface of any section of text on a Web page.

Table 6.2 summarizes the tags and attributes discussed in this hour. Don't feel like you have to memorize all these tags, by the way! That's why you have this book: so you can look them up when you need them. Remember that all the HTML tags are listed in Appendix C, "Complete HTML 4.0 Quick Reference," and all the special character codes can be found in Appendix D.

TABLE 6.3 HTML TAGS AND ATTRIBUTES COVERED IN HOUR 6.

Tag/Attribute	Function
<EM>...</EM>	Emphasis (usually italic).
<STRONG>...</STRONG>	Stronger emphasis (usually bold).
<B>...</B>	Boldface text.

Tag/Attribute	Function
`<I>...</I>`	Italic text.
`<TT>...</TT>`	Typewriter (monospaced) font.
`<PRE>...</PRE>`	Preformatted text (exact line endings and spacing will be preserved—usually rendered in a monospaced font).
`<BIG>...</BIG>`	Text is slightly larger than normal.
`<SMALL>...</SMALL>`	Text is slightly smaller than normal.
`<SUB>...</SUB>`	Subscript.
`<SUP>...</SUP>`	Superscript.
`<STRIKE>...</STRIKE>`	Puts a strikethrough line in text.
`<FONT>...</FONT>`	Controls the appearance of the enclosed text.
Attributes:	
`SIZE="..."`	The size of the font, from 1 to 7. Default is 3. Can also be specified as a value relative to the current size; for example, +2 or -1.
`COLOR="..."`	Changes the color of the text.
`FACE="..."`	Name of font to use if it can be found on the user's system. Commas can separate multiple font names, and the first font on the list that can be found will be used.
`<BASEFONT>`	Sets the default size of the font for the current page.
Attributes:	
`SIZE="..."`	The default size of the font, from 1 to 7.

Q&A

Q **Other books talk about some text-formatting tags that you didn't cover in this chapter, such as `<CODE>` and `<ADDRESS>`. Shouldn't I know about them?**

A There are a number of tags in HTML to indicate what kind of information is contained in some text. The `<ADDRESS>` tag, for example, was supposed be put around addresses. The only visible effect of `<ADDRESS>` in most browsers, however, is making the text italic. So Web page authors today usually just use the `<I>` tag instead. Similarly, `<CODE>` and `<KBD>` do essentially the same thing as `<TT>`. You may also read about `<VAR>`, `<SAMP>`, or `<DFN>` in some older HTML references, but nobody uses them in ordinary Web pages.

6

One tag that you might occasionally find handy is `<BLOCKQUOTE>`, which indents all the text until the closing `</BLOCKQUOTE>`. Some Web page authors use `<BLOCKQUOTE>` on all or part of a page as a quick and easy way to widen the left and right margins.

Q How do I find out the exact name for a font I have on my computer?

A On a Windows or Macintosh computer, open the control panel and click the Fonts folder. The TrueType fonts on your system will be listed. Use the exact spelling of font names when specifying them in the `<FONT FACE>` tag. To find the name of PostScript fonts in Windows if you use Adobe Type Manager, run the ATM Control Panel.

Q How do I put Kanji, Arabic, Chinese, and other non-European characters on my pages?

A First of all, everyone who you want to be able to read these characters on your pages must have the appropriate language fonts installed. They must also have selected that language character set and font under Options, General Preferences, Fonts in Netscape Navigator or View, Options, General, Fonts in Microsoft Internet Explorer. You can use the Character Map accessory in Windows 95 (or a similar program in other operating systems) to get the numerical codes for each character in any language font. If the character you want has a code of 214, use `&#214;` to place it on a Web page.

The best way to include a short message in an Asian language (such as `We speak Tamil—Call us!`) is to include it as a graphics image. That way everyone will see it, even if they use English as their primary language for Web browsing.

Workshop

Quiz

1. Write the HTML to produce the following:

   Come for ~~cheap~~ free H$_2$O on May 7th at 9:00PM

2. What's the difference between the following two lines of HTML?

   ```
   Deep <TT>S p  a   a  c e</TT> Quest
   Deep <PRE>S p  a   a  c e</PRE> Quest
   ```

3. How would you say, "We're having our annual Nixon Impeachment Day SALE today," in normal-sized blue text, but with the word *SALE* at the largest possible size in bright red?

4. How do you say "© 1996, Webwonks Inc." on a Web page?

Answers

1. ```
   Come for <STRIKE>cheap</STRIKE> free H<SUB>2</SUB>O on May
   7<SUP><U>th</U></SUP> at 9:00<SMALL>PM</SMALL>
   ```

2. The line using `<TT>` will look like this:

   Deep S p a c e Quest

   The line using `<PRE>` will produce the following three lines of text on the Web page.

   ```
   Deep
   S p   a    a   c e[sr]
   Quest
   ```

3. ```
   <FONT COLOR="blue">We're having our annual Nixon Impeachment Day
   <FONT COLOR="red" SIZE=7>SALE</FONT> today!</FONT>
   ```

4. ```
   &copy; 1996, Webwonks Inc.
   ```

   The following would also produce the same result:

   ```
   &#169; 1996, Webwonks Inc.
   ```

Exercises

- Professional typesetters use small capitals for the "AM" and "PM" in clock times. They also use superscripts for dates like the "7th" or "1st". Use the `<SMALL>` and `<SUP>` tags to typeset important dates and times correctly on your Web pages.

- Go through all the Web pages you've created so far, and ask yourself if they would look significantly better if you used a different typeface or font color. Use the `<FONT>` tag to enhance the pages that would benefit from it most, and leave the rest alone.

6
   ```

Hour 7

Email Links and Links within a Page

In Hour 3, "Linking to Other Web Pages," you learned to use the <A> tag to create links between HTML pages. This hour shows you how to use the same tag to allow readers to jump between different parts of a single page. This gives you a convenient way to put a table of contents at the top of a long document, or put a link at the bottom of a page that returns you to the top. You'll see how to link to a specific point within a separate page, too.

This hour also tells you how to embed a live link to your email address in a Web page, so readers can instantly compose and send messages to you from within most Web browsers.

Using Named Anchors

Figure 7.1 demonstrates the use of intra-page links. To see how such links are made, take a look at the first <A> tag in Figure 7.1:

```
<A NAME="top"></A>
```

This is a different use of the <A> anchor tag; all it does is give a name to the specific point on the page where the tag occurs. The </A> tag must be included, but no text is necessary between <A> and </A>.

Now look at the last <A> tag in Figure 7.1:

```
<A HREF="#top">Return to Index.</A>
```

The # symbol means that the word "top" refers to a named anchor point within the current document, rather than a separate page. So when a reader clicks Return to Index, the Web browser will display the part of the page starting with the <A NAME="top"> tag.

Here's an easy way to remember the difference between these two different types of <A> tags: <A HREF> is what you click, and <A NAME> is where you go when you click there.

New Term An *anchor* is a named point on a Web page. The same tag is used to create Hypertext links and anchors (which explains why the tag is named <A>).

Similarly, each of the <A HREF> links in Figure 7.1 makes an underlined link leading to a corresponding <A NAME> anchor. Clicking the letter *B* under Alphabetical Index in Figure 7.2, for instance, takes you to the part of the page shown in Figure 7.3.

To Do

Now that you have several pages of your own linked together, you might want to add an index at the top of your home page so people can easily get an overview of what your pages have to offer.

- Place <A NAME> tags in front of each major topic on your home page or any longish page you make.

- Copy each of the major topic headings to a list at the top of the page, and enclose each heading in an <A HREF> linking to the corresponding <A NAME> tag.

One of the most common uses for the <A NAME> tag is creating an alphabetical index. The bad news for anyone with an alphabetical list that they want to index is that typing out 26 links to 26 anchors is a rather tedious endeavor. The good news is that I've already done it for you and dropped off the indexed page at the 24 Hour HTML Café:

```
http://24hourHTMLcafe.com/hour7/
```

Click the Instant Alphabetical Index link and select File, Save As to save the document to your hard drive. You can then cut-and-paste your own alphabetical information after each letter.

FIGURE 7.1.

An <A> tag with a NAME attribute acts as a marker, so <A> tags with HREF attributes can link to that specific point on a page.

```
<HTML><HEAD><TITLE>Alphabetical Shakespeare</TITLE></HEAD>
<BODY>
<A NAME="top"></A>
<H2>First Lines of Every Shakespearean Sonnet</H2>
Don't ya just hate when you go a-courting, and there you are
down on one knee about to rattle off a totally romantic
Shakespearean sonnet, and zap! You space it. <I>"Um... It was,
uh... I think it started with a B..."</I><P>
Well, appearest thou no longer the dork. Simply pull this
page up on your laptop computer, click on the first letter of
the sonnet you want, and get an instant reminder of the first
line to get you started. <I>"Beshrew that heart that makes my
heart to groan..."</I> She's putty in your hands.<P>
<H3 ALIGN="center">
Alphabetical Index<BR>(click on a letter)<BR>
<A HREF="#A">A</A> <A HREF="#B">B</A> <A HREF="#C">C</A>
<A HREF="#D">D</A> <A HREF="#E">E</A> <A HREF="#F">F</A>
<A HREF="#G">G</A> <A HREF="#H">H</A> <A HREF="#I">I</A>
<A HREF="#J">J</A> <A HREF="#K">K</A> <A HREF="#L">L</A>
<A HREF="#M">M</A> <A HREF="#N">N</A> <A HREF="#O">O</A>
<A HREF="#P">P</A> <A HREF="#Q">Q</A> <A HREF="#R">R</A>
<A HREF="#S">S</A> <A HREF="#T">T</A> <A HREF="#U">U</A>
<A HREF="#V">V</A> <A HREF="#W">W</A> <A HREF="#X">X</A>
<A HREF="#Y">Y</A> <A HREF="#Z">Z</A>
</H3><P><HR><P>
<A NAME="A"></A><H2>A</H2>
A woman's face with nature's own hand painted,<BR>
Accuse me thus, that I have scanted all,<BR>
Against my love shall be as I am now<BR>
Against that time (if ever that time come)<BR>
Ah wherefore with infection should he live,<BR>
Alack what poverty my muse brings forth,<BR>
Alas 'tis true, I have gone here and there,<BR>
As a decrepit father takes delight,<BR>
As an unperfect actor on the stage,<BR>
As fast as thou shalt wane so fast thou grow'st,<BR>
<P><A HREF="#top"><I>Return to Index.</I></A><HR>
<A NAME="B"></A><H2>B</H2>
Be wise as thou art cruel, do not press<BR>
Being your slave what should I do but tend,<BR>
Beshrew that heart that makes my heart to groan<BR>
Betwixt mine eye and heart a league is took,<BR>
But be contented when that fell arrest,<BR>
But do thy worst to steal thy self away,<BR>
But wherefore do not you a mightier way<BR>
<P><A HREF="#top"><I>Return to Index.</I></A><HR>
```

...Sonnets starting with C through X go here...

```
<A NAME="Y"></A><H2>Y</H2>
Your love and pity doth th' impression fill,<BR>
<P><A HREF="#top"><I>Return to Index.</I></A><HR>
<A NAME="Z"></A><H2>Z</H2>
(No sonnets start with Z.)<BR>
<P><A HREF="#top">Return to Index.</A><HR><P>
</BODY></HTML>
```

7

FIGURE 7.2.

The <A NAME> tags in Figure 7.1 don't appear at all on the Web page. The <A HREF> tags appear as underlined links.

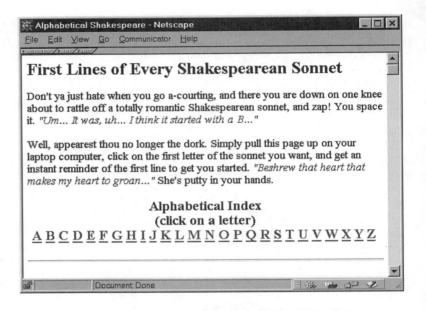

FIGURE 7.3.

Clicking the letter B in Figure 7.2 takes you down to the appropriate section of the same page.

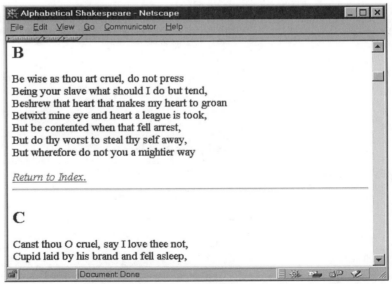

Linking to a Specific Part of Another Page

You can even link to a named anchor on another page by including the address or name of that page followed by # and the anchor name.

Figure 7.4 shows several examples, such as the following:

```
<A HREF="sonnets.htm#131">You're ugly and smelly, but I still
love you.</A>
```

Clicking You're ugly and smelly, but I still love you. (in Figure 7.5) will bring up the page named sonnets.htm, and goes directly to the point where
<A NAME="131"></A> occurs on that page (see Figure 7.6). (The HTML for sonnets.htm is not listed here because it is quite long. It's just a bunch of sappy old sonnets with anchor name tags in front of each one.) Note that anchor names can be numbers, words, or any combination of letters and numbers. In this case, I used the sonnet number.

FIGURE 7.4.

To link to a specific part of another page, put both the page address and anchor name in the <A HREF> tag.

```
<HTML><HEAD><TITLE>Topical Shakespeare</TITLE></HEAD>
<BODY>
<H2>Shakespearean Sonnets for Every Occasion</H2>
Choose your message for a genuine Shakespearean sonnet which
expresses your feelings with tact and grace.
<P><I>
<A HREF="sonnets.htm#131">
You're bossy, ugly and smelly, but I still love you.</A><BR>
<A HREF="sonnets.htm#2">
Life is short. Let's make babies.</A><BR>
<A HREF="sonnets.htm#140">
Say you love me or I'll tell lies about you.</A><BR>
<A HREF="sonnets.htm#31">
You remind me of all my old girlfriends.</A><BR>
<A HREF="sonnets.htm#57">
You abuse me, but you know I love it.</A><BR>
<A HREF="sonnets.htm#141">
I think you're hideous, but I'm desperate.</A><BR>
<A HREF="sonnets.htm#150">
You don't deserve me, but take me anyway.</A><BR>
<A HREF="sonnets.htm#36">
I feel bad about leaving, but see ya later.</A></I>
</BODY></HTML>
```

Be sure to only include the # symbol in <A HREF> link tags. Don't put a # symbol in the <A NAME> tag, or links to that name won't work.

7

FIGURE 7.5.

The page listed in Figure 7.4. All the links on this page go to different parts of a separate page named sonnets.htm.

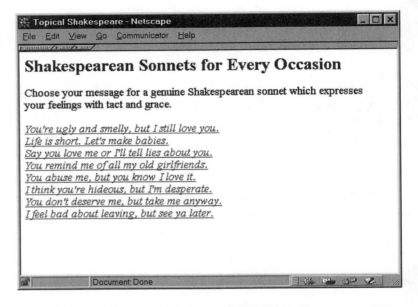

FIGURE 7.6.

Clicking You're ugly and smelly, but I still love you. *in Figure 7.4 brings you directly to this part of the* sonnets.htm *page. (HTML for this page isn't shown.)*

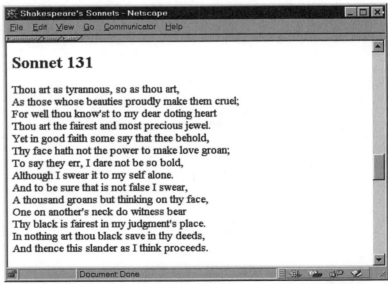

Linking Your Email Address into a Web Page

In addition to linking between pages and between parts of a single page, the <A> tag allows you to link to your email address. This is a the simplest way to enable readers of your Web pages to "talk back" to you. Of course, you could just tell them your email address and trust them to type it into whatever email program they use if they want to say something to you. But you can make it almost completely effortless for them to send you a message by providing a clickable link to your email address instead.

An HTML link to my email address would look like the following:

```
<A HREF="mailto:dicko@netletter.com">Send me an e-mail message.</A>
```

The words Send me an e-mail message will appear just like any other <A> link (as underlined text in the color you set for links in the LINK or VLINK attributes of the <BODY> tag). In most Web browsers, when someone clicks the link, he or she gets a window in which to type a message that will be immediately sent to you.

If you want people to see your actual email address (so they can make note of it or send a message using a different email program), type it both in the HREF attribute and as part of the message between the <A> and </A> tags.

For example, the HTML in Figure 7.7 is an email directory page for a club of aging German philosophers. (Yes, I know, Wittgenstein's English. But he was born in Austria, so they let him in the club anyway.) The resulting page in Figure 7.8 lists the club officers with a clickable email link for each.

FIGURE 7.7.

Links to email addresses use the same <A> tag as links to Web pages.

```
<HTML><HEAD><TITLE>GPC E-Mail Directory</TITLE></HEAD>
<BODY>
<H2>German Philosopher's Club<BR>E-Mail Directory</H2>
<UL>
<LI><A HREF="mailto:manny@netletter.com">
    <I>Emmanuel Kant, President</I>
    <BR>manny@netletter.com</A><P>
<LI><A HREF="mailto:@martynetletter.com">
    <I>Martin Heidegger, Secretary</I>
    <BR>marty@netletter.com</A><P>
<LI><A HREF="mailto:will-fred@netletter.com">
    <I>Georg Wilhelm Friedrick Hegel, Senior Officer</I>
    <BR>will-fred@netletter.com</A><P>
<LI><A HREF="mailto:fred-will@netletter.com">
    <I>Friedrick Wilhelm Nietzche, Junior Officer</I>
    <BR>fred-will@netletter.com</A><P>
<LI><A HREF="mailto:jj@netletter.com">
    <I>Ludwig J.J. Wittgenstein, Administrative Assistant</I>
    <BR>jj@netletter.com</A><P>
</UL>
</BODY></HTML>
```

7

FIGURE **7.8.**

FIGURE **7.8.**

The `mailto:` *links in Figure 7.6 look just like* `http://` *links on the page.*

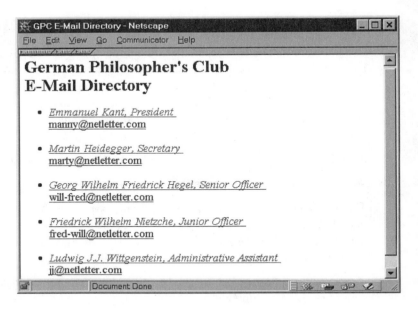

When someone clicks the top link in Figure 7.8 in Netscape Navigator (or any other e-mail capable Web browser), a separate window (see Figure 7.9) will open with spaces for him or her to enter a subject line and email message. The email address from the link will be automatically entered, and he or she can simply click the mail button to send the message.

FIGURE **7.9.**

Clicking the top link in Figure 7.8 brings up this email window within Netscape Navigator.

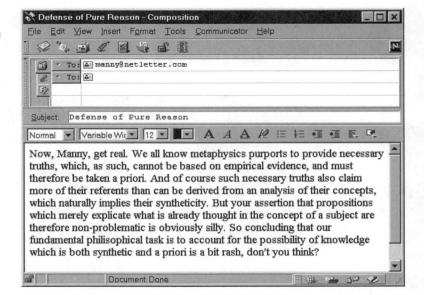

It is customary to put an email link to the Web page author at the bottom of every Web page. Not only does this make it easy for customers or others to contact you, it also gives them a way to tell you about any problems with the page that your testing may have missed.

Summary

This hour has shown you two uses for the <A> tag not covered in Hour 3. You saw how to create named anchor points within a page and how to create links to a specific anchor. You also saw how to link to your email address so readers can easily send you messages.

Table 7.1 summarizes the two attributes of the <A> tag discussed in this hour.

TABLE 7.1. HTML TAGS AND ATTRIBUTES COVERED IN HOUR 7.

Tag/Attribute	Function
<A>...</A>	With the HREF attribute, creates a link to another document or anchor; with the NAME attribute, creates an anchor that can be linked to
	Attributes:
HREF="..."	The address of the document and/or anchor point to which to link
NAME="..."	The name for this anchor point in the document

Q&A

Q Can I put both HREF and NAME in the same <A> tag? Would I want to for any reason?

A You can, and it might save you some typing if you have a named anchor point and a link right next to each other. But it's generally better to use <A HREF> and <A NAME> separately to avoid confusion because they play very different roles in an HTML document.

Q What happens if I accidentally spell the name of an anchor wrong, or forget to put the # in front of it?

A If you link to an anchor name that doesn't exist within a page (or you misspell the anchor name), the link just goes to the top of that page.

7

Q When I test my intra-page links with Netscape Navigator 2.0 or 3.0, they don't seem to work quite right. Was there a change in the HTML standard or something?

A   The proper HTML hasn't changed, but there was a known bug in some older versions of Navigator that prevented links to anchors from working correctly in some (not all) situations. There's not much you can do about that other than encouraging people to upgrade to the latest version of their Web browser.

Q What if I use a different company to handle my email than my Web pages? Will my email links still work?

A   Yes. You can put any email address on the Internet into a link, and it will work fine. The only situation where email links won't work is when the person who clicks the link hasn't set up the email part of his or her Web browser properly, or is using an older version that isn't capable of sending email.

Workshop

Quiz

1. Write the HTML to make it possible for someone clicking the words *About the authors* at the top of the page to skip down to a list of credits at the bottom of the page.

2. Suppose your company has three employees, and you want to create a company directory page listing some information about each of them. Write the HTML for that page and the HTML to link to one of the employees from another page.

3. If your email address is bon@soir.com, how would you make the text *goodnight greeting* into a link that people can click to compose and send you an email message?

Answers

1. At the top of the page, put

   ```
   <A HREF="#credits">About the authors</A>
   ```

   And at the beginning of the credits section, put

   ```
   <A NAME="credits"></A>
   ```

2. The company directory page would look like the following:

   ```
   <HTML><HEAD><TITLE>Company Directory</TITLE></HEAD>
   <BODY><H1>Company Directory</H1>
   <A NAME="jones"><H2>Jane Jones</H2>
   Ms. Jones is our accountant... etc.
   ```

```
<A NAME="smith"><H2>Sam Smith</H2>
Mr. Smith is our salesman.. etc.
<A NAME="bharwaniji"><H2>R.K. Satjiv Bharwahniji</H2>
Mr. Bharwahniji is our president... etc.
</BODY></HTML>
```

A link to one employee's information from another page would look like the following (if the above file was named `directory.htm`):

```
<A HREF="directory.htm#bharwaniji">About our president</A>
```

3. Type the following on your Web page:

```
Send me a <A HREF="mailto:bon@soir.com">goodnight greeting</A>!
```

Exercises

- When you link back to your home page from other pages, you might want to skip some of the introductory information at the top of the home page. Using a link to a named anchor just below that introductory information will avoid presenting it to people who have already read it, making your pages seem less repetitive. Also, if any pages on your site are longer than two screens of information when displayed in a Web browser, consider putting a link at the bottom of the page back up to the top.

- Look through your Web pages and consider whether there are any places in the text where you'd like to make it easy for people to respond to what you're saying. Include a link right there to your email address. You can never provide too many opportunities for people to contact you and tell you what they need or think about your products, especially if you're running a business.

7

HOUR 8

Creating HTML Forms

Up to this point, everything in this book has focused on getting information out to others. (Email links, introduced in Hour 7, "Email Links and Links Within a Page," are the one exception.) But HTML is a two-way street; you can use your Web pages to gather information from the people who read them as well.

Web forms allow you to receive feedback, orders, or other information from the readers of your Web pages. If you've ever used a Web search engine such as HotBot or Yahoo!, you're familiar with HTML forms. Product order forms are also an extremely popular use of forms.

This chapter shows you how to create your own forms and the basics of how to handle form submissions.

NEW TERM An HTML *form* is part of a Web page that includes areas where readers can enter information to be sent back to you, the publisher of the Web page.

Creating a Form

Every form must begin with a `<FORM>` tag, which can be located anywhere in the body of the HTML document. The `<FORM>` tag normally has two attributes, METHOD and ACTION:

```
<FORM METHOD="post" ACTION="mailto:me@mysite.com">
```

Nowadays, the METHOD is almost always "post", which means to send the form entry results as a document. (In some special situations, you may need to use METHOD="get", which submits the results as part of the URL header instead. For example, "get" is sometimes used when submitting queries to search engines from a Web form. If you're not yet an expert on forms, just use "post"—unless someone tells you to do otherwise.)

The ACTION attribute specifies the address to which to send the form data. You have two options here:

- You can type mailto: followed by your email address, and the form data will be send directly to you whenever someone fills out the form.
- You can type the location of a form-processing program or script on the Web server computer, and the form data will then be sent to that program. You'll read more about this option at the end of this hour. For now, however, we'll just use mailto: because it's simpler.

The form in Figures 8.1 and 8.2 includes every type of input you can currently use on HTML forms (with one exception: the `<BUTTON>` tag is discussed in Hour 19, "Web Page Scripting for Non-Programmers"). Figure 8.3 shows how the form in Figure 8.2 might look after someone fills it out. Refer to these figures as you read the following explanations of each type of input element.

Notice that some of the text in Figures 8.2 and 8.3 is monospaced, meaning that every letter is the same width. Monospaced text makes it easy to line up a form input box with the box above or below it and can make your forms look neater. To use monospaced text in all or part of a form, enclose the text between `<PRE>` and `</PRE>` tags. Using these tags also relieves you from having to put `<BR>` at the end of every line because the `<PRE>` tag puts a line break on the page at every line break in the HTML document.

FIGURE 8.1.

All parts of a form must fall between the <FORM> *and* </FORM> *tags.*

8

```
<HTML><HEAD><TITLE>Guest Book</TITLE></HEAD>
<BODY>
<H1>My Guest Book</H1>
Please let me know what you think of my Web pages. Thanks!
<FORM METHOD="POST" ACTION="mailto:me@mysite.com">
<INPUT TYPE="hidden" NAME="noseeum"
VALUE="the user won't see this">
<PRE>
   What is your name? <INPUT TYPE="text"
NAME="fullname" SIZE=25>
Your e-mail address: <INPUT TYPE="text"
NAME="e-address" SIZE=25>
</PRE>
Check all that apply:<BR>
<INPUT TYPE="checkbox" NAME="likeit" CHECKED>
I really like your Web site.<BR>
<INPUT TYPE="checkbox" NAME="best">
One of the best sites I've seen.<BR>
<INPUT TYPE="checkbox" NAME="envy">
I sure wish my pages looked as good as yours.<BR>
<INPUT TYPE="checkbox" NAME="love">
I think I'm in love with you.<BR>
<INPUT TYPE="checkbox" NAME="idiot">
I have no taste and I'm pretty dense,
so your site didn't do much for me.
<P>
Choose the one thing you love best about my pages:<BR>
<INPUT TYPE="radio" NAME="payment" VALUE="me" CHECKED>
That gorgeous picture of you and your cats.<BR>
<INPUT TYPE="radio" NAME="payment" VALUE="cats">
All those moving poems about your cats.<BR>
<INPUT TYPE="radio" NAME="payment" VALUE="burbs">
The inspiring recap of your suburban childhood.<BR>
<INPUT TYPE="radio" NAME="payment" VALUE="treasures">
The detailed list of all your Elvis memorabilia.
<P>
Imagine my site as a book, video, or album.<BR>
Select the number of copies you think it would sell:<BR>
<SELECT SIZE=3 NAME="potential">
<OPTION SELECTED>Million copy bestseller for sure!
<OPTION>100,000+ (would be Oprah's favorite)
<OPTION>Thousands (an under-appreciated classic)
<OPTION>Very few: not banal enough for today's public
</SELECT>
<P>
How do you think I could improve my site?
<SELECT NAME="suggestion">
<OPTION SELECTED>Couldn't be better
<OPTION>More about the cats
<OPTION>More Elvis stuff
<OPTION>More family pictures
</SELECT>
<P>
Feel free to type more praise, marriage proposals,
gift offers, etc. below:<BR>
<TEXTAREA NAME="comments" ROWS=4 COLS=55>
I just want to thank you so much for touching my life.
</TEXTAREA>
<INPUT TYPE="submit" VALUE="Click Here to Submit">
<INPUT TYPE="reset"  VALUE="Erase and Start Over">
</FORM>
</BODY></HTML>
```

FIGURE 8.2.

*The form listed in
Figure 8.1 uses every
type of HTML form
input element.*

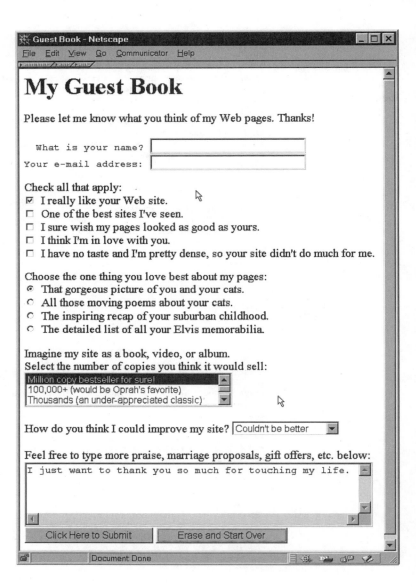

FIGURE 8.2.

*The form listed in
Figure 8.1 uses every
type of HTML form
input element.*

FIGURE 8.3.

Visitors to your Web site fill out the form with their mouse and/or keyboard, and then click the Click Here to Submit button.

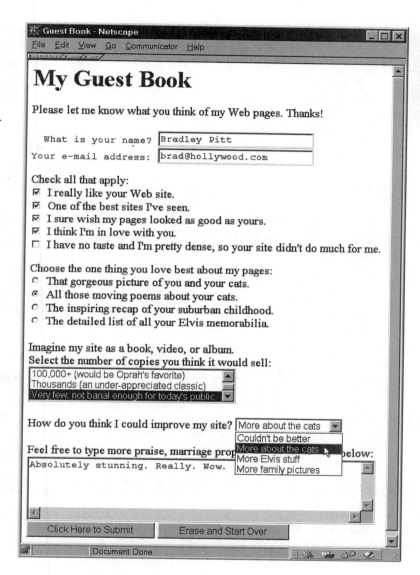

Text Input

To ask the user for a specific piece of information within a form, use the <INPUT> tag. This tag must fall between the <FORM> and </FORM> tags, but it can be anywhere on the page in relation to text, images, and other HTML tags. For example, to ask for some-one's name you could type the following:

```
What's your first name? <INPUT TYPE="text" SIZE=20 MAXLENGTH=30 NAME
="firstname">
What's your last name? <INPUT TYPE="text" SIZE=20 MAXLENGTH=30 NAME
="lastname">
```

The TYPE attribute indicates what type of form element to display—a simple one-line text entry box in this case. (Each element type is discussed individually in the following sections.)

The SIZE attribute indicates approximately how many characters wide the text input box should be. If you are using a proportionally spaced font, the width of the input will vary depending on what the user enters. If the input is too long to fit in the box, most Web browsers will automatically scroll the text to the left.

MAXLENGTH determines the number of characters the user is allowed to type into the text box. If someone tries to type beyond the specified length, the extra characters won't appear. You can specify a length that is longer, shorter, or the same as the physical size of the text box. SIZE and MAXLENGTH are used only for TYPE="text" because other input types (check boxes, radio buttons, and so on) have a fixed size.

 If you want the user to enter text without it being displayed on the screen, you can use <INPUT TYPE="password"> instead of <INPUT TYPE="text">. Asterisks (***) are then displayed in place of the text the user types. The SIZE, MAXLENGTH, and NAME attributes work exactly the same for TYPE="password" as for TYPE="text".

Identifying Each Piece of Form Data

No matter what type an input element is, you must give a name to the data it gathers. You can use any name you like for each input item, as long as each one on the form is differ-ent. When the form is sent to you (or to your form-processing script), each data item is identified by name.

For example, if someone entered Jane and Doe in the text box defined in the section "Text Input," you would see the following two lines in the email message you get when she submits the form.

```
firstname=Jane
lastname=Doe
```

Figure 8.4 is a sample email message from the form in Figure 8.3. Notice that each data element is identified by the name given to it in Figure 8.1.

> Depending on how your email software handles attachments, you might see the data in a different format than that shown in Figure 8.4. Usually, in fact, you'll see it all in one big long line, and you'll have to insert a line break before each & symbol to make it (sort of) readable. You'll also notice that spaces appear as plusses and punctuation appears as ASCII code numbers. The final section in this chapter talks about setting up a server script to wrangle the form data into a more readable format before it comes to you.

FIGURE 8.4.

Clicking the submit button in Figure 8.3 causes this information to be sent to me@mysite.com.

```
From: dicko@netletter.com
Date: Sun, 24 May 1998 22:15:29 -0500 (EST)
To: me@mysite.com
Subject: Form posted from Mozilla

Attachment type: application/x-www-form-urlencoded

&noseeum=the+user+won%27t+see+this
&fullname=Bradley+Pitt
&e-address=brad@hollywood.com
&likeit=on
&best=on
&envy=on
&love=on
&payment=cats
&potential=Very+few%3A+not+banal+enough+for+today%27s+public
&suggestion=More+about+the+cats
&comments=Absolutely+stunning.+Really.+Wow.%0D%0A
```

Check Boxes

The simplest input type is a check box, which appears as a small square the user can select or deselect by clicking. You must give each check box a NAME. If you want a check box to be checked by default when the form comes up, include the CHECKED attribute. For example, the following would make two check boxes.

```
<INPUT TYPE="checkbox" NAME="baby" CHECKED> Baby Grand Piano
<INPUT TYPE="checkbox" NAME="mini"> Mini Piano Stool
```

The check box labeled "Baby Grand Piano" would be checked. (The user would have to click in it to turn it off if he didn't want a piano.) The one marked "Mini Piano Stool" would be unchecked at first, so the user would have to click in it to turn it on if he wanted a piano stool.

When the form is submitted, selected check boxes appear in the form result as follows:

`baby=on`

Blank (deselected) check boxes do not appear in the form output at all.

> You can use more than one check box with the same name, but different values, as in the following code:
> ```
> <INPUT TYPE="checkbox" NAME="pet" VALUE="dog"> Dog
> <INPUT TYPE="checkbox" NAME="pet" VALUE="cat"> Cat
> <INPUT TYPE="checkbox" NAME="pet" VALUE="iguana"> Iguana
> ```
> If the user checked both cat and iguana, the submission result would include the following:
> ```
> pet=cat
> pet=iguana
> ```

Radio Buttons

Radio buttons, where only one choice can be selected at a time, are almost as simple to implement as check boxes. Just use `TYPE="radio"` and give each of the options its own `INPUT` tag, but use the same `NAME` for all of the radio buttons in a group:

```
<INPUT TYPE="radio" NAME="card" VALUE="v" CHECKED> Visa
<INPUT TYPE="radio" NAME="card" VALUE="m"> MasterCard
```

The `VALUE` can be any name or code you choose. If you include the `CHECKED` attribute, that button will be selected by default. (No more than one radio button with the same `NAME` can be checked.)

If the user selected MasterCard from the preceding radio button set, the following would be included in the form submission to the server script:

`card=m`

If the user didn't change the default `CHECKED` selection, `card=v` would be sent instead.

Selection Lists

Both scrolling lists and pull-down pick lists are created with the `<SELECT>` tag. You use this tag together with the `<OPTION>` tag:

```
<SELECT NAME="extras" SIZE=3 MULTIPLE>
<OPTION SELECTED> Electric windows
<OPTION> AM/FM Radio
<OPTION> Turbocharger
</SELECT>
```

8

No HTML tags other than <OPTION> should appear between the <SELECT> and </SELECT> tags.

Unlike the text input type, the SIZE attribute here determines how many items show at once on the selection list. If SIZE=2 had been used in the preceding code, only the first two options would be visible, and a scrollbar would appear next to the list so the user could scroll down to see the third option.

Including the MULTIPLE attribute allows users to select more than one option at a time, and the SELECTED attribute makes an option selected by default. The actual text accompanying selected options is returned when the form is submitted. If the user selected Electric windows and Turbocharger, for instance, the form results would include the following lines:

```
extras=Electric+windows
extras=Turbocharger
```

> If you leave out the SIZE attribute or specify SIZE=1, the list will create a pull-down pick list. Pick lists cannot allow multiple choices; they are logically equivalent to a group of radio buttons. For example, another way to choose between credit card types would be
>
> ```
> <SELECT NAME="card">
> <OPTION> Visa
> <OPTION> Mastercard
> </SELECT>
> ```

Text Areas

The <INPUT TYPE="text"> attribute mentioned earlier only allows the user to enter a single line of text. When you want to allow multiple lines of text in a single input item, use the <TEXTAREA> and </TEXTAREA> tags instead. Any text you include between these two tags will be displayed as the default entry. Here's an example:

```
<TEXTAREA NAME="comments" ROWS=4 COLS=20>
Please send more information.
</TEXTAREA>
```

As you probably guessed, the ROWS and COLS attributes control the number of rows and columns of text that fit in the input box. Text area boxes do have a scrollbar, however, so the user can enter more text than fits in the display area.

Some older browsers do not support the placement of default text within the text area. In these browsers, the text may appear outside the text input box.

Submit!

Every form must include a button that submits the form data to the server. You can put any label you like on this button with the VALUE attribute:

```
<INPUT TYPE="submit" VALUE="Place My Order Now!">
```

A gray button will be sized to fit the label you put in the VALUE attribute. When the user clicks it, all data items on the form are sent to the email address or program script specified in the FORM ACTION attribute.

You can also optionally include a button that clears all entries on the form so users can start over again if they change their minds or make mistakes. Use the following:

```
<INPUT TYPE="reset" VALUE="Clear This Form and Start Over">
```

Creating a Custom Submit Button

You can combine forms with all the HTML bells and whistles you learn from this book, including backgrounds, graphics, text colors, tables, and frames. When you do so, however, the standard submit and reset buttons may start looking a little bland.

Fortunately, there is an easy way to substitute your own graphics for those buttons. To use an image of your choice for a submit button, type

```
<INPUT TYPE="image" SRC="button.gif">
```

The image named button.gif will appear on the page, and the form will be submitted whenever someone clicks that image. You can also include any attributes normally used with the <IMG> tag, such as BORDER or ALIGN. (Chapter 10, "Putting Graphics on a Web Page" introduces the <IMG> tag.)

The exact pixel coordinates where the mouse clicked an image button will be sent along with the form data. For example, if someone entered bigjoe@chicago.net in the form in Figure 8.6, the resulting form data might look like the following:

Anotherone=bigjoe@chicago.net
&x=75
&y=36

Normally you should ignore the x and y coordinates, but some server scripts use them to make the button into an imagemap.

Figures 8.5 and 8.6 show a very simple form that uses a customized submit button. (You'll see how to make graphics like the signup.gif button in Hour 9, "Creating Your Own Web Page Graphics.")

FIGURE 8.5.

The <INPUT> tag on this page uses a custom graphical submit button.

```
<HTML><HEAD><TITLE>FREE!</TITLE></HEAD>
<BODY>
<H1>Free Electronic Junk Mail!</H1>
To start receiving junk e-mail from us daily*, enter your
e-mail address below and click on the <I>SignUP!</I> button.
<FORM METHOD="POST" ACTION="mailto:suckerlist@ripoff.com">
<INPUT TYPE="text" NAME="anotherone" SIZE=25>
<INPUT TYPE="image" SRC="signup.gif" BORDER=0 ALIGN="top">
</FORM>
*<SMALL>By clicking the above button, you also agree to the
terms of our Marketing Agreement, which is available upon
request at our offices in Bangkok, Thailand. A fee may be
charged for removal from our list if you elect at a later
date not to receive additional sales literature.</SMALL>
</BODY></HTML>
```

You can make a button that cancels the form and proceeds to another page (ignoring all information the user has entered so far) simply by linking to that other page. For example:

<A HREF="nodice.htm">Click here to cancel.</A>

There is no specific form type for a graphical reset button, but you can achieve the same effect by putting an image link to the current page, like this:

<A HREF="thispage.htm"><IMG SRC="cancel.gif"></A>

(Don't worry if you don't really understand the last line yet. You'll learn all about the <IMG> tag in Hour 10.)

FIGURE 8.6.

Forms don't need to be complex to be effective. (They might need to be a little less blunt, though.)

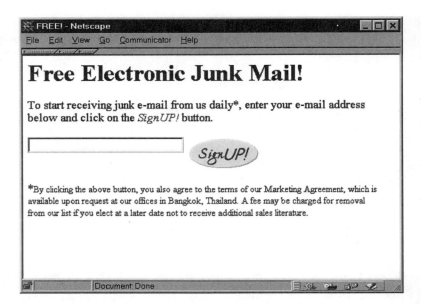

Using Server Scripts to Process Forms

All the form examples in this chapter used a `mailto:` address in the FORM ACTION attribute. As mentioned earlier, this isn't the only way to handle form processing. In fact, it isn't very commonly used, for five reasons:

- Only Netscape Navigator (versions 3.0 and later), Microsoft Internet Explorer (versions 3.0 and later), and other HTML 3.2 or 4.0 browsers support `mailto:` forms. For anyone using an older Web browser, the form won't work if it has `mailto:` in the FORM ACTION attribute.

- As you saw in Figure 8.4, the email data you get from a `mailto:` form is difficult to read, especially for long forms.

- Using a server script to pre-process form data is quite easy, and gives you much more flexibility in how you handle the information.

- When someone clicks the submit button of a `mailto:` form, she will see a warning message like the one in Figure 8.7. Any kind of message like this can scare people away from submitting the form, even if they are not submitting sensitive or secret information.

- The `mailto:` form action doesn't generate any kind of confirmation that the form data has been sent. It simply leaves the form there in front of the person who submitted it. Without any further confirmation, the user is often left thinking, "Did it really work? Should I push the button again?"

FIGURE 8.7.

Microsoft Internet Explorer displays a message almost identical to this one from Netscape Navigator whenever a form is submitted via email.

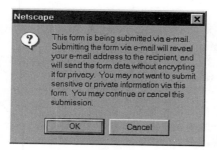

8

For all these reasons, most forms on the Internet today use a more complicated procedure for processing the data. Instead of sending form data directly to an email address, it's usually sent to a special forms-processing program (called a *script*) on the Web server computer itself.

To do this, you'll probably need help from the person or company who runs your Web server. Someone will need to either write a program for you or set up a prewritten form-processing program to work on the Web server computer. The most common thing such a script would do is reformat the form data to make it easier for you to read before forwarding it to your email address. (Of course, if you are happen to be a programmer, you can write your own scripts in any language supported on the server.)

Normally, a form-processing script also generates some sort of reply page and sends it back to be displayed for the user. However, if no such page is generated, the form remains visible.

It's also possible to set things up so that much of the form information can be interpreted and processed automatically. For example, server software exists to authorize a credit card transaction automatically over the Internet, confirm an order to the customer's email address, and enter the order directly into your company's in-house database for shipment. Obviously, setting up that sort of thing can get quite complex, and it's beyond the scope of this book to explain all the things you could do with form data once it has been submitted.

Once the script program is in place, you need to ask the person who set it up what address you should put in the ACTION attribute of the FORM tag. Depending on the script, you will probably also have to include some additional secret incantations after the <FORM> tag in your HTML page to tell the script things like what to say back when someone submits a form ("Thanks for your order. . .") and what to do with the data once it has been processed.

Most Internet service providers that host Web pages already have a "generic" form-processing script set up, and will happily tell you the exact HTML to use it. If your ISP can't do this, or charges you an extra fee for it, well, to be quite frank you are probably not using a very good ISP! In that case, you have the following choices:

- Switch to a more helpful Web hosting service.
- Learn advanced server programming.
- Use a `mailto:` address in the `ACTION` attribute and handle any necessary data processing on your own computer.

To Do

Before you put a form online that requires a script to process the results, you should do the following:

- Ask your Internet service provider what they offer for form-processing scripts and what exact address to which your forms should send their information. Later in this chapter, you'll see where and how to put that address into your forms.

- If you run your own Web server computer, the server software probably came with some basic form-processing scripts. Consult your documentation to set them up properly and find out the address on your server where each is located.

- If you have a choice of several form-processing scripts, I recommend starting with the script to simply send the "raw" form data to your email address. The example in this chapter uses such a script. You can experiment with fancier scripts later.

- Once you have the address of your form-processing script, put that in the `ACTION` attribute of the `FORM` tag and upload the form just like any other Web page. For example, if the script was in the `htbin` directory folder on the server computer and the script was named `generic` you would use the following `FORM` tag:

```
<FORM METHOD="post" ACTION="/htbin/generic">
```

Including Hidden Data

If you want to send certain data items to the server script that processes a form but you don't want the user to see them, you can use the `INPUT TYPE="hidden"` attribute. This attribute has no effect on the display at all; it just adds any name and value you specify to the form results when they are submitted.

You might use this attribute to tell a script where to email the form results. For example, type

```
<INPUT TYPE="hidden" NAME="mail_to" VALUE="dicko">
```

which adds the following line to the form output:

```
mail_to=dicko
```

For this attribute to have any effect, someone must create a script or program to read this line and do something about it. My Internet service provider's form script uses this hidden value to determine where to email the form data. (My account name with them is dicko.)

Most scripts require at least one or two hidden input elements. Consult the person who wrote or provided you with the script for details. You can also use hidden items to indicate which of the many similar forms a particular result came from, or simply to include a note to yourself in the form data reminding you from which form it came.

The most common mistake many companies make when putting a first order form on the Internet is the same one all too often made on paper order forms: leaving out a key piece of information. To avoid yourself the embarrassment of an incomplete order form, visit the HTML Café site at http://24hourHTMLcafe.com/hour8/

Click the Sample Form link to bring up a sample order form. This is a just your basic, run-of-the-mill product order form with credit card information, name, address, and so forth. Use it as a starting template and then add your own products, graphics, and unique information. Don't forget to change the <FORM ACTION> to the address of your own server script (or mailto: followed by your email address)!

Summary

This hour demonstrated how to create HTML forms, which allow readers of your Web pages to enter specific information and send it back to you via email.

You also found that you can set up a script or program to process form data. Your Internet service provider (ISP) or server software vendor can help you do this.

You will learn how to make an order form add up its own totals automatically in Hour 19, "Web Page Scripting for Non-Programmers."

Table 8.1 summarizes the HTML tags and attributes covered in this hour.

TABLE 8.1. HTML TAGS AND ATTRIBUTES COVERED IN HOUR 8.

Tag/Attribute	Function
<FORM>...</FORM>	Indicates an input form.
	Attributes:
ACTION="..."	The address of the script to process this form input.
METHOD="..."	How the form input will be sent to the server. Normally set to POST, rather than GET.
<INPUT>	An input element for a form.
	Attributes:
TYPE="..."	The type for this input widget. Possible values are CHECKBOX, HIDDEN, RADIO, RESET, SUBMIT, TEXT, or IMAGE.
NAME="..."	The name of this item, as passed to the script.
VALUE="..."	For a text or hidden item, the default value; for a check box or radio button, the value to be submitted with the form; for reset or submit buttons, the label for the button itself.
SRC="..."	The source file for an image.
CHECKED	For check boxes and radio buttons, indicates that this item is checked.
SIZE="..."	The width, in characters, of a text input region.
MAXLENGTH="..."	The maximum number of characters that can be entered into a text region.
ALIGN="..."	For images in forms, determines how the text and image will align (same as with the <IMG> tag—see Chapter 10).
<TEXTAREA>...</TEXTAREA>	Indicates a multiline text entry form element. Default text can be included.
	Attributes:
NAME="..."	The name to be passed to the script.
ROWS="..."	The number of rows this text area displays.
COLS="..."	The number of columns (characters) this text area displays.
<SELECT>...</SELECT>	Creates a menu or scrolling list of possible items.

Tag/Attribute	Function
	Attributes:
NAME="..."	The name that is passed to the script.
SIZE="..."	The number of elements to display. If SIZE is indicated, the selection becomes a scrolling list. If no SIZE is given, the selection is a pop-up menu.
MULTIPLE	Allows multiple selections from the list.
<OPTION>	Indicates a possible item within a <SELECT> element.
	Attributes:
SELECTED	With this attribute included, the <OPTION> will be selected by default in the list.
VALUE="..."	The value to submit if this <OPTION> is selected when the form is submitted.

Q&A

Q I've heard that it's dangerous to send credit card numbers over the Internet. Can't thieves intercept form data on its way to me?

A It is possible to intercept form data (and any Web pages or email) as it travels through the Internet. If you ask for credit card numbers or other sensitive information on your forms, you should ask the company that runs your Web server about "secure" forms processing. There are several reliable technologies for eliminating the risk of high-tech eavesdroppers, but it may cost you quite a bit to implement the security measures.

To put the amount of risk in perspective, remember that it is *much* more difficult to intercept information traveling through the Internet than it is to look over someone's shoulder in a restaurant or retail store.

Q I'm not set up to take credit cards or electronic payments. How do I make an order form for people to print out on paper and mail to me with a check?

A Any form can be printed out. Just leave off the submit button if you don't want any email submissions, and instruct people to fill out the form and select File, Print. Remember to include a link to some other page so they can go back to the rest of your Web site after they print the form. And don't forget to tell them where they should send the check!

Q Can I put forms on a CD-ROM, or do they have to be on the Internet?

A You can put a form anywhere you can put a Web page. If it's on a disk or CD-ROM instead of a Web server, it can be filled out by people whether they are connected to the Internet or not. Of course, they must be connected to the Internet (or your local intranet) when they click the submit button, or the information won't get to you.

Q I've seen sites on the Internet that use pick lists to link between multiple pages, kind of like a navigation menu. How do they do that?

A All things are possible if you have a professional programmer to write custom scripts for you. Even if you don't, you can find some sample prewritten scripts for this sort of thing on the Internet (search under "CGI Scripts" in any major search engine such as www.yahoo.com). Even after you locate a prewritten script, however, you may still need some assistance installing it and getting it to work properly on your Web server.

Workshop

Quiz

1. What do you need to get from the people who administer your Web server computer before you can put a form on the Internet?

2. Write the HTML to create a "guestbook" form that asks someone for his or her name, sex, age, and email address. Assume that you want the results mailed to jane@calamity.com.

3. If you had created an image named sign-in.gif, how would you use it as the submit button for the guestbook in question 2?

Answers

1. The Internet address of a script or program which is set up specifically to process form data.

2.
```
<HTML><HEAD><TITLE>My Guestbook</TITLE></HEAD>
<BODY>
<H1>My Guestbook: Please Sign In</H1>
<FORM METHOD="post" ACTION="mailto:jane@calamity.com">
Your name: <INPUT TYPE="text" NAME="name" SIZE=20><P>
Your sex:
<INPUT TYPE="radio" NAME="sex" VALUE="male"> male
<INPUT TYPE="radio" NAME="sex" VALUE="female"> female<P>
Your age: <INPUT TYPE="text" NAME="age" SIZE=4><P>
```

```
Your e-mail address:
<INPUT TYPE="text" NAME="email" SIZE=30><P>
<INPUT TYPE="submit" VALUE="Sign In">
<INPUT TYPE="reset" VALUE="Erase">
</FORM>
</BODY></HTML>
```

3. Replace

```
<INPUT TYPE="submit" VALUE="Sign In">
```

with

```
<INPUT TYPE="image" SRC="sign-in.gif">
```

Exercise

- You should make a form using all of the different types of input elements and selection lists to make sure you understand how each of them works.

PART III
Web Page Graphics

Hour

HOUR 9

Creating Your Own Web Page Graphics

You don't have to be an artist to put high-impact graphics and creative type on your Web pages. You don't need to spend hundreds or thousands of dollars on software, either. This hour tells you how to create the images you need to make visually exciting Web pages. Though the sample figures in this chapter use a popular Windows graphics program (Paint Shop Pro from JASC Software), you can easily follow along with any major Windows or Macintosh graphics application.

This hour is only concerned with creating the actual graphics files, so it doesn't discuss any HTML tags at all. In Hour 10, "Putting Graphics on a Web Page," you'll see how to integrate your graphics with your HTML pages.

One of the best ways to save time creating the graphics and media files is, of course, to avoid creating them altogether. Any graphic or media clip you see on any site is instantly reusable as soon as the copyright holder grants (or sells) you the right to copy it.

Grabbing a graphic from any Web page is as simple as clicking it with the right mouse button (or the button held down, on a Macintosh mouse), and selecting Save Image As in Netscape Navigator or Save Picture As in Microsoft Explorer. Extracting a background image from a page is just as easy: Right-click it and select Save Background As.

Choosing Graphics Software

You can use almost any computer graphics program to create graphics images for your Web pages, from the simple paint program that comes free with your computer's operating system to an expensive professional program, such as Adobe Photoshop. If you have a digital camera or scanner attached to your computer, it probably came with some graphics software capable of creating Web page graphics.

If you already have some software you think might be good for creating Web graphics, try using it to do everything described in this chapter. If it can't do some of the tasks covered here, it probably won't be a good tool for Web graphics.

To Do

One excellent and inexpensive program that does provide everything you're likely to need is Paint Shop Pro from JASC, Inc. If you are using a Windows computer, I highly recommend that you download a free, fully functional evaluation copy of Paint Shop Pro 5.0 before reading the rest of this chapter.

(Macintosh users should download BME at http://www.softlogik.com instead, because Paint Shop Pro is currently available for Windows only.)

1. Start your Web browser and go to http://www.jasc.com/.
2. Click the Downloads link and choose Paint Shop Pro.
3. Click the download site nearest you, and the file will transfer to your hard drive. You'll be asked to confirm where you want to put the file on your hard drive; be sure to remember which folder it goes into!
4. Once the download transfer is complete, use Windows Explorer to find the file you downloaded and double-click it to install Paint Shop Pro.

The Paint Shop Pro software you can get online is a fully functional share-ware evaluation copy. If you agree with me that it's essential for working with Web page images, please be prompt about sending the $99 registration fee to the program's creators at JASC Software. (The address is in the online help in the software.) I'm confident that you're not going to find any other graphics software even close to the power and usability of Paint Shop Pro for anywhere near $99. (In fact, I have—and know how to use—all the leading super-expensive commercial graphics programs from Photoshop on down, and Paint Shop Pro is the best by far for day-to-day work with Web graphics.)

Almost all the graphics you'll see in this book were created with Paint Shop Pro, and this chapter uses Paint Shop Pro to illustrate several key Web graphics techniques you'll need to know. Of course, there are so many ways to produce images with Paint Shop Pro, I can't even begin to explain them all. If you'd like a quick but complete tutorial on using Paint Shop Pro to make high-impact Web page graphics, I recommend the book *Creating Paint Shop Pro Web Graphics* by Andy Shafran et al. (yes, I'm one of the "al."). You can order this book directly from JASC when you register the software.

Graphics Basics

Two forces are always at odds when you post graphics and multimedia on the Internet. Your eyes and ears want everything to be as detailed and accurate as possible, but your clock and wallet want files to be as small as possible. Intricate, colorful graphics mean big file sizes, which can take a long time to transfer, even over a fast connection.

So how do you maximize the quality of your presentation while minimizing file size? To make these choices, you need to understand how color and resolution work together to create a subjective sense of quality.

NEW TERM   The *resolution* of an image is the number of individual dots, or *pixels*, that make up an image. Large, high-resolution images generally take longer to transfer and display than small, low-resolution images. Resolution is usually written as the width times the height; a 300×200 image, for example, is 300 pixels wide and 200 pixels high.

NEW TERM   You might be surprised to find that resolution isn't the most significant factor determining the storage size (and transfer time) of an image file. This is because images used on Web pages are always stored and transferred in *compressed* form. *Image compression* is the mathematical manipulation that images are put through to squeeze out repetitive patterns. The mathematics of image compression is complex, but the basic idea is that repeating patterns or large areas of the same color can be squeezed out when the image is stored on a disk. This makes the image file much smaller, and allows it to be transferred faster over the Internet. The Web browser program can then restore the original appearance of the image when the image is displayed.

In the rest of this chapter you'll learn exactly how to create graphics with big visual impact and small file sizes. The techniques you'll use to accomplish this depend on the contents and purpose of each image. There are as many uses for Web page graphics as there are Web pages, but four types of graphics are by far the most common:

- Photos of people, products, or places
- Graphical banners and logos, for the top of pages
- Snazzy-looking buttons or icons to link between pages
- Background textures or "wallpaper" to go behind pages

The last of these will be covered in Hour 11, "Custom Backgrounds and Colors." But you can learn to create the other three kinds of graphics right now.

Preparing Photographic Images

To put photos on your Web pages, you'll need some kind of scanner or digital camera. You'll often need to use the custom software that comes with your scanner or camera to save pictures on your hard drive. Note, however, that you can control any scanner that is compatible with the TWAIN interface standard directly from Paint Shop Pro and most other graphics programs—see the software documentation for details.

> If you don't have a scanner or digital camera, any Kodak film-developing store can transfer photos from 35mm film to a CD-ROM for a modest fee. You can then use Paint Shop Pro to open and modify the Kodak Photo-CD files. Some large photo developers other than Kodak also offer similar digitizing services.

Once you have the pictures, you can use Paint Shop Pro (or another similar graphics program) to get them ready for the Web.

You want Web page graphics to be as compact as possible, so you'll usually need to crop the size of your digital photos. Follow these steps to crop a picture in Paint Shop Pro:

1. Click the rectangular selection tool on the tools palette. (The tools palette is shown in the left in Figure 9.1. You can drag it wherever you want it, so it may be in a different place on your screen.)

2. Click the top-left corner of the part of the image you want to keep and hold down the mouse button while you drag down to the lower-right corner (see Figure 9.1).

3. Select Image, Crop to Selection.

FIGURE 9.1.

Use the rectangular selection tool to crop images as tightly as possible.

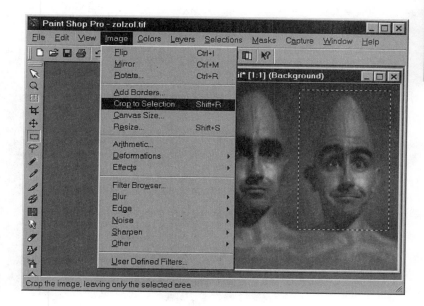

9

Even after cropping, your image may be larger than it needs to be for a Web page. Generally, a complex photograph should be no more than 300×300 pixels, and a simpler photo can look fine at 100×50 or so.

Notice that in Paint Shop Pro the resolution of the current image is shown at the bottom-right corner of the window. The image may look larger or smaller than it really is, because Paint Shop Pro automatically adjusts the image to fit in the window while you're working on it. (The current magnification ratio is shown just above each image, in the title bar.) To see the image at the size it will appear on a Web page, select View, Normal Viewing (1:1).

To change the resolution of an image, and therefore its apparent size, use the Image, Resize command. (Notice that in some software, including earlier versions of Paint Shop Pro, this option is called Resample.) You'll get the Resize dialog box shown in Figure 9.2.

You'll almost always want Smart Size, Resize all Layers, and Maintain Aspect Ratio selected. When you enter the width (in pixels or a percentage of the original) you'd like the image to be, the height will be calculated automatically to keep the image from squishing out of shape.

FIGURE 9.2.

To change the size of an image, select Image, Resize to get this dialog box.

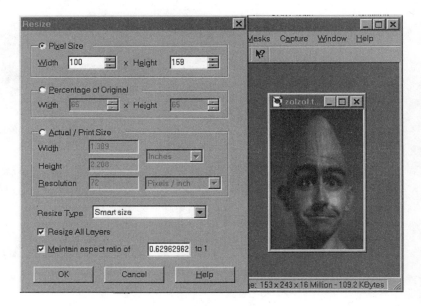

Many photographs will require some color correction to look their best on a computer screen. Like most photo-editing programs, Paint Shop Pro offers many options for adjusting the brightness, contrast, and color balance of an image.

Most of these options are pretty intuitive to use, but the most important and powerful one may be unfamiliar if you're not an old graphics pro. Whenever an image appears too dark or too light, select Colors, Adjust, Gamma Correction. For most images, this works better than Colors, Adjust, Brightness and Contrast, because it doesn't "wash out" bright or dark areas.

As shown in Figure 9.3, you can move the sliders in the Gamma Correction dialog box to adjust the correction factor until the image looks about right. (Numbers above 1 make the image lighter, and numbers between 1 and 0 make the image darker.) If the color in the image seems a little off, try deselecting the Link checkbox, which allows you to move the Red, Green, and Blue sliders separately and adjust the color balance.

FIGURE 9.3.

Gamma correction is the best way to fix images that are too dark or too light.

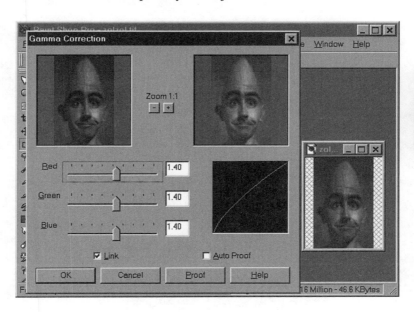

Most of the other image-editing tools in Paint Shop Pro offer small preview windows like the one in Figure 9.3, so a little playful experimentation is the best way to find out what each of them does.

Controlling JPEG Compression

Photographic images look best when saved in the JPEG file format. When you're finished adjusting the size and appearance of your photo, select File, Save As and choose the JPEG-JFIF Compliant file type with Standard Encoding, as shown in the bottom half of Figure 9.4.

Figure 9.4 also shows the Save Options dialog box you'll see when you click the Options button. You can control the compression ratio for saving JPEG files by adjusting the compression level setting between 1 percent (high quality, large file size) and 99 percent (low quality, small file size).

You may want to experiment a bit to see how various JPEG compression levels affect the quality of your images, but 25% compression is generally a good compromise between speed and quality for most photographic images.

FIGURE 9.4.

Paint Shop Pro allows you to trade reduced file size for image quality when saving JPEG images.

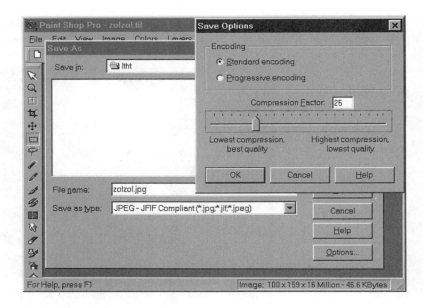

Creating Banners and Buttons

Graphics that you create from scratch, such as banners and buttons, involve different considerations than photographs.

The first decision you need to make when you produce a banner or button is how big it should be. Almost everyone accessing the Web now (or in the foreseeable future) has a computer with one of three screen sizes. The most common resolution for palm-sized computers and televisions is 640×480 pixels. The resolution of most laptop computers today is 800×600 pixels, and 1024×768 pixels is the preferred resolution of most new desktop computers and future laptops. You should generally plan your graphics so that they will always fit in the smallest of these screens, with room to spare for scrollbars and margins.

This means that full-sized banners and title graphics should be no more than 600 pixels wide. Photos and large artwork should be from 100 to 300 pixels in each dimension, and smaller buttons and icons should be 20 to 100 pixels tall and wide.

Figure 9.5 shows the dialog box you get when you select File, New to start a new image. You should always begin with 16.7 million colors (24-bit) as the image type. You can always change the size of the image later with Image, Crop or Image, Enlarge Canvas, so don't worry if you aren't sure exactly how big it needs to be.

For the background color, you should usually choose white to match the background that most Web browsers ordinarily use for Web pages. (You'll see how to change the background color of a page in Hour 11.) When you know you'll be making a page with a non-white background, you can choose a different background color, as shown in Figure 9.5.

FIGURE 9.5.

You need to know the approximate size of an image before you start working on it.

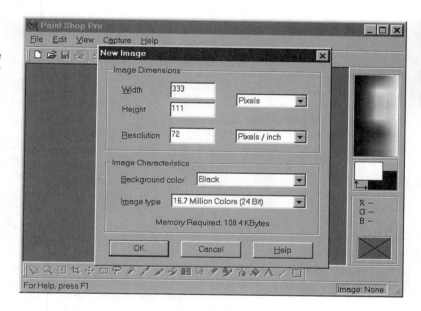

When you enter the width and height of the image in pixels and click OK, you are faced with a blank canvas—an intimidating sight if you're as art-phobic as most of us! Fortunately, computer graphics programs such as Paint Shop Pro make it amazingly easy to produce professional-looking graphics for most Web page applications.

Often, you will want to incorporate some fancy lettering into your Web page graphics. For example, you might want to put a title banner at the top of your page that uses a decorative font with a drop-shadow or other special effects. To accomplish this in Paint Shop Pro, do the following:

1. Choose the color you want the lettering to be from the color palette on the right edge of the Paint Shop Pro window. (Press the letter C to make the color palette appear if you don't see it.)

2. Click the "A" tool on the toolbar, and then click anywhere on the image. The Add Text dialog box in Figure 9.6 will appear.

3. Choose a font and size for the lettering, and make sure Antialias is selected under Text Effects. (This smoothes the edges of the text, so that it won't look "blocky.) Click OK.

4. Click anywhere in the image, and then grab and drag the text with the mouse to position it where you want it (usually in the center of the image).

FIGURE 9.6.

Use Paint Shop Pro's text tool to create elegant lettering in a graphics image.

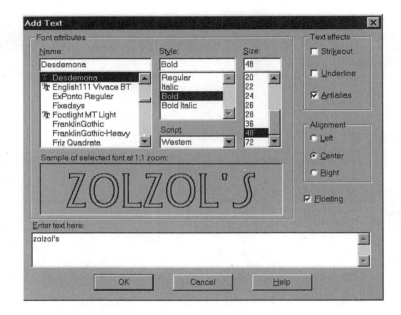

The list of fonts you see when you use the text tool will almost certainly be different than those shown in Figure 9.6. You will see only the fonts previously installed on your computer.

When you first put the text onto the image, it will shimmer with a moving dotted outline. This means it is selected, and that any special effects you now choose from the menu will apply to the shape of the letters you just made. For example, you might select Image, Effects, Chisel to add a chiseled outline around the text. Figure 9.7 shows the dialog box that would appear.

Notice that you can adjust the chisel effect and see the results in a small preview window before you actually apply them to the image. This makes it very easy to learn what various effects do simply by experimenting with them. Using only the text tool and the four choices on the Image, Effects submenu (Buttonize, Chisel, Cutout, and Drop Shadow), you can create quite a variety of useful and attractive Web graphics.

FIGURE 9.7.

Like most menu choices in Paint Shop Pro, the Image, Effects, Chisel command gives you an easy-to-use preview of the effects.

You may also want to deform, blur, sharpen, or otherwise play around with your text after you've applied an effect to it. To do so, simply select Image, Deformations, Deformation Browser (to warp the shape of the letters) or Image, Filter Browser (to apply an image-processing filter). You will get a dialog box like the one shown in Figure 9.8, which lets you pick from a list of effects and preview each one to see which one you want to try.

In Figure 9.8, I chose the Edge Enhance filter from the Filter Browser, which adds a sparkly effect to the chiseled lettering. You can have a lot of fun playing around with all the different options in the filter and deformation browsers!

Reducing the Number of Colors

One of the most effective ways to reduce the download time for an image is to reduce the number of colors. This can drastically reduce the visual quality of some photographic images, but works great for most banners, buttons, and other icons.

FIGURE 9.8.

Select Image, Filter Browser to play with all the image processing filters available, and then choose the one you want.

In Paint Shop Pro, you can do this by selecting Colors, Decrease Color Depth. (Most other graphics programs have a similar option.) Choose 16 Colors (4-bit) when your image has very few colors in it. If the image has lots of colors (or the image didn't look good when you tried 16 Colors), select Colors, Decrease Color Depth, 256 Colors (8-bit) instead. The software will automatically find the best palette of 16 or 256 colors for approximating the full range of colors in the image.

Even if you only use two or three colors in an image, you should still select Colors, Reduce Color Depth, 16 Colors before you save it. If you don't, the image file will waste some space "leaving room for" lots of colors even though very few are actually in use.

When you reduce the number of colors in an image, you will see a dialog box with several choices (see Figure 9.9). For Web page images, you will almost always want to choose an Optimized Octree and Nearest Color. Leave all the Options on the right side of the dialog box unchecked; they will seldom improve the quality of an image noticeably.

FIGURE 9.9.

Reducing the number of colors in an image can dramatically decrease file size without changing the appearance of the image much.

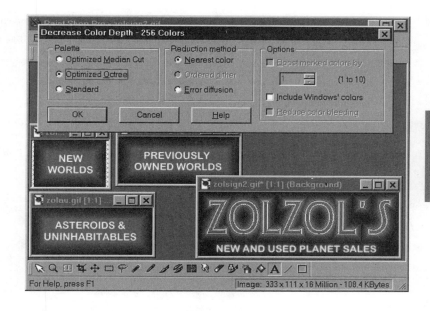

9

 Dithering (also called *error diffusion* in Paint Shop Pro) means using random dots or patterns to intermix palette colors. This can make images look better in some cases, but should usually be avoided for Web page graphics. Why? Because it substantially increases the information complexity of an image, and that almost always results in much larger file sizes and slower downloads. So, listen to your Great Uncle Oliver and "don't dither!"

There is a special file format for images with a limited number of colors, called the Graphics Interchange Format (GIF). To save a GIF image in Paint Shop Pro, select File, Save As and choose GIF-CompuServe as the image type.

Interlaced GIFs and Progressive JPEGs

Both the GIF and JPEG image file formats offer a nifty feature to make images appear faster than they possibly could. An image can be stored in such a way that a "rough draft" of the image appears quickly, and then the details are filled in as the download finishes. This has a profound psychological effect, because it gives people something to look at instead of drumming their fingers waiting for a large image to pour slowly onto the screen.

A file stored with this feature is called an *interlaced GIF* or *progressive JPEG*. Despite the two different names, the visual results are similar with either format.

NEW TERM An *interlaced GIF* file is an image that will appear blocky at first, and then more and more detailed as it finishes downloading. Similarly, a *progressive JPEG* file appears blurry at first, and then gradually comes into focus.

Most graphics programs that can handle GIF files enable you to choose whether to save them interlaced or noninterlaced. In Paint Shop Pro, for example, you can choose Version 89a and Interlaced by clicking the Options button in the Save As dialog box just before you save a GIF file (see Figure 9.10).

FIGURE 9.10.

Paint Shop Pro lets you save interlaced GIF images, which appear to display faster when loading.

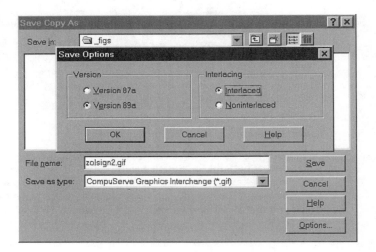

To save a progressive JPEG file, select Save As (or Save Copy As), choose the JPEG-JFIF Compliant image type, click the Options button, and select Progressive Encoding. The progressive JPEG standard is quite new and is only supported by Netscape Navigator version 2.0 or later and Microsoft Internet Explorer version 3.0 or later.

Browsers that don't support progressive JPEG will not display the file as if it were just a regular JPEG—they will display nothing at all or a message saying the file isn't recognizable. Interlaced GIFs, on the other hand, will appear correctly even in older browsers that don't support two-stage display.

Image files smaller than about 3KB will usually load so fast that nobody will ever see the interlacing or progressive display anyway. In fact, very small images may actually load *more slowly* when interlaced. Save these tricks for larger images only.

Summary

In this hour you learned the basics of preparing graphics for use on Web pages. You saw how to download and use the popular graphics program Paint Shop Pro to work with photos, banners, buttons, and other Web page images (though the techniques you learned will work with many other graphics programs as well). You also found out how to decide between the various graphics file formats used for Web page graphics, and how to make images that appear in stages for the illusion of speed.

Q&A

Q **Shouldn't I just hire a graphics artist to design my pages for me instead of learning all this stuff?**

A If you have plenty of money and need a visually impressive site—or if you think that ugly building with chartreuse trim that people are always complaining about actually looks pretty nice—hiring some professional help might not be a bad idea. But remember that you probably know what you want more than anyone else does, which often counts more than artistic skills when producing a good Web page.

Q **I've produced graphics for printing on paper. Is making Web page graphics much different?**

A Yes. In fact, many of the rules for print graphics are reversed on the Web. Web page graphics have to be low-resolution, while print graphics should be as high-resolution as possible. White washes out black on computer screens, while black bleeds into white on paper. Also, someone may stop a Web page when only half the graphics are done. So try to avoid falling into old habits if you've done a lot of print graphics design.

Workshop

Quiz

1. Suppose you have a scanned picture of a horse that you need to put on a Web page. How big should you make it, and in what file format should you save it?

2. Your company logo is a black letter Z with a red circle behind it. What size should you draw (or scan) it, and what file format should you save it in for use on your Web page?

3. Should you save a 100×50 pixel button graphic as an interlaced GIF file?

Answers

1. Depending on how important the image is to your page, as small as 100×40 pixels or as large as 300×120 pixels. The JPEG format, with about 50 percent compression, would be best.

2. About 100×100 pixels is generally good for a logo, but a simple graphic like that will compress very well so you could make it up to 300×300 pixels if you want. Save it as a 16-color GIF file.

3. No. A small file like that will load just as fast or faster without interlacing.

Exercises

- If you have an archive of company (or personal) photos, look through it to find a few that might enhance your Web site. Scan them (or send them out to be scanned) so that you'll have a library of graphics all ready to draw from as you produce more pages in the future.

- Before you start designing graphics for an important business site, try spicing up your own personal home page. This will give you a chance to learn Paint Shop Pro (or your other graphics software) so you'll look like you know what you're doing when you tackle it at work.

HOUR 10

Putting Graphics on a Web Page

In Hour 9, "Creating Your Own Web Page Graphics," you started making some digital images for your Web pages. This hour shows you how easy it is to put those graphics on your pages with HTML.

To Do

You should get two or three images ready now so you can try putting them on your own pages as you follow along with this hour.

If you have some image files already saved in the GIF or JPEG format (the filenames will end in .gif or .jpg), use those. Otherwise, you can just grab some graphics I've put on the Internet for you to practice with. Here's how:

1. Enter the following address into your Web browser:

   `http://24hourHTMLcafe.com/hour10/images.htm`

   You should see a page with four images of hats and stars at the bottom.

2. Click Sample Images. You should see a magic hat and some stars.

▼   3. Save each of the graphics to your computer's hard drive by clicking each image with the right mouse button (or holding down the mouse button if you use a Macintosh computer), and then selecting Save Image As from the pop-up menu.

Put the graphics on your hard drive in the folder you use for creating Web pages.

     4. As you read this chapter, use these image files to practice putting images on your pages. (It's also fine to use any graphics you created while reading the previous ▲   chapter.)

At the 24-Hour HTML Café, you'll find live links to many graphics and multi-media hotlists and hot sites where you can find ready-to-use graphics. To access these links, go to http://www.mcp.com/resources/webpub.

The familiar Web search engines and directories such as Yahoo! (http://www.yahoo.com/), Excite (http://www.excite.com), and InfoSeek (http://www.infoseek.com/) can become a gold mine of graphics images, just by leading you to sites related to your own theme. They can also help you discover the oodles of sites specifically dedicated to providing free and cheap access to reusable media collections.

Placing an Image on a Web Page

To put an image on a Web page, first move the image file into the same directory folder as the HTML text file. Insert the following HTML tag at the point in the text where you want the image to appear (use the name of your image file instead of *myimage.gif*):

```
<IMG SRC="myimage.gif">
```

Figure 10.1, for example, inserts several images at the top and bottom of the page. Whenever a Web browser displays the HTML file in Figure 10.1, it will automatically retrieve and display the image files as shown in Figure 10.2.

If you guessed that IMG stands for "image," you're right. SRC stands for "source," which is a reference to the location of the image file. (As discussed in Hour 1, "Understanding HTML and the Web," a Web page image is always stored in a file separate from the text, even though it will appear to be part of the same page.)

Just as with the <A HREF> tag (covered in Hour 3, "Linking to Other Web Pages"), you can specify any complete Internet address as the <IMG SRC>—or you can specify just the filename if an image will be located in the same directory folder as the HTML file. You may also use relative addresses, such as photos/birdy.jpg or ../smiley.gif.

FIGURE 10.1.

Use the <IMG> tag to place graphics images on a Web page.

```
<HTML>
<HEAD><TITLE>ZOLZOL's New &amp; Used Planets</TITLE></HEAD>
<BODY>
<IMG SRC="zolzol2.jpg" ALT="Friendly Fen">
<IMG SRC="zolsign2.gif" ALT="ZOLZOL's New and Used Planets">
<IMG SRC="zolzol1.jpg" ALT="Honest Han">
<H1><IMG SRC="zolmodel.gif" ALT="HomeStar 12">
The HomeStar Model 12</H1>
<H3><I>Manufactured Home Planets for Today's Lifeforms</I></H3>
Tired of sinking endless time and resources into the same old
run-down ecosystem? Maybe it's time to think about the
<B>modern solution</B> to all your environmental problems!
Why spend a forture on another filthy, volcano-stained planet
riddled with unsightly hurricanes and lightning storms, when
you can own a <B>factory new</B> manufactured planet for a
fraction of the price? We custom-build each HomeStar Model 12
to your race's specifications, with your choice of sky and
ground colors, synthetic Sim-Veg landscaping, and odor-free
Quick-Gro hydroponic agricultural systems. Call ZOLZOL's for a
<B>free quotation</B> today!<P>
<SMALL>(Orbital installation may incur additional fees,
and may require local zoning permits.)</SMALL><P>
<DIV ALIGN="center">
<A HREF="zolzol.htm"><IMG SRC="zolhome.gif" BORDER=0
 ALT="ZOLZOL's Home Page"><BR>Click here for more bargains!</A>
</DIV>
</BODY></HTML>
```

Theoretically, you can include an image from any Internet Web page within your own pages. For example, you could include a picture of my family by putting the following on your Web page:

`<IMG SRC="http://netletter.com/dicko/olivers.gif">`

The image would be retrieved from my server computer whenever your page was displayed.

However, even though you could do this, you shouldn't! Not only is it bad manners (it often costs people money whenever you pull something from their server computer), it can also make your pages display more slowly. You also have no way of controlling whether the image has been changed or deleted. If someone gives you permission to use an image from one of their pages, always transfer a copy of that image to your computer and use a local file reference such as `<IMG SRC="olivers.gif">`.

FIGURE 10.2.

When a Web browser displays the HTML page in Figure 10.1, it adds the images named `zolzol2.jpg,` `zolsign.gif,` `zolzol1.jpg,` `zolmodel.gif,` *and* `zolzol.gif.`

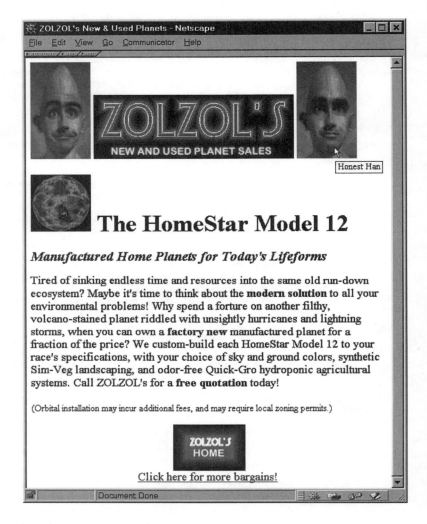

Labeling an Image

Each `<IMG>` tag in Figure 10.1 includes a short text message, such as `ALT="Friendly Fen"`. The `ALT` stands for alternate text because this message will appear in place of the image in older Web browsers that don't display graphics, or for those users who choose to turn off automatic image downloading in their Web browser preferences settings.

People who are using the latest Web browser software will see the message you put in the `ALT` attribute too. Because graphics files sometimes take a while to transfer over the Internet, most Web browsers show the text on a page first with the `ALT` messages in place of the graphics, as shown in Figure 10.3.

FIGURE 10.3.

People will see the ALT *messages while they wait for the graphics to appear.*

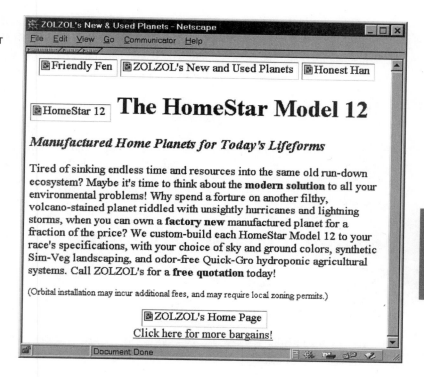

Even after the graphics replace the ALT messages, the ALT message still appears in a little box whenever the mouse pointer passes over an image. In Figure 10.2, for example, the mouse arrow is over the photo of Han Zol, and the ALT message "Honest Han" is showing.

You should generally include a suitable ALT attribute in every <IMG> tag on your Web pages, keeping in mind the variety of situations where people might see that message. A very brief description of the image is usually best, but Web page authors sometimes put short advertising messages or subtle humor in their ALT messages. For small or unimportant images, it's fine to omit the ALT message altogether.

Images That Are Links

With the same <A HREF> tag used to make text links, you can make any image into a clickable link to another page. Figures 10.1 and 10.2 show an example; clicking the big button at the bottom of the page (or the words Click here for more bargains!) retrieves the page named zolzol.htm.

Normally, Web browsers draw a colored rectangle around the edge of each image link. Like text links, the rectangle will usually appear blue to people who haven't visited the link recently, and purple to people who have visited it. Since you will seldom, if ever, want this unsightly line around your beautiful buttons, you should always include BORDER=0 in any <IMG> tag within a link. (You'll learn more about the BORDER attribute in Hour 13, "Page Design and Layout.")

Hour 11, "Custom Backgrounds and Colors," explains how to change the link colors. All the same rules and possibilities discussed in Hour 3 and Hour 7, "Email Links and Links within a Page," apply to image links exactly as they do for text links. (You can link to another part of the same page with <A HREF="#name"> and <A NAME="name">, for example.)

Horizontal Image Alignment

As discussed in Hour 5, "Text Alignment and Lists," you can use <DIV ALIGN= "center">, <DIV ALIGN="right">, and <DIV ALIGN="left"> to align part of a page to the center, right margin, or left margin. These tags affect both text and images.

For example, the last <IMG> tag in Figure 10.1 occurs between the <DIV ALIGN="center"> tag and the closing </DIV> tag. You can see in Figure 10.2 that this causes the image (as well as the text below it) to be centered on the page. Like text, images are normally lined up with the left margin unless a <DIV ALIGN="center"> or <DIV ALIGN="right"> tag indicates that they should be centered or right-justified.

As the first three images in Figures 10.4 and 10.5 demonstrate, you can also use <DIV ALIGN="center"> to center more than one image at a time. Since there are no <BR> or <P> tags between them, the three images all appear on one line, and the entire line is centered horizontally in the browser window.

You can also make text wrap around images, as the paragraph around the pictures of Mars and Venus in the lower-middle part of Figure 10.5 does. You do this by including an ALIGN attribute within the <IMG> tag itself, as shown in the fifth and sixth <IMG> tags in Figure 10.4.

<IMG ALIGN="left"> aligns the image to the left and causes text to wrap around the right side of it. And as you'd expect, <IMG ALIGN="right"> aligns the image to the right and causes text to wrap around the left side of it.

You can't use <IMG ALIGN="center"> because text won't wrap around a centered image. You must use <DIV ALIGN="center"> if you want an image to be centered on the page, as I did with the top image in Figures 10.4 and 10.5.

FIGURE 10.4.

This page contains examples of both horizontal and vertical image alignment, as well as automatic wrapping of text around images.

```html
<HTML>
<HEAD><TITLE>ZOLZOL's New &amp; Used Planets</TITLE></HEAD>
<BODY>
<DIV ALIGN="center">
<IMG SRC="zolzol2.jpg">
<IMG SRC="zolsign2.gif" ALIGN="top">
<IMG SRC="zolzol1.jpg">
</DIV>
<H1><IMG SRC="zolsol3.gif" ALIGN="middle"> Sol III</H1>
<H3><I>A real water planet at a desert planet price!</I></H3>
This baby has its <B>original ecosystem</B> still installed,
and comes pre-populated by a technologically-savvy <B>ideal
slave species</B>! <I>PLUS:</I> <B>atmospheric oxygen</B>,
plenty of hydrocarbons, <B>H<SUB>2</SUB>O by the gigaton</B>,
and a wide range of metals, all pre-mined and ready for
off-planet shipment as an <B>immediate source of income</B>
for you and your families! So pack up the kids, hop in the
battlecruiser, and move onto this barely-used world today!
Did we mention the huge, close moon?
<IMG SRC="zolmoon.gif" ALIGN="absmiddle">
<B>What a space base!</B> Don't let this once-in-a-millenium
opportunity pass you buy: <B>call ZOLZOL's</B> to place your
bid for Sol III* <B>right now!</B><P>
<IMG SRC="zolsol2.gif" ALIGN="left">
<IMG SRC="zolsol4.gif" ALIGN="right">
(And don't forget to bid on Sol III's sister planets, Sol II
and Sol IV! With a little investment in these great
fixer-uppers, you could have the <B>three-planet home of your
dreams</B> for one low price. <B>Call NOW!</B>)
<BR CLEAR="all"><HR>
<SMALL><B>*Disclaimer:</B> One or more races on this planet may
possess chemical and/or nuclear weapons. All sales are final.
Invasion and enslavement of native species is the sole
responsibility of the customer and ZolZol's makes no warrantees,
expressed or implied. ZolZol believes this planet to be in
inhabititable condition, but some environmental degradation
is normal for speciated worlds.</SMALL><P>
<DIV ALIGN="center">
<A HREF="zolzol.htm"><IMG SRC="zolhome.gif" BORDER=0></A>
<A HREF="zolnew.htm"><IMG SRC="zolnew.gif" BORDER=0></A>
<A HREF="zoljunk.htm"><IMG SRC="zoljunk.gif" BORDER=0></A>
</DIV>
</BODY></HTML>
```

10

Notice that ALIGN means something different in an <IMG> tag than it does in a <DIV> tag. <IMG ALIGN="right"> will align an image to the right and cause any text that follows to wrap around the image. <DIV ALIGN="right">, on the other hand, just controls the alignment and never causes text to wrap around images.

FIGURE 10.5.

*The HTML page listed
in Figure 10.4, as it
appears in a Web
browser.*

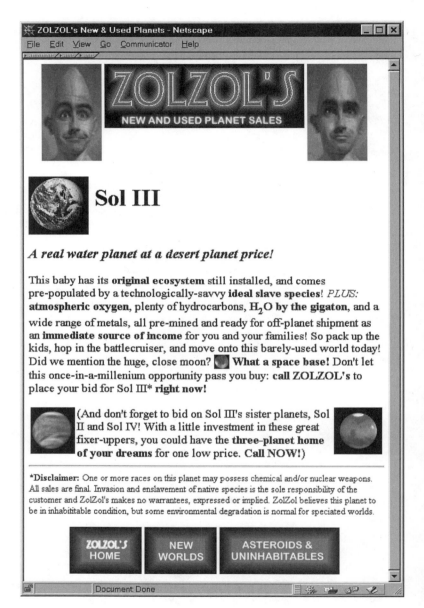

Vertical Image Alignment

You may want to insert a small image right in the middle of a line of text or you might like to put a single line of text next to an image as a caption. In either case, it would be handy to have some control over how the text and images line up vertically. Should the bottom of the image line up with the bottom of the letters? Should the text and images all be arranged so their middles line up? You can choose between these and several other options:

- To line up the top of an image with the top of the tallest image or letter on the same line, use `<IMG ALIGN="top">`.
- To line up the bottom of an image with the bottom of the text, use `<IMG ALIGN="bottom">`.
- To line up the bottom of an image with the bottom of the lowest image or letter on the same line, use `<IMG ALIGN="absbottom">`. (If there are some larger images on the same line, `ALIGN=absbottom` might place an image lower than `ALIGN=bottom`.)
- To line up the middle of an image with the baseline of the text, use `<IMG ALIGN="middle">`.
- To line up the middle of an image with the overall vertical center of everything on the line, use `<IMG ALIGN="absmiddle">`. This might be higher or lower than `ALIGN="middle"`, depending on the size and alignment of other images on the same line.

10

Three of these options are illustrated in Figures 10.4 and 10.5. The ZOLZOL's logo is aligned with the top of the photos on either side of it by using `ALIGN="top"`, the picture of the water planet uses `ALIGN="middle"` to line up the baseline of the words *Sol III* with the center of the Earth, and the little image of the moon is lined up in the exact center of the text around it using `ALIGN="absmiddle"`.

If you don't include any `ALIGN` attribute in an `<IMG>` tag, the image will line up with the bottom of any text next to it. That means you never actually have to type in `ALIGN="bottom"` because it does the same thing.

In fact, you probably won't use any of the vertical alignment settings much; the vast majority of Web page images use either `ALIGN="left"`, `ALIGN="right"`, or no `ALIGN` attribute at all. So don't worry about memorizing all these options—you can always refer to this book if you ever do need them.

FIGURE 10.6.

You can control the vertical alignment of images with the ALIGN *attribute.*

```
<HTML><HEAD><TITLE>ZOLZOL's New &amp; Used Planets</TITLE>
</HEAD>
<BODY BACKGROUND="zolstars.jpg" TEXT="white">
<DIV ALIGN="center">
<IMG SRC="zolzol2.jpg" ALIGN="left" ALT="Friendly Fen">
<IMG SRC="zolzol1.jpg" ALIGN="right" ALT="Honest Han">
<IMG SRC="zolsign2.gif" ALT="ZOLZOL's New and Used Planets">
<P><I>"Make us an offer, we'll make you a deal!"</I>
<BR CLEAR="all">
<IMG SRC="zolfen.gif" ALIGN="left">
<IMG SRC="zolhan.gif" ALIGN="right">
<BR CLEAR="all">
</DIV><P>
ZOLZOL's: the <B>best planets</B> at the <B>best prices</B>
in the galaxy! And have we got a zee-binger for you <B>right
now</B>! This <B>special exclusive</B> is a nine-planet
system out on a quiet spiral arm by a pretty little star the
locals call <I>Sol</I>. (Not <I>Zol</I>, ha ha! That's us!)
So <B>escape the chaos</B> of galactic downtown! Buy these
peaceful, out-of-the-way planets as a complete
<B>ready-to-invade</B> star system, or if you're short on
cash just pick the rock you like the best! Click below to
see <B>what a find</B> and <B>what a bargain</B> this system
really is! (But click quick, these premium spheres are sure
to <B>sell fast!</B>) <P>
<DIV ALIGN="center">
<A HREF="zolused.htm"><IMG SRC="zolused.gif" BORDER=0
 ALT="Previously Owned Worlds"></A>
<A HREF="zolnew.htm"><IMG SRC="zolnew.gif" BORDER=0
 ALT="New Worlds"></A>
<A HREF="zoljunk.htm"><IMG SRC="zoljunk.gif" BORDER=0
 ALT="Asteroids and Uninhabitables"></A>
</DIV>
</BODY></HTML>
```

You may have noticed that Figure 10.7 has a custom background instead of the standard white background. You'll learn all about this sort of thing in Hour 11, but you can probably figure out how it's done just by looking at the <BODY> tag in Figure 10.6.

To Do

Try adding some images to your Web pages now, and experiment with all the different values of ALIGN. To get you started, here's a quick review of how to add the magic hat image to any Web page. (See the To Do box at the beginning of this hour for help downloading the magic hat image.)

• Copy the magic.gif image file to the same directory folder as the HTML file.

▼

- With a text editor, add `<IMG SRC="magic.gif">` where you want the image to appear in the text.

- If you want the image to be centered, put `<DIV ALIGN="center">` before the `<IMG>` tag, `</DIV>` after it. To wrap text around the image instead, add `ALIGN="right"` or `ALIGN="left"` to the `<IMG>` tag.

▲

If you have time for a little more experimentation, try combining multiple images of various sizes (such as the stars and the magic hats) with various vertical alignment settings for `<IMG ALIGN>`.

FIGURE 10.7.

The top, middle, and bottom of each line depends on the size of the text and images on that line. Notice that the words "Friendly Fen" Zol and "Honest Han" Zol are actually two small image files, not text.

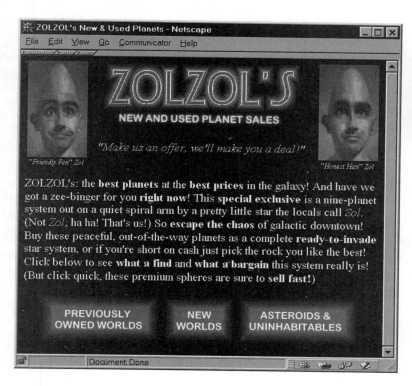

10

Summary

This hour has shown you how to use the `<IMG>` tag to place graphics images on your Web pages. You learned to include a short text message to appear in place of the image as it loads, and whenever someone moves their mouse pointer over the image. You also learned to control the horizontal and vertical alignment of each image, and how to make text wrap around the left or right of an image.

Finally, you learned how to make images into "buttons" that link to other pages by using the same <A> tag introduced in Hour 3. And you got a sneak preview of the kind of custom page backgrounds you'll learn to use in Hour 11.

Table 10.1 summarizes the attributes of the <IMG> tag covered in this hour.

TABLE 10.1. HTML TAGS AND ATTRIBUTES COVERED IN HOUR 10.

Tag/Attribute	Function
Attributes:	
SRC="..."	The address or filename of the image.
ALT="..."	A text message that may be displayed in place of the image.
ALIGN="..."	Determines the alignment of the given image. If LEFT or RIGHT, the image is aligned to the left or right column, and all following text flows beside that image. All other values, such as TOP, MIDDLE, BOTTOM, ABSMIDDLE, or ABSBOTTOM, determine the vertical alignment of this image with other items in the same line.

Q&A

Q **I found a nice image on a Web page on the Internet. Can I just use Save Image As to save a copy and then put the image on my Web pages?**

A It's easy to do that, but unfortunately it's also illegal in most countries. You should get written permission from the original creator of the image first. Most Web pages include the email address of their author, which makes it a simple matter to ask for permission—a lot simpler than going to court!

Q **How long a message can I put after ALT= in an <IMG> tag?**

A Theoretically, as long as you want. But practically, you should keep the message short enough so that it will fit in less space than the image itself. For big images, 10 words may be fine. For small images, a single word is better.

Q **I used the <IMG> tag just like you said, but all I get is a little box with an X or some shapes in it when I view the page. What's wrong?**

A The "broken image" icon you're seeing can mean one of two things: either the Web browser couldn't find the image file, or the image isn't saved in a format the browser can understand. To solve either one of these problems, open the image file by using Paint Shop Pro (or your favorite graphics software), select Save As, and be sure to save the file in either the GIF or JPEG format. Also make sure you save it in the same folder as the Web page that contains the `<IMG>` tag referring to it, and that the filename on the disk precisely matches the filename you put it the `<IMG>` tag (including capitalization).

Q How do I control both the horizontal and vertical alignment of an image at once?

A The short answer is that you can't. For example, if you type `<IMG ALIGN="right" ALIGN="middle" SRC="myimage.gif">`, the `ALIGN="middle"` will be ignored.

There are ways around this limitation, however. In Part IV, "Web Page Design," you will discover several techniques for positioning text and images exactly where you want them in both the horizontal and vertical directions.

Workshop

10

Quiz

1. How would you insert an image file named `elephant.jpg` at the very top of a Web page?

2. How would you make the word *Elephant* appear whenever the actual `elephant.jpg` image couldn't be displayed by a Web browser?

3. Write the HTML to make the `elephant.jpg` image appear on the right side of the page, with a big headline reading *Elephants of the World Unite!* on the left side of the page next to it.

4. Write the HTML to make a tiny image of a mouse (named `mouse.jpg`) appear between the words *Wee sleekit, cow'rin,* and the words *tim'rous beastie*.

5. Suppose you have a large picture of a standing elephant named `elephant.jpg`. Now make a small image named `fly.jpg` appear to the left of the elephant's head, and `mouse.jpg` appear next to the elephant's right foot.

Answers

1. Copy the image file into the same directory folder as the HTML text file, and type `<IMG SRC="elephant.jpg">` immediately after the `<BODY>` tag in the HTML text file.

2. Use the following HTML:

   `<IMG SRC="elephant.jpg" ALT="Elephant">`

3. `<IMG SRC="elephant.jpg" ALIGN="right">`
   `<H1>Elephants of the World Unite!</H1>`

4. `Wee sleekit, cow'rin,<IMG SRC="mouse.jpg">tim'rous beastie`

5. `<IMG SRC="fly.jpg" ALIGN="top">`

   `<IMG SRC="elephant.jpg">`
   `<IMG SRC="mouse.jpg">`

Exercises

- Try using any small image as a "bullet" to make lists with more flair. If you also want the list to be indented, use the `<DL>` definition list and `<DD>` for each item (instead of `<UL>` and `<LI>`, which would give the standard boring bullets). Here's a quick example, using the `star.gif` file from my sample images page:

  `<DL><DD><IMG SRC="star.gif">A murder of crows[sr]`

  `<DD><IMG SRC="star.gif">A rafter of turkeys[sr]`

  `<DD><IMG SRC="star.gif">A muster of peacocks</DL>`

Hour 11

Custom Backgrounds and Colors

Nearly every example Web page in Hours 1 through 10 has a white background and black text. In this hour, you'll find out how to make pages with background and text colors of your choosing. You'll also discover how to make your own custom background graphics, and how to let the background show through parts of any image you put on your Web pages.

To Do

The black-and-white figures printed in this book obviously don't convey colors very accurately, so you may want to view the example pages online. You can also try the colors on your own Web pages as you read about how to make them.

To find all the examples from this hour online, go to
http://24hourHTMLcafe.com/hour11/.

Background and Text Colors

To specify the background color for a page, put BGCOLOR="blue" inside the <BODY> tag. Of course, you can use many colors other than blue. You can choose from the 16 standard Windows colors: black, white, red, green, blue, yellow, magenta, cyan, purple, gray, lime, maroon, navy, olive, silver, and teal. (You can call magenta by the name "fuchsia", and cyan by the name "aqua" if you want to feel more artsy and less geeky.)

You can also specify colors for text and links in the <BODY> tag. For example, in Figure 11.1 you'll notice the following <BODY> tag:

```
<BODY BGCOLOR="teal" TEXT="fuchsia" LINK="yellow" VLINK="lime"
ALINK="red">
```

As you probably guessed, TEXT="fuchsia" makes the text yellow. There are three separate attributes for link colors:

- LINK="yellow" makes links that haven't been visited recently yellow.
- VLINK="lime" makes recently visited links lime green.
- ALINK="red" makes links briefly blink red when someone clicks them.

> Here's a neat trick: If you make the VLINK color the same as the BGCOLOR color, links to pages that a visitor has already seen will become invisible. This can make your page seem "smart"—offering people only links to places they haven't been. (Note, however, that it may also annoy anybody who wants to return to a page they've already seen!)

Figures 11.1 and 11.2 illustrate how color can be used in combination with links. Because I used pure, beautiful teal as the background color in the graphics images, they blend right into the background of the Web page. (I didn't need to use *transparent* images, which you'll learn about later in this hour.)

Creating Custom Colors

If the 16 named colors don't include the exact hue you're after, you can mix your own custom colors by specifying how much red, green, and blue light should be mixed into each color.

FIGURE 11.1.

You can specify colors for the background, text, and links in the <BODY> tag of any Web page.

```html
<HTML><HEAD><TITLE>The Teal and the Fuchsia</TITLE></HEAD>
<BODY BGCOLOR="teal" TEXT="fuchsia"
 LINK="yellow" VLINK="lime" ALINK="red">
<IMG SRC="c.gif" ALIGN="right">
<H1><A HREF="credley.htm">CREDLEY HIGH SCHOOL</A></H1>
<H2>"The Old Teal and Fuchsia"</H2>
<DIV ALIGN="center">
<I><B>Oh, hail! Hail! Sing Credley!<BR>
Our colors jump and shout!<BR>
Deep teal like ocean's highest waves,<BR>
Fuchsia like blossoms bursting out!<P>
<IMG SRC="cheer.gif" ALIGN="left">
As Credley conquers every team<BR>
So do our brilliant colors peal<BR>
From mountain tops &amp; florist shops<BR>
Sweet sacred fuchsia, holy teal!<P>
Our men are tough as vinyl siding<BR>
Our women, strong as plastic socks<BR>
Our colors tell our story truly<BR>
We may be ugly, but we rock!</B></I>
</DIV></BODY></HTML>
```

FIGURE 11.2.

On a color screen, this ever-so-attractive page has a teal background, fuchsia body text, and yellow link text, as specified in Figure 11.1.

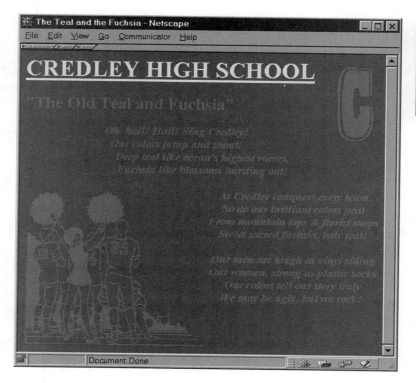

11

The format is *#rrggbb* where *rr*, *gg*, and *bb* are two-digit hexadecimal values for the red, green, and blue components of the color. If you're not familiar with hexadecimal numbers, don't sweat it. Just remember that FF is the maximum, 00 is the minimum, and use one of the following codes for each component:

- FF means full brightness
- CC means 80 percent brightness
- 99 means 60 percent brightness
- 66 means 40 percent brightness
- 33 means 20 percent brightness
- 00 means none of this color component

For example, bright red is #FF0000, dark green is #003300, bluish-purple is #660099, and medium-gray is #999999. To make a page with a red background, dark green text, and bluish-purple links that turn white when you click them and gray when you've visited them, the HTML would look like the following:

```
<BODY BGCOLOR="#FF0000" TEXT="#003300" LINK="#660099" ALINK="#FFFFFF"
VLINK="#999999">
```

Though the colors you specify in the <BODY> tag apply to all text on the page, you can also use either color names or hexadecimal color codes to change the color of a particular word or section of text by using the <FONT> tag. This is discussed in Hour 6, "Text Formatting and Font Control."

> For a very handy chart showing the 216 most commonly used hexadecimal color codes, along with the colors they create, go to:
>
> http://24hourHTMLcafe.com/colors
>
> Click the "Color Code Reference."
>
> You can then choose any of the standard 16 text colors to see how each of them looks over every color in the table.

Keep in mind that even though you can specify millions of different colors, some computers are set to display only the 16 named colors. Other computers only reliably display the 216 colors in the color code reference mentioned in the previous tip. All others will be approximated by dithered patterns, which can make text look messy and difficult to read.

Also, you should be aware that different computer monitors may display colors in very different hues. I recently designed a page with a beautiful blue background for a company I work for, only to find out later that the president of the company saw it on his computer as a lovely purple background! Neutral, earth-tone colors such as medium gray, tan, and ivory can lead to even more unpredictable results on many computer monitors, and may even seem to change color on one monitor depending on lighting conditions in the room and the time of day.

The moral of the story: Stick to the named colors and don't waste time mucking with hexadecimal color codes, unless you have precise control over the computer displays of your intended audience.

You can set the color of an individual link to a different color than the rest by putting a <FONT> tag with a COLOR attribute *after* the <A HREF>. (Also include a </FONT> tag before the </A> tag.) For example, the following would make a green link:

Visit the <A HREF="thumb.htm"><FONT COLOR="green">Green Thumb page</FONT></A> to become a better gardener.

However, older versions of some browsers (including Microsoft Internet Explorer 3.0), will always display all links with the colors set in the <BODY> tag. Very old browsers may completely ignore some or all of your color specifications.

11

Background Image Tiles

Background tiles let you specify an image to be used as a wallpaper pattern behind all text and graphics in a document. You put the image file name after BACKGROUND= in the <BODY> tag like the following:

```
<BODY BACKGROUND="image.jpg">
```

Like other Web graphics, background tiles must be in either the GIF or JPEG file format, and you can create them by using Paint Shop Pro or any other graphics software. For example, the tile.gif file referred to by the <BODY> tag in Figure 11.3 is an image of one small tile. As you can see in Figure 11.4, most Web browsers will repeat the image behind any text and images on the page, like floor tile.

Tiled background images should be implemented with great care to avoid distracting from the main content of the page itself. The text in Figure 11.4, for example, would be very difficult to read if I hadn't made it all bold-face—and may still be hard to decipher on some computer monitors. Many pages on the Web are almost impossible to read due to overdone backgrounds.

So before you include your company logo or baby pictures as wallpaper behind your Web pages, stop and think. If you had an important message to send someone on a piece of paper, would you write it over the top of the letterhead logo or on the blank part of the page? Backgrounds should be like fine papers: attractive, yet unobtrusive.

FIGURE 11.3.

You can specify a background image to tile behind a page in the BACKGROUND attribute of the <BODY> tag.

```
<HTML><HEAD><TITLE>Motawi Tileworks</TITLE></HEAD>
<BODY BACKGROUND="tile.gif">
<IMG SRC="mtworks.gif"><P>
<IMG SRC="motawis.gif" ALIGN="left">
<B>Karim and Nawal Motawi (brother and sister) welcome you
to <A HREF="http://www.motawi.com">Motawi Tileworks</A>, an art
tile studio specializing in the Arts & Crafts style. We create
low-relief and polychrome tiles for accents and as art pieces,
as well as many varieties of flat tiles, architectural borders,
trims, and custom pieces.</B>
<DIV ALIGN="center">
<H2><A HREF="http://www.motawi.com">www.motawi.com</A></H2>
33 North Staebler, Suite 2, Ann Arbor, MI 48103<BR>
tel.:(734) 213-0017 fax:(734) 213-2569<BR>
</DIV></BODY></HTML>
```

FIGURE 11.4.

The tile.gif *file (specified in Figure 11.3 and shown in Figure 11.5) is automatically repeated to cover the entire page.*

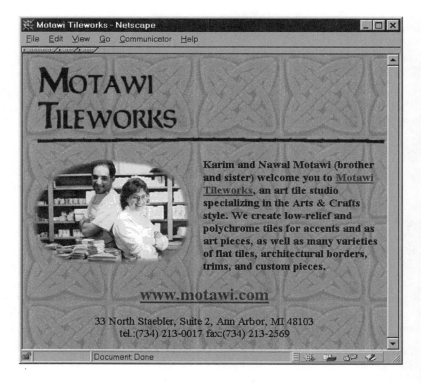

Transparent Images

You will see how to make your own background tiles later in this hour, but first a word about how to let the background show through parts of your foreground graphics.

Web page images are always rectangular. However, the astute observer of Figure 11.4 (that's you) will notice that the background tiles show through portions of the images, and therefore the title and picture don't look rectangular at all. You'll often want to use partially transparent images to make graphics look good over any background color or background image tile.

Figure 11.5 shows the images from Figure 11.4, as they looked in Paint Shop Pro when I created them. (Figure 11.5 also shows the single tile used for the background in Figure 11.4.)

FIGURE 11.5.

When I saved two of these images in Paint Shop Pro, I made the background color transparent. (The third image, at the top left, is the background tile.)

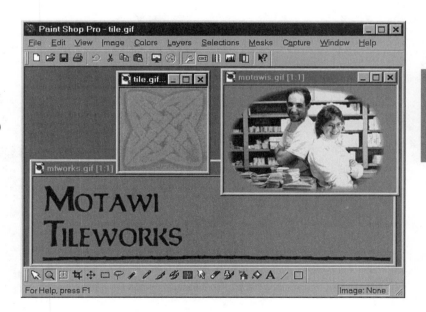

To make part of an image transparent, the image must have 256 or fewer colors, and you must save it in the GIF file format. (JPEG images can't be transparent.) Most graphics programs that support the GIF format allow you to specify one color to be transparent.

To Do

To save a transparent GIF in Paint Shop Pro follow these steps:

1. Select Colors, Decrease Color Depth, 256 Colors (8-bit) or Colors, Decrease Color Depth, 16 Colors (4-bit), and check the Optimized Octree and Nearest color boxes (as recommended in Hour 9, "Creating Your Own Web Page Graphics").

2. Choose the eyedropper tool, and right-click the color you want to make transparent.

3. Select Colors, View Palette Transparency. If any part of the image is already set to be transparent, you will see a gray checkered pattern in that part now.

4. Select Colors, Set Palette Transparency, as shown in Figure 11.6.

5. You should see the dialog box in Figure 11.7. Choose Set the Transparency Value to the Current Background Color, and click OK.

6. As in Figure 11.8, you will now see the transparent parts of the image turn to a gray checkerboard pattern. You can use any of the painting tools to touch up parts of the image where there is too little or too much of the transparent background color.

7. When everything looks right, select File, Save As (or File, Save Copy As) and choose the CompuServe Graphics Interchange (*.gif) as the file type.

FIGURE 11.6.

Use the View Palette Transparency and Set Palette Transparency commands on Paint Shop Pro's Colors menu to make the background show through parts of an image.

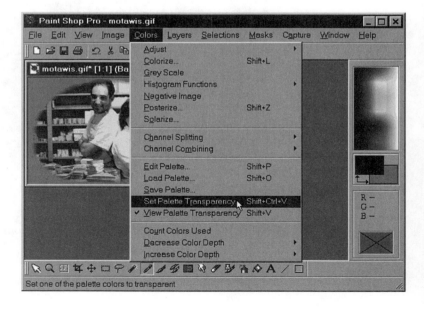

FIGURE 11.7.

FIGURE 11.7.

*When you select
Colors, Set Palette
Transparency, this dia-
log box appears. You
will usually want the
middle option.*

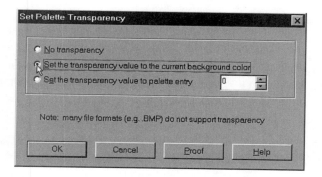

FIGURE 11.8.

*Paint Shop Pro shows
transparent regions of
an image with a gray
checkerboard pattern.
(You can change the
grid size and colors
used under File,
Preferences, General
Program Preferences,
Transparency).*

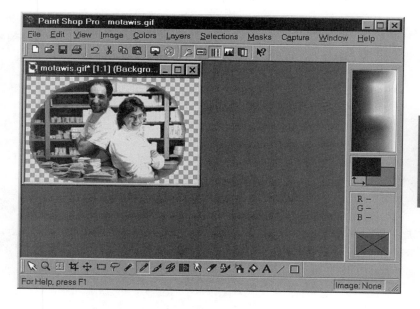

11

In earlier versions of Paint Shop Pro, and in some other software, transparency control is implemented very differently. In Paint Shop Pro 3.11 and
4.0, for example, you would find transparency settings under Options in the
Save As dialog box when saving a GIF file.

Creating Your Own Backgrounds

Any GIF or JPEG image can be used as a background tile. But pages look best when the
top edge of a background tile matches seamlessly with the bottom edge, and the left edge
matches up with the right.

If you're clever and have some time to spend on it, you can make any image into a seamless tile by meticulously cutting and pasting, while touching up the edges. But Paint Shop Pro provides a much easier way to automatically make any texture into a seamless tile. You simply use the rectangular selection tool to choose the area you want to make into a tile, and then select Selections, Convert to Seamless Pattern. Paint Shop Pro crops the image and uses a sophisticated automatic procedure to overlay and blur together opposite sides of the image.

In Figure 11.9 I did this with part of an image of the planet Jupiter, taken from a NASA image archive. The resulting tile, shown as the background of a Web page in Figure 11.10, tiles seamlessly but has the tone and texture of the eye of Jove himself.

You'll find similar features in other graphics programs, including Photoshop (use Filter, Other, Offset with Wrap Turned On), Kai's Power Tools, and the Macintosh programs Mordant and Tilery.

FIGURE 11.9.

Paint Shop Pro can automatically take any region of an image and make it into a background pattern that can be easily made into tiles.

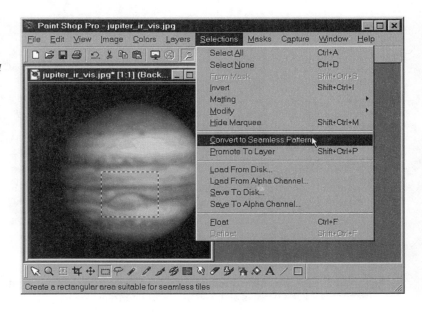

FIGURE 11.10.

The results of Figure 11.9 used as a background image for a Web page.

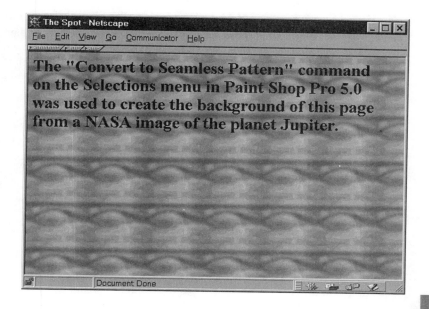

To Do

Here some tips for making your own background tiles with Paint Shop Pro.

- If you have a scanner or digital camera, try using some textures from around the house or office, such as the top of a wooden desk, leaves of houseplants, or clothing.

- Using the Image, Blur, Blur More filter on an image (as I did with the Jupiter picture in Figures 11.9 and 11.10) before you make it into a seamless tile will help it look better as a background. Using Colors, Adjust, Brightness and Contrast is usually also necessary to keep the background subtle in color variation.

- When you select an area to make into a tile, try to choose part of the image that is fairly uniform in brightness from side to side. Otherwise, the tile may not look seamless even after you use Convert to Seamless Pattern.

- You must also use a big enough image so that you can leave at least the width and height of the tile on either side of your selection. If you don't, when you select Convert to Seamless Pattern you'll get a message saying `Your selection is too close to the edge to complete this operation`.

- You can also make some almost-automatic textures with the paper texture feature in the paintbrush style palette in Paint Shop Pro. You can make great paper textures too by selecting Image, Noise, Add followed by Image, Blur, Blur and Colors, Colorize.

11

If you just cannot seem to get the pattern you want, there are hundreds of sites on the Internet that offer public domain background images that you are free to use or inexpensive professionally designed backgrounds. A good starting place is the Background Underground lounge at the 24-Hour HTML Café:

`http://24hourHTMLcafe.com/bgu/`

This page presents several flashy backgrounds (tone them down with Colors, Adjust before using them on your pages), and links to hundreds more.

If you happen to see a background image on someone else's page that you wish you could use on your own page, it is a simple matter to click on the background with the right mouse button and select Save Background As to save a copy of it. Be careful, though, to ask the person who created the image for permission before you use it.

Summary

In this hour, you learned how to set the background and text colors for a Web page. You also found out how to make a tiled background image appear behind a Web page, how to make foreground images partially transparent so the background shows through, and how to create seamless image tiles for use as backgrounds.

Table 11.1 summarizes the attributes of the <BODY> tag discussed in this hour.

TABLE 11.1. ATTRIBUTES OF THE <BODY> TAG COVERED IN HOUR 11.

Attributes	Function
`<BODY>...</BODY>.`	Encloses the body (text and tags) of the HTML document
`BACKGROUND="..."`	The name or address of the image to tile on the page background
`BGCOLOR="..."`	The color of the page background
`TEXT="..."`	The color of the page's text
`LINK="..."`	The color of unfollowed links
`ALINK="..."`	The color of activated links
`VLINK="..."`	The color of followed links

Q&A

Q Doesn't Netscape Navigator let people choose their own background and text color preferences?

A Yes, and so does Microsoft Internet Explorer. Both programs allow users to override the colors you (as a Web page author) specify. So some may see your white-on-blue page as green-on-white, or their own favorite colors, instead. But very few people use this option, so the colors specified in the <BODY> tag will usually be seen.

Q I've heard that there are 231 "magic colors" that I should use to look good in Netscape Navigator. Is that true?

A Here's the real story: There are 231 colors that will appear less "fuzzy" to people who operate their computers in a 256-color video mode (the other 25 colors are used for menus and stuff like that). So some Web page authors try to stick to those colors. However, true color or high color computer displays are increasingly common, and they show all colors with equal clarity. On the other hand, lots of people still use a 16-color video mode, which makes most of the 231 "magic" colors look fuzzy too. I recommend sticking to the 16 named colors for text and using whatever colors you want for graphics.

Q My background image looks okay in my graphics editing program, but has weird white or colored gaps or dots in it when it comes up behind a Web page. Why?

A There are two possibilities: If the background image you're using is a GIF file, it probably has transparency turned on which makes one of the colors in the image turn white (or whatever color you specified in the BODY BGCOLOR attribute). The solution is to open the file with your graphics program, and turn off the transparency (in Paint Shop Pro, select Colors, Set Palette Transparency, and pick No Transparency). Then re-save the file.

If a JPEG (or .jpg) image, or a non-transparent GIF image, seems to look spotty when you put it on a Web page, it may just be the Web browser's "dithering." That's the method the software uses to try to show more colors than your system is set up to display at once by mixing colored dots together side-by-side. There's not much you can do about it, though you'll find hints for minimizing the problem in Hour 9, "Creating Your Own Web Page Graphics."

11

Workshop

Quiz

1. How would you give a Web page a black background and make all text, including links, bright green?

2. How would you make an image file named `texture.jpg` appear as a repeating tile behind the text and images on a Web page with white text and red links that turn blue after being followed?

3. If `elephant.jpg` is a JPEG image of an elephant standing in front of a solid white backdrop, how do you make the backdrop transparent so only the elephant shows on a Web page?

4. Which menu choice in Paint Shop Pro automatically creates a background tile from part of any image?

Answers

1. Put the following at the beginning of the Web page:

   ```
   <BODY BGCOLOR="black"
   TEXT="lime" LINK="lime" VLINK="lime" ALINK="black">
   ```

   Or the following would do exactly the same thing:

   ```
   <BODY BGCOLOR="#000000"
   TEXT="#00FF00" LINK="#00FF00" VLINK="#00FF00" ALINK="#000000">
   ```

2. ```
   <BODY BACKGROUND="texture.jpg"
   TEXT="white" LINK="red" VLINK="blue" ALINK="black">
   ```

3. Open the image in Paint Shop Pro, and then use Colors, Decrease Color Depth, 256 Colors to pick the best 256 colors for the image. Right-click the white area, select Colors, Set Palette Transparency and elect to make the background color transparent. Touch up any off-white spots that didn't become transparent, and then use File, Save As to save it in the GIF 89a format.

4. Selections, Convert to Seamless Pattern. See the Paint Shop Pro documentation if you need a little more help using it than this hour provided.
   ```

Exercises

- Try getting creative with some background tiles that *don't* use Convert to Seamless Pattern. You'll discover some sneaky tricks for making background tiles that don't look like background tiles in Hour 14, "Graphical Links and Imagemaps," but I bet you can figure out some interesting ones on your own right now. (Hint: What if you made a background tile 2,000 pixels wide and 10 pixels tall?)
- If you have some photos of objects for a Web-based catalog, consider taking the time to paint a transparent color carefully around the edges of them. (Sometimes the magic wand tool can help automate this process.) You can also use Paint Shop Pro's Image, Effects, Drop Shadow feature to add a slight shadow behind or beneath each object, so they appear to stand out from the background.

11

Hour **12**

Creating Animated Graphics

There are several ways to add some movement to a Web page, and most of them are covered in the two most advanced chapters of this book: Hour 20, "Setting Pages in Motion with Dynamic HTML," and Hour 17, "Embedding Multimedia in Web Pages." However, you can actually add animation to standard GIF images, and it's so easy to do that the technique doesn't even qualify as "advanced."

GIF animations are a great way to make simple animated icons and add a little motion to spice up any Web page. They also transfer much faster than most video or multimedia files. In this chapter, you'll learn how to create GIF animations and how to optimize them for the fastest possible display.

Software for Making Web Page Animations

The latest version of Paint Shop Pro from JASC software includes a module called Animation Shop, which is designed especially for creating Web page GIF animations. There are a few other GIF animation programs available, including both freeware and advanced commercial software packages. But Animation Shop offers the best mix of great features, ease of use, and low price.

(For Macintosh users, I recommend GifBuilder, which is available free at http://www.shareware.com. Another good GIF animation program for the Macintosh is Gif.g1F.giF at http://www.cafe.net/peda/ggg/.)

As mentioned in Hour 9, "Creating Your Own Web Page Graphics," you can download a free evaluation copy of Paint Shop Pro 5.0, which includes Animation Shop 1.0, from the Internet at www.jasc.com. If you haven't already, I recommend that you download and install it now so you can try your hand at building an animation or two as you read this chapter.

Creating the Pictures You Want to Animate

The first step in creating a GIF animation is to create a series of images to be displayed one after the other. Each of these images is called a *frame*. (By the way, this use of the word "frame" has nothing whatsoever to do with the "frames" you'll learn about in Hour 21, "Multipage Layout with Frames.") You can use any graphics software you like to make the images, though Paint Shop Pro is an obvious choice if you plan on using Animation Shop to put the animation together.

Figure 12.1 shows three pictures I drew with Paint Shop Pro. In each picture, the icon of the man and the "NO" symbol around him are exactly identical, but the flames and smoke on his body are slightly different. When these three images are put together into an animation, the flames will seem to flicker.

Notice that the images in Figure 12.1 are transparent (the checkerboard background isn't part of the picture, it's how Paint Shop Pro indicates transparency). The animation made from them will therefore be transparent, too, and will look great over any light-colored Web page background. (See Hour 11, "Custom Backgrounds and Colors," for more on making transparent GIF images.)

FIGURE 12.1.

Use Paint Shop Pro or any other graphics program to produce the individual "frames" of your animation.

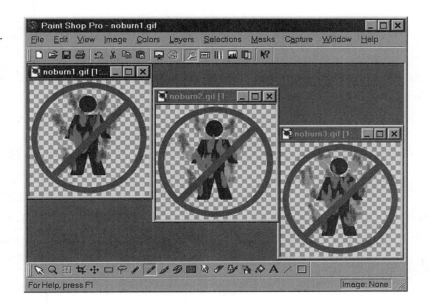

If you know how to use the Layers feature of Paint Shop Pro (or any other advanced graphics software), you'll find that creating animation frames is easier because you can easily turn on and off parts of a picture to make variations, or move layers to simulate motion. For example, I actually created one image with separate transparent layers for the man, the NO symbol, and the flame and smoke variations. I then used Edit, Copy Merged and Edit, Paste, As New Image to make the three individual images in Figure 12.1, each with different opacity settings for each layer.

Don't fret, however, if all that layer manipulation is a bit beyond you still. You can easily make very effective animations by copying an ordinary one-layer image and painting on some variations, or moving some parts of it around to make the next frame.

When you have the individual frames of your animation ready, use Colors, Decrease Color Depth to limit them to 256 or 16 colors, and then save each of them as a separate GIF file. (Refer to Hour 9 for more detailed instructions if you need a refresher on creating and saving GIF files.)

To Do

You might want to create a few frames for your own animation, and use them to follow along with the numbered steps below.

You'll find it easier to build and modify animations if you give the images for each animation similar names. You might name the images for a dog animation dog1.gif, dog2.gif, dog3.gif, and so on.

12

▼ If you would like to work with the same three animation frames I use for the first example in this chapter, you'll find them at:

`http://24hourHTMLcafe.com/hour12/noburn1.gif`

`http://24hourHTMLcafe.com/hour12/noburn2.gif`

▲ `http://24hourHTMLcafe.com/hour12/noburn3.gif`

Assembling the Pictures into an Animation

Once you have the individual GIF files saved, select File, Run Animation Shop from
within Paint Shop Pro to start putting them together into a single animation file.

> The fastest way to create a simple GIF animation with Animation Shop is to
> select File, Animation Wizard. This will start an "interview" that leads you
> through all the steps discussed next.
>
> In this hour, however, I show you how to create animations "by hand," with-
> out using the Animation Wizard. This will give you a head start when you
> want to use the advanced animation tricks discussed toward the end of the
> chapter.

The basic idea here couldn't be simpler: you just need to tell Animation Shop which pictures to show, and in what order. There are also a couple of other picky details you need
to specify: how long to show each picture before moving on to the next one, and how
many times to repeat the whole sequence. Follow this step-by-step procedure to assemble an animation:

1. Select File, Open (in Animation Shop, not in Paint Shop Pro), and choose the
   image file that you want to be the first frame of the animation. It will appear with
   blank cross-hatched frames on either side of it, as shown in Figure 12.2. Notice
   that the transparency is preserved, as indicated by the gray checkerboard pattern
   showing through.

2. Select Edit, Insert Frames, From File to get the dialog box in Figure 12.3. Click
   the Add File button and choose the image you want to appear second in the animation. Click Add File again to add the third frame, and so forth until the list contains all the images you made for this animation. Then click OK.

FIGURE 12.2.

A single-frame GIF image as it first appears when opened in Animation Shop.

FIGURE 12.3.

Selecting Edit, Insert Frames, From File gives you this dialog box. The Add File button lets you choose an image to add to the animation.

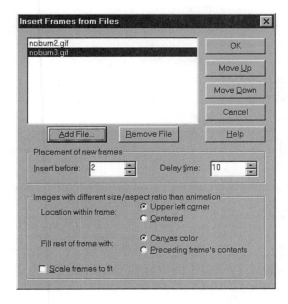

12

FIGURE 12.4.

Animation Shop displays all the frames of an animation side-by-side, like a filmstrip.

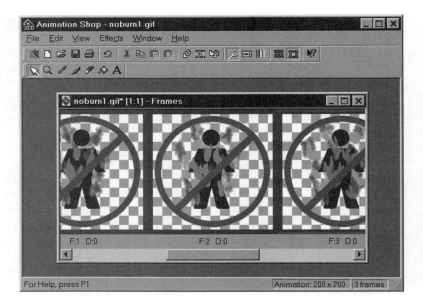

3. You should now see all the frames layed out next to each other like a filmstrip (see Figure 12.4). You can use the scroll bar to move forward and back through the filmstrip if all the frames aren't visible at once. If you'd like to see a preview of the animation, select View, Animation. If any frames are in the wrong order, you simply grab and drag them into the proper positions with the mouse.

   If you don't tell it any different, Animation Shop normally puts a tenth of a second between each frame of the animation. That was actually about right for my little burning-man icon. However, you will often want to control the length of time each individual frame is displayed before the next one replaces it.

4. To set the timing for a frame, click it (the border around it will turn blue and red) and then select Edit, Frame Properties. (Alternatively, you can right-click the frame and pick Properties from the pop-up menu.) You'll get the dialog box shown in Figure 12.5, where you can specify the Display Time in hundredths of a second.

> Notice that there is also a Delay Time setting in Figure 12.3. This allows you to adjust the timing of all the frames at once, when you first put the animation together. This can save you a lot of work, if all or most of your frames will have the same delay, because it saves you from having to change the Frame Properties of them all one by one.

FIGURE 12.5.

Right-click a frame and choose Properties to set the amount of time that frame should be displayed.

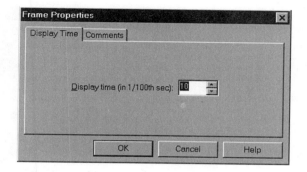

5. One final detail, and your animation will be done! Select Edit, Animation Properties (or, alternatively, right-click on the gray area below the filmstrip and pick Properties from the pop-up menu) to get the dialog box in Figure 12.6. I wanted my flames to keep flickering as long as someone is viewing my animation, so I chose Repeat the Animation Indefinitely. In some cases, however, you might only want your animation sequence to play once (or some other number of times) before stopping to display the last frame as a still image. In that case, you'd select the second choice and enter the number of times to repeat.

FIGURE 12.6.

Right-click the gray bar below the frames and choose Properties to set the number of times the entire animation will repeat.

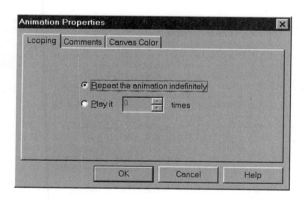

12

6. Your animation is complete. Select File, Save As to save it. You will be presented with a control like the one in Figure 12.7, which allows you to choose a balance between good image quality and small file size.

The long list of optimizations may seem bewildering—and all the choices you'd have to make if you clicked the Customize button would be even more mind-boggling. But fortunately, Animation Shop usually does an excellent job of choosing the most appropriate optimizations for you based on the slider setting. Move the slider up for better image quality, and down for smaller file size.

FIGURE 12.7.

When you save a GIF animation, Animation Shop automatically figures out which optimizations will work best.

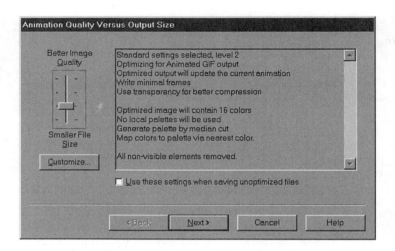

How do you decide where it goes? Animation Shop helps there, too. When you pick a setting and click Next>, after some chugging and crunching, you'll see a report like the one in Figure 12.8. This makes it much easier for you to decide "how big is too big," and go back to adjust the slider by clicking <Back. When the file size seems acceptable, click Finish.

FIGURE 12.8

When you set the slider in Figure 12.7 and click Next>, you get this report to help you decide if you found the right balance.

	Current File	Optimized File	% Change
Size of file:	n/a	9.4K bytes	n/a
Time to download at 14.4K baud:	n/a	7 seconds	
Time to download at 28.8K baud:	n/a	4 seconds	
Time to download at 56K baud:	n/a	2 seconds	
Time to download over ISDN:	n/a	< 1.0 second	

Putting a GIF Animation onto a Web Page

In Hour 10, "Putting Graphics on a Web Page," you learned to use the <IMG> tag to make GIF images appear on your Web pages. To put a GIF animation on a Web page, you use exactly the same tag in exactly the same way. For example, suppose I gave my animated anti-flaming icon the name `noburn.gif` when I saved it in Animation Shop. The HTML to put it on a Web page would be as follows.

```
<IMG SRC="noburn.gif">
```

Just as with any other graphic, you can include `ALT=` if you want a text message to be associated with the image. You can also include the `ALIGN` attribute to line up the animation with other graphics or text next to it, or to wrap text to the left or right of the animation. All the `<IMG>` tag attributes discussed in Hour 10 also work with GIF animations.

Figure 12.9 is a simple HTML page incorporating `noburn.gif` along with a few other animations and still images. Figure 12.10 doesn't move because this book is made out of boring old paper, but if you view the file on your computer you'll see the flames fly. (Go to `http://24hourHTMLcafe.com` and click "An Animated Warning.")

FIGURE 12.9.

Some of the .gif files specified in the <IMG> tags are still images, and some are animations. The HTML is the exactly same, either way.

```
<HTML><HEAD><TITLE>NO SMOKING OR FLAMING</TITLE></HEAD>
<BODY>
<DIV ALIGN="center">
<IMG SRC="noburn.gif" ALT="Defense de Combustion"><BR>
<IMG SRC="rgt.gif"><IMG SRC="no.gif"><IMG SRC="lft.gif"><BR>
<IMG SRC="awarn.gif"><BR>
The Webmaster General has determined that spontaneous
combustion may be hazardous to your health and the health
of those around you.<BR>Please refrain from smoking or
flaming while visiting this Web site.
</DIV></BODY></HTML>
```

FIGURE 12.10.

Viewed online, this page contains a burning icon, a scrolling marquee, and an animated special-effect title.

12

Generating Transitions and Text Effects

Animation Shop (like some other GIF animation programs) can do much more than just collect multiple GIF images into a single animation file. It can also generate some impressive special effects, and even create scrolling text banners all by itself. I don't have room in this book to explain in detail how to use these features, but they're easy enough so that you can probably pick it up on your own with a little help from the Animation Shop online help system.

Just to get you started, Figures 12.11 and 12.12 show how I made the two bottom animations shown in Figure 12.10. One uses the Effects, Image Transitions feature to dissolve between a picture of the word ATTENTION and a picture of the word WARNING (I made these two pictures in Paint Shop Pro ahead of time). The other uses the Effects, Text Transitions to scroll the words NO SPONTANEOUS COMBUSTION smoothly across a white background. This didn't require any images at all, since the text transition effects generate their own pictures of the text as they do their magic.

FIGURE 12.11.

Use Effects, Image Transitions to generate fades, wipes, dissolves, and other automatic transitions between images.

Once you get started with Web page animation, it's hard not to get carried away. I couldn't resist adding a flashing neon sign to the 24-Hour HTML Café. In the examples page for this hour (http://24hourHTMLcafe.com/hour10/), you'll also find links to several other animations that you are welcome to reuse for your own pages. (The book that turns its own pages is especially popular.)

FIGURE 12.12.

Use Effects, Text Transitions to generate moving text and special-effect text over a frame or set of frames.

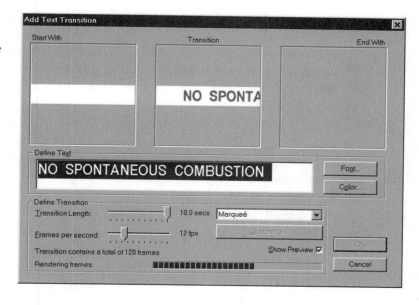

Summary

This hour introduced you to animated GIF images, which are the easiest and quickest way to add some action to your Web pages. You found out how to use Animation Shop 1.0, the animation module for putting together GIF animations for Paint Shop Pro 5.0. You also saw how to control how many times an animation repeats and the timing of each frame in an animation, as well as how to make animations partially transparent by using transparent GIF images in them.

GIF animations can be placed on Web pages by using the same <IMG> tag as ordinary, unmoving images. All the <IMG> attributes and options discussed in Hour 10 also work with animated images.

Like some other graphics programs, Animation Shop has the capability of generating some or all frames of an animation using a variety of special effects and automatic transitions.

Q&A

Q I've seen quite a few animations on the Web that show a three-dimensional object rotating. Can I make those with Animation Shop?

A Yes, but you'll also need some kind of 3D modeling and rendering software to create the individual frames.

You may have also seen interactive, three-dimensional virtual reality scenes and objects embedded in Web pages. Those are something completely different than GIF animations, made with a special language called the Virtual Reality Modeling Language, or VRML. For more information on VRML, refer to *Web Page Wizardry: Wiring Your Site for Sound and Action*, from Sams Publishing.

Q I've seen moving marquee-type signs on Web pages. Are those GIF animations?

A Sometimes they are and sometimes they aren't. There are several ways to make text move across an area on a Web page. One of the easiest is to use Animation Shop, which can make fancy marquees from a simple string of text that you type. See the Animation Shop online help for details.

Note that GIF animations are only one way to make marquees. They are often Java applets or ActiveX controls (see Hour 18, "Interactive Pages with Applets and ActiveX"). Some versions of Microsoft Internet Explorer even support a special <MARQUEE> tag, but this tag is now obsolete.

Q I have a Windows AVI video clip. Can I turn it into a GIF animation?

A Yes. You can download a little program called Microsoft GIF Animator that will do the trick from the Microsoft Web site (http://www.microsoft.com/). A more advanced video editing program that supports AVI and GIF files is the commercial program VideoCraft from Andover Advanced Technologies (http://www.anda-tech.com/).

You can also embed AVI files directly into Web pages, as discussed in Chapter 17, "Embedding Multimedia in Web Pages."

Workshop

Quiz

1. If you want your logo to bounce up and down on your Web page, how would you do it?

2. How would you make a quarter-of-a-second pause between each frame of the animation?

3. How would you modify a GIF animation that repeats forever to play only three times before stopping instead?

Answers

1. Use Paint Shop Pro or another graphics program to make a few images of the logo at various heights (perhaps squishing when it reaches a line at the bottom). Then assemble those images using Animation Shop, and save them as a multi-image GIF animation file named `bounce.gif`. You can then place that animation on a Web page using the `<IMG SRC="bounce.gif">` tag, just like any GIF image.

2. When you build the animation in Animation Shop, enter 25 as the time delay (in centiseconds).

3. Open the animation in Animation Shop, select Edit, Animation Properties, choose Play it and enter the number 3.

Exercises

- Animation Shop can make slide shows of dissimilar images by automatically generating transition effects, such as fading between pictures. It can also automatically add a number of special effects to still or moving text. If you take a little time to explore the advanced features of this program, I'm sure you'll find it time well spent.

- Don't forget that the free copy of Paint Shop Pro and Animation Shop you can download from www.jasc.com is an evaluation copy only. If you like it (and who wouldn't!?), be sure to send JASC Inc. their well-earned registration fee to purchase the software.

12

PART IV
Web Page Design

Hour

HOUR 13

Page Design and Layout

You've learned in earlier hours how to create Web pages with text and images on them. This hour goes a step further by showing you some HTML tricks to control the spaces *between* your text and images. These tricks are essential for making your pages attractive and easy to read. This hour provides practical advice to help you design attractive and highly readable pages, even if you're not a professional graphics designer.

This hour also teaches you how to ensure that your Web pages will appear as quickly as possible when people try to read them. This is essential for making a good impression with your pages, especially for people who will be accessing them through modem connections to the Internet.

To Do

The techniques covered in this hour are intended to help you make the pages you've already created better and faster. So select some of the most important and/or impressive pages that you've made to date, and see if you can make them look even better.

- Choose pages with some graphics on them, because almost all tricks in this hour involve images.

▼
- If you have a page you think might especially benefit from a creative layout or unique background, start with that one.
- You might have some text and images that you haven't gotten around to putting on a Web page yet. If so, this hour can help make those new pages your best yet.
▲
- Copy the pages you select into their own directory folder, and play with new design possibilities for them as you read through this hour.

Web Page Design

So far, this book has focused mostly on the exact mechanics of Web page creation. But before getting into the nitty-gritty of spacing and layout tricks, you should take a moment now to step back and think about the overall visual design of your Web pages. Now that you know basic HTML, you need to learn how to apply it wisely.

Every aspect of a Web page should reflect the goals that led you to create the page in the first place. Not only should the text and graphics themselves communicate your message, but the way you fit those elements together can itself make an enormous impact on readers' perceptions of you and/or your company.

Table 13.1 is a checklist to help you think about the key design elements of a Web page. You should aim for most of your pages to meet the recommendations in this table, though some individual pages will undoubtedly need to "break the rules."

TABLE 13.1. KEY ELEMENTS OF WEB PAGE DESIGN.

Things to Consider	Suggested Guidelines
Text Content	Between 100 and 500 words per page
Text Breaks	A headline, rule, or image every 40 to 100 words (except in long articles or stories)
Page Length	Two to four screens (at 640×480 resolution)
File Size	No more than 50KB per page, including images (animated GIFs can be up to 100KB per page)
Speed	First screen of text and key images appear in under 3 seconds over a 28.8Kbps modem
Colors	Two to four thematic colors dominant
Fonts	No more than three fonts (in graphics and text)
Blank Space	Background should show on at least 50 percent of page
Contrast	No color in background should be close to text color
Tone and Style	All text and graphics consistent in mood and theme
Overall Impact	Page as a whole should appear balanced and attractive

Most of the tips in Table 13.1 are common to any page design, on paper or electronic. But some of them are particularly tricky to control on Web pages.

The next section of this chapter presents some HTML commands for handling the blank space and overall visual impact of your pages. Then this chapter wraps up with some techniques for meeting the speed requirements of today's Web, even when you use relatively large images.

Image Spacing and Borders

Figures 13.1 through 13.3 show the HTML text, images, and final appearance of a well-designed Web page. It meets all the criteria outlined in Table 13.1.

FIGURE 13.1.

This page uses several techniques for adding blank space between images and text.

```
<HTML><HEAD><TITLE>The Varieties of Proboscis</TITLE></HEAD>
<BODY BACKGROUND="wainscot.gif"
 TEXT="green" LINK="maroon" VLINK="green" ALINK="white">
<DIV ALIGN="center">
<IMG SRC="vofp.gif" ALIGN="top" WIDTH=400 HEIGHT=100>
<IMG SRC="bosc.gif" ALIGN="top" WIDTH=125 HEIGHT=135>
<BR><IMG SRC="spacer.gif" WIDTH=20 HEIGHT=20><BR></DIV>
<A HREF="point.htm" ><H2>
<IMG SRC="point.gif" ALIGN="left"
 WIDTH=120 HEIGHT=120 BORDER=3 HSPACE=20 VSPACE=5>
The Needle</H2></A>
Being perhaps the most refined and coveted variety, this
proboscis is favoured by accountants, lawyers, librarians,
and all persons of great intellect and bile.<BR CLEAR="left">
<IMG SRC="spacer.gif" WIDTH=20 HEIGHT=20><BR>
<A HREF="arch.htm"><H2 ALIGN="right">
<IMG SRC="arch.gif" ALIGN="right"
 WIDTH=140 HEIGHT=100 BORDER=3 HSPACE=20 VSPACE=5>
The Arch</H2></A>
An original inspiration for both Roman and Gothic
archetectural motifs, this well-loved proboscis boasts
an extensive history in the fine arts.<BR CLEAR="right">
<IMG SRC="spacer.gif" WIDTH=20 HEIGHT=20><BR>
<A HREF="bulb.htm"><H2><IMG SRC="bulb.gif" ALIGN="left"
 WIDTH=140 HEIGHT=100 BORDER=3 HSPACE=20 VSPACE=5>
The Bulb</H2></A>
A long-standing favourite of politicians and food service
professionals, this is the traditional proboscis of good
cheer and prolific oration.<BR CLEAR="left">
<IMG SRC="spacer.gif" WIDTH=20 HEIGHT=20><BR>
<A HREF="hook.htm"><H2 ALIGN="right">
<IMG SRC="hook.gif" ALIGN="right"
 WIDTH=120 HEIGHT=120 BORDER=3 HSPACE=20 VSPACE=5>
The Hook</H2></A>
This most visible and respected proboscis type commands
prompt attention and high regard in both religous and
secular circles.<BR CLEAR="right">
```

13

```
<IMG SRC="spacer.gif" WIDTH=20 HEIGHT=20><P>
<DIV ALIGN="center">
<IMG SRC="flourish.gif" WIDTH=136 HEIGHT=30><P>
<A HREF="home.htm"><I>Return to the European Anatomy
Home Page.</I></A>
</DIV></BODY></HTML>
```

FIGURE 13.2.

Five of the nine image files referred to in Figure 13.1.

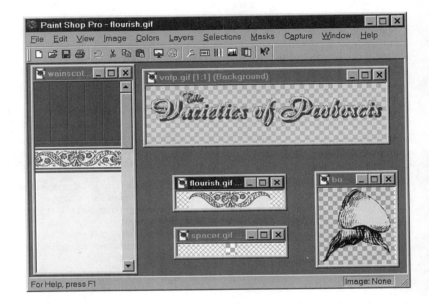

 When you look at Figure 13.2, remember that Paint Shop Pro uses cross-hatching to indicate that a window is bigger than the image it contains, and a checkerboard pattern to indicate which regions of an image are transparent. For example, spacer.gif is actually a very small, entirely transparent square.

Notice the generous amount of space between images and paragraphs in Figure 13.3. Web browsers tend to crowd everything together, but you can easily add space three different ways:

- Use small, totally transparent images to leave room between other things. The spacer.gif file (shown in Figure 13.2 and referred to in Figure 13.1) creates 20 pixels of blank space between each of the main parts of this page.

FIGURE 13.3.

Thanks to generous spacing and a carefully premeditated layout, the HTML in Figure 13.1 looks great as a Web page.

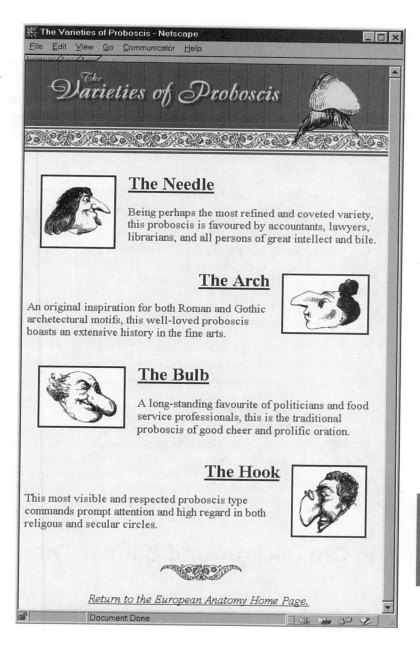

- When you wrap text around an image by using `<IMG ALIGN="right">` or `<IMG ALIGN="left">`, you can skip down past the bottom of that image at any time with `<BR CLEAR="right">` or `<BR CLEAR="left">`. If you have images on both the right and left, you can type `<BR CLEAR="all">` to go past both of them.
- You can add extra space on the left and right sides of any image with `<IMG HSPACE>`. To add space on the top and bottom sides, use `<IMG VSPACE>`. For example, each image in Figure 13.3 has 20 pixels of blank space to the left and right of it, and 5 pixels above and below it. This is because each `<IMG>` tag in Figure 13.1 includes the attributes `HSPACE=20 VSPACE=5`.

You'll read about the `WIDTH` and `HEIGHT` attributes of the `<IMG>` tag later in this chapter, in the "Specifying Image Width and Height" section.

The `<IMG>` tags in Figure 13.1 also include a `BORDER=3` attribute, which enlarges the rectangular border around the images. The border is normally 1 pixel thick for any image inside an `<A>` link, but `BORDER=3` makes it 3 pixels thick.

The most popular use of the `BORDER` attribute is to make the image border disappear completely by typing `BORDER=0`. This is especially handy with transparent images, which often look funny with a rectangle around them.

The color of the border will be the same as the color of any text links. In this page, images that link to pages someone hasn't visited yet will have maroon borders. Images that link to a recently visited page will have green borders.

If you include a `BORDER` attribute in an `<IMG>` that isn't between `<A>` and `</A>` link tags, all versions of Netscape Navigator and version 4.0 of Microsoft Internet Explorer will draw the border by using the regular body text color. However, earlier versions of Microsoft Internet Explorer will never draw a border around an image that isn't a link, even if you include a `BORDER` attribute.

The Old Background Banner Trick

One of the most prominent tricks employed in Figure 13.3 is the use of a 1,000-pixel high background image (named `wainscot.gif`). Because the entire page is unlikely to be more than 1,000 pixels high, the background only appears to repeat in the horizontal direction. And since the bottom part of the image is all the same color, it looks like the background is only a banner at the top of the page.

Unlike a foreground image used as a banner, however, this wainscoting will automatically size itself to go from "wall to wall" of any sized window. It takes up less space on a disk and transfers over the Internet faster, because only one repetition of the pattern needs to be stored.

If you use this trick to make background banners on your own Web pages, you should make them at least 2,000 pixels high. The page in Figure 13.3 can actually become longer than 1,000 pixels when someone uses a very large font size setting, in which case the wainscoting shows up again at the very bottom or middle of the page.

"Hang on," you say. "143×1000 is 143,000 pixels! Won't that make an enormous image file and take forever to download?" The answer is no; large areas of uniform color take up virtually no space at all when compressed in the GIF file format. (Wainscot.gif is only a 3KB file.)

By using a very wide background that repeats vertically, you can easily make a repeating banner that runs down the left side of a page, too. If you don't want text to obscure the banner, put a very large, totally transparent image at the beginning of the HTML page with <IMG ALIGN="left">.

Figures 13.4 through 13.6 show the HTML, graphics, and resulting Web pages to implement a left-side banner.

Note that I made the other graphics all right-justified, both for aesthetic reasons and so that I could avoid using <BR CLEAR="left">, which would skip all the way to the bottom of the left-justified banner graphic.

If you use a left-aligned transparent banner, be sure to add enough blank space around the actual foreground image to fill the area on the page you want to cover. The "Varieties of Proboscis" title graphic in Figures 13.5 and 13.6, for example, is 170×1200 pixels.

Because almost nobody views Web pages in a window larger than 1600×1200 pixels, vertically tiled background banners can safely be 2,000 pixels wide.

FIGURE 13.4.

With a few strategic changes, you could put the top banner in Figure 13.3 to the left side.

```
<HTML><HEAD><TITLE>The Varieties of Proboscis</TITLE></HEAD>
<BODY BACKGROUND="wainsco2.gif"
 TEXT="green" LINK="maroon" VLINK="green" ALINK="white">
<IMG SRC="vofp2.gif" ALIGN="left" WIDTH=170 HEIGHT=1200>
<IMG SRC="spacer.gif" WIDTH=20 HEIGHT=20><BR>
<A HREF="point.htm" ><H2>
<IMG SRC="point.gif" ALIGN="right"
 WIDTH=120 HEIGHT=120 BORDER=3 HSPACE=20 VSPACE=5>
The Needle</H2></A>
Being perhaps the most refined and coveted variety, this
proboscis is favoured by accountants, lawyers, librarians,
and all persons of great intellect and bile.<BR CLEAR="right">
<IMG SRC="spacer.gif" WIDTH=20 HEIGHT=20><BR>
<A HREF="arch.htm"><H2 ALIGN="right">
<IMG SRC="arch.gif" ALIGN="right"
 WIDTH=140 HEIGHT=100 border=3 HSPACE=20 VSPACE=5>
The Arch</H2></A>
An original inspiration for both Roman and Gothic
archetectural motifs, this well-loved proboscis boasts
an extensive history in the fine arts.<BR CLEAR="right">
<IMG SRC="spacer.gif" WIDTH=20 HEIGHT=20><BR>
<A HREF="bulb.htm"><H2><IMG SRC="bulb.gif" ALIGN="right"
 WIDTH=140 HEIGHT=100 BORDER=3 HSPACE=20 VSPACE=5>
The Bulb</H2></A>
A long-standing favourite of politicians and food service
professionals, this is the traditional proboscis of good
cheer and prolific oration.<BR CLEAR="right">
<IMG SRC="spacer.gif" WIDTH=20 HEIGHT=20><BR>
<A HREF="hook.htm"><H2 ALIGN="right">
<IMG SRC="hook.gif" ALIGN="right"
 WIDTH=120 HEIGHT=120 border=3 HSPACE=20 VSPACE=5>
The Hook</H2></A>
This most visible and respected proboscis type commands
prompt attention and high regard in both religous and
secular circles.<BR CLEAR="right">
<IMG SRC="spacer.gif" WIDTH=20 HEIGHT=20><P>
<DIV ALIGN="center">
<IMG SRC="flourish.gif" WIDTH=136 HEIGHT=30><P>
<A HREF="home.htm"><I>Return to the European Anatomy
Home Page.</I></A>
</DIV></BODY></HTML>
```

FIGURE 13.5.

The rotated graphics for a left-side banner. (Notice how I changed the direction of the light source and shadowing, too.)

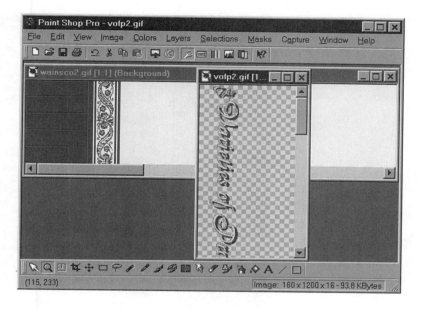

Sometimes, you'll choose to push the limits of HTML layout. The home page of the 24-Hour HTML Café (http://24hourHTMLcafe.com) does exactly that, combining several tricks from this and other hours into a flexible layout that adjusts itself to the size of the browser window gracefully.

If you view the page in a small enough window (less than about 600 pixels wide), you'll notice that the images start crawling all over each other in ways God obviously never intended them to try. I could have solved this problem with tables (see Hour 15) or other advanced tricks, but I went for simplicity at the risk of annoying the very few people who look at the Web through extremely small windows.

13

FIGURE **13.6.**

FIGURE **13.6.**

The HTML from Figure 13.4 and the banner from Figure 13.5, as they appear in Netscape Navigator.

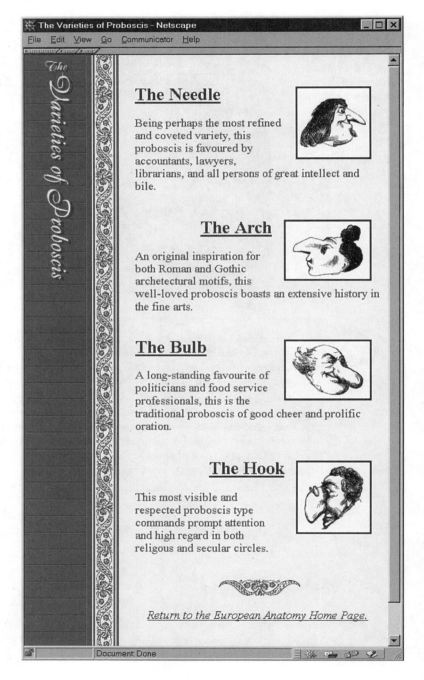

Specifying Image Width and Height

Because text moves over the Internet much faster than graphics, most Web browsers will display the text on a page before the images. This gives people something to read while they're waiting to see the pictures, which makes the whole page seem to come up much faster.

You can make sure that everything on your page appears as quickly as possible and in the right places by explicitly stating the width and height of each image. That way, a Web browser can leave the right amount of space for that image as it lays out the page and come back to get the actual image file later.

For each image on your page, use Paint Shop Pro or another graphics program to find out the exact width and height in pixels. (In Paint Shop Pro, this information appears at the bottom-right corner of the main window when you move the mouse over any part of an image.) Then include those dimensions in the <IMG> tag like this:

```
<IMG SRC="myimage.gif" WIDTH=200 HEIGHT=100>
```

The width and height you specify for an image don't have to match the actual width and height of the image. The Web browser program will try to squish or stretch the image to whatever size you specify.

This usually makes images look very ugly, but there is one excellent use for it: You can save a very small, totally transparent image and use it as any size "spacer" by specifying the WIDTH and HEIGHT of the blank region you want to create on your page.

Summary

This hour provided some guidelines for designing attractive, highly readable Web pages. It also explained how to create and control blank space on your pages, as well as how to put borders around images. You saw how to use backgrounds to create banners across the top or left edge of a page, and how to make sure people always have text to look at while waiting for the images on your page.

Table 13.2 summarizes the tags and attributes discussed in this chapter.

13

TABLE 13.2. HTML TAGS AND ATTRIBUTES COVERED IN HOUR 13.

Tag/Attribute	Function
`<IMG>`	Inserts an inline image into the document.
	Attributes:
`SRC="..."`	The address of the image.
`ALIGN="..."`	Determines the alignment of the given image (see Hour 10, "Putting Graphics on a Web Page").
`VSPACE="..."`	The space between the image and the text above or below it.
`HSPACE="..."`	The space between the image and the text to its left or right.
`WIDTH="..."`	The width, in pixels, of the image. If `WIDTH` is not the actual width, the image is scaled to fit.
`HEIGHT="..."`	The width, in pixels, of the image. If `HEIGHT` is not the actual height, the image is scaled to fit.
`BORDER="..."`	Draws a border of the specified value in pixels to be drawn around the image. In case the images are also links, `BORDER` changes the size of the default link border.
` `	A line break.
	Attributes:
`CLEAR="..."`	Causes the text to stop flowing around any images. Possible values are `RIGHT`, `LEFT`, `ALL`.

Q&A

Q I'd like to know exactly how wide the margins of a page are so I can line up my background and foreground images the way I want.

A Unfortunately, different browsers (and even the same browser on different types of computers) leave different amounts of space along the top and left side of a page, so you can't precisely line up foreground graphics with background images. Generally, you can expect the top and left margins to be 8 to 12 pixels.

The good news is that you'll learn an elegant and precise way to control margin width in Hour 16, "Using Style Sheets."

Q I've seen pages on the Web with multiple columns of text, wide margins, and other types of nice layouts you didn't discuss. How were those pages made?

A Probably with the HTML table tags, which are discussed in Hour 15, "Advanced Layout with Tables."

Workshop

Quiz

1. How would you wrap text around the right side of an image, leaving 40 pixels of space between the image and the text?

2. How could you insert exactly 80 pixels of blank space between two paragraphs of text?

3. If you have a circular button that links to another page, how do you prevent a rectangle from appearing around it?

4. What four attributes should you always include in every `<IMG>` tag as a matter of habit?

Answers

1. ```
   <IMG SRC="myimage.gif" HSPACE=40 VSPACE=40 ALIGN="left">
   Text goes here.
   ```

2. Create a small image that is all one color, and save it as `nothing.gif` with that color transparent. Then put the following tag between the two paragraphs of text:
   ```
   <IMG SRC="nothing.gif" WIDTH=1 HEIGHT=80>
   ```

3. Use the `BORDER=0` attribute, like the following:
   ```
   <A HREF="another_page.htm"><IMG SRC="circle.gif" BORDER=0></A>
   ```

4. `SRC`, `ALT`, `WIDTH`, and `HEIGHT`. For example:
   ```
   <IMG SRC="fred.jpg" ALT="Fat Fred" WIDTH=300 HEIGHT=100>
   ```

Exercises

- Try creating a page with the wildest layout you can manage with the HTML tags you've learned so far. If you're resourceful, you should be able to create a staggered diagonal line of images, or place short sentences of text almost anywhere on the page.

- Make a very large background—so big that people will see only one "tile" and you don't have to worry about it being seamless. Most Web browsers will display all foreground content (in front of the BGCOLOR you specify in the `<BODY>` tag) while the background image loads. So go ahead and play around with the creative possibilities that large backdrops open up.

13
   ```

Hour 14

Graphical Links and Imagemaps

If you've read Hour 10, "Putting Graphics on a Web Page," you know how to make an image link to another document. (If you don't quite recall how to do it right now, it looks like this: `<A HREF="gohere.htm"><IMG SRC="image.gif"></A>`.)

You can also subdivide an image into regions that link to different documents, depending on where someone clicks. This is called an *imagemap*, and any image can be made into an imagemap. A Web site with medical information might show an image of the human body and bring up different pages of advice for each body part. Or a map of the world could allow people to click any country for regional information. Many people use imagemaps to create a "navigation bar" that integrates icons for each page on their Web site into one cohesive imagemap.

Netscape Navigator and Microsoft Internet Explorer allow you to choose between two different methods for implementing imagemaps. Nowadays, all your imagemaps should be done by using the latest method, which is called a client-side imagemap. You may also want to make them work the old-fashioned server-side way for users of older browser programs. I explain both kinds of imagemaps in this hour.

NEW TERM An *imagemap* is an image on a Web page that leads to two or more different links, depending on which part of the image someone clicks. Modern Web browsers use *client-side imagemaps,* but you can also create *server-side imagemaps* for compatibility with old browsers.

How and Why to Avoid Using Imagemaps

The first thing I must say about imagemaps is that you probably won't need, or want, to use them! It's almost always easier, more efficient, and more reliable to use several ordinary images, placed right next to one another, with a separate link for each image.

For example, imagine that you wanted to make a Web page that looked like Figure 14.1, with each of the glowing words leading to a different link. The "obvious" approach would be to use a single imagemap for the entire central graphic. You'll see how to do that later in this hour.

However, the better solution is to cut the graphic into pieces by using Paint Shop Pro (or any other graphics program), and make each piece a separate image on the Web page. This way, the page is compatible with all versions of all Web browsers without requiring any server scripting or advanced HTML. Figure 14.2 shows how to cut the picture up so that each link area is a separate image. Figure 14.3 shows the HTML to make the page in Figure 14.1, using the images in Figure 14.2.

Notice that I was very careful not to put any spaces or line breaks between the bottom two <IMG> tags in Figure 14.3. A space or line break between <IMG> tags would create a small space between the images on the page, and the illusion of everything fitting together into one big image would be totally destroyed.

For the same reason, it's important not to put several images whose widths add up to more than about 580 pixels on a single line. The result might look good on your 800×600 screen, but someone looking at the page in a 640×480 window would see the images break apart onto separate lines.

FIGURE 14.1.

You can create this page using ordinary <IMG> tags and <A HREF> links. Imagemaps aren't necessary.

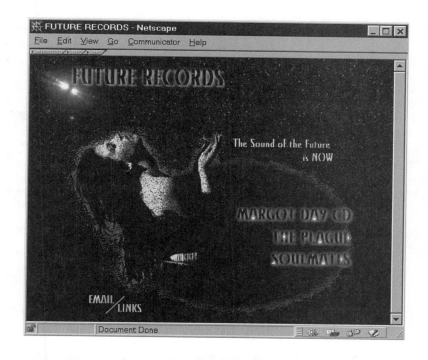

FIGURE 14.2.

To avoid using imagemaps, you would need to cut the image on the top left up into the seven images on the right. (Cut and paste using the rectangular selection tool.)

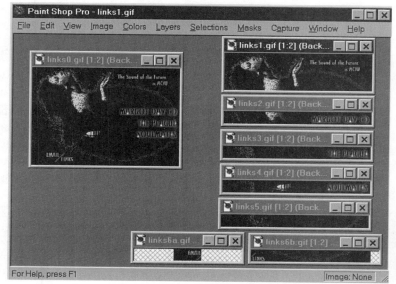

14

FIGURE 14.3.

This is one way to implement the page in Figure 14.1, by using the images in Figure 14.3. (Note that the big image in Figure 14.3, links0.gif, *isn't used.)*

```
<HTML><HEAD><TITLE>FUTURE RECORDS</TITLE>
</HEAD>
<BODY BGCOLOR="#000008" BACKGROUND="fade2.gif"
 TEXT="F0F0F0" LINK="F000FF" VLINK="8000F0" ALINK="8080FF">
<IMG SRC="future2.gif"
 WIDTH=320 HEIGHT=108 ALT="FUTURE RECORDS">
<DIV ALIGN="center">
<IMG SRC="links1.gif" WIDTH=490 HEIGHT=127
 ALT="The Sound of the Future is NOW"><BR>
<A HREF="margotcd.htm"><IMG SRC="links2.gif"
 WIDTH=490 HEIGHT=40 ALT="MARGOT DAY CD" BORDER=0></A><BR>
<A HREF="plague.htm"><IMG SRC="links3.gif"
 WIDTH=490 HEIGHT=40 ALT="THE PLAGUE" BORDER=0></A><BR>
<A HREF="soulmate.htm"><IMG SRC="links4.gif"
 WIDTH=490 HEIGHT=40 ALT="SOULMATES" BORDER=0></A><BR>
<IMG SRC="links5.gif" WIDTH=490 HEIGHT=40><BR>
<A HREF="mailto:margot@together.net"><IMG SRC="links6a.gif"
 WIDTH=93 HEIGHT=40 ALT="EMAIL" BORDER=0></A><A
 HREF="links.htm"><IMG SRC="links6b.gif"
 WIDTH=397 HEIGHT=40 ALT="LINKS" BORDER=0></A>
</DIV></BODY></HTML>
```

When *would* you want to use an imagemap, then? Only when the parts of an image you want to link are so numerous or oddly arranged that it would be a big hassle to chop the image up into smaller images.

That does happen from time to time, so it's a good idea to know how to create imagemaps when you truly need to. The rest of this hour shows you how.

Mapping Regions Within an Image

To make any type of imagemap, you'll need to figure out the numerical pixel coordinates of each region within the image that you want to be a clickable link. An easy way to do this is to open the image with Paint Shop Pro and watch the coordinates at the bottom of the screen as you use the rectangle selection tool to select a rectangular region of the image (see Figure 14.4). When the mouse button is down, the coordinates at the bottom of the screen show both the top-left and bottom-right corners of the rectangle. When the mouse button isn't down, only the x,y position of the mouse is shown.

> There are fancy programs that let you highlight a rectangle with your mouse and automatically spew out imagemap coordinates into a file, but they are rather cumbersome to use. You'll save the most time by ignoring the "time-saver" programs and just locating the pixel coordinates in Paint Shop Pro or your favorite general-purpose graphics program and jotting them down on a scrap of paper.

FIGURE 14.4.

Paint Shop Pro can easily tell you the coordinates for imagemap regions without mucking about with special image-mapping utilities.

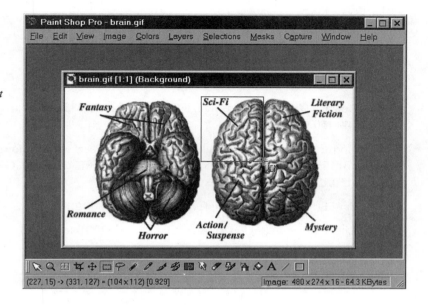

You could use the whole image in Figure 14.4 as an imagemap, linking to seven Web pages about the various literary genres. To do so, you would first need to decide which region of the image should be linked to each Web page. You can use rectangles, circles, and irregular polygons as regions. Figure 14.5 shows an example of how you might divide up the image by using these shapes.

FIGURE 14.5.

You don't actually have to draw anything that looks like this. I just made it to show you which regions in Figure 14.1 will become clickable links.

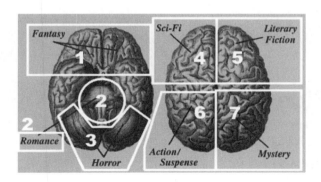

To create the imagemap, first jot down the pixel coordinates of the top-left and bottom-right corners of each rectangular region shown in Figure 14.5. You also need to locate and record the center point and radius of the circle, and the coordinates of each corner of the irregularly shaped regions. (If you want to follow along with this by using an image

14

of your own, just write the coordinates on a piece of paper for now. You'll see exactly how to put them into an HTML file momentarily.)

These coordinates are

Fantasy (region 1): A rectangle from 15,15 to 220,100.

Romance (region 2): A rectangle from 0,200 to 75,235 and a circle centered at 140,150 with radius 40.

Horror (region 3): An irregular polygon with corners at the following eight points: (70,175), (90,155), (125,195), (160,195), (190,160), (220,185), (185,270), and (110,270).

Sci-Fi (region 4): A rectangle from 225,10 to 330,120.

Literary Fiction (region 5): A rectangle from 330,10 to 475,120.

Action/Suspense (region 6): An irregular polygon with corners at the following five points: (230,130), (330,130), (330,270), (210,270), and (210,230).

Mystery (region 7): A rectangle from 330,130 to 475,270.

To Do

▼ To Do

You'll remember how to make imagemaps better if you get an image of your own and turn it into an imagemap as you read the following explanation.

- For starters, it's easiest to choose a fairly large image that is visually divided into roughly rectangular regions.

- If you don't have a suitable image handy, use Paint Shop Pro (or your favorite graphics program) to make one. One easy and useful idea is to put a word or icon for each of your important pages together into a button bar or signpost.

▲

Client-Side Imagemaps

Once you have the coordinates written down, you're ready to create an HTML imagemap. Just after the <BODY> tag in your Web page, put

`<MAP NAME="brainmap">`

(You can use whatever name you want if `"brainmap"` doesn't describe the image you're using very well.)

Now you need to type an <AREA> tag for each region of the image. Figure 14.6 shows how you would define the eight regions of the brain image.

FIGURE 14.6.

The <MAP> and <AREA> tags define the regions of an imagemap.

```
<HTML><HEAD><TITLE>Best Seller Brain</TITLE></HEAD>
<BODY>
<MAP NAME="brainmap">
<AREA SHAPE="rect" COORDS="15,15,220,100" HREF="fantasy.htm">
<AREA SHAPE="rect" COORDS="0,200,75,235" HREF="romance.htm">
<AREA SHAPE="circle" COORDS="140,150,40" HREF="romance.htm">
<AREA SHAPE="poly" COORDS="70,175, 90,135, 125,195, 160,195,
   190,160, 220,185, 185,270, 110,270" HREF="horror.htm">
<AREA SHAPE="rect" COORDS="225,10,330,120" HREF="scifi.htm">
<AREA SHAPE="rect" COORDS="330,10,475,120" HREF="litfi.htm">
<AREA SHAPE="poly" COORDS="230,130, 330,130, 330,270,
   210,270, 210,230" HREF="action.htm">
<AREA SHAPE="rect" COORDS="330,130,475,270" HREF="mystery.htm">
</MAP>
<DIV ALIGN="center">
<H1>The Best Seller Brain</H1>
<IMG SRC="brain.gif" USEMAP="#brainmap" BORDER=0><P>
<I>"Only a person with a Best Seller mind
can write Best Sellers."</I></DIV>
<DIV ALIGN="right">-Aldous Huxley</DIV>
</BODY></HTML>
```

Each <AREA> tag in Figure 14.3 has three attributes:

- SHAPE indicates whether the region is a rectangle (SHAPE="rect"), a circle (SHAPE="circle"), or an irregular polygon (SHAPE="poly").

- COORDS gives the exact pixel coordinates for the region. For rectangles, give the x,y coordinates of the top-left corner followed by the x,y coordinates of the bottom-right corner. For circles, give the x,y center point followed by the radius in pixels. For polygons, list the x,y coordinates of all the corners, in connect-the-dots order.

- HREF specifies the page that clicking the region will link to. You can use any address or filename that you would use in an ordinary <A HREF> link tag.

After the <AREA> tags, you are done defining the imagemap, so you insert a closing </MAP> tag.

To place the actual imagemap on the page, you use an ordinary <IMG> tag, and add a USEMAP attribute:

```
<IMG SRC="brain.gif" USEMAP="#brainmap">
```

Use the name you put in the <MAP> tag (and don't forget the # symbol). In Figure 14.6, I also included the BORDER attribute, as you should for any image on a Web page.

14

It is also possible to put the map definition in a separate file by including that file's name in the USEMAP attribute, like the following:

`<IMG SRC="thisthat.gif" USEMAP="maps.htm#thisthat">`

For instance, if you used an imagemap on every page in your Web site, you could just put the <MAP> and <AREA> tags for it on one page instead of repeating it on every single page where the imagemap appeared.

Figure 14.7 shows the imagemap in action. Notice that Netscape Navigator displays the link address for whatever region the mouse is moving over at the bottom of the window, just as it does for "normal" links. If someone clicked where the mouse cursor (the little hand) is shown in Figure 14.7, the page named `fantasy.htm` would come up.

FIGURE 14.7.

The imagemap defined in Figure 14.6 as it appears on the Web page.

Mouse over imagemap link

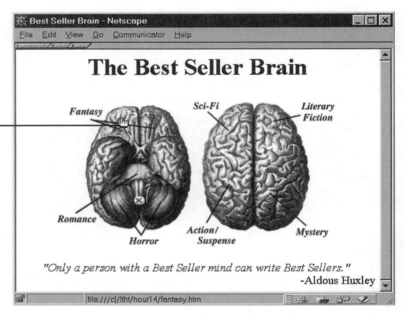

> You may want to include text links at the bottom of your imagemap leading
> to the same pages the map itself links to. This allows people who have older
> Web browsers—or who don't want to wait for the image to finish loading—
> to access those pages.
>
> For an example—and a little tongue-in-cheek history lesson thrown into the
> bargain—click on "The Immortal Presidents" at:
>
> `http://24hourHTMLcafe.com/hour14/`

Server-Side Imagemaps

The old-fashioned way to do an imagemap is to let the server computer where the Web
page resides do all the work. Most Web authors don't bother with server-side imagemaps
anymore, because it's easier and just as effective to provide text links for people using
older browsers. But there are still an awful lot of people out there using pre-1995 Web
browsers, and it isn't really *that* hard to make your imagemaps work for them. You can
read the following explanation of what's involved and decide for yourself whether it's
worth your time to provide server-side imagemaps.

When the user clicks an image that has been mapped this way, the browser program just
sends the x,y coordinates of the mouse pointer's location to a special script on the server.
Usually, this script is located in some subdirectory of `cgi-bin` on the server, and the
HTML to implement the imagemap is just a normal anchor link.

```
<A HREF="/cgi-bin/imagemap/thisthat"><IMG SRC="thisthat.gif" ISMAP></A>
```

Simple. But when you install a Web page including such a link, you need to tell the
imagemap script which parts of the image should be associated with which link addresses. This is normally done in a *map file*. Each line in the map file is simply the word
`rect` followed by an URL address and two sets of x,y coordinates representing the top-
left corner and the bottom-right corner of a region of the image. Some server scripts also
support non-rectangular regions with the word `poly` and `circle` (or `round`).

The first line in a map file begins with the word `default` followed by the URL address
that should be used if the user happens to click outside any rectangular region defined by
a `rect` line. A map file named `thisthat.map` might look like the following:

```
default /top/this.htm
rect /top/this.htm 0,0,102,99
rect /top/that.htm 103,0,205,99
```

14

The final step in setting up a server-side imagemap is telling the imagemap script which map file to use for which image by adding a line to a system file named imagemap.conf. This file will already exist and includes entries for every imagemap defined on the server. You simply add a line with the name used in the HREF attribute of the <A> tag, a colon, and then the actual location and name of the associated map file. For example, the previous reference is HREF="/cgi-bin/imagemap/thisthat", and the preceding map file is named thisthat.map. If this map file were in a directory named /mapfiles, the line in imagemap.conf would read

```
thisthat : /mapfiles/thisthat.map
```

All this isn't nearly as difficult as it may sound if you've never set up an imagemap before, but it can be a hassle, especially if your pages reside on somebody else's server and you don't have the rights to modify system files such as imagemap.conf yourself. What's worse, server-side imagemaps don't work at all on Web pages located on your hard drive, a CD-ROM, or most local networks.

There are also some variations in the exact syntax for imagemap implementation, depending on the software installed on your server. So if you move your pages to a different server, the imagemaps may not work anymore. Yuck.

Fortunately, the latest versions of all the major browsers support the client-side imagemaps discussed earlier in this hour, where the association of links with specific regions in an image is handled by the browser itself instead of a server script. This means that you can include imagemaps in your HTML files without imposing an additional burden on your Internet service provider's server, and you can be more certain that they will be processed correctly and dependably.

Combined Client/Server Imagemaps

There is a way for you to provide client-side imagemaps that automatically switch to server-side imagemaps if the user's browser doesn't support client-side maps. With a single line of code, you can allow an imagemap to be interpreted either by the end user's software or by the server by including the ISMAP attribute in the <IMG> tag, and then including both a USEMAP= attribute and cgi-bin/imagemap reference.

```
<MAP "#thisthat">
<AREA SHAPE="rect" COORDS="0,0,102,99" HREF="this.htm">
<AREA SHAPE="rect" COORDS="103,0,205,99" HREF="that.htm"></MAP>
<A HREF="/cgi-bin/imagemap/thisthat">
<IMG SRC="thisthat.gif" USEMAP="#thisthat" ISMAP></A>
```

Here, as with any unrecognized tag, browsers that don't support client-side imagemaps will simply ignore the USEMAP and ISMAP tags and treat the preceding code like an old-fashioned server-side imagemap.

Summary

This hour explained how to create imagemaps—links that lead to more than one place, depending on where you click an image—as well as why and how to avoid using them whenever possible. You saw how to define rectangular and circular link regions within an image, as well as irregularly shaped polygonal regions. You also learned to provide an alternate link just for people using older browsers that don't support the current imagemap standard. Finally, you got a quick run-down on providing server-side imagemaps on most types of Web servers—just in case you want to provide the best possible experience for users of outdated browsers.

Table 14.1 is a summary of the tags and attributes covered in this hour.

TABLE 14.1. HTML TAGS AND ATTRIBUTES COVERED IN HOUR 14.

Tag/Attribute	Function
`<IMG>`	Inserts an image into the document.
Attributes:	
`ISMAP`	This image is a clickable imagemap.
`SRC="..."`	The URL of the image.
`USEMAP="..."`	The name of an imagemap specification for client-side image mapping. Used with `<MAP>` and `<AREA>`.
`<MAP>...</MAP>`	A client-side imagemap, referenced by `<IMG USEMAP="...">`. Includes one or more `<AREA>` tags.
`<AREA>`	Defines a clickable link within a client-side imagemap.
Attributes:	
`SHAPE="..."`	The shape of the clickable area. Currently, RECT, POLY, and CIRCLE (or ROUND) are the valid options.
`COORDS="..."`	The left, top, right, and bottom coordinates of the clickable region within an image.
`HREF="..."`	The URL that should be loaded when the area is clicked.

14

Q&A

Q I'd like to know exactly which browsers support client-side imagemaps, and which ones support server-side imagemaps.

A All browsers that display graphics support server-side imagemaps. All versions of Netscape Navigator and Microsoft Internet Explorer with version numbers 2.0 or higher also support client-side imagemaps. Any other Web browser produced after 1995 probably supports client-side imagemaps, too.

Q My imagemaps with polygonal and circular regions don't seem to work right in Netscape 2.0. Why?

A Netscape Navigator version 2.0 and Microsoft Internet Explorer version 2.0 only support rectangular regions in client-side imagemaps. Only people using version 3.0 or later of these browsers will be able to click non-rectangular regions.

Q I don't have Paint Shop Pro and my graphics software doesn't tell me x,y coordinates. How do I figure out the coordinates for my imagemaps?

A Here's a sneaky way to do it using Netscape Navigator. Put the image on a page with the ISMAP attribute and an <A> tag around it, like the following:

```
<A HREF="nowhere"><IMG SRC="myimage.gif" ISMAP></A>
```

When you view that page with Navigator, move the mouse over the image. You will see the coordinates in the message box at the bottom of the window.

Workshop

Quiz

1. You have a 200×200-pixel image named `quarters.gif` for your Web page. When viewers click the top-left quarter of the image, you want them to get a page named `toplft.htm`. When they click the top-right quarter, they should get `toprgt.htm`. Clicking the bottom left should bring up `btmlft.htm`, and the bottom right should lead to `btmrgt.htm`. Write the HTML to implement this as a client-side imagemap.

2. If you wanted people using older browsers that don't support client-side imagemaps to get a page named `oldies.htm` when they click any part of the imagemap, how would you modify the HTML you wrote for Question 1?

3. How could you implement the effect described in Question 1 without using imagemaps at all?

Answers

1.
```
<MAP NAME="quartersmap">
<AREA SHAPE="rect" COORDS="0,0,99,99" HREF="toplft.htm">
<AREA SHAPE="rect" COORDS="100,0,199,99" HREF="toprgt.htm">
<AREA SHAPE="rect" COORDS="0,100,99,199" HREF="btmlft.htm">
<AREA SHAPE="rect" COORDS="100,100,199,199" HREF="btmrgt.htm">
</MAP>
<IMG SRC="quarters.gif" WIDTH=200 HEIGHT=200
USEMAP="#quartersmap">
```

2. Replace the `<IMG>` tag above with
```
<A HREF="oldies.htm">
<IMG SRC="quarters.gif" WIDTH=200 HEIGHT=200 ISMAP
USEMAP="#quartersmap"></A>
```

3. Use a graphics program such as Paint Shop Pro to chop the image into the four quarters, and save them as separate images named `toplft.gif`, `toprgt.gif`, `btmlft.gif`, and `btmrgt.gif`. Then write
```
<A HREF="toplft.htm"><IMG SRC="toplft.gif"
WIDTH=100 HEIGHT=100 BORDER=0></A>
<A HREF="toprgt.htm"><IMG SRC="toprgt.gif"
WIDTH=100 HEIGHT=100 BORDER=0></A><BR>
<A HREF="btmlft.htm"><IMG SRC="btmlft.gif"
WIDTH=100 HEIGHT=100 BORDER=0></A>
<A HREF="btmrgt.htm"><IMG SRC="btmrgt.gif"
WIDTH=100 HEIGHT=100 BORDER=0></A>
```

(Be careful to break the lines of the HTML *inside* the tags as shown in this code, to avoid introducing any spaces between the images.)

Exercises

- If you have some pages containing short lists of links, see if you can cook up an interesting imagemap to use instead.

- Imagemaps are usually more engaging and attractive than a row of repetitive-looking icons or buttons. Can you come up with a visual metaphor related to your site that would make it easier—and maybe more fun—for people to navigate through your pages? (Thinking along these lines is a good preparation for the issues you'll be tackling in Part VI, "Building a Web Site," by the way.)

14

HOUR **15**

Advanced Layout with Tables

One of the most powerful tools for creative Web page design is the *table,* which allows you to arrange text and graphics into multiple columns and rows. This hour shows you how to build HTML tables and how to control the spacing, layout, and appearance of the tables you create.

NEW TERM   A *table* is an orderly arrangement of text and/or graphics into vertical *columns* and horizontal *rows*.

To Do

As you read this hour, think about how arranging text into tables could benefit your Web pages. The following are some specific ideas to keep in mind:

- Of course, the most obvious application of tables is to organize tabular information, such as a multi-column list of names and numbers.
- If you want more complex relationships between text and graphics than the `<IMG ALIGN="left">` or `<IMG ALIGN="right">` can provide, tables can do it.

- Tables can be used to draw borders around text or around several graphics images.
- Whenever you need multiple columns of text, tables are the answer.

For each of your pages that meets one of these criteria, try adding a table modeled after the examples in this hour. The Exercises section at the end of this hour offers a couple of detailed suggestions along these lines, as well.

Creating a Simple Table

To make tables, you have to start with a `<TABLE>` tag. Of course you end your tables with the `</TABLE>` tag. If you want the table to have a border, use a `BORDER` attribute to specify the width of the border in pixels. A border size of `0` (or leaving the `BORDER` attribute out entirely) will make the border invisible, which is often handy when you are using a table as a page layout tool.

With the `<TABLE>` tag in place, the next thing you need is the `<TR>` tag. `<TR>` creates a table row, which contains one or more *cells* of information. To create these individual cells, you use the `<TD>` tag. `<TD>` stands for table data; you place the table information between the `<TD>` and `</TD>` tags. The closing `</TD>` tag is always optional, since one cell of the table clearly must end when the next one begins. Likewise, no `</TR>` tags are required since each row must end when the next row begins (or when the table itself ends).

NEW TERM   A *cell* is a rectangular region that can contain any text, images, and HTML tags. Each row in a table is made up of at least one cell.

There is one more basic tag involved in building tables: The `<TH>` tag works exactly like a `<TD>` tag, except that it indicates that the cell is part of the heading of the table. Some Web browsers render `<TH>` and `<TD>` cells exactly the same, but Netscape Navigator 4.0 and Microsoft Internet Explorer 4.0 both display the text in `<TH>` cells as centered and boldface.

You can create as many cells as you want, but each row in a table should have the same number of columns as the other rows. The example in Figures 15.1 and 15.2 show a simple table using only these four tags.

As you know, HTML ignores extra spaces between words and tags. However, you might find your HTML tables easier to read (and less prone to time-wasting errors) if you use spaces to indent `<TD>` tags, as I did in Figure 15.1.

FIGURE 15.1.

*The <TABLE>, <TR>,
and <TD> tags are all
you need to create
simple tables. The
<TH> tag can also be
used to specify a
heading.*

```
<HTML><HEAD><TITLE>Things to Fear</TITLE></HEAD>
<BODY>
<TABLE>
<TR><TH>Description <TH>Size          <TH>Weight
<TR><TD>.38 Special  <TD>Five-inch barrel <TD>Twenty ounces
<TR><TD>Rhinoceros   <TD>Twelve feet    <TD>Up to two tons
<TR><TD>Broad Axe    <TD>Thirty-inch blade<TD>Twelve pounds
</TABLE>
</BODY></HTML>
```

FIGURE 15.2.

*The HTML table in
Figure 15.1 has four
rows and three
columns.*

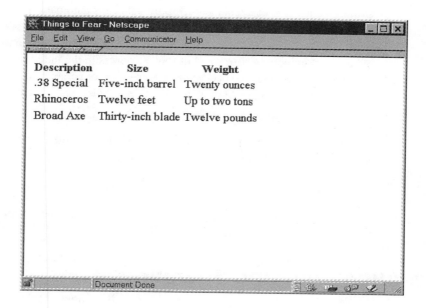

You can place virtually any other HTML element into a table cell. However, tags used in
one cell don't carry over to other cells, and tags from outside the table don't apply within
the table. For example, if you wrote

```
<B>
<TABLE><TR>
 <TD><I>Hello
 <TD>There
</TABLE>
</B>
```

the word *There* would be neither boldface nor italic because neither the <B> tag outside
the table nor the <I> tag from the previous cell affect it.

15

To make both the words *Hello* and *There* boldface, you would need to type

```
<TABLE><TR>
 <TD><B>Hello</B>
 <TD><B>There</B>
</TABLE>
```

Table Size

Ordinarily, the size of a table and its individual cells automatically expand to fit the data you place into it. However, you can choose to control the exact size of the entire table by putting WIDTH and/or HEIGHT attributes in the <TABLE> tag. You can also control the size of each cell by putting WIDTH and HEIGHT attributes in the individual <TD> tags. The WIDTH and HEIGHT can be specified as either pixels or percentages. For example, the following HTML makes a table 500 pixels wide and 400 pixels high:

```
<TABLE WIDTH=500 HEIGHT=400>
```

To make the first cell of the table 20 percent of the total table width and the second cell 80 percent of the table width, you would type the following:

```
<TABLE><TR><TD WIDTH=20%>Skinny cell
<TD WIDTH=80%>Fat cell</TABLE>
```

When you use percentages instead of fixed pixel sizes, the table will resize automatically to fit any size browser window, while still maintaining the aesthetic balance you're after.

Alignment and Spanning

By default, anything you place inside a table cell is aligned to the left and vertically centered. You can align the contents of table cells both horizontally and vertically with the ALIGN and VALIGN attributes.

You can apply these attributes to any <TR>, <TD>, or <TH> tag. Alignment attributes assigned to a <TR> tag apply to all cells in that row. Depending on the size of your table, you can save yourself a considerable amount of time and effort by applying these attributes at the <TR> level and not in each individual <TD> or <TH> tag. The HTML code in Figure 15.3 uses VALIGN="top" to bring the text to the top of each cell. Figure 15.4 shows the result.

At the top of Figure 15.4, a single cell spans two columns. This is accomplished with the COLSPAN=2 attribute in the <TH> tag for that cell. As you might guess, you can also use the ROWSPAN attribute to create a cell that spans more than one row.

15

FIGURE 15.3.

*You can use align-
ment, cell spacing,
borders, and back-
ground colors to bring
clarity and elegance to
your tables.*

```
<HTML><HEAD><TITLE>Things to Fear</TITLE></HEAD>
<BODY>
<TABLE BORDER=2 CELLPADDING=8 CELLSPACING=3>
<TR BGCOLOR="silver">
<TH COLSPAN=2>Description<TH>Size<TH>Weight<TH>Speed
<TR VALIGN="top">
<TD><IMG SRC="handgun.gif"><TD><H2>.38 Special</H2>
<TD>Five-inch barrel.<TD>Twenty ounces.
<TD>Six rounds in four seconds.
<TR VALIGN="top">
<TD><IMG SRC="rhino.gif"><TD><H2>Rhinoceros</H2>
<TD>Twelve feet, horn to tail.<TD>Up to two tons.
<TD>Thirty-five miles per hour in bursts.
<TR VALIGN="top">
<TD><IMG SRC="axeman.gif"><TD><H2>Broad Axe</H2>
<TD>Thirty-inch blade.<TD>Twelve pounds.
<TD>Sixty miles per hour on impact.
</TABLE>
</BODY></HTML>
```

FIGURE 15.4.

*The COLSPAN attribute
in Figure 15.3 allows
the top-left cell to
span multiple columns.*

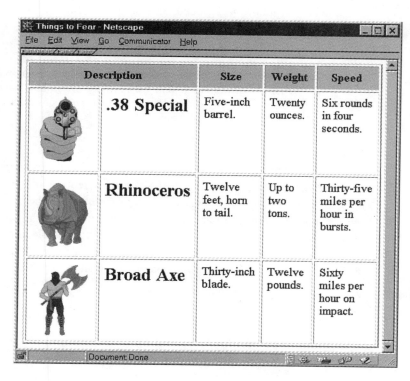

Keeping the structure of rows and columns organized in your mind can be the most difficult part of creating tables with cells that span multiple columns or rows. The tiniest error can often throw the whole thing into disarray. You'll save yourself time and frustration by sketching your tables out on graph paper before you start writing the HTML to implement them.

Backgrounds and Spacing

There are a few tricks in Figures 15.3 and 15.4 that haven't been mentioned yet. You can give an entire table—and each individual row or cell in a table—its own background, distinct from any background you might use on the Web page itself. You do this by placing a BGCOLOR or BACKGROUND attribute in the <TABLE>, <TR>, <TD>, or <TH> tags exactly as you would in the <BODY> tag (see Hour 11, "Custom Backgrounds and Colors"). To give an entire table a yellow background, for example, you would use <TABLE BGCOLOR= "yellow"> or the equivalent <TABLE BGCOLOR="#FFFF00">.

Only users of Netscape Navigator and Microsoft Internet Explorer versions 3.0 or higher will see table background colors. Table background images are supported by Microsoft Internet Explorer versions 3.0 and 4.0, and Netscape Navigator version 4.0 only.

You can also control the space around the borders of a table with the CELLPADDING and CELLSPACING attributes. The CELLSPACING attribute sets the amount of space (in pixels) between table borders and between table cells themselves. The CELLPADDING attribute sets the amount of space around the edges of information in the cells. Setting the CELLPADDING value to 0 causes all the information in the table to align as closely as possible to the table borders, possibly even touching the borders. CELLPADDING and CELLSPACING give you good overall control of the table's appearance.

You saw the effect of background color and spacing attributes in Figures 15.3 and 15.4.

You can place an entire table within a table cell, and that separate table can possess any and all the qualities of any table you might want to create. In other words, you can "nest" tables inside one another.

Nested tables open up a vast universe of possibilities for creative Web page layout. For example, if you wanted a column of text to appear to the left of a table, you could create a two-column table with the text in one column and the sub-table in the other column, like the following:

```
<TABLE>
<TR><TD>
To the right, you see all our telephone numbers.
<TD>
<TABLE BORDER=1>
<TR><TD>Voice<TD>802-888-2828
<TR><TD>Fax   <TD>802-888-6634
<TR><TD>Data  <TD>802-888-3009
</TABLE>
</TABLE>
```

Notice that the inner table has borders, but the outer table does not.

Creative Page Layout with Tables

The boring, conventional way to use tables is for tabular arrangements of text and numbers. But the real fun begins when you make the borders of your tables invisible and use them as guides for arranging graphics and columns of text any which way you please. For an example, take a look at Figures 15.5 and 15.6.

While I worked on building this table, I left the borders visible so I could make sure everything was placed the way I wanted. Then, before incorporating this table into the final Web page, I removed the BORDER=1 attribute from the <TABLE> tag to make the lines invisible.

I used two different tables in Figures 15.5 and 15.6. The top one allowed me to arrange the images and text into four columns. The bottom one let me confine the text to the middle 400 pixels of the screen, essentially giving me extra-wide margins. Remember both of these applications of tables, because you'll probably find uses for them often!

Figure 15.5.

*Use tables whenever
you want multiple
columns of text and/or
wide margins.*

```
<HTML><HEAD><TITLE>Marvin Osgood, D.D.E.</TITLE></HEAD>
<BODY><DIV ALIGN="center">
<TABLE CELLSPACING=10>
<TR VALIGN="top">
<TD><IMG SRC="handgun.gif"><BR>
Five-inch barrel. Twenty ounces.
Six rounds in four seconds.
<TD><IMG SRC="rhino.gif"><BR>
Twelve feet, horn to tail. Up to two tons.
Thirty-five miles per hour.
<TD><IMG SRC="axeman.gif"><BR>
Thirty-inch blade. Twelve pounds.
Sixty miles per hour on impact.
<TD><IMG SRC="dentist.gif"><BR>
<B>Quarter-inch bit. Under an ounce.
Fifty revolutions per second.</B>
</TABLE>
<TABLE WIDTH=400>
<TR><TD ALIGN="center">
<H1>Visit the Dentist.</H1>
<H2>It's Really Not So Bad.</H2><P>
Getting yourself to go to the dentist shouldn't be like
pulling teeth. Modern oral care is relatively painless and
inexpensive, compared to some of the alternatives. So make
an appointment today.<P>
<B>1-800-PAINLESS</B><BR>
<I>Dr. Marvin T. Osgood, D.D.E.</I>
</TABLE>
</DIV></BODY></HTML>
```

Tabular arrangements of text and numbers is the visual table-building
method. Making the borders invisible and using them as guides for graphics
and text is fun. You can see an example of this by clicking on "LOOK: The
Site of the '90s" at

http://24hourHTMLcafe.com/hour15/

While I worked on building this table, I left the borders visible so I could
make sure everything was placed the way I wanted. Then, before incorporating this table into the final Web page, I changed to BORDER=0 to make
the lines invisible.

Your real-world site will probably be a bit more tame than the "LOOK"
site—but of course some of you will start getting even crazier ideas....

FIGURE 15.6.

HTML tables give you greater flexibility and control in how you lay out your Web pages.

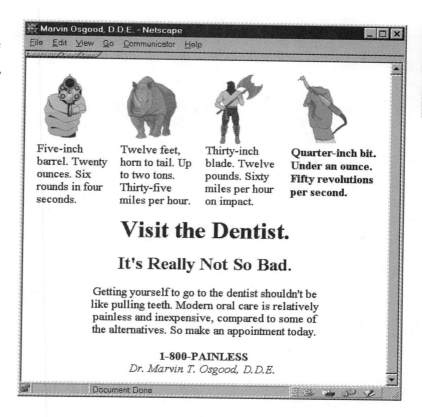

Summary

In this hour you learned to arrange text and images into organized arrangements of rows and columns, called *tables*. You learned the three basic tags for creating tables, and many optional attributes for controlling the alignment, spacing, and appearance of tables. You also saw that tables can be used together and nested within one another for an even wider variety of layout options.

Table 15.1 summarizes the tags and attributes covered in this hour.

TABLE 15.1. HTML TAGS AND ATTRIBUTES COVERED IN HOUR 15.

Tag/Attribute	Function
`<TABLE>...</TABLE>`	Creates a table that can contain any number of rows (`<TR>` tags).
	Attributes:
`BORDER="..."`	Indicates the width in pixels of the table borders. (`BORDER=0`, or omitting the `BORDER` attribute, makes borders invisible.)
`CELLSPACING="..."`	The amount of space between the cells in the table.
`CELLPADDING="..."`	The amount of space between the edges of the cell and its contents.
`WIDTH="..."`	The width of the table on the page, in either exact pixel values or as a percentage of page width.
`BGCOLOR="..."`	Background color of all cells in the table that do not contain their own `BACKGROUND` or `BGCOLOR` attributes.
`BACKGROUND="..."`	Background image to tile within all cells in the table that do not contain their own `BACKGROUND` or `BGCOLOR` attributes (Microsoft Internet Explorer 3.0 only).
`<TR>...</TR>`	Defines a table row, containing one or more cells (`<TD>` tags).
	Attributes:
`ALIGN="..."`	The horizontal alignment of the contents of the cells within this row. Possible values are `LEFT`, `RIGHT`, and `CENTER`.
`VALIGN="..."`	The vertical alignment of the contents of the cells within this row. Possible values are `TOP`, `MIDDLE`, and `BOTTOM`.
`BGCOLOR="..."`	Background color of all cells in the row that do not contain their own `BACKGROUND` or `BGCOLOR` attributes.
`BACKGROUND="..."`	Background image to tile within all cells in the row that do not contain their own `BACKGROUND` or `BGCOLOR` attributes.
`<TD>...</TD>`	Defines a table data cell.
	Attributes:
`ALIGN="..."`	The horizontal alignment of the contents of the cell. Possible values are `LEFT`, `RIGHT`, and `CENTER`.
`VALIGN="..."`	The vertical alignment of the contents of the cell. Possible values are `TOP`, `MIDDLE`, and `BOTTOM`.
`ROWSPAN="..."`	The number of rows this cell will span.
`COLSPAN="..."`	The number of columns this cell will span.

Tag/Attribute	Function
WIDTH="..."	The width of this column of cells, in exact pixel values or as a percentage of the table width.
BGCOLOR="..."	Background color of the cell.
BACKGROUND="..."	Background image to tile within the cell.
<TH>...</TH>	Defines a table heading cell. (Takes all the same attributes as *<TD>*.)

15

Q&A

Q **I made a big table, and when I load the page nothing appears for a long time. Why the wait?**

A Because the Web browser has to figure out the size of everything in the table before it can display any part of it, complex tables can take a while to appear on the screen. You can speed things up a bit by always including WIDTH and HEIGHT attributes for every graphics image within a table. Using WIDTH attributes in the <TABLE> and <TD> tags also helps.

Q **I've noticed that a lot of pages on the Web have tables where one cell will change while other cells stay the same. How do they do that?**

A Those sites are using *frames*, not tables. Frames are similar to tables except that each frame contains a separate HTML page and can be updated independently of the others. The new "floating frames" can actually be put inside a table, so they can look just like a regular table even though the HTML to create them is quite different. You'll find out how to make frames in Hour 21, "Multipage Layout with Frames."

Q **I read in another book that there is a table <CAPTION> tag, but you didn't mention it in this book. Why not?**

A The <CAPTION> tag is hardly ever used, and considering how much you're learning at once here, I didn't think you needed an extra tag to memorize! But since you asked, all the <CAPTION> does is center some text over the top of the table. You can easily do the same thing with the <DIV ALIGN="center"> tag you're already familiar with, but the idea behind <CAPTION> is that some highly intelligent future software might associate it with the table in some profound and meaningful way, thus facilitating communication with higher life-forms and saving humanity from cosmic obscurity and almost-certain destruction. Obviously, this doesn't matter to your short-term quarterly profits, so you can safely pretend the <CAPTION> tag doesn't exist.

Q Weren't there some new table tags in HTML 4.0? And isn't this a book about HTML 4.0?

A The HTML 4.0 standard introduced several new table tags not discussed in this book. The primary practical uses of these extensions are to prepare the ground for some advanced features that no Web browser yet offers, such as tables with their own scrollbars and more reliable reading of tables for visually impaired users. If either of these things is of direct concern to you, you can find out about the new tags at the www.w3c.org Web site. The new tags do not directly affect how tables are displayed in any existing Web browser.

But don't worry; the new tags do not and will not make any of the table tags covered in this hour obsolete. They will all continue to work just as they do now.

Workshop

Quiz

1. You want a Web page with two columns of text side-by-side. How do you create it?

2. You think the columns you created for Question 1 look too close together. How do you add 30 pixels of space between them?

3. Write the HTML to create the table shown in the following figure:

Answers

1. With the following table:
```
<TABLE><TR><TD ALIGN="top">
...First column of text goes here...
</TD><TD ALIGN="top">
...Second column of text goes here...
</TD></TR></TABLE>
```

2. Add `CELLSPACING=30` to the `<TABLE>` tag. (Or you could use `CELLPADDING=15` to add 15 pixels of space inside the edge of each column.)

3.
```
<TABLE BORDER=5>
<TR>
 <TD ROWSPAN=3>A</TD>
 <TD COLSPAN=3>B</TD>
</TR>
<TR>
 <TD>E</TD>
 <TD>F</TD>
 <TD ROWSPAN=2>C</TD>
</TR>
<TR>
 <TD COLSPAN=2>D</TD>
</TR>
</TABLE>
```

Exercises

- You can use a simple one-celled table with a border to draw a rectangle around any section of text on a Web page. By nesting that single-cell table in another two-column table, you can put a "sidebar" of text to the left or right side of your Web page. Outlined sections of text and sidebars are very common on printed paper pages, so you'll probably find uses for them on your Web pages, too.

- Do you have any pages where different visitors might be interested in different information? Use a table to present two or three columns of text, each with its own heading (and perhaps its own graphic). Then something of interest to everyone will be visible at the top of the page when it first appears.

HOUR 16

Using Style Sheets

Style sheets are without a doubt the "Next Big Thing" in the fast-paced world of the Web. The concept is simple: You create a single style sheet document that specifies the fonts, colors, backgrounds, and other characteristics that establish a unique look. Then you link every page that should have that look to the style sheet, instead of specifying all those style elements over and over again in each document separately. Then when you decide to change your official corporate typeface or color scheme, you can modify all your Web pages at once by changing one or two style sheets.

NEW TERM A *style sheet* is a single page of formatting instructions that can control the appearance of many HTML pages at once.

If style sheets accomplished this and nothing else, they'd save millions of dollars worth of Webmasters' time and become an integral part of most Web publishing projects. But they aim to do this and much more as well. The HTML style sheet standard enables you to set a great number of formatting characteristics that it was never possible to modify before with any amount of effort. These include exacting typeface controls, letter and line spacing, margins and page borders, and expanded support for non-European languages and characters. They also enable sizes and other measurements to be specified in familiar units such as inches, millimeters, points, and picas. You can also use style sheets to precisely position graphics and text anywhere on a Web page.

In short, style sheets bring the sophistication level of paper-oriented publishing to the Web. And they do so—you'll pardon the expression—"with style."

 If you have three or more Web pages that share (or should share) similar formatting and fonts, you may want to create a style sheet for them as you read this hour.

A Basic Style Sheet

Despite their intimidating power, style sheets can be very simple to create. Consider the document in Figures 16.1 and 16.2. These documents share several properties that could be put into a common style sheet.

- They use the Book Antiqua font for body text and Prose Antique for headings.
- They use an image named parchmnt.jpg as a background tile.
- All text is maroon (on a color screen, not in this book!).
- They have wide margins and indented body text.
- There is lots of vertical space between lines of text.
- The footnotes are centered and in small print.

Some of these properties, such as text color, the background tile, and centered small print, are easy to achieve with ordinary HTML tags. Others, such as line spacing and wide margins, are beyond the scope of standard HTML. However, they can now be achieved easily with style sheets.

Figure 16.3 shows an HTML style sheet that specifies how these properties should look.

The first thing you'll undoubtedly notice about this style sheet is that it doesn't look anything like normal HTML. Style-sheet specifications are really a separate language in and of themselves.

Of course, there are some familiar HTML tags in there. As you might guess, BODY, P, H1, and H2 in the style sheet refer to the corresponding tags in the HTML documents to which the style sheet will be applied. In braces after each tag name are the specifications for how all text within that tag should appear.

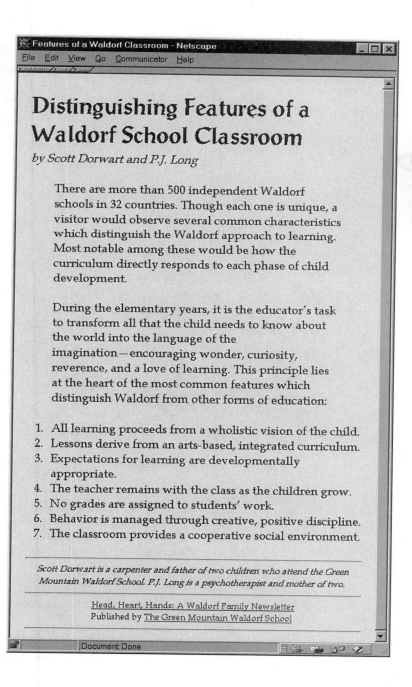

16

Distinguishing Features of a Waldorf School Classroom

by Scott Dorwart and P.J. Long

There are more than 500 independent Waldorf schools in 32 countries. Though each one is unique, a visitor would observe several common characteristics which distinguish the Waldorf approach to learning. Most notable among these would be how the curriculum directly responds to each phase of child development.

During the elementary years, it is the educator's task to transform all that the child needs to know about the world into the language of the imagination—encouraging wonder, curiosity, reverence, and a love of learning. This principle lies at the heart of the most common features which distinguish Waldorf from other forms of education:

1. All learning proceeds from a wholistic vision of the child.
2. Lessons derive from an arts-based, integrated curriculum.
3. Expectations for learning are developmentally appropriate.
4. The teacher remains with the class as the children grow.
5. No grades are assigned to students' work.
6. Behavior is managed through creative, positive discipline.
7. The classroom provides a cooperative social environment.

Scott Dorwart is a carpenter and father of two children who attend the Green Mountain Waldorf School. P.J. Long is a psychotherapist and mother of two.

Head, Heart, Hands: A Waldorf Family Newsletter
Published by The Green Mountain Waldorf School

FIGURE 16.2.

*This page uses the
same style sheet as the
one in Figure 16.1.*

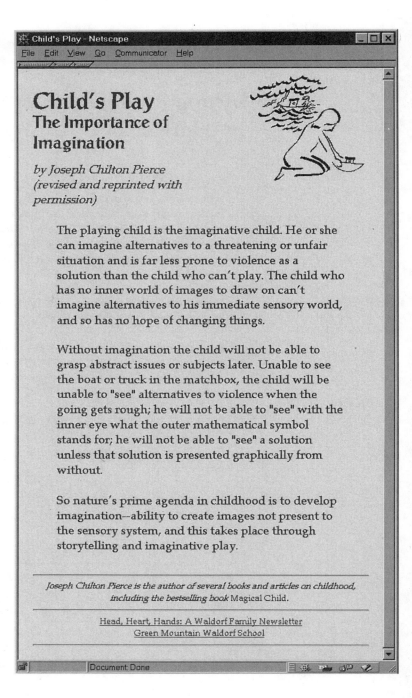

Figure 16.3.

A single style sheet can specify the properties of any number of pages. Figures 16.1 and 16.2 both use this one.

```
BODY {font-size: 12pt;
      font-family: "Book Antiqua";
      color: maroon;
      background: url(parchmnt.gif);
      line-height: 16pt;
      margin-left: 10pt;
      margin-right: 10pt;}

P {margin-left: 24pt;
   margin-right: 24pt;}

H1 {font: 24pt "Prose_Antique" "Lucida Handwriting";
    font-weight: bold;
    line-height: 30pt;}

H2 {font: 18pt "Prose_Antique" "Lucida Handwriting";
    font-weight: bold;
    line-height: 22pt;}

DIV.footnote {font-size: 9pt;
              line-height: 12pt;
              text-align: center}
```

16

In this case, all BODY text that isn't within some other tag should be rendered at a size of 12 points, in the Book Antiqua font if possible, and with the color maroon and 16 points between lines. The page should have 10-point margins, and the background should be the image found at the relative URL parchmnt.jpg.

Any paragraph starting with a <P> tag will be indented an additional 24 points.

Any text within <H1> or <H2> tags should be rendered in boldface Prose have Antique at a size of 24 points and 18 points, respectively. If a user doesn't have a font named Prose Antique installed, the Lucida Handwriting font will be used instead.

The pt after each measurement in Figure 16.3 means "points" (there are 72 points in an inch). If you prefer, you can specify any style sheet measurement in inches (in), centimeters (cm), pixels (px), or widths-of-a-letter-m, which are called ems (em).

The point sizes used in the HTML <FONT> tag are *not* the same as the point sizes specified in style sheets. <FONT SIZE=3> corresponds to approximately 12pt text, <FONT SIZE=1> is about 6pt text, and <FONT SIZE=7> (the maximum size for the FONT tag) is about 24pt text. You can specify font sizes as large as you like with style sheets, although most display devices and printers will not correctly handle fonts over 200 points.

To link this style sheet to the HTML documents, you include a `<LINK>` tag in the `<HEAD>` section of each document. Figure 16.4 is the HTML for the page in Figure 16.1. It contains the following `<LINK>` tag.

```
<LINK REL=STYLESHEET TYPE="text/css" HREF="hhh.css">
```

This assumes the style sheet was saved under the name `hhh.css` in the same directory folder as the HTML document. Netscape Navigator 4.0 and Internet Explorer 4.0 will then give the body and heading text the properties specified in the style sheet, without the need for any `<FONT>` tags or `<BODY BACKGROUND>` attribute in the document itself.

In most Web browsers, you can see the commands in a style sheet by opening the `.css` file and choosing Notepad or another text editor as the helper application to view the file. (To find out the name of the `.css` file, look at the HTML source of any document that links to it.)

Unfortunately, Netscape Navigator 4.0 refuses to let you view style sheet files. There's not even an easy way to download them to your hard drive with Navigator 4.0 to view them with another application. So if you want to have a peek at other people's style sheets that you find on the Internet, you'll need to use a different Web browser than Navigator 4.0.

CSS1 Versus CSS2

There are actually two different languages to choose from when you make a style sheet. The one I recommend you use is called *Cascading Style Sheets, Level 1 (CSS1),* since it is compatible with both Netscape Navigator 4.0 and Microsoft Internet Explorer 4.0. The new CSS2 standard is only partially implemented in the current crop of browsers, and neither Netscape nor Microsoft is currently claiming that its next version will fully support CSS2. They do already support some parts of CSS2, such as the ability to precisely position text and graphics on the page (discussed under "Specifying Inline Styles" later in this hour).

You'll find a complete reference guide to both the CSS1 and CSS2 style sheet languages at www.w3c.org. The rest of this hour explains how to put the information from those reference documents to use in a way that is compatible with the current generation of Web browsers.

If you are a JavaScript programmer, and the only browser you need to support is Netscape Navigator 4.0, you may prefer the *JavaScript Style Sheets* language instead. It has all the same capabilities as CSS1, but uses a slightly different syntax. See the Netscape Developer's Edge Online Web site (http://developer.netscape.com/) for a reference guide to that language.

FIGURE 16.4.

When viewed in Netscape Navigator 4.0 or Microsoft Internet Explorer 4.0, this page looks like Figure 16.1. In older browsers that don't support style sheets, it looks like Figure 16.5.

```
<HTML>
<HEAD>
<TITLE>Features of a Waldorf Classroom</TITLE>
<LINK REL=STYLESHEET TYPE="text/css" HREF="hhh.css">
</HEAD>
<BODY>
<H1>Distinguishing Features of a Waldorf School Classroom</H1>
<I>by Scott Dorwart and P.J. Long</I>
<P>There are more than 500 independent Waldorf schools in 32
countries. Though each one is unique, a visitor would observe
several common characteristics which distinguish the Waldorf
approach to learning. Most notable among these would be how
the curriculum directly responds to each phase of
child development.<P>
During the elementary years, it is the educator's task to
transform all that the child needs to know about the world
into the language of the imagination-encouraging wonder,
curiosity, reverence, and a love of learning. This
principle lies at the heart of the most common features
which distinguish Waldorf from other forms of education:<P>
<OL>
<LI>All learning proceeds from a wholistic vision of the child.
<LI>Lessons derive from an arts-based, integrated curriculum.
<LI>Expectations for learning are developmentally appropriate.
<LI>The teacher remains with the class as the children grow.
<LI>No grades are assigned to students' work.
<LI>Behavior is managed through creative, positive discipline.
<LI>The classroom provides a cooperative social environment.
</OL>
<P>
<DIV CLASS="footnote">
<HR>
<I>Scott Dorwart  is a carpenter and father of two children
who attend the Green Mountain Waldorf School.
P.J. Long is a psychotherapist and mother of two.</I>
<HR>
<A HREF="http://netletter.com/GMWS/HHH.htm">
Head, Heart, Hands: A Waldorf Family Newsletter</A><BR>
Published by
<A HREF="http://netletter.com/GMWS/GMWS.htm">
The Green Mountain Waldorf School</A>
<HR>
</DIV>
</BODY></HTML>
```

16

Older Web Browsers

Style sheets are only supported by Netscape Navigator version 4.0 or later and Microsoft Internet Explorer version 3.0 or later. Older browsers, and many HTML viewers built into word processors or other business software applications, will simply ignore the `<LINK>` tag and display the page without any special formatting. Figure 16.5, for example, shows how the HTML from Figure 16.4 looks in Netscape Navigator 3.0.

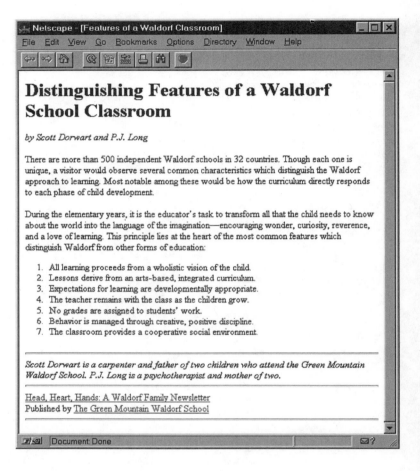

You should always test your style-sheet enhanced pages without the style sheet (use an
older browser, or just change the name of the style sheet temporarily so the browser can't
find it) to make sure they still look acceptable.

There is also a special "problem case" you should be aware of: Microsoft implemented
rudimentary style sheet support in Internet Explorer version 3.0. Since it did this before
the official style sheet specification had been released and didn't try to support the full
specification anyway, the results are sometimes quite different than what you would see
with a more modern browser.

Figure 16.6 shows how Microsoft Internet Explorer 3.0 displays the page from Figures
16.1, 16.4, and 16.5. Notice the strange spacing and gray background. It's a good idea
for Web page authors to keep a copy of Internet Explorer 3.0 for testing, to make sure

your pages don't look too weird to users of this problematic browser. Other than that, there isn't much you can do about it except to encourage readers of your pages to upgrade quickly to either Microsoft Internet Explorer 4.0 or Netscape Navigator 4.0.

The style specifications supported by Internet Explorer 3.0 are explained in the following list. For maximum compatibility, make sure you design your pages to look all right if only these style elements show up and all the other style specifications are ignored.

- `font:` Lets you set many font properties at once. You can specify a list of font names separated by commas; if the first is not available, the next will be tried, and so on. You can also include the words `bold` and/or `italic` and a font size. Each of these font properties can be specified separately with `font-family:`, `font-size:`, `font-weight: bold`, and `font-style: italic` if you prefer.

- `text-decoration:` Is useful for turning link underlining off—simply set text decoration to `none`. The values of `underline`, `italic`, and `line-through` are also supported.

- `line-height:` Is also known in the publishing world as leading. This sets the height of each line of text, usually in points.

- `background:` Places a color or image behind text, either with a color or a `url(address)` where *address* points to a background image tile. Note that this can be assigned not only to the `<BODY>` tag, but to any tag or span of text to "highlight" an area on a page. (Also note that it doesn't always work quite right in Microsoft Internet Explorer 3.0, though it works fine in version 4.0 browsers.)

Style Classes

This is a "teach yourself" book, so you don't have to go to a single class to learn how to give your pages great style. But you do need to learn what a *style class* is. Whenever you want some of the text on your pages to look different than the other text, you can create what amounts to a custom-built HTML tag. Each type of specially formatted text you define is called a *style class*.

NEW TERM A *style class* is a custom set of formatting specifications that can be applied to any passage of text in a Web page:

For example, suppose you wanted two different kinds of `<H1>` headings in your documents. You would create a style class for each one by putting the following text in the style sheet:

```
H1.silly {font: 36pt "Comic Sans";}
H1.serious {font: 36pt "Arial";}
```

FIGURE **16.6.**

Microsoft Internet Explorer version 3.0 had an incomplete implementation of style sheets, which makes most style sheet pages look a bit strange. (This is the same page shown in Figures 16.1, 16.4, and 16.5.)

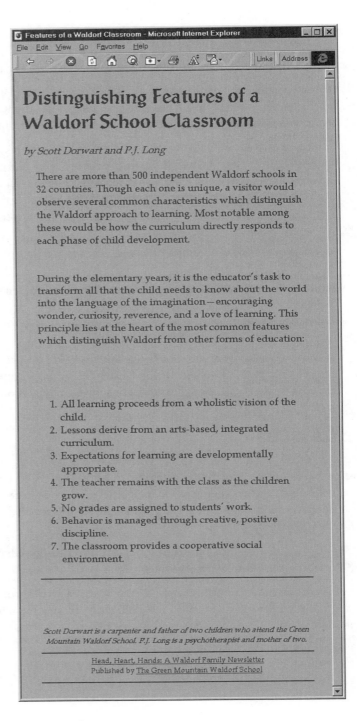

To choose between the two style classes in an HTML page, you would use the CLASS attribute, as follows.

```
<H1 CLASS="silly">Marvin's Munchies Inc.</H1>
Text about Marvin's Muchies goes here.
<H1 CLASS="serious">MMI Investor Information</H1>
Text for business investors goes here.
```

The words "Marvin's Munchies Inc." would appear in 36-point Comic Sans to people whose browsers support style sheets (assuming you include a <LINK> to the style sheet at the top of the Web page, and assuming they have the Comic Sans font installed). But the words "MMI Investor Information" would appear in the 36-point Arial font instead.

What if you want to create a style class that could be applied to any text, rather than just headings or some other particular tag? You can associate a style class with the <DIV> tag (which, as you may recall from Hour 5, "Text Alignment and Lists," can enclose any text but doesn't do anything except what its ALIGN or other attributes indicate).

By using DIV. followed by any style class name you make up and any style specifications you choose, you can essentially create your own custom HTML tag to control any number of font, spacing, and margin settings all at once. Wherever you want to apply your custom tag in a page, use a <DIV> tag with the CLASS= attribute followed by the class name you created.

For example, the style sheet in Figure 16.3 includes the following style class specification:

```
DIV.footnote {font-size: 9pt;
              line-height: 12pt;
              text-align: center}
```

This style class is applied in Figure 16.4 with the following tag:

```
<DIV CLASS="footnote">
```

Everything between that tag and the accompanying </DIV> tag in Figure 16.1 appears in 9-point centered text with 12-point vertical line spacing. The same style class was also used on the footnote in Figure 16.2.

Specifying Inline Styles

In some situations, you might want to specify styles that will be used in only one Web page. You can then enclose a style sheet between <STYLE> and </STYLE> tags and include it in the beginning of an HTML document, between the </HEAD> and <BODY> tags. No <LINK> tag is needed, and you cannot refer to that style sheet from any other page (unless you copy it into the beginning of that document, too).

If you want to specify a style for only a small part of a page, you can go one step further and put a STYLE attribute within a <P>, <DIV>, or <SPAN> tag.

> <SPAN> and </SPAN> are "dummy" tags that do nothing in and of them-
> selves, except specify a range of text to apply any STYLE attributes that you
> add. The only difference between <DIV> and <SPAN> is that <DIV> forces a
> line break, while <SPAN> doesn't. Therefore, you should use <SPAN> to modi-
> fy the style of any portion of text shorter than a paragraph.

Here's how a sample STYLE attribute might look:

```
<P STYLE="color: green">This text is green, but
<SPAN STYLE="color: red"> this text is red.</SPAN>
Back to green again, but...</P>
<P>...now the green is over, and we're back to the default color for
this page.
```

Although the effect of this example could be achieved as easily with the <FONT COLOR> tag (see Hour 6, "Text Formatting and Font Control"), many style specifications have no corresponding HTML tag. Generally, you should avoid inline styles except when there is no way to do what you're after in HTML, and you feel that using an external style sheet would be too cumbersome.

> To give the pages at the 24-Hour HTML Café a consistent look and feel, I cre-
> ated a style sheet that is linked to every page in the site. For your edifica-
> tion and convenience, I copied the text of that style sheet into an HTML
> page, which you can access from http://24hourHTMLcafe.com/hour16.
>
> Here's a little trick to notice in the htmlcafe.css style sheet: I gave the <P>
> tag a style with a left margin of 40 pixels. This means that every <P> tag in
> the HTML Café pages doesn't just start a new paragraph, but also indents
> the text 40 pixels. Whenever I don't want indentation, I can start a para-
> graph with <P></P>, which still skips a line but doesn't indent.

Positioning and Layers

Here's the bad news: Neither the official HTML 4.0 standard nor the official Cascading Style Sheets Level 1 (CSS1) standard gives you any direct way to control the exact position of the images and text on your Web pages. The closest thing you can do is adjust the margins of your page. For example, the following HTML would position the first image on the page exactly 50 pixels to the left and 40 pixels down from the top-left corner of the browser window. It would then indent the text exactly 60 pixels from the left edge of the browser window.

```
<BODY>
<SPAN STYLE="margin-left: 50px; margin-top: 40px">
<IMG SRC="pretty.gif"></SPAN>
<SPAN STYLE="margin-left: 60px;">
This is a pretty picture.</SPAN>
```

A lot of Web page designers have prayed to the HTML gods for the power to be more direct about where they want an image to be. Overlapping layers of images and text are high on a lot of wish lists, too. Unfortunately, there is no officially sanctioned way to say, "Put this image at pixel position 100,50 and this text at 200,52."

The good news is that the new Cascading Style Sheets Level 2 (CSS2) standard includes positioning, and both Netscape Navigator 4.0 and Microsoft Internet Explorer 4.0 already conform to part of that standard. It's a simple, elegant extension to the CSS1 style sheet standard, so you'll find it quite easy to use.

> Netscape has also created its own unique way of handling positioning and layering: a new tag called <LAYER>. I don't cover that tag here because it isn't likely to be accepted as a standard. The style-based positioning technique achieves the same results in a way that's more likely to be compatible with non-Netscape browsers.

The following line of HTML shows how to position an image with the top-left corner exactly 50 pixels to the left and 40 pixels down from the top edge of the browser window. Though I use a <SPAN> tag here, you can include a similar STYLE attribute in almost any HTML tag to position some text precisely where you want it.

```
<SPAN STYLE="position: absolute; left: 50px; top: 40px">
<IMG SRC="pretty.gif"></SPAN>
```

> If you leave out the position: absolute part, measurements will be relative to wherever the text or image would normally appear on the page, rather than relative to the top-left corner of the browser window.

Along with left: and top: positioning, you can also optionally include width: and height: for text blocks.

16

Figure 16.7 is a simple HTML document with style-based positioning included. You can see the resulting Web page, as displayed by Netscape Navigator version 4.0, in Figure 16.8. The page would look exactly the same in Microsoft Internet Explorer 4.0.

Notice that elements are drawn onto the page in the order that they occur in the HTML document. For example, the white streak appears to be layered on top of the logo, but underneath the body text because of the order in which they were drawn.

FIGURE 16.7.

This HTML page uses inline styles to precisely position images and text.

```
<HTML><HEAD><TITLE>Refractal Design Inc.</TITLE></HEAD>
<BODY TEXT="yellow" BACKGROUND="gradcom4.jpg">
<SPAN STYLE="position: absolute; left: 390px; top: 40px">
 <IMG SRC="spianim.gif" HEIGHT=140 WIDTH=140>
</SPAN>
<SPAN STYLE="position: absolute; left: 16px; top: 110px;">
 <IMG SRC="streak.gif" HEIGHT=260 WIDTH=444>
</SPAN>
<DIV STYLE="position: absolute; left: 300px; top: 60px;">
<H2>Refractal</H2></DIV>
<DIV STYLE="position: absolute; left: 510px; top: 120px;">
<H2>Design</H2></DIV>
<DIV STYLE="position: absolute; left: 55px; top: 130px;
            width: 340px;">
Refractal Design Inc. produces heirloom quality limited
edition fine jewelry, jewelry accessories, and other related
items. We are both a design house and a manufacturing facility.
</DIV></BODY></HTML>
```

FIGURE 16.8.

This is how Netscape Navigator 4.0 displays the HTML from Figure 16.7.

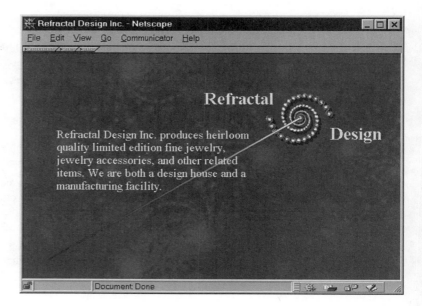

According to the proposed standard, STYLE specifications can go in any tag you like. For example, the following:

`<DIV STYLE="position: absolute; left: 300px; top: 60px;">`
`<H2>Refractal</H2></DIV>`

does exactly the same thing as

`<H2 STYLE="position: absolute; left: 300px; top: 60px;">Refractal</H2>`

In Netscape Navigator 4.0, these two approaches are indeed equivalent. However, in Microsoft Internet Explorer 4.0, putting the positioning information in the `<H2>` tag doesn't work. Presumably, this will be corrected in future versions of Internet Explorer, but for maximum compatibility you should always use `<SPAN>` or `<DIV>` tags for positioning.

16

Though exact positioning control is a great idea, always remember that anyone using Netscape Navigator version 3.0 or earlier, Microsoft Internet Explorer version 3.0 or earlier, or almost any other Web browser will not see any of your fancy positioning. The HTML from Figure 16.7, for example, looks like Figure 16.9 when displayed in Netscape Navigator 3.0.

Also remember that changes in font or window size can easily destroy the appearance of your carefully positioned elements. As with all style sheet stuff, I strongly recommend that you use style-based positioning only for fine tuning—at least until most of your intended audience has moved up to version 4.0 or later browsers.

Summary

In this hour, you learned that a style sheet can control the appearance of many HTML pages at once. It can also give you extremely precise control over typography, spacing, and the positioning of HTML elements. You also learned that, by adding a STYLE attribute to almost any HTML tag, you can control the style of any part of an HTML page without referring to a separate style sheet document.

Table 16.1 summarizes the tags discussed in this hour. Refer to the CSS1 and CSS2 style sheet standards at www.w3c.org for details on what options can be included after the `<STYLE>` tag or STYLE attribute.

Figure 16.9.

The HTML from Figure 16.7 doesn't look very artistic in Netscape Navigator 3.0 because none of the positioning shows up.

Table 16.1. HTML tags and attributes covered in Hour 16.

Tag	Attribute	Function
`<STYLE>...</STYLE>`		Allows an internal style sheet to be included within a document. Used between `<HEAD>` and `</HEAD>`.
`<LINK>`		Links to an external style sheet (or other document type). Used in the `<HEAD>` section of the document.
	`HREF="..."`	The address of the style sheet.
	`TYPE="..."`	The Internet content type (always "text/css" for a style sheet).
	`REL="..."`	The link type (always "stylesheet" for style sheets).
`<SPAN>...</SPAN>`		Does nothing at all, except provide a place to put `STYLE` or other attributes. (Similar to `<DIV>...</DIV>`, but does not cause a line break.)
	`STYLE="..."`	Includes inline style specifications. (Can be used in `<SPAN>`, `<DIV>`, `<BODY>`, and most other HTML tags.)

Q&A

Q How do I use positioning and layers to make text and graphics fly around the page? Isn't that what they call "Dynamic HTML"?

A "Dynamic HTML" is a general term (used mostly for marketing purposes) meaning anything that makes Web pages move. You'll learn more about all that in Hour 19, "Web Page Scripting for Non-Programmers," and Hour 20, "Setting Pages in Motion with Dynamic HTML."

In a nutshell, scripting lets you use a simple programming language called JavaScript to modify any HTML or style sheet information (including positioning) on-the-fly in response to the mouse movements and clicks of people who visit your pages.

Q Say I link a style sheet to my page that says all text should be blue, but there's a `<SPAN STYLE="font-color: red">` tag in the page somewhere. Will that text come out blue or red?

A Red. Local inline styles always take precedence over external style sheets. Any style specifications you put between `<STYLE>` and `</STYLE>` tags at the top of a page will also take precedence over external style sheets (but not over inline styles later in the same page).

Q Can I link more than one style sheet to a single page?

A Sure. For example, you might have a sheet for font stuff and another one for margins and spacing. Just include a `<LINK>` for both.

Workshop

Quiz

1. Create a style sheet to specify half-inch margins, 30-point blue Arial headings, and all other text in double-spaced 10-point blue Times Roman (or the default browser font).

2. If you saved the style sheet you made for question 1 as `corporat.css`, how would you apply it to a Web page named `intro.htm`?

3. Write the HTML to make Netscape Navigator 4.0 or Microsoft Internet Explorer 4.0 display the words "What would you like to" starting exactly at the top left corner of the browser window, and "THROW TODAY?" in large type exactly 80 pixels down and 20 pixels to the left of the corner.

Answers

1. ```
   BODY {font: 10pt blue;
   line-height: 20pt;
   margin-left: 0.5in;
   margin-right: 0.5in;
   margin-top: 0.5in;
   margin-bottom: 0.5in}
   H1 {font: 30pt blue Arial}
   ```

2. Put the following tag between the `<HEAD>` and `</HEAD>` tags of the `intro.htm` document:

   ```
   <LINK REL=STYLESHEET TYPE="text/css" HREF="corporat.css">
   ```

3. ```
   <SPAN STYLE="position: absolute; left: 0px; top: 0px">
   What would you like to</SPAN>
   <H1 STYLE="position: absolute; left: 80px; top: 20px">
   THROW TODAY?</H1>
   ```

Exercises

- Develop a standard style sheet for your Web site and link it into all your pages. (Use inline styles for pages that need to deviate from it.) If you work for a corporation, chances are it has already developed font and style specifications for printed materials. Get a copy of those specifications and follow them for company Web pages, too.

- Be sure to explore the official style sheet specs at www.w3c.org and try some of the more esoteric style controls I didn't mention in this hour.

Part V
Dynamic Web Pages

Hour

Hour 17

Embedding Multimedia in Web Pages

Multimedia is a popular buzzword for sound, motion video, and interactive animation. This hour shows you how to include multimedia in your Web pages.

The first thing you should be aware of is that computer multimedia is still in its youth, and Internet multimedia is barely in its infancy. The infant technology's rapid pace of growth creates three obstacles for anyone who wants to include audiovisual material in a Web page:

- There are many incompatible multimedia file formats from which to choose, and none has emerged as a clear "industry standard" yet.

- Most people do not have fast enough Internet connections to receive high-quality audiovisual data without a long wait.

- Each new Web browser version that comes out uses different HTML tags to include multimedia in Web pages.

The moral of the story: Whatever you do today to implement a multimedia Web site, plan on changing it before too long.

The good news is that you can sidestep all three of these obstacles to some extent today, and they are all likely to become even easier to overcome in the near future. This hour shows you how to put multimedia on your Web pages for maximum compatibility with the Web browser versions that most people are now using. It also introduces you to the new standard way that Web page multimedia will be handled in the future.

> The Microsoft ActiveX controls and Java applets discussed in Hour 18, "Interactive Pages with Applets and ActiveX," can be used with many of the same types of media files discussed in this chapter. Be sure to read Hour 18 before you make any final decisions about how you will incorporate multimedia into your Web site.

To Do

Before you see how to place multimedia on your Web pages in any way, you need to have some multimedia content to start with.

Creating multimedia of any kind is a challenging and complicated task. If you're planning to create your own content from scratch, you'll need far more than this book to become the next crackerjack multimedia developer. Once you've got some content, however, this hour will show you how to place your new creations into your Web pages.

For those of us who are artistically challenged, a number of alternative ways to obtain useful multimedia assets are available. Aside from the obvious (hire an artist), here are a few suggestions:

1. The Web itself is chock-full of useful content of all media types, and stock media clearinghouses of all shapes and sizes now exist online. See the hotlist at the 24-Hour HTML Café (`http://24hourHTMLcafe.com/hotsites.htm#multimedia`) for links to some of the best stock media sources on the Web.

2. Don't feel like spending any money? Much of the material on the Internet is free. Of course, it's still a good idea to double-check with the accredited author or current owner of the content; you don't want to get sued for copyright infringement. In addition, various offices of the U.S. government generate content which, by law, belongs to all Americans. (Any NASA footage found online, for instance, is free for you to use.)

▼

▲

3. Check out the online forums and Usenet newsgroups that cater to the interests of videographers. As clearly as possible, describe your site and what you want to do with it. Chances are you'll find a few up-and-coming artists who'd be more than happy to let thousands of people peruse their work online.

Putting Multimedia on a Web Page

The following sections show you how to add some audio and video to a Web page in three different ways:

1. The "old way" for maximum compatibility with all Web browsers.

2. The "today way" that's best for Netscape Navigator 2.0, 3.0, and 4.0 and Microsoft Internet Explorer 3.0 and 4.0.

3. The "new way" that doesn't work well with any existing Web browser, but will be the official standard technique for the future.

In the ActiveX section of Hour 18, you'll discover an alternative approach to embedding multimedia that works especially well with Microsoft Internet Explorer.

17

In this hour's sample pages, I use Windows AVI video and MIDI sound files. For better compatibility with non-Windows computers, you could use Apple's QuickTime audio/video/format, the RealAudio/RealVideo/format, or any other video format supported by today's Web browsers. The procedures shown in this hour for incorporating the files into your Web pages are the same, no matter which file format you choose.

Multimedia the Old-fashioned Way

The simplest and most reliable option for incorporating a video or audio file into your Web site is to simply link it in with <A HREF>, exactly as you would link to another HTML file. (See Hour 3, "Linking to Other Web Pages," for coverage of the <A> tag.)

For example, the following line could be used to offer an AVI video of a Maine lobster:

```
<A HREF="lobstah.avi">Play the lobster video.</A>
```

When someone clicks the words "Play the lobster video," the lobstah.avi video file will be transferred to their computer. Whichever helper application or plug-in the user has installed will automatically start as soon as the file has finished downloading. If no AVI-compatible helper or plug-in can be found, the Web browser will offer the user a chance to save the video on the hard drive for later viewing.

> In case you're not familiar with *helper applications* (or *helper apps* for short), they are the external programs that a Web browser calls on to display any type of file it can't handle on its own. (Generally, the helper application that is associated with a file type in Windows will be called on whenever a Web browser can't display that type of file.) *Plug-ins* are special helper applications that are specifically designed for tight integration with Netscape Navigator.

Embedding Sound in a Web Page

Over the past few years, Microsoft and Netscape have offered various conflicting solutions to the problem of how to put multimedia on a Web page. Some of these, such as Microsoft's proprietary extensions to the <IMG> tag, are now completely obsolete.

One non-standard tag has endured, however; Netscape's <EMBED> tag is now actually more compatible with both Netscape and Microsoft browsers than the official HTML 4.0 <OBJECT> tag, which was supposed to replace it.

The <EMBED> tag enables you to place any type of file directly into your Web page. For the media to appear on the Web page, however, every user must have a plug-in or OLE-compatible helper application that recognizes the incoming data type and knows what to do with it. The plug-ins that come bundled with Netscape Navigator 3.0 can handle most common media types, including WAV, AU, MPEG, MID, EPS, VRML, and many more. Many other plug-ins are also available from other companies to handle almost any type of media file.

> Netscape maintains a Web page that lists all registered plug-ins and plug-in developers. To check out the current assortment, head to http://home.netscape.com/comprod/products/navigator/version_2.0/plugins/index.html.
>
> The Plug-Ins Development Kit, available for free from Netscape, allows developers to create new plug-ins for their own products and data types (for more information, see Netscape's Web site at http://home.netscape.com/).

The following line of HTML would embed a sound clip named hello.wav and display the playback controls at the current position on the page, as long as visitors to the page have a WAV-compatible plug-in or helper app.

```
<EMBED SRC="hello.wav">
```

Notice that, like the <IMG> tag, <EMBED> requires an SRC attribute to indicate the address of the embedded media file. Also like <IMG>, the <EMBED> tag can take ALIGN, WIDTH, and HEIGHT attributes. The SRC, WIDTH, HEIGHT, and ALIGN attributes are interpreted by the browser just as they would be for a still image. However, the actual display of the data is handled by whichever plug-in or helper application each user may have installed. In the case of sound files, the sound is played and some controls are usually displayed. Which controls actually appear depend on which plug-in or helper application each individual user has installed, so you, as a Web page author, can't know ahead of time exactly what someone will see.

The <EMBED> tag also enables you to set any number of optional parameters, which are specific to the plug-in or player program. For instance, the page in Figure 17.1 includes the following:

```
<EMBED SRC="atune.mid" WIDTH=1 HEIGHT=1 AUTOSTART="true" LOOP="true"
HIDDEN="true">
```

This causes the music file atune.mid to play whenever the page is displayed. As you can see in Figure 17.2, this has no visual effect on the page whatsoever. (Since this book doesn't have any speakers, you can't hear the auditory effect unless you pull the page up online at http://24hourHTMLcafe.com/hour17/.)

FIGURE 17.1.

The <EMBED> tag embeds multimedia files directly into a Web page in Netscape Navigator.

```
<HTML><HEAD><TITLE>Music</TITLE></HEAD>
<BODY BACKGROUND="wiggles.jpg">
<A HREF="nosound.htm">
<IMG SRC="shutup.gif" BORDER=0 ALIGN="right" ALT="Stop music">
</A>
<TABLE WIDTH=500>
<TR><TD><IMG SRC="piano.gif" WIDTH=200 HEIGHT=172>
<TR><TD><B>Roaming through the jungle of 'oohs' and 'ahs,'
searching for a more agreeable noise, I live a life of
primitivity with the mind of a child and an unquenchable
thirst for sharps and flats.</B>
&#151;Duke Ellington, <I>Music Is My Mistress</I>
</TABLE>
<EMBED SRC="atune.mid" WIDTH=1 HEIGHT=1
 AUTOSTART="true" LOOP="true" HIDDEN="true">
<NOEMBED>
  <A HREF="atune.mid">Click here to hear.</A>
</NOEMBED>
</BODY></HTML>
```

17

FIGURE 17.2.

If you were looking at this page (from Figure 17.1) on a computer with a sound card and speakers, you would hear the atune.mid *file playing.*

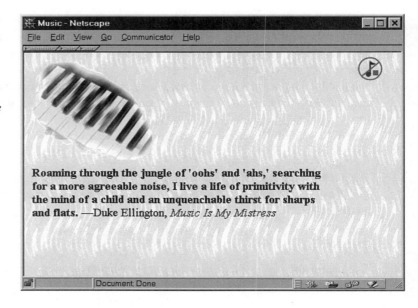

AUTOSTART, LOOP, and HIDDEN are not standard attributes of the <EMBED> tag, so the browser simply hands them over to the plug-in program to interpret. AUTOPLAY="true", LOOP="true", and HIDDEN="true" are specific to the LiveAudio plug-in that comes built-in to Netscape Navigator 3.0 and 4.0. (These attributes tell the plug-in to play the video automatically as soon as it loads, to play it over again each time it finishes, and not to display any controls on the Web page.) If a user has a different AVI plug-in, or no plug-in at all for handling MIDI (Musical Instrument Digital Interface) files, these attributes will do nothing at all. Refer to the Web pages of each plug-in developer for information on the commands that its plug-in will accept as attributes in the <EMBED> tag.

If a suitable plug-in can't be found for an <EMBED> tag, the Windows 95 versions of both Netscape Navigator and Microsoft Internet Explorer may embed an OLE-compliant application (such as the Media Player application that comes with Windows) to play the media file. Therefore, the sound will play successfully in both Netscape Navigator and Microsoft Internet Explorer.

Whenever you set up a Web page to play a sound automatically, it's a good idea to give people some way to turn the sound off. (There's nothing more annoying than surfing the Web with your favorite CD-ROM on and hitting a musical Web page that can't be turned off!) The easiest way to turn off a sound is simply to link to a page with no sounds embedded in it. For example, clicking the shutup.gif icon in the upper-right corner of Figure 17.2 loads the silent but otherwise identical page shown in Figures 17.3 and 17.4. When someone wants to turn the sound back on, he can click the rockon.gif icon to link back to the original page.

FIGURE 17.3.

This page is identical to Figure 17.1, but with no sound.

```
<HTML><HEAD><TITLE>No Music</TITLE></HEAD>
<BODY BACKGROUND="wiggles.jpg">
<A HREF="sound.htm">
<IMG SRC="rockon.gif" BORDER=0 ALIGN="right" ALT="Play music">
</A>
<TABLE WIDTH=500>
<TR><TD><IMG SRC="piano.gif" WIDTH=200 HEIGHT=172>
<TR><TD><B>Roaming through the jungle of 'oohs' and 'ahs,'
searching for a more agreeable noise, I live a life of
primitivity with the mind of a child and an unquenchable
thirst for sharps and flats.</B>
&#151;Duke Ellington, <I>Music Is My Mistress</I>
</TABLE>
</BODY></HTML>
```

17

FIGURE 17.4.

Clicking the crossed-out musical note in Figure 17.2 takes you to this silent page. Clicking the circled note on this page takes you back to the musical page again.

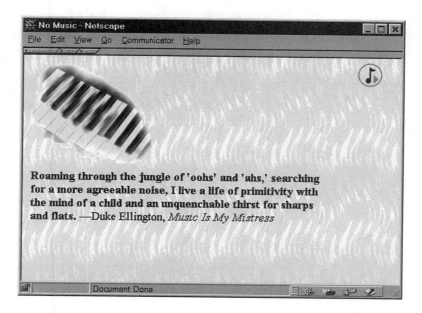

Embedding Video in a Web Page

The HTML page in Figure 17.5 demonstrates the use of <EMBED> with a video clip in the Windows AVI (Audio-Video Interleave) format. The <EMBED> tag in Figure 17.5 also includes the AUTOSTART and LOOP attributes, which tell Netscape's LiveVideo plug-in to start playing the video when the page loads and to repeat it over and over again as long as the page is being displayed. Figure 17.6 shows the resulting page as viewed with Netscape Navigator 4.0.

FIGURE 17.5.

You can embed a video into a Web page with the same <EMBED> tag used to embed sound.

```
<HTML><HEAD><TITLE>Fractal Video Clip</TITLE></HEAD>
<BODY>
  <EMBED SRC="3dtetra2.avi" AUTOSTART="true" LOOP="true"
    WIDTH=160 HEIGHT=120 VSPACE=10 HSPACE=20 ALIGN="left">
  <NOEMBED>
    <A HREF="3dtetra2.avi">
      <IMG SRC="3dtetra.jpg" BORDER=0
        WIDTH=160 HEIGHT=120 VSPACE=10 HSPACE=20 ALIGN="left">
    </A>
  </NOEMBED>
<H2>A Spinning 3-D Fractal</H2>
If the video clip to the left doesn't start on its own,
click on it to make it play. Once it starts, you can
right-click on it and choose Pause to make it stop.
</BODY></HTML>
```

FIGURE 17.6.

The page in Figure 17.5, seen in Netscape Navigator 4.0. If this page were a computer screen, the fractal would be spinning and a soundtrack would be playing.

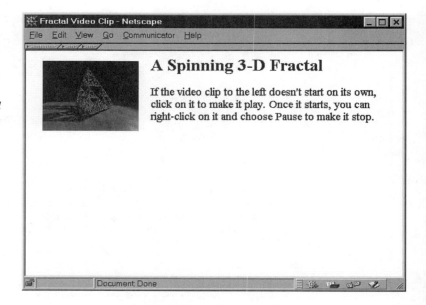

Microsoft Internet Explorer will recognize the <EMBED> tag and try to find an OLE-compliant Windows application to display the media file. In the case of AVI video, the Windows Media Player application will usually be embedded into the Web page, as shown in Figure 17.7.

Notice that the size of the video is reduced to make room for the Media Player controls. This isn't ideal, since it makes the video appear differently in Internet Explorer than it does in Netscape Navigator. In the next section of this hour, you'll learn how to remedy this problem.

FIGURE 17.7.

The page in Figure 17.5, seen in Microsoft Internet Explorer 4.0. The Windows Media Player is automatically embedded in the Web page.

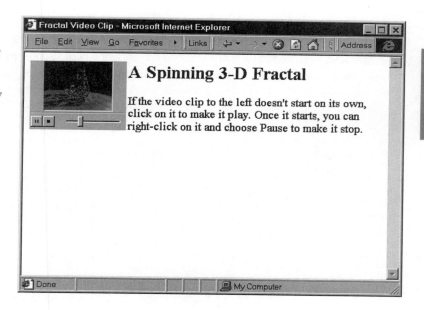

17

Basically, when Navigator and Explorer encounter an <EMBED> tag, they try their hardest to find some way to embed the media file directly in the Web page. As a Web page author, you can't predict what plug-in or helper application will be selected, but you can at least try to put some instructions on the Web page telling your audience where to download a suitable player.

Embedded helper apps only work in Windows 95 and Windows NT. They will not function for Macintosh or UNIX users.

Also, you should not confuse this use of Windows object linking and embedding (OLE) with the ActiveX controls discussed in the next section—even though they do rely on the same underlying OLE technology.

You can use <EMBED> with any type of audio, video, or interactive multimedia files as long as your audience has the correct player software installed.

Unfortunately, you as a Web page author have no control over or knowledge of which file types and applications people who visit your pages will have configured on their computers, or even how many visitors will be using a Microsoft Windows operating system. So the exotic uses of <EMBED> are probably best left to corporate intranets or other situations where the page publisher has some control over the intended audience's computer setup.

Trying to Please Everybody

Because Netscape knew that not all Web browsers would support its non-standard <EMBED> tag, it provided an easy way to include alternate content for other browsers. Immediately following an <EMBED> tag, you can specify any amount of HTML code for other browsers, between the <NOEMBED> and </NOEMBED> tags. For example, Figure 17.5 contains the following code:

```
<EMBED SRC="3dtetra2.avi" AUTOSTART="true" LOOP="true"
  WIDTH=160 HEIGHT=120 VSPACE=10 HSPACE=20 ALIGN="left">
  <NOEMBED>
    <A HREF="3dtetra2.avi">
      <IMG SRC="3dtetra.jpg" BORDER=0
       WIDTH=160 HEIGHT=120 VSPACE=10 HSPACE=20 ALIGN="left">
    </A>
  </NOEMBED>
```

Here's how this will work in various browsers:

- Netscape Navigator 3.0 or 4.0 sees only the <EMBED> tag and ignores everything between <NOEMBED> and </NOEMBED>. (If the Netscape LiveMedia plug-in is installed, it interprets AUTOSTART and LOOP as discussed earlier.)

- In Netscape Navigator 2.0, if no AVI-compatible plug-in is installed, users may see an unsightly puzzle-piece icon and a message saying Plug-in Not Loaded. If they click the Get the Plug-in button, they will be taken to a page on Netscape Corporation's Web site explaining how to get and install plug-ins and helper apps.

- Microsoft Internet Explorer 3.0 or 4.0 looks in the Windows file type registry for a player for the <EMBED> tag. It will usually find mplayer.exe, the Windows Media Player, and embed it into the Web page.

- Microsoft Internet Explorer 2.0, and most other older browsers, sees only the <A> and <IMG> tags. It displays the 3dtetra.jpg image, so that users with an AVI-compatible helper application can click the image to play the 3dtetra2.avi video clip in a separate window.

- Netscape Navigator version 1.2 is actually a special problem case because it recognizes the <EMBED> tag, but not the <NOEMBED> tag. It displays both the image specified in IMG SRC and an embedded OLE display or, more often, a broken image icon resulting from a failed attempt to display the <EMBED> tag. Clicking the 3dtetra.jpg image will still launch an AVI helper application if one is available.

To thicken the plot, some people who already have the software they need to view your EMBED media files may see a message announcing boldly Warning: There is a possible security hazard here. What this message really means is that the user has a helper application available on his system that can display the media file, and Netscape Navigator (version 2.0 or higher) is about to run it. The alarmist tone of the message is very unfortunate, because the likelihood of having any security risk is actually no greater than any other time a helper application is invoked or a page is displayed.

Some novice users are sure to become convinced that they must click Cancel or risk having the monitor blow up, but what you really want them to do is click Continue, so they can watch a totally harmless video clip. Unfortunately, there's really nothing you can do as a Web page author to control whether this message appears. Most people with current browser versions won't see it. However, you should still be aware of what some users may see so you can intelligently choose if and when to use the <EMBED> tag, and what sort of caveats to offer along with your embedded media.

Multimedia the New Way

Netscape's <EMBED> tag has come under fire for a number of reasons, both technical and political. Officially, it has already been made obsolete by a new tag called <OBJECT>, which has the blessing of Netscape, Microsoft, and the official World Wide Web Consortium (W3C) standards-setting committee. The <OBJECT> tag will do everything Netscape wants the <EMBED> tag to do, plus a lot more.

Unfortunately, the 4.0 version of Microsoft Internet Explorer interprets the <OBJECT> tag somewhat unreliably because it was released before the official standard for the tag was approved. The fact that most people are still using earlier browser versions has also slowed widespread use of the <OBJECT> tag. Alas, support of <OBJECT> in the preview release of Microsoft Internet Explorer 5.0 isn't any better, nor does it look likely that the next maintenance update of Netscape Navigator will support the standard fully.

You can read more about the <OBJECT> tag, including an example of its current use, under "ActiveX Controls" in Hour 18.

Another beacon of hope has appeared on the Web multimedia horizon as well. The W3C has officially sanctioned SMIL 1.0, the Synchronized Multimedia Integration Language.

17

When Web browsers start conforming to this new standard, you will have a reliable way to synchronize multiple sound, video, and animation sources on your Web pages. (Assuming, that is, that your intended audience has high-speed network connections capable of delivering multiple media streams by then.) You can dream of the possibilities as you read about SMIL at the www.w3c.org Web site.

In this hour you have struggled with a turgid tangle of incompatible HTML extensions and media formats. And if you, the Web page author, find it a bit confusing (as I assure you that I, the book author, sometimes do), just think how confusing it might be to your audience when your Web page video encounters an uncooperative browser.

My bottom-line advice is this: For now, avoid embedded multimedia if you possibly can. Most people would rather have a good old-fashioned clickable link to the multimedia file. `<A HREF="hotvideo.avi">Hot Video (AVI format, 240K)</A>` allows people to play the video if and when they want to, or download it and play it from their hard drive. If you have software that can convert between AVI and QuickTime, offer links to the same video in both formats to accommodate both Windows and Macintosh users. (Offer both WAV and AU formats if it's a sound clip.)

To experience both the new and old-fashioned approaches to Web page multimedia yourself, kick back, grab an appropriate beverage, and tune your browser to `http://24hourHTMLcafe.com/hour17`.

Summary

In this hour, you've seen how to embed video and sound into a Web page. But remember that the `<EMBED>` tag (and its successor, the `<OBJECT>` tag) can be used to include a vast array of media types besides just AVI and MIDI files. Some of these media types are alternative audio and video formats that aim to achieve greater compression, quality, or compatibility than the Windows standard formats. Others, such as Shockwave and QuickTime VR, add a variety of interactive features that old-fashioned audiovisual media types lack.

Table 17.1 summarizes the tags discussed in this hour.

TABLE 17.1.   HTML TAGS AND ATTRIBUTES COVERED IN HOUR 17.

Tag	Attribute	Function
<EMBED>		Embeds a file to be read or displayed by a Netscape plug-in application.
	SRC="..."	The URL of the file to embed.
	WIDTH="..."	The width of the embedded object in pixels.
	HEIGHT="..."	The height of the embedded object in pixels.
	ALIGN="..."	Determines the alignment of the media window. Values are the same as for the <IMG> tag.
	VSPACE="..."	The space between the media and the text above or below it.
	HSPACE="..."	The space between the media and the text to its left or right.
	BORDER="..."	Draws a border of the specified size in pixels around the media.
<NOEMBED>...</NOEMBED>		Alternate text or images to be shown to users who do not have a plug-in installed or are using browsers that don't recognize the <EMBED> tag.
<OBJECT>		Inserts images, videos, Java applets, ActiveX controls, or other objects into a document. (See Hour 18 for attributes of the <OBJECT> tag.)

17

In addition to the <EMBED> attributes listed in Table 17.1, you can designate applet-specific attributes to be interpreted by the plug-in that displays the embedded object.

Q&A

Q I hear a lot about "streaming" video and audio. What does that mean?

A In the past, video and audio files took minutes and sometimes hours to retrieve through most modems, which severely limited the inclusion of video and audio on Web pages. The goal that everyone is moving toward is streaming video or audio, which will play while the data is being received. This is to say that you will not have to download the clip completely before you can start to watch it.

Streaming playback is now widely supported through Microsoft Internet Explorer's built-in features and Netscape Navigator plug-ins. The examples in this hour use Windows AVI and WAV audio files to demonstrate both streaming and the old-fashioned download-and-play methods of delivering audiovisual media.

Q **How do I choose between audiovisual file formats such as QuickTime, Windows AVI/WAV, RealVideo/RealAudio, and MPEG? Is there any significant difference between them?**

A QuickTime is the most popular video format among Macintosh users, though QuickTime players are available for Windows 3.1 and Windows 95 as well. Similarly, AVI and WAV are the video and audio formats of choice for Windows users, but you can get AVI and WAV players for the Macintosh. However, all these are almost certain to be eclipsed by MPEG as the online audio and video standard of choice within the next couple of years. MPEG-1 video is best for Internet transmission because it is far more compact than MPEG-2. MPEG-3 is already gaining ground as the high-fidelity audio standard of choice. Unfortunately, relatively few people have MPEG-compatible players installed now.

So how do you choose? If your audience is mostly Windows users, pick AVI or WAV. If it includes a significant number of Macintosh users, pick QuickTime or at least offer it as an alternative. If cross-platform compatibility is essential, consider the RealVideo or RealAudio format—although only those who download special software from www.real.com will be able to see that format. In any case, plan to switch to MPEG eventually.

Workshop

Quiz

1. What's the simplest way to let the widest possible audience see a video on your Web site?

2. Write the HTML to embed a video file named `myvideo.avi` into a Web page so that both Netscape Navigator and Microsoft Internet Explorer users will be able to see it, and users of other browsers would see an image linking to it.

3. What tag will soon replace `<EMBED>` and work with future versions of all major Web browsers?

Answers

1. Just link to it, like this:

```
<A HREF="myvideo.avi">My Video</A>
```

2. Use the following HTML:

```
<EMBED SRC="myvideo.avi">
<NOEMBED>
<A HREF="myvideo.avi"><IMG SRC="theimage.gif"></A>
</NOEMBED>
```

3. `<OBJECT>`

Exercises

- If you include multimedia elements that require special players, you might need a special page to help people understand and set up what they need to make the most of your site. A link to that page should be prominently located near the top of your home page, steering newcomers aside just long enough to give them a clue.

- The techniques and tags covered in this hour for embedding media also work with Virtual Reality Modeling Language (VRML) files. To find out how you can use VRML to put interactive three-dimensional scenes and objects in your Web pages, check out the VRML home page at

  `http://home.netscape.com/eng/live3d/howto/vrml_primer_index.html`.

17

HOUR 18

Interactive Pages with Applets and ActiveX

Congratulations. You've got HTML under your belt, and you're ready to graduate from the school of Web publishing and enter the real world of Web development. The World Wide Web of the past was simply a way to present information, and browsing wasn't too different from sitting in a lecture hall, watching a blackboard, or staring at an overhead projector screen. But today's Web surfer is looking for interactive, animated sites that change with each viewer and each viewing.

To achieve that level of interactivity, this hour introduces a number of ways you can go beyond passive text and graphics into the dynamic world of modern Web site development.

It would take a book many times the length of this one to teach you all the scripting and programming languages that can be used to create interactive programs for the Web. However, you can easily learn the HTML to incorporate prewritten programs into your Web pages.

To Do

To Do

Reading this hour will give you enough information to decide what types of programs or scripts might be best for your Web site. If you decide to take the leap into actually using some (or even creating your own) on your pages, you should look to the following resources:

- You'll find a list of online sources for prewritten scripts and reusable program components in the 24-Hour HTML Café hotlist page at `http://24hourHTMLcafe.com/hotsites.htm`.

- If you want to write your own interactive programming for Web pages, I recommend *Dynamic Web Publishing Unleashed* by Sams Publishing. You'll also find some online tutorials in the 24-Hour HTML Café hotlist.

The Old Way

Until very recently, there were only two ways to enhance the functionality of a Web browser. You could write and place programs on the Web server computer to manipulate documents as they were sent out, or you could write and install programs on the user's computer to manipulate or display documents as they were received.

You can still do both of these things, and they may still be the most powerful and flexible means of enhancing Web pages. Unfortunately, both involve a high level of expertise in traditional programming languages (such as C++) and knowledge of Internet transfer protocols and operating system architecture. If you're not fortunate enough to already be an experienced UNIX or Windows programmer, as well as something of a Net guru, you're not going to start cranking out cool Web applications tomorrow (or the next day, or the next...).

On the server side, simplified scripting languages like Perl can flatten the learning curve quite a bit. Many people who don't consider themselves real programmers can hack out a Common Gateway Interface (CGI) script to process Web forms or feed animations to a Web page without too many false starts. With visual programming tools such as Visual Basic, you can learn to produce a respectable client-side helper application fairly quickly as well.

But there is an easier way, and because this hour is intended to take you on the fast track to Web development, I have to recommend that you avoid the old ways until you run into something that you just can't accomplish any other way.

Before dashing into the inside lane, I do need to tell you about one way to enhance the Web that is not easier than server programming. It is, however, even more powerful when used well. Netscape Navigator plug-ins are custom applications designed especially to extend Netscape's capabilities.

You're probably familiar with some of the more popular plug-ins, such as Shockwave and Acrobat. Because these programs are usually written in C++ and have direct access to both the client computer's operating system and Netscape's data stream, developing plug-ins is not for the faint of heart or inexperienced. Still, if you can call yourself a "programmer" without blushing, you may find it well worth the effort. All in all, writing and debugging a plug-in is still considerably less daunting than developing a full-blown business application.

Internet Programming for the Rest of Us

Suppose you just want your Web order form to add up totals automatically when customers check off which products they want. This is not rocket science. Implementing it shouldn't be either. You don't want to learn UNIX or C++ or the Windows 95 Applications Programming Interface. You don't want to compile and install half a dozen extra files on your Web server, or ask the user to download your handy-dandy calculator application. You just want to add up some numbers. Or maybe you just want to change a graphic depending on the user's preferences, or the day of the week, or whatever. Or maybe you want to tell a random joke every time somebody logs on to your home page. Until now, there really was no simple way to do these simple things.

Scripting languages such as JavaScript (which you'll learn about in Hour 19, "Web Page Scripting for Non-Programmers"), give you a way. Okay, so it's still programming. But it's the kind of programming you can learn in an afternoon, or in an hour if you've fooled around with BASIC or Excel macros before. It's programming for the rest of us. Scripts go right into the HTML of your Web pages, wherever you want something intelligent to happen.

Strong Java

JavaScript and its competitors do have drawbacks and limitations. For any high-volume data or image-processing work, scripting would be too slow. And complex applications of any kind are poorly suited for direct inclusion in the text of an HTML document. After all, there are only so many lines of code you want to wade through to see the HTML itself.

When you outgrow JavaScript, does that mean you'll need to return to server-side scripting or applications programming? No. JavaScript is just the baby sister of a more robust and powerful language called Java. Like JavaScript, Java is especially designed for the Web. And like JavaScript scripts, Java programs install and run automatically whenever a Web page is loaded. However, unlike JavaScript, Java programs are compiled into a more compact and efficient form (called bytecodes) and stored in a separate file from the Web pages that may call them.

Java also includes a complete graphics drawing library, security features, strong type checking, and other professional-level programming amenities that serious developers need. The biggest limiting factor with Java mini-applications (called *applets*) is that they must be small enough that downloading them won't delay the display of a Web page by an intolerable amount of time. Fortunately, Java applets are extremely compact in their compiled form and are often considerably smaller than the images on a typical Web page.

A Java program will work equally well on both Windows and Macintosh computers. Best of all, the syntax of Java is nearly identical to JavaScript, so you can cut your teeth on JavaScript and easily move to Java when you need or want to.

You'll find many ready-to-use Java applets on the Web, and Figure 18.1 shows how to include them in a Web page. The two <APPLET> tags in Figure 18.1 insert two separate Java applets named Bounce.class and RnbText.class. (These class files must be placed in the same directory as the Web page.) The Bounce applet makes a graphical icon hop up and down, and the RnbText applet below it makes some text wiggle like a wave while rainbow colors flow through it. Figure 18.2 is a snapshot of these animated effects.

FIGURE 18.1.

Java applets are pre-written programs that you place on your Web page with the <APPLET> *tag.*

```
<HTML><HEAD><TITLE>Oh Happy Day</TITLE></HEAD>
<BODY><DIV ALIGN="center">
<APPLET CODE="Bounce.class" WIDTH=500 HEIGHT=300>
No Java? How sad.
</APPLET>
<APPLET CODE="RnbText.class" WIDTH=500 HEIGHT=50>
<PARAM NAME="text"
 VALUE="B E  H A P P Y , L IK E  M  E !!!">
</APPLET>
</DIV></BODY></HTML>
```

FIGURE 18.2.

The <APPLET> tags in Figure 18.1 insert programs to draw a bouncing happy face and some wiggly, colorful animated text on the page.

18

In the new HTML 4.0 standard, the <APPLET> tag is officially obsolete. The <OBJECT> tag that replaces it is discussed at the end of this hour. However, most people are still using earlier versions of Web browsers that require the <APPLET> tag, and the current (4.0) versions of both Netscape Navigator and Microsoft Internet Explorer still support <APPLET>. So you should continue to use <APPLET> until all of your intended audience switches to HTML 4-compatible browsers—which isn't likely to happen for quite some time.

The WIDTH and HEIGHT attributes in the <APPLET> tag do just what you'd expect them to—specify the dimensions of the region on the Web page that will contain the applet's output. The <PARAM> tag is used to supply any information that a specific applet needs to do its thing. The NAME identifies what information you're supplying to the applet, and VALUE is the actual information itself. In this example, the RnbText applet is designed to display some text, so you have to tell it what text to display. The Bounce applet doesn't require any <PARAM> tag, because it was designed to do just one thing, with no optional settings.

Every applet will require different settings for the NAME and VALUE attributes, and most applets require more than one <PARAM> tag to set all their options. Whoever created the applet will tell you (usually in some kind of readme.txt or other documentation file) what NAME attributes you need to include and what sort of information to put in the VALUE attributes for each NAME.

> Note that you can use the same applet more than once on the page. This is quite efficient, because it will only need to be downloaded once, and the Web browser will then create two copies of it automatically. For example, you could use RnbText to display two different lines of animated, rainbow-colored text on a page.

ActiveX Controls

For quite some time, Microsoft Windows has included a feature called object linking and embedding (OLE), which allows all or part of one program to be embedded in a document that you are working on with another program. For example, you can use OLE to put a spreadsheet in a word-processing document.

When the Internet explosion rocked the world in the mid-90s, Microsoft adapted its OLE technology to work with HTML pages online and renamed it ActiveX. Everybody likes to invent his own jargon, so ActiveX programs are called controls rather than applets.

Though ActiveX is touted as the main competitor of Java, it actually isn't a specific programming language. It's a standard for making programs written in any language conform to the same protocols, so that neither you, the Web page author, nor the people who view your pages need to be aware of the language in which the control was written. It just works, whether the programmer used Visual Basic, VBScript (a simplified version of Visual Basic), C++, or even Java.

It's not surprising that support for the Microsoft ActiveX protocol is built into Microsoft Internet Explorer (versions 3.0 and later). For users of Netscape Navigator to be able to see ActiveX controls, they need to download and install a plug-in from Ncompass Labs (http://www.ncompasslabs.com).

> Note that ActiveX controls will only work on Windows and Macintosh computers. Also, ActiveX controls must be separately compiled for each different operating system.

Because ActiveX is the newest of the technologies discussed in this hour, you must use the new <OBJECT> tag to insert it into a page.

As Figure 18.3 shows, an ActiveX <OBJECT> tag looks rather bizarre.

FIGURE 18.3.

The <OBJECT> *tag on this page embeds an ActiveX control.*

```
<HTML><HEAD><TITLE>Label Control </TITLE></HEAD>
<BODY>
<OBJECT ID="labelA"
  CLASSID="clsid:99B42120-6EC7-11CF-A6C7-00AA00A47DD2"
  TYPE="application/x-oleobject"
  WIDTH=240 HEIGHT=240 ALIGN="left">
<PARAM NAME="Angle" VALUE="30">
<PARAM NAME="Alignment" VALUE="4" >
<PARAM NAME="BackStyle" VALUE="0" >
<PARAM NAME="Caption" VALUE="Wowza!">
<PARAM NAME="FontName" VALUE="Arial">
<PARAM NAME="FontSize" VALUE="36">
<PARAM NAME="ForeColor" VALUE="#9900FF" >
</OBJECT>
With the ActiveX Label Control, you can draw text of
any size, in any color, at any angle, without waiting
for great big graphics files to download.<P>
Best of all, the Label Control is already installed
on your computer if you have Microsoft Internet Explorer
version 4.0 or higher.
</BODY></HTML>
```

18

The bizarre part is the CLASSID attribute, which must include a unique identifier for the specific ActiveX control you are including. If you use an automated program such as Microsoft's ActiveX Control Pad to create your ActiveX pages, it will figure out this magic number for you. Otherwise, you'll need to consult the documentation that came with the ActiveX control to find the correct CLASSID.

As if the long string of gibberish in CLASSID wasn't enough, the ID attribute must include another unique identifier, but this time you get to make it up. You can use any label you want for ID, as long as you don't use the same label for another ActiveX control in the same document. (ID is used for identifying the control in any scripts you might add to the page.)

If you are something of a whiz with Windows, you can use regedit.exe to look in the Windows class Registry for the CLSID in HKEY_CLASSES_ROOT. If the previous sentence makes no sense to you, you'll need to rely on the person who wrote the ActiveX control (or an automated Web page authoring tool) to tell you the correct CLASSID.

The <PARAM> tags work the same with <OBJECT> as they do with the <APPLET> tag, discussed earlier in this hour. They provide settings and options specific to the particular ActiveX control you are placing on the Web page, with NAME identifying the type of information and VALUE giving the information itself. In the example from Figure 18.3, <PARAM> tags are used to specify the alignment, orientation, font, and color of some text to be displayed by the Label control. This is one of many ActiveX controls built into Microsoft Internet Explorer 4.0, and documented at the Microsoft Developer Network Web site at www.microsoft.com.

Notice that nothing in the HTML itself gives any clue as to what the ActiveX control on that page actually looks like or does. Only when you view the page, as in Figure 18.4, do you see that it is a nifty little program to display rotated text.

FIGURE 18.4.

The ActiveX control on this page is a program for displaying fancy text, though you wouldn't know it by looking at the HTML in Figure 18.3.

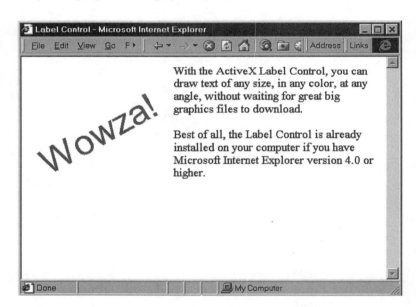

Using ActiveX to Embed a Video

ActiveX controls can do anything a programmer can cook up, but there is one specific ActiveX control included with Microsoft Internet Explorer that you should definitely know how to use. The ActiveMovie control is the Microsoft equivalent of Netscape's LiveVideo plug-in. Using ActiveMovie is currently the most reliable way to play a video in Microsoft Internet Explorer without displaying the klunky controls you get when the Windows Media player is embedded in a Web page.

Figure 18.5 shows the CLASSID and <PARAM> options you'll need to know to use the ActiveMovie control. (The parameters are pretty self explanatory, as long as you know that "1" means yes/on and "O" means no/off.) As Figure 18.6 demonstrates, this ActiveX object creates exactly the same effect in Microsoft Internet Explorer 4.0 as the <EMBED> example from Hour 17, "Embedding Multimedia in Web Pages," did for Netscape Navigator 4.0.

FIGURE 18.5.

You can use the ActiveMovie control to play a video with the <OBJECT> *tag shown here.*

```
<HTML><HEAD><TITLE>Fractal Video Clip</TITLE></HEAD>
<BODY>
<OBJECT ID="ActiveMovie1"
 CLASSID="CLSID:05589FA1-C356-11CE-BF01-00AA0055595A"
 WIDTH=160 HEIGHT=120 VSPACE=10 HSPACE=20 ALIGN="left">
<PARAM NAME="ShowDisplay" VALUE="0">
<PARAM NAME="ShowControls" VALUE="0">
<PARAM NAME="AutoStart" VALUE="1">
<PARAM NAME="PlayCount" VALUE="10">
<PARAM NAME="FileName" VALUE="3dtetra2.avi">
  <EMBED SRC="3dtetra2.avi" AUTOSTART="true" LOOP="true"
   WIDTH=160 HEIGHT=120 VSPACE=10 HSPACE=20 ALIGN="left">
  <NOEMBED>
    <A HREF="3dtetra2.avi">
      <IMG SRC="3dtetra.jpg" BORDER=0
       WIDTH=160 HEIGHT=120 VSPACE=10 HSPACE=20 ALIGN="left">
    </A>
  </NOEMBED>
</OBJECT>
<H2>A Spinning 3-D Fractal</H2>
If the video clip to the left doesn't start on its own,
click on it to make it play. Once it starts, you can
right-click on it and choose Pause to make it stop.
</BODY></HTML>
```

18

FIGURE 18.6.

The page listed in Figure 18.5 will look the same in both Netscape Navigator and Microsoft Internet Explorer.

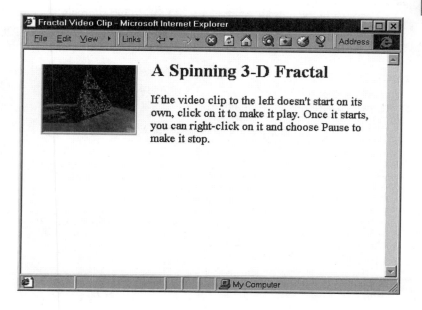

Notice that I included the Netscape `<EMBED>` tag between the `<OBJECT>` and `</OBJECT>` tags in Figure 18.5. If an `<OBJECT>` tag is successful in embedding the object it refers to (in this case, the ActiveMovie control), it will ignore all the HTML up to its closing `</OBJECT>` tag (except of course any `<PARAM>` tags). However, if the requested object can't be found or displayed for any reason, the rest of the HTML in front of the closing `</OBJECT>` tag will not be ignored. In this case, that means that if the `<OBJECT>` tag doesn't work (probably because the user isn't using Microsoft Internet Explorer as his browser), the `<EMBED>` tag will be called on instead. Therefore, the page will work nicely in both Microsoft Internet Explorer and Netscape Navigator.

As a last resort, an image linked to the video is included between `<NOEMBED>` and `</NOEMBED>` tags. This won't be seen by any recent version of Microsoft Internet Explorer or Netscape Navigator; it's just there for other Web browsers that don't support either ActiveX or embedded multimedia.

Summary

This hour gives you a brief outline of the three types of interactive programming that are easiest to add to your Web site: JavaScript, Java applets, and ActiveX controls. It also discusses the difference between these technologies and more traditional server-side scripting and Netscape plug-ins.

You didn't get enough technical stuff in this short hour to write your own programs and scripts, but you did learn the basic HTML to insert prewritten ones into your Web pages. You also saw how to use an ActiveX control to embed video in a page, and how to combine that with what you learned in Hour 17 for maximum compatibility.

In Hour 19, "Web Page Scripting for Non-Programmers," you'll learn to write some of your own simple JavaScripts to do some of the easiest—and most useful—tasks for which scripting is commonly used.

Table 18.1 summarizes the tags covered in this hour.

TABLE 18.1. HTML TAGS AND ATTRIBUTES COVERED IN HOUR 18.

Tag	Attribute	Function
<APPLET>		Inserts a self-running Java applet.
	CLASS="..."	The name of the applet.
	SRC="..."	The URL of the directory where the compiled applet can be found (should end in a slash / as in "http://mysite/myapplets/"). Do not include the actual applet name, which is specified with the CLASS attribute.
	ALIGN="..."	Indicates how the applet should be aligned with any text that follows it. Current values are TOP, MIDDLE, and BOTTOM.
	WIDTH="..."	The width of the applet output area in pixels.
	HEIGHT="..."	The height of the applet output area in pixels.
<PARAM>		Program-specific parameters. (Always occurs within <APPLET> or <OBJECT> tags.)
	NAME="..."	The type of information being given to the applet or ActiveX control.
	VALUE="..."	The actual information to be given to the applet or ActiveX control.
<OBJECT>		Inserts images, videos, Java applets, or ActiveX OLE controls into a document.
	CLASSID="..."	The address of a Java applet or identification code for an ActiveX program.
	ID="..."	Gives an identifying name for a Microsoft ActiveX program (Microsoft only).
	DATA="..."	Can be used in some situations to tell an applet or program where to find some data that it needs.
	TYPE="..."	Can indicate the type of data referred to by a DATA attribute.
	STANDBY="..."	Lets you specify a text message to be displayed while an applet or program object is being loaded and initialized.

18

In addition to the standard <APPLET> attributes in Table 18.1, you can specify applet-specific attributes to be interpreted by the Java applet itself.

Q&A

Q So just what exactly is the difference between "scripting" and "programming," anyway?

A Usually, the word "scripting" is used for programming in relatively simple computer languages that are integrated directly into an application (or into HTML pages). However, the line between scripting and "real programming" is pretty fuzzy.

Q I've used Visual Basic before, and I heard I could use it in Web pages. Is that true?

A Yes, but only if you want to limit the audience for your pages to users of Microsoft Internet Explorer version 3.0 or later. So far the rest of the world is sticking to JavaScript. Visit the Microsoft Web site (http://www.microsoft.com) for details about the differences between VBScript and Visual Basic.

Q I've heard about ActiveX scripting and ActiveX documents. How are these different from ActiveX controls?

A In Microsoft-speak, "ActiveX scripting" means VBScript or JavaScript linking to a page as an ActiveX control. ActiveX documents are HTML pages that use an ActiveX control to view a word processing document or spreadsheet within a Web page. (Career tip: If you want a job at Microsoft, consider listing your first name as "ActiveX" on the application form. They like that.)

Q Most of the Java applets I find on the Internet have two files, one ending with .java and one ending with .class. Which one do I put on my Web page, and what do I do with the other one?

A Put the file ending with .class on your Web page with the <APPLET> tag. The .java file is the actual Java source code, provided in case you are a Java programmer and you want to change it. You don't need the .java file to use the applet.

Workshop

Quiz

1. Suppose you found a cool Java game on the Internet and the documentation with it says it's free for anyone to use. It says you need to give the applet two parameters: the "speed" should be between 1 and 100, and the "skill" should be between 1 and 5. The applet itself is named `roadkill.class`. Write the HTML to display it in a 400×200-pixel area in the middle of a Web page.

2. The ActiveX Label control displays some text in any orientation you choose. Write the HTML to insert the ActiveX control in a Web page, given the following information:

   The class ID is

   `clsid:{99B42120-6EC7-11CF-A6C7-00AA00A47DD2}`

   Confine the display area to 300×300 pixels.

   Specify the following parameter values:

   Caption: "New and Exciting!"

   Angle: 45

   FontName: Arial Black

   FontSize: 18

Answers

1.
```
<APPLET CODE="roadkill.class" WIDTH=400 HEIGHT=200>
<PARAM NAME="speed" VALUE=50>
<PARAM NAME="skill" VALUE=2>
</APPLET>
```

2.
```
<OBJECT CLASSID="clsid:99B42120-6EC7-11CF-A6C7-00AA00A47DD2"
ID="label" WIDTH=300 HEIGHT=300>
<PARAM NAME="caption" VALUE="New and Exciting!">
<PARAM NAME="angle" VALUE="45">
<PARAM NAME="fontname" VALUE="Arial Black">
<PARAM NAME="fontsize" VALUE="18">
</OBJECT>
```

18

Exercise

You'll find many more reusable applets and controls by visiting
`http://24hourHTMLcafe.com/hotlist.htm#developer` and checking out the
developer resources links. If you find one that actually adds enough value to your
site from the visitor's perspective to be worth the install-and-initialize waiting time,
try incorporating it into your pages.

HOUR 19

Web Page Scripting for Non-Programmers

"Scripting" is a polite word for "computer programming," and that's obviously an enormous topic you're not going to learn much about in a one-hour lesson. Still, there are some awfully handy things you can do in a snap with scripting—and which you can't do any other way. So with a spirit of bold optimism, this hour aims to help you teach yourself just enough Web page scripting to make your pages stand out from the "non-de-script" crowd.

Specifically, you'll learn in this hour how to make the images (or multimedia objects) on your Web pages change in response to mouse movements or mouse clicks, as well as how to automatically add up totals on an order form. Using the JavaScript language, you can do these tasks in a way that is compatible with versions 3.0 or later of both Netscape Navigator and Microsoft Internet Explorer. Other Web browsers won't respond to your scripting, but will still display the pages properly.

You'll learn some additional JavaScript tricks in Hour 20, "Setting Pages in Motion with Dynamic HTML." If the ease and power of the few JavaScript commands you learn in these two hours whet your appetite for more (as I think they will), I encourage you to turn to a book such as Sams Publishing's *Sams Teach Yourself JavaScript in a Week*.

Interactive Highlighting

If you've used any graphical CD-ROM software application, you have probably seen buttons that light up or change when your mouse passes over them. This looks cool, and gives you some visual feedback before you click something, which research shows can reduce confusion and errors.

You can add the same sort of visual feedback to the links on your Web pages, too. The first step toward achieving that effect is to create the graphics for both the dark and "lit up" icons. Figure 19.1 shows some pumpkin faces I created in Paint Shop Pro. I made two copies of each pumpkin; one darkened, and one illuminated as if it had a candle inside.

FIGURE 19.1.

Four graphics images, each with a highlighted version to replace it when the mouse points to it.

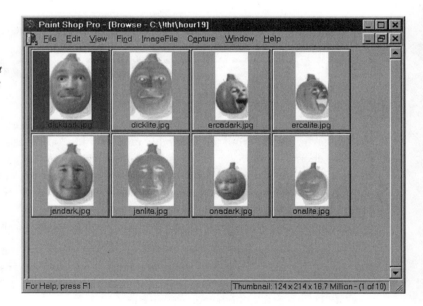

To Do

Do you have any pages that would look flashier or be easier to understand if the navigation icons or other images changed when the mouse passed over them? If so, try creating some "highlighted" versions of the images on them, and try modifying your own page as you read the following few paragraphs. Here are a few ideas to get you started:

▼
- Use Paint Shop Pro's text tool to make graphical titles that change color when the mouse points to them.
- Use the Image, Effects, Buttonize command in Paint Shop Pro with various background colors to make buttons that light up just before they're pressed.
- Use the techniques you learned in Hour 12, "Creating Animated Graphics," to make icons that rotate, wiggle, or blink when the mouse passes over them. (You can use a regular, non-animated GIF for the image to present when the mouse isn't pointing to the icon.)
▲
- If you have a list of choices, put a blank (totally transparent) image in front of each one, and make an arrow or bullet icon appear in front of the item to which the mouse is pointing.

Here's how the HTML for a graphical link would look before any scripting is added. This should all look easy and familiar to you. (If it doesn't, review Hour 10, "Putting Images on a Web Page," and Hour 13, "Page Design and Layout.")

```
<A HREF="erica.htm"><IMG SRC="ercadark.jpg"
 WIDTH=98 HEIGHT=214 BORDER=0 ALT="Erica"></A>
```

The first thing you need to do is give this particular <IMG> tag its own unique name. You'll use this name to refer to this specific spot on the page when you want to change which image will be displayed in that spot. We'll name this spot "erica" by putting a NAME attribute in the <IMG> tag, like the followings:

```
<A HREF="erica.htm"><IMG NAME="erica" SRC="ercadark.jpg"
 WIDTH=98 HEIGHT=214 BORDER=0 ALT="Erica"></A>
```

Now for the magic part. You can add JavaScript commands to any link on a Web page by including two special attributes called OnMouseOver and OnMouseOut. With OnMouseOver, you tell the Web browser what to do when the mouse passes over any text or images within that link. With OnMouseOut, you indicate what to do when the mouse moves out of the link area.

In this case, we want the image to change to ercalite.jpg when the mouse passes over the corresponding link, and change back to ercadark.jpg when the mouse moves away.

Here's what that looks like in HTML and JavaScript:

```
<A HREF="erica.htm" ONMOUSEOVER="erica.src='ercalite.jpg'"
ONMOUSEOUT="erica.src='ercadark.jpg'"><IMG NAME="erica"
SRC="ercadark.jpg" WIDTH=98 HEIGHT=214 BORDER=0 ALT="Erica"></A>
```

Notice that you need to enclose the name of the image file in single quotes (apostrophes), but the whole JavaScript command gets enclosed by double quotes (inch marks).

19

When you do this on your Web pages, just follow my example closely, substituting your own image names and graphics files.

Figure 19.2 shows the complete HTML for a Web page using the pumpkin images as links. You can see how the pumpkins light up when the mouse passes over them in Figures 19.3 and 19.4, or online at `http://24hourHTMLcafe.com/hour19`.

FIGURE 19.2.

The JavaScript-enhanced HTML for the page shown in Figures 19.3 and 19.4.

```
<HTML><HEAD><TITLE>The Olivers</TITLE></HEAD>
<BODY><DIV ALIGN="center">
<H1>The Oliver Family</H1>
<A HREF="erica.htm" ONMOUSEOVER="erica.src='ercalite.jpg'"
                    ONMOUSEOUT="erica.src='ercadark.jpg'"
><IMG NAME="erica" SRC="ercadark.jpg"
  WIDTH=98 HEIGHT=214 BORDER=0 ALT="Erica"></A
><A HREF="dick.htm" ONMOUSEOVER="dick.src='dicklite.jpg'"
                    ONMOUSEOUT="dick.src='dickdark.jpg'"
><IMG NAME="dick" SRC="dickdark.jpg"
  WIDTH=124 HEIGHT=214 BORDER=0 ALT="Dick"></A
><A HREF="jan.htm" ONMOUSEOVER="jan.src='janlite.jpg'"
                   ONMOUSEOUT="jan.src='jandark.jpg'"
><IMG NAME="jan" SRC="jandark.jpg"
  WIDTH=136 HEIGHT=214 BORDER=0 ALT="Jan"></A
><A HREF="ona.htm" ONMOUSEOVER="ona.src='onalite.jpg'"
                   ONMOUSEOUT="ona.src='onadark.jpg'"
><IMG NAME="ona" SRC="onadark.jpg"
  WIDTH=100 HEIGHT=214 BORDER=0 ALT="Ona"></A><P>
Click on a family member to find out all about us.
</DIV></BODY></HTML>
```

FIGURE 19.3.

When the mouse passes over the pumpkin with my daughter's face, it lights up and her name (from the ALT attribute) appears.

FIGURE 19.4.

When you move the mouse to my pumpkin, my face lights up instead of Erica's.

Usually, you will want the image that the mouse is passing over to light up or change. But you aren't limited to doing it that way. For example, if you wanted all the pumpkins to light up whenever the mouse moved over one of them, you could put the following JavaScript in each <A> tag:

```
<A HREF="erica.htm" ONMOUSEOVER="erica.src='ercalite.jpg';
dick.src='dicklite.jpg'; jan.src='janlite.jpg'; ona.src='onalite.jpg'"
ONMOUSEOUT="erica.src='ercadark.jpg'";
dick.src='dickdark.jpg'; jan.src='jandark.jpg'; ona.src='onadark.jpg'">
```

As you can see, modifying multiple images is as simple as putting a semicolon (;) after the first JavaScript command and then following it with another command. You can put as many commands as you need in the same OnMouseOver (or OnMouseOut) attribute, as long as you separate them by semicolons.

Preloading Images for Speed

The code in Figure 19.2 will work flawlessly with both Microsoft Internet Explorer and Netscape Navigator (versions 3.0 and later of both browsers). There is only one minor problem: the "lit up" images won't be downloaded from your Web site until someone actually moves the mouse over the image. This can cause a significant delay before the highlighted image appears, possibly lowering the all-important Gee Whiz Factor (GWF).

19

You can avoid this annoyance by including some JavaScript telling the browser to pre-load the images as soon as possible when the page is displayed. That way, by the time the slow human reader gets around to passing his or her mouse over the link, those images will usually be immediately ready to pop onto the screen. This makes the animations seem to appear without any download delay, giving the page a snappy feel and pumping the GWF back up to truly nerdly levels. Figure 19.5 shows how it's done.

FIGURE 19.5.

This page looks and acts exactly like the page in Figure 19.2, except that all the "lite" images are pre-loaded for enhanced responsiveness.

```
<HTML><HEAD><TITLE>The Olivers</TITLE>
<SCRIPT LANGUAGE="JavaScript">
<!--
  ercalite=new Image(98,214);  ercadark=new Image(98,214);
  dicklite=new Image(124,214); dickdark=new Image(124,214);
  janlite=new Image(136,214);  jandark=new Image(136,214);
  onalite=new Image(100,214);  onadark=new Image(100,214);
  ercalite.src="ercalite.jpg"; ercadark.src="ercadark.jpg";
  dicklite.src="dicklite.jpg"; dickdark.src="dickdark.jpg";
  janlite.src="janlite.jpg";   jandark.src="jandark.jpg";
  onalite.src="onalite.jpg";   onadark.src="onadark.jpg";
//-->
</SCRIPT></HEAD>
<BODY><DIV ALIGN="center">
<H1>The Oliver Family</H1>
<A HREF="erica.htm" ONMOUSEOVER="erica.src=ercalite.src"
                    ONMOUSEOUT="erica.src=ercadark.src"
><IMG NAME="erica" SRC="ercadark.jpg"
   WIDTH=98 HEIGHT=214 BORDER=0 ALT="Erica"></A
><A HREF="dick.htm" ONMOUSEOVER="dick.src=dicklite.src"
                    ONMOUSEOUT="dick.src=dickdark.src"
><IMG NAME="dick" SRC="dickdark.jpg"
   WIDTH=124 HEIGHT=214 BORDER=0 ALT="Dick"></A
><A HREF="jan.htm" ONMOUSEOVER="jan.src=janlite.src"
                   ONMOUSEOUT="jan.src=jandark.src"
><IMG NAME="jan" SRC="jandark.jpg"
   WIDTH=136 HEIGHT=214 BORDER=0 ALT="Jan"></A
><A HREF="ona.htm" ONMOUSEOVER="ona.src=onalite.src"
                   ONMOUSEOUT="ona.src=onadark.src"
><IMG NAME="ona" SRC="onadark.jpg"
   WIDTH=100 HEIGHT=214 BORDER=0 ALT="Ona"></A><P>
Click on a family member to find out all about us.
</DIV></BODY></HTML>
```

There are a couple of things worthy of note in Figure 19.5. The most important is the <SCRIPT> tag. This is used whenever you need some JavaScript that doesn't go in an attribute of some other tag. You can put <SCRIPT> tags anywhere in the <HEAD> or <BODY> section of a document. (The forms example later in this hour will mention more about that.)

The <!-- and //--> tags just inside the <SCRIPT> and </SCRIPT> tags are actually comment tags, which have the effect of hiding the script from older browsers that otherwise might become confused and try to display the code as text on the page. You should always put each of these comment tags on a line by itself, as I did in Figure 19.5.

I won't go too deep into an explanation of the JavaScript in Figure 19.5, since that would get us into a course on computer programming. But you don't need to understand exactly how this works to copy it in your own pages, using your own image names and graphics files. When you do try this on your pages, don't overlook the fact that I had to use the names from the JavaScript definitions at the top of the page instead of the actual graphics file names. For example, the `OnMouseOver` attribute of the `NAME="erica"` image now looks like this:

```
ONMOUSEOVER="erica.src=ercalite.src"
```

(without any single-quotes) instead of this:

```
ONMOUSEOVER="erica.src='ercalite.jpg'"
```

You can also use the `OnMouseOver` and `OnMouseOut` attributes with imagemaps (which are covered in Hour 14, "Graphical Links and Imagemaps"). For an example of a large interactive imagemap, using no less than 24 separate images, move your mouse cursor around the pocket watch at the completed *24-Hour HTML Café* site at `http://24hourHTMLcafe.com`.

Peeking at the source code will show you exactly how to incorporate JavaScript commands into an imagemap. (It will also reveal that the clock is actually five separate images—four imagemaps and the changing image in the center. They don't call me "Tricky Dicky" for nuthin.)

Also, don't forget that you can use animated GIFs with JavaScripts too! For an example, check out the "Predictions and Fictions" link at `http://24hourHTMLcafe.com/hour19`.

19

Adding Up an Order Form

One of the most common uses of scripting is making an order form that adds up its own totals based on what items the customer selects. Figure 19.6 is an example that you can copy to create self-totaling forms yourself.

Though the code in Figure 19.6 is unrealistically simple for any real company's order form (most companies would like at least the address and phone number of the person placing the order), it is a completely functional JavaScript-enhanced Web page. Figure 19.7 demonstrates what the form would look like after a user entered the number 3 in the first box and the number 1 in the third box of the Qty column. The numbers in the Totals column are computed automatically.

FIGURE **19.6.**

A simple order form that uses JavaScript to automatically compute totals.

```
<HTML><HEAD><TITLE>Parts</TITLE>
<SCRIPT LANGUAGE="JavaScript">
<!--
  function CalculateTotals(){
    f=document.orderform;
    f.total1.value=parseInt(f.qty1.value)*50;
    f.total2.value=parseInt(f.qty2.value)*295;
    f.total3.value=parseInt(f.qty3.value)*395;
    f.total4.value=parseInt(f.qty4.value)*750;
    f.grandtotal.value=parseInt(f.total1.value)
                        +parseInt(f.total2.value)
                        +parseInt(f.total3.value)
                        +parseInt(f.total4.value);}
//-->
</SCRIPT></HEAD>
<BODY>
<H1>Parts Order Form</H1>
Indicate how many of each part you wish to order in the
"Qty" column. The total amount of your order will be
calculated automatically. When you are ready to submit your
order, click on the <B>Make Purchase</B> button.
<FORM NAME="orderform" METHOD="POST" ACTION="/htbin/generic">
<TABLE BORDER=3>
<TR><TH>Qty<TH>Part #<TH>Description<TH>Price<TH>Total
<TR>
<TD><INPUT NAME="qty1" SIZE=3 ONBLUR="CalculateTotals()">
<TD>25791<TD>Chromated Flywheel Knob<TD ALIGN="right">$50
<TD><INPUT NAME="total1" SIZE=7
    ONFOCUS="document.orderform.qty2.select();
                document.orderform.qty2.focus();">

<TR>
<TD><INPUT NAME="qty2" SIZE=3 ONBLUR="CalculateTotals()">
<TD>17557<TD>Perambulatory Dramograph<TD ALIGN="right">$295
<TD><INPUT NAME="total2" SIZE=7
    ONFOCUS="document.orderform.qty3.select();
                document.orderform.qty3.focus();">

<TR>
<TD><INPUT NAME="qty3" SIZE=3 ONBLUR="CalculateTotals()">
<TD>98754<TD>Triple-Extruded Colorizer<TD ALIGN="right">$395
<TD><INPUT NAME="total3" SIZE=7
    ONFOCUS="document.orderform.qty4.select();
                document.orderform.qty4.focus();">

<TR>
<TD><INPUT NAME="qty4" SIZE=3 ONBLUR="CalculateTotals()">
<TD>47594<TD>Rediculation Kit (Complete)<TD ALIGN="right">$750
<TD><INPUT NAME="total4" SIZE=7
    ONFOCUS="document.orderform.qty1.select();
                document.orderform.qty1.focus();">

<TR>
<TD><TD><TD ALIGN="right"><B>GRAND TOTAL:</B>
<TD><INPUT NAME="grandtotal" SIZE=7
    ONFOCUS="document.orderform.qty1.select();
                document.orderform.qty1.focus();">

</TABLE><BR>
<INPUT TYPE="submit" VALUE="Make Purchase">
</FORM>
<SCRIPT LANGUAGE="JavaScript">
<!--
  f=document.orderform;
  f.qty1.value=0; f.qty2.value=0;
  f.qty3.value=0; f.qty4.value=0;
  f.total1.value=0; f.total2.value=0;
  f.total3.value=0; f.total4.value=0;
  f.grandtotal.value=0:
//-->
</SCRIPT>
</BODY></HTML>
```

FIGURE 19.7.

The JavaScript in Figure 19.6 produces this form. Here, the customer has entered some desired quantities and the form has figured out the total cost.

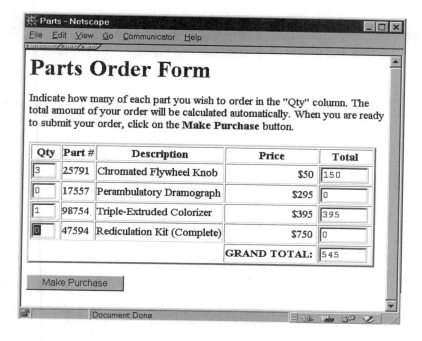

Most programmers could probably customize and expand the page in Figure 19.6 quite a bit without knowing anything whatsoever about JavaScript. What's more, this page works on any server and any JavaScript-enabled browser on any operating system.

Even if you don't do programming at all, you can easily adapt the code in Figure 19.6 to your own uses. The following list highlights the key elements of this JavaScript that you'll need to understand.

If you're not already familiar with HTML forms, you should review Hour 8, "Creating HTML Forms," before you try to understand or modify this example.

- As in the earlier example, I started by giving a name to all the parts of the page I would need to modify. Using the NAME attribute, I named the <FORM> itself "orderform". I also gave each input element in the form a name, such as "qty1", "qty2", "total1", "total2", and so on.
- The HTML page itself is always named "document", so I refer to the form as "document.orderform". The first input item on that form as

"document.orderform.qty1", the "grandtotal" input item is "document.order-form.grandtotal", and so forth. You'll notice that at the beginning of each <SCRIPT>, I put f=document.orderform. This just saved me some typing, since I could then use the letter f from then on instead of typing out document.orderform as part of every name.

- The *function* near the top of the page, which I chose to name ComputeTotals(), is the part of the script that actually does the computations. This function is pretty straightforward: it multiplies the quantities the user entered by the prices to get the totals, then adds up the totals to make a grand total. The only tricky thing here is all that parseInt() business. You have to use parseInt() to indicate that something is a number whenever you want to do computations. (This isn't necessary in most other programming languages. JavaScript is a little weird that way.) If you want to allow numbers that aren't integers, such as 12.5 or 13.333, use parseFloat() instead of parseInt().

- The <SCRIPT> at the bottom of the page just sets all the input elements to zero when the page first appears. This has to be done after the form itself is defined on the page with the <FORM> and </FORM> tags.

- The actual action happens in the <INPUT> tags. Just as the earlier example in this hour used ONMOUSEOVER to respond to a mouse movement, this example responds to ONFOCUS and ONBLUR. The ONFOCUS stuff happens when the user first clicks in (or tabs to) an input box to enter some data. The ONBLUR commands are triggered when the user is done entering data in a box and moves on to the next one.

- Take a look at the <INPUT> tags named qty1, qty2, qty3, and qty4. In each of these, you'll see ONBLUR="CalculateTotals()" which simply does all the math in the CalculateTotals function in the top <SCRIPT> every time the user enters a number in the Qty column. (JavaScript takes care of displaying the totals and grand total automatically, so you don't see any explicit command to "print" these numbers.)

- Now look at all the other <INPUT> tags. Each of them contains two commands, similar to the following:

```
ONFOCUS="document.orderform.qty2.focus();
document.orderform.qty2.select()"
```

This causes the cursor to skip to the next input box, so that the user doesn't get a chance to modify the totals. It also causes whatever data is in that next input box to be selected, so whatever the user types will replace the old data instead of being tacked onto the end of it.

Whew! That may seem like a lot to figure out, especially if you've never done any programming before! But with a little experimentation, and a few careful readings of this explanation, you should be able to put together a simple automatic order form of your own without any further knowledge of JavaScript.

> Time for a confession: There's a form-input tag I didn't tell you about in Hour 8. The <BUTTON> tag creates a button—sort of like <INPUT TYPE="submit">, except that a <BUTTON> button doesn't actually do anything. Not until you tell it what to do with some JavaScript, that is. If a programmable button sounds like something you'd like to use on your forms, hop on over to the "JavaScript Button" example at http://24hourHTMLcafe.com/hour19 to see one in action, and check out the HTML that makes it work.

The Wide World of JavaScript

You've learned enough in this hour to have a head start on JavaScript, and add some snazzy interaction to your Web pages. You've probably also gotten the idea that there's a lot more you can do, and it isn't as hard as you may have thought.

You may also find some scripts online that can be incorporated into a Web page of your own with little or no modification. (Check out the JavaScript-related links at http://24hourHTMLcafe.com/hotsites.htm#developer for good places to find scripts.)

When you find scripts you'd like to reuse or experiment with, use Figure 19.6 as a guide for placing the JavaScript elements where they should go; generally, functions go in the <HEAD> area, preceded by <SCRIPT LANGUAGE="JavaScript">, and followed by </SCRIPT>. The parts of the script that actually carry out the actions when the page is loaded go in the <BODY> part of the page, but still need to be set aside with the <SCRIPT> tag. Sections of script that respond to specific form entries go in the <A> or <INPUT> tags, with special attributes such as ONMOUSEOVER or ONBLUR.

You can also put JavaScript into a separate file by putting the name of that file in an SRC attribute within the <SCRIPT> tag, like the following:

```
<SCRIPT LANGUAGE="JavaScript" SRC="bingo.htm"></SCRIPT>
```

This is especially handy when you are using a script that someone else wrote and you don't want it cluttering up your HTML. Some parts of the script, such as JavaScript attributes of form <INPUT> tags, may still have to go in your HTML document, however.

19

Note that Netscape and Microsoft have slightly different—and often incompatible—implementations of JavaScript (Microsoft officially calls its implementation JScript, and its browser also supports a completely different scripting language called VBScript). The Web sites at http://home.netscape.com and http://www.microsoft.com are the best places to find out about the exact differences. Many simple scripts, including all those in this book, will work the same in both browsers.

Summary

In this hour, you've seen how to use scripting to make the images on your Web pages respond to mouse movements. You've also seen how similar JavaScript commands can be used to change multiple images at once, and to perform automatic calculations on form data. None of these tasks require much in the way of programming skills, though they may inspire you to learn the JavaScript language to give your pages more complex interactive features.

Q&A

Q Are there other "secret" attributes besides OnMouseOver, OnMouseOut, OnBlur, and OnFocus that I can use just as easily? And can I put them anyplace other than in an <A> or <INPUT> tag?

A Yes, and yes. Each HTML tag has an associated set of JavaScript attributes, which are called "events." For example, OnClick can be used within the <A> tag and some forms tags to specify a command to be followed when someone clicks that link or form element. Refer to Appendix C, "Complete HTML 4.0 Quick Reference," for a complete listing of the events you can use in each tag.

Q Doesn't Microsoft use a different scripting language for Internet Explorer?

A Yes, Microsoft recommends using a scripting language based on Visual Basic called VBScript, but Microsoft Internet Explorer version 3.0 or later also supports JavaScript. Many commands work slightly differently in the Microsoft implementation of JavaScript than they do in Netscape Navigator, however. Fortunately, the simple commands covered in this hour work exactly the same in both browsers so you can use them with confidence.

Q I tried using the tricks from this hour with images that were arranged in a table, but they didn't always work. Why?

A There's a bug in Netscape Navigator 3.0 that causes problems when you dynamically change images in a table. The trouble was corrected in Netscape Navigator 4.0, and was never an issue with Microsoft Internet Explorer. But, because so many people still use Navigator 3.0, it's safer to avoid changing any image within a table using JavaScript.

Q You said it was `OnMouseOver`, but in the example HTML file you used `ONMOUSEOVER` instead. Doesn't the capitalization matter?

A Nope. `ONMOUSEOVER` would do the same thing, too. Note, however, that capitalization *does* matter when you make up your own names for things in JavaScript. `GrandTotal=5` and `grandtotal=5` are not equivalent commands, since `GrandTotal` doesn't refer to the same item as `grandtotal`.

Workshop

Quiz

1. Say you've made a picture of a button and named it `button.gif`. You also made a simple GIF animation of the button flashing green and white, named `flashing.gif`. Write the HTML and JavaScript to make the button flash whenever someone moves the mouse pointer over it, and link to a page named `gohere.htm` when someone clicks the button.

2. How would you modify what you wrote for Question 1 so that the button starts flashing when someone moves the mouse over it, and keeps flashing even if he or she moves the mouse away?

3. Write the HTML for a form that will automatically calculate a total order cost, based on the number of widgets the user wants and a price of $25 per widget.

Answers

1.
```
<A HREF="gohere.htm"
ONMOUSEOVER="flasher.src='flashing.gif';
ONMOUSEOUT="flasher.src='button.gif'">
<IMG NAME="flasher" SRC="button.gif" BORDER=0></A>
```

2.
```
<A HREF="gohere.htm"
ONMOUSEOVER="flasher.src='flashing.gif'">
<IMG NAME="flasher" SRC="button.gif" BORDER=0></A>
```

19

```
3. <HTML><HEAD><TITLE>Widget Order Form</TITLE>
   <SCRIPT LANGUAGE="JavaScript">
   <!--
   function CalculateTotal() {
   document.orderform.total.value=
   parseInt(document.orderform.qty.value)*25}
   //-->
   </SCRIPT></HEAD><BODY>
   <FORM NAME="orderform" METHOD="post"
   ACTION="/htbin/generic">
   Please send me
   <INPUT NAME="qty" SIZE=3 ONBLUR="CalculateTotal()">
   widgets at $25 each = TOTAL:
   <INPUT NAME="total" SIZE=5>
   <INPUT TYPE="submit" VALUE="Order Now">
   </FORM>
   <SCRIPT LANGUAGE="JavaScript">
   <!--
   document.orderform.qty.value=0;
   document.orderform.total.value=0;
   //-->
   </SCRIPT>
   </BODY></HTML>
```

Exercise

Hey, what are you waiting for? Now that you're an HTML expert, get yourself a copy of the new *Sams Teach Yourself JavaScript in 24 Hours* or *Sams Teach Yourself JavaScript in a Week* and take the next quantum leap in Web publishing!

Hour 20

Setting Pages in Motion with Dynamic HTML

As we all know, in order to qualify as genuine computer jargon a word must be spelled with all capital letters and no vowels. The latest unpronounceable buzzword along this line is *DHTML*, which stands for *Dynamic HTML*. Like all the best tech-talk, this term means quite a few different things, depending on whom you ask.

Everyone agrees that Dynamic HTML brings a new level of power and excitement to Web pages. And everyone agrees that it has something to do with scripting, animation, and interactivity. Unfortunately, nobody yet agrees exactly how you get to have all this fun. Microsoft, Netscape, and the World Wide Web Consortium (the folks who set the standards) all still disagree about the details of what you can do with Dynamic HTML and how you should go about doing it. Creating Dynamic HTML pages therefore currently requires a certain amount of fortitude, cleverness, and perhaps foolhardiness.

Since I am obviously well endowed with all of these attributes, in this hour I will bravely lead you into the wilds of Dynamic HTML. Don't expect to become a DHTML guru in the next 60 minutes, but you can count on coming away with some reusable scripts to animate the contents of your Web pages in ways you couldn't do before. You will also emerge with the know-how necessary to put these scripts to work, and modify them for your own purposes.

To Do

Since the example for this hour involves interactive animation, it will be easier to see how everything works if you have the actual page on your computer, instead of just the static pictures in this book. I therefore recommend that you download the example files from the 24 Hour HTML Café before you continue reading. Here's how:

- If you don't already have version 4.0 or later of Netscape Navigator (for Windows PCs or the Macintosh) or version 4.0 or later of Microsoft Internet Explorer (for Windows only), go to Netscape at `http://home.netscape.com` or Microsoft at `http://www.microsoft.com/ie/` and follow the instructions for downloading and installing the latest browser version.

- Start your Web browser and go to the 24 Hour HTML Café at `http://24hourHTMLcafe.com/hour20`.

- Under "The XYZ Files" example, you will see a list of seven filenames. Use the right mouse button (or hold down the button if you're using a Macintosh) to click each of these, choosing Save Link As from the pop-up menu each time. Save all seven files in a new folder on your hard drive.

   (The files are `xyfiles.htm`, `slide.js`, `nodhtml.htm`, `xfolder.gif`, `yfolder.gif`, `zfolder.gif`, and `empty.gif`. The last of these GIF images is invisible, so don't worry if you try to look at it after you save it and don't see anything. You also won't see anything if you try to view `slide.js` with a Web browser.)

   Once you have those seven files on your hard drive, you can use your favorite text editor and Web browser to look at them (and, if you're bold, modify them to work with your own graphics and text) as you read the rest of this hour.

Learning How to Fly

For the first part of this hour, your noble quest will be to make some text "fly in" from the edge of a page when that page first comes up in the browser window. Just to make the quest more worthy of pursuit, you'd better make the text slide diagonally, instead of straight left-to-right. Naturally, what you really want (and shall no doubt soon gain) is a general-purpose script that you can use to slide any text and/or graphics any which way you want.

And while you're at it, why not go wild and ask for a script that can slip things underneath the edge of other things, or slide one layer of text and graphics behind or in front of any number of other layers?

Figures 20.1 and 20.2 are snapshots of a Dynamic HTML Web page with flying text. This is the `xyzfiles.htm` document you were just instructed to download from the 24 Hour HTML Café, so you may want to look at it on your computer screen now. See how the text glides in from behind the file folders as soon as you pull up the page? Pretty cool, huh.

FIGURE 20.1.

Dynamic HTML lets you animate overlapping layers of text and graphics. This text is emerging from behind some images.

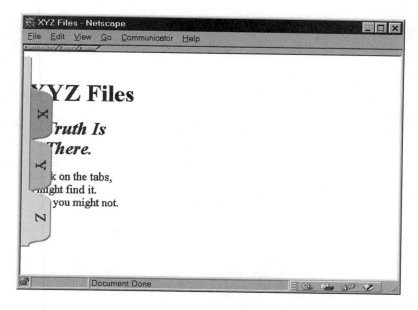

To achieve the effect shown in Figures 20.1 and 20.2, your HTML and JavaScript code will need to do all of the following:

1. Check to make sure that the user's Web browser can handle Dynamic HTML, and provide some alternative content if it can't.

2. Define and name the layer containing the text, and hide it out of sight beyond the edge of the page.

3. Define and name the layers containing the file tab images. (Each tab is actually assigned its own layer, because later in this hour they will all be animated separately.)

4. Animate the text layer sliding onto the page.

20

FIGURE 20.2.

The text that was moving in Figure 20.1 has now settled into place and stopped.

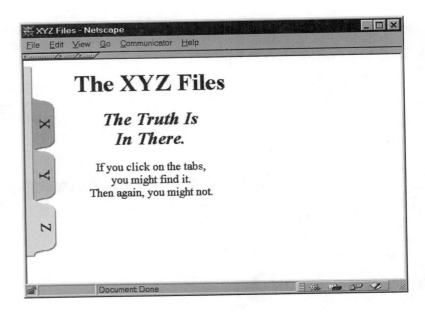

Figure 20.3 shows the HTML to do all these things. The following sections explain how each of these four tasks is accomplished.

All text between <!-- and --> tags in Figure 20.3 (or any other HTML page) will be completely ignored by the Web browser. These comments are just reminders the Web page author has written to himself (that's me) and anyone else who might need some hints to understand how the page works (that's you).

Dividing a Web Page into Layers

Shortly, you'll learn how to detect whether a page is being viewed with a DHTML-compatible Web browser. But first, you need to know an essential secret of all Dynamic HTML: how to define layers of text and/or graphics so you can move them around.

But wait—you already know how to do that! Remember way back in Hour 5, "Text Alignment and Lists," when you learned to use the <DIV ALIGN="center"> tag to center a bunch of text and/or graphics on the page? The whole purpose of the <DIV> and </DIV> tags is to define a region of the page (also called a *division* or *layer*) so you can then do something with that whole region at once.

FIGURE 20.3.

This is the HTML for the page in Figures 20.1 and 20.2. The JavaScript that does the animation is in a separate file (see Figure 20.6), named slide.js.

```html
<HTML><HEAD><TITLE>XYZ Files</TITLE>
<SCRIPT SRC="slide.js" LANGUAGE="JavaScript">
</SCRIPT></HEAD>

<!-- Check for DHTML compatibility and if it's okay,
     then fly in the headings and body text -->
<BODY ONLOAD="if (checkDHTML()) {
 layername=makeName('intro');
 yhop=-2; ygoal=20; xhop=10; xgoal=80; slide() }">

<!-- Tell users of non-JavaScript browsers to go away,
     but hide the message from DHTML-compatible browsers -->
<DIV STYLE="position: absolute;
            left: -250px; top: 10px; width: 250">
Your browser can't cope with this DHTML page.<P>
<A HREF="nodhtml.htm">Click here for a regular HTML page.</A>
<P></DIV>

<!-- Get the headings and body text ready to fly in -->
<DIV ID="intro" STYLE="text-align: center; z-index: 0;
 position: absolute; left: -260px; top: 88px; width: 260px">
<H1>The XYZ Files</H1>
<H2><I>The Truth Is<BR>In There.</I></H2>
If you click on the tabs,<BR>you might find it.<BR>
Then again, you might not.</DIV>

<!-- Give each file folder image its own layer -->
<DIV ID="layer1" STYLE="position: absolute;
 left: -250px; top: 10px; width: 300; z-index: 1">
<IMG SRC="xfolder.gif" WIDTH=300 HEIGHT=330></DIV>
<DIV ID="layer2" STYLE="position: absolute;
 left: -250px; top: 10px; width: 300; z-index: 2">
<IMG SRC="yfolder.gif" WIDTH=300 HEIGHT=330></DIV>
<DIV ID="layer3" STYLE="position: absolute;
 left: -250px; top: 10px; width: 300; z-index: 3">
<IMG SRC="zfolder.gif" WIDTH=300 HEIGHT=330></DIV>
```

As you found out in Hour 16, "Using Style Sheets," centering the contents of a <DIV> region is only one of many possibilities for playing with it. You could also turn all the text in the region red with <DIV STYLE="color: red">, or put a red background behind the region with <DIV STYLE="background-color: red">, or even pick up the whole region and move it to the top-left corner of the browser window with <DIV STYLE="position: absolute; left: 0px; top: 0px">.

Now you're about to learn how to do all these things dynamically, in response to user-initiated events such as mouse movements and link clicks. Of course, you'll need a name for each <DIV> region you want to order around. In some older versions of JavaScript, you would use the familiar NAME attribute for this purpose but, for reasons beyond my ken, a new attribute called ID is now used instead.

20

For example, the following code from Figure 20.3 defines a layer named "intro".

```
<DIV ID="intro" STYLE="text-align: center; z-index: 0;
 position: absolute; left: -260px; top: 88px; width: 260px">
<H1>The XYZ Files</H1>
<H2><I>The Truth Is<BR>In There.</I></H2>
If you click on the tabs,<BR>you might find it.<BR>
Then again, you might not.</DIV>
```

The STYLE attribute positions this layer 88 pixels down from the top edge of the browser window, and *negative* 260 pixels from the left edge. Negative means to the left, so in other words you won't actually be able to see this layer (until you move it) because it's completely outside the viewing window, off to the left side. The STYLE attribute also specifies the width of the layer as 260 pixels and indicates that the text should be centered in that 260-pixel-wide region.

Each of the last three <DIV> tags in Figure 20.3 contains a single <IMG> tag, placing a 300×330-pixel image of a file folder on the page. If you look carefully at the STYLE attributes for these <DIV> tags, you'll notice that each layer is positioned 250 pixels outside the left edge of the browser window, so that only the rightmost 50 pixels of the image are visible in Figures 20.1 and 20.2. The rest is hidden beyond the edge of the viewing window, and will not be revealed until later this hour when I show you how to interactively animate the file folder images.

You'll also notice that all three of these <DIV> layers are placed in exactly the same spot, right on top of one another. The only reason you can see the bottom two folder tabs is that the images covering them are partially transparent GIFs, allowing parts of the image and background beneath to show through.

With all these semi-transparent layers piled on top of one another, you need some way to determine which layer appears in front, which one is in the back, and the stacking order of the layers in between. You can do this by including z-index: followed by a number in the STYLE attribute of each layer. Higher numbered layers will appear in front of lower numbered layers. In Figure 20.3, the intro layer gets a z-index of 0 (the very bottom layer), and the X, Y, and Z file tabs get z-indexes of 1, 2, and 3 respectively. Figure 20.1 clearly shows the result of this stacking order. (If you gave the intro layer a z-index of 4 or more, the text would appear in front of the file tabs instead of behind them.)

Offering Alternate Content in Plain HTML

There's one more <DIV> layer in Figure 20.3 that I haven't mentioned yet. The code for it looks like the following:

```
<DIV STYLE="position: absolute;
 left: -250px; top: 10px; width: 250">
Your browser can't cope with this DHTML page.<P>
<A HREF="nodhtml.htm">Click here for a regular HTML page.</A>
<P></DIV>
```

Like the intro layer mentioned earlier, this layer is nothing more than a little text positioned completely out of view beyond the edge of the browser window. The point here is that older browsers that don't support style sheet positioning won't know enough to hide this layer, and so users of those browsers will see the text telling them how lame their browser is, and offering a link to an alternative page—presumably one that doesn't use any Dynamic HTML jugglery.

Figure 20.4 shows what the page from Figures 20.1–20.3 looks like when viewed with the Opera browser, which doesn't support style sheets or JavaScript. The STYLE and ID attributes of the <DIV> tags have no effect at all in Opera, so the contents of all the layers are displayed one after the other down the page.

FIGURE 20.4.

When the page in Figures 20.1–20.3 is viewed in Opera 3.21, a link to an alternate page appears.

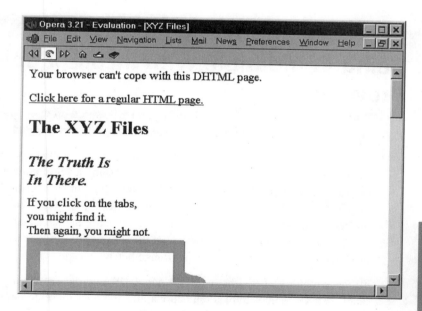

When a user follows the "Clicks here for a regular HTML page" link in Figure 20.4, he or she gets the nodhtml.htm document shown in Figure 20.5. You can make any page you want and name it nodhtml.htm (or change the "nodhtml.htm" reference to the page of your choice). Instead of telling the user that his or her browser isn't advanced enough for your state-of-the-art pages, you might choose instead to simply present equivalent content without the fancy DHTML animation.

20

FIGURE 20.5.

Clicking the link in Figure 20.4 takes the user to a plain-vanilla HTML page, with no DHTML enhancements.

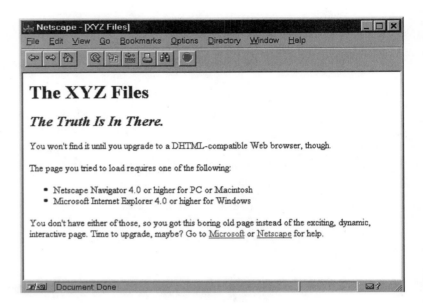

Being Compatible with Incompatible Browsers

With all the layers in place, and users of under-powered browsers properly warned, the only thing left to do is write a little JavaScript to slide the `intro` layer onto the page.

Well, unfortunately, that's not quite true. There are still some ugly browser-compatibility issues to resolve first. You've seen how to offer some level of compatibility with browsers that support neither style sheet positioning nor JavaScript. But if you want a page that works out in the real world, you also need to be ready for Web browsers that understand older versions of JavaScript but still can't handle advanced stuff like layer animation. If you don't detect and divert those browsers, anyone using them to view your DHTML pages may see all sorts of strange behavior and error messages.

To make matters worse, the two most popular Web browsers use incompatible scripting languages. For some simple applications, like the ones presented in Hour 19, "Web Page Scripting for Non-Programmers," Netscape Navigator and Microsoft Internet Explorer are compatible enough to write simple scripts that work in both browsers. But when you try to do more interesting things, such as moving overlapping layers of text and graphics around, Netscape's JavaScript and Microsoft's JScript are just not talking the same language.

None of this would be a big deal if you were creating Web pages for a corporate intranet where all employees always used exactly the same software. (Such corporations do exist, I'm told, though I'm not sure I believe it.) But most of us want our pages to look good to anyone who pulls them off the Internet, no matter what Web browser he is using. At the very least, we'd like our fancy interactive bells and whistles to work with the latest browsers from Netscape and Microsoft, and perhaps gracefully offer a less exciting page to users of any other Web browser.

Time for the bad news: achieving this level of compatibility is a huge headache. Ah, but the good news is that I already got the headache for you, had a beer, got over it, and wrote the necessary scripts so you don't have to. I won't even try to teach you enough to understand how I did it, but if you take a look at Figure 20.6, I will tell you what the JavaScript does, and why.

As mentioned in Hour 19, you can either type a script directly into a Web page, between the <SCRIPT> and </SCRIPT> tags, or you can put the script in a separate file and indicate the filename with an SRC attribute in the <SCRIPT> tag. The Web page in Figure 20.3 uses the latter approach to include the slide.js script listed in Figure 20.6. This allows you to use the same script in as many Web pages as you want without having to maintain multiple copies of the script itself.

Any line starting with // is ignored by the JavaScript interpreter, the same way anything between <!-- and --> tags is ignored by HTML browsers. The lines starting with // in Figure 20.6 are just comments by the Web page author, reminding anyone who reads the code what each function does.

As you may remember from Hour 19, a *function* is a piece of JavaScript code that can be called on to do a specific task. The first function in Figure 20.6 checks to see if a Web page is being viewed with a DHTML-compatible Web browser. In order to qualify as DHTML-compatible (according to me on this particular Thursday, anyway), a browser must understand some version of JavaScript advanced enough to group text and graphics into layers and dynamically position those layers anywhere on a Web page. The following are the only browsers that meet these criteria:

- Netscape Navigator 4.0 or later for Windows or Macintosh (but not UNIX)
- Microsoft Internet Explorer 4.0 or later for Windows (but not Macintosh or UNIX)

20

Figure 20.6.

You can link this JavaScript file (named slide.js) *to your own pages to give them instant cross-browser Dynamic HTML compatibility.*

```
// Define all variables and set the default delay to 5ms
var layername, xgoal, ygoal, xhop, yhop, delay=5;

// Check to see if the browser is DHTML-compatible
function checkDHTML() {
  if ((parseInt(navigator.appVersion)>=4) &&
     ((navigator.appName!="Netscape" &&
       navigator.appVersion.indexOf("X11") == -1) ||
      (navigator.appName!="Microsoft Internet Explorer" &&
       navigator.appVersion.indexOf("Macintosh") == -1)))
    { return 1 }
   else
    { document.location="nodhtml.htm"; return 0 }
}

// Construct a valid reference to a layer
// in either Netscape JavaScript or Microsoft JScript
function makeName(layerID) {
  if (navigator.appName=="Netscape")
   { refname = eval("document." + layerID) }
   else
   { refname = eval("document.all." + layerID + ".style") }
  return refname
}

// Slide over xhop,yhop pixels every delay milliseconds
// until the layer reaches xgoal and ygoal
function slide() {
  if ((parseInt(layername.left) != xgoal) ||
     (parseInt(layername.top) != ygoal))
    { layername.left = parseInt(layername.left) + xhop;
      layername.top = parseInt(layername.top) + yhop;
      window.setTimeout("slide()", delay) }
}
```

You'll see how to use the checkDHTML function on your Web pages momentarily, but first you should know what it does when it detects an incompatible browser. The following line of JavaScript deals with this eventuality:

```
{ document.location="nodhtml.htm"; return 0 }
```

This takes the user to the nodthtml.htm page in Figure 20.5, while sending a signal back to the original page to let it know that it shouldn't try to do any DHTML tricks.

The next function in Figure 20.6, called makeName, is pure black magic. To understand the need for it, you have to realize exactly how Microsoft and Netscape's implementations of JavaScript differ when it comes to handling layers.

To change the position of a layer (for example, the layer named "intro"), you need some way to say "the top of the layer named "intro"," and "the left side of the layer named "intro"" in JavaScript. And that's where the trouble starts. To move the layer down so its top edge is 200 pixels from the top edge of the browser window, you need a different command in Netscape Navigator than in Microsoft Internet Explorer. The Netscape way would be the following:

```
document.intro.top = 200
```

The Microsoft way to say the same thing would be the following:

```
document.all.intro.style = 200
```

This clearly makes it a pain in the proverbial back button to write a script that works with both browsers.

Now for the black magic. If you give the makeName function in Figure 20.1 the name "intro", it will give you back either "document.intro" or "document.all.intro.style", depending on which browser you are using. If you put this result to refer to a layer, it works nicely for Netscapians and Microsofters alike. You will soon see exactly how this works in practice, because you're finally ready to see how the Dynamic HTML layer animation is accomplished.

Moving a Layer Around with JavaScript

The only two sections of code in Figures 20.3 and 20.6 I haven't explained yet in this hour are the <BODY> tag in Figure 20.3 and the slide function in Figure 20.6. Together, these create the effect seen in Figures 20.1 and 20.2, the text layer flying onto the page. The <BODY> tag looks like this:

```
<BODY ONLOAD="if (checkDHTML()) {
 layername=makeName('intro');
 yhop=-2; ygoal=20; xhop=10; xgoal=80; slide() }">
```

Any JavaScript commands you put after ONLOAD= in the <BODY> tag will be carried out as soon as the Web page is displayed. (ONLOAD will also be triggered every time the user hits the Reload button in Netscape Navigator, or the Refresh button in Microsoft Internet Explorer.)

So what does the JavaScript in this ONLOAD attribute do? First, it starts the checkDHTML function. If this function detects a DHTML-compatible browser, the following steps are carried out:

1. The makeName function is given the layer ID "intro", so that it can construct the appropriate Netscape or Microsoft version of the layer name. The result is saved as layername.

20

2. The numbers -2, 20, 10, and 80 are put into storage boxes (or, if you speak math, *variables*) named yhop, ygoal, xhop, and xgoal. The point of this is to tell the slide function where you want the layer moved to, and how fast to move it. (More on that shortly.)

3. The slide function is called on to "fly in" the layer.

Here's the slide function from Figure 20.6:

```
function slide() {
  if ((parseInt(layername.left) != xgoal) ||
    (parseInt(layername.top) != ygoal))
  {  layername.left = parseInt(layername.left) + xhop;
     layername.top = parseInt(layername.top) + yhop;
     window.setTimeout("slide()", delay) }
}
```

I can't teach you enough JavaScript in this hour for you to be able to write your own functions like this, but you can probably get the general gist of how this function works. First, it checks to see if the layer referred to by layername is already at the location specified by xgoal and ygoal. If the layer isn't there yet, it moves the layer xhop pixels horizontally and yhop pixels vertically. Then it waits for a short time, and goes back to the beginning of the function. It keeps on hopping over and over again until it reaches the goal.

If xhop is a negative number, the layer will hop to the left instead of the right. Likewise, if yhop is negative the layer will move up instead of down. The bigger the values of xhop and yhop, the faster the layer will get where it's going. You can also control the length of the pause between hops by changing the value of delay. For example, adding delay=100; to the ONLOAD commands just before the slide() would cause a 100 millisecond (1/10th of a second) delay between each step in the layer movement.

In the example page from Figure 20.3, the <DIV STYLE> attribute initially places the intro layer at the x,y pixel location (-260,88). In the <BODY ONLOAD> attribute, xgoal and ygoal are set to (80,20), while xhop and yhop are set to (10,-2). So the slide moves the layer from (-260,88) to each of the following positions, one after the other:

(-250,86) (-240,84) (-230,82) (-220,80) ... etc.

until it finally reaches (80,20). I had to be very careful when I chose the values for xhop and yhop, because they must reach the xgoal and ygoal in exactly the same number of steps. If I had used (9,-3) instead of (10,-2), the layer would never land on the spot (80,20) and therefore it would never stop moving! When you use the slide function for your own animations, be sure to grab a calculator and make sure the two sides of the following equation come out to the same number (using the initial x,y position of the layer for xstart and ystart):

```
(xgoal - xstart) / xhop = (ygoal - ystart) / yhop
```

I could have added some JavaScript to the slide function to check this automatically, but the whole point is that Dynamic HTML functions can be pretty simple and still get the job done.

> If you've done any programming in other languages, it may seem strange to you that there aren't any explicit commands in Figure 20.6 to draw anything on the screen. JavaScript takes care of updating the display automatically as soon as you change the position settings for anything on the Web page.

Interactive Layer Animation

The rest of this hour will demonstrate another application of the slide function, and show you how Dynamic HTML can respond to user-initiated events. The goal this time will be to modify the XYZ Files example page so that the user can click any of the three file tabs to "pull out" the hidden part of that graphic.

Figures 20.7 and 20.8 show an example: The user clicks the file tab marked X, and that image slides to the right. If the user clicked the tab again, it would slide back into its original location. You could achieve this interactive animation by adding the Dynamic HTML code in Figure 20.9 to the end of the page presented earlier (in Figure 20.3).

FIGURE 20.7.

You can make layers respond to the user's actions. Here, the image of the X file slides out in response to a mouse click.

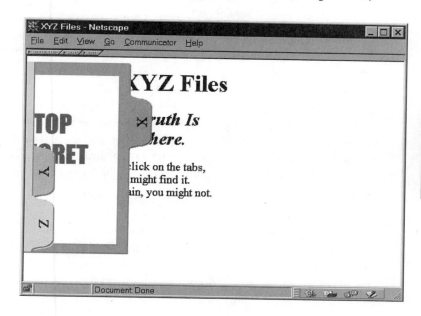

20

FIGURE 20.8.

Notice here and in Figure 20.7 that the moving image stays in front of the text but behind the other two images as it slides.

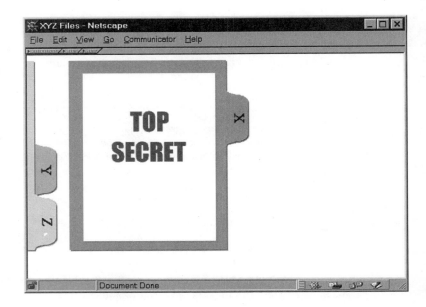

The first <DIV> layer defined in Figure 20.9 enables the file tab marked X to display the behavior you see in Figures 20.7 and 20.8 (and which you can see on your computer screen by clicking the X tab).

```
<DIV STYLE="position: absolute;
 left: 10px; top: 65px; z-index: 4">
<A HREF="#" ONCLICK="layername=makeName('layer1');
 yhop=0; ygoal=10; xhop=40; xgoal=70; slide()">
<IMG SRC="empty.gif" WIDTH=35 HEIGHT=85 BORDER=0></A></DIV>
```

This layer doesn't change the appearance of the page at all, because it contains only a single image (`empty.gif`), which I made completely transparent before saving it in Paint Shop Pro. The purpose of the invisible image is to give the user something on which to click, so the <DIV STYLE> positions it directly over the tab of the X file image. (It took some trial and error to find exactly the right spot, and the best WIDTH and HEIGHT for the image. To make it easier, I left out the BORDER=0 attribute of the <IMG> tag, making a visible border around the image, until I had found the correct pixel coordinates for it.)

The ONCLICK attribute lets you specify some JavaScript to respond when the mouse clicks something. In future versions of JavaScript, you'll be able to put an ONCLICK, ONMOUSEOVER, or ONMOUSEOUT attribute in an <IMG> tag, but for now that doesn't work, so you have to make the image a link and put the attribute in the <A> tag. In this case, I didn't want the link to actually go anywhere so I just used HREF="#" to make a link to the top of the current page. (A bit silly, but it works.)

FIGURE 20.9.

Adding this to the end of the page in Figure 20.3 enables the interactive behavior shown in Figures 20.7 and 20.8.

```html
<!-- Use invisible image links to nowhere as triggers
     to pull out and put away the file folders -->
<DIV STYLE="position: absolute;
 left: 10px; top: 65px; z-index: 4">
<A HREF="#" ONCLICK="layername=makeName('layer1');
 yhop=0; ygoal=10; xhop=40; xgoal=70; slide()">
<IMG SRC="empty.gif" WIDTH=35 HEIGHT=85 BORDER=0></A></DIV>
<DIV STYLE="position: absolute;
 left: 330px; top: 65px; z-index: 5">
<A HREF="#" ONCLICK="layername=makeName('layer1');
 yhop=0; ygoal=10; xhop=-40; xgoal=-250; slide()">
<IMG SRC="empty.gif" WIDTH=35 HEIGHT=85 BORDER=0></A></DIV>
<DIV STYLE="position: absolute;
 left: 10px; top: 155px; z-index: 6">
<A HREF="#" ONCLICK="layername=makeName('layer2');
 yhop=0; ygoal=10; xhop=40; xgoal=70; slide()">
<IMG SRC="empty.gif" WIDTH=35 HEIGHT=85 BORDER=0></A></DIV>
<DIV STYLE="position: absolute;
 left: 330px; top: 155px; z-index: 7">
<A HREF="#" ONCLICK="layername=makeName('layer2');
 yhop=0; ygoal=10; xhop=-40; xgoal=-250; slide()">
<IMG SRC="empty.gif" WIDTH=35 HEIGHT=85 BORDER=0></A></DIV>
<DIV STYLE="position: absolute;
 left: 10px; top: 245px; z-index: 8">
<A HREF="#" ONCLICK="layername=makeName('layer3');
 yhop=0; ygoal=10; xhop=40; xgoal=70; slide()">
<IMG SRC="empty.gif" WIDTH=35 HEIGHT=85 BORDER=0></A></DIV>
<DIV STYLE="position: absolute;
 left: 330px; top: 245px; z-index: 9">
<A HREF="#" ONCLICK="layername=makeName('layer3');
 yhop=0; ygoal=10; xhop=-40; xgoal=-250; slide()">
<IMG SRC="empty.gif" WIDTH=35 HEIGHT=85 BORDER=0></A></DIV>
</BODY></HTML>
```

You can also use ONCLICK and other events in the <AREA> tag of an image-map (see Hour 14, "Graphical Links and Imagemaps"), which might have been a more elegant way of achieving the result I was after in this example.

And don't forget that you can initiate JavaScript events, including Dynamic HTML animations, in response to form input, too (see Hour 19).

20

The JavaScript commands in the <A ONCLICK> attribute are very similar to those you saw earlier in the <BODY ONLOAD> attribute. The makeName function is used to make a valid layer name. Then xgoal and ygoal are set to the destination of the layer, while xhop and yhop are set to the size of each hop on the way there. (Notice that yhop is 0 and ygoal is the same as the initial top: setting, since the image only moves horizontally.) Finally, slide is called on to do the actual animation.

The second <DIV> layer in Figure 20.9 is almost the same, but located 320 pixels further to the right. The xgoal is also 320 pixels further to the left, and xhop is -40 instead of 40. This gives the user a place to click to "put away" the file folder image after it has been "pulled out."

The remaining four <DIV> layers provide exactly the same interactive behavior for the file tabs marked Y and Z.

Summary

This was undoubtedly the most challenging hour in the book. Don't be surprised or discouraged if you need to read through it more than once, and experiment for a while with the sample page, to understand what's going on and begin to successfully adapt the Dynamic HTML code to your own purposes.

If you have any experience with computer programming, you probably gleaned enough from this hour and the previous one to start writing your own JavaScript enhancements to your pages. And even if you have never written a line of computer-language code before in your life, you can still copy the code in the book and use it on your own pages.

In this hour, you've seen how to combine HTML, style sheets, and JavaScript to animate independent layers of text and graphics. You learned how to initiate an animation when a page first loads, or in response to a mouse click on any region of the page.

Of course, all this is only the tip of the Dynamic HTML iceberg. Current scripting languages allow you to modify any of the content or formatting of your pages on-the-fly, in response to a wide variety of events. Future versions of JavaScript are likely to make it much easier to do so in a way that is fully compatible with all major Web browsers. The promising future of Dynamic HTML is discussed in Hour 24, "Planning for the Future of HTML."

Q&A

Q Isn't there some way to make layers without using the STYLE attribute?

A Only in Netscape Navigator versions 3.0 and 4.0. Netscape invented its own <LAYER> tag, which is unlikely to ever become part of the HTML standard or be supported by other browsers. For more information on this tag, visit http://developer.netscape.com.

Q In Hour 16, "Using Style Sheets," you stressed the concept of keeping style specifications in a separate document, but in this hour you put all the style stuff right in with the HTML. Aren't you being hypocritical?

A Sort of. It is often a good idea to keep styles in a separate document, and you can combine true style sheets and Dynamic HTML. For example, I could have made a style sheet that included a style like the following:

```
DIV.peekaboo {position: absolute; left: -250px; top: 10px; width:
300;}
```

Then I could have applied that style to each of the three file tab layers with `<DIV CLASS="peekaboo">`. But doing so would probably have just made the page harder to understand and maintain. When you are working with JavaScript and style-based positioning, I usually find it easier and more efficient to use inline styles than separate style sheets.

Q **I'm a professional programmer, and I think it was inelegant of you to employ global variables instead of parameter passing in your implementation of the recursive function `slide()`. Furthermore...**

A Was that a question? I didn't think so. Get over it, okay?

Workshop

Quiz

1. Modify this Web page so that the "Balzout Skydiving" heading and `fall.gif` image drop into place together from above the top edge of the browser window. (Use the `slide.js` script presented in this hour.)

```
<HTML><HEAD><TITLE>Take a Dive</TITLE>
</HEAD><BODY>
<IMG SRC="diver.gif" ALIGN="left" WIDTH=100 HEIGHT=200>
<H1>Balzout Skydiving</H1>
Join Richard Balzout for a free chute-packing lesson
on June 15th at the Sewerside Memorial Airfield.
</BODY></HTML>
```

2. Now modify the page from Question 1 some more, so that clicking the `fall.gif` image makes it leap back up out of sight.

Answers

1. The following is one possibility. You could change the speed of the fall by adjusting the value of yhop. (This quiz answer is included in the online examples at `http://24hourHTMLcafe.com/hour20`, by the way.)

```
<HTML><HEAD><TITLE>Take a Dive</TITLE>
<SCRIPT SRC="slide.js" LANGUAGE="JavaScript">
</SCRIPT></HEAD><BODY>
<BODY ONLOAD="if (checkDHTML()) {
```

20

```
layername=makeName('ComeOnDown');
yhop=5; ygoal=10; xhop=0; xgoal=10; slide() }">
<DIV ID="ComeOnDown"
STYLE="position: absolute; left: 10px; top: -210px;">
<IMG SRC="diver.gif" ALIGN="left" WIDTH=100 HEIGHT=200>
<H1>Balzout Skydiving</H1></DIV>
<DIV STYLE="position: absolute; left: 10px; top: 220px;">
Join Richard Balzout for a free chute-packing lesson
on June 15th at the Sewerside Memorial Airfield.</DIV>
</BODY></HTML>
```

2. Replace the <IMG> tag with the following.

```
<A HREF="#" ONCLICK="layername=makeName('ComeOnDown');
yhop=-10; ygoal=-210; xhop=0; xgoal=10; slide()">
<IMG SRC="diver.gif" ALIGN="left"
WIDTH=100 HEIGHT=200 BORDER=0></A>
```

Exercise

Try combining the techniques you learned in this hour with the JavaScript examples in Hour 19. For example, you might create a graphical meter by moving an image up and down on the page in response to a number entered in a form input box. The possibilities are endless, so grab your imagination and get creative!

PART VI

Building a Web Site

Hour

Hour **21**

Multipage Layout with Frames

One major limitation of HTML in the old days was that you could see only one page at a time. *Frames* overcome this limitation by dividing the browser window into multiple HTML documents.

Frames are like tables (covered in Hour 15, "Advanced Layout with Tables") in that they allow you to arrange text and graphics into rows and columns. But unlike a table cell, any frame can contain links that change the contents of other frames (or itself). For example, one frame could display an unchanging index page while another frame could change based on which links the reader clicks.

Frames are only supported by Netscape Navigator version 2.0 or later and Microsoft Internet Explorer version 3.0 or later. However, you'll see how to provide alternative content for other browsers that don't display frames.

To Do

▼ To Do

Frames are basically a way of arranging and presenting several Web pages at once. You'll be able to learn the material in this hour faster if you have a few interrelated Web pages all ready before you continue.

- If you have an index page or table of contents for your Web site, copy it to a separate directory folder so you can experiment with it without changing the original. Copy a few of the pages that the index links to as well.

▲
- As you read this hour, try modifying the sample frames I present to incorporate your own Web pages.

What Are Frames?

At first glance, Figure 21.1 may look like an ordinary Web page, but it is actually two separate HTML pages, both displayed in the same Netscape Navigator window. Each of these pages is displayed in its own frame, separated by a horizontal bar.

NEW TERM   A *frame* is a rectangular region within the browser window that displays a Web page, alongside other pages in other frames.

FIGURE 21.1.

Frames allow more than one Web page to be displayed at once.

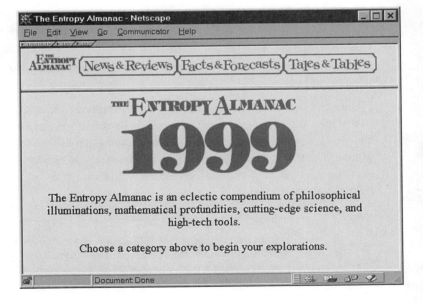

The main advantage of using frames becomes apparent when a reader clicks one of the links in the bottom frame of Figure 21.1. The top frame will not change at all in this example, but a new page will be loaded and displayed in the bottom frame, as in Figure 21.2.

FIGURE 21.2.

Clicking "Facts & Forecasts" in Figure 21.1 brings up a new bottom page, but leaves the top frame the same.

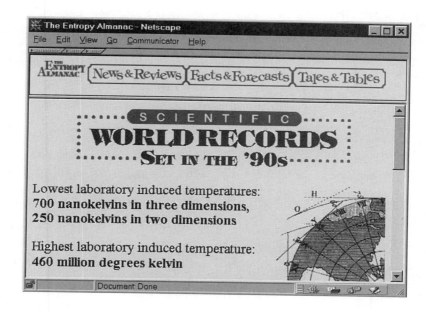

Creating a Frameset Document

How did I make the site in Figures 21.1 and 21.2? First, I created the contents of each frame as an ordinary HTML page. These pages (listed in Figure 21.4) don't contain any tags you haven't already seen in other hours.

To put them all together, I used a special kind of page called a *frameset document*.

A frameset document actually has no content. It only tells the browser which other pages to load and how to arrange them in the browser window. Figure 21.3 shows the frameset document for the Entropy Almanac site in Figures 21.1 and 21.2.

NEW TERM A *frameset document* is an HTML page that instructs the Web browser to split its window into multiple frames, and specifies which Web page should be displayed in each frame.

In Figure 21.3, instead of a `<BODY>` tag, there is a `<FRAMESET>` tag. No tags that would normally be contained in a `<BODY>` tag can be within the `<FRAMESET>` tag. The `<FRAMESET>` tag in Figure 21.3 includes a ROWS attribute, meaning that the frames should

21

be arranged on top of each other like the horizontal rows of a table. If you want your frames to be side-by-side, use a COLS attribute instead of ROWS.

FIGURE 21.3.

If you load this frame-set document in Netscape Navigator, you'll see the site in Figure 21.1.

```
<HTML><HEAD><TITLE>The Entropy Almanac</TITLE></HEAD>
<FRAMESET ROWS="74,*">
   <FRAME SRC="banner.htm" NAME="top">
   <FRAME SRC="greeting.htm" NAME="main">
</FRAMESET>
<NOFRAMES><BODY>
<H1>The Entropy Almanac</H1>
Your browser does not support frames.
Please <A HREF="noframes.htm">click here</A> for
the frameless version of this Web site.
</BODY></NOFRAMES>
</HTML>
```

You must specify the sizes of the ROWS or COLS, either as precise pixel values or as percentages of the total size of the browser window. You can also use an asterisk (*) to indicate that a frame should fill whatever space is available in the window. If more than one frame has an * value, the remaining space will be divided equally between them.

In Figure 21.3, <FRAMESET ROWS="74,*"> means to split the window vertically into two frames. The top frame will be exactly 74 pixels tall, and the bottom frame will take up all the remaining space in the window. The top frame contains the document banner.htm, and the bottom frame contains greeting.htm (both of which are listed in Figure 21.4).

After the framesets in Figure 21.3, I included a complete Web page between the <BODY> and </BODY> tags. Notice that this doesn't appear at all in Figures 21.1 or 21.2. All Web browsers that support frames will ignore anything between the <NOFRAME> and </NOFRAME> tags.

Because some browsers still do not support frames, it is probably wise to include alternative content with the <NOFRAME> tag. If nothing else, just include a note recommending that people get either Microsoft or Netscape's browser to see the frames.

Some Web page publishers actually produce two versions of their site—one with frames, and one without. You can save yourself that hassle by simply including links between all the pages that will appear in your primary frame.

Because you can't predict the size of the window that someone will view your Web page in, it is often convenient to use percentages rather than exact pixel values to dictate the size of the rows and columns. For example, to make a left frame 20 percent of the width of the browser window with a right frame taking up the remaining 80 percent, you would type the following:

```
<FRAMESET COLS="20%,80%">
```

An exception to this rule would be when you want a frame to contain graphics of a certain size; then you would specify that size in pixels and add a few pixels for the margins and frame borders. This is the case in Figure 21.3, where the images in the top frame are each 42 pixels tall. I allowed 32 extra pixels for margins and borders, making the entire frame 74 pixels tall.

In any case, if you specify any frame size in pixels, there must also be at least one frame in the same frameset with a variable (*) width so that the document can be displayed in a window of any size.

The <FRAME> Tag

Within the <FRAMESET> and </FRAMESET> tags, you should have a <FRAME> tag indicating which HTML document to display in each frame. (If you have fewer <FRAME> tags than the number of frames defined in the <FRAMESET> tag, any remaining frames will be left blank.) You don't need to specify a closing </FRAME> tag.

Include an SRC attribute in each <FRAME> tag with the address of the Web page to load in that frame. (You can put the address of an image file instead of a Web page if you just want a frame with a single image in it.)

You can include any HTML page you want to in a frame. For smaller frames, however, it's a good idea to create documents specifically for the frames with the reduced display area for each frame in mind. The top frame in Figure 21.1, for instance, is listed first in Figure 21.4. It is much shorter than most Web pages, because it was designed specifically to fit in a frame under 75 pixels tall.

You may notice that the <A> and <IMG> tags in the banner.htm document in Figure 21.4 are arranged a bit strangely. Since I didn't want any space between the graphics, I had to make sure there were no spaces or line breaks between any of the tags. Therefore, I had to put all the line breaks inside the tags, between attributes. This makes the HTML a bit hard to read, but keeps the images right next to each other on the page.

21

FIGURE 21.4.

These two Web pages were designed specifically to fit in frames of Figure 21.1. (The bottom document in Figure 21.2 is not listed here.)

The banner.htm document:

```
<HTML><HEAD><TITLE>The Entropy Almanac</TITLE></HEAD>
<BODY BACKGROUND="back.gif">
<A HREF="greeting.htm"
 TARGET="main"><IMG SRC="eatiny.gif"
 BORDER=0 ALIGN="left"></A><A HREF="news.htm"
 TARGET="main"><IMG SRC="news.gif"
 BORDER=0></A><A HREF="facts.htm"
 TARGET="main"><IMG SRC="facts.gif"
 BORDER=0></A><A HREF="tales.htm"
 TARGET="main"><IMG SRC="tales.gif" BORDER=0></A>
</DIV></BODY></HTML>
```

The greeting.htm document:

```
<HTML><HEAD><TITLE>The Entropy Almanac</TITLE></HEAD>
<BODY BACKGROUND="back.gif">
<DIV ALIGN="center">
<IMG SRC="easmall.gif"><BR><IMG SRC="1999.gif"><P>
The Entropy Almanac is an eclectic compendium of
philosophical illuminations, mathematical profundities,
cutting-edge science, and high-tech tools.<P>
Choose a category above to begin your explorations.
</DIV></BODY></HTML>
```

Linking Between Frames and Windows

The real fun begins when you give a frame a name with the FRAME NAME attribute. You can then make any link on the page change the contents of that frame by using the A TARGET attribute. For example, Figure 21.3 includes the following tag:

```
<FRAME SRC="greeting.htm" NAME="main">
```

This displays the greeting.htm page in that frame when the page loads, and names the frame "main".

In the top frame, listed in Figure 21.4, you will see the following link:

```
<A HREF="facts.htm" TARGET="main"><IMG SRC="facts.gif" BORDER=0></A>
```

When the user clicks this link, the facts.htm page is displayed in the frame named main (the lower frame). To accomplish this sort of interactivity before the invention of frames, you would have had to use complex programming or scripting languages. Now you can do it with a simple link!

If the TARGET="main" attribute hadn't been included, the facts.htm page would be displayed in the current (top) frame instead.

To save space, I haven't listed the `facts.htm` page in a figure; it's just a regular Web page with no special frame-related features. You can see what the top of it looks like in Figure 21.2, and you can see this whole frameset online at `http://24hourHTMLcafe.com/hour21`.

When you include the TARGET attribute in a link, you can use a few special frame names in addition to the names you have defined with FRAME NAME.

- _blank loads the link into a new, unnamed window.
- _self loads the link into the current frame, replacing the document now being displayed in this frame.
- _top loads the link into the entire browser window. Use this when you want to get rid of all frames or replace the entire window with a whole new set of frames.
- _parent loads the link over the parent frame if the current frame is nested within other frames. (This name does the same thing as _top unless the frames are nested more than one level deep.)

Note that all other names beginning with an underscore (_) will be ignored.

Nested Frames

By nesting one <FRAMESET> within another, you can create rather complex frame layouts. For example, the document shown in Figure 21.5 and listed in Figure 21.6 has a total of nine frames. A COLS frameset is used to split each row of the ROWS frameset into three pieces.

Figure 21.7 lists the HTML for all nine of the separate Web pages shown in Figure 21.5. The corners and side frames contain blank HTML documents, showing nothing more than specially designed background tiles. The top frame is a permanent title graphic, and the bottom frame is a navigation bar similar to the one shown in the previous example. The net effect is to surround the middle frame within a sort of "picture frame" border. Figure 21.8 shows thumbnails of all the background tiles and other graphics incorporated into the pages.

21

FIGURE 21.5.

This window contains nine frames, some of which are nothing more than blank pages with custom background tiles.

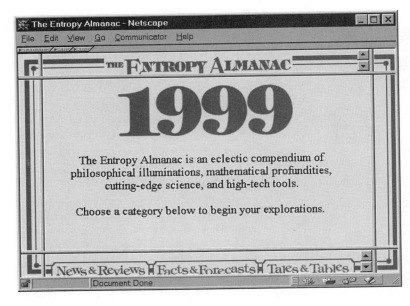

FIGURE 21.6.

To create Figure 21.5, I used three horizontal <FRAMESET>s within a vertical <FRAMESET>.

```
<HTML><HEAD><TITLE>The Entropy Almanac</TITLE></HEAD>
<FRAMESET ROWS="43,*,43">
  <FRAMESET COLS="43,*,43">
    <FRAME SRC="ctoplft.htm" NAME="toplft">
    <FRAME SRC="bordtop.htm" NAME="top">
    <FRAME SRC="ctoprgt.htm" NAME="toprgt">
  </FRAMESET>
  <FRAMESET COLS="43,*,43">
    <FRAME SRC="bordlft.htm" NAME="left">
    <FRAME SRC="main.htm" NAME="main">
    <FRAME SRC="bordrgt.htm" NAME="right">
  </FRAMESET>
  <FRAMESET COLS="43,*,43">
    <FRAME SRC="cbtmlft.htm" NAME="btmlft">
    <FRAME SRC="bordbtm.htm" NAME="btm">
    <FRAME SRC="cbtmrgt.htm" NAME="btmrgt">
  </FRAMESET>
</FRAMESET>
</HTML>
```

FIGURE 21.7.

The nine separate HTML documents shown in Figure 21.5, and referred to in Figure 21.6.

The ctoplft.htm document:
```
<HTML><BODY BACKGROUND="ctoplft.gif"></BODY></HTML>
```

The bordtop.htm document:
```
<HTML><HEAD><TITLE>The Entropy Almanac</TITLE></HEAD>
<BODY BACKGROUND="bordtop.gif">
<DIV ALIGN="center">
<A HREF="main.htm" TARGET="main">
<IMG SRC="easmall.gif" BORDER=0></A>
</DIV></BODY></HTML>
```

The ctoprgt.htm document:
```
<HTML><BODY BACKGROUND="ctoprgt.gif"></BODY></HTML>
```

The bordlft.htm document:
```
<HTML><BODY BACKGROUND="bordlft.gif"></BODY></HTML>
```

The main.htm document:
```
<HTML><HEAD><TITLE>The Entropy Almanac</TITLE></HEAD>
<BODY BACKGROUND="back.gif">
<DIV ALIGN="center"><IMG SRC="1999.gif"><P>
The Entropy Almanac is an eclectic compendium of
philosophical illuminations, mathematical profundities,
cutting-edge science, and high-tech tools.<P>
Choose a category below to begin your explorations.
</DIV></BODY></HTML>
```

The bordrgt.htm document:
```
<HTML><BODY BACKGROUND="bordrgt.gif"></BODY></HTML>
```

The cbtmlft.htm document:
```
<HTML><BODY BACKGROUND="cbtmlft.gif"></BODY></HTML>
```

The bordbtm.htm document:
```
<HTML><HEAD><TITLE>The Entropy Almanac</TITLE></HEAD>
<BODY BACKGROUND="bordbtm.gif"><DIV ALIGN="center">
<A HREF="news.htm" TARGET="main">
<IMG SRC="news.gif" BORDER=0></A>
<A HREF="facts.htm" TARGET="main">
<IMG SRC="facts.gif" BORDER=0></A>
<A HREF="tales.htm" TARGET="main">
<IMG SRC="tales.gif" BORDER=0></A>
</DIV></BODY></HTML>
```

The cbtmrgt.htm document:
```
<HTML><BODY BACKGROUND="cbtmrgt.gif"></BODY></HTML>
```

21

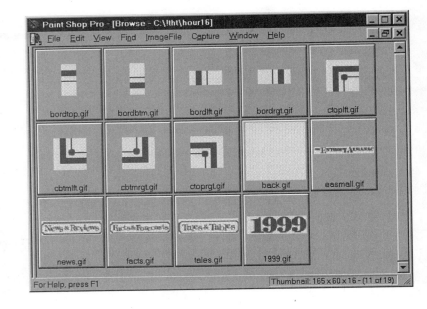

FIGURE 21.8.

To create the border effect in Figures 21.5 and 21.9, I designed several custom background tiles and matching title graphics.

Margins, Borders, and Scrolling

The problem with the nine-frame arrangement in Figure 21.5 is that it looks ugly and stupid. We can fix that.

The ugly parts are the gray dividers between the frames, which completely ruin the effect of surrounding the center frame with nicely designed graphics. There also isn't enough room in the top and bottom frames to display the graphics without scrollbars. Fortunately, there are HTML commands to get rid of the frame dividers, make more space in small frames by reducing the size of the margins, and force frames not to have scrollbars.

Before you read about these HTML magic tricks, take a look at the dramatic results they can achieve. Figure 21.9 is a nine-frame window displaying the same Web pages shown in Figure 21.5. Obviously, Figure 21.9 looks much nicer! In Figure 21.10, You can see the anti-ugliness medication I gave to the frameset code from Figure 21.6.

In addition to the NAME attribute, the <FRAME> tag can take the following special frame-related attributes:

- MARGINWIDTH   Left and right margins of the frame (in pixels).
- MARGINHEIGHT   Top and bottom margins of the frame (in pixels).
- SCROLLING   Display scrollbar for the frame? ("yes" or "no")

FIGURE 21.9.

Like Figure 21.5, this is actually nine separate Web pages being displayed in nine frames.

```
<HTML><HEAD><TITLE>The Entropy Almanac</TITLE></HEAD>
<FRAMESET ROWS="43,*,43" BORDER=0>
  <FRAMESET COLS="43,*,43" BORDER=0>
    <FRAME SRC="ctoplft.htm" NAME="toplft"
     SCROLLING=NO FRAMEBORDER=0>
    <FRAME SRC="bordtop.htm" NAME="top"
     SCROLLING=NO FRAMEBORDER=0 MARGINHEIGHT=1>
    <FRAME SRC="ctoprgt.htm" NAME="toprgt"
     SCROLLING=NO FRAMEBORDER=0>
  </FRAMESET>
  <FRAMESET COLS="43,*,43" BORDER=0>
    <FRAME SRC="bordlft.htm" NAME="left"
     SCROLLING=NO FRAMEBORDER=0>
    <FRAME SRC="main.htm" NAME="main" FRAMEBORDER=0>
    <FRAME SRC="bordrgt.htm" NAME="right"
     SCROLLING=NO FRAMEBORDER=0>
  </FRAMESET>
  <FRAMESET COLS="43,*,43" BORDER=0>
    <FRAME SRC="cbtmlft.htm" NAME="btmlft"
     SCROLLING=NO FRAMEBORDER=0>
    <FRAME SRC="bordbtm.htm" NAME="btm"
     SCROLLING=NO FRAMEBORDER=0 MARGINHEIGHT=1>
    <FRAME SRC="cbtmrgt.htm" NAME="btmrgt"
     SCROLLING=NO FRAMEBORDER=0>
    <FRAME SRC="cbtmrgt.htm" NAME="btmrgt"
     SCROLLING=NO FRAMEBORDER=0>
  </FRAMESET>
</FRAMESET>
</HTML>
```

FIGURE 21.10.

The frameset document shown in Figure 21.9. By adding some attributes to the <FRAME> tags, I was able to make the frames look much nicer.

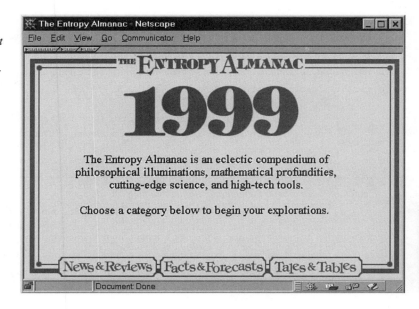

21

- FRAMEBORDER Display dividers between this frame and adjacent frames? (1 means yes, 0 means no.)

- NORESIZE Don't allow this frame to be resized by the user.

MARGINWIDTH and MARGINHEIGHT are pretty self-explanatory, but each of the other attributes is discussed in detail in the next few paragraphs.

Normally, any frame that isn't big enough to hold all of its contents will have its own scrollbar(s). The top and bottom frames in Figures 21.5 are examples. If you don't want a particular frame to ever display scrollbars, you can put SCROLLING=NO in the <FRAME> tag. Conversely, SCROLLING=YES forces both horizontal and vertical scrollbars to appear, whether they are needed or not.

When graphics just fit within a small frame, Netscape Navigator and Microsoft Internet Explorer often display scrollbars that only scroll a few pixels down and have no real purpose. Rather than make the frame bigger (and take up valuable window real estate with empty margin space), you will often want to just turn off the scrollbars with SCROLLING=NO.

The only situation I can think of where you might want to use SCROLLING=YES is if some graphics won't line up right unless you can count on the scrollbars always being there. Chances are, you'll probably never need SCROLLING=YES.

People viewing your frames can ordinarily resize them by grabbing the frame border with the mouse and dragging it around. If you don't want anyone messing with the size of a frame, put NORESIZE in the <FRAME> tag.

Both Microsoft Internet Explorer and Netscape Navigator allow you to control the size of the frame borders, or eliminate the borders altogether. This makes a frame document look just like regular Web page, with no ugly lines breaking it up.

Unfortunately, for maximum compatibility you need to use need to use three different sets of HTML tags.

- For Netscape Navigator and Microsoft Internet Explorer 4.0, use BORDER=0 in the <FRAMESET> tag to eliminate borders, or BORDER= followed by a number of pixels to change the size of the frame borders.

- If you want borderless frames to show up in all recent versions of both popular browsers, type FRAMEBORDERS=NO BORDER=0 in your <FRAMESET> tag.

And guess what? The official HTML 4.0 standard actually specifies yet another method for eliminating frame borders. To be compatible with that standard, you need to put a FRAMEBORDER=0 attribute in every single <FRAME> tag (not just the <FRAMESET> tags). This doesn't have any effect in any existing browser, but it's a good idea to include it now to avoid future compatibility problems.

The frameset document in Figure 21.10 uses all these methods, just to be thorough. I recommend you do the same.

Borderless frames, when used together with custom graphics, can allow you to create sites that are easier to navigate and more pleasant to visit. For example, when someone visits the site in Figure 21.9 and clicks one of the navigation choices in the bottom frame, the page she chose comes up in the middle frame quickly, because the title graphic, navigation buttons, and border graphics all remain in place. The frames will also automatically adapt to changes in the size of the browser window, so the nice "picture frame" effect looks just as good at 1024×768 resolution as it does at 640×480.

Figure 21.11 shows the result of clicking the "Facts & Forecasts" link in Figure 21.10. Note that the middle frame gets its own scrollbar whenever the contents are too big to fit in the frame.

FIGURE 21.11.

Clicking a link at the bottom of Figure 21.10 brings up a new page in the middle frame, without redrawing any of the other frames.

21

The official HTML 4.0 standard includes a tag, <IFRAME>, for embedding a frame into an HTML page. For example, the following would display the page mybio.htm in a 200×200-pixel region, underneath the heading "Short Bios." (If the document mybio.htm didn't fit in that small region, it would have its own little scrollbar(s) next to it.)

```
<HTML><HEAD><TITLE>Bios</TITLE></HEAD><BODY>
<H1>Short Bios</H1>
<IFRAME NAME="bioframe" SRC="mybio.htm" WIDTH=200 HEIGHT=200>
</IFRAME><P>
<A HREF="yourbio.htm" TARGET="bioframe" >Your Bio</A><P>
<A HREF="mybio.htm" TARGET="bioframe">My Bio</A>
</BODY></HTML>
```

Clicking the "Your Bio" link would replace the contents of the 200×200-pixel region with yourbio.htm. Clicking "My Bio" would put mybio.htm back into that region.

Unfortunately, the only browser that currently understands the <IFRAME> tag is Microsoft Internet Explorer. The tag will be ignored by Netscape Navigator and all other current Web browsers, so it isn't of much practical use today unless *all* your intended audience will be using Internet Explorer version 3.0 or later. Other browsers should support it in the future. (You can view an <IFRAME> example online at http://24hourHTMLcafe.com/hour21 if you have Microsoft Internet Explorer.)

Summary

In this hour, you learned how to display more than one page at a time by splitting the Web browser window into *frames*. You learned to use a *frameset document* to define the size and arrangement of the frames, as well as which Web page or image will be loaded into each frame. You saw how to create links that change the contents of any frame you choose, while leaving the other frames unchanged. You also discovered several optional settings that control the appearance of resizable borders and scrollbars in frames. Finally, you saw how to nest framesets to create complex frame layouts.

Table 21.1 summarizes the tags and attributes covered in this hour.

TABLE 21.1. HTML TAGS AND ATTRIBUTES COVERED IN HOUR 21.

Tag/Attribute	Function
`<FRAMESET>...</FRAMESET>`	Divides the main window into a set of frames that can each display a separate document.
	Attributes:
`ROWS="..."`	Splits the window or frameset vertically into a number of rows specified by a number (such as 7), a percentage of the total window width (such as 25%), or as an asterisk (*) indicating that a frame should take up all the remaining space, or divide the space evenly between frames (if multiple * frames are specified).
`COLS="..."`	Works similar to ROWS, except that the window or frameset is split horizontally into columns.
`FRAMESPACING="..."`	Space between frames, in pixels (Microsoft Internet Explorer 3.0 only).
`FRAMEBORDER="..."`	Specifies whether to display a border for the frames. Options are YES and NO. (Microsoft Internet Explorer 3.0 only.)
`BORDER="..."`	Size of the frame borders in pixels (Netscape Navigator only.)
`<FRAME>`	Defines a single frame within a `<FRAMESET>`.
	Attributes:
`SRC="..."`	The URL of the document to be displayed in this frame.
`NAME="..."`	A name to be used for targeting this frame with the TARGET attribute in `<A HREF>` links.
`<MARGINWIDTH>`	The amount of space (in pixels) to leave to the left and right side of a document within a frame.
`<MARGINHEIGHT>`	The amount of space (in pixels) to leave above and below a document within a frame.
`SCROLLING="..."`	Determines whether a frame has scrollbars. Possible values are YES, NO, and AUTO.
`NORESIZE`	Prevents the user from resizing this frame (and possibly adjacent frames) with the mouse.
`<NOFRAMES>...</NOFRAMES>`	Provides an alternative document body in `<FRAMESET>` documents for browsers that do not support frames (usually encloses `<BODY>...</BODY>`).
`<IFRAME>...</IFRAME>`	Creates an inline frame. Currently only works in Microsoft Internet Explorer version 3.0 or later.
	(`<IFRAME>` *accepts all the same attributes as* `<FRAME>`.)

21

Q&A

Q **Can I display other people's Web pages from the Internet in one frame, and my own pages in another frame at the same time? What if those sites use frames, too?**

A You can load any document from anywhere on the Internet (or an intranet) into a frame. If the document is a frameset, its frames will be sized to fit within the existing frame into which you load it.

For example, you could put a "hotlist" of your favorite links in one frame, and have the pages that those links refer to appear in a separate frame. This makes it easy to provide links to other sites without risking that someone will "get lost" and never come back to your own site. Note, however, that if any link within that site has TARGET="_top" it will replace all your frames.

You should also be aware that "framing" somebody else's pages so that they appear to be part of your own site may get you in legal trouble. Several major lawsuits are pending on this exact issue, so be sure to get explicit written permission from anyone whose pages you plan to put within one of your frames (just as you would if you were putting images or text from their site on your own pages).

Q **Can I prevent people from putting my pages in their frames, and making my lovely pages look like part of their sleazy site?**

A Yes. To "frame-proof" any page, put the following JavaScript "secret code" in the <BODY> tag:

```
<BODY ONLOAD="if (self != top) top.location = self.location">
```

The page will then always appear by itself, with no other frames visible, even if the link that called it up was within a frame.

Q **Do I need to put a <TITLE> in all my frames? If I do, which title will be displayed at the top of the window?**

A The title of the frameset document is the only one that will be displayed. <HEAD> and <TITLE> tags are not required in framed documents, but it's a good idea to give all your pages titles just in case somebody opens one by itself outside any frame.

Workshop

Quiz

1. Write the HTML to list the names Mickey, Minnie, and Donald in a frame taking up the left 25 percent of the browser window. Make it so that clicking each name brings up a corresponding Web page in the right 75 percent of the browser window.

2. Write a frameset document to make the frame layout pictured here:

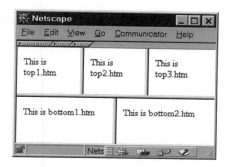

Answers

1. You need five separate HTML documents. The first document is the frameset:

```
<HTML><HEAD><TITLE>Our Friends</TITLE></HEAD>
<FRAMESET COLS="25%,75%">
<FRAME SRC="index.htm">
<FRAME SRC="mickey.htm" NAME="mainframe">
</FRAMESET>
</HTML>
```

Next, you need the index.htm document for the left frame:

```
<HTML><HEAD><TITLE>Our Friends Index</TITLE></HEAD>
<BODY>
Pick a friend:<P>
<A HREF="mickey.htm" TARGET="mainframe">Mickey</A><P>
<A HREF="minnie.htm" TARGET="mainframe">Minnie</A><P>
<A HREF="donald.htm" TARGET="mainframe">Donald</A><P>
</BODY></HTML>
```

Finally, you need the three HTML pages named mickey.htm, minnie.htm, and donald.htm. Those would contain the information about each friend.

21

2.
```
<HTML><HEAD><TITLE>Nested Frames</TITLE></HEAD>
<FRAMESET ROWS="*,*">
 <FRAMESET COLS="*,*,*">
 <FRAME SRC="top1.htm">
 <FRAME SRC="top2.htm">
 <FRAME SRC="top3.htm">
 </FRAMESET>
 <FRAMESET COLS="*,*">
 <FRAME SRC="bottom1.htm">
 <FRAME SRC="bottom2.htm">
 </FRAMESET>
</FRAMESET>
</HTML>
```

Exercise

In Hour 23, "Helping People Find Your Web Pages," you'll find out how to make a page that loads another page automatically after a specified time interval. When you combine that trick with frames, you can create all sorts of interesting animated layout effects.

HOUR 22

Organizing and Managing a Web Site

The first twenty-one hours of this book led you through the design and creation of your own Web pages and the graphics to put on them. Now it's time to stop thinking about individual Web pages and start thinking about your Web site as a whole.

This hour shows you how to organize and present multiple Web pages, so that people will be able to navigate among them without confusion, and ways to make your Web site memorable enough to visit again and again.

Because Web sites can be (and usually should be) updated frequently, creating pages that can be easily maintained is essential. This hour shows you how to add comments and other documentation to your pages so that you—or anyone else on your staff—can understand and modify your pages.

To Do

By this point in the book, you should have enough knowledge of HTML to produce most of your Web site. You have probably made a number of pages already, and perhaps even published them online.

As you read this hour, think about how your pages are organized now and how you can improve that organization. Don't be surprised if you decide to do a "redesign" that involves changing almost all of your pages—the results are likely to be well worth the effort!

When One Page Is Enough

Building and organizing an attractive and effective Web site doesn't always need to be a complex task. In some cases, you can effectively present a great deal of useful information on a single page, without a lot of flashy graphics. In fact, there are several advantages to a single-page site:

- All the information on the site downloads as quickly as possible.
- The whole site can be printed out on paper with a single print command, even if it is several paper pages long.
- Visitors can easily save the site on their hard drive for future reference, especially if it uses a minimum of graphics.
- Links between different parts of the same page usually respond more quickly than links to other pages.

Figure 22.1 shows the first part of a Web page that serves its intended audience better as a single lengthy page than it would as a multipage site. It contains about eight paper pages worth of text explaining how to participate in a popular email discussion list.

The page begins, as most introductory pages should, with a succinct explanation of what the page is about and who would want to read it. Then a detailed table of contents allows readers to skip directly to the reference material in which they are most interested. (Refer to Hour 7, "Email Links and Links Within a Page," for a refresher on how to build a table of contents.)

As Figure 22.2 shows, each short section of the page is followed by a link back up to the table of contents, so navigating around the page feels much the same as navigating around a multipage site. Since the contents of the page are intended as a handy reference, its readers will definitely prefer the convenience of being able to bookmark or save a single page instead of eight or ten separate pages.

FIGURE 22.1.

A good table of contents can make a lengthy page easy to navigate.

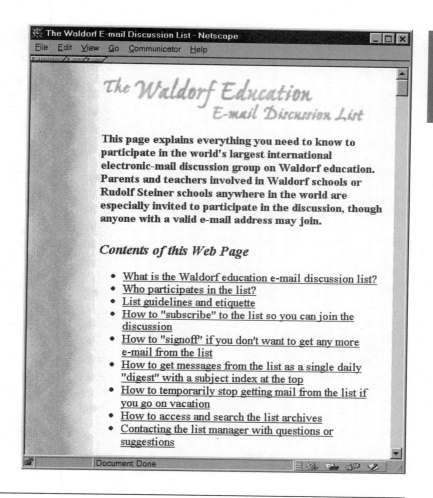

Having seen all the fancy graphics and layout tricks in the book, you may be tempted to forget that a good old-fashioned outline is often the most clear and efficient way to organize a Web site. Even if your site does require multiple pages, a list like the table of contents in Figure 22.1 may be the best way to guide people through a relatively small Web site——or subsections of a larger one.

FIGURE 22.2.

Always provide a link back to the table of contents after each section of a long Web page.

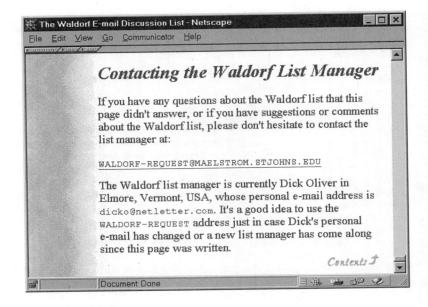

Organizing a Simple Site

Though single-page sites have their place, most companies and individuals will serve their readers better by dividing their site into short, quick-read pages with graphical navigation icons to move between the pages. That way, the entire site doesn't have to be downloaded by someone seeking specific information.

The goal of the home page in Figure 22.3, like the goal of many Web sites today, is simply to make the organization "visible" on the Internet. Many people today immediately turn to the World Wide Web when they want to find out about an organization, or find out whether a particular type of organization exists at all. A simple home page should state enough information so that someone can tell whether they want to find out more. It should then provide both traditional address and telephone contact information and an electronic mail address, either directly on the home page or via a prominent link (like the ABOUT NEW VISIONS button in Figure 22.3).

One of the most common mistakes that beginning Web site producers make is making each page on the site look different than the one before. Another equally serious mistake is using the same, publicly available "clip art" that thousands of other Web authors are also using. Remember that on the Internet, one click can take you around the world. The only way to make your pages memorable and recognizable as a cohesive site is to make all your pages adhere to a unique, unmistakable visual theme.

FIGURE 22.3.

This small-business home page uses distinctive graphics and no-nonsense text to quickly convey the intended mood and purpose of the site.

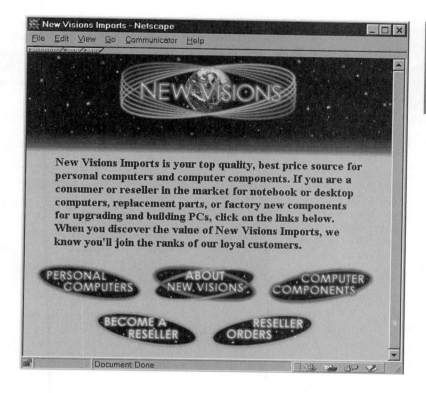

For example, when someone clicks the COMPUTER COMPONENTS link in Figure 22.3, he is taken to the page in Figure 22.4. The visual reiteration of the link as a title, and the repetition of the background, logo, and link graphics all make it immediately obvious that this page is part of the same site as the previous page. (Reusing as many graphics from the home page as possible also speeds display, since these images are already cached on the reader's computer.)

The page in Figure 22.4 avoids another common disease that beginning Web authors too often catch; I call it the "construction site" syndrome. If you've looked around the Internet very much, I'm sure you're as sick as I am of cute little road worker icons and dead-end pages that say nothing but "Under Construction." Please remember that when you put your pages on the Internet, you are publishing them just as surely as if a print shop were running off 10,000 copies. No publisher would ever annoy readers by printing a brochure, book, or newspaper with useless pages saying only "Under Construction." Don't annoy your readers, either: If a page isn't ready to go online, *don't put it online* until it is ready, and don't put any links to it on your other pages yet.

Even though the page in Figure 22.4 does let the reader know that the site will offer an online parts database in the future, it also makes it clear how to price and order components today.

FIGURE 22.4.

Clicking COMPUTER COMPONENTS in Figure 22.3 takes you here. The graphical theme makes it instantly clear that this is part of the same site.

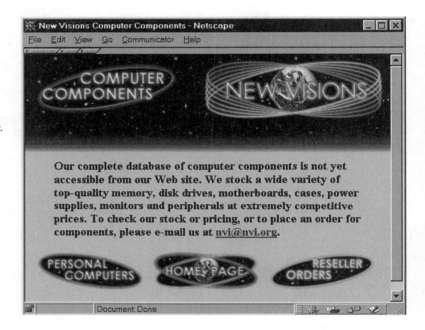

Organizing a Larger Site

For complex sites, sophisticated layout and graphics can help organize and improve the looks of your site when used consistently throughout all of your pages. To see how you can make aesthetics and organization work hand-in-hand, let's look at a site that needs to present a large volume of information to several different audiences.

Figure 22.5 shows the top part of the Center for Journal Therapy home page. This site currently provides access to the equivalent of about 75 paper pages of text, in the form of 25 electronic documents. As the Center for Journal Therapy continues to publish newsletters, directories, and instructional materials, the site is likely to expand to hundreds of paper pages worth of information. (If you would like to view this site online, go to http://www.journaltherapy.com.)

FIGURE 22.5.

The four links at the top of this page lead to a surprising wealth of information.

The first page a visitor sees should always begin by explaining what the site is about, and providing enough introductory information to "hook" the intended audience while getting rid of anyone who really has no interest. The Center for Journal Therapy site does this with a photo and note from Kay Adams, whose face and name are well known by much of the target audience. After the welcome note, the home page offers brief sections with the headings, "What is Journal Therapy?," "About the Center for Journal Therapy," and "About Kathleen Adams," followed by the address, telephone numbers, and email address of the organization. This is a worthy model for any organization's home page to imitate, though in cases where a prominent personality is not a main feature of the site it's usually best to skip the "Welcome" and go straight into the "What is..." introduction.

If there's one thing I would change about the page in Figure 22.5, it would be the lack of emphasis on benefits to the reader. It is absolutely essential, especially for commercial sites or any site intending to serve the needs of some audience, to make the very first words on the page explain *why* it would benefit a reader to look further. Research shows that you have 3 to 5 seconds to convince visitors that your site is worth their attention before they head elsewhere, possibly never to return. Use those seconds wisely! (Hint: Is the phrase "Welcome to the Home Page of..." worth wasting two of those precious seconds on?)

The Center for Journal Therapy site is intended to serve at least three distinct groups: therapists and laypersons just discovering journal therapy, professionals who already use journal therapy in their practice, and journal therapy instructors. Many other Web sites are similar in that they need to address both newcomers and people who are already knowledgeable about the subject of the site.

The site in Figures 22.5 and 22.6 is organized into four main categories of pages, accessible through the four "hand written" link icons that appear at the top of each page. It's important to notice that these icons were chosen to give each of the three different audiences a choice that would clearly meet their needs. Always organize the main links on your site according to the questions or desires of your readers, not the structure of the information itself. For example, some of the same information is available in the "Resource Center" and in the "Instructor Center" on this site. This redundancy serves both audiences well, because it gives them a place to find everything they need without wading through material they aren't interested in.

Figure 22.6 is the page you would get if you clicked Instructor Center, the imagemap in Figure 22.5. The graphics at the top provide a strong visual relationship to the original page, and provide quick access to the rest of the site, including the home page. All the contact information is also repeated at the bottom of the page; it's almost never a bad idea to put your name, address, and phone number on all the major pages of your site if you want to encourage readers to contact you.

The page in Figure 22.6 serves as a "passage" from the home page to all the resources on the site that are likely to be of interest to journal therapy instructors. Providing topic-specific link pages like this one is a much less confusing way of organizing large quantities of information than some of the alternatives beginning Web publishers often choose instead. It's all too common to see home pages with a dozen or more links arranged in a long list or string of buttons. That many links all in one group will inevitably confuse readers and make your site hard to use.

FIGURE 22.6.

If you click Instructor Center in Figure 22.5, you get this page.

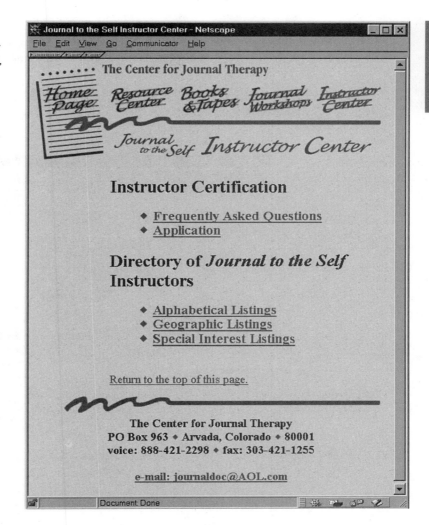

In all aspects of your site design, keep in mind the following fact: studies have repeatedly shown that people become confused and annoyed when presented with more than seven choices at a time, and people feel most comfortable with five of fewer choices. Therefore, you should avoid presenting more than five links (either in a list, or as graphical icons) next to one another, and never present more than seven at once. When you need to present more than seven text links, break them up into multiple lists with a separate heading for each five to seven items.

It will also help your readers navigate your site without confusion if you avoid putting any page more than two (or at most three) links away from the home page, and always send readers back to a main category page (or the home page) after reading a subsidiary page. Figure 22.7 shows the page you would get by clicking the Alphabetical Listings link in Figure 22.6. This page, like all pages in the Center for Journal Therapy site, is never more than two clicks away from the home page, even though it can be reached by multiple routes.

FIGURE 22.7.

Subsidiary pages don't include all the graphics links in Figures 22.5 and 22.6, but they do follow the same visual theme.

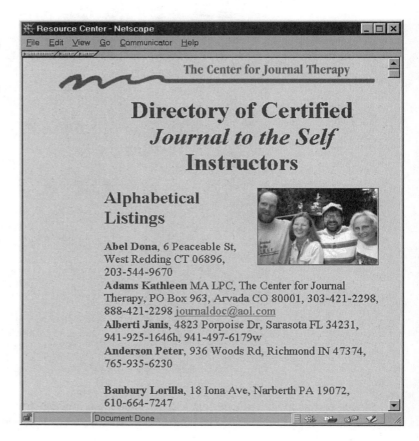

Clicking The Center for Journal Therapy at the very top of Figure 22.7 will take the reader back to the home page. The link uses an absolute address (`http://www.journaltherapy.com/`) instead of a relative address (`welcome.htm`), so that anyone who saves the page on his hard drive can still go to the online site by clicking this link. See Hour 3, "Linking to Other Web Pages," for a review of absolute and relative addresses.

Including Comments in a Page

Whenever you type an HTML page, keep in mind that you or someone else will almost certainly need to make changes to it someday. Simple text pages are easy to read and revise, but complex Web pages with graphics, tables, and other layout tricks can be quite difficult to decipher.

As you saw in Hour 20, "Setting Pages in Motion with Dynamic HTML," you can enclose comments to yourself or your co-authors between <!-- and --> tags. These comments will not appear on the Web page when viewed with a browser, but can be read by anyone who examines the HTML code with a text editor, word processor, or the a Web browser's View, Source command.

> To include comments in a JavaScript script, put // at the beginning of each comment line (no "closing tag" is needed for JavaScript comments). In style sheets, start comments with /* and end them with */. The HTML <!-- and --> tags will *NOT* work properly in scripts or style sheets!
>
> You can and should, however, include one <!-- tag just after a <SCRIPT> or <STYLE> tag, with a --> tag just before the matching </SCRIPT> or </STYLE>. This will hide the script or style commands from older browsers that would otherwise treat them as regular text and display them on the page.

To Do

It will be well worth your time now to go through all the Web pages, scripts, and style sheets you've created so far and add any comments that you or others might find helpful when revising them in the future.

1. Put a comment explaining any fancy formatting or layout techniques before the tags that make it happen.

2. Use a comment just before an <IMG> tag to briefly describe any important graphic whose function isn't obvious from the ALT message.

3. Always use a comment (or several comments) to summarize how the cells of a <TABLE> are supposed to fit together visually.

4. If you use hexadecimal color codes (such as <FONT COLOR="#8040B0">), insert a comment indicating what the color actually is ("blueish-purple").

5. Indenting your comments helps them to stand out, and makes both the comments and the HTML easier to read. Don't forget to use indentation in the HTML itself to make it more readable, too.

Summary

This hour has given you examples and explanations to help you organize your Web pages into a coherent site that is informative, attractive, and easy to navigate.

This hour also discussed the importance of making your HTML easy to maintain by adding comments and indentation to your HTML code.

Q&A

Q I've seen pages that ask viewers to change the width of their browser window or adjust other settings before proceeding beyond the home page. Why?

A The idea is that the Web page author can offer a better presentation if they have some control over the size of reader's windows or fonts. Of course, nobody ever bothers to change their settings, so these sites always look weird or unreadable. You'll be much better off using the tips you learn in this book to make your site readable and attractive at any window size and a wide variety of browser settings.

Q Won't lots of comments and spaces make my pages load slower when someone views them?

A All modems compress text when transmitting it, so adding spaces to format your HTML doesn't usually change the transfer time at all. You'd have to type hundreds of words of comments to cause even one extra second of delay when loading a page. It's the graphics that slow pages down, so squeeze your images as tightly as you can (refer to Hour 13, "Page Design and Layout"), but use text comments freely.

Q Will you look at my site and give me some suggestions on how to improve it?

A I'd like to, really. Truly I would. But if I looked at all my readers' sites and offered even a tiny bit of wisdom for each, I would be at it for hours every day. (Go to http://24hourHTMLcafe.com/mysite.htm for a form to tell me your site address. No promises, but I usually find time to take a peek.) I have looked at hundreds of reader sites, and usually, my advice always amounts to this: "Your site looks pretty and/or ugly, and you've got the basic idea of HTML, but you need to make it more clear (a) who your site is intended for—right in the first sentence or heading, (b) what earthly good your site is going to do them, and (c) what you want them to do as a result of visiting your site." All the great graphics and HTML-manship in the world can't substitute for clearly and consistently answering those three questions for yourself and your site's visitors.

Workshop

Quiz

1. What are three ways to help people stay aware that all your pages form a single "site"?

2. What two types of information should always be included in the first home page that people encounter at your site?

3. If you wanted to say, "Don't change this image of me. It's my only chance at immortality," to future editors of a Web page, but you didn't want people who view the page to see that message, how would you do it?

Answers

1. (a) Using consistent background, colors, fonts, and styles.

   (b) Repeat the same link words or graphics on the top of the page the link leads to.

   (c) Repeat the same small header, buttons, or other element on every page of the site.

2. (a) Enough identifying information so that they can immediately tell the name of the site and what the site is about.

   (b) Whatever the most important message you want to convey to your intended audience is, stated directly and concisely.

3. Put the following just before the <IMG> tag:

   ```
   <!-- Don't change this image of me.
        It's my only chance at immortality. -->
   ```

Exercise

Grab a pencil (the oldfangled kind) and sketch out your Web site as a bunch of little rectangles with arrows between them. Then sketch a rough overview of what each page will look like by putting squiggles where the text goes and doodles where the images go. Each arrow should start at a doodle-icon that corresponds to the navigation button for the page the arrow leads to. This can give you a good intuitive grasp of which pages on your site will be easy to get to, and how the layout of adjacent pages will work together—all before you invest time in writing the actual HTML to connect the pages together.

Hour 23

Helping People Find Your Pages

The HTML tags and techniques you'll discover in this hour won't make any visible difference in your Web pages, but they will help make your Web pages much more visible to your intended audience. For most Web authors, this may be the easiest—but most important—hour in the book. You will learn how to make links to your pages appear at all the major Internet search sites whenever someone searches for words related to your topic or company. There are no "magic secrets" to guarantee that you'll be at the top of every search list, but there are many reliable and effective techniques you can employ to make sure your site is as easy to find as possible.

This chapter also shows you how to make one page automatically load another, how to forward visitors to pages that have moved, and how to document the full Internet address of a page.

Publicizing Your Web Site

Presumably, you want your Web pages to attract someone's attention or you wouldn't bother to create them. If you are placing your pages only on a local network or corporate intranet, or distributing your pages exclusively on disk or by email, helping people find your pages may not be much of an problem. If you are adding your pages to the millions upon millions of others on the Internet, however, bringing your intended audience to your site is a very big problem indeed.

To tackle this problem, you need a basic understanding of how most people decide which pages they will look at. There are basically three ways that people can become aware of your Web site:

- Somebody tells them about it and gives them the address, and they enter that address directly into their Web browser.
- They follow a link to your site from someone else's site.
- They find your site listed in a search site such as Yahoo! or HotBot.

You can make all three of them happen more often if you invest some time and effort into it. To increase the number of people who hear about you through word-of-mouth, well, use your mouth! And every other channel of communication available to you; if you have an existing contact database or mailing list, announce your Web site to those people. Add the site address to your business cards or company literature. Heck, go buy TV ads broadcasting your Internet address if you've got the money. In short, do the marketing thing.

Getting links to your site from other sites is also pretty straightforward—though that doesn't mean it isn't a lot of work. Find every other Web site related to your topic, and offer to add a link to their site if they add one to yours. If there are specialized directories on your topic, either online or in print, be sure you are listed. There's not much I can say in this book to help you with that, except to go out and do it.

What I can help you with in this book is the third item above, being visible at the major Internet search sites. I'm sure you've used at least one or two of the "big six" search sites: Yahoo!, AltaVista, HotBot, Excite, Infoseek, and Lycos. (The addresses of these sites are just what you'd think: `yahoo.com`, `altavista.digital.com`, `hotbot.com`, and so on.)

These sites are basically huge databases that attempt to catalog as many pages on the Internet as possible. They all use automated processing to build the databases, though some (such as Yahoo!) emphasize quality by having each listing checked by a human. Others (such as HotBot) prefer to go for quantity, and rely almost entirely on programs called *robots* or *spiders* to crawl around the Internet hunting for new pages to index.

NEW TERM A *robot* (also called a *spider*) is an automated computer program that spends all day looking at Web pages all over the Internet and building a database of the contents of all the pages it visits.

As the spiders and/or humans constantly add to the database, another program called a search engine processes requests from people who are looking for Web pages on specific topics. The search engine looks in the database for pages that contain the key words or phrases that someone is looking for, and sends that person a list of all the pages that contain those terms.

23

NEW TERM A *search engine* is an automated computer program that looks in a database index for pages containing specific words or phrases. Some people use the term *Internet directory* to mean a search engine whose database was built mostly by people instead of robots. (Lately, it's become the vogue in some circles to call search engines *portals*.)

Listing Your Pages with the Major Search Sites

If you want people to find your pages, you absolutely must submit a request to each of the six major search sites to index your pages. Each of these sites has a form for you to fill out with the address, a brief description of the site, and in some cases a category or list of keywords with which your listing should be associated. These forms are easy to fill out; you can easily do all six of them in an hour with time left over to list yourself at one or two specialized directories you might have found as well. (How did you find the specialized directories? Through the major search sites, of course!)

There are sites that provide one form that automatically submits itself to all the major search engines, plus several minor ones (www.submit-it.com and http://www.liquidimaging.com/submit/ are popular examples). Many of these sites attempt to sell you a "premium" service that gets you listed in many other directories and indexes as well. Depending on your target audience, these services may or may not be of value, but I strongly recommend that you go directly to each of the six most popular search sites and use their own forms to submit your requests to be listed. That way you can be sure to answer the questions (which are slightly different at every site) accurately, and you will know exactly how your site listing will appear at each of them.

But wait! Before you rush off this minute to submit your listing requests, read the rest of this hour. Otherwise, you'll have a very serious problem, and you will have already lost your best opportunity to solve it.

To see what I mean, imagine this scenario: You publish a page selling automatic cockroach flatteners. I have a roach problem, and I'm allergic to bug spray. I open up my laptop, brush the roaches off the keyboard, log on to my favorite search site, and enter "cockroach" as a search term. The search engine promptly presents me with a list of the first 10 out of 10,254 Internet pages containing the word "cockroach." You have submitted your listing request, so you know your page is somewhere on that list.

Did I mention that I'm rich? And that two roaches are mating on my foot? You even offer same-day delivery in my area. So do you want your page to be number 3 on the list, or number 8,542? Okay, now you understand the problem.

Providing Hints for Search Engines

Fact: There is absolutely nothing you can do to guarantee that your site will appear in the top ten search results for a particular word or phrase in any major search engine (short of buying ad space from the search site, that is). After all, if there was, why couldn't everyone else who wants to be #1 on the list do it too? What you *can* do is avoid being last on the list, and give yourself as good a chance as anyone else of being first.

Each search engine uses a slightly different method for determining which pages are likely to be most relevant, and should therefore be sorted to the top of a search result list. You don't need to get too hung up about the differences, though, because they all use some combination of the same basic criteria. The following list includes almost everything any search engine considers when trying to evaluate which pages best match one or more keywords. The first three of these criteria are used by every major search engine, and all of them also use at least one or two of the other criteria.

- Do the keywords appear in the <TITLE> tag of the page?
- Do the keywords appear in the first few lines of the page?
- How many times do the keywords appear in the entire page?
- Do the keywords appear in a <META> tag in the page?
- How many other pages in my database link to the page?
- How many times have people chosen this page from a previous search list result?
- Is the page rated highly in a human-generated directory?

Clearly, the most important thing you can do to improve your position on search lists is to consider what word combinations your intended audience is most likely to enter when they go hunting for your type of site. I'd recommend that you don't even concern yourself with common single-word searches; the lists they generate are usually so long that trying to make it to the top is like playing the lottery. Focus instead on uncommon words and two- or three-word combinations that are most likely to indicate relevance to your topic. Make sure those terms and phrases occur several times on your page, and be certain to put the most important ones in the <TITLE> tag and the first heading or introductory paragraph.

> Some over-eager Web page authors put dozens or even hundreds of repetitions of the same word on their pages, sometimes in small print or a hard-to-see color, just to get the search engines to sort that page to the top of the list whenever someone searched for that word. This practice is called *search engine spamming*.
>
> Don't be tempted to try this sort of thing, because all the major search engines immediately delete any page from their database that sets off a "spam detector" by repeating the same word or group of words in a suspicious pattern. It's still fine (and quite beneficial) to have several occurrences of important search words on a page. Just use the words in normal sentences or phrases, and the spam police will leave you alone.

Of all the search engine evaluation criteria I just listed, the use of <META> tags is probably the most poorly understood. Some people rave about <META> tags as if using them could instantly move you to the top of every search list. Other people dismiss <META> tags as ineffective and useless. Neither of these extremes is true.

A <META> tag is a general-purpose tag you can put in the <HEAD> portion of any document to specify some information about the page that doesn't belong in the <BODY> text. Most major search engines allow you to use <META> tags to give them a short description of your page and some keywords to identify what your page is about. For example, your automatic cockroach flattener order form might include the following two tags anywhere between <HEAD> and </HEAD>.

```
<META NAME="description"
 CONTENT="Order form for the SuperSquish cockroach flattener.">
<META NAME="keywords"
 CONTENT="cockroach, roaches, kill, squish, supersquish">
```

The first of these tags ensures that the search engine has an accurate description of your page to present on its search results list. The second slightly increases your page's ranking on the list whenever any of your specified keywords are included in a search query.

You should always include NAME="description" and NAME="keywords"<META> tags in any page that you request a search engine to index. Doing so may not have a dramatic effect on your position in search lists, and not all search engines look for <META> tags, but it can only help so there's no reason not to do it.

> In the unlikely even that you don't want a page to be included in search engine databases at all, you can put the following <META> tag in the <HEAD> portion of that page.
>
> <META NAME="robots" CONTENT="noindex">
>
> This causes some search robots to ignore the page. For more robust protection from prying robot eyes, ask the person who manages your Web server computer to include your page address in their robots.txt file. (They'll know what that means and how to do it.) Then all major search spiders will be sure to ignore your pages.

To give you a concrete example of how to improve search engine results, consider the page in Figures 23.1 and 23.2. This page should be fairly easy to find, since it deals with a specific topic and includes several occurrences of some uncommon technical terms for which people interested in this subject would be likely to search. However, there are several things you could do to improve the chances of this page appearing high on a search engine results list.

To a human being, the contents of the page in Figures 23.3 and 23.4 look almost the same as the page in Figures 23.1 and 23.2. To search robots and search engines, however, these two pages appear quite different. The following list summarizes the changes, and explains why I made each modification.

1. I added some important search terms to the <TITLE> tag and the first heading on the page. The original page didn't even include the word "fractal" in either of these two key positions.

2. I added <META> tags to assist some search engines with a description and keywords.

3. I added an ALT attribute to the first <IMG> tag. Not all search engines read and index ALT text, but some do.

4. I took out the quotation marks around technical terms (such as "fractal" and "iterated") because some search engines consider *"fractal"* to be a different word than *fractal*. I could have used the HTML character entity " to make the quotation marks, in which case the search robot would have disregarded them, but I chose instead to simply italicize the words.

FIGURE 23.1.

There's nothing wrong with this page, but it presents some problems to people who might try to find it from an Internet search site.

```
<HTML><HEAD><TITLE>Fractal Central</TITLE></HEAD>
<BODY BACKGROUND="bacfrac.jpg" TEXT="#003399">
<DIV ALIGN="center">
<IMG SRC="fraccent.gif" HEIGHT=149 WIDTH=320>
<TABLE CELLSPACING=10><TR><TD VALIGN="top">
  <TABLE BORDER=2 CELLPADDING=10 WIDTH=133>
  <TR><TD ALIGN="center">
  Discover the latest software, books and more at our
  online store.<BR><A HREF="ordform.htm">
  <IMG SRC="ordform.gif" BORDER=0 HEIGHT=55 WIDTH=111></A>
  </TABLE>
<TD VALIGN="top"><H2>A Comprehensive Guide to the<BR>
Art and Science of Chaos and Complexity</H2></DIV>
What's that? You say you're hearing about "fractals" and
"chaos" all over the place, but still aren't too sure what
they are? How about a quick summary of some key concepts:
<OL><LI>Even the simplest systems become deeply complex and
richly beautiful when a process is "iterated" over and over,
using the results of each step as the starting point of the
next. This is how Nature creates a magnificently detailed
300-foot redwood tree from a seed the size of your fingernail.
<P><LI>Most "iterated systems" are easily simulated on
computers, but only a few are predictable and controllable.
Why? Because a tiny influence, like a "butterfly flapping it's
wings," can be strangely amplified to have major consequences
such as completely changing tomorrow's weather in a distant
part of the world.
<P><LI>Fractals can be magnified forever without loss of
detail, so mathematics that relies on straight lines is
useless with them. However, they give us a new concept
called "fractal dimension" which can measure the texture
and complexity of anything from coastlines to storm clouds.
<P><LI>While fractals win prizes at graphics shows,
their chaotic patterns pop up in every branch of science.
Physicists find beautiful artwork coming out of their
plotters. "Strange attractors" with fractal turbulence
appear in celestial mechanics. Biologists diagnose "dynamical
diseases" when fractal rhythms fall out of sync. Even pure
mathematicians go on tour with dazzling videos of their
research.</OL>Think all these folks may be on to something?<P>
<DIV ALIGN="center"><A HREF="http://netletter.com/nonsense/">
<IMG SRC="findout.gif" HEIGHT=20 WIDTH=150 BORDER=0></A></DIV>
</TABLE></BODY></HTML>
```

23

5. I added the keyword "fractal" twice to the text in the order form box. I also rearranged the table so this box didn't appear in the HTML code before the <H1> heading or the main body text. Since search sites give special importance to words occurring early in the HTML document, it's important not to put table columns (or <SCRIPT> or <STYLE> tags) before the text containing your most important search words.

FIGURE 23.2.

The first part of the page in Figure 23.1, as it appears in a Web browser.

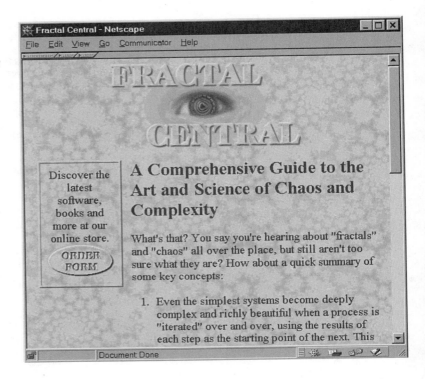

It would be impossible to quantify how much more frequently people searching for information on fractals and chaos were able to find the page in Figure 23.3 versus the page in Figure 23.1. But it's a sure bet that none of the changes could do anything but improve the page's visibility to search engines. As is often the case, the improvements made for the benefit of the search spiders probably made the subject of the page easier for humans to recognize and understand as well.

Loading Another Page Automatically

When you are managing a Web site, it may become necessary to move some pages from one address to another. You might decide, for example, to change the service provider or domain name of your whole site. Or you might just reorganize things and switch some pages in a different directory folder.

What happens, then, when someone comes to the address of her favorite Web page on your site after you've moved it? If you don't want her to be stranded with a Not Found error message, you should put a page at the old address which says "This page has moved to…" with the new address (and a link to it).

FIGURE 23.3.

This page will be easier for people interested in fractals and chaos to find than the page in Figure 23.1.

23

```
<HTML><HEAD>
<TITLE>Fractal Central:
        A Guide to Fractals, Chaos, and Complexity</TITLE>
<MEAT NAME="description"
 CONTENT="A comprehensive guide to fractal geometry,
            chaos science and complexity theory.">
<META NAME="keywords"
 CONTENT="fractal, fractals, chaos science, chaos theory,
            fractal geometry, complexity, complexity theory">
</HEAD>
<BODY BACKGROUND="bacfrac.jpg" TEXT="#003399">
<DIV ALIGN="center">
<IMG SRC="fraccent.gif" HEIGHT=149 WIDTH=320
 ALT="Fractal Central">
<H2>A Comprehensive Guide to Fractal Geometry,
Chaos Science and Complexity Theory</H2></DIV>
<TABLE CELLSPACING=10><TR><TD VALIGN="top">
What's that? You say you're hearing about <I>fractals</I> and
<I>chaos</I> all over the place, but still aren't too sure what
they are? How about a quick summary of some key concepts:
<OL><LI>Even the simplest systems become deeply complex and
richly beautiful when a process is <I>iterated</I> over and
over, using the results of each step as the starting point of
the next. This is how Nature creates a magnificently detailed

    ...blah, blah, blah...

mathematicians go on tour with dazzling videos of their
research.</OL>Think all these folks may be on to something?<P>
<DIV ALIGN="center"><A HREF="http://netletter.com/nonsense/">
<IMG SRC="findout.gif" HEIGHT=20 WIDTH=150 BORDER=0></A></DIV>
<TD VALIGN="top">
  <TABLE BORDER=2 CELLPADDING=10 WIDTH=133>
  <TR><TD ALIGN="center">
  Discover the latest fractal software, books and more at the
  <B>Fractal Central</B> online store.<BR>
  <A HREF="ordform.htm">
  <IMG SRC="ordform.gif" BORDER=0 HEIGHT=55 WIDTH=111></A>
  </TABLE>
</TABLE>
</BODY></HTML>
```

Chances are, you've encountered similar messages on the Internet from time to time yourself. Some of them probably employed the neat trick you're about to learn; they automatically transferred you to the new address after a few seconds, even if you didn't click a link.

In fact, you can make any page automatically load any other page after an amount of time you choose. The secret to this trick is the <META> tag, which goes in the <HEAD> section of a page and looks like the following:

```
<META HTTP-EQUIV="Refresh" CONTENT="5; nextpage.htm">
```

FIGURE 23.4.

The first part of the page in Figure 23.3, as it appears in a Web browser.

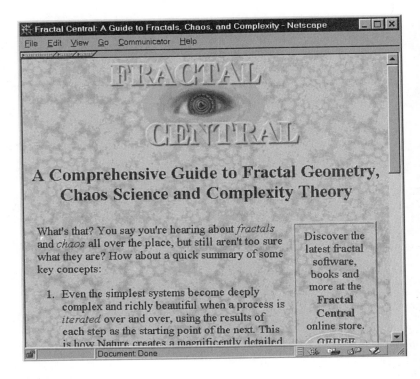

Put the number of seconds to wait before loading the next page where I put 5 in the line above, and put the address of the next page to load instead of *nextpage.htm*.

For example, the page listed in Figure 23.5 looks like Figure 23.6 when viewed in a Web browser. After 5 seconds (during which a GIF animation counts down from 5 to 0), the <META> tag causes the page at http://netletter.com/nicholas/ (Figures 23.7 and 23.8) to appear.

For the impatient, I also included a link to the netletter.com/nicholas page, which someone could click before the 5 seconds is up. Also, some very old Web browsers don't recognize <META>, so you should always put a normal link on the page leading to the same address as the <META> refresh tag.

FIGURE 23.5.

The <META> tag causes the Web browser to automatically load the page in Figure 23.7 after 5 seconds.

```
<HTML><HEAD><TITLE>New Address Notice</TITLE></HEAD>
<META HTTP-EQUIV="Refresh"
        CONTENT="6; URL=http://netletter.com/nicholas">
<BODY BGCOLOR="black" TEXT="silver" LINK="red" VLINK="white">
<DIV ALIGN="center">
Nicholas' home page is now located at
<A HREF="http://netletter.com/nicholas/">
netletter.com/nicholas</A>.
<H2><FONT COLOR="red">You will arrive in<P>
<IMG SRC="countdn.gif"><P>seconds.</FONT></H2>
</DIV></BODY></HTML>
```

23

FIGURE 23.6.

The page listed in Figure 23.5. I used a GIF animation (countdn.gif) to entertain readers while they're waiting for the next page.

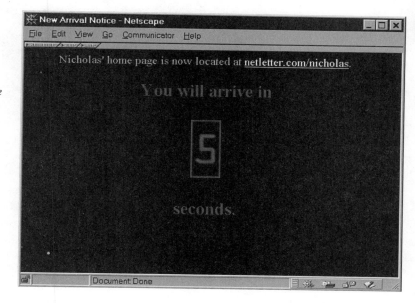

FIGURE 23.7.

The <BASE> tag in this page has nothing to do with page forwarding. (<BASE> is discussed in the next section of this hour.)

```
<HTML><HEAD><TITLE>New Arrival Notice</TITLE>
<BASE HREF="http://netletter.com/nicholas/welcome.htm">
</HEAD>
<BODY BGCOLOR="black" TEXT="silver" LINK="red" VLINK="white">
<DIV ALIGN="center">
<H2><FONT COLOR="red">You have arrived.<P>
<IMG SRC="nicholas.jpg"><P>So has Nicholas.<BR>
(Age zero and counting.)</FONT></H2>
</DIV></BODY></HTML>
```

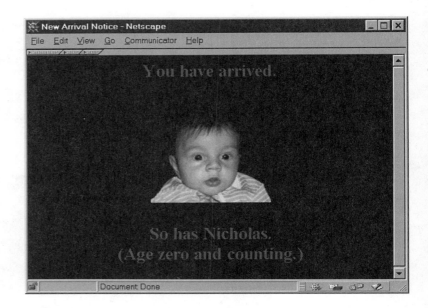

FIGURE 23.8.

The page listed in Figure 23.7. The page in Figures 23.5 and 23.6 forward to this page automatically after the 5-second delay.

Advanced Header Tags

The <META> tag can actually be used for a wide variety of purposes besides automatically loading a new page and giving hints to search engines. You can use it to specify any information you like about the document, such as the author or a page ID number. How and why you do this is beyond the scope of this introductory book, and very few Web page authors ever use the <META> tag for anything other than page forwarding and making their pages easier to find on the Internet.

There are also three other advanced tags for locating and interlinking documents that you may occasionally see in the <HEAD> section of Web pages. Two of them, <ISINDEX> and <NEXTID>, are considered obsolete and are almost never used by Web page authors today. <LINK> is most often used to link a style sheet to a Web page (see Hour 16, "Using Style Sheets"), but can also theoretically be used to document an association between one Web page and another.

The final section of this hour discusses one more tag that goes in the <HEAD> section of a document, and which you may sometimes find useful.

Documenting the Full Address of a Page

Suppose you create a Web page advertising your business, and a customer likes your page so much that she saves it on her hard drive. A couple of days later, she wants to show a friend your cool site, but... guess what? She forgot to bookmark it, and of course the page doesn't contain a link to itself. She clicks the links to your order form, but they are only filename links (like <A HREF="orderform.htm">) so they don't work from her hard drive unless the order form is on her hard drive, too. So you lose two eager customers.

One way to avoid this heartbreaking scenario is to always use complete addresses starting with http:// in all links. However, this makes your pages difficult to test and maintain.

You could also include a link to the full address of your home page on every page, including the home page itself. Yet there's a more elegant way to make a page remember where it came from.

The <BASE> tag lets you include the address of a page within the <HEAD> section of that page, like this:

```
<HTML><HEAD>
 <BASE HREF="http://www.myplace.com/mypage.htm">
 <TITLE>My Page</TITLE>
</HEAD>
<BODY> ...the actual page goes here... </BODY>
</HTML>
```

For the HTML authors whose job is to maintain this page, the <BASE> tag provides convenient documentation of where this page should be put.

Even more importantly, all links within the page behave as if the page were at the <BASE> address, *even if it isn't*. For example, if you had the page in Figure 23.7 on your hard drive and you opened it with a Web browser, all images on the page would be loaded from the online site at http://netletter.com/nicholas/ rather than from the hard drive. The links would also lead to pages in the nicholas directory at http://netletter.com, instead of pages on the hard drive.

Few Web page authors use (or even know about) the <BASE> tag. Many who do know about it don't like the hassle of changing it when they want to test a page (including images and links) on their hard drive. I've tried to give you enough information in this chapter to choose for yourself whether the <BASE> tag is worthwhile for you.

If you do choose to use the <BASE> tag, don't put it in your pages until you're ready to upload them to the Web server. That way you can test them with all the images and link pages on your hard drive, and then add the <BASE> tag at the last minute, to enjoy the benefits it offers once your pages are online.

Summary

This hour showed you how to make a page remember its own address, and how to make a page load another page automatically. It also taught you how to provide hints to search engines (such as HotBot, AltaVista, Lycos, Infoseek, and so on) so that people can find your pages more easily on the Internet. Table 23.1 lists the tags and attributes covered in this hour.

TABLE 23.1.   HTML TAGS AND ATTRIBUTES COVERED IN HOUR 23.

Tag/Attribute	Function
`<META>`	Indicates meta-information about this document (information about the document itself). Most commonly used to make a page automatically load another page, or reload itself. Used in the document `<HEAD>`.
	Attributes:
`HTTP-EQUIV="..."`	Gives a command to the Web browser or server. For example, `HTTP-EQUIV="Refresh"` will cause a new page to load automatically.
`NAME="..."`	Can be used to specify which type of information about the document is in the `CONTENT` attribute. For example, `NAME="Author"` means the author's name or ID is in `CONTENT`.
`CONTENT="..."`	The actual message or value for the information specified in `HTTP-EQUIV` or `NAME`. For example, if `HTTP-EQUIV="Refresh"` then `CONTENT` should be the number of seconds to wait, followed by a semi-colon and the address of the page to load.
`<BASE>`	Indicates the full URL of the current document. This optional tag is used within `<HEAD>`.
	Attributes:
`HREF="..."`	The full URL of this document.
`<ISINDEX>`	Indicates that this document is a gateway script that allows searches. (Very seldom used.)
`<NEXTID>`	Indicates the "next" document to this one (as might be defined by a tool to manage HTML documents in series). `<NEXTID>` is considered obsolete.
`<LINK>`	Indicates a link from this entire document to another (as opposed to `<A>`, which can create multiple links in the document). (Refer to see Hour 16.)

Q&A

Q I have lots of pages in my site. Do I need to fill out a separate form for each of them at each search site that I want to index them?

A No. If you submit just your home page (which is presumably linked to all the other pages), the search spider will crawl through all the links on the page (and all the links on the linked pages, and so on) until it has indexed all the pages on your site.

Q I submitted a request to be listed with a search engine, but my page never comes up, even when I enter the unique name of my company. What can I do?

A All the big search engines offer a form you can fill out to instantly check whether a specific address is included in their database. If you find that it isn't, about all you can do is submit another request form. Sometimes it takes days or even weeks for the spiders to get around to indexing your pages after you submit a request. Yahoo! is particularly infamous for being way behind on index requests, because it employs human beings to check every page it lists.

Q When I put keywords in a `<META>` tag, do I need to include every possible variation of spelling and capitalization?

A Don't worry about capitalization, because almost all searches are entered in all-lowercase. Do include any obvious variations or common errors in spelling as separate keywords, though.

Q Can I use the `<META>` tag to make a page automatically reload itself every few seconds or minutes?

A Yes, but there's no point in doing that unless you have some sort of program or script set up on your Web server computer to provide new information on the page.

Workshop

Quiz

1. If you publish a page about puppy adoption, how could you help make sure the page can be found by people who enter "puppy", "dog", and/or "adoption" at all the major Internet search sites?

2. Suppose you recently moved a page from `http://mysite.com/oldplace/thepage.htm` to `http://mysite.com/newplace/thepage.htm`, but you're not quite sure if you're going to keep it there yet. How would you automatically send people who try the old address to the new address, without any message telling them there was a change?

3. What are three ways to make sure that people who save one of your pages on your hard drive can find your site online from it, even if they forget to add it to their Bookmarks or Favorites list?

Answers

1. First, make sure "puppy", "dog", and "adoption" all occur frequently on your main page (as they probably already do), and title your page something like "Puppy dog adoption." While you're at it, put the following <META> tags in the <HEAD> portion of the page:

```
<META NAME="description"
CONTENT="Dog adoption information and services">
<META NAME="keywords" CONTENT="puppy, dog, adoption">
```

Finally, put your page online and go to yahoo.com, hotbot.com, altavista. digital.com, lycos.com, excite.com, and infoseek.com to fill out each of their page submission forms.

2. Put the following page at

```
http://mysite.com/oldplace/thepage.htm
<HTML><HEAD><META HTTP-EQUIV="Refresh" CONTENT="0;
http://mysite.com/newplace/thepage.htm></HEAD>
</HTML>
```

To accommodate people using older browsers that don't support <META>, it would be a good idea to also include the following just before the </HTML> tag:

```
<BODY><A HREF="http://mysite.com/newplace/thepage.htm">
Click here to get the page you're after.</A></BODY>
```

3. (a) Include a link to the site, using the full Internet address, on every page. Example:

```
The address of this page is:
<A HREF="http://mysite.com/home.htm">
http://mysite.com/home.htm</A>
```

(b) Use full Internet addresses in all links between your pages. Example:

```
This is my home page. From here you can
<A HREF="http://mysite.com/personal.htm">
find out about my exciting personal life</A>, or
<A HREF="http://mysite.com/work.htm">
find out about my boring work life</A>.
```

(c) Use the <BASE> tag to specify the full Internet address of a page. Example:

```
<HEAD><BASE HREF="http://mysite.com/home.htm">
<TITLE>My Home Page</TITLE></HEAD>
```

Exercises

- Can you think of some fun and/or useful ways to employ automatically changing pages (with the `<META HTTP-EQUIV="Refresh">` tag)? I bet you can.

- Now that you've made it through all the HTML tutorials in this book, you probably have some fantastic Web pages online. So get on over to those search sites and let the world know you exist!

23

Hour 24

Planning for the Future of HTML

Almost everything you have learned in this book is likely to work flawlessly with HTML-compatible software for many years to come. There are tens of millions of pages of information written in standard HTML, and even as that standard evolves, tomorrow's Web browsers and business software will retain the capability to view today's Web pages.

Some of the most exciting applications of HTML, however, are still rapidly developing. This hour introduces the latest HTML extensions and helps you understand what these new capabilities will enable you to do.

To Do

When this hour was written, "now" meant mid-1998. Because you are living in "the future," you can check to make sure my crystal ball wasn't too cloudy, with the help of the following Web sites.

- Your best two sources for the latest HTML standards (and proposed future standards) are the World Wide Web Consortium site

▼ To Do

▼

    (`http://www.w3.org`) and the HTML Compendium
    (`http://www.htmlcompendium.org`.

- To see how the standards are actually implemented in the latest Web browsers, and to see what nonstandard HTML extensions might be available, visit the Microsoft Web site (`http://www.microsoft.com`) and the Netscape Web Site

▲

    (`http://home.netscape.com`).

You can also get copies of the latest Web browser updates from these two Web sites.

HTML Beyond the Web

The intimate familiarity with HTML you gained from this book will be one of the most important (and profitable) skills that anyone can have in the next few years. However, most of the HTML pages you create in your lifetime will probably not be Web pages.

To understand why, and to see the big picture of where HTML is headed, consider the following features of the latest HTML standard:

- Through style sheets and scripting, HTML now gives you precise control over the appearance and functionality of virtually any textual and graphical information.
- All major programming languages, interactive media, and database formats can also be seamlessly integrated with HTML.
- HTML's extended character sets and fonts can now be used to communicate in the native script of almost any human language in the world.
- New data security standards are finally making it practical to carry out financial and other sensitive transactions with HTML, and to manage confidential or restricted-access information.
- All future versions of the Microsoft Windows operating system will use HTML as a fundamental part of the user interface. Nearly all current versions of office productivity software also support HTML.

All this adds up to a very near future where HTML will without a doubt play a central role—it might even be accurate to say *the* central role—in the display and exchange of almost all information across all computers and computer networks on Earth. If this sounds important, well, it is. However, this hour will make a case that HTML will have an even more important role than that to play. To understand how that can be so, we'll need to take another step back to see an even bigger picture: the changing role of the computer itself in our society.

From Calculators to Communicators

The computer was once considered a device for accounting and number crunching. Then it evolved into a device for crunching all types of information, from words and numbers to graphics and sounds. Today and tomorrow, the computer is above all a communications device; its primary use is the transmission of information between people.

In many workplaces today, you can use a computer to access business information every day without knowing much more than how to click links and scroll down through long pages. And you can do so without being at all sure which information is coming from your computer, which is coming from the server down the hall, and which is coming from other servers perhaps thousands of miles away.

Users who become used to seeing highly readable and attractive pages of information on their computer screens are losing the tiny bit of tolerance they have left for cryptic icons, unadorned text messages, and idiosyncratic menu mazes. They will soon expect their computer screens to *always* be as easy to read and interact with as the Web.

Those who make their millions supplying computer software are well aware of that expectation, and are expending an unprecedented amount of research and development effort toward fulfilling it. Along the way, the central metaphor for interacting with computers has changed from the "window" of the 1980s "desktop," to the "page" of the 1990s "World Wide Web."

HTML as the New User Interface

As the role of the computer evolves, HTML is becoming more and more central to nearly everything we do with computers. HTML is the de facto global standard for connecting all types of information in a predictable and presentable way.

HTML gives you a painless and reliable way to combine and arrange text, graphics, sound, video, and interactive programs. Unlike older proprietary page layout standards, HTML was originally designed for efficient communication between all kinds of computers worldwide.

The prominence of HTML, however, does *not* mean that Web browsers will be a major category of software application in the coming years. In fact, the "Web browser" as a distinct program has already nearly disappeared. Microsoft Internet Explorer 5.0, for instance, does much more than retrieve pages from the World Wide Web. It lets you use HTML pages as the interface for organizing and navigating through the information on your own computer, including directory folders and the Windows Desktop itself. In conjunction with HTML-enabled software such as Office 98, HTML becomes the common standard interface for word processing, spreadsheets, and databases. Netscape Communicator is also much more than a Web browser. It uses HTML to integrate all types of media into email, discussion groups, schedule management, business documents, and collaborative project management.

Meanwhile, HTML support is being included in every major software release so that every program on your computer will soon be able to import and export information in the form of HTML pages. In a nutshell, HTML is the glue that holds together all the diverse types of information on our computers and ensures that it can be presented in a standard way that will look the same to anyone in the world.

In a business world that now sees fast, effective communication as the most common and most important task of its workers, the "information glue" of HTML has the power to connect more than different types of media. It is the hidden adhesive that connects a business to its customers and connects individual employees to form an efficient team. Knowing how to apply that glue—the skills you gained from this book—puts you in one of the most valuable roles in any modern organization.

The Digital Media Revolution

The most important changes in the next few years might not be in HTML itself, but in the audience you can reach with your HTML pages. Many Web site developers hope that Internet-based content will have enough appeal to become the mass-market successor to television and radio. Less optimistic observers note that the global communications network has a long way to go before it can even deliver television-quality video to most users, or reach a majority of the worlds' populace at all.

I won't pretend to have a magic mirror that lets me see how and when HTML becomes a mass-market phenomenon, but one thing is certain: All communication industries, from television to telephony, are moving rapidly toward exclusively digital technology. As they do so, the lines between communication networks are blurring. New Internet protocols promise to optimize multimedia transmissions at the same time that new protocols allow wireless broadcasters to support two-way interactive transmissions. The same small satellite dish can give you both Internet access and high-definition TV.

Add to this trend the fact that HTML is the only widely supported worldwide standard for combining text content with virtually any other form of digital media. Whatever surprising turns the future of digital communication takes, it's difficult to imagine that HTML won't be sitting in the driver's seat.

Over a million people can already access the Internet without a "real computer" through TV set-top boxes and from WebTV, Inc., cable TV companies, and digital satellite services. These devices are only the first wave of much more ubiquitous appliances that provide HTML content to people that wouldn't otherwise use computers.

The prospect of mass-market HTML access is obviously a great opportunity for HTML page authors. However, it can also present a number of challenges when designing HTML pages, because many people might see your pages on low-resolution TV screens or on small hand-held devices. See the "What You Can Do Today to Be Ready for Tomorrow" section for some pointers on making sure your HTML pages can be enjoyed and understood by the widest possible audience.

From HTML to XML: Unity in Diversity

24

So far in this hour, I've noted how HTML is in the right place at the right time to enable several key changes in business and interpersonal communication. As the people and companies of the world become more interconnected and interdependent, HTML's ability to make all information technology easier to use and less constrained by geography seems almost magical.

Even more magically, HTML has enabled an explosion of new media formats and incompatible file types, while at the same time providing the first truly universal format for exchanging all types of information. The limitations of the HTML language itself have stood in the way of it truly fulfilling this important role, however. To address these limitations, the World Wide Web Consortium has created a new language called *XML*, or *eXtensible Markup Language*.

Before you can understand what XML is, and why it may be a key to the future of computer communication, you first have to meet its mother. Her name is *SGML*, or *Standard General Markup Language*. She is a venerable, time-worn standard for describing other markup languages. HTML is just one of many languages that can be defined in SGML. Others include specialized languages for library indexing, print publications management, mathematical formulas, molecular chemistry, and so on. Though no one SGML browser can render all these specialized document types, any SGML browser can read the *document type definition* (*DTD*) and figure out how to render those elements of the document type that it understands while ignoring the rest.

It would be ideal if Web browsers could read any SGML document type instead of being limited only to HTML documents. The problem with this idea is the SGML is so complex and powerful that it can be very difficult to learn and implement. If this book were about SGML, the title would be something like "Sams Teach Yourself SGML in a Year and a Half."

XML was created to bridge the gap between HTML, which is easy to learn but kinda wimpy, and SGML, which gives you God-like powers, but may require several reincarnations to master. Like SGML, XML allows you to define your own special-purpose tags and implement complex link relationships between documents. Like HTML, XML is a simple enough to learn fairly quickly because it avoids all the more esoteric (and least commonly used) aspects of SGML.

XML is a general-purpose language, which includes all the HTML tags but also allows specialized extensions of the language to be easily defined without losing compatibility with the core language. XML standardizes the format of the most common types of information while freely allowing unlimited special cases for proprietary formats and new technology. This means that you can both ensure complete compatibility between the widest variety of software and easily develop unique information formats to meet your individual needs.

The ability to extend HTML pages with custom data types is far more than a way to embed a nifty movie or virtual reality scene into your Web page. To show how much more, the next section of this hour highlights some of the most exciting up-and-coming uses of HTML and XML.

 Microsoft Internet Explorer 5.0 will be the first widely used Web browser to support some XML capabilities. Netscape is working on a version of its browser which also implements some or all of the XML 1.0 standard. For more information on XML, its capabilities, and its implementations, go to the World Wide Web Consortium Web site at www.w3c.org.

HTML Applications of the Future

The near-universal compatibility of HTML and XML provides a big incentive to format any important document as a Web page—even if you have no immediate plans for putting it on the World Wide Web. You can create a single page that can be printed on paper, sent as an email message, displayed during a board meeting presentation, and posted for reference on the company intranet. Or you can take the traditional route and format the page separately for each of these applications—and edit each file with a different software program when the information needs to be updated. Now that most business software supports the HTML standard, many organizations are trying to get employees to consistently use it for all important documents.

Yet the great migration to HTML goes beyond what you might have thought of as "documents" in the old days. Combined with Java, ActiveX, and other new technologies,

HTML-based presentations can in many cases replace what was once done with proprietary data formats, specialized software, or more traditional programming languages. Here are a few of the other areas where HTML is finding application beyond the Web:

- Kiosks with HTML-based interactive content are popping up everywhere. They look like ATM machines on steroids, and they're helping sell records and theme park tickets, expand department store displays, and even automate the paying of parking tickets. The number of kiosks using intranet and HTML technology is projected to soar from under 90,000 today to over 500,000 by the end of 1998.

- Information-rich CD-ROM titles are migrating to HTML fast. Encyclopedia Brittanica is already entirely HTML-based, which enables it to offer its content on CD-ROM, the Web, or a combination of both for maximum speed and up-to-the-minute currency. Because CD-ROM drives display multimedia so much faster than most Internet connections, dynamic HTML presentations become possible that just couldn't be done on today's World Wide Web. The new DVD-ROM drives will be even faster and will hold much more information, making them ideally suited to large multimedia "sites."

24

- Corporate newsletters are now often created in HTML for the company internet, and then printed on paper for delivery to employees or customers who wouldn't see them on the Web. The traditional difference between online and paper presentations was that graphics needed to be high-resolution black-and-white for printing and low-resolution color for computer screens. Today's inexpensive color printers, however, do a great job making low-res color images look great in am HTML-based newsletter.

- Teachers are finding that tests and educational worksheets are easier to administer as HTML pages and can include many types of interactive content that wouldn't be possible on paper. Even for students that lack access to the Internet, simple HTML documents can be passed out on floppy disks.

- Vertical market users often buy a computer specifically to run a certain custom-designed application or set of applications. The VARs and systems integrators that provide these systems are delivering machines configured to start up displaying HTML pages. This can help step users through the use of the machine or replace old-fashioned *idiot menus* with a more attractive and sophisticated interface without sacrificing ease of use.

I could list many more creative and beneficial uses of HTML beyond run-of-the-mill Web pages, but the point should be clear: If you need to present any type of information, seriously consider HTML as an alternative to the specialized software or programming tools that you would have used for the job a couple of years ago.

What You Can Do Today to Be Ready for Tomorrow

If you've made your way through most of the hours of this book, you already have one of the most important ingredients for future success in the new digital world: a solid working knowledge of HTML.

Chances are that your primary reason for learning HTML at this time was to create some Web pages, but I hope this hour has convinced you that you'll be using HTML for far more than that in the future. The following are some of the factors you should consider when planning and building your Web site today so that it will also serve you well tomorrow:

- Whenever you run into something that you'd like to do on a Web page, but can't with HTML as it stands today, include a comment in the page so you can add that feature when it becomes possible in the future. The multimedia and interactive portions of your site are likely to need more revisions to keep up with current technology than will the text and graphics portions. When possible, keep the more cutting edge elements of your site separate and take especially good care to document them well with the <!-- and --> comment tags.

- Though new technologies such as Java and ActiveX might be the wave of the future, avoid them today except when developing for disk-based media or a fast local intranet. Even when everyone is using 56Kbps or faster modems, many people still will move on to a different site before they'll wait for an applet or interactive movie to download, initialize, and start working.

- Because style sheets give you complete control over the choice and measurements of type on your Web pages, it would be a good idea to study basic typography now, if you aren't familiar with it. Understanding and working with things such as *leading*, *kerning*, *em-spaces,* and *drop caps* have long been essential for producing truly professional-quality paper pages. It will soon be essential for producing outstanding Web pages, too.

- The potential of JavaScript and other Web page scripting languages is currently hobbled by incompatible and buggy implementations. This should change fast when the new *Document Object Model* (*DOM*) standard comes out in 1999. Learning basic scripting now will put you one step ahead when the first truly standardized version of the language makes a much greater variety of interactive scripting applications possible.

- When you design your pages, don't assume that everyone who sees them will be using a computer. Televisions, video-telephones, game consoles, and many other devices might have access to them as well. Some of these devices have very low-resolution screens (with as few as 320×200 pixels). Though it's difficult to design a Web page to look good at that resolution, you'll reach the widest possible audience if you do.

- As older Web browsers fall out of general use, you will be able to layer images and text on top of each other more reliably. That means that many things you need large images for today you will be able to do much more efficiently with several small image elements tomorrow. Always keep copies of each individual image element that goes into a larger graphic, without any text. This will let you easily optimize the graphics later without re-creating everything from scratch.

- Several new standards have been issued or are about to be issued by the World Wide Web Consortium. These include the *Synchronized Multimedia Interface Language* (*SMIL*), the *Mathematics Markup Language* (*MathML*), the *eXtensible Style Sheet Language* (*XSL*), and some early proposals for a graphics markup language. On the privacy and security front, new standards include the *Platform for Internet Content Selection* (*PICS*), the *Platform for Privacy Preferences* (*P3P*), and the *Digital Signature* standard (*Dsig*). Since these advances are likely to both expand the potential capabilities of your Web site and change some of the methods you now use to build Web pages, you should visit the www.w3c.org site and take the time to learn at least a little about each of them.

24

You'll find links to several online reference and learning resources at the 24-Hour HTML Café at http://24hourHTMLcafe.com.

In addition to providing an easy way to review all the sample pages and HTML techniques covered in this book, this site offers many example pages this book didn't have room for.

You'll also find links to hundreds of Web sites created by readers of this book. You're sure to pick up some great ideas for your own pages!

Summary

This hour has provided a bird's-eye view of the future of HTML. It discussed the new roles that HTML will play in global communications, and briefly introduced how HTML relates to the new *eXtensible Markup Language* (*XML*) standard. Finally, it offered some advice for planning and constructing Web pages today that will continue to serve you well into the future.

Q&A

Q So what is the difference between *digital communication* and other communication, anyway? Does *digital* mean it uses HTML?

A When information is transferred as distinct bits of information, which are essentially numbers, it's called *digital*. It's much easier to store, retrieve, and process information without losing or changing it when it is transferred digitally. Any information from a computer (including HTML) is by its nature digital, and in the not-too-distant future, telephone, television, radio, and even motion picture production will be digital.

Q How soon can I start designing Internet Web pages that aren't limited by what I can transfer over a 28.8Kbps modem?

A That depends on who you want to read your pages. There will be millions of 28.8Kbps modems (and the marginally faster 33.6Kbps and 56Kbps modems) in use for many years to come. But more and more people will have 128Kbps ISDN lines, 400Kbps satellite dishes, and 1Mbps (1,000Kbps) or faster cable, copper-optic, and wireless connections, too. Before long, the number of 1.4Mbps users will just about match the number of 14.4Kbps users. That difference of 100× in speed will lead more and more Web page publishers to offer separate high-speed and low-speed sites.

Q Man, I'm ashamed of you for not mentioning VRML in a hour about the future of the Internet! What gives?

A Hey everyone, did I mention that interactive, immersive three-dimensional worlds will be the future of the Internet? Virtual Reality Modeling Language (VRML) 2.0 is the current standard for making it happen, and it's compatible with your Web browser today. Unfortunately, VRML isn't quite ready for mass consumption and it's well beyond the scope of this book. But if you don't think it's going to change the world, think again. Go to `http://www.vrml.org` to read all about it.

Workshop

Quiz

Hey, you've had twenty-three quizzes in twenty-four hours! Instead of taking another one, may I suggest that you congratulate yourself for a job well done, take a break, and treat yourself to something special? You deserve it.

Exercise

Back from your break yet? Now that you've learned HTML and have your Web site online, this book can still help you make it better and better. You may want to review the Q&A sections throughout the book and Appendix A, "Readers' Most Frequently Asked Questions." And be sure to stick a bookmark at the beginning of Appendix C, "Complete HTML 4.0 Quick Reference." Exploring the "Exercises" sections that you might have skipped the first time around will help build your HTML skills as well.

And I'm sure you haven't yet explored all the oodles and oodles of entertaining examples and tutorial tips at the 24-Hour HTML Café. That's 24hourHTMLcafe.com, where the JavaScript is hot and the HTML never stops flowing... See you there!

24

APPENDIX A

Readers' Most Frequently Asked Questions

I have read and carefully collated over 1,000 questions and suggestions sent to me by readers of previous editions of this book. This feedback has influenced everything in this edition, from the overall outline to the specific notes, tips, and quiz questions. I've tried to incorporate the answers to readers' questions into the text at just the point in each hour when you would have found yourself asking those questions.

This appendix is for those times when you may have overlooked or forgotten a key point in the book. It's also a chance for me to answer those questions that didn't fit under any particular topic. These questions are presented in order of frequency: Number 1 is the most commonly asked question, number 2 is the next, and so on down to number 24. (A good number. I had to stop somewhere!)

In cases where the answer is clearly explained in the book, I just refer you to the relevant part of that hour. In cases where you might need a little more from me, I provide a succinct answer here and may also refer to an online resource that can help.

If you have a question that isn't answered here (or in the rest of the book), please email it to me at askme@netletter.com. I can't promise a personal response to every reader (there are a lot of you!), but I will add new questions to the online version of this appendix at the 24-Hour HTML Café site at (http://24hourHTMLcafe.com/faq.htm).

The 24 Top Questions from Readers of *Sams Teach Yourself HTML in 24 Hours*

1. **What should I read next?**

   Try *Sams Teach Yourself JavaScript in 24 Hours* (due for publication in late 1998) or *Dynamic Web Publishing Unleashed*. You can find out more about both books and buy them online at www.mcp.com.

2. **I'm stuck on my first page. It didn't work. What did I do wrong?**

   The first page is always the hardest. If you see all the HTML when you try to view the file (by selecting File, Open in your Web browser), or if you see some weird-looking characters at the top of the page, you haven't saved the file in plain text or ASCII text format. If you can't figure out how to do that in your word processor, use the Notepad or SimpleText editor that came with your computer instead. (WordPad is especially problematic in this regard.)

   For more guidance on making your first page, carefully go over the first **To Do** box and the "A Simple Sample Page" section in Hour 2, "Create a Web Page Right Now."

   Also, remember that you don't have to be connected to the Internet to edit and view Web pages on your hard drive. (If your Web browser tries to connect to the Internet every time you start it up, change the home page in the Edit, Preferences settings to a page on your hard drive.)

3. **Graphics or media files don't work/don't show online.**

   There are several common pitfalls you may encounter when putting graphics on a Web page:

   - Make sure the graphics file is in the same folder as the HTML document that refers to it. (Or if you're trying to refer to it in a different folder, review the "Relative Addresses" section in Hour 3, "Linking to Other Web Pages.")

- Make sure the graphics file is saved in GIF or JPEG format. Open the file with Paint Shop Pro (or another graphics program) and use File, Save As to save it again just to be sure.

- Make sure the capitalization of the filename and the `<IMG SRC>` tag match. `MyImage.gif` and `myimage.GIF` are not the same to most Web servers!

- To get rid of the blue line around a graphic, put `BORDER=0` in the `<IMG>` tag.

- This one's unlikely, but possible: Do you have Automatically load images turned off under Edit, Preferences, Advanced in Netscape Navigator 4.0, or Show Pictures turned off under View, Internet Options, Advanced in Microsoft Internet Explorer 4.0?

- True story: One reader spent four days trying to figure out why none of his images worked. He was typing `<IMG SCR=` instead of `<IMG SRC=` every single time. Don't laugh—just check *your* page for typos.

Refer to Hour 10, "Putting Graphics on a Web Page." If you're having trouble arranging graphics on the page, you'll find many helpful hints in all four chapters of Part IV, "Web Page Design."

Audio and video files are trickier and more prone to problems. There's no practical way to make them work in every version of every popular browser, but refer to Hour 17, "Embedding Multimedia in Web Pages," for as much help as I can give.

4. How do I get forms to work on my server?

Ask your Internet Service Provider to help you set up a forms-processing script. If they can't do it, you either need to find a service provider who is willing to actually provide some service or use the `ACTION=mailto:` option as described in the beginning of Hour 8, "Creating HTML Forms."

5. How do I put a counter on my page?

You probably don't need one, since most Internet Service Providers will send you a detailed report each week summarizing exactly how many times each of your pages was accessed. You should expect (read: demand) this, but some Web hosting services (especially free ones, or those outside North America) just won't provide it. In that case, you'll need to set up a CGI script on your server. That isn't too terribly difficult, and you'll find the code and some advice on how to do it at `www.developer.com` and other Web development sites.

6. I'm confused about frames. Mine don't work, and I don't quite understand why. Do you?

A

Frames are tricky. It may take a couple readings of Hour 21, "Multipage Layout with Frames" and some experimentation before something "clicks" for you and you see how the whole thing works. Here are some tips that may help:

- Remember that you can right-click in any frame and pick View Frame Source in Netscape Navigator or View Source in Microsoft Internet Explorer to see the HTML for that frame. Selecting View, Source from the main menu shows you the HTML for the frameset document.

- The only way to make a link change the contents of two or more frames at once is to link to a new frameset and include TARGET="_top" in the <A> link tag.

- You also use TARGET="_top" when you want to "break out" of all the frames and go back to a regular single-page document.

7. How do I pursue a career in Web page design, and how much should I charge to make someone a Web page?

As in any competitive business (and Web page design is a *very* competitive business), you'll need a solid marketing plan to be successful. If you've already found some clients, the amount you charge them is obviously up for negotiation. As a general rule, the going rate for experienced Web developers is between $25 and $50 per hour. If you are still learning, expect to charge less than that, unless you are already a professional graphics or publications designer with a loyal client base.

8. How do I make password-protected pages?

The easiest way is to make up a weird directory name, put the pages in that directory folder on the Web server, and only tell the address of the pages to those who are authorized to access them. More secure methods abound, but all of them require some kind of prewritten script or advanced server software. Consult your Internet Service Provider to see what kinds of security options they may have available.

9. Where can I find Java applets/prewritten Javascript?

Try www.developer.com and www.infohiway.com/javascript/indexf.htm, or look in any of the major Internet search sites under Java or JavaScript.

10. I can't get a link to work. What could be wrong?

Check the spelling and capitalization of the HREF link and the file to which you're trying to link. Some links will work on your hard drive but fail on the Web server if the capitalization doesn't match. (This is because Windows doesn't care about capitalization of filenames, and UNIX does.) Also, review Hour 3 to make sure you understand the finer points of relative and absolute addressing.

11. I am having trouble getting JavaScript/Java/ActiveX code to work, even though I'm pretty sure I got the syntax right.

Please don't imagine for a moment that Microsoft or Netscape could possibly have bugs in their Web browsers, especially in the sacred Java and JavaScript modules. You are the problem. To redeem yourself, you must build a shrine next to your computer, paste gilt-edged pictures of Bill Gates and Marc Andreessen to it, and humbly offer it cold pizza thrice daily. If you do this with a clean heart and pure mind, all problems with code implementation will still be your own darn fault, but at least Microsoft may decide not to take legal action against you for it.

12. Where can I get more help creating graphics and multimedia?

If you use Paint Shop Pro for graphics, try the tutorials at www.jasc.com or read the *Creating Paint Shop Pro Web Graphics* book available through the JASC online store. Learning to work with audio and video is a more ambitious endeavor, but my book *Web Page Wizardry: Wiring Your Site for Sound and Action* will give you a good head start. I also contributed chapters on working online audio and video to *Web Publishing Unleashed: Professional Reference Edition*. Both books can be purchased at www.mcp.com.

13. How do I make a pull-down list of links?

You need JavaScript or CGI Scripting (advanced stuff) to make it work.

14. How do I get a message to scroll along the bottom?

You'll find JavaScript for that at both www.developer.com and www.infohiway.com/javascript/indexf.htm.

15. How do I put files on a Web site for people to download?

Just upload the file in the same place you put your Web pages and use a regular HTML link, like the following:

```
<A HREF="bigfile.zip">Click here to download bigfile.zip.</A>
```

16. How do I put a browser on a disk? Do I need to if I publish Web pages on a disk?

Most people have a Web browser on their computer these days, but if you want to provide one just in case, you'll need permission from the browser company. I recommend Opera (www.opera.no), which is small enough to fit on a single 1.4MB floppy disk and allows distribution of free time-limited evaluation copies.

17. When I try to download Paint Shop Pro or the FTP software you recommended, the download is deathly slow or stops altogether. Can you help?

I'm afraid there's not much I (or you) can do, except recommend that you try again later. And you thought you needed a car to get in a traffic jam?

A

18. Should I use Java applets and other advanced stuff?

Not unless you need to do something you can't do any other way. Basic HTML is faster, more widely compatible, and easier to maintain.

19. How do I make a form for people to fill out and print?

They can fill out and print any HTML form. Just tell them to do it. See the Q&A section at the end of Hour 8, "Creating HTML Forms."

20. How do I full justify text so it lines up with both margins?

If you have a flat-panel screen, you could try scissors and glue. The CSS2 style sheet standard does support "text-align: justify" as a style specification, but none of the popular Web browsers can display full justified text yet.

21. How do I publicize my site, and how do I find advertisers for my site?

The first section of Hour 23, "Helping People Find Your Web Pages," will help some, but mostly you'll need to come up with your own marketing/PR plan tailored to your specific situation.

There are a number of Web advertising services and companies that will pay independent Web publishers like you to run ads or affiliate with them in other potentially profitable ways. Most pay you a small amount each time a visitor to your site clicks one of their ads. (See http://www.sitecash.com/guide.htm for some possibilities.)

22. How do I create HTML pages or links within email messages?

Just type regular HTML like you would to make a Web page. Most advanced email programs nowadays (especially those bundled with Microsoft Internet Explorer and Netscape Communicator) allow you to create and view "HTML Mail." You format it just as you would a document—no HTML experience required.

23. How do I open a link in a new window?

Use TARGET="_blank" in your <A HREF> link tag.

24. How do I link to a database and/or let people search my site?

You'll need to give a software company some money for a good answer to that one. NetObjects Fusion is one of the more popular and powerful options. Microsoft and Netscape also offer advanced Web server extensions that allow for database access and searching. One of many online stores where you can comparison shop for this type of software is www.developerdirect.com.

APPENDIX B

HTML Learning Resources on the Internet

General HTML Information

The 24-Hour HTML Café (The companion site to *Sams Teach Yourself HTML 4 in 24 Hours*, Third Edition, including an online version of this appendix.):

    http://24hourHTMLcafe.com

The MCP Web Publishing Resource Center:

    http://www.mcp.com/resources/webpub/

The World Wide Web Consortium (W3C):

    http://www.w3.org/

The Compendium of HTML Elements:

    http://www.htmlcompendium.org/

Microsoft Internet Explorer Web Browser:

```
http://www.microsoft.com/ie/
```

Microsoft Internet Magazine:

```
http://www.microsoft.com/internet
```

Netscape Communications Home Page:

```
http://home.netscape.com
```

Netscape DevEdge Online:

```
http://developer.netscape.com
```

The Developer's JumpStation:

```
http://oneworld.wa.com/htmldev/devpage/dev-page.html
```

The HTML Writer's Guild:

```
http://www.hwg.org/
```

The Web Developer's Virtual Library:

```
http://WWW.Stars.com/
```

HTML for Rookies:

```
http://members.tripod.com/~larrydoz/html4rookies.html
```

Web Page Design

Author's Little Helper (design and editorial services for Web page authors):

```
http://netletter.com/helper/
```

Creating Graphics for the Web:

```
http://www.widearea.co.uk/designer/
```

Web Page Design Tips:

```
http://stoopidsoftware.com/tips/
```

Web Page Design Decisions:

```
http://www.wilsonweb.com/articles/12design.htm
```

Sun Guide to Web Style:

```
http://www.sun.com/styleguide/
```

A Guide to Creating a Successful Web Site:

http://www.hooked.net/~larrylin/web.htm

Web Pages that Suck:

http://www.webpagesthatsuck.com/

Software

Paint Shop Pro (a highly recommended Windows graphics and animation editor):

http://www.jasc.com

GIF Construction Set (another alternative for creating animated graphics):

http://www.mindworkshop.com/alchemy/gcsdemo.html

Perl Library to Manage CGI and Forms:

http://www.bio.cam.ac.uk/cgi-lib/

Mapedit: A Tool for Windows and X11 for Creating Imagemap Map Files:

http://www.boutell.com/mapedit/

Shareware.com (best source for almost any type of free or inexpensive software for all types of computers):

http://www.shareware.com

The Ultimate Collection of Winsock Software:

http://www.tucows.com/

Dave Central Software Archive:

http://www.davecentral.com/

WinSite Windows Software Archive:

http://www.winsite.com/

B

Graphics

Cool Graphics on the Web:

http://little.fishnet.net/~gini/cool/

Barry's Clip Art Server:

http://www.barrysclipart.com

256 Color Square:

http://www59.metronet.com/colors/

Color Triplet Chart:

http://www.phoenix.net/~jacobson/rgb.html

Imaging Machine:

http://www.vrl.com/Imaging/

Frequently Asked Questions from comp.graphics:

http://www.primenet.com/~grieggs/cg_faq.html

Multimedia and Virtual Reality

RealAudio and RealVideo:

http://www.real.com

StreamWorks and XingMPEG:

http://www.xingtech.com

QuickTime:

http://quicktime.apple.com

VDOLive:

http://www.clubvdo.net/

Macromedia's Shockwave:

http://www.macromedia.com/

Multimedia Authoring:

http://www.mcli.dist.maricopa.edu/authoring/

The VRML Repository:

http://www.sdsc.edu/vrml/

Advanced Developer Resources

Webreference (tutorials and references to HTML and related technologies):

http://www.webreference.com

Cut N' Paste JavaScript (200+ scripts to cut and paste into your pages):

http://www.infohiway.com/javascript/indexf.htm

Netscape's JavaScript Guide:

```
http://developer.netscape.com/docs/manuals/communicator/jsguide4/index.htm
```

JavaSoft:

```
http://www.javasoft.com/
```

Developer.com Resource Directories:

```
http://www.developer.com/directories/
```

Tech Tools for Developers:

```
http://www.techweb.com/tools/developers/
```

NCompass ActiveX Plug-in for Netscape Navigator:

```
http://www.ncompasslabs.com/
```

A Webmaster's Guide to Search Engines:

```
http://searchenginewatch.com/webmasters/index.html
```

The TrueDoc Web Typography Center:

```
http://www.truedoc.com/webpages/intro/
```

Microsoft's TrueType Typography Pages:

```
http://www.microsoft.com/truetype/
```

HTML Validators

HTML Validation Service (checks your pages for HTML 4.0 compatibility):

```
http://www.webtechs.com/html-val-svc/
```

Htmlchek (checks compatibility with older HTML 2.0 and 3.0 standards):

```
http://uts.cc.utexas.edu/~churchh/htmlchek.html
```

Weblint (paid-subscription HTML validation service):

```
http://www.unipress.com/cgi-bin/WWWeblint
```

Directories with HTML Information

Yahoo! World Wide Web:

```
http://www.yahoo.com/Computers/Internet/World_Wide_Web/
```

B

HotWired's WebMonkey:

http://www.webmonkey.com/

Cool Site of the Day:

http://cool.infi.net/

Lycos Web Publishing Index:

http://a2z.lycos.com/Internet/Web_Publishing_and_HTML/

InfoSeek HTML Index:

http://www.infoseek.com/Internet/HTML

TechWeb's HTML Authoring Tools:

http://www.techweb.com/tools/html/

Web Site Services

The List (Internet Service Providers Buyer's Guide):

http://thelist.internet.com/

PointGuide's Partners Program (free personal search engine for your site):

http://www.pointguide.com/partners/

GuestPage (free guestbook service):

http://www.GuestPage.com/

The Counter (free Web counter/tracker):

http://www.TheCounter.com/

Affiliate Guide (info on companies that pay you to promote them on your site):

http://www.sitecash.com/guide.htm

CreditNet (accept and process credit card payments online):

http://www.creditnet.com/

BannerAd Network (advertise your site/exchange ads with other sites):

http://www.banneradnetwork.com/

Add It (register your pages with multiple search sites, free):

http://www.liquidimaging.com/submit/

Submit It! (register your pages with hundreds of search sites, paid service):

http://www.submit-it.com/

Free Web Site Hosting

Geocities:

```
http://www.geocities.com/
```

Angelfire:

```
http://www.angelfire.com/
```

Cybercities:

```
http://www.cybercities.com/
```

Tripod:

```
http://www.tripod.com/
```

Yahoo! Free Home Page Service Listings:

```
http://www.yahoo.com/Business_and_Economy/Companies/Internet_Services
/Web_Services/Free_Web_Pages/
```

B

APPENDIX C

Complete HTML 4.0 Quick Reference

HTML 4.0 is an ambitious attempt to meet the needs of Web developers worldwide, both casual and professional. This appendix provides a quick reference to all the elements and attributes of the language.

This appendix is based on the information provided in the *HTML 4.0 Specification W3C Recommendation,* revised on 24-Apr-1998. The latest version of this document can be found at http://www.w3.org/TR/REC-html40/.

To make the information readily accessible, this appendix organizes HTML elements by their function in the following order:

- Structure
- Text phrases and paragraphs
- Text font elements
- Lists

- Links
- Tables
- Frames
- Embedded content
- Style
- Forms
- Scripts

The elements are listed alphabetically within each section, and the following information is presented:

- Usage—A general description of the element
- Start/End Tag—Indicates whether these tags are required, optional, or illegal
- Attributes—Lists the attributes of the element with a short description of their effect
- Empty—Indicates whether the element can be empty
- Notes—Relates any special considerations when using the element and indicates whether the element is new, deprecated, or obsolete

 Several elements and attributes have been *deprecated*, which means they have been outdated by the current HTML version, and you should avoid using them. The same or similar functionality is provided by using new features.

Following this, the common attributes and intrinsic events are summarized.

 HTML 4.0 introduces several new attributes that apply to a significant number of elements. These are referred to within each element listing as core, i18n, and events.

Structure

HTML relies on several elements to provide structure to a document (as opposed to structuring the text within) as well as provide information that is used by the browser or search engines.

<BDO>...</BDO>

Usage	The bidirectional algorithm element used to selectively turn off the default text direction.
Start/End Tag	Required/Required.
Attributes	core.
	lang="..." The language of the document.
	dir="..." The text direction (ltr, rtl). Mandatory attribute.
Empty	No.
Notes	Strict DTD.

There are, in fact, 3 versions of HTML 4: Strict (pure HTML 4), Transitional (elements within the Strict DTD plus additional elements held over from HTML 3.2), and Frameset (Transitional plus frames). Each one relies upon a Document Type Definition to specify which elements and attributes are to be used, and the DTD is noted here.

<BODY>...</BODY>

Usage	Contains the content of the document.
Start/End Tag	Optional/Optional.
Attributes	core, i18n, events.
	background="..." Deprecated. URL for the background image.
	bgcolor="..." Deprecated. Sets background color.
	text="..." Deprecated. Text color.
	link="..." Deprecated. Link color.
	vlink="..." Deprecated. Visited link color.
	alink="..." Deprecated. Active link color.
	onload="..." Intrinsic event triggered when the document loads.
	onunload="..." Intrinsic event triggered when document unloads.

C

Empty	No.
Notes	Strict DTD. There can be only one BODY, and it must follow the HEAD. The BODY element can be replaced by a FRAMESET element. The presentational attributes are deprecated in favor of setting these values with style sheets.

Comments <!-- ... -->

Usage	Used to insert notes or scripts that are not displayed by the browser.
Start/End Tag	Required/Required.
Attributes	None.
Empty	Yes.
Notes	Comments are not restricted to one line and can be any length. The end tag is not required to be on the same line as the start tag.

<DIV>...</DIV>

Usage	The division element is used to add structure to a block of text.
Start/End Tag	Required/Required.
Attributes	core, i18n, events.
	align="..." Deprecated. Controls alignment (left, center, right, justify).

You will notice that the oft-used align attribute has been deprecated. This affects a large number of elements whose rendered position was controlled by setting the alignment to a suitable value, such as right or center. Also deprecated is the <CENTER> element. The W3C strongly encourages users to begin using Style Sheets to modify the visual formatting of an HTML document.

Empty	No.
Notes	Strict DTD. Cannot be used within a P element. The align attribute is deprecated in favor of controlling alignment through style sheets.

`<!DOCTYPE...>`

Usage   Version information appears on the first line of an HTML document and is a Standard Generalized Markup Language (SGML) declaration rather than an element.

`<H1>...</H1>` through `<H6>...</H6>`

Usage   The six headings (H1 is the uppermost, or most important) are used in the BODY to structure information in a hierarchical fashion.

Start/End Tag   Required/Required.

Attributes   core, i18n, events.

align="..." Deprecated. Controls alignment (left, center, right, justify).

Empty   No.

Notes   Strict DTD. Visual browsers will display the size of the headings in relation to their importance, with H1 being the largest and H6 the smallest. The align attribute is deprecated in favor of controlling alignment through style sheets.

`<HEAD>...</HEAD>`

Usage   This is the document header and contains other elements that provide information to users and search engines.

Start/End Tag   Optional/Optional.

Attributes   i18n.

profile="..." URL specifying the location of META data.

Empty   No.

Notes   Strict DTD. There can be only one HEAD per document. It must follow the opening `<HTML>` tag and precede the BODY.

`<HR>`

Usage   Horizontal rules are used to separate sections of a Web page.

C

Start/End Tag	Required/Illegal.
Attributes	core, events.
	align="..." Deprecated. Controls alignment (left, center, right, justify).
	noshade="..." Displays the rule as a solid color.
	size="..." Deprecated. The size of the rule.
	width="..." Deprecated. The width of the rule.
Empty	Yes.
Notes	Strict DTD.

<HTML>...</HTML>

Usage	The HTML element contains the entire document.
Start/End Tag	Optional/Optional.
Attributes	i18n.
	version="..." URL of the document type definition specifying the HTML version used to create the document.
Empty	No.
Notes	Strict DTD. The version information is duplicated in the <!DOCTYPE...> declaration and is therefore not essential.

<META>

Usage	Provides information about the document.
Start/End Tag	Required/Illegal.
Attributes	i18n.
	http-equiv="..." HTTP response header name.
	name="..." Name of the meta information.
	content="..." Content of the meta information.
	scheme="..." Assigns a scheme to interpret the meta data.
Empty	Yes.
Notes	Strict DTD.

<SPAN>...</SPAN>

Usage	Organizes the document by defining a span of text.
Start/End Tag	Required/Required.
Attributes	core, i18n, events.
Empty	No.
Notes	Strict DTD. This element is new to HTML 4.

<TITLE>...</TITLE>

Usage	This is the name you give your Web page. The TITLE element is located in the HEAD element and is displayed in the browser window title bar.
Start/End Tag	Required/Required.
Attributes	i18n.
Empty	No.
Notes	Strict DTD. Only one title allowed per document.

Text Phrases and Paragraphs

Text phrases (or blocks) can be structured to suit a specific purpose, such as creating a paragraph. This should not be confused with modifying the formatting of the text.

<ABBR>...</ABBR>

Usage	Used to define abbreviations.
Start/End Tag	Required/Required.
Attributes	core, i18n, events.
Empty	No.
Notes	Strict DTD. This element is new to HTML 4. The material enclosed by the tag is the abbreviated form, whereas the long form is defined by attributes within the tag.

<ACRONYM>...</ACRONYM>

Usage	Used to define acronyms.
Start/End Tag	Required/Required.
Attributes	core, i18n, events.

C

Empty	No.
Notes	Strict DTD. This element is new to HTML 4.

`<ADDRESS>...</ADDRESS>`

Usage	Provides a special format for author or contact information.
Start/End Tag	Required/Required.
Attributes	`core, i18n, events.`
Empty	No.
Notes	Strict DTD. The `BR` element is commonly used inside the `ADDRESS` element to break the lines of an address.

`<BLOCKQUOTE>...</BLOCKQUOTE>`

Usage	Used to display long quotations.
Start/End Tag	Required/Required.
Attributes	`core, i18n, events.`
	`cite="..."` The URL of the quoted text.
Empty	No.
Notes	Strict DTD.

`<BR>`

Usage	Forces a line break.
Start/End Tag	Required/Illegal.
Attributes	`core, i18n, events.`
	`clear="..."` Sets the location where next line begins after a floating object (`none, left, right, all`).
Empty	Yes.
Notes	Strict DTD.

`<CITE>...</CITE>`

Usage	Cites a reference.
Start/End Tag	Required/Required.
Attributes	`core, i18n, events.`

Empty	No.
Notes	Strict DTD.

<CODE>...</CODE>

Usage	Identifies a code fragment for display.
Start/End Tag	Required/Required.
Attributes	`core, i18n, events`.
Empty	No.
Notes	Strict DTD.

<DEL>...</DEL>

Usage	Shows text as having been deleted from the document since the last change.
Start/End Tag	Required/Required.
Attributes	`core, i18n, events`.
	`cite="..."` The URL of the source document.
	`datetime="..."` Indicates the date and time of the change.
Empty	No.
Notes	Strict DTD. This element is new to HTML 4.

<DFN>...</DFN>

Usage	Defines an enclosed term.
Start/End Tag	Required/Required.
Attributes	`core, i18n, events`.
Empty	No.
Notes	Strict DTD.

<EM>...</EM>

Usage	Emphasized text.
Start/End Tag	Required/Required.
Attributes	`core, i18n, events`.

C

Empty	No.
Notes	Strict DTD.

`<INS>...</INS>`

Usage	Shows text as having been inserted in the document since the last change.
Start/End Tag	Required/Required.
Attributes	`core`, `i18n`, `events`.
	`cite="..."` The URL of the source document.
	`datetime="..."` Indicates the date and time of the change.
Empty	No.
Notes	Strict DTD. This element is new to HTML 4.

`<KBD>...</KBD>`

Usage	Indicates text a user would type.
Start/End Tag	Required/Required.
Attributes	`core`, `i18n`, `events`.
Empty	No.
Notes	Strict DTD.

`<P>...</P>`

Usage	Defines a paragraph.
Start/End Tag	Required/Optional.
Attributes	`core`, `i18n`, `events`.
	`align="..."` Deprecated. Controls alignment (`left`, `center`, `right`, `justify`).
Empty	No.
Notes	Strict DTD.

`<PRE>...</PRE>`

Usage	Displays preformatted text.
Start/End Tag	Required/Required.

Attributes	core, i18n, events.
	width="..." The width of the formatted text.
Empty	No.
Notes	Strict DTD.

`<Q>...</Q>`

Usage	Used to display short quotations that do not require paragraph breaks.
Start/End Tag	Required/Required.
Attributes	core, i18n, events.
	cite="..." The URL of the quoted text.
Empty	No.
Notes	Strict DTD. This element is new to HTML 4.

`<SAMP>...</SAMP>`

Usage	Identifies sample output.
Start/End Tag	Required/Required.
Attributes	core, i18n, events.
Empty	No.
Notes	Strict DTD.

`<STRONG>...</STRONG>`

Usage	Stronger emphasis.
Start/End Tag	Required/Required.
Attributes	core, i18n, events.
Empty	No.
Notes	Strict DTD.

`<SUB>...</SUB>`

Usage	Creates subscript.
Start/End Tag	Required/Required.
Attributes	core, i18n, events.

C

Empty	No.
Notes	Strict DTD.

\<SUP\>...\</SUP\>

Usage	Creates superscript.
Start/End Tag	Required/Required.
Attributes	core, i18n, events.
Empty	No.
Notes	Strict DTD.

\<VAR\>...\</VAR\>

Usage	A variable.
Start/End Tag	Required/Required.
Attributes	core, i18n, events.
Empty	No.
Notes	Strict DTD.

Text Formatting Elements

Text characteristics such as the size, weight, and style can be modified using these elements, but the HTML 4.0 specification encourages you to use style instead.

\<B\>...\</B\>

Usage	Bold text.
Start/End Tag	Required/Required.
Attributes	core, i18n, events.
Empty	No.
Notes	Strict DTD.

\<BASEFONT\>

Usage	Sets the base font size.
Start/End Tag	Required/Illegal.

Attributes	`size="..."` The font size (1 through 7 or relative, that is +3).
	`color="..."` The font color.
	`face="..."` The font type.
Empty	Yes.
Notes	Transitional DTD. Deprecated in favor of style sheets.

`<BIG>...</BIG>`

Usage	Large text.
Start/End Tag	Required/Required.
Attributes	`core, i18n, events`.
Empty	No.
Notes	Strict DTD.

`<FONT>...</FONT>`

Usage	Changes the font size and color.
Start/End Tag	Required/Required.
Attributes	`size="..."` The font size (1 through 7 or relative, that is, +3).
	`color="..."` The font color.
	`face="..."` The font type.
Empty	No.
Notes	Transitional DTD. Deprecated in favor of style sheets.

`<I>...</I>`

Usage	Italicized text.
Start/End Tag	Required/Required.
Attributes	`core, i18n, events`.
Empty	No.
Notes	Strict DTD.

C

\<S>...\</S>

Usage	Strikethrough text.
Start/End Tag	Required/Required.
Attributes	core, i18n, events.
Empty	No.
Notes	Transitional DTD. Deprecated.

\<SMALL>...\</SMALL>

Usage	Small text.
Start/End Tag	Required/Required.
Attributes	core, i18n, events.
Empty	No.
Notes	Strict DTD.

\<STRIKE>...\</STRIKE>

Usage	Strikethrough text.
Start/End Tag	Required/Required.
Attributes	core, i18n, events.
Empty	No.
Notes	Transitional DTD. Deprecated.

\<TT>...\</TT>

Usage	Teletype (or monospaced) text.
Start/End Tag	Required/Required.
Attributes	core, i18n, events.
Empty	No.
Notes	Strict DTD.

\<U>...\</U>

Usage	Underlined text.
Start/End Tag	Required/Required.
Attributes	core, i18n, events.

Empty	No.
Notes	Transitional DTD. Deprecated.

Lists

You can organize text into a more structured outline by creating lists. Lists can be nested.

<DD>...</DD>

Usage	The definition description used in a DL (definition list) element.
Start/End Tag	Required/Optional.
Attributes	core, i18n, events.
Empty	No.
Notes	Strict DTD. Can contain block-level content, such as the <P> element.

<DIR>...</DIR>

Usage	Creates a multi-column directory list.
Start/End Tag	Required/Required.
Attributes	core, i18n, events.
	compact Deprecated. Compacts the displayed list.
Empty	No.
Notes	Transitional DTD. Must contain at least one list item. This element is deprecated in favor of the UL (unordered list) element.

<DL>...</DL>

Usage	Creates a definition list.
Start/End Tag	Required/Required.
Attributes	core, i18n, events.
	compact Deprecated. Compacts the displayed list.
Empty	No.
Notes	Strict DTD. Must contain at least one <DT> or <DD> element in any order.

C

`<DT>...</DT>`

Usage	The definition term (or label) used within a DL (definition list) element.
Start/End Tag	Required/Optional.
Attributes	core, i18n, events.
Empty	No.
Notes	Strict DTD. Must contained text (which can be modified by text markup elements).

`<LI>...</LI>`

Usage	Defines a list item within a list.
Start/End Tag	Required/Optional.
Attributes	core, i18n, events.
	type="..." Changes the numbering style (1, a, A, i, I), ordered lists, or bullet style (disc, square, circle) in unordered lists.
	value="..." Sets the numbering to the given integer beginning with the current list item.
Empty	No.
Notes	Strict DTD.

`<MENU>...</MENU>`

Usage	Creates a single-column menu list.
Start/End Tag	Required/Required.
Attributes	core, i18n, events.
	compact Deprecated. Compacts the displayed list.
Empty	No.
Notes	Transitional DTD. Must contain at least one list item. This element is deprecated in favor of the UL (unordered list) element.

`<OL>...</OL>`

Usage	Creates an ordered list.
Start/End Tag	Required/Required.

Attributes	core, i18n, events.
	type="..." Sets the numbering style (1, a, A, i, I).
	compact Deprecated. Compacts the displayed list.
	start="..." Sets the starting number to the chosen integer.
Empty	No.
Notes	Strict DTD. Must contain at least one list item.

\<UL>...\</UL>

Usage	Creates an unordered list.
Start/End Tag	Required/Required.
Attributes	core, i18n, events.
	type="..." Sets the bullet style (disc, square, circle).
	compact Deprecated. Compacts the displayed list.
Empty	No.
Notes	Strict DTD. Must contain at least one list item.

Links

Hyperlinking is fundamental to HTML. These elements enable you to link to other documents, other locations within a document, or external files.

\<A>...\</A>

Usage	Used to define links and anchors.
Start/End Tag	Required/Required.
Attributes	core, i18n, events.
	charset="..." Character encoding of the resource.
	name="..." Defines an anchor.
	href="..." The URL of the linked resource.
	target="..." Determines where the resource will be displayed (user-defined name, _blank, _parent, _self, _top).
	rel="..." Forward link types.

C

`rev="..."` Reverse link types.

`accesskey="..."` Assigns a hotkey to this element.

`shape="..."` Enables you to define client-side imagemaps using defined shapes (`default`, `rect`, `circle`, `poly`).

`coords="..."` Sets the size of the shape using pixel or percentage lengths.

`tabindex="..."` Sets the tabbing order between elements with a defined `tabindex`.

Empty	No.
Notes	Strict DTD.

<BASE>

Usage	All other URLs in the document are resolved against this location.
Start/End Tag	Required/Illegal.
Attributes	`href="..."` The URL of the linked resource.

`target="..."` Determines where the resource will be displayed (user-defined name, `_blank`, `_parent`, `_self`, `_top`).

Empty	Yes.
Notes	Strict DTD. Located in the document HEAD.

<LINK>

Usage	Defines the relationship between a link and a resource.
Start/End Tag	Required/Illegal.
Attributes	`core`, `i18n`, `events`.

`href="..."` The URL of the resource.

`rel="..."` The forward link types.

`rev="..."` The reverse link types.

`type="..."` The Internet content type.

`media="..."` Defines the destination medium

(screen, print, projection, braille, speech, all).

target="..." Determines where the resource will be displayed (user-defined name, _blank, _parent, _self, _top).

Empty	Yes.
Notes	Strict DTD. Located in the document HEAD.

Tables

Tables are meant to display data in a tabular format. Before the introduction of HTML 4.0, tables were widely used for page layout purposes, but, with the advent of style sheets, this is being discouraged by the W3C.

<CAPTION>...</CAPTION>

Usage	Displays a table caption.
Start/End Tag	Required/Required.
Attributes	core, i18n, events.
	align="..." Deprecated. Controls alignment (left, center, right, justify).
Empty	No.
Notes	Strict DTD. Optional.

<COL>

Usage	Groups columns within column groups in order to share attribute values.
Start/End Tag	Required/Illegal.
Attributes	core, i18n, events.
	span="..." The number of columns the group contains.
	width="..." The column width as a percentage, pixel value, or minimum value.
	align="..." Horizontally aligns the contents of cells (left, center, right, justify, char).
	char="..." Sets a character on which the column aligns.

C

charoff="..." Offset to the first alignment character on a line.

valign="..." Vertically aligns the contents of a cell (top, middle, bottom, baseline).

Empty	Yes.
Notes	Strict DTD.

`<COLGROUP>...</COLGROUP>`

Usage	Defines a column group.
Start/End Tag	Required/Optional.
Attributes	core, i18n, events.

span="..." The number of columns in a group.

width="..." The width of the columns.

align="..." Horizontally aligns the contents of cells (left, center, right, justify, char).

char="..." Sets a character on which the column aligns.

charoff="..." Offset to the first alignment character on a line.

valign="..." Vertically aligns the contents of a cell (top, middle, bottom, baseline).

Empty	No.
Notes	Strict DTD. This element is new to HTML 4.

`<TABLE>...</TABLE>`

Usage	Creates a table.
Start/End Tag	Required/Required.
Attributes	core, i18n, events.

align="..." Deprecated. Controls alignment (left, center, right, justify).

bgcolor="..." Deprecated. Sets the background color.

width="..." Table width.

cols="..." The number of columns.

border="..." The width in pixels of a border around the table.

frame="..." Sets the visible sides of a table (void, above, below, hsides, lhs, rhs, vsides, box, border).

rules="..." Sets the visible rules within a table (none, groups, rows, cols, all).

cellspacing="..." Spacing between cells.

cellpadding="..." Spacing in cells.

Empty	No.
Notes	Strict DTD.

`<TBODY>...</TBODY>`

Usage	Defines the table body.
Start/End Tag	Optional/Optional.
Attributes	core, i18n, events.

align="..." Horizontally aligns the contents of cells (left, center, right, justify, char).

char="..." Sets a character on which the column aligns.

charoff="..." Offset to the first alignment character on a line.

valign="..." Vertically aligns the contents of cells (top, middle, bottom, baseline).

Empty	No.
Notes	Strict DTD. This element is new to HTML 4.

`<TD>...</TD>`

Usage	Defines a cell's contents.
Start/End Tag	Required/Optional.
Attributes	core, i18n, events.

axis="..." Abbreviated name.

C

axes="..." axis names listing row and column headers pertaining to the cell.

nowrap="..." Deprecated. Turns off text wrapping in a cell.

bgcolor="..." Deprecated. Sets the background color.

rowspan="..." The number of rows spanned by a cell.

colspan="..." The number of columns spanned by a cell.

align="..." Horizontally aligns the contents of cells (left, center, right, justify, char).

char="..." Sets a character on which the column aligns.

charoff="..." Offset to the first alignment character on a line.

valign="..." Vertically aligns the contents of cells (top, middle, bottom, baseline).

| Empty | No. |
| Notes | Strict DTD. |

\<TFOOT\>...\</TFOOT\>

Usage	Defines the table footer.
Start/End Tag	Required/Optional.
Attributes	core, i18n, events.

align="..." Horizontally aligns the contents of cells (left, center, right, justify, char).

char="..." Sets a character on which the column aligns.

charoff="..." Offset to the first alignment character on a line.

valign="..." Vertically aligns the contents of cells (top, middle, bottom, baseline).

Empty	No.
Notes	Strict DTD. This element is new to HTML 4.

<TH>...</TH>

Usage	Defines the cell contents of the table header.
Start/End Tag	Required/Optional.
Attributes	core, i18n, events.

axis="..." Abbreviated name.

axes="..." axis names listing row and column headers pertaining to the cell.

nowrap="..." Deprecated. Turns off text wrapping in a cell.

bgcolor="..." Deprecated. Sets the background color.

rowspan="..." The number of rows spanned by a cell.

colspan="..." The number of columns spanned by a cell.

align="..." Horizontally aligns the contents of cells (left, center, right, justify, char).

char="..." Sets a character on which the column aligns.

charoff="..." Offset to the first alignment character on a line.

valign="..." Vertically aligns the contents of cells (top, middle, bottom, baseline).

Empty	No.
Notes	Strict DTD.

<THEAD>...</THEAD>

Usage	Defines the table header.
Start/End Tag	Required/Optional.
Attributes	core, i18n, events.

C

align="..." Horizontally aligns the contents of cells (left, center, right, justify, char).

char="..." Sets a character on which the column aligns.

charoff="..." Offset to the first alignment character on a line.

valign="..." Vertically aligns the contents of cells (top, middle, bottom, baseline).

Empty	No.
Notes	Strict DTD. This element is new to HTML 4.

`<TR>...</TR>`

Usage	Defines a row of table cells.
Start/End Tag	Required/Optional.
Attributes	core, i18n, events.

align="..." Horizontally aligns the contents of cells (left, center, right, justify, char).

char="..." Sets a character on which the column aligns.

charoff="..." Offset to the first alignment character on a line.

valign="..." Vertically aligns the contents of cells (top, middle, bottom, baseline).

bgcolor="..." Deprecated. Sets the background color.

Empty	No.
Notes	Strict DTD.

Frames

Frames create new "panels" in the Web browser window that are used to display content from different source documents.

<FRAME>

Usage	Defines a FRAME.
Start/End Tag	Required/Illegal.
Attributes	name="..." The name of a frame.
	src="..." The source to be displayed in a frame.
	frameborder="..." Toggles the border between frames (0, 1).
	marginwidth="..." Sets the space between the frame border and content.
	marginheight="..." Sets the space between the frame border and content.
	noresize Disables sizing.
	scrolling="..." Determines scrollbar presence (auto, yes, no).
Empty	Yes.
Notes	Frameset DTD. This element is new to HTML 4.

<FRAMESET>...</FRAMESET>

Usage	Defines the layout of FRAMES within a window.
Start/End Tag	Required/Required.
Attributes	rows="..." The number of rows.
	cols="..." The number of columns.
	onload="..." The intrinsic event triggered when the document loads.
	onunload="..." The intrinsic event triggered when the document unloads.
Empty	No.
Notes	Frameset DTD. This element is new to HTML 4. FRAMESETs can be nested.

C

<IFRAME>...</IFRAME>

Usage	Creates an inline frame.
Start/End Tag	Required/Required.

Attributes	name="..." The name of the frame.
	src="..." The source to be displayed in a frame.
	frameborder="..." Toggles the border between frames (0, 1).
	marginwidth="..." Sets the space between the frame border and content.
	marginheight="..." Sets the space between the frame border and content.
	scrolling="..." Determines scrollbar presence (auto, yes, no).
	align="..." Deprecated. Controls alignment (left, center, right, justify).
	height="..." Height.
	width="..." Width.
Empty	No.
Notes	Transitional DTD. This element is new to HTML 4.

<NOFRAMES>...</NOFRAMES>

Usage	Alternative content when frames are not supported.
Start/End Tag	Required/Required.
Attributes	None.
Empty	No.
Notes	Frameset DTD. This element is new to HTML 4.

Embedded Content

Also called inclusions, embedded content applies to Java applets, imagemaps, and other multimedia or programmed content that is placed in a Web page to provide additional functionality.

<APPLET>...</APPLET>

Usage	Includes a Java applet.
Start/End Tag	Required/Required.

Attributes

`codebase="..."` The URL base for the applet.

`archive="..."` Identifies the resources to be pre-loaded.

`code="..."` The applet class file.

`object="..."` The serialized applet file.

`alt="..."` Displays text while loading.

`name="..."` The name of the applet.

`width="..."` The width of the displayed applet.

`height="..."` The height of the displayed applet.

`align="..."` Deprecated. Controls alignment (`left`, `center`, `right`, `justify`).

`hspace="..."` The horizontal space separating the image from other content.

`vspace="..."` The vertical space separating the image from other content.

Empty   No.

Notes   Transitional DTD. Applet is deprecated in favor of the `OBJECT` element.

\<AREA\>

Usage   The `AREA` element is used to define links and anchors.

Start/End Tag   Required/Illegal.

Attributes   `shape="..."` Enables you to define client-side imagemaps using defined shapes (`default`, `rect`, `circle`, `poly`).

`coords="..."` Sets the size of the shape using pixel or percentage lengths.

`href="..."` The URL of the linked resource.

`target="..."` Determines where the resource will be displayed (user-defined name, `_blank`, `_parent`, `_self`, `_top`).

`nohref="..."` Indicates that the region has no action.

C

                                                `alt="..."` Displays alternative text.

`tabindex="..."` Sets the tabbing order between elements with a defined `tabindex`.

Empty	Yes.
Notes	Strict DTD.

`<IMG>`

Usage	Includes an image in the document.
Start/End Tag	Required/Illegal.
Attributes	`core`, `i18n`, `events`.

`src="..."` The URL of the image.

`alt="..."` Alternative text to display.

`align="..."` Deprecated. Controls alignment (`left`, `center`, `right`, `justify`).

`height="..."` The height of the image.

`width="..."` The width of the image.

`border="..."` Border width.

`hspace="..."` The horizontal space separating the image from other content.

`vspace="..."` The vertical space separating the image from other content.

`usemap="..."` The URL to a client-side imagemap.

`ismap` Identifies a server-side imagemap.

Empty	Yes.
Notes	Strict DTD.

`<MAP>...</MAP>`

Usage	When used with the AREA element, creates a client-side imagemap.
Start/End Tag	Required/Required.
Attributes	`core`.

`name="..."` The name of the imagemap to be created.

Empty	No.
Notes	Strict DTD.

<OBJECT>...</OBJECT>

Usage	Includes an object.
Start/End Tag	Required/Required.
Attributes	`core`, `i18n`, `events`.

`declare` A flag that declares but doesn't create an object.

`classid="..."` The URL of the object's location.

`codebase="..."` The URL for resolving URLs specified by other attributes.

`data="..."` The URL to the object's data.

`type="..."` The Internet content type for data.

`codetype="..."` The Internet content type for the code.

`standby="..."` Show message while loading.

`align="..."` Deprecated. Controls alignment (`left`, `center`, `right`, `justify`).

`height="..."` The height of the object.

`width="..."` The width of the object.

`border="..."` Displays the border around an object.

`hspace="..."` The space between the sides of the object and other page content.

`vspace="..."` The space between the top and bottom of the object and other page content.

`usemap="..."` The URL to an imagemap.

`shapes=` Enables you to define areas to search for hyperlinks if the object is an image.

`name="..."` The URL to submit as part of a form.

`tabindex="..."` Sets the tabbing order between elements with a defined `tabindex`.

C

Empty	No.
Notes	Strict DTD. This element is new to HTML 4.

\<PARAM>

Usage	Initializes an object.
Start/End Tag	Required/Illegal.
Attributes	`name="..."` Defines the parameter name.
	`value="..."` The value of the object parameter.
	`valuetype="..."` Defines the value type (`data`, `ref`, `object`).
	`type="..."` The Internet media type.
Empty	Yes.
Notes	Strict DTD. This element is new to HTML 4.

Style

Style sheets (both inline and external) are incorporated into an HTML document through the use of the STYLE element.

\<STYLE>...\</STYLE>

Usage	Creates an internal style sheet.
Start/End Tag	Required/Required.
Attributes	`i18n`.
	`type="..."` The Internet content type.
	`media="..."` Defines the destination medium (`screen`, `print`, `projection`, `braille`, `speech`, `all`).
	`title="..."` The title of the style.
Empty	No.
Notes	Strict DTD. Located in the HEAD element.

Forms

Forms create an interface for the user to select options and submit data back to the Web server.

\<BUTTON>...\</BUTTON>

Usage	Creates a button.
Start/End Tag	Required/Required.
Attributes	core, i18n, events.

`name="..."` The button name.

`value="..."` The value of the button.

`type="..."` The button type (button, submit, reset).

`disabled="..."` Sets the button state to disabled.

`tabindex="..."` Sets the tabbing order between elements with a defined tabindex.

`onfocus="..."` The event that occurs when the element receives focus.

`onblur="..."` The event that occurs when the element loses focus.

Empty	No.
Notes	Strict DTD. This element is new to HTML 4.

\<FIELDSET>...\</FIELDSET>

Usage	Groups related controls.
Start/End Tag	Required/Required.
Attributes	core, i18n, events.
Empty	No.
Notes	Strict DTD. This element is new to HTML 4.

\<FORM>...\</FORM>

Usage	Creates a form that holds controls for user input.
Start/End Tag	Required/Required.
Attributes	core, i18n, events.

`action="..."` The URL for the server action.

`method="..."` The HTTP method (get, post). get is deprecated.

C

enctype="..." Specifies the MIME (Internet media type).

onsubmit="..." The intrinsic event that occurs when the form is submitted.

onreset="..." The intrinsic event that occurs when the form is reset.

target="..." Determines where the resource will be displayed (user-defined name, _blank, _parent, _self, _top).

accept-charset="..." The list of character encodings.

Empty	No.
Notes	Strict DTD.

\<INPUT\>

Usage	Defines controls used in forms.
Start/End Tag	Required/Illegal.
Attributes	core, i18n, events.

type="..." The type of input control (text, password, checkbox, radio, submit, reset, file, hidden, image, button).

name="..." The name of the control (required except for submit and reset).

value="..." The initial value of the control (required for radio and checkboxes).

checked="..." Sets the radio buttons to a checked state.

disabled="..." Disables the control.

readonly="..." For text password types.

size="..." The width of the control in pixels except for text and password controls, which are specified in number of characters.

maxlength="..." The maximum number of characters that can be entered.

`src="..."` The URL to an image control type.

`alt="..."` An alternative text description.

`usemap="..."` The URL to a client-side imagemap.

`align="..."` Deprecated. Controls alignment (`left`, `center`, `right`, `justify`).

`tabindex="..."` Sets the tabbing order between elements with a defined `tabindex`.

`onfocus="..."` The event that occurs when the element receives focus.

`onblur="..."` The event that occurs when the element loses focus.

`onselect="..."` Intrinsic event that occurs when the control is selected.

`onchange="..."` Intrinsic event that occurs when the control is changed.

`accept="..."` File types allowed for upload.

Empty	Yes.
Notes	Strict DTD.

`<ISINDEX>`

Usage	Prompts the user for input.
Start/End Tag	Required/Illegal.
Attributes	`core`, `i18n`.

`prompt="..."` Provides a prompt string for the input field.

Empty	Yes.
Notes	Transitional DTD. Deprecated.

`<LABEL>...</LABEL>`

Usage	Labels a control.
Start/End Tag	Required/Required.
Attributes	`core`, `i18n`, `events`.

for="..." Associates a label with an identified control.

disabled="..." Disables a control.

accesskey="..." Assigns a hotkey to this element.

onfocus="..." The event that occurs when the element receives focus.

onblur="..." The event that occurs when the element loses focus.

| Empty | No. |
| Notes | Strict DTD. This element is new to HTML 4. |

\<LEGEND\>...\</LEGEND\>

Usage	Assigns a caption to a FIELDSET.
Start/End Tag	Required/Required.
Attributes	core, i18n, events.

align="..." Deprecated. Controls alignment (left, center, right, justify).

accesskey="..." Assigns a hotkey to this element.

| Empty | No. |
| Notes | Strict DTD. This element is new to HTML 4. |

\<OPTGROUP\>...\</OPTGROUP\>

Usage	Used to group form elements within a SELECT element.
Start/End Tag	Required/Required.
Attributes	core, i18n, events.

disabled Not used.

label="..." Defines a group label.

| Empty | No. |
| Notes | Strict DTD. This element is new to HTML 4. |

\<OPTION\>...\</OPTION\>

| Usage | Specifies choices in a SELECT element. |

Start/End Tag	Required/Optional.
Attributes	core, i18n, events.
	selected="..." Specifies whether the option is selected.
	disabled="..." Disables control.
	value="..." The value submitted if a control is submitted.
Empty	No.
Notes	Strict DTD.

`<SELECT>...</SELECT>`

Usage	Creates choices for the user to select.
Start/End Tag	Required/Required.
Attributes	core, i18n, events.
	name="..." The name of the element.
	size="..." The width in number of rows.
	multiple Allows multiple selections.
	disabled="..." Disables the control.
	tabindex="..." Sets the tabbing order between elements with a defined tabindex.
	onfocus="..." The event that occurs when the element receives focus.
	onblur="..." The event that occurs when the element loses focus.
	onselect="..." Intrinsic event that occurs when the control is selected.
	onchange="..." Intrinsic event that occurs when the control is changed
Empty	No.
Notes	Strict DTD.

C

<TEXTAREA>...</TEXTAREA>

Usage	Creates an area for user input with multiple lines.
Start/End Tag	Required/Required.
Attributes	core, i18n, events.
	name="..." The name of the control.
	rows="..." The width in number of rows.
	cols="..." The height in number of columns.
	disabled="..." Disables the control.
	readonly="..." Sets the displayed text to read-only status.
	tabindex="..." Sets the tabbing order between elements with a defined tabindex.
	onfocus="..." The event that occurs when the element receives focus.
	onblur="..." The event that occurs when the element loses focus.
	onselect="..." Intrinsic event that occurs when the control is selected.
	onchange="..." Intrinsic event that occurs when the control is changed.
Empty	No.
Notes	Strict DTD. Text to be displayed is placed within the start and end tags.

Scripts

Scripting language is made available to process data and perform other dynamic events through the SCRIPT element.

<SCRIPT>...</SCRIPT>

Usage	The SCRIPT element contains client-side scripts that are executed by the browser.
Start/End Tag	Required/Required.

Attributes	`type="..."` Script language Internet content type.
	`language="..."` Deprecated. The scripting language, deprecated in favor of the `type` attribute.
	`src="..."` The URL for the external script.
Empty	No.
Notes	Strict DTD. You can set the default scripting language in the `META` element.

`<NOSCRIPT>...</NOSCRIPT>`

Usage	The `NOSCRIPT` element provides alternative content for browsers unable to execute a script.
Start/End Tag	Required/Required.
Attributes	None.
Empty	No.
Notes	Strict DTD. This element is new to HTML 4.

Common Attributes and Events

Four attributes are abbreviated as `core` in the preceding sections. They are:

- `id="..."` A global identifier
- `class="..."` A list of classes separated by spaces
- `style="..."` Style information
- `title="..."` Provides more information for a specific element, as opposed to the `TITLE` element, which entitles the entire Web page

Two attributes for internationalization (i18n) are abbreviated as `i18n`:

- `lang="..."` The language identifier
- `dir="..."` The text direction (`ltr`, `rtl`)

The following intrinsic events are abbreviated `events`:

- `onclick="..."` A pointing device (such as a mouse) was single-clicked.
- `ondblclick="..."` A pointing device (such as a mouse) was double-clicked.
- `onmousedown="..."` A mouse button was clicked and held down.
- `onmouseup="..."` A mouse button that was clicked and held down was released.
- `onmouseover="..."` A mouse moved the cursor over an object.

C

- `onmousemove="..."` The mouse was moved.
- `onmouseout="..."` A mouse moved the cursor off an object.
- `onkeypress="..."` A key was pressed and released.
- `onkeydown="..."` A key was pressed and held down.
- `onkeyup="..."` A key that was pressed has been released.

APPENDIX D

HTML Character Entities

Table D.1 contains the possible numeric and character entities for the ISO-Latin-1 (ISO8859-1) character set. Where possible, the character is shown.

Not all browsers can display all characters, and some browsers might even display characters different from those that appear in the table. Newer browsers seem to have a better track record for handling character entities, but be sure to test your HTML files extensively with multiple browsers if you intend to use these entities.

TABLE D.1. ISO-LATIN-1 CHARACTER SET.

Character	Numeric Entity	Character Entity (if any)	Description
	&#00;–&#08;		Unused
	&#09;		Horizontal tab
	&#10;		Line feed
	&#11;–&#31;		Unused
	&#32;		Space
!	&#33;		Exclamation mark
"	&#34;	&quot;	Quotation mark
#	&#35;		Number sign
$	&#36;		Dollar sign
%	&#37;		Percent sign
&	&#38;	&amp;	Ampersand
'	&#39;		Apostrophe
(	&#40;		Left parenthesis
)	&#41;		Right parenthesis
*	&#42;		Asterisk
+	&#43;		Plus sign
,	&#44;		Comma
-	&#45;		Hyphen
.	&#46;		Period (fullstop)
/	&#47;		Solidus (slash)
0–9	0–9		Digits 0–9
:	&#58;		Colon
;	&#59;		Semicolon
<	&#60;	&lt;	Less than
=	&#61;		Equal sign
>	&#62;	&gt;	Greater than
?	&#63;		Question mark
@	&#64;		Commercial "at"
A–Z	A–Z		Letters A–Z
[	&#91;		Left square bracket
\	&#92;		Reverse solidus (backslash)

Character	Numeric Entity	Character Entity (if any)	Description
]	&#93;		Right square bracket
^	&#94;		Caret
—	&#95;		Horizontal bar
`	&#96;		Grave accent
a–z	a–z		Letters a–z
{	&#123;		Left curly brace
|	|		Vertical bar
}	&#125;		Right curly brace
~	&#126;		Tilde
	&#127;–		Unused
¡	&#161;	&iexcl;	Inverted exclamation
¢	&#162;	&cent;	Cent sign
£	&#163;	&pound;	Pound sterling
¤	&#164;	&curren;	General currency sign
¥	&#165;	&yen;	Yen sign
¦	&#166;	¦ or brkbar;	Broken vertical bar
§	&#167;	&sect;	Section sign
¨	&#168;	&uml;	Umlaut (dieresis)
©	&#169;	&copy;	Copyright (Netscape only)
ª	&#170;	&ordf;	Feminine ordinal
‹	&#171;	&laquo;	Left angle quote, guillemot left
¬	&#172;	&not;	Not sign
-	&#173;	&shy;	Soft hyphen
®	&#174;	&reg;	Registered (trademark Netscape only)
¯	&#175;	&hibar;	Macron accent
°	&#176;	&deg;	Degree sign
±	&#177;	&plusmn;	Plus or minus
2	&#178;	&sup2;	Superscript two
3	&#179;	&sup3;	Superscript three
´	&#180;	&acute;	Acute accent

continues

D

TABLE D.1. CONTINUED

Character	Numeric Entity	Character Entity (if any)	Description
µ	µ	µ	Micro sign
¶	¶	¶	Paragraph sign
·	·	·	Middle dot
¸	¸	¸	Cedilla
¹	¹	¹	Superscript one
º	º	º	Masculine ordinal
›	»	»	Right angle quote, guillemot right
¼	¼	¼	Fraction one-fourth
½	½	½	Fraction one-half
¾	¾	¾	Fraction three-fourths
¿	¿	&iquest	Inverted question mark
À	À	À	Capital A, grave accent
Á	Á	Á	Capital A, acute accent
Â	Â	Â	Capital A, circumflex accent
Ã	Ã	Ã	Capital A, tilde
Ä	Ä	Ä	Capital A, dieresis or umlaut mark
Å	Å	Å	Capital A, ring
Æ	Æ	Æ	Capital AE diphthong (ligature)
Ç	Ç	Ç	Capital C, cedilla
È	È	È	Capital E, grave accent
É	É	É	Capital E, acute accent
Ê	Ê	Ê	Capital E, circumflex accent
Ë	Ë	Ë	Capital E, dieresis or umlaut mark
Ì	Ì	Ì	Capital I, grave accent
Í	Í	Í	Capital I, acute accent
Î	Î	Î	Capital I, circumflex accent
Ï	Ï	Ï	Capital I, dieresis or umlaut mark
Ð	Ð	Ð	Capital Eth, Icelandic

Character	Numeric Entity	Character Entity (if any)	Description
Ñ	&#209;	&Ntilde;	Capital N, tilde
Ò	&#210;	&Ograve;	Capital O, grave accent
Ó	&#211;	&Oacute;	Capital O, acute accent
Ô	&#212;	&Ocirc;	Capital O, circumflex accent
Õ	&#213;	&Otilde;	Capital O, tilde
Ö	&#214;	&Ouml;	Capital O, dieresis or umlaut mark
×	&#215;		Multiply sign
Ø	&#216;	&Oslash;	Capital O, slash
Ù	&#217;	&Ugrave;	Capital U, grave accent
Ú	&#218;	&Uacute;	Capital U, acute accent
Û	&#219;	&Ucirc;	Capital U, circumflex accent
Ü	&#220;	&Uuml;	Capital U, dieresis or umlaut mark
Ý	&#221;	&Yacute;	Capital Y, acute accent
þ	&#222;	&THORN;	Capital THORN, Icelandic
ß	&#223;	&szlig;	Small sharp s, German (sz ligature)
à	&#224;	&agrave;	Small a, grave accent
á	&#225;	&aacute;	Small a, acute accent
â	&#226;	&acirc;	Small a, circumflex accent
ã	&#227;	&atilde;	Small a, tilde
ä	&#228;	&aauml;	Small a, dieresis or umlaut mark
å	&#229;	&aring;	Small a, ring
æ	&#230;	&aelig;	Small ae diphthong (ligature)
ç	&#231;	&ccedil;	Small c, cedilla
è	&#232;	&egrave;	Small e, grave accent
é	&#233;	&eacute;	Small e, acute accent
ê	&#234;	&ecirc;	Small e, circumflex accent
ë	&#235;	&euml;	Small e, dieresis or umlaut mark
ì	&#236;	&igrave;	Small i, grave accent

continues

D

TABLE D.1.   CONTINUED

Character	Numeric Entity	Character Entity (if any)	Description
í	&#237;	&iacute;	Small i, acute accent
î	&#238;	&icirc;	Small i, circumflex accent
ï	&#239;	&iuml;	Small i, dieresis or umlaut mark
ð	&#240;	&eth;	Small eth, Icelandic
ñ	&#241;	&ntilde;	Small n, tilde
ò	&#242;	&ograve;	Small o, grave accent
ó	&#243;	&oacute;	Small o, acute accent
ô	&#244;	&ocirc;	Small o, circumflex accent
õ	&#245;	&otilde;	Small o, tilde
ö	&#246;	&ouml;	Small o, dieresis or umlaut mark
÷	&#247;		Division sign
ø	&#248;	&oslash;	Small o, slash
ù	&#249;	&ugrave;	Small u, grave accent
ú	&#250;	&uacute;	Small u, acute accent
û	&#251;	&ucirc;	Small u, circumflex accent
ü	&#252;	&uuml;	Small u, dieresis or umlaut mark
ý	&#253;	&yacute;	Small y, acute accent
þ	&#254;	&thorn;	Small thorn, Icelandic
ÿ	&#255;	&yuml;	Small y, dieresis or umlaut mark

GLOSSARY

ActiveX   A relatively new technology invented by Microsoft for embedding animated objects, data, and computer code on Web pages.

anchor   A named point on a Web page. (The same HTML tag is used to create hypertext links and anchors, which explains why the tag is named <A>).

animated GIF   An animated graphic exploiting looping and timing features in the GIF89a format.

ASCII file   A text file that conforms to the American Standard Code for Information Interchange. All HTML files must be saved as ASCII text files (not in any other word processor format), or they will not appear correctly in Web browsers.

attributes   Special code words used inside an HTML tag to control exactly what the tag does.

bandwidth   The maximum information-carrying capacity of an electronic connection or network.

binary file   An executable file or a file that is not in ASCII text format.

bookmarks   In Netscape Navigator, a list of your favorite Web pages and Internet resources. You can add items to this menu at any time. Bookmarks are equivalent to favorites in Microsoft Internet Explorer.

browse   To wander around a portion of the Internet looking for items of interest. Also known as surfing or cruising.

browser   A software program for viewing HTML pages.

cache   A temporary storage area that a Web browser uses to store pages and graphics that it has recently opened. The cache enables the browser to quickly load the same pages and images if they are opened again soon.

cascading style sheets   A new addition to HTML that allows page designers to have greater control over the rendering of a document. Browsers that support style sheets will allow font and color attributes to be specified. CSS1 is the first phase of cascading style sheets, and CSS2 is the second phase that includes layer positioning and other new features.

client-side imagemaps   A new HTML method for linking an image to more than one address. The advantage of this approach is that the browser can display the destination URL of a region when the mouse passes over it, and some network traffic is saved because the browser can directly request the new document when a click is made.

code   Anything written in a language intended for computers to interpret. *See* **script** and **source code**.

comment   Text in an HTML document (or computer program) that will be seen only by the people who edit the source for that page. Comments are normally invisible when a page is viewed with a Web browser. Comments in HTML begin with <!-- and end with -->. Comments in JavaScript begin with //.

Common Gateway Interface (CGI)   An interface for external programs to talk to a Web server. Programs that are written to use CGI are called CGI programs or CGI scripts, and are commonly used for processing HTML forms.

compression   The process of making a computer file smaller so that it can be copied more quickly between computers.

cyberspace   A broad expression used to describe the activity, communication, and culture happening on the Internet and other computer networks.

definition list   An indented list without a number or symbol in front of each item. *See* **ordered list** and **unordered list**.

DHTML   *See* **Dynamic HTML**.

digital   Electronic circuits generally considered to use an on or off sequence of values to convey information.

digitized   Converted to a digital format suitable for storage.

direct connection   A permanent, 24-hour link between a computer and the Internet. A computer with a direct connection can use the Internet at any time.

directory service   An Internet service that maintains a database on individuals, including email, fax, and telephone numbers, that is searchable by the public.

DOM (Document Object Model)   A standard under development by the W3C that will govern the way scripting and programming languages refer to the elements on a Web page. Currently, Microsoft and Netscape use incompatible methods for referencing elements. It is hoped that the DOM standard will make it more practical to develop scripts and programs that work with all available Web browsers.

domain   The address of a computer on the Internet. A user's Internet address is made up of a username and a domain name.

domain name system (DNS)   An Internet addressing system that uses a group of names that are listed with dots (.) between them, working from the most specific to the most general group. In the United States, the top (most general) domains are network categories such as edu (education), com (commercial), and gov (government). In other countries, a two-letter abbreviation for the country is used, such as ca (Canada) and au (Australia).

download   To retrieve a file or files from a remote machine to your local machine.

DSig (Digital Signature)   A proposed standard from the World Wide Web Consortium for one organization or individual to vouch for the identity of another, which is about the best that can be done to verify identities or statements online. May be used in conjunction with PICS or P3P for verification purposes.

Dynamic HTML   A somewhat loosely defined term for the integration of scripting, style sheets, and HTML to create animated, interactive Web pages.

email (electronic mail)   A system that enables a person to compose a message on a computer and transmit that message through a computer network, such as the Internet, to another computer user.

email address   The word-based Internet address of a user, typically made up of a username, an at sign (@), and a domain name (that is, user@domain). Email addresses are translated from the numeric IP addresses by the domain name system (DNS).

encryption   The process of encoding information so that it is secure from other Internet users.

FAQ   Short for frequently asked questions, a computer file containing the answers to frequently asked questions about a particular Internet resource.

favorites   In Microsoft Internet Explorer, a list of your favorite Web pages and Internet resources. You can add items to this menu at any time. Favorites are equivalent to book-marks in Netscape Navigator.

firewall   A security device placed on a LAN to protect it from Internet intruders. This can be a special kind of hardware router, a piece of software, or both.

form   A page that includes areas to be filled out by the reader. HTML forms allow information to be sent back to the company or individual who made (or maintains) the page.

frame   A rectangular region within the browser window that displays a Web page alongside other pages in other frames.

freeware   Software available to anyone, free of charge, unlike shareware, which requires payment.

FTP (File Transfer Protocol)   The basic method for copying a file from one computer to another through the Internet.

graphics   Digitized pictures and computer-generated images.

graphical editor   A program that allows you to edit an approximation of what a Web page will look like when viewed with a Web browser. Graphical editors usually hide the actual HTML tags they are creating from view. It is not recommended that you use a graphical editor when learning HTML with this book.

helper application   An application that is configured to launch and view files that are unreadable to a Web browser.

HTML (Hypertext Markup Language)   The document formatting language used to create pages on the World Wide Web.

HTTP (Hypertext Transfer Protocol)   The standard method for exchanging informa-tion between HTTP servers and clients on the Web. The HTTP specification lays out the rules of how Web servers and browsers must work together.

hypertext   Text that allows readers to jump spontaneously among onscreen documents and other resources by selecting highlighted keywords that appear on each screen. Hypertext appears most often on the World Wide Web.

image compression   The mathematical manipulation that images are put through to squeeze out repetitive patterns. It makes them load and display much faster.

imagemap   An image on a Web page that leads to two or more different links, depending on which part of the image someone clicks. Modern Web browsers use client-side imagemaps, but you can also create server-side imagemaps for compatibility with old browsers.

interlaced GIF   An image file that will appear blocky at first, then more and more detailed as it continues downloading. (Similar to a progressive JPEG file.)

Internet   A large, loosely organized integrated network connecting universities, research institutions, government, businesses, and other organizations so that they can exchange messages and share information.

Internet Explorer   A popular Web browser created by Microsoft Corporation and integrated with the Windows operating system.

Internet service provider (ISP)   The company that provides you or your company with access to the Internet. ISPs usually have several servers and a high-speed link to the Internet backbone.

intranet   A private network with access restricted to one organization, but which uses the same standards and protocols as the global public Internet.

ISDN (Integrated Services Digital Network)   Essentially operates as a digital phone line. ISDN delivers many benefits over standard analog phone lines, including multiple simultaneous calls and higher-quality data transmissions. ISDN data rates are 56Kbps to 128Kbps.

Java   The Web-oriented language developed by Sun Microsystems.

JavaScript   A Web page scripting language originally developed by Netscape. Many JavaScript commands are similar (but not identical) to Java commands. Unlike Java, however, you can include JavaScript directly in the text of HTML pages.

JScript   The version of JavaScript implemented by Microsoft in Internet Explorer. JScript is almost-but-not-quite compatible with Netscape's JavaScript.

Kbps (kilobits per second)   A rate of transfer of information across a connection such as the Internet.

LAN (local area network)   A computer network limited to a small area.

link   An icon, a picture, or a highlighted string of text that connects the current Web page to other Web pages, Internet sites, graphics, movies, or sounds. On the Web, you skip from page to page by clicking links.

Mbps (megabits per second)   A rate of transfer of information across a connection such as the Internet. (Equal to approximately 1,000Kbps.)

modem (modulator/demodulator)   A device to convert the digital signals of a computer to an analog format for transmission across telephone lines.

multimedia   A description for systems capable of displaying or playing text, pictures, sound, video, and animation.

navigation   Movement within a computer environment (for example, navigation of a Web site).

Netscape   Short for Netscape Communications Corporation, a software company that developed and markets a popular World Wide Web browser called Navigator, which is part of a software suite called Communicator. Some people casually refer to Navigator as Netscape.

network   A set of computers interconnected so that they can communicate and share information. Most major networks are connected to the global network-of-networks, called the Internet.

online   A general term referring to anything connected to or conveyed through a communications network.

ordered list   An indented list that has numbers or letters in front of each item. *See* **definition list** and **unordered list**.

P3P (Platform for Privacy Preferences)   A recent W3C standard concerning the security and privacy restrictions associated with Web pages.

Paint Shop Pro (PSP)   A popular graphics program from JASC software for creating Web page images. PSP is used for the graphics examples in this book, though you can achieve the same results with many other graphics programs.

password   A secret code, known only to the user, that allows that user to access a computer that is protected by a security system.

PICS (Platform for Internet Content Selection)   A new W3C standard protocol for rating Web page content according to any criteria a rating authority or company might choose. Applications include restricting access to confidential or adult-oriented material. *See* **DSig**.

pixel   An individual dot of color in a computer graphics image.

POTS   Plain old telephone service.

PPP (Point-to-Point Protocol)   A communications protocol that enables a dial-up Internet connection.

progressive JPEG   An image file that appears blurry at first, and then gradually comes into focus. (Similar to an interlaced GIF file.)

protocol   Specific rules and conventions defining how data can be exchanged between any two devices.

provider   A general reference to an Internet service provider.

public domain   Material that is freely usable by anyone, but still could be copyrighted.

relative address   An address describing the path from one Web page to another, instead of a full (or absolute) URL address.

resolution   The number of individual dots, or pixels, that make up an image.

resource   A generic term to describe the varied information and activities available to Internet users.

robot   An automated program that indexes Web pages for a search engine, or carries out other repetitive tasks that humans would otherwise have to do.

search engine   A program that provides a way to search for specific information. Often used to refer to popular sites such as AltaVista or HotBot, where you can search for pages on the Internet containing certain keywords.

server   A networked computer that "serves" a particular type of information to users. *See* **Web server**.

server-side imagemaps   A technique for implementing Web page images that lead to more than one link, so that the server computer determines which link to go to. This method is now less commonly used than client-side imagemaps.

script   A short computer program written in a simplified programming language such as JavaScript, VBScript, or Perl.

SGML (Standard General Markup Language)   A well-established international standard for defining text-based markup languages. HTML is one example of the types of languages that can be defined in SGML. *See* **XML**.

shareware   Software programs that users are permitted to acquire and evaluate for free. Shareware is different from freeware in that, if a person likes the shareware program and plans to use it on a regular basis, he is expected to send a fee to the programmer.

Shockwave   An interactive multimedia system for the Web that views applications developed by Macromedia Director.

SMIL (Synchronized Multimedia Integration Language)   A new W3C-recommended standard for controlling the timing of multiple audio, video, and interactive media presentations on a Web page. SMIL is not yet implemented in any Web browser software.

source or **source code**   The actual text and commands stored in an HTML file (including tags, comments, and scripts) that may not be visible when the page is viewed with a Web browser.

spider   An automated program that indexes Web pages for a search engine. Also called a robot.

surfing   Another term for browsing.

T-1 line   A digital circuit capable of transferring data at 1.544Mbps.

T-3 line   A digital circuit equivalent to 28 T-1 lines.

table   Text and/or images arranged into orderly rows and columns. HTML provides several tags specifically for creating tables.

tag   A coded HTML command used to indicate how part of a Web page should be displayed.

TCP/IP (Transmission Control Protocol/Internet Protocol)   The agreed-on set of computer communications rules and standards that allows communications between different types of computers and networks that are connected to the Internet.

text editor   Any program that allows you to edit text with your computer.

unordered list   An indented list with a special bullet symbol in front of each item. *See* **definition list** and **ordered list**.

URL (uniform resource locator)   Also commonly called a location or address. This is an addressing system that locates documents on the Internet.

username   Used with a password to gain access to a computer. A dial-up IP user typically has a username and password for dialing the access provider's Internet server.

VBScript   A script language developed by Microsoft. A technical competitor to Java and JavaScript applications.

visitor   A person who is viewing one of your Web pages. Also called a user or reader.

VRML (Virtual Reality Modeling Language)   A three-dimensional navigation specification used to simulate three-dimensional objects or worlds online.

W3C   *See* **World Wide Web Consortium**.

Web   Can be used to refer to the entire World Wide Web or to a particular Web site.

Web browser   A software program used for viewing Web pages, such as Netscape Navigator or Microsoft Internet Explorer.

Web page   An HTML document made available through the World Wide Web, along with any associated graphics or multimedia files.

Web server   A computer on the Internet that hosts data that can be accessed by Web browsers using the HTTP protocol.

Web site   One or more Web pages that are intended to be viewed and explored together as a cohesive presentation.

World Wide Web (WWW or the Web)   A set of Internet computers and services that provide an easy-to-use system for finding information and moving among resources. WWW services feature hypertext, hypermedia, and multimedia information, which can be explored through browsers such as Netscape Navigator or Microsoft Internet Explorer.

World Wide Web Consortium (W3C)   The organization that drafts and recommends technical standards for the World Wide Web. HTML 4.0 and CSS2 are examples of W3C-recommended standards.

XSL (eXtensible Stylesheet Language)   The W3C style sheet standard for XML. (XSL is related to XML in exactly the same way that CSS is related to HTML.)

XML (eXtensible Markup Language)   A W3C-recommended standard for defining new document types, as well as user-defined or application-specific tags to extend the capabilities of HTML. Basically, a less powerful version of SGML.

Index

Symbols

A

C

X-Y-Z

Presenting XML

Richard Light

Presenting XML will teach users about the XML language and how it will be used to speed up the Web through greater use of client-side processing; better indexing; search and retrieval; richer link types; and more complex structures. The book will cover what the XML language is, how it relates to HTML and SGML, how it will affect the Web, and the kinds of applications possible. It will go over in detail what the XML specification is and will describe the basics of writing XML code and creating XML-aware applications. It also contains an introduction to XML-extensible Markup Language—the slimmed down, Web-enabled version of SGML from which HTML was created.

The XML standard is being advanced by the World Wide Web Consortium (W3C) as an alternative and complement to HTML. XML is neutral with respect to vendor, application, and platform, just like HTML.

$24.99 US/$35.95 CDN	*Sams*
ISBN: 1-57521-334-6	*350 pp.*

Net Results: Web Marketing that Works

US Web and Rick Bruner

Net Results: Web Marketing that Works is an insightful guide for small and large businesses wishing to launch a successful Web marketing campaign. It will explore the strategies and tactics that have shown proven results in driving effective ROI. The book will cover return on investment goals; design optimization; online promotions; online ad placement utilizing and creating online communities. US Web is one of the leading Web development firms in the world with an extensive list of distinguished clients—thus prompting strong media and consumer interest in this project. US Web's senior management team is made up of individuals with significant reputations in digital entertainment and commerce.

A Web site is a destination, yet until you've built the roads that lead to it, it's nothing but a ghost town. This book shows you how to build the road, and get the returns you expect from your site. Reveals the unique methodologies used by US Web that have brought success to its Fortune 1000 clients and companies like Netscape, Avon, Procter & Gamble, and Viacom. Shows online marketers how to increase their effectiveness through several case studies and techniques.

$29.99 US/$42.95 CDN	*Intermediate —Advanced*
ISBN: 1-56830-414-5	*416 pp.*
Internet-Business	*Hayden Books*

Dynamic HTML Unleashed

Michael Van Hoozer

Dynamic HTML Unleashed is an all-in-one guide to using Dynamic HTML and Web scripting languages to create Web pages and Web applications that change in response to user actions. It covers the following:

- Dynamic Styles—Showing or hiding elements, changing the size or color of fonts, changing the position of elements
- The Dynamic HTML Object Model—Describing an object model and explaining how to use it on a page
- Positioning—Placing elements anywhere on x, y, and z planes
- Dynamic Content—Changing, inserting, or deleting elements
- Filter, Transition and Animation—Adding multimedia controls
- Data awareness—Making HTML a better environment for displaying and collecting data

This book contains a comprehensive look at all of the technologies collectively referred to as Dynamic HTML. It also covers Microsoft Internet Explorer 4 and the Netscape Communicator technologies. Real-world examples show how Dynamic HTML enhances static web pages.

$39.99 US/$56.95 CDN   *Casual—Accomplished*

ISBN: 1-57521-353-2   *800 pp.*

Maximum Security, Second Edition

Anonymous

Security continues to be the predominant concern for any company or organization either on the Internet now or considering it. Hardly a week passes without a new report of crackers breaking into computer systems at some government agency, trashing some Fortune 500 company's Web site, or stealing user passwords or credit card numbers. When the first edition of this book was published in June 1997, its popularity caught everyone by surprise. It immediately shot to the top of several computer security bestseller lists, surpassing even established security books from O'Reilly, Wiley, and Addison-Wesley. While undoubtedly some bought the book to learn how to hack, the book's most enthusiastic fans were computer security managers who appreciated the book's comprehensive coverage and clear, to-the-point descriptions of the most common techniques hackers use to penetrate systems. The hacking community, however, hasn't stood still. A thoroughly updated and revised edition of this book is now required to discuss the hundreds of new computer system holes that have been discovered over the course of the past year, and to cover the latest techniques that hackers are now using to crack into computers and networks. A controversial, comprehensive guide to Internet security—written by a reformed hacker. Fully revised, updated and expanded to cover hundreds of new system holes, new developments in hacking techniques, and the latest security technologies. The first edition is currently the most popular computer security book on the market today.

$49.99 US/$71.95 CDN   *Intermediate—Advanced*

ISBN: 0-672-31341-3   *1,000 pp.*

Sams

JavaScript Unleashed, Second Edition

Richard Wagner, et al.

JavaScript Unleashed, Second Edition helps the reader thoroughly understand and apply JavaScript, which, because of its simplicity, has been dubbed "the scripting language for the masses." This complete reference's clear instructions and easy-to-follow examples will appeal to everyone from the hobbyist programmer to the power user. This book teaches how to work with JavaScript style sheets and manipulate content layering and positioning on the HTML page. It also covers Netscape Navigator 4.0, Netscape Plug-ins, auto-installs and applets, digital signature verification, browser screen manipulation without the use of menu options or toolbars, absolute positioning and content layering. The CD-ROM includes code from the book, sample applications and third-party products.

Covers JavaScript

$49.99 USA/$70.95 CAN   *Casual—Experienced*

1-57521-306-0   *1,000 pp.*

Internet-Programming, JavaScript

Sams Teach Yourself CGI Programming in a Week, Third Edition

Rafe Colburn

Sams Teach Yourself CGI Programming in a Week, Third Edition follows the same format and uses the same learning tools as other books in the Sams Teach Yourself Series. This new edition covers implementing CGI with C and Active Server Page technology, in addition to Perl. Also covered are Windows CGI programming and how to use CGI to interact with Java, VBScript, and JavaScript. The book takes the reader from the basics of CGI learning; for example, how to implement and customize existing CGI programs that have been written by others to create his own programs from scratch. The book will also provide numerous real-life examples of CGI scripts—database search tools, survey forms, interactive games, order forms, guest books, and more. The final sections of the book will cover advanced CGI programming debugging techniques, solutions for common CGI problems, and so on. CGI is the next step beyond simple HTML, allowing users to add forms and other types of interactivity to Web pages. This book has been updated and revised to cover Active Server Pages, Perl 5, C, Windows CGI, JavaScript, VBScript, AppleScript, and new CGI development tools. Learn how to add interactivity and pro-grams to Web pages with CGI.

$29.99 US/$42.95 CDN   *Intermediate—Accomplished*

1-57521-381-8   *500 pp.*

Internet-Programming   *Sams*

Dynamic Web Publishing Unleashed, Second Edition

Shelly Powers, et al.

Over 1,400 pages of information and solutions, this book is the most comprehensive guide to Web publishing on the market. Expert authors provide thorough coverage of advanced Web publishing technologies, including HTML, Java, CGI, VBScript, and JavaScript. This book is loaded with information on the following topics: Hypertext Markup Language; Web page design; style sheets; Dynamic HTML; HTML forms; advanced layout with tables and frames; client side scripting (JavaScript, VBScript, image maps, and so on); Java 1.1; ActiveX; CGI server side scripting; and push technologies (Castanet, CDF, and Netcaster). It includes all the information readers need to publish on the World Wide Web. It provides in-depth coverage of HTML 4, Java, ActiveX, JavaScript, VBScript, CGI, Dynamic HTML, and also explains how to integrate technologies such as cascading style sheets into Web publications.

$39.99 US/$57.95 CDN   *Casual—Experienced*

1-57521-363-X   *844 pp.*

Sams Teach Yourself Java 1.2 in 21 Days, Third Edition

Laura Lemay and Rogers Cadenhead

Sams Teach Yourself Java 1.2 in 21 Days continues to be the most popular, best-selling Java tutorial on the market. It has been acclaimed for its clear and personable writing, for its extensive use of examples, and for its logical and complete organization. The third edition of the book will maintain and improve upon all these qualities while updating the material to cover the latest developments in the Java language such as using Java Foundation Classes, Java 2D Classes, and JavaBeans. It provides step-by-step lessons for the most popular network-oriented, cross-platform programming language. This is a thoroughly revised, updated, and improved edition of the market's leading Java tutorial. It includes new coverage of Java Foundation Classes, Java 2D Classes, JavaBeans, and the new security model.

$29.99 US/$42.95 CDN   *Beginner—Intermediate—Advanced*

1-57521-390-7   *Sams*

Internet-Programming

Add to Your Sams Library Today with the Best Books for Programming, Operating Systems, and New Technologies

To order, visit our Web site at www.mcp.com or fax us at

1-800-835-3202

ISBN	Quantity	Description of Item	Unit Cost	Total Cost
1-57521-334-6		Presenting XML	$29.99	
1-56830-414-5		Net Results Web Marketing that Works	$29.99	
1-57521-353-2		Dynamic HTML Unleashed	$39.99	
0-672-31341-3		Maximum Security, Second Edition	$49.99	
1-57521-306-0		JavaScript Unleashed, Second Edition	$49.99	
1-57521-381-8		Sams Teach Yourself CGI Programming in a Week	$29.99	
1-57521-363-X		Dynamic Web Publishing Unleashed, Second Edition	$39.99	
1-57521-390-7		Sams Teach Yourself Java 1.2 in 21 Days, Third Edition	$29.99	
		Shipping and Handling: See information below.		
		TOTAL		

Shipping and Handling

Standard	$5.00
2nd Day	$10.00
Next Day	$17.50
International	$40.00

201 W. 103rd Street, Indianapolis, Indiana 46290   1-800-835-3202 — FAX

Book ISBN 0-672-31347-2

THE CRITICS HAIL

APRIL FOOLS

AN INSIDER'S ACCOUNT OF THE RISE AND COLLAPSE OF DREXEL BURNHAM

* * *

"Mr. Stone writes well [and] poses some intriguing questions . . . *April Fools* tells how Mr. Milken was both admired and loathed, and how Drexel employees suffered greatly from the junk bond scandal."
—**Andrew Blum,** *Wall Street Journal*

*

"A balanced and thorough portrait. . . . He nicely summarizes the complex charges . . . and notes the huge impact this one man had on a whole sector of the financial markets. . . . Explores the much-debated potential application of the RICO law to financial cases."
—*Baltimore Sun*

*

"The Götterdämmerung has been succinctly but nonetheless ruddily illuminated."
—**Murray Kempton,** *New York Newsday*

*

"The first and only inside look at the Drexel Burnham debacle. Stone, a former vice president . . . uses his personal experience to shed light on not only Michael Milken, the financial whiz, but also on the man."
—*Library Journal*

*   *more . . .*

"Although there has been plenty of media coverage of Milken and Drexel, this work presents for the first time an inside view."
—*Akron Beacon Journal*

*

"A witty and instructive account of the debacle . . . a valuable account."
—*Lexington Herald-Leader*

*

"Milken, Boesky, and Giuliani are strikingly silhouetted against the yo-yo years of Wall Street in the late 1980s. A fascinating glimpse of the unreal."
—**Trans Pacific News Service**

*

DAN G. STONE was vice president of Institutional Equity Sales at Drexel Burnham during its decline. He is also the author of *How to Invest in the Market*.

APRIL FOOLS

An Insider's Account of the Rise and Collapse of Drexel Burnham

DAN G. STONE

WARNER BOOKS

A Time Warner Company

Warner Books Edition

Copyright © 1990, 1991 by Dan G. Stone

Warner Books, Inc., 666 Fifth Avenue, New York, NY 10103

 A Time Warner Company

Printed in the United States of America

First Warner Books Printing: October 1991

10 9 8 7 6 5 4 3 2 1

Stone, Dan G.
    April fools : an insider's account of the rise and collapse of
Drexel Burnham / Dan G. Stone.—Warner Books ed.
        p.   cm.
    Includes index.
    ISBN 0-446-39344-4
    1. Drexel Burnham Lambert Incorporated.   2. Stockbrokers—New York
(N.Y.)   3. Securities fraud—New York (N.Y.)   4. Drexel Burnham
Lambert Incorporated—Employees—Dismissal of.   I. Title.
HG4928.5.S76   1991
332.63'2'0973—dc20   91-25630
                                                                       CIP

Cover design by Tom Tafuri
Cover photo of Michael Milken by Terry Ashe/SYGMA
Cover photo of Rudolph Giuliani by Alan Tannenbaum/SYGMA
Cover photo of Drexel Burnham Lambert employee by Nina Berman/SIPA press

ACKNOWLEDGMENTS

My sincere thanks to two great editors, David Gibbons and Don Fine, and to those who were willing to talk about an unhappy subject.

I would also like to acknowledge the wealth of information provided by *The Predators' Ball*, *Takeover*, *The Wall Street Journal*, *The New York Times*, *The Washington Post*, *New York Magazine*, and *Fortune*, among others. In particular, I would like to highlight the first-class reporting of Connie Bruck, Moira Johnston, James Stewart, Daniel Hertzberg, Laurie Cohen, Kurt Eichenwald, David Vise, and Christopher Byron, as well as the legal insights of L. Gordon Crovitz and Prof. G. Robert Blakey.

To Drs. Emilita and Thomas Stone
who always offered the best advice
and never sent a bill.

CONTENTS

DBL GROUP—1989
(HOLDING COMPANY)

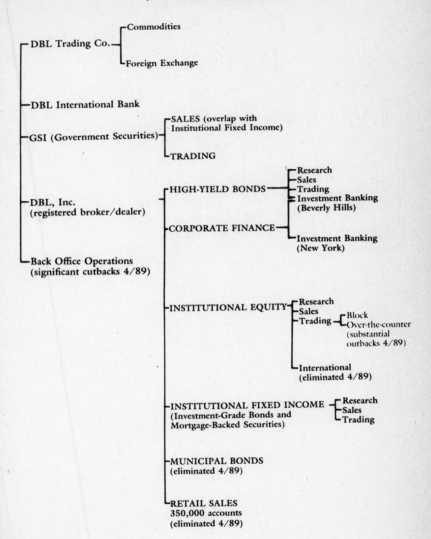

- DBL Trading Co.
  - Commodities
  - Foreign Exchange
- DBL International Bank
- GSI (Government Securities)
  - SALES (overlap with Institutional Fixed Income)
  - TRADING
- DBL, Inc. (registered broker/dealer)
  - HIGH-YIELD BONDS
    - Research
    - Sales
    - Trading
    - Investment Banking (Beverly Hills)
  - CORPORATE FINANCE
    - Investment Banking (New York)
  - INSTITUTIONAL EQUITY
    - Research
    - Sales
    - Trading
      - Block
      - Over-the-counter (substantial cutbacks 4/89)
    - International (eliminated 4/89)
  - INSTITUTIONAL FIXED INCOME (Investment-Grade Bonds and Mortgage-Backed Securities)
    - Research
    - Sales
    - Trading
  - MUNICIPAL BONDS (eliminated 4/89)
  - RETAIL SALES 350,000 accounts (eliminated 4/89)
- Back Office Operations (significant cutbacks 4/89)

CHRONOLOGY
OF EVENTS

1935
Burnham & Co. is founded by I. W. Burnham.

1970
Michael Milken, a twenty-three-year-old student at the Wharton business school, joins Drexel Firestone, a Philadelphia-based investment banking firm.

1973
Drexel Firestone is acquired; the new company is called Drexel Burnham.

1974
Fred Joseph is hired as a corporate finance officer; a decade later, he will become the chief executive officer of the firm.

1976
Drexel Burnham acquires William D. Witter, which is connected to the Brussels-based Groupe Bruxelles Lambert; the official name of the firm becomes Drexel Burnham Lambert Inc.

1977
Lehman Brothers raises money for three companies through the sale of high-yield bonds; Drexel Burnham will soon dominate the market for original-issue junk bonds, selling $100 billion worth of these bonds by 1990.

1978
Michael Milken moves Drexel's junk-bond operation to Beverly Hills.

1981

Conoco is purchased by du Pont, the first of the mega–acquisitions of the 1980s.

1982

Boone Pickens's Mesa Petroleum attempts a *hostile* takeover of Cities Service, an oil company twenty times its size; Occidental Petroleum steps in as a white knight.

1983

The leveraged buyout of Gibson Greetings provides its new owners, including former Secretary of State William Simon, a 20,000 percent profit in eighteen months; with the help of junk bonds and kind markets, LBOs will become the success story of the decade.

1984

Mesa Petroleum, backed by Drexel, attempts a takeover bid of Gulf Oil; Chevron purchases Gulf for $13.3 billion.

Saul Steinberg's Reliance Group makes a hostile bid for Disney, backed by a $700 million commitment from Drexel's clients; Steinberg accepts greenmail from Disney.

Carl Icahn makes a hostile bid for Phillips Petroleum; Drexel introduces the "highly confident" letter.

1985

April 1; Drexel Burnham celebrates its fiftieth anniversary.
November 1; Delaware Supreme Court rules in favor of Ron Perelman's $1.8 billion hostile takeover of Revlon, financed with $1.1 billion in junk bonds.

1986

April 20; Drexel raises $2.5 billion through high-yield debt for Kohlberg Kravis's $6.2 billion acquisition of Beatrice, the largest leveraged buyout to date.
May 12; Dennis Levine is arrested on insider trading charges.
November 14; Ivan Boesky pleads guilty to one felony count and pays a $100 million fine; within a week, Drexel Burnham is reported to be under "formal order of investigation" by the Securities and Exchange Commission and criminal investigation by the U.S. Attorney's Office; the focus is on Michael Milken and his high-yield bond operation.

December 31; The firm earns $525 million for the year, the highest profits of any Wall Street firm before or since.

1987
February 12; Three arbitrageurs—Robert Freeman of Goldman Sachs, Richard Wigton of Kidder Peabody, and Timothy Tabor of Merrill Lynch—are arrested on insider trading charges, implicated by investment banker Martin Siegel.
February 19; Staley Continental sues Drexel for alleged extortion and manipulation by one of its salesmen; the case is eventually settled out of court.

1988
April 28; Fred Joseph testifies before the House Oversight and Investigations Subcommittee regarding Drexel's employee partnerships.
September 7; The Securities and Exchange Commission files a civil suit against Drexel Burnham, Michael Milken, and four other employees.
December 21; Drexel Burnham, under threat of a RICO indictment, agrees to plead guilty to six felonies and pay $650 million.

1989
March 29; Michael Milken is indicted on ninety-eight counts of securities fraud.
April 13; Drexel settles its civil case with the Securities and Exchange Commission.
April 18; Fred Joseph announces a restructuring that involves the loss of four thousand jobs, Drexel's staff being trimmed from 9,400 to 5,400.
May 12; The firm raises the $5 billion junk-bond portion of the $26.2 billion takeover of RJR Nabisco, the largest leveraged buyout in history.
August 5; Congress passes the savings and loan bailout bill, requiring thrifts to sell all junk bonds within five years.
December 31; The firm loses $40 million for 1989, its first operating loss.

1990
February 13; Drexel Burnham files for bankruptcy.

APRIL
FOOLS

CHAPTER ONE

APRIL FOOLS

I couldn't be fonder of you if
you were my own son, but . . .
—*The Maltese Falcon*

T he rumor spread across the trading floor in minutes, and like most
negative rumors, it was true. Drexel Burnham, my firm for almost
eight years, was about to announce massive layoffs for the first time
in more than fifty years—four thousand people would be out of a job.
It was April 18, 1989, less than one week after we had finally settled
the most extensive and expensive securities fraud investigation in the
history of Wall Street.

Fred Joseph, the chairman and chief executive officer of Drexel,
came over the "hoot-and-holler" phone system that connected all of
the firm's branches together. For two and a half years, Fred, still
fighting trim at fifty-two, had done an admirable job of holding up
morale—and, in many ways it seemed, of holding together the firm.

When one of Wall Street's most visible figures, Ivan Boesky, was
arrested in late 1986 and, in turn, pointed his finger our way, Fred
had become the spokesman and chief negotiator for ten thousand
employees. Now the negotiations were over, and Fred was here to tell
us that, in effect, he was becoming the spokesman for less than six
thousand employees. Which, of course, wasn't well received by those
who were being fired.

1

The survivors, he told us, would be high-yield (junk) bonds, corporate finance, institutional equity and fixed income, and risk arbitrage. No surprises there. Drexel's junk-bond department dominated its market, doing as much business as all of its competitors. And it was some of the highest-paying business to be done.

The corporate finance department arranged mergers, acquisitions, and the sale of stocks and bonds for corporations. Companies produced goods and services; corporate finance produced deals. These deals were designed to allow a company to become more effective, or in the case of hostile takeovers, to force it along that path. Whether the investment bankers of corporate finance did more good than harm to the economy is still in dispute; what is clear, however, is that they made a great deal of money, and no firm on Wall Street was about to ditch this department.

Tied in with the corporate finance effort was the institutional equity department, which was where I worked. (Officially, we were called the Professional Investor Group, giving us the disconcerting acronym of PIG.) We gave advice to the institutions that invested over a trillion dollars in the stock market. These institutions included banks, mutual funds, insurance companies, and investment advisers; their money came from individuals' savings and, more prominently, from their pension funds. In return for our advice, institutions executed their buy-and-sell orders through our trading desk, and Drexel received commissions on each trade. We didn't make much money; in fact, after deducting all the expenses involved, we lost money. Still, we were important to the firm because we were needed to sell the equity deals that our investment bankers put together.

The institutional fixed-income department was in essentially the same position as my department. The people there traded high-quality bonds for their customers, which was a more competitive and, therefore, less profitable business than selling high-yield bonds. But, like institutional equity, they were useful in placing deals.

The risk arbitrage department took positions in the stocks of companies that were in the process of being bought out by other companies. As long as there were plenty of takeovers being announced, there was usually a nice profit to be made by arbitrageurs.

These were the survivors. Fred Joseph moved on to the departments that were facing the abyss: international research, municipal bonds, and retail sales.

The demise of our effort to research foreign stocks was consistent with Wall Street's general retreat from overseas expansion, a concept that had been in vogue only a few years earlier. Too many costs, too little expertise.

The termination of the municipal bond department was easily understood. In the best of circumstances, it was a highly competitive, low-margin business. But Drexel already had two strikes against it—namely, the felony counts it had agreed to plead guilty to as part of its settlements with the U.S. Attorney's Office and with the Securities and Exchange Commission (SEC). State and local governments don't look kindly on felonies, especially those in which they aren't directly involved. Drexel's chances of getting much business from them were slim to none.

The focus of Fred's comments was on the elimination of the retail system. Eleven hundred salespeople and their entire support staff were out of a job. The mood shifted from grim to ugly. Someone somewhere picked up the phone connecting him with Fred and the rest of the world. "This sucks," he said. And then everyone realized: Their soon-to-be ex-boss was only as far away as that phone in front of them, and they could just reach out and touch him, anonymously.

The professionalism and dignity that had always set the tone in these Drexeline conference calls were gone. In their place was a new bluntness normally reserved for loved ones. If the firm now believed in a brave new world of massive layoffs, then those being pushed out weren't about to leave gracefully.

"Thanks for nothing," said one. "We don't have enough Vaseline," said another. Among the harsh questions, sound effects. It was as if the lions in the circus had looked at the tamer and asked, "Why the hell are we afraid of *him*?

Fred ended the meeting.

The salespeople made the most noise—and they certainly had a right to be angry—but they had less at risk than others. A retail broker is effectively a manager of his own business, relying on the ideas of his firm but selling by force of personality. A retail salesperson can change employers and his clients will follow. Successful salespeople have no trouble finding new jobs because they—actually, their clients—are immediately profitable to their new firm.

The retail salespeople who stayed with Drexel during the twenty-nine-month investigation by and large fell into two camps. Those who were successful would simply move to another firm. Those who were unsuccessful would be in trouble, but until now, many of them had actually benefited from Drexel's ordeal, because the firm was loath to fire anyone while the government was breathing down its neck—bad for morale, bad for its image.

The employees who were really hurt were the back-office personnel, the people who handled the buy-and-sell orders, processed the paperwork, and made sure that everything was done correctly. These unglamorous jobs, which paid the bills for thousands of employees and their families, were already filled at every other firm. New people weren't needed.

Regardless of who you were—back office or line, employed or not—you felt taken advantage of. The firm had always emphasized the importance of its employees; in one advertisement under the heading "10,000 Strong," each employee had been listed by name. Now you had to wonder: How long ago did they decide to fire thousands?

That's not to say that it was the wrong decision at the time. Even though Drexel felt that it had been strong-armed into an unfair settlement with the government, the world would see only that it was an admitted felon. Which would make a retail salesperson's job difficult, at best. The average American, whose view of the business world has been shaped by "Dallas" and "Dynasty," is just not interested in taking investment advice from a firm that he or she considers a den of thieves.

But the question remained: When did management realize that the retail system was marked for extinction? Fred Joseph told us that management had only recently received the recommendations of its strategic consultants, but that answer came across as a lame denial, bordering on evasive. When did management *know*? When did it realize that a retail system reaching every community and a corporate image of paternalism were assets in negotiating with the government, assets that would become liabilities once a settlement was reached?

Fred was not a popular guy that afternoon. If his reputation could be valued like a stock, its price would be in a free-fall, with few buyers and thousands of sellers. His employees were pissed off—most of them felt cheated and many were facing unemployment as well.

But let's be fair. The first responsibility of the managers of a corporation is to maximize the value of the shares that its stockholders own. (In the case of Drexel, a private corporation, most of the shares were owned by employees.) The maximization of shareholders' net worth seems like a cold priority, but it is the basis of our economic system. And to misquote Winston Churchill: "It's the worst system except for all the others."

Assume for a minute that you were the head of Drexel. Your choices were to jettison the retail system while negotiations are under way and risk a public backlash that could wipe out the firm; wait until the settlement is completed before eliminating retail, which would alienate everyone; or keep the retail system (and municipal bonds, for that matter) with the knowledge that it would probably become a significant drain on a firm that was already in financial trouble.

The problem with making this decision was that there were no good options. The best decision was to avoid taking a job in which you have to make a decision such as this.

Perhaps management's choice shouldn't have been such a shock; after all, less than four months earlier, Drexel had agreed to fire Michael Milken—the key figure in the firm's unbelievable success— once he was indicted. But in that decision there was a big fat mitigating circumstance: The government evidently had the weapon, and the willingness, to put us out of business if it didn't get what it wanted. And it wanted Milken out.

The weapon was the Racketeer Influenced Corrupt Organizations (RICO) statute, designed primarily to combat Mafia-controlled businesses. In the hands of Rudolph Giuliani, the politically ambitious U.S. Attorney for the Southern District Court, RICO was held over Drexel's head. The common wisdom, right or wrong, was that an indictment would finish off Drexel long before it ever had its day in court. The firm was in a jam.

At what point was the cost of settling too great, even if it meant the probable liquidation of the firm and the loss of ten thousand jobs? On December 19, 1988, that point had been reached. Two days later, the world turned and a settlement was signed. Drexel agreed to choose six felony counts from a list of allegations that the government had collected.

There was also money involved: $650 million, equal to the earnings of twenty thousand families. As a stockholder in the firm, I took a beating. My share of the settlement with the government amounted to the equivalent of five hundred M-16 rifles with enough firepower to retake Rockefeller Plaza from the Japanese. It seemed like a great deal of money at the time, and it seems like even more now.

As for Mike Milken, he would "remain for the moment." Several months later, he would be indicted by the government and would leave the firm. In addition, his $100 million bonus for 1988 was withheld at the insistence of the prosecutors. He had earned the money and he wasn't accused of any wrongdoing in that year, but still, no dice.

The firing of Milken was treated with mixed emotions on the trading floor. He was the man who had put Drexel in the big leagues, the brilliant workaholic who had sold America on high-yield bonds. He had made his firm the most feared and the most profitable on Wall Street. You had to respect the abilities and the achievements of this guy.

Still, respect didn't mean popularity. Milken and those he had hired weren't exactly the Trapp Family Singers; they fought for every dollar as if it were their first. More important, every accusation against Drexel involved the high-yield bond department. Michael may have been the primary reason for our past successes, but he was also the primary reason for our current troubles.

And then there was the disdain factor. It had come across in a magnificent speech Milken had made to the equity department in October 1986, a time when seemingly nothing could slow him down. In addition to outlining his view of the future, he made some remarks about our lack of effort and intensity, remarks that probably annoyed people more than they would ever admit.

So when Milken was fired, the rest of us could say that the firm had little choice, without feeling too bad. We could say that he had, to some extent, brought it on himself with his take-no-prisoners tactics. We could say that Michael was extraordinary, certainly, but that the firm had exceptional talent, regardless—an argument akin to praising your Lincoln Town Car after the Lamborghini has been recalled.

But when management fired the little people—thousands of them—well, that was different. After all, the government didn't force this decision. And this was close to home. The one-big-family concept at Drexel was history. Whether or not management's decision had merit, few employees now trusted their firm. A new attitude had emerged: No one is going to look after you but you.

By April 1989, I had been with Drexel Burnham for nearly eight years. During that time, Wall Street had changed more rapidly than in any period since the mid-1930s. The unwritten rule that who you knew was perhaps more important than what you knew—that relationships were more important than ideas—had shifted, to the dismay of those with the right connections. Uncivil behavior such as hostile takeovers became fashionable. Wall Street firms took on more and more risk; their profits soared and then collapsed, while their vulnerability to bad times just kept increasing.

Ambitious prosecutors redefined the importance of rules that had sat dormant—and were progressively abused—for fifty years. Parking stock, an infraction that had been treated like parking tickets, became a major felony. Meanwhile, insider trading, a serious crime that deserved serious attention, was never defined in any way that even experts could understand.

The Justice Department unleashed the racketeering laws on the financial community. To many it was a move long overdue, but to others this weapon threatened to negate the most important rule we have: You're innocent until proven guilty. The RICO statute, arguably, is legalized extortion when used to negotiate with financial institutions, which are dependent on public confidence for their survival.

Working on Wall Street in the 1980s provided some unusually good memories and some particularly bad ones. The growth of the junk-bond market, which catapulted Drexel to the top, forced many lousy managers to pay attention to the interests of their stockholders—most of them small investors—or risk losing their coveted positions. My firm, however, also contributed to and benefited from the United States' newfound love affair with debt, as well as with greed.

It was a decade when the stock market tripled, while suffering its worst decline in history along the way; when the average person on the street became more skeptical about most everyone on the Street; and when the financial community created billionaires that ranged in character from a modest midwestern value investor to a New York real estate self-promoter in an age of self-promotion.

It was a time when most people worked hard to make a living, and a few made an absolute killing. Among the many I remember with respect are the vast majority of the employees at Drexel, who gave their jobs their best effort, and the clients with whom I dealt, who cared deeply about the pensions and savings entrusted to them. These people stood out in sharp contrast to the immoral minority of corporate managers who squandered their shareholders' money for their private agenda, of savings and loan owners who gambled with federally insured funds, and of Wall Streeters who worried too much about their commissions and too little about their customers.

Perhaps my best memory of the 1980s was in being a part of a system that worked—and worked well—despite the abuses at every level. Meanwhile, a system that didn't work was collapsing, done in by its bloated goals and false promises. "Russia is a country that is burying their troubles," Will Rogers wrote sixty years ago. "Your criticism is your epitaph." But if a government cheats its people long enough, leaving them in poverty, without hope, their troubles will bury it. At least that's the way it should be. And, finally, that's the way it was.

In April of 1989, however, the impending victory of capitalism didn't mean squat to the employees of Drexel Burnham. Some were trying to figure out what to do with their lives; the rest were trying to figure out what this all meant to them. The top management of my department called a meeting to explain the world to us.

As the salespeople and traders wondered about their future prospects, their mortgage payments, and their kids' tuition bills, one senior manager noted that "a circle exists in a continuous and continuous manner" [sic]. He said that there were "only degrees of difficulty and unhappiness," and he offered some additional drivel about an "unholy alliance."

He spoke of "agony" and "doing our darnedest."

He spoke of Macbeth, of Drexel's need to move quickly. He seemed oblivious to the insult of comparing our firm to a homicidal nut who would end up with his head on a stick.

And yet, ironically, this analogy from hell was prophetic. Within a year, Drexel Burnham Lambert would collapse into bankruptcy. The end, when it came, was swift, unnerving—as if the house you had lived in for years was suddenly swallowed up by a swamp that you didn't even know existed.

The destruction of Drexel raised some unsettling questions. How could the firm disappear less than two weeks after one senior manager assured certain employees that the financial condition was sound—

more than that, strong? How could any firm with $800 *million* in net worth go bankrupt? What good was Drexel's $1 billion in excess regulatory capital (whatever that meant) if it couldn't prevent defaulting on a $100 million loan?

Why didn't the government step in to help the firm and its employees? Was Drexel's crisis that much less important than Hayden, Stone's twenty years earlier, or Lockheed's fifteen years earlier, or Chrysler's ten years earlier, or Continental Illinois's six years before?

Perhaps, and not just for financial reasons. In its prime, the firm had cultivated enemies in high places. "The old Drexel Burnham Lambert that everyone knew and hated for the last ten years is gone," a Bush administration official told *The Wall Street Journal*. Good riddance, many thought.

Did the dislike for Drexel even reflect a certain degree of anti-Semitism? Its leaders, it was said, were "the new breed" of Jews—aggressive and arrogant and effective. They not only didn't belong to the right clubs, they made these clubs less influential in American business.

Would it have made any difference if the firm had kept its retail system? Would the thought of three hundred and fifty thousand investors with accounts at Drexel, all screaming for their money, have made a sufficient impression on the SEC and the Federal Reserve? Would the government have found a way to keep the firm in business, twisting a few well-chosen arms in the banking community?

But this is just speculation. The reality was that approximately five thousand employees came to work on Monday, February 12, 1990, and most were out of a job by Friday. Some exacted a petty revenge by purchasing computers from the firm for twenty cents on the dollar, then canceling the checks once the equipment was out of the building. Morale, already brain dead, was subsequently dealt another blow by the news that management had paid out $260 million in bonuses—over $10 million in one case—only weeks before the end.

"I don't think it's sad for those jerks on Wall Street," takeover expert Theodore Forstmann told the *Journal*. But it was. For every "jerk" whose glorious lifestyle was knocked down a few notches, there were a hundred decent people who found themselves putting their possessions in boxes and leaving their firm for the last time.

And everyone wondered, How could this happen?

CHAPTER TWO

ON THE STREET

It was great when it all began . . .
—*Rocky Horror Picture Show*

The firm I joined in 1981 had been in business for more than forty-five years and had little in common with the firm that it would become in the next five. The underlying culture of Drexel Burnham, however, did lay the groundwork for its almost inconceivable success and collapse, and for its continuing influence on Wall Street.

To understand Drexel, you need to understand its industry. The Street is essentially in the business of selling ideas. It advises corporations on what businesses to buy and sell, and on how to raise money and how to spend it. It advises investors on where to put their money to get the best return without taking on too much risk. It tries to put together the people who have funds with the people who need them; it helps make money flow efficiently. And, as the money flows smoothly from one hand to another, Wall Street keeps a small percentage for its efforts.

This may not sound like a noble cause, but in some ways it is. Certainly, it's an important one. Our economic system is based on the freedom to produce what you want and to purchase what you want.

Supply and demand determine prices, and prices determine what is supplied and demanded in the future. The financial markets allow companies to raise money so they can afford to produce what's wanted; at the same time, the markets give those with excess cash the opportunities to invest it.

Everybody does what is in their own self-interest, and it works out pretty well, in general. The free enterprise system has a great advantage over its competition: It recognizes human nature. From each according to his abilities, to each according to his needs is an admirable sentiment, but it's one that reads better than it plays. An expert in Leninism once noted, according to George Will, that it is a measure of Vladimir Lenin's foresight that none of his predictions have come true yet.

If Wall Street's product is ideas, its raw materials are people and capital. Between a firm's brains and its money, ideas can be created, disseminated, and executed. Thinking up ideas is not easy work, but getting corporations and individuals to believe in them and to put their own money behind them can be harder still.

Drexel Burnham was always a place where employees were given a good deal of freedom to generate ideas or implement them, or both. "People made a very nice living being free in the market, which is what this business is all about," said Allan McCarthy, a salesman who joined in 1976. The firm was organized around profit centers, whereby individual departments were compensated based on their own performance, rather than that of the entire firm. It was, noted one executive, a bunch of businesses under a big tent.

The ringmaster was Isaac Wolfe ("I.W.") Burnham, named after a relative who left his father money. I.W., known by the odd nickname of "Tubby," was—and is—respected by virtually everyone on the Street, and you don't have to work here long to know how rare that is. He founded the firm on April 1, 1935 with mostly borrowed money, and was its chief executive until 1976. "Tubby Burnham was regarded as being there when it counted," according to McCarthy. "If it was a tough time to trade gold, he was trading gold; if it was a tough time to trade treasuries, he was trading treasuries. He was always there."

When an employee was found to have a brain tumor, back before the days of comprehensive health insurance, Burnham saw to it that the firm took care of the bills. When a longtime employee left his wife for a walk on the wild side, he personally interceded. Until 1961 or 1962, he knew everyone by their first name.

Burnham and Co., as the firm was called at that time, had a few hundred employees and a few million dollars in net worth. It had struggled through the Wall Street doldrums of 1959 and 1960, when a busy day in the stock market meant three million shares. The company had only barely avoided a layoff.

Fortunately, the 1960s were great for stocks and better still for brokers. The Nixon administration, however, ushered in an awful era for Wall Street, a time marked by continuing declines in the bond market and two severe declines in the stock market—during 1969 and, brutally, during 1973–1974. Brokerage firms suffered both from their inability to deal with the increased volume of business from the "go-go" years of the 1960s and from the lousy markets that inevitably followed that boom.

One firm that fell on hard times was Drexel Firestone, a Philadelphia investment bank that traced its roots back to the bluest bloods of turn-of-the-century Wall Street—Edward Harriman and J. P. Morgan among them. The firm's problem was simple: A noticeable number of its top investment bankers had left for greener pastures.

The atmosphere there in the early 1970s was somewhat reminiscent of a proper British club twenty years earlier. The Empire was yesterday's news, but nobody was quite up to acknowledging it. According to one Drexel banker, the firm had lost all its significant clients except two local utilities, Philadelphia Electric and Penn Power and Light.

Drexel Firestone did maintain its style, however. One senior partner was described as the perfect model for a life-size FAO Schwarz investment banker doll. One morning, surrounded by the boardroom's beautiful mahaghony walls and under the watchful portraits of the firm's founders, he let loose a brainstorm: Firestone Tire, which had a financial interest in the firm, should acquire Campbell Soup.

Never mind that Campbell was four times larger than Firestone, that there was no strategic reason for them to merge, that Firestone was already on the brink of having the safety rating on its bonds downgraded, or that the Dorrance family, which controlled Campbell could—and would—stop any acquisition attempt. Never mind that this idea was doomed from birth. It was on the table, and some poor MBA would waste a day doing the requisite analysis before this proposal could be politely put to sleep.

In later years, this senior partner would find his niche when he became the chairman of the Finance Committee, a committee that had only one member and which never met.

Drexel did retain one great advantage, nevertheless. In the clubby world of Wall Street, it was still given a prime piece of the syndicates that were formed to sell stocks and bonds. Burnham and Co., meanwhile, wanted to be a major-bracket firm, which was unlikely to happen in anyone's lifetime unless it acquired a major. And so, in 1973, it bought Drexel.

The two firms that joined to form Drexel Burnham (the Drexel name got lead billing to avoid risking its major-bracket status) had about as much in common as the Union and the Confederacy. In the corporate finance department, the predominantly Jewish Burnham group felt that the Drexel people had memories instead of clients, and the predominantly WASP Drexel investment bankers thought the Burnham team would've been better off with memories instead of the clients they had.

This problem was largely resolved by the catastrophic bear markets of the next two years. By the end of 1974, the ranks of corporate finance had been decimated from forty to eleven. "Everyone was thinking M&A [mergers and acquisitions]," recalled a senior Drexel investment banker. "but we were getting nowhere."

In the depths of the 1974 Wall Street death march, Fred Joseph was hired. He had been the head of Shearson's retail system and, before that, had been an assistant to John Shad, the vice-chairman of E. F. Hutton. Shad had hired Joseph out of Harvard Business School, impressed with this young man's background and attitude.

Joseph was the son of a Boston cabdriver; he grew up in a lower-middle-class family, Jewish in an Irish town. Not surprisingly, he became a good amateur boxer. Less predictably, he was accepted into Harvard College; he was the last student from P. T. Campbell High School to make the Ivy League until his brother graduated six years later.

Tony Meyer, a senior investment banker who met Fred after his arrival at Drexel Burnham remembered: "He produced a little hand-written list of companies that he thought he could deliver [as clients]; I could only recognize three of them." Fred rose quickly in the firm to senior vice-president, then to cohead of corporate finance, then to the chief of the department.

Among Fred's strengths was a great charm—he was extremely like-able and articulate and, well, decent. People just disagreed on how sincere his image was.

"He was very, very clever at figuring out what it took to get what he wanted," said Meyer. "He never said anything that I didn't want to hear." According to another former senior officer of the firm who likely bears a grudge, Fred was "a bright, able, attractive investment banker," but cold and aloof on a personal level, a go-getter who "suffered from the Little Man Syndrome." A more generous senti-ment was voiced by a young investment banker who joined many years later, "Fred Joseph was a nice guy who set the example, then hired people who had the same point of view."

On a professional level, that point of view was straightforward, one that hadn't changed since the day he walked in the door: Fred wanted to build a highly respected Wall Street powerhouse. And he did, with more than a little help from a friend.

The final piece of the Drexel Burnham structure was the 1976 acquisition of William D. Witter, a small "research boutique," which focused on the analysis of a few industries and their stocks. William D. Witter was controlled by Groupe Bruxelles Lambert, a Brussels-based investment banking firm. As a result of the acquisition of Wit-ter, the Groupe received more than 20 percent of Drexel's stock and the firm officially became Drexel Burnham Lambert Inc.

When I came on board in June 1981, Drexel Burnham was about halfway between the firm that was struggling to meet its bills in the mid-1970s and the firm that would revolutionize American finance in the mid-1980s. It was still a second-tier shop on Wall Street, but the entrepreneurial culture and the people were already in place. To an unusually perceptive business-school student, the hidden potential of Drexel made it the place to go, the opportunity to get in early on what would become the hottest firm on the Street.

I was not that student. Not only didn't I recognize the possibilities for the firm, I didn't even realize what they were interviewing me for:

"Why do you want to work in investment banking?"

"I don't. I want to work in investment *management.*"

"Then why are you here?"

"The letter said investment management."

"No, it said investment banking."

"No, it didn't."

"Yes, it did."

I checked the letter. No, it didn't.

The interviewer was pleasant, considering that he was dealing with Wharton's only illiterate grad student.

"Look," he said. "We have a half hour left. I can catch an earlier train, or we can just sit and chat for a while."

"No, why don't you catch the earlier train."

"We'll be in touch."

A few days later, the odds makers took a beating as I got a call from Drexel:

"What positions would you be interested in?"

"What are you hiring for?" I asked. (I certainly could carry a conversation.)

"Everything. What are you interested in?"

I was interviewing for an institutional sales position at Merrill Lynch, so I suggested that.

Again, I was told that they would get back to me, and again they did.

I eventually spent a grueling day of interviews with analysts, salesmen, and officers at Drexel. Because I didn't know quite what the job involved, the early interviews went poorly. By the afternoon, I had a good idea of the drill and, probably for the first time in the process, I sounded like someone that someone would want to hire.

This is not meant as a criticism of the people who decided to give me a job and pay me the exorbitant (in my eyes, at least—at first) salary of $35,000 a year. I did have the Wharton name behind me, and I was finishing up my undergraduate and graduate studies in five years. On paper, I looked pretty strong, which may have encouraged everyone to downplay my occasional confusion in person.

My first assignment of any real importance was to analyze for the sales force a new offering that Drexel was about to sell to the public. It was an odd thing to ask a kid fresh out of school to spend a night reading a one-hundred-page prospectus that explained everything that could go wrong with a company trying to raise $100 million and then expect him to summarize it for a group of pros who genuinely knew what they were doing.

Also, it was the responsibility of corporate finance to explain the strengths and weaknesses of a deal that it had put together and which it wanted the salesmen to sell to their clients. In later years, corporate finance would handle these presentations, providing us with detailed memos and access to the managements of the companies we were trying to finance. But at this stage, the investment bankers just sent the prospectuses to us and expected us to sell whatever it was that these documents told us was for sale.

Churchill once commented in reviewing a book on penguins, "This book tells me more about penguins than I care to know"—a complaint that certainly applied to reading a prospectus. But this first deal that I read at least had the advantage of being in an interesting industry, an industry that Drexel Burnham would raise billions of dollars for in the upcoming years: cable television.

The company itself managed—by mismanagement—to go down the tubes. But it did introduce the firm to a wonderful group of companies that needed to borrow a great deal of money and produced a great deal of cash to pay off that debt. And it did introduce me to a fellow who would become a pseudolegend at Drexel Burnham: The Great Acquisitor.

The Great One was the top investment banker on this cable deal. According to a senior corporate finance officer, "Fred Joseph used to think he was very bright, hardworking, extremely quick at sizing up situations and thinking on his feet." Others had a somewhat different point of view. "I wouldn't hire him to hold my horse," said another senior banker. "My guess is to know him is to hate him." "A big, fat guy with a wimpy, namby-pamby voice" was one salesman's description. "Unless the guy's changed, I always thought he was a moron." One analyst viewed him simply as "a great investment banker and an enormous pig."

I met with The Great Acquisitor once to review some figures that one of the salesmen had requested, and he impressed me with his self-confidence and his apparent thoroughness (unfortunately, I can be a lousy judge of character). He assured me that he had gone over the numbers about twenty times the previous night.

Based on what I learned later about the Acquisitor's analytic ability, his assurance was probably a crock. Someone who had supervised him briefly in an earlier time on an earlier deal mentioned that The Great One's responsibility was to provide the analysis on which to judge that deal. Instead, he assigned it to a junior person, who proceded to botch up the numbers. When his superior on the deal noticed the errors, The Great One did the analysis himself. Wrong again. He redid the numbers. Different results, but still wrong.

My next important assignment was, for me, a several-month walk through the valley of the shadow. Another new salesman and I became the liaisons between our institutional equity department and the convertible bond group. A convert, as you might know, is a hybrid security: a bond (a loan to a company) that entitles you to a fixed rate of interest, which can be exchanged into a certain number of shares of stock (a piece of ownership in that company).

The job was a peach, sort of a Wall Street version of *The Island of Lost Souls,* with its restless natives and House of Pain. It was my first direct contact with any of the boys on the West Coast, and it was the first and last time in my eight years that I would go home most nights with knots in my stomach.

When people at Drexel spoke of the West Coast, they were actually referring to one small office in Beverly Hills. This was the home of the high-yield bond department and, less important, of the convertible bond group. Over the next five years, this so-called branch office, three thousand miles from Wall Street, would become the center of the universe for corporate America.

Of course, I didn't know that. What I did know was that I was a twenty-two-year-old rookie who was out of his league. At first, I had hoped that my new assignment would live up to its billing—a great opportunity, etc. The first phone call my partner and I had with our main contact on the Coast, however, made it clear that we weren't in Kansas anymore. I was obsequious, striving for unctuous. At the end of the conversation, the Gray Prince, a senior vice-president, asked us if we had any questions before he came to New York to meet us.

"No," my partner responded. "But I'm sure we'll think of some by the time you get out here."

Good answer—banal and professional.

"Well," responded the voice on the line. "I don't want to get blindsided."

Huh?

Blindsided by us? Why? Weren't we on the same side?

Maybe, maybe not.

We soon learned that our primary responsibility was to get the salesmen in the equity department to fill out questionaires. These questionaires would tell the boys on the Coast, the portfolio managers with the authority, to buy convertible bonds. Now, no salesman in his right mind is eager to tell anyone else who to call at his accounts to generate business. That's his job; more important, that's his livelihood. If there are stocks or convertible bonds (which are, after all, a form of stock) to be sold to his accounts, he wants to write the tickets. To tell someone three thousand miles away the best contacts is to risk losing those commissions.

Which increasingly seemed like a very likely risk.

Our conversations with the Coast had more in common with the Paris Peace Talks than with two departments of the same firm working toward the greater good. The equity salesmen didn't want to give away their contacts without some ground rules on how commissions on convert trades would be divided, and the Coast preferred vague assurances. They argued that whoever got the order should get the commission, which seemed fair on the surface. The problem was that every transaction would potentially create a battle, and two parts of Drexel would be fighting each other.

The greater problem was that we didn't trust them. Our West Coast contacts were selling machines; what they said always seemed to be geared to moving the merchandise. You didn't get a sense that you were hearing both sides of the story, or perhaps even the correct story.

Every morning, we would be told the list of converts that the Coast had in inventory and wanted to sell. The morning rundown was delivered by our other contact, who we had nicknamed "Bodo," based on the *Lord of the Rings*. Of course, we never called him that on the phone, because we were scared shitless of him—he was the nastiest fuckin' hobbit on Middle Earth.

One morning after he had given us the dozen or so names that we should encourage the equity salesmen to sell to their clients, we asked him for his three favorite converts, the three from the total universe of hundreds of publicly traded convertible bonds that he thought were the best value. He quickly gave us three names from that morning's sell list.

Say it ain't so, Bodo.

The greatest excitement—and tension—was reserved for the deals, when new convertible bonds were offered to the public, and commissions were about ten times higher than those to be earned on converts already trading in the market. The equity salesmen were at a great disadvantage, because the West Coast controlled "the books," deciding which clients would receive these convertible bonds as well as how many they would get. Not surprisingly, on deals where the demand for converts exceeded the number being offered, the lion's share would go to accounts that had ordered the bonds through the convert salesmen on the Coast.

This was frustrating, but this was life. What was unacceptable was the concept of "running ahead," which emerged on one huge and important convertible offering. The Coast tried a popular approach among totalitarian governments: the sham democracy. We were told not to discuss the deal until it was officially filed with the SEC. Fine, that's the rule. As soon as the deal was filed, however, orders started pouring in through the West Coast by the tens of millions. And, by the way, orders would be filled on a first-come, first-served basis.

Somehow, the salesmen out there had managed to educate their clients on the intricacies of the deal and receive orders in a matter of seconds, or for the more sluggish among them, in minutes. It was extraordinary. It was unprecedented. It was bullshit.

We arranged a phone call—my partner, my boss, and I—with the Prince.

"Did any of your salespeople call any of the accounts before the deal was filed?" I asked.

Short pause.

"No."

"Well," I replied like a good/nasty lawyer who never asks a question without knowing the answer, "we were told by two accounts that they were told about the deal a week before it was filed."

Long pause.

Pure venom: "Don't you *ever* ask me a leading question like that again."

And the clouds parted, and the angels hid, and I realized: Welcome to the real world.

A meeting was finally called to hash out our differences, to decide once and for all how to get the two coasts working together in selling converts. I was prepared; I was psyched. In New York, my partner and I joined up with my sales manager, and we filed into his boss's office.

At the other end of the conference line, in Beverly Hills, were the Prince, Bodo, and a mystery guest.

The meeting began.

A voice from the Coast: "Eddie, this is Mike. Can we take care of this another time, you and I?"

"Sure, Mike."

End of meeting.

For me, this was a frustrating nonevent. For the guy at the other end of the line, this was just another of several hundred details he had dealt with that day. At thirty-five, he was already a major force in the financial world and was well on his way to building an empire.

CHAPTER THREE

THE WORLD ACCORDING TO MIKE

You say you want a revolution,
well, you know, we all want to change the world . . .

—THE BEATLES

Michael Milken did what should be all but impossible: He found a gold mine lying under Wall Street virtually ignored. Our financial markets had been in existence for at least a century, and had been operating under modern regulations for forty years. Any extraordinary opportunities should have been exploited by the tens of thousands of bright, ambitious financiers who had spent their careers looking for the overlooked and the undervalued.

Milken did find such an opportunity—or perhaps more accurately, he created one. As a college student at Berkeley in the late 1960s, Milken read about the systematic undervaluation of low-quality bonds. These were bonds that the rating agencies—Moody's and Standard & Poor's (S&P), in particular—felt were speculations instead of investments. They were assigned a rating of BB ("double-B") or less, well below the top-grade rating of AAA ("triple-A").

These "speculative" bonds had historically offered a high yield that more than offset the risks. Certainly, some high-yield bonds had defaulted, leaving their holders with pieces of paper that no longer

21

paid the interest promised. Still, a well-diversified portfolio provided a better return to investors than they would have received from owning Treasury bonds.

On average, about 3 percent of high-yield bonds had missed an interest payment each year. The prices of these defaulted bonds naturally tumbled, losing some 50 percent of their original value. Therefore, the loss rate on all junk bonds averaged 1.5 percent a year. This loss rate is less than the 3 to 4 percent high-yield premium—the amount by which high-yield interest rates exceed Treasury bond interest rates. The gains from the extra interest are higher than the losses from the occasional disasters.

And it was with this thesis as inspiration that Milken turned corporate America on its head and built a billion-dollar personal fortune from scratch. It is difficult to comprehend the influence he would eventually wield: He became the driving force (some would say the controlling factor) in the most potent market of the 1980s.

Whether he had any idea of the impact he would have when he joined Drexel's nascent high-yield bond department in 1970 is anyone's guess. If anyone could have imagined his future, it was Milken himself. But even he probably couldn't envision what would be accomplished in the next fifteen years, and he certainly wouldn't have believed what could happen in the following five.

What was obvious to him—and to everyone who met him—was that he was no ordinary guy. He was a genius: not in the sense that most people mean when they throw the term around, but in the lights-out, unbelievable category. He was also an extraordinary salesman with a work ethic that would have finished off most motivated young men in six months.

Physically, he was unimposing, about six-feet tall and thin to the point of gaunt, as if food was just an afterthought. In a business known for gray temples and ponderous voices, he had neither. But his youthful appearance didn't matter; his force of intelligence and personality were overwhelming.

At Drexel, Milken was an oddity, a rare Jew among WASPs, trading junk bonds at a firm that still fancied itself among the elite. These junk bonds fell into two camps: "fallen angels," bonds that had once been considered high grade, but whose ratings had been downgraded as the fortunes of the underlying companies had floundered, and "Chinese paper," low-quality bonds that had been issued to pay for some of the wild-and-woolly acquisitions of the 1960s.

He created an active high-yield bond market, and an active market is a necessary condition for a successful market. Buyers want to know that they can sell their holdings at will. Milken was eager to take the role of market maker, because he understood better than his clients and his competitors how much these bonds were worth. The more he traded, the more he would able to earn, buying low and selling high.

He would think up interesting trading ideas and go to his head trader, Charlie Causey, to put them to work. Charlie was one of the only people that Michael ever dealt with who didn't hesitate to criticize him. "Who the hell are you?" someone overheard Causey yell at Milken. "You don't know one side of a bond from another." The two worked together for many years, until Charlie, who had earned all he would need, left for a fishing trip in the late 1970s, and stayed.

Milken earned his first million-dollar bonus before he was thirty. He made his first fortune buying the junk bonds of real estate investment trusts (REITs). These REITs, which invested in income-producing properties and raw land, were the darlings of the market in the late 1960s, but fell out of favor in the 1970s.

The recession of 1974 certainly hurt the value of the bonds, as the underlying properties suffered in a poor economy. But more important, the *price* of REIT bonds was beaten down out of proportion to the decline in their value, as investors' greed was replaced by fear. Milken recognized that at ten or twenty cents on the dollar, these bonds were great buys.

Trading junk bonds was clearly not the extent of Milken's ambition, even early on. According to senior investment banker Tony Meyer, "Michael used to wander into my office in the early to mid-1970s and he'd say, 'Listen, why don't we try to develop some underwriting business peddling bond issues of BB and B companies. I'm very active in this market and we really need a source of business. We're never going to do any business with GM or GE.'

"And I'd say, 'Michael, don't be crazy.'"

In 1977, Milken's idea became a reality: For the first time since the days of J. P. Morgan, bonds of a noninvestment-grade company were sold to the public. The underwriter of these new bonds, however, was not Drexel, it was Lehman Brothers. In fact, Lehman did the first four original-issue junk bonds; after that, it basically abandoned its newly created franchise, a decision that cost it perhaps a billion dollars in potential fees during the subsequent decade.

If Lehman was leery about underwriting high-yield bonds, Drexel was not. For one thing, it didn't need to worry about offending a large number of high-grade corporate clients, because it didn't have many to offend. For another, it had a young trader in-house who knew the junk-bond market and its customers better than anyone on the Street.

And there was a huge pool of possible clients among the approximately 20,000 companies that were large enough to finance in the public markets, but that didn't qualify for an investment-grade rating from Moody's or S&P. These companies, representing 95 percent of the country's total, had been forced to rely primarily on bank debt to finance their growth.

The major problems with borrowing from banks were the restrictive covenants, which told you what you couldn't do in running your business, and the floating interest rate, which allowed the cost of the loan to rise in a recession just when you could least afford it. As Ralph Ingersoll of Ingersoll Publications told *The Wall Street Journal,* "I don't sleep at nights when I have bank debt."

It was a nice fit all around: Drexel needed a franchise of its own, a lot of companies needed financing, a lot of money was looking for high returns, and Michael Milken knew how to bring together the sellers and the buyers. Drexel became the leading firm in high-yield bond financings in 1978 and proceeded to maintain its domination of this market from that time on, doing as many deals as all of its competitors *combined.*

Around this time, Milken moved his operation from New York to Beverly Hills. The senior members of the firm, from Burnham on down, opposed the move, but they couldn't prevent it. Milken, at thirty-one, was already too important; if the firm said no, he could have gotten what he wanted anywhere on Wall Street in just a bit longer than it takes to dial the phone.

He had several reasons for the move to the West Coast. He wanted to return to his hometown, where his parents still lived. He wanted his family to enjoy a better quality of life than they currently had in New Jersey, as inconceivable as that might seem. He wanted his competitors to have as little knowledge of what he was doing as possible. Perhaps he wanted the same for his firm.

(Milken's passion for secrecy was highlighted in confidential depositions taken many years later in conjunction with a lawsuit by Green Tree Acceptance Inc., accusing Drexel of mishandling an offering of bonds and stock. In one of these depositions, obtained by *The Washington Post*, Paul Boyum of Green Tree spoke of his attempt to get the list of those who had bought his company's stock:

"[Gerald Koerner, a first vice-president in Drexel's corporate finance department] said Milken wouldn't give it to them. The West Coast wouldn't tell the East Coast who they were selling stock to, which to me was unbelievable. I simply didn't believe him."

"Did you say so?" asked an attorney.
"Yes.
"What did he say?
"He said Drexel is a funny institution.")

By 1980, it was obvious that the high-yield bond market was for real. "Every deal that got done made it easier to get the next one done," remembered Keith Hartley, a corporate finance officer who had joined the firm in 1973. "We really felt like we were accomplishing something." Another veteran recalled the mood: "Everybody began to feel very affluent, very good about life, very smart. Guys thought they were really great because they were innovative."

Milken's operation had, by then, branched out to convertible bonds, which would haunt me less than two years later. A new wrinkle on junk bonds emerged as well, which would become the focus of a serious controversy—debt with warrants. The idea was simple: Encourage companies that were selling junk bonds to include warrants, which allow a holder to buy shares of stock at a set price, to make the deals more attractive. These warrants would give bond buyers—who were only lenders to a company—a piece of ownership with its upside potential if the company did well.

The use of warrants, known as "equity kickers," did highlight a basic fact in the junk-bond market: Its growth was more dependent on the buyers than the sellers. There was a virtually unlimited list of companies that would be eager to raise long-term capital at fixed interest rates, which is what these bonds allowed them to do. The hard part was in convincing people, particularly those who made the decisions at institutions such as insurance companies, savings and loans (S&Ls), and advisory firms, to invest billions of dollars in bonds that until recently had been ridiculed or ignored or treated with suspicion.

This was Milken's real challenge, and nobody was better. Even late in his career, when he had become the main man on the Street, he was still willing to make his sales pitch in person. A large insurance company in New Jersey had decided to begin investing in junk bonds; Milken showed up with Jim Dahl, his top salesman. The meeting began a bit after 9:00 A.M. and lasted for five hours. "He would look at a name, and give you the whole history," said a participant. "They just looked at him like he was the Messiah."

A limosine picked him up at 2:15 to drive him to New York for a 3:00 meeting; after that, he had another one at 4:00, and a flight out of La Guardia Airport at 5:15. Someone expressed concern that he would miss his plane. "I'll make it," he replied.

"He was a man who had every fact and figure in order," observed a young investment banker. "He knew the particulars, every covenant, every uptick and downtick. He had the unusual talent of being very technically proficient in a presentation, then being able to step back and talk about the world, the global village."

"He had incredible thoughts, fascinating points of view," a banker from the Coast recalled. "He could sit in a meeting and explain to the chairman of a company why the Germans raising the bundesbank rate would affect snow peas, or why real estate prices in Japan were affecting your mortgage."

Michael Milken had the ability to make the clichéd seem profound because coming from him, it was. When he asked the heads of corporations to tell him their dreams, they knew that here was a man who could make those dreams happen.

Milken almost single-handedly built—and perhaps controlled—a huge financial market. He convinced buyers to abandon their prejudices against junk bonds, and he convinced sellers to pay the price that he said was necessary to place the merchandise. By the beginning of the 1980s, the high-yield bond market, his market, was poised to show the world that it was not only big, it was powerful.

The 1980s on Wall Street was an era of junk-financed takeovers, conjuring up images of anemic dweebs trading inside information and dragging suitcases of cash through lower Manhattan. The reality was a bit different. To begin with, most buyouts were friendly, with both the buyer and the seller agreeing on a fair price without hiring detective firms to dig up dirt on each other.

The times were ripe for a takeover boom. The 1960s' religion of bigger is better had left its followers ill-prepared for the 1970s. The problem was stock prices: They went down when they were supposed to go up. During the good days, big conglomerates could buy high-growth companies and pay for them with shares of their own stock; these holding companies would then look better to investors, because they owned a stable of fast-growing (but unrelated) businesses.

When stock prices headed south, conglomerates could no longer afford to pay up for acquisitions, because their currency—their stock—didn't buy as much anymore. More important, investors began to question the attractiveness of big companies composed of businesses with little or nothing in common. The financial fashion statement of the late 1960s went the way of the Nehru jacket, both for good reason.

Meanwhile, inflation was rising, and the values of corporate assets were increasing, as well. The land that companies owned, the plants that produced their products, and the prices of these products all rose sharply in the 1970s. The investment community, its former optimism rewarded with painful bear markets, preferred to focus instead on the dismal economy and the sorry state of the world, from the U.S. perspective, at least.

The election of Ronald Reagan to the presidency was a turning point. His landslide victory gave him the mandate to get inflation down, and he did. He was willing to accept a price that most politicians would never have: the worst economic downturn since the Great Depression. Following this recession, the economy would grow for almost a decade. Reagan also spearheaded the 1981 Tax Act, which increased the value of corporations by reducing their tax payments.

The stage was set for takeovers. Companies were selling for significantly less than they were worth, and the future was looking brighter. Investors were either unaware of the values, or skeptical that they would ever be realized. All that was needed was the money to pay for the buyouts.

Banks were willing to finance the least-risky part of the acquisitions: the senior debt. They would put up about half the cost of the deal, provided that they had a claim on all the assets in the event that anything went wrong. That way they were fairly certain to get their money back, even if the company went bankrupt.

The people buying the company would contribute a small amount in return for all the equity. Should the acquisition be a successful one, these stockholders would receive the full benefit of the company's increased value; potential profits could be enormous.

The hard part was finding investors who were willing to fill in the middle, to buy the debt that was too risky for the banks but that didn't offer the home-run possibilities of the equity. In order for buyouts to happen easily and efficiently, there had to be a market for this junk debt. And once Milken came around, there was.

In the early years of the takeover boom, the businesses being bought were often the divisions of conglomerates. For example, a small company that didn't have much in common with the other parts of the corporation and whose performance wasn't contributing greatly to the overall results might be divested. The buyers, usually consisting of the small company's management and a group of financiers, would borrow most of the agreed on purchase price.

The success of this leveraged buyout (LBO) would depend in large part on the ability of management, which now had a substantial vested interest in the company's future, to do what it had often been unable to do before: turn the company around. This might involve decisions that it had been prevented from making before by its conglomerate parent, such as entering a new market, or decisions that it had been unwilling to make, such as cutting back on its work force. There was also the question of luck: Would the demand for the company's products exceed expectations, or not?

The potential rewards for a successful LBO were enormous, because the upside went to the stockholders who had put up only a small fraction of the money. Just how great that potential was became apparent to the world in 1983 when Gibson Greetings sold shares of its stock to the public.

Gibson, whose most famous employee was Garfield the Cat, had been purchased from RCA for $80 million, of which $79 million was borrowed. The buyer was Wesray, a buyout firm headed by former Secretary of the Treasury William Simon. When the company went public only eighteen months later, Simon's investment of $330,000 had risen to a market value of $66 million—a gain of 20,000 percent!

Profits like that are not ignored for long, and LBOs became the rage. Acquisitions financed primarily with debt would rise from $11 billion in the 1978–1983 period to $182 billion in the following five years. And at the center of the action was Mike Milken—to some extent helping the process; to some extent feeding it—placing the junk bonds that Wall Street had considered unplaceable.

Takeovers evolved from the unwanted divisions of conglomerates to the conglomerates themselves. Because these companies were selling well below the total value of their subsidiaries—the sum of the parts was worth more than the whole—why not buy the undervalued package, and sell off the pieces?

The leveraged buyout of Beatrice Companies highlighted this strategy. Completed in April 1986, it was the largest LBO to that time; the buyer was Kohlberg Kravis Roberts and Company (KKR), the granddaddy of the leveraged buyout firm. Drexel Burnham financed the junk-bond portion of this $6.2 billion deal, raising $2.5 billion through four different types of securities, from 11% ten-year senior notes (11% interest annually for ten years; strong claim on assets) to fifteen-year floating rate junior subordinate debentures (uncertain interest rate; uncertain claim).

Donald Kelly, a veteran of the food industry and the new chief executive of Beatrice, was able to reduce $100 million in annual costs, according to a July, 1989 *Fortune* article.

As for selling the pieces of this far-flung conglomerate, the new owners were able to find buyers for its Avis car rental, Tropicana juices, Playtex hosiery, Coca-Cola bottling, and international food operations—with total proceeds of approximately $4.4 billion.

The non-food businesses were packaged into a separate company called E-II, in recognition of Kelly's previous company, Esmark. A small percentage of E-II was sold through a 1987 public offering of stock, in which my department played a role; in 1988, American Brands, the tobacco company, purchased all the shares for some $800 million.

The remaining Beatrice businesses—boasting such familiar consumer names as Butterball, Hunt's, La Choy, Peter Pan, and Swiss Miss—were sold to ConAgra on June 7, 1990 for $1.3 billion. In four years, all the bank debt and junk bonds from the Beatrice acquisition was repaid, and KKR more than tripled its $420 million equity investment.

The buy-out of Beatrice, which probably would not have happened if Michael Milken had not made the high-yield market happen, was a friendly transaction—the people running the company were willing to sell. This was not always the case with takeovers in the 1980s. And that is where the real excitement began.

Hostile takeovers are dependent on one basic fact: A company is owned by its shareholders, not its management. When you buy stock in a public corporation, you become a partial owner, entitled to your share of its future profits. You and the other stockholders have the right to choose the board of directors, which then hires the managers. These managers are your employees, responsible for running the company for your benefit, by maximizing the long-term value of your stock.

This system of means and ends works beautifully in theory, but it gets muddled in practice. Managers usually choose their own bosses, the board of directors. The election of the board of directors is, in turn, rubber-stamped by *their* bosses, who are the stockholders. More important, managers tend to run a company as if it were theirs, which can cause conflicts of interest with the real owners.

Most managers want their company to grow—it's only natural. But bigger isn't necessarily better; expanding may just waste money, which will hurt the value of the stock. Or the managers may run the company like a private fiefdom. This too will hurt the shareholders' investments. The managers may also receive a bid to buy the entire company, which is usually bad for them, but good for the stockholders.

Managers are not very flattered when an outside party believes that it can afford to pay significantly more for a company than its stock-market value and still have itself a bargain. A takeover bid tells the world that this company is probably undermanaged, so much so that even at a price 50 percent or more above the current one, better management can make the numbers work.

Not surprisingly, most managers resent the implication that they've been mediocre in doing their job, which is to make the most of a company's assets for the benefit of its owners. They also dislike the thought of losing their jobs. If they reject the takeover bid, however, the story is not over; the final decision rests with the shareholders. And between the first bid and the last tender offer, hostile takeovers can get ugly.

The first large takeover battle of the 1980s didn't involve junk bonds or Drexel Burnham, but it did remind everyone who the owners were. In 1981, Conoco, an oil company, was pursued by both Seagram's, the Canadian liquor company, and du Pont, the Delaware chemical giant. Eventually, du Pont won majority control, Seagram's bought a minority position, and Conoco's shareholders made a very nice profit.

The takeover front was generally quiet as the stock market fell—most people are more comfortable buying when prices are rising, based on the suspect logic that prices will keep rising. The bear market of 1981–1982 created a great deal of concern about the present and the future, which discouraged buyers of both stocks and companies.

In 1982, Boone Pickens and his small exploration company, Mesa Petroleum, made a run at Cities Service, an oil company some *twenty times* Mesa's size. It brought back memories of thirteen years earlier, when Saul Steinberg's leasing company tried to buy Chemical Bank; Steinberg failed, but allegedly not without receiving some insight from President Richard Nixon: "We're not ready for you yet, sonny."

Boone introduced the 1980s to a new character that would take center stage for several years: the raider. At various times, the title would be worn by Steinberg—evidently all grown up—and by men as different in style and skills as Carl Icahn, Ron Perelman, Sir James Goldsmith, Irv "The Liquidator" Jacobs, and Nelson Peltz. Their stories ranged from the almost inevitable success of the brilliant Icahn, whose name would create a healthy dose of fear in corporate America, to the seemingly improbable success of the tenacious Peltz, whose name . . . well, whatever.

Some of these raiders would present themselves as the vanguard of change, the saviors of this country's small stockholders—some forty million of them. They would propose their hostile bids in the language of truth and justice, their motive to free the owners of public corporations from the mediocracy and tyranny of self-interested managers.

Eventually, those who wrapped themselves in lily white would prove more interested in personal profit than in protecting the oppressed. But no one hired them for the role of Sir Galahad, and nothing required them to live up to their rhetoric. More important, their actions didn't negate their argument; some shaking of the status quo wasn't a bad idea.

Boone Pickens was the ideal role model for a raider/crusader, from his folksy name to his sophisticated understanding of takeover strategy. His attempt to buy Cities Service failed, but shareholders, including himself, made a 50 percent profit when Occidental Petroleum acquired the company.

Boone's next target was the mammoth Gulf Oil, and his weapon was the proxy vote. The shareholders were asked to decide whether their company should sell off some of its assets and return the proceeds to them, rather than leave the decision up to the management. In December 1983, the stockholders voted down the proposal, but not by much.

The next step was a hostile bid, and for this, Boone called in Drexel to put the money where his mouth was. Within forty-eight hours, Milken raised $1.7 billion in commitments from various institutions. One point of view that has emerged in later years is that Milken opposed Drexel's move into financing hostile takeovers. As one senior executive noted, "He just flat-out didn't. If Michael had been opposed, it never would have been launched as a major strategy."

Regardless, Pickens's plan to bid for Gulf was shot to hell as the stock price rose sharply before the offer to buy was announced. The reason was simple: Some person(s) started trading on the inside information that a tender offer was in the works.

Boone cut back his takeover plan to a more modest offer for 20 percent of Gulf's shares. In time, the company found a "white knight" in Chevron, another of oil's seven sisters, which purchased Gulf in a friendly transaction for a staggering $13.3 billion. The shareholders reaped a windfall: Their stock had doubled in less than a year.

Drexel, however, was in a pickle. The firm knew it could raise previously unheard of sums to finance takeovers; the problem was in raising the money without alerting the world to the target.

The next major deal raised a different problem: greenmail. Saul Steinberg returned to center stage in 1984, with a hostile bid for Disney. Milken's group raised $700 million in commitments to finance the deal, while a few of us tried to get involved by pressing a trader who did a terrific Donald Duck imitation to call up the Coast, telling them how ticked off he and Mickey were about the whole thing.

No matter. Disney bought out Steinberg's shares—and only his shares—at a premium price, leaving the other shareholders to watch the value of their stock plummet. To many, the repurchase of Steinberg's position suggested the financial equivalent of "Don't go away mad, just go away."

Later that year, Boone Pickens attempted a takeover of Phillips Petroleum that ended on December 23, when he accepted a recapitalization plan. Specifically, Phillips bought back his stock for cash at $53 per share, while the other shareholders were offered a share repurchase that the stock market valued at approximately $46.

On the heels of the Pickens situation, Carl Icahn entered the picture, buying up shares in Phillips. He then made a hostile bid for the whole company, an $8 billion transaction. Shareholders would get half in cash, half in bonds. The cash portion would be raised by Milken from his junk-bond buyers.

An interesting feature of this tender offer was that none of the financing was in place. Drexel simply assured the world that it was "highly confident" it could raise the money; this was the solution to Drexel's problem of financing a takeover without giving anyone advance notice of the target.

Once the offer was on the table, Icahn asked Milken to get immediate commitments for $1.5 billion of the $4 billion that he had said he could raise. It was done in two days.

"His word didn't mean a whole lot until he was able to do it," said Keith Hartley, a Drexel investment banker. But now that Milken had shown he was more than able, his word was gold.

The takeover boom was on. In 1985, acquisitions totaled $180 billion, up sharply from an impressive $122 billion the previous year. Among the deals that Drexel backed were Icahn's $900 million buyout of TWA, Peltz's $1 billion purchases of both National Can and American Can, Perelman's $1.8 billion acquisition of Revlon, Sam Heymann's $5 billion attempt at GAF, and Kohlberg Kravis's $6.2 billion takeover of Beatrice.

Corporate America realized that, for the first time in decades, it was accountable to its owners. Managers recognized that if they didn't improve the value of the shareholders' investment, someone else might. In the summer of 1985 alone, fifty corporations voluntarily restructured, according to Ivan Boesky, an active figure on Wall Street at that time. These corporations had sold off assets and had bought back shares, trying to maximize the stock price. It was nice to see.

Michael Milken didn't introduce takeovers to Wall Street, but more than anyone, he made them an important part of its business. He didn't create an environment where companies were selling for substantially less than they were worth, but he did take advantage of it with a passion—some would say with a vengeance. By the mid-1980s, he was the Street's leading player, with some powerful enemies watching from the wings.

CHAPTER FOUR

THE NEW WAY

You don't have to be nice to
people on the way up if you're
not planning to come back down.

The financial community is a loose collection of firms very different in image and approach, from white-shoe genteel to street-tough down and dirty. These firms have little in common beyond a desire to make money by moving money. By 1986, however, they did see eye to eye on at least one point: They all wished Drexel would curl up and die.

The banks, already taking a beating in the back pocket by the late seventies, were hurt further by the rise of the junk-bond market. Their low-cost passbook deposits were leaving for the greener pastures of newly created money market funds, and their blue-chip clients like IBM and AT&T were able to borrow money at lower cost by selling short-term loans, known as commercial paper, directly to the public.

The most attractive business left for the banks was in lending to medium-size companies that needed money to grow, but that were too unproven to sell commercial paper. Unfortunately for the Citibanks and the Mellons, high-yield bonds gave these borrowers another route to take. "We robbed the banks of all their best loans," a Drexel officer boasted.

Investment bankers from the firm approached the chief execs of corporate America's middle class with a compelling sales pitch. They pointed out that these companies were paying a lot more for their bank loans than the stated rate, due to the restrictive covenants attached and the gimmicks such as compensating balances whereby a borrower must leave a certain portion of the loan on deposit with the bank.

Just as important, these bank loans were short term, which left the companies at risk that the loans might be called in the near future. Drexel, on the other hand, could get them long-term loans—by selling their bonds to the public—which would leave them free to focus on building a successful long-term business.

The basic problem that the banks faced was their own shortsightedness; as Milken noted in an interview with *New Perspectives Quarterly:* "The tendency of our financial structure has been to channel loans to industries of the past rather than of the future." Bankers gave their best rates to those who had prospered in the inflationary 1970s, such as oil explorers, real estate developers, and commodity-rich Third World countries.

It was these borrowers, however, who were most at risk—they were already leveraged to the hilt with earlier loans, and the prices of their products had risen to the point where they were killing demand. In effect, the best deals went to the worst borrowers, setting the stage for massive loan losses that the banks are still trying to deal with a decade later.

This country's corporate elite disliked Drexel for a simple reason: The firm was sticking its nose where it didn't belong. Investment bankers were supposed to give advice, gentleman to gentleman, on financing and friendly acquisitions; they were supposed to be charming, well bred, and low handicapped. They weren't supposed to raise money for hostile takeover artists. And they sure as hell weren't supposed to think up hostile takeovers, and then go looking for someone to replace the current managers.

If you were the chief executive of a large corporation, one in which you had spent thirty years climbing the ranks, Michael Milken was your worst nightmare. He couldn't be dismissed as another Ralph Nader or as a peddler of junk; he was a man who had a nasty vision and an ability to see it through. His was the face that you woke up with at two in the morning; his was the name that a fleet of Drexelites used to convince potential acquirers that anything was possible.

And if that wasn't bad enough, these Drexel people were brash and contemptuous, and . . . well, you know. Jews had played an important, if often unwelcomed, role on Wall Street for many decades before Drexel entered the limelight, but most had wanted to become a part of the establishment, not take it apart.

Anti-Semitism is a subtle thing, because prejudice is carefully handled by those intelligent enough to know how disgusting it is. No chief exec whose firm is threatened by a sanctimonious raider backed by an arrogant upstart Jewish firm, as Drexel was perceived to be, is likely to sit down with his therapist and explain, "Well, Doc, the reason I'm ready to kill somebody is fourfold: I've got this bastard out there telling the world what a lousy job he thinks I've been doing—let's give the ego factor . . . say, 20 percent. Meanwhile, he's trying to take over my company and put me on the street—that's a good 50 percent. The shareholders deserve a lot more than he's offering—give that 10 percent. And this whole thing wouldn't have happened in the first place if it wasn't for those pushy Jews—20 percent, easy."

But if anti-Semitism was a factor in Drexel's unpopularity, it certainly wasn't the driving factor. After all, Boone Pickens was a good ole boy, and he was deeply disliked by many oil company executives. What primarily earned Drexel its enemies in high places was its willingness, even eagerness, to aggressively shake up some powerful interests that didn't want to be shaken.

That eagerness was nowhere more apparent than in the firm's relationship with its competitors on Wall Street. Drexel created deals that hurt their businesses, it backed deals that hurt their clients, and whenever possible, it dealt them out of the game. This was a fun place to work: even on the East Coast, there was a certain warm feeling about aggravating people you didn't particularly admire.

Hostile takeovers were an obvious source of confrontation, because the battle lines were usually clear and the stakes involved more than money. Perhaps the costliest from Drexel's point of view was the failed attempt by its client, Boone Pickens, to take over Unocal, which was represented by its investment banker of thirty years, Dillon Read. It was trouble on several levels. For one thing, the Delaware Supreme Court rejected the idea of offering more for the first 50 percent of the shares than for the rest, which it rightly viewed as arm-twisting. For another, it upheld a Unocal plan that could discourage hostile bids in general. But, most important, the Unocal battle created bad blood with Dillon's chairman, Nicholas Brady, who would later become secretary of the treasury.

Drexel's ability to irritate its competition extended far beyond take-overs, and with no apologies. "What really pissed off people," argued an investment banker who came over from First Boston, "was that Drexel could do better deals." At First Boston, he had worked on a huge deal for Navistar—formally International Harvester—to replace high-yield debt with new shares of stock. The lead guy on the transaction, whose last big deal hadn't been a great success, "was just swigging down Pepto-Bismol; he had a little bottle."

When they got to Navistar headquarters in Chicago, the Pepto Man almost had a coronary. The chairman told them that he had been called by Drexel, which had heard about the deal and was suggesting that the company just swap some new debt for the old debt, a transaction known as an exchange offer. First Boston and the comanager on the deal, Shearson, convinced Navistar to stick with the current plan, but as the investment banker recalled, Drexel's recommendation "was, in retrospect, a better idea for the company."

During Wall Street's glory days, First Boston was extremely successful in winning over new clients and generating deals. Their top gun was the brilliant and controversial Bruce Wasserstein, who understood the importance of humility—to him, it had little. His sales approach to potential clients was described by this former investment banker as, "We're First Boston. Do yourself a favor and let us do a deal for you."

Many did themselves a favor, although at least two of the biggest probably wish they hadn't. With Wasserstein as an adviser, Texaco acquired Getty from Pennzoil and Campeau bested Macy's for the rights to Federated. A few years later, Texaco agreed to pay Pennzoil $3 billion for ignoring its agreement with Getty, and Campeau filed for bankruptcy. Of course that is not to suggest that Wasserstein had any foreknowledge that the deals would fall apart.

The investment banker from First Boston told another story of his earlier days with Piper Jaffrey, a Midwest brokerage firm, when he worked on a deal for Apache Petroleum with three other Street firms. One of the investment bankers joined Drexel, which then bid for the whole deal at a lower cost to the company. The upshot was that Drexel didn't get the deal for itself, but it was invited to participate;

the other firms now found themselves sharing a smaller commission five ways instead of four. Apache, however, paid less for the deal than it would have if Drexel had never arrived.

Another example involved the chief executive of a casino company, a down-to-earth guy who described the decor in his hotels as "bordello modern." This exec found himself in the odd situation of having one investment banker too many. He had asked Bear Stearns to raise a chunk of money for him, and was promised an answer by noon. Too nervous to wait quietly, he decides to call Fred Joseph and find out if Drexel might be able to step up if necessary. Fred says fine.

Bear Stearns calls: The answer is yes. The exec tells the investment banker that he spoke with Joseph and asks would Bear Stearns do the deal with Drexel. The response: "Not with those assholes."

The exec calls Fred back to tell him, sorry, but Bear Stearns had first choice, and they sure don't want Drexel on board. Fred's response: "I already told Michael."

All hell breaks loose. For two days, Milken berates this exec, reminding him of the last deal that Drexel had underwritten for him, and that Milken himself had invested in that offering.

"Fred's a pretty persuasive guy," the exec noted. "But if Fred was a three, Michael was a ten." The result was that Bear Stearns kept the deal, but Drexel did the lion's share of future underwriting.

No matter how poorly Drexel got along with most of the Street, nothing matched the relationship between our firm and Salomon Brothers. It was pure—they hated each other on both a professional and personal level.

Salomon was a Wall Street powerhouse. It dominated the markets for treasury bonds, municipal bonds, high-quality corporate bonds, and mortgage-backed securities. Solly was also a major factor in the stock market. It commanded respect; if nothing else, it demanded respect. From Drexel, it got very little.

Salomon particularly resented Milken's unwillingness to share on deals, a process known as syndication. For almost a century, when a firm sold stocks or bonds, it put together a syndicate of other Wall Street firms and everyone got a piece. The biggest pieces went to major bracket firms, then smaller to middle bracket firms, and less to each of the remaining selling group. (The reason that Burnham bought Drexel in 1973, you might remember, was to buy its way into the syndicate big leagues.)

The syndicate system favored Salomon. Its reputation in the high-grade bond market made it a natural to be lead manager on those deals, giving it the biggest piece of the pie and the right to allocate the bonds to whomever it wished. In equity deals, it had a compelling sales pitch to convince companies to choose it as lead manager: It could get wider distribution of the company's stock among both institutions and individuals than could a firm that primarily dealt with individuals. This wider distribution would allow the shares to trade with less volatility once public and would encourage more Wall Street analysts to follow the company on a research basis.

Milken, however, had no interest in the syndicate approach. Simply put, he didn't need any help finding buyers for his high-yield bonds, and he wasn't about to give away commissions just because that's the way things had always been done. Also, junk-bond commissions—averaging 3 to 4 percent of the deal's total size—were the highest on the Street, as much as ten times greater than those in the more competitive, more homogeneous high-grade and government bond markets.

By 1986, Drexel Burnham absolutely dominated the most important financial market and had transformed itself into the most profitable firm on Wall Street. Its net worth had more than doubled in under two years, to the benefit of its employees who owned over 70 percent of the stock. The number of employees had grown from three thousand in 1979 to ten thousand in 1986. The firm held equity positions in 150 of the companies that it had financed, and had created an aura that there was no transaction that it couldn't finance. Drexel was arguably the most influential company in the country.

Milken's operation, with only three hundred people, was obviously the tail that wagged the dog. How much of the firm's profit was generated from the high-yield bond department is open to debate. Management argues that it never exceeded 50 percent of the total, although some people believe the figure was more on the order of 100 percent. One analyst, who thinks the higher number is closer to the truth, half-seriously mentioned to me in 1986 that "Drexel Burnham is a subsidiary of Mike Milken, Inc." The Securities and Exchange

Commission, the most objective of the sources, put the figure for the 1983-1987 period at approximately 50 percent, in line with management's estimate.

If people on Wall Street or Main Street let themselves forget that all roads led to Wilshire Boulevard, there was always the annual High-Yield Bond Conference to remind them. The conference, which came to be known as "The Predators' Ball," brought together thousands of money managers and dozens of company leaders. Held each April, it celebrated the incredible growth of the high-yield bond market, which by the mid-1980s represented 20 percent of all bonds issued by American corporations. It preached the gospel of activist management and served as a catalyst for new deals. At its finale, when all the work was done, it showcased, among others, Diana Ross, Kenny Rogers, and the Chairman of the Board himself.

It was a hot ticket on the East Coast, and those who went returned in awe. The level of professionalism, the cutting-edge thinking, the attention to detail were beyond what anyone had ever seen.

Critics would later charge that among the details attended to involved some young ladies, professionals in their own right. This may have been true, or perhaps not. If it happened, it was wrong—but so what? From the street corners to the occasional honeymoon suite, prostitution is a fact of life, and hardly the worst.

But, of course, this has nothing to do with the reordering of American business, the reason that three thousand people crammed themselves into the ballroom of the Beverly Wilshire at 6:00 A.M. These junk-bond buyers and sellers would have some breakfast, waiting until exactly 6:50 when Michael Milken would take the podium to introduce the first speaker of the day. In his introductions, recalled one listener, he liked to focus on the speakers' rise from humble beginnings and their large personal investments in the companies they managed.

The next twelve to fifteen hours would include company presentations, panel discussions, and guest speakers ranging from raiders to regulators. There were even videos to lighten the mood, including J. R. Ewing advertising a new titanium card for takeovers and Madonna improbably admitting in a dubbed version of her pop hit "Material Girl" that she was a "double-B" girl. And through it all, there was no doubt that Milken was the man in charge, not to be taken lightly.

My department got a small taste of Michael's heavy side in October

1986 at our equity conference, a Friday to Sunday deal at the Vista Hotel in lower Manhattan. It was, in effect, the celebration of our coming of age on Wall Street, even though we recognized that the rites of passage had happened three thousand miles away.

The firm had earned over $600 million between 1982 and 1985, and was well on its way to the most profitable year the Street would ever see. In 1986, Drexel would earn $525 million and be the lead manager on 188 offerings that raised $47.2 billion, more than twice its 1985 record total. Even those of us who didn't know the figures knew the feeling of being part of the most successful firm on Wall Street.

Different speakers, from Fred Joseph to various department heads, outlined where we were heading—namely, further up. Any rational person, and we were very rational about great news, could see that Drexel was unstoppable, with a large backlog of deals just waiting to be processed and an unlimited potential deal flow waiting to be created.

Milken had revolutionized finance or, at least, he had popularized the concept of revolution. His successes were apparent in each morning's *Wall Street Journal,* which carried the announcement of yet another high-yield financing. These announcements, known as tombstones, were the highlight of my morning. Squeezed into a seat on the Long Island Railroad for my daily, dismal commute, I would scan the back pages of the *Journal,* admiring the number of Drexel tombstones and the size of our deals. It even occurred to me that one morning I would go through the paper and find *only* Drexel deals.

And now, Brother Michael was here to explain it all to us, and the room was packed. The first thing that struck me when he arrived that Saturday afternoon was that he looked awfully young to be who he was. (Around the eyes, however, as someone said later, he looked a good deal older.)

Milken didn't have a set speech, referring to notes or speaking from memory. His manner was quiet, serious, and at times even disdainful, as if he were a teacher talking to a few of his lagging students. His comments moved back and forth between investment generalities and company specifics. He told us that we must think in broad, conceptual terms, to take a long-term view.

He gave us his view. Companies, from GM to the local phone system, want change, he said. He touched on one of his favorite themes: Money is not a scarce commodity. You didn't need to read between the lines; you only had to read the lines: The restructuring of American business was going to continue.

The big losers of the future would be the big losers of the past—the people who owned the bonds of investment-grade companies. To him, these bonds had nowhere to go but down, and their holders were saying to the world, "Help me lose as much as possible."

The winners, Milken implied, would be those backing the managers who understood value, and knew how to realize it. "The most important factor in credit and equity analysis is the manager," he argued, not a company's balance sheet or its income statement.

He spoke of individual companies, drawing lessons from their current state of affairs. Macy's, he said, had used the wrong financial structure in their leveraged buyout, a mistake that he predicted would raise the cost to its shareholders by $800 million over a decade. Beatrice, which had recently gone private as well, could boost the value of the company by $1.5 billion just by eliminating $200 million a year in excess expenses. Safeway could improve its profits by cutting back on low-margin private label products, which the customers didn't want anyway.

Warner Communications would benefit from the new technologies created by others, because these meant new markets for its library of recordings. Texas Air was part of an industry that hadn't made money for two decades, but now it was one of five airlines that controlled 75 percent of air traffic. Electric utilities were "changed and changing," with opportunities for stockholders in a deregulated industry.

And so on.

He spoke of market share, pointing out that "the lowest [share] is best in lousy businesses"—for example, in the equity business, the business from which everyone in the audience made their living. We gave advice and put together buyers and sellers, receiving in return a minuscule commission of less than ten cents a share. The opportunity, he said, was in finding ideas that we believed in, stocks that the firm could buy for its own account and that its sales force could resell for a large profit.

Salesmanship: He hit this issue hard. "Getting the idea around is almost as important as getting the idea," he observed. "You must make people make decisions. . . . Your only obligation is to give your best advice, not to eliminate risk. . . . If you can't sell the business, you let down the firm." No equivocating here.

He criticized our efforts: "I get depressed when I go to Sixty Broad," referring to the home office in lower Manhattan where we worked. His comments reflected a general attitude on the West Coast that we couldn't sell insulin to diabetics; our attitude was that, at the right price, his people would sell diabetes. Regardless, he was the man pushing the buttons, and some listeners sensed that he was preparing to take control of the East Coast, as well. It seemed logical, and it probably would've been inevitable if the world didn't collapse on the firm less than a month later.

"What do you want to do with your life?" he asked us, not realizing that his was about to change drastically. What level did we want to attain? He spent some time talking about what it took to be a success on Wall Street. "You must understand value," he advised. "Don't get too caught up in emotion. . . . Don't let ego get in the way. Why not go on making money with our mouths shut? Let the other guy be real big. . . . The rest of the world will come to us eventually if we have the best ideas."

One of his ideas was to restructure the massive Third World debt, known on the Street as "toxic waste." "Our financial establishment bought the mythology that lending to countries was less risky than lending to American business," was how he phrased his viewpoint years later in a magazine interview. Now he was ready to clean up some of the mess that the banks had created, and on a for-profit basis.

Another of his ideas was to introduce Japan's $100 billion a year surplus to U.S. corporations; the American financial revolution could be enhanced and then exported.

The possibilities were staggering. The mood at a corporate finance lunch on November 14, 1986—what would become a fateful day for the firm—was recalled by an investment banker who was in attendance: "We really had the world by the balls."

THE HARDEST-WORKING PEOPLE IN AMERICA

> Legend tells of the traveler who went into a country store and found the shelves lined with bags of salt.
>
> "You must sell a lot of salt," said the traveler.
>
> "Nah," said the storekeeper. "I can't sell no salt at all. But the feller who sells me salt—boy, can *he* sell salt."
>
> —Martin Mayer

To have the world in your hand is no small achievement, especially when you got it there in ten years. Most people wouldn't even dream the possibility, and of those who would, most wouldn't have a prayer. But Mike Milken had done it, at least in his world. By the mid-1980s, he was arguably the most influential financier in the free world.

Over drinks one evening in 1985, a trader and I discussed Milken's rumored income of *$30 million* in the previous year (not realizing at the time that the estimate was low by almost $100 million). The trader pointed out the obvious: If he'd made that kind of money, he'd quit. I pointed out the equally obvious: Anyone satisfied with that kind of money would not be the type of person capable of earning such huge sums in the first place.

Milken wanted a lot more than $30 million or $130 million, raising the question: Why? How could he keep pushing himself, and everyone around him, so relentlessly when he had already earned more than he would need for several lifetimes?

What made Michael tick?

"He loved what he was doing," observed one investment banker. "He got joy from the adrenaline, from the action."

"He was a consummate competitor," noted one of the more astute people I know. "He gave no quarter; he asked no quarter. Eventually, it overcame him, it started to consume him—the need to compete."

There was greed, of course. "Money was his mistress," was one bond trader's colorful phrase, although he would no doubt agree that, for Milken, money was primarily a means of keeping score. "He enjoys winning the game of making money," was a point of view that most observers would agree with.

Milken certainly wasn't materialistic. The yuppie fest of new cars, new houses, new spouses, and self-aggrandizing charity events didn't appeal to him. After he graduated from college, he married his junior-high-school girlfriend. He was the father of three, and his family lived modestly, giving more to charity in a week than it spent on itself in a year. Milken had no interest in the noveau riche hobby of buying a place in high society; more likely, he felt little attraction for the establishment, for the comfortable status quo.

He did have an ego. "He had to in order to convince people," argued one arbitrageur. "He never wavered. You had the sense that he had every answer." One West Coast trader put Milken at the top of the scale for ego, but at the absolute bottom for arrogance.

Fame was unimportant to him—he avoided the press like the plague and remained surprisingly anonymous outside of Wall Street. By his choice, he wasn't on Drexel's board of directors or its executive committee, and he never even received mention in any of the firm's annual reports.

As for power . . . well, that was a different story.

In the final analysis, no one knows what really put the fire in Mike Milken, but Burt Siegel, a senior vice-president at Drexel, was probably closest when he said that Michael's motives "ran the gamut from wanting to do something extraordinarily good to pure greed." Essentially, he had every quality that almost all successful businessmen have—by a factor of ten.

Milken was a bit driven, much as Othello was a bit jealous. It wasn't that he was intense—everybody who's anybody on the Street is intense—it's that he was *so* intense. Maybe when *Webster's* is updated, it'll recognize what the financial community learned a long time ago: **in•tense** (in-'tens) *adj.* **1.** existing or occurring in a high or extreme degree: an *intense* individual. [See M. R. MILKEN.]

His stamina was legendary: He made crucial decisions day after day on less sleep than most people need to figure out what day it is. He created a pressure cooker around himself that he worked in eighteen hours a day; he would've appreciated the comment by Jeffrey Katzenberg of Disney Studios to an employee: "If you're not willing to come in on Saturday, don't even *bother* coming in on Sunday." He never drank caffeine or liquor. He had no intention of burning out.

From the beginning, Milken was able to see the world differently from the crowd, to see opportunity where others saw risk, to keep his emotions in check. He also had an underlying confidence in his own judgment, an ability to believe that his view was not only different, it was right.

That confidence was already apparent by the time he was a college student at Berkeley; he managed money for friends with a fee structure that would've scared most investment managers silly: He got half the profits, but was responsible for *all* the losses.

While other students protested the war, he studied business. Eventually, many of them joined the mainstream, but he stayed on the outside. In retrospect, he did more than most in shaking up the establishment.

He was an inventor, according to Phil Birsch, a Drexel investment banker much as Henry Ford or Thomas Edison. "He invented a new product, and benefited from it." And if, as Chris Ryder, an institutional salesman at Morgan Stanley argues, Henry Ford created this country's middle class, Michael Milken deserves some credit for helping to create a middle class for American business.

It's interesting that Milken began his career with junk bonds as a profitable pursuit and developed in time a fanatical zeal about their possibilities. He was attracted to them in the 1970s because they were underloved and undervalued; in the 1980s, he was able to use them as catalysts for change. This overlooked corner of the bond market gave him the opportunity to achieve what are perhaps his two favorite goals: To make a bundle and to make a difference.

Michael Milken and Fred Joseph shared some characteristics, certainly—after all, they were able to work closely together for almost ten years. They both were ambitious, aggressive, driven; they both wanted to have an impact: Joseph to build a first-rate firm; Milken to build an empire. Neither cared about money in the way that most people do. Both were uncomfortable with the established order—one more for intellectual reasons; the other perhaps more for personal reasons.

Fred was "a multifaceted kind of guy," observed Tony Meyer, who knew Joseph at Drexel for more than a decade. "He loves farming and hunting, and welds metal in his basement. A guy like that can't be all bad." To a young investment banker, Fred was "a nice guy . . . a gloss-over type of guy," and borrowing a line from playwright Arthur Miller: He was "the kind of guy that liked to be liked."

Michael, on the other hand, "didn't give a shit what anyone thought of him," according to one East Coast banker. Sadly for him, Milken would eventually have to start worrying about his image. He would become front-page news for years, and his kids—and their schoolmates—would find themselves reading about him in the same sentence as Boesky, Ponzi, and even Capone. "He and his wife were devastated by the negative publicity," a senior officer remembered.

Both Milken and Joseph were exceptional leaders in their own right. They chose people based on the bottom line, rather than on the right bloodline; in the early 1980s, Fred told *Fortune* magazine half-jokingly that he preferred fat, ugly hirees. "He didn't care what they looked like," said his brother, Steve Joseph, who headed Drexel's mortgage-backed securities department. "He cared an awful lot about how bright they were, how hard they worked, how their ethics were."

An exaggerated example of the Drexel look was offered by Michel Bergerac, the former chairman of Revlon who lost his job to a Milken-financed takeover: "I'll never forget those twenty or thirty guys coming off the elevators," he told Connie Bruck, author of *The Predators' Ball*. "All short, bald, with big cigars! It was incredible! If central casting had had to produce thirty guys like that, they couldn't do it. They looked like they were in a grade-D movie that took place in Mississippi or Louisiana, about guys fixing elections in a back room."

The main man himself didn't spend much energy cultivating the *GQ* look, either, with his "polyester shirts . . . tie too short . . . bad rug" (the toupee was his only concession to vanity). Milken wasn't opposed to dressing well—he didn't wear K-Mart specials to black-tie affairs—but he probably just found the whole thing irrelevant.

Fred was a strong motivator, but as usual, nobody could do it like Michael. He set an example for his personnel that they couldn't beat, but that they tried to join. "He was a one-man factory," said one West

Coast member, who doesn't go in for hyperbole. "He did the work of forty people."

The heart of his operation was on the fourth floor of an office building he owned on Wilshire Boulevard, just off of Rodeo Drive. His key salesmen and traders sat at a long X-shaped desk, more famous on Wall Street than King Arthur's round table. Where the cross hairs met sat Milken.

For the high-yield bond group, the day began with "a traffic jam at five-thirty, six o'clock on Rodeo and Wilshire." By then, Milken was completing an hour or two of meetings with companies that wanted to raise money. As traders, salesmen, and others arrived, they would find a man already deep in work, a man more likely to greet them with a question than with a hello. "He'd ask, 'What about the sixteen and five-eighths Resorts bond? Tell me about that trade.'"

"There were about twenty guys on the floor . . . very tight . . . very familylike . . . very casual in a real tense atmosphere," recalled one trader. From six-thirty to one in the afternoon, West Coast time, the major financial markets were open, and the floor was controlled chaos, salesmen and traders yelling at each other, everyone going on all cylinders.

A client of mine from an insurance company once defined a bond salesman as someone who calls and says, "You need tickets for the game tonight?" Not these guys—they worked hard for the money.

As for Milken, "his eyes were all over that floor. . . . Every decision was second-guessed by him. He knew every position." Meanwhile, he was on the phone constantly, sometimes for only ten seconds a call, and not only to push the merchandise. "He understood the nature of people, relationships, keeping in touch," one person observed. In front of him were folders containing lists on notebooked green accounting sheets—details to be taken care of, thousands of them, written up and down the pages in impeccable handwriting.

Often, the main order of business was to find buyers for a new junk-bond offering. "I want it all sold today," he would say. "He was very good at motivating, pushing a deal over the hump," recalled a West Coast investment banker. "He would call Iowa, if necessary."

After trading hours, there were corporate finance meetings, when company managements explained why they wanted to sell high-yield bonds and why the West Coast's clients should buy them. "You were expected to participate in these meetings," said one trader, and then in summarizing the day: "You had to be on the ball from five to five." There's an old saying: It's not the years, it's the miles; for the guys on the Coast, it wasn't just the hours, it was the pressure.

Following the meetings, Milken might remain to develop new deals with the West Coast investment bankers, who were more likely to work a later schedule, perhaps until ten or eleven at night. When he returned to his home in Encino, a trunkload of documents accompanied him, and, of course, a phone was always waiting.

His employees viewed him with a mixture of admiration, awe, envy, and fear. "When he said do something, you did it," someone said, a comment that was probably a good rule of thumb for all. Milken wanted an atmosphere of confrontation, and that's what he got. He wanted his people to fight, and they did—for a trade, for an order, for a bigger bonus. Joe Garagiola's observation about Billy Martin ("He could get into a fight in an empty elevator") would've felt pretty much at home on the fourth floor of 9560 Wilshire Boulevard.

There were questions about the quality of the people that Milken hired, questions that would figure heavily in Milken's downfall and that of his firm. "Nobody out there was smart enough to do a crossword puzzle, except Michael," said a Drexel East investment banker. "A lot of mediocre people made incredible amounts of money," said a New York–based security analyst, although he had earlier pointed out that "Milken was able to attract . . . phenomenal people." A West Coast trader made a similar argument, saying that he "hired really talented people," while also noting that "Milken surrounded himself with s——s." (Not a compliment, believe me.)

In reality, everyone was right—to a degree. There were those who were extremely bright and those who were better at their jobs than most on the Street. And there were those who weren't. The great ones made more money than they ever thought possible, and the rest made more than they ever thought likely.

Even in an aggressive business such as this, they were unusual. When I spoke with them, there was a familiar defensive/combative intensity at the other end of the line, an unpleasantness, almost as a point of honor. They gave the impression that they were dealing with an idiot, and nothing could possibly annoy them more.

Let's say a client of mine wanted to sell 200 convertible bonds of Batguano Industries, which have a 9 percent yield and mature in 1998:

I am depressed. I pick up the phone and dial 44444, the number for the West Coast when calling internally. The phone rings and rings. How can it ring so long, I wonder—they can't possibly know who's calling.

"Drexel." (Woman's voice, harried)

"Yeah, who trades the Batguanos, nines of '98?

"Hold on."

(Time passes. Treaties are concluded. . . .)

"Drexel." (Woman again, maybe the same one.)

"I'm waiting for the trader on the Batguanos."

(Yelling) "Who does the Batguanos? (Then) "Hold on."

(. . . and ignored.)

"Drexel."

"Are you the trader on the Batguanos?"

"Yeah."

"This is Dan Stone, New York Institutional Equity. Who's this?"

"Archie Rice."

"Hey, Archie, how are you doing?"

(Silence.)

"I've got a client that wants the market on the Batguanos, nines of '98."

"Who's the client?"

(Pause.) "First Guaranty." (Wish I hadn't told him.)

"How many bonds?"

"Two hundred."

"Buying or selling?"

"He wants both sides." (I know that answer will piss him off, but it makes certain my client gets a reasonable bid for the bonds.)

"One oh two, one oh three." (He's pissed.)

"Thanks, Archie. I'll get right back to you if he wants to do 'em."

(Click.)

(Well, my guy can sell at least one hundred bonds at 102, or $1,020 per bond. If I'd only asked for the bid, it might've been only 101. Or for that matter, if I'd only asked for the offer, it might've been 104 instead of 103. By asking for both sides of the market—by not saying whether my client is a seller or a buyer—Archie has to give me a reasonable number at either end.)

I couldn't blame the West Coast for trying to make the most profit possible, even on an insignificant chump-change trade like this, but

I'd bet that they'd blame me for putting my client's interests ahead of theirs. Or, as they might put it, ahead of *our* firm—our firm, their pocket.

"The culture was to keep all the money on the West Coast," according to a trader. There was a vindictive sense of fairness involved: This was Mike's franchise, no one else's. There was also Mike himself, with his photographic memory, his attention to just about every detail, and his "piercing, laserlike eyes," wondering why one of his traders or salesmen or investment bankers let some of their money slip away. It's hard to imagine anyone looking forward to finessing an explanation.

The common wisdom was that Milken wanted 100 percent market share. Closer to the truth was Milken's comment to a company president in the late 1970s, as recalled by an investment banker who sat in on the conversation: "Mike said he didn't want to do one hundred percent of the business; he wanted to do seventy-five percent of the business with a hundred percent of the profit." Someone suggested that his two favorite words were *more* and *next,* two words that went a long way in defining the man. Regardless, his competitors didn't stand a chance, and those that put up a good fight sometimes became employees.

Milken controlled the high-yield market, from the data on a decade of bond trading to the location of every junk bond in public and private hands to the pricing of new offerings. And everybody who serviced him got a piece of the largest pie in captivity. Some committed their lives to getting an obscenely large and wonderful slice; others were content to be overfed for a reasonable effort.

Drexel's investment bankers were in heaven. "You could do whatever you wanted," said one from the Coast. "A company would say, 'Can you do this, this, this?' Yeah, we can do anything."

"It was one of the most fun places to work since it was so unstructured," recalled one from New York. "You could work on different types of projects. . . . There was a sense of freedom, of creativity."

"There was a remarkable pulse to the place," said another. He spoke of "Drexel-speak shorthand," putting together deals rapid-fire: "I've got a private company, seventy-five million dollars; you've got a public company, bleeding, can't get its act together."

"All right, we'll put 'em together. I'll get this guy to do the mezzanine [buy the junk bonds]."

"I've got the senior debt done."

Slam, bam—a new company, probably a better one. According to this officer, "Every other investment bank I've ever witnessed would masturbate on the subject for two weeks."

And for obvious reasons. They didn't have Drexel's entrepreneurial nature, they didn't have its personnel, and let's face it, they didn't have Milken. "He had the relationships," noted an East Coast manager, "and the others in corporate finance were more in the processing role." "He was heavily relied on to think up deals," said a corporate finance officer. "He created them, then stepped aside." "Toward the end, many of the deals came in through Milken," said Tony Meyer. "If you are with a firm that has an edge, and you're assigned to process a deal, you look good."

The Great Acquisitor "was a classic example among Drexel people," one officer said of the firm's heyday. "He's dragging a hundred mega-ton bomb in a cart, with a device in a box to set it off, and he can't figure out why he's so important. Then he begins to believe it."

By late 1986, the rainmakers at the firm found it easy to believe anything, and those who weren't here found it easier to justify joining. At the top business schools in the country, the best and brightest were eager to climb aboard, as well; one graduate of Harvard Business School described Drexel as "the absolutely, one hundred percent shop to get into."

Those who got the call, the rookies and the elite, found themselves in the middle of the action, with unlimited opportunities and occasional temptations. "There was a tremendous free flow of information," said one officer, "because there was a strong feeling that everyone knew what the rules were." In case people forgot—or tried to forget—Fred Joseph would remind his investment bankers every four to six weeks, according to this person, with a speech to the effect of: "I know I'm a broken record, but we have a lot of sensitive information; if anyone violates the law, you're not only out of the company, you're out of the industry, and we'll do whatever we can to see that you don't work again in this business."

Unfortunately, not everyone in the firm heard the message—or chose to listen. Some crossed the line into the unethical, a few into the illegal. It was wrong, it was unnecessary, and finally, it was fatal.

CHAPTER SIX

THE DARK SIDE
OF THE FORCE

Just win, baby

—LOS ANGELES RAIDERS' MOTTO

"Without exception, everything that he wanted to do was with a view toward either screwing the client . . . or was illegal," recalled a senior East Coast investment banker of a young West Coast trader. "He never had a single honest thought in the whole three-week period—not a one. Everything was: 'Here's the way we make the most money for Drexel,' and every time I would say, 'But we can't do that, it's against the law; it's against the spirit of the underwriting contract,' this, that, and the other thing. He'd say, 'Who the *fuck* are you working for anyway; are you working for Drexel or the SEC?'

"They were all trying to please Michael, and they knew that the way to please Michael was to make a lot of money. . . . If at the end of the day, they could say, 'Michael, we made twenty-three thousand dollars on ABC, seventy-eight thousand on DEF, one hundred and two thousand on XYZ,' he'd be pleased with them, pat them on the head, maybe give them a Mercedes."

There were those who were so eager for approval or money that they stepped into the gray, and a few that stepped over the line. They made a lot more for themselves, a little more for their firm, and they hurt the reputations—and futures—of ten thousand other people who didn't have any interest in being associated with the unethical or the illegal.

These buccaneers on the coast were a minority, but one to steer clear of. There was, of course, the Gray Prince, who had helped to make my first several months at the firm such fun. "There wasn't anything that he wouldn't have done to sell a deal," a New York-based salesman commented. "No holds barred—anything it took to sell it he would use, whether it was accurate or inaccurate." This salesman also remembers telling the Prince that some customers were interested in selling stock, when the West Coast wanted buyers. "They'll carry them out in a stretcher," was his absurd, but otherwise charming, message for the clients.

In negotiating a $25 million deal, the differential between what the client company wanted to pay and what the West Coast wanted it to pay had been narrowed to only $15,000. "You've gotten ninety-five percent of what you wanted," an investment banker argued. "Let him leave with a good taste in his mouth." When the Prince refused, the banker offered to pay the difference out of his own pocket, rather than try to twist the last 5 percent out of his client.

There was also Cadillac Man, a supersalesman who landed in a lawsuit for selling, allegedly with the help of a selective memory, a half-interest in a company destined for bankruptcy. The buyer, a nearby savings and loan, purchased a phenomenal $300 million of junk bonds in less than a year and eventually went bankrupt, as well. (But there's a happy side to the story: It was their real estate, not their bonds, that was primarily responsible for the bailout from taxpayers.)

There was the Young Turk, who would later turn state's evidence to protect himself, and Bruce Newberg, who would refuse even though it meant an indictment. And there were the lesser players who would rather face their maker than face their boss—Mr. One Hundred Percent—the man they deeply admired and feared.

"I had great trouble with their techniques and tactics and ethics," a top institutional equity salesman said. He recalled a trade that he had suggested to a client: Sell shares of Occidental Petroleum (Oxy), and buy Oxy's preferred, which had a 17 percent yield and was convertible into Oxy common stock. The Coast had the Oxy preferreds for sale, and the client bought 250,000 shares during the day from a trader out there.

"At the end of the day, the trader says, 'Okay, what's this account number?'

" 'Well, you'll find out tomorrow when you see the ticket.'

" 'Oh, no, no, no. We're gonna write the ticket out here.'

" 'Oh, no, no, no. We're writing the buy side here. You may want to write the sell side out there.'

"Back and forth. So I put him on hold, and I called Billy who was handling the trade for me. And I said, 'Bill, take those Oxy trades and get them key punched right now. So he went over there and put them in. A minute or so, he signaled me, so I called back [the trader on the Coast] and said, 'So, what did you say?'

" 'We're gonna write the ticket out here.'

" 'You're not writing the ticket out there.' (They would've taken all the commission).

" 'You want me to get Michael involved in this?"

"I did tense just a bit, but I said, 'Put him on the phone.'

"Never put him on.

"If I had explained to Milken what had happened, he would've said, 'Fine, you deserve that side of it; we'll take this side of it.' But this trader was so worried that the next day—and it happened—Milken would say, 'Where's the other side of this Oxy trade?'

"That was his mentality. They didn't want to let it get away. He set that tone, but the underlings took it to an even further degree."

"There were an awful lot of people who spent an awful lot of time saying, 'Michael says,' " remembered Steve Joseph. "They would try to please Michael and anticipate what he wanted." They would also stand a much better chance of winning any battle if they could use Milken's name in their behalf—how could anyone outside of that office know whether or not he had actually said whatever he was supposed to have said.

Which raises the big question: Were the ethics of the buccaneers the ethics of their boss? They didn't have his strengths so they had to rely more on their swords. Still they weren't renegades—they were on his ship, at his side by his choice.

It's difficult to believe that Milken was unaware of conversations a few feet from him, when by his own admission he had trained himself to listen in on almost every conversation on the floor. Perhaps, as one Milken supporter argued, those who crossed the line made a point of doing it when he wasn't around to hear. But if he did hear, then he condoned it, for reasons both obvious and obscure.

"Michael had major blind spots that developed as things went along," argued an East Coast investment banker. "He very much had a trader's mentality, as far as rules and laws and regulations were concerned. He viewed them as impediments to the free flow of trading activity that should be regarded with contempt; I don't think he took securities regulations seriously.

"I think we've been trained as a nation to admire guys who say, 'Don't sit there talking about obstacles all day—just get 'em the fuck out of the way so we can move forward.' At the same time, some things are not mindless laws; some things deserve your attention, like the law against rolling your mother-in-law down the stairs. That really isn't something that you have to figure out a way around; that's something that you really have to observe."

Some would argue that Milken observed all the regulations and laws, and that even his eventual admissions of guilt were only made with a loaded, although entirely legal, gun at his head.

Others might agree with one East Coast salesman's description of Milken as "a benevolent king sitting on his throne, giving out munificent benefits. And yet, lo and behold, there's the tax collector and the executioner and the judge advocate and the inquisitor—there are all these folks running around" in the king's name, with the king's blessing.

And there are others who would argue that the king didn't mind knocking around a few peasants himself or getting his own hands dirty.

One thing is certain: Milken played to win—with his competitors, with his clients, with his employees, with the East Coast, and with the market.

"You didn't do business with a Drexel competitor unless Drexel said okay," a former executive of Columbia Savings and Loan told *Institutional Investor Magazine.* "Mike was an animal in terms of the other Wall Street houses." The complaints that surfaced from competitors over the years focused on the usual suspects of bad manners and bad ethics—primarily, misleading and mistreating them on the increasingly rare deals where Drexel and other firms were supposed to work together.

There was also the issue of last-minute adjustments to a deal, which hurt both the competitors and the clients. In this case, the terms of a deal are changed almost at the end, too late for the company to hire a different firm. One East Coast investment banker mentioned Milken's willingness to tell a company that he had "bought the deal," committing him to completing the deal on the terms discussed; one variable was left undecided, however, leaving a loophole to make later changes.

Companies selling junk bonds were asked to pay huge fees—three times greater, proportionally, than on high-grade bond deals—to compensate for the difficulty in selling these deals, even if that difficulty was not always apparent. In 1983, MCI Communications, the long-distance telephone company that was Drexel's most celebrated high-yield bond client, filed a $500 million offering. The company was asked to pay a commission of 2 percent or $10 million, the reason being that such a large deal would be hard to sell. On the day of the deal, Milken asked the company if they want to *double* the size to $1 billion—but he still wanted that 2 percent fee.

When Rupert Murdoch's Newscorp hired Drexel to sell $1.1 billion in bonds to finance its acquisition of television stations from Metromedia, it agreed to an unusual compensation schedule. The commission on bonds that were sold to the former holders of Metromedia would be 2 percent; that on bonds sold to new buyers would be 4 percent. Milken and the Great Acquisitor gave Newscorp their estimate: The breakdown of buyers would be half old, half new. After the bonds were placed, however, the company was informed that more than 90 percent of the buyers were new bondholders, implying a much higher commission. Not surprisingly, the company asked for the list of buyers, and it's still waiting for the names.

As part of a junk bond offering, a company might be asked to provide warrants which would give the holder a potentially lucrative piece of the company's stock. These warrants might be used to "sweeten the deal," making it more attractive to possible junk-bond buyers—no problem with that. Or these warrants might be used as partial payment to the Wall Street firm underwriting the deal—again, no problem. The potential for abuse occurs when a client is asked to provide a package of warrants to be used as sweetner *and* payment. In this case, the warrants might not find their way to the buyers—they might not be necessary to sell the bonds. But the client might not know that.

To clear up any misunderstanding, Fred Joseph told the high-yield department in 1985 that all clients must be told explicitly which warrants were intended for the buyers and which for the firm. How well this rule worked in practice is open to some question. The $6.2 billion Beatrice deal, discussed in Chapter 3, included $33.4 million warrants at a bargain price of $.25 each. A proxy statement provided to Beatrice shareholders, and quoted by Abraham Briloff in *Barron's* (December 5, 1988), indicated that these warrants were to be sold "in connection with the sale of debt securities other than senior notes"— presumably, as sweeteners to the $1.9 billion worth of subordinated bonds.

Ninety-nine percent of these warrants, however, showed up in the hands of BCP Partners some fourteen months later, according to a public document review by Briloff. The partners of BCP were Drexel and certain of its employees.

Drexel contends that the warrants were meant to be sold *only* to the buyers of the most speculative bond issue—the $150 million floating rate subordinated debentures. More than that, this bond issue was offered *first* to Drexel; in effect, it was an additional payment—above and beyond the $86 million cash fee—to the firm for its investment banking efforts, allegedly with the approval of the client, Kohlberg Kravis. (Kohlberg Kravis, through a public relations representative, declined to comment.)

But that is not the end of the story. The firm chose to buy some 10 percent of the junior bonds with the accompanying warrants. The balance of the warrants—which were destined to produce a 5,000 percent profit—and the bonds apparently were bought by private partnerships put together by Milken, and available only by invitation.

The invites went to employees on the West Coast, selected investment bankers on the East Coast, and even some executives from client companies. These partnerships, eventually numbering in the hundreds, gave Milken leverage over those people that he relied on most. In effect, these desirable partnerships allowed him to dole out favors to a selected group, favors that could only be collected far in the future when the partnerships cashed out.

The result was the creation of a superclass within Drexel, without the knowledge of most of us in the firm. Lucrative merchandise, such as warrants, which should have gone to all the employees, went instead to the ruling class. (I'm talking about the stuff that was *earned*; anything that was obtained by deception wasn't needed or wanted.) Allegations would later surface in congressional hearings that these partnerships engaged in self-dealing on junk bond offerings and trades that were possibly illegal, and unquestionably unethical.

If Milken was generous with those in the firm who helped his business, he could be intimidating to those who occasionally hurt it. Once when a research analyst prepared a report on a corporate client with a neutral conclusion on its stock, his boss received a phone call from Michael. The analyst recalls Milken's message, as relayed by the research director: "There is no such thing as an unhappy corporate finance client. There is such a thing as an unemployed analyst."

Actually, the neutral opinion on the stock turned out to be optimistic, as its price fell by 60 percent in subsequent years. Bear in mind, however, that Milken's attitude on this one may have been influenced by personal factors: The chief exec of this company had helped a member of Michael's family in a time of crisis—this may not be a valid excuse, but it certainly qualifies as a damn good reason.

One investment banker remembered a "very direct experience that had a lot to do with becoming at least partially disenchanted with Michael, and it also had a lot to do with my decision that as soon as I saved enough pennies in the jar, I was getting my ass out of Drexel. . . . My phone rang one afternoon." It was the treasurer of an important client company. "He said, 'I'm on the phone with Michael,' and Michael said, 'Hi, ———, how are you?'

"[The exec] went on to say, 'There's something that we've been kicking around that we want to talk to you about.' I said, 'Shoot,' and he said, 'We've be talking about the possibility of making a tender offer for the warrants [that had been sold to the public]. They're trading for around one and one-quarter bid; Michael is of the opinion that we can bring in the whole issue for a dollar fifty. [These warrants were given to buyers of the high-yield bonds in an offering several years earlier. They gave the holders the right to buy stock in the company at a set price; accordingly, if the stock price rose above this price, these warrants would be profitable to holders. The price of the stock, however, had declined sharply—the warrants would remain out of the money unless the stock quadrupled in the two years before they would expire. Because of this, the warrants were selling for about $1.25 each; Milken felt that the company could purchase all of them for $1.50 per warrant.] That way we would get rid of the overhang on the common stock. What do you think?'

"And I said, 'This is kind of a hip-shoot since I haven't been thinking about this, but if you want a quick reaction: Why bother?' [He went on to explain the business and tax reasons that argued against using the company's cash to repurchase the warrants.]

"And [the exec] said, 'Yeah, I was sort of coming to the same conclusion myself, but we'll keep thinking about it and I wish you would, too'—and bye, bye, bye, and everyone hung up.

"Thirty seconds later, the phone rings, and it was Michael. He said, 'I don't think that was very polite'—those were his first words.

" 'What?'

" '[Criticizing] my idea.'

" 'How was I supposed to know it was your idea? He called up—I had no way of knowing whose idea it was. I feel compelled to honestly respond to a client if he asks me a question. If you had wanted to set the stage for maybe trying to persuade the company that they should do it, why the hell didn't you call me up?'

"He said, 'I just wanted you to know that I don't think it was very polite, and that's my message for today.'

"And with that he hung up."

"Mike's whole pattern was to push the wall," said another corporate finance officer. The days of stodgy investment bankers waiting for their clients to call when they needed financing were over—for better and worse. This banker spoke of the pressure to get clients to maintain the junk-bond momentum. Such pressure inevitably led to questionable practices.

One allegation against the firm involved coercing companies to become clients. "People did business because they had to," said an East Coast investment banker. But this was a two-edged sword.

The most notorious allegation of coercion involved some conversations between employees of A.E. Staley, a food processing concern, and Jim Dahl. Staley was told that Drexel owned 1.5 million shares—over 5 percent of the total—and that it "wanted to be Staley's investment banker." Dahl allegedly told Robert Hoffman, Staley's chief financial officer, "It is very important for us to sit down and talk before you do something that hurts me and before I do something that hurts you." The company had other plans: It sued Drexel. Turnabout being fair play, the suit, which included the allegations just mentioned and was widely reported in the media, including *The Wall*

Street Journal, was eventually dropped after Drexel agreed to buy a division from Staley for $35 million, which one competitor valued at $10 million.

The other side of the sword was that some companies were willing, even eager, to hire Drexel as their investment banker to protect themselves from the possibility that a corporate raider might want Drexel to help them finance a takeover bid. In effect, they were buying insurance against Milken showing up on the other side of the table.

One of America's premier companies, a rumored takeover candidate, tried to co-opt the firm, according to a corporate finance officer. Fred Joseph refused, telling the company that Drexel "wasn't in the business of raider protection. Joseph's behavior was absolutely exemplary," he added.

Certainly, Drexel was interested in advising blue-chip companies on how to defend themselves against hostile takeovers—the best defense being to raise the perceived value, and therefore, the stock price, so that no one could afford to pay up for the shares. In this officer's view, however, the firm wanted to be hired for its talents in helping a company, not as a payoff to keep it from helping a company's potential enemy.

Along this line, Drexel scored a coup when Marty Siegel of white-shoed Kidder Peabody agreed to join the firm in 1986. He brought enormous respectability and a long list of corporate clients—and as it would turn out, a few skeletons in his closet.

The firm's interest in representing, and defending, blue-chip companies was good business—steady fees, powerful clients, improved image. It did not reflect, however, a change of heart regarding the merits of hostile takeovers. These takeovers were shaking up the status quo to the benefit of the actual owners of American business: some forty million stockholders.

But takeovers also had negative consequences that received less publicity from Drexel. Companies were leveraged to the hilt: If they pulled through, the greatest benefits accrued to the buyers who put up a small investment; if they failed, the greatest harm fell on the employees and the bondholders. In addition, the old stockholders, who received a premium price for their shares, often learned that they still had been bought out on the cheap. And managers, afraid to plan for a future that they might never survive long enough to see, allowed their companies to become less competitive. (Whether a short-term focus made their companies more vulnerable to takeovers, rather than less, is an issue worth considering.)

Serious questions arose as well from friendly takeovers. Consider management-led leveraged buyouts, in which Drexel played the lead financing role on the Street. The buyers here are the folks who are supposed to make money for their stockholders, not for themselves. If their companies are undervalued, their management skills are often the primary reason. Regardless, they are morally—and legally—responsible to do something about it, and that something doesn't involve hiring an investment banker to help them lock in the profit for themselves. And yet they did.

Drexel had no obligation to appoint itself the conscience of the free market, but it could have done a better job in choosing its champions. The concept of the entrepreneurial owner-manager, dedicated to the interests of the stockholders, often read better than it played. Perhaps the most extreme case involved a fellow who would eventually be convicted of tax evasion in overvaluing a gift to a church; as one investment banker asked, "Why would anyone want to do business with him?"

In the high-yield market, everyone wanted to do business with Milken—or, more accurately, they needed to. He was the market. He developed it and he sustained it. His competition in the 1970s and early 1980s was weak. "First Boston had had a bad experience," said a corporate finance officer. "Salomon didn't want to touch it. . . . Morgan Stanley was not interested. . . . Bache was doing the deals we turned down."

Milken and his department were, in effect, responsible for controlling an increasingly important market. To their credit, according to an investment banker, "They took such good care of their constituents—Milken always seemed to make them whole." But there was a flip side: "A lot of deals were made on the trading side," said a West Coast banker. "You scratch my back; I'll scratch yours."

The idea of trading favors is an integral part of business and personal life. On Wall Street, it was a part of every market. For example, a client might want to get rid of some stocks or bonds that a firm doesn't want to buy, but the firm does and takes a loss. The client is told of the loss and is expected to make it up with additional commissions on other trades or on new deals.

The quid pro quo concept, in some cases, carries with it a sour smell. Most people on the Street are small players and, if they wish, can steer clear of these cases without affecting the markets in which they work. Milken, however, was the lead player in his market, which like all markets, relied on confidence; this sense of confidence, in turn, was dependent at any given time on a perception of health.

Perhaps this point of view justifies an attitude that, as long as the favors are balanced out over the long haul, it doesn't matter whether every trade is a fair one. Perhaps not. It certainly doesn't justify an inner circle of favored clients who bought the hard-to-place deals and who enjoyed a place in the partnerships.

Another concern involved the issue of overfunding. "A lot of companies were overfinanced to create additional currency for high-yield bonds," noted a young East Coast officer. In these cases, client companies were encouraged to raise more money than they needed, and to put the excess cash in junk bonds. "Some of these companies were so small and naive, they relied on Drexel . . . they needed Drexel . . . Drexel was totally in control."

There is, however, a simple argument in favor of overfunding. Because a small company, unlike an IBM or AT&T, can never be certain that it will be able to raise money in the future, and because raising that money is a time-consuming and even expensive process for the company, there is a great deal to say for financing as much debt as possible. Eventually, the additional funds will be needed, and the company won't have to try raising more cash at that time.

Be that as it may, there was criticism of this practice, and from no less a source than I. W. Burnham. "It's wrong for an underwriter to say to a company that needs fifty million dollars, 'We can get you a hundred million,' " he told Connie Bruck. "I am always telling my guys, it's wrong."

By the mid-1980s, however, Burnham's influence on his firm's policies was insignificant. He was in his seventies and had not been Drexel's chief exec for almost a decade, having been eased aside by those senior officers more in agreement with Milken's aggressive philosophy—"He gave an inch at a time," according to a Drexel veteran. "Had I. W. been in charge, things would've been different," argued one research analyst. "He asked too many questions," said a longtime trader, after noting that "the old man loved Michael, too."

Regardless of how any of us in the firm felt about Milken, not too many questioned his success or his tactics. There were reasons, some better than others. One salesman pointed out that Drexel Burnham's stock, owned primarily by its employees, rose about 1,000 percent between 1982 and 1986. "That's why everyone turned their heads," he argued.

In fairness, the employees on the East Coast were in the dark about what was happening in the high-yield department three thousand miles away. (The same point can be made as well about the majority of employees in that office.) The guys on the Coast were a tough group, but there was no law against that.

Wall Street prides itself on playing hardball—even though the high-yield bond department was more likely than most to steal second base, spikes flying, or put a fastball in someone's ear, their tactics seemed more a matter of degree than of good versus evil. If being an occasional asshole was illegal, the Street might start resembling Love Canal; for that matter, if greed alone bought you a ticket to jail, every state would probably have more people making license plates than using them.

Rationalizations? Maybe. One thing's for sure, senior management should have had a clearer picture of what was happening in its most important department, which represented anywhere from half to all of the firm's income. So why didn't it? There's the obvious argument: "They didn't care what Milken was doing since he was making them rich," said a trader.

Another argument is that Milken didn't want to be watched more closely, and that by the mid-1980s, what he didn't want didn't happen. As one executive noted, Milken had moved to the West Coast but management hadn't.

There's also a different point of view: Why would Milken cheat, especially in the most regulated business in the world? He didn't need to. His brilliance and foresight, and even ambition, should have been the best defense against him breaking the law. Why would he do anything that stupid?

"My feeling was, with that department sailing as close to the wind as it was, that sooner or later, something was likely to happen," said a senior investment banker, "something that would blow them into the water." The first explosion occurred on May 12, 1986, at Drexel's New York headquarters. Dennis Levine, a thirty-three-year-old investment banker, was charged with insider trading. His arrest was easily dismissed as isolated and unimportant, which it was and wasn't.

As Levine explained in a May 1990 *Fortune* article, he had joined Drexel in early 1985 after his former firm, the investment banking powerhouse Lehman Brothers, merged with Shearson—a retail brokerage house and, since 1981, a subsidiary of American Express. "Levine was considered a great get at the time," recalled a former Drexel exec, who added, "Wall Street is very famous for not checking out its people very well."

Dennis Levine was a role model for ambitious B-school graduates: young, personable, rich. After years of power breakfasts, working lunches, and four-star dinners, he wasn't likely to win any race that relied on more than gravity, but then again, who cared? He was an important investment banker, a man in the action, involved in several of the most exciting battles of the 1980s: Carl Icahn against Phillips, Oscar Wyatt (of Coastal) against American Natural Resources, Sir James Goldsmith against Crown Zellerbach, and Ron Perelman against Revlon.

His 1985 bonus was more than $1 million, a healthy increase from his 1978 salary of $19,000 as a Citibank trainee. He was also well on his way to making over $11 million in illegal profits from trading on inside information. He traded by making collect calls from a pay phone to a secret Swiss account at Pictet & Cie and, later, to the Bahamian subsidiary of Geneva-based Bank Leu.

Levine's unraveling was a bit convoluted. Executives at his bank, more than impressed by his unerring stock picking, were copying his decisions for their own accounts and placing the bulk of the buy-and-sell orders through a Merrill Lynch office in Venezuela. One or more employees there jumped on the insider trading bandwagon, as well. In mid-1985, an anonymous letter was sent to Merrill, accusing two of them. Merrill called the SEC, which began investigating Bank Leu.

After ten months, the bank decided that immunity was more important than confidentiality, and Levine's name was turned over to U.S. authorities. To make matters worse for him, he found out that his partner, Robert Wilkis of Lazard Freres, had ignored a number of agreed-on precautions. Levine decided to settle with the government, pleading guilty to four felonies and disgorging his $11.5 million in illegal gains; he also implicated his friend, Wilkis, and his more recent partner, Ivan Boesky.

Boesky was a very big fish, the most successful of Wall Street's arbitrageurs. In earlier days, these arbs had searched for inefficiencies in the financial markets, where they could buy one security and simultaneously sell an identical, or nearly identical, security. This would lock in a profit at no risk.

Takeovers had created a new twist: "risk arbitrage." Risk arbs made bets on mergers. If a deal was announced, the shares of the target company would rise toward the price being offered. The stock price would rarely reach the offer price, however, because there was always a chance that the deal would fall through, particularly a hostile takeover. Risk arbs made their living by deciding what price to pay for a stock following the announcement of a deal.

For example, if IBM receives a bid of $150 per share from The Pep Boys (Manny, Moe & Jack), its price might only rise from 100 to 140. If an arb bought the shares at 140 and the deal went through three months later, his or her profit would be $10 per share; on a percentage basis, the return would be about 7 percent ($10 divided by the $140 investment) for three months. If you annualize this figure, the return is four times greater, or some 30 percent.

Of course, the deal might fall through. These three boys might have trouble raising the $90 billion purchase price. If this happened, the arb would lose $40 per share when the price of IBM fell back to 100. On the other hand, another bidder might enter the fray, offering more than $150 per share and giving the arb an even greater profit.

The final result is dependent on a number of factors, from a bidder's ability to pay to a target's willingness to sell to the personalities of the players to the opinions of various courts. The stock and bond markets, meanwhile, might influence a deal by rising or falling. Also, management might decide to hold out for a higher price, or raise the price itself, or fight to stay independent, no matter what it did to the price.

A risk arb tries to determine the odds that an announced takeover attempt will succeed, or even to determine which deals will be announced. He relies on information from public statements, court decisions, past history, proxy filings, company analyses, educated guesses, and contacts on Wall Street. The occasional arbitrageur takes this process a step too far, steering a shortcut through the law by seeking out the most accurate information out there: inside information.

Risk arbitrage in general is neither well understood nor well liked. It is viewed by the public as the financial community's equivalent of white slavery, selling corporations to the tender mercies of the highest bidder. In fact, arbs serve a valid role, giving shareholders an opportunity to sell their shares before a deal might fall through. Still, arbitrageurs are usually viewed as the heavies; Carl Icahn, himself a former arbitrageur, captured the popular view with a comment to author Moira Johnston, author of *Takeover:* "I've told my wife, if I need surgery, get me the heart of an arb. It's never been used."

Boesky rode the takeover wave of the 1980s, which produced deals—and risk arbitrage profits—of unprecedented size. As he became a great success and a minor celebrity, he tried to make risk arbitrage respectable, even enviable. "I think greed is healthy," he told students at Columbia Business School. "You can be greedy and still feel good about yourself."

He also wrote a book, *Merger Mania,* with the intriguing subtitle: *Arbitrage: Wall Street's Best Kept Money-Making Secret.* Not surprisingly, he neglected to mention that the secret ingredient of the best kept secret was inside information.

The book is interesting on several levels. There's the following line at the end of the foreword: "This book is dedicated to ending the tall tales about risk arbitrage." Or the admission in chapter four: "A great deal of information is available from Wall Street research firms." It just may not be legal.

Or the Cheshire Cat smile, chiseled features, and intense eyes facing you on the front cover. You have to wonder: What was going on in this guy's head? He knew he was a fraud. Were fame and fortune more important than self-respect or were they his basis for self-respect?

During the glory days of 1985 and 1986, Boesky appeared to relish his role among the rich and famous—the king of the arbs. He certainly seemed right for the part. He worked too hard, slept three to four hours a night, dressed in dark suits, owned a pink Rolls Royce, lunched at Lutece, spoke with a deep, formal voice, and produced extraordinary results.

"I can't predict my demise," he told *The Washington Post* in 1985, "but I suspect it will occur abruptly."

For most employees at Drexel Burnham, Ivan Boesky's past successes and future prospects were, well, irrelevant. He was a distant figure, operating in a world far removed. That is, until the news of his settlement with the government was released—one sentence on the Quotron machine after the market closed on Friday, November 14, 1986: Boesky had pleaded guilty to one felony and agreed to pay $100 million in fines and restitutions.

For my firm, it was the beginning of the end.

CHAPTER SEVEN

MEANWHILE, BACK AT THE STOCK EXCHANGE...

> Life is pain. Anyone who tells you different
> is trying to sell you something.
>
> —*The Princess Bride*

While Drexel's high-yield bond department and its investment bankers were restructuring corporate America in the first half of the 1980s, the firm's equity business was prospering as well, existing almost in a parallel universe. We contributed modestly to the firm's spectacular rise, although we never produced the kind of impact and money that Milken's troops made. Still, outside of monarchs and dictators, nobody else did either.

Compared to the real world, we were pretty lucky. We worked hard and smart, we were overpaid, and we had a great boss: the stock market. When most people think of Wall Street, they think of the market—not bonds or commodities, but the market: stocks. Even junk bonds, which put a torch under the financial community, were never more interesting than when they affected the stock market. They made page one when they financed takeovers that drove up the stock prices of target companies, putting the fear of Mike into the managers of undervalued companies.

The high-yield bond department was certainly involved in the market, but the equity department lived it, and that was fine with me. The stock market is a fascinating challenge, one designed to make most people miserable, where the experts gravitate toward the obvious, and the obvious is obviously wrong.

The most bizarre aspect of Wall Street is that it has managed to attract the best and brightest to the challenge and then forced them to play under a set of conditions that almost guarantees lousy results. You couldn't have thought up this system if you tried.

The problem begins with the priority: To make money. No problem yet; certainly, no surprise. The folks who give the advice and manage the money, however, have created the problem by adding one requirement: They want to make money *quickly*. This little addition to the priority has managed to muck up the process.

But what a process, especially during the rising markets and rising profits of the 1980s. It began each day with the morning meeting, a thirty- to sixty-minute drill that occurred simultaneously throughout Wall Street. When I joined Drexel Burnham, the meeting started at eight-thirty; by the time I left, it was starting almost an hour earlier.

For most of that time, the institutional equity sales force would walk down from their desks on the ninth floor of 60 Broad Street to the conference room on the eighth, where the research department was based. (A senior exec once described the department to a veteran analyst as a bunch of prima donnas linked up by an air-conditioning system.) Joining us at the morning meeting were the research analysts who would be speaking, other analysts who were just sitting in, research support staff, and those retail salesmen who, to their credit, weren't content to rely on the ideas fed to them by their sales managers.

The conference room, modestly furnished by anyone's standards, seated about a hundred, and was equipped with microphones. When the conference call system was hooked up, all the branch offices could listen in on the meeting. The system had been with the firm longer than most people in the room, and seemed to have a mind of its own, sometimes abandoning our branch offices from Boston to Century City.

The morning meeting was normally run by the director of research, who had the primary responsibility of deciding which analysts should speak and in which order. A change in the firm's rating on a stock, particularly from hold to buy, was a top priority. An important event at a company—a large new order or a downbeat forecast from management, for example—was another priority. Lower down the list was a minor change in an earnings estimate or the reemphasis of an existing recommendation.

For eight years, people complained about the morning meeting, particularly its length. In time, the meetings ran more efficiently, with analysts hitting the key points quickly and comprehensibly. This was offset, however, by the growth of the equity research department, which probably doubled in size while I was at the firm. The result was that the presentations became tighter, but there were more analysts vying for the mike. The killer weeks were those following the end of each quarter, when companies reported their earnings for the previous three months, and fifteen to twenty analysts would show up each morning.

I certainly couldn't blame them. The success of a "sell-side" analyst was, in large part, dependent on being heard and listened to by our clients. The best way to leverage a message, whatever that message might be on a given day, was to get the sales force involved. When thirty salesmen are making calls on a particular stock, the analyst gets exposure and, sometimes, immediate impact. If thirty salesmen each convince a few clients to buy shares in a new recommendation, the price of that stock will rise with its opening price.

For example, in January 1985, David Healy, our respected copper analyst, added Phelps Dodge to the buy list, his first recommendation in the group since 1979. The outlook for copper prices, by his calculations, was favorable—the inventory-to-consumption ratio, a measure of supply and demand, was approaching shortage conditions. If prices rose as expected, Phelps Dodge would be a prime beneficiary. The salesmen, and the clients, recognized the importance of this call, and the shares rose more than a point on the opening. Phelps would triple before Dave would pull his recommendation.

The impact of a major call can be felt on the downside as well. In April 1985, Arthur Kirsch removed Philip Morris from the buy list, after strongly—and successfully—recommending it for years. The concern, highlighted in the previous day's *Wall Street Journal,* was that tobacco litigation would become a major cloud over the stock for the first time since the early 1960s. Arthur's rating change became everyone's first call, and not surprisingly, Morris's share price plummeted, dropping 7 percent on the first trade that morning.

Naturally, the analysts who had the greatest impact were those who had earned the respect of the salesmen and the clients. Regardless, every analyst stood to benefit from the sales force's support. If I'd been a research analyst, I would've found a reason to speak at the morning meeting three days a week.

But as a salesman, I was a listener, and time moves slowly when other people get to do the talking. Occasionally, time would seem to stop in its tracks. The morning meetings, however, were for information not entertainment, although there were some lively moments every so often. In one 1983 meeting, an analyst spoke about Paradyne's new computer-related something or other and was asked to explain how it worked (a good question because salesmen, and investors, have a tendency to get caught up in a story even if they don't completely understand it). Following the Paradyne analyst was the Tampax analyst, who began his presentation with: "I hope nobody is going to ask me how this works."

The best comment at a meeting was made during the wild 1980 run-up in gold prices. When asked how high the price might reach, the analyst quoted Adam's first words to Eve: "Stand back, honey, I don't know how big this is gonna get."

Enjoyable or not, the morning meeting was crucial: It provided the sales force with ammunition for the day, the ideas and names to discuss—the new recommendation, the stock that was removed from our buy list, a notable increase in an earnings estimate, a significant new development in an industry. For the balance of the day, we would be on the phone, as would salesmen from all the brokerage houses, with the clients—the institutions that invested people's savings and pensions in the stock market.

We would provide these professional investors with an edited version of what our analysts had said—what had happened at a company, what we expected to happen in the market, what our best stocks were, what our favorite analysts liked, whatever. We also discussed the stocks they were buying and selling and asked them their favorite ideas.

The tone and content of the sales presentation depended on the individual salesperson and, of course, on the individual client. Some were interested in ways to make money that day, most focused on a three- to six-month horizon, and some even thought in terms of several years.

There were the gunslingers trading in and out of large blocks of stock based on the latest piece of news or rumor; these were the funds that fire the imaginations of small investors when they think of the pros. A rumor that the Federal Reserve will provide more money to the economy? They buy stocks. An announcement from the chief financial officer of a company that earnings in the quarter will rise by less than expected? They sell shares in that company.

My clients didn't include the gunslingers, and I didn't mind. Investing is done best by investors, not speculators, gifted or not. More important, as a salesman, I wasn't particularly interested in being a well-paid rumormonger, trading bits of the latest and the hottest. Bear in mind, good information can sometimes be too good, and the dividing line isn't always clear.

Other salesmen were better at dealing with this issue, and several others were just better at this job. I may never have asked to cover a gunslinger account, but then again, no sales manager ever offered me one either.

The gunslingers were usually a part of a larger group known as "hedge funds." A hedge fund, by definition, simply has the right to "short stocks": selling shares that they don't own, with the intention of repurchasing those shares at a lower price, and pocketing the difference. This permits them to hedge their exposure to the stock market. Some stocks are bought, hoping for a rise in their prices; others are shorted, hoping for a decline in their prices. A portfolio of "long" winners and "short" losers allows a great stock picker to make money no matter which direction the stock market heads.

Not all hedge funds are gunslingers—far from it. In fact, one of the best investors I know runs a hedge fund focused on long-term performance. He recognizes that even if you buy the cheap ones and short the expensive ones, you may have to wait a while for the market to come to its senses.

Most institutional investors can't short stocks and are considered more conservative. These institutions include bank trust departments, insurance companies, mutual funds, and most investment advisers. These were my clients, from Rochester to Baltimore and New York to Cedar Rapids.

Because my accounts were not among the big boys like Citibank and IDS and Alliance Capital, they primarily relied on me to tell them what Drexel was saying and what was worth paying attention to. The larger buy-side players could count on phone calls from our research analysts directly, in addition to the sales calls. Our analysts spoke with their analysts and their portfolio managers, as did all the analysts from all the other Wall Street firms.

Sell-side analysts also had to stay in touch with the companies they followed, usually ten to twenty of them in one or two industries. They had to be on top of everything that was happening, and they had to have an expert opinion on what was about to happen. They had to understand industry trends, and recognize or anticipate new ones.

They had to write morning meeting notes, and weekly research abstracts, and stand-alone company/industry reports. They had to translate all this information into conclusions about whether each stock should be bought and sold, and then convince the sales force and the clients that they were right. And then they had to be right.

Analysts essentially had to work their butts off if they wanted to be well respected and not just well paid.

They also faced pressure of a different sort: the possibility that a negative analysis of a company would invite retaliation. The retaliation that most analysts face is the loss of access to one of the companies they're covering. Because their best source for information about what's going on at a company is management, no analyst is eager to be critical. The world of an analyst is a lonely place when nobody returns his or her phone calls.

Accordingly, sell recommendations are like black holes: They exist in theory, but try finding one. Analysts prefer to rate the lemons as "neutral," "long-term hold," "okay to hold," or in rare cases, "okay to sell." If a brokerage firm is covering seven hundred stocks as we were in 1986, half of them might be buy rated, or some variation of *buy,* and the overwhelming majority of the rest might be various types of *hold.* The remaining four names are *sells.*

These pressures on analysts might raise a question in your mind: Why not be a salesman instead? For one thing, salesmen—the good ones—work pretty damn hard, as well. They spend their days on the phone, and their nights and weekends reading material about the companies their firms follow and about the economy and the market in general. As with analysts, their jobs require repetitive, often boring sales calls, ongoing administrative tasks, and the patient development of relationships; their success is based on the football principle of four yards and a cloud of dust.

In one respect, analysts have a great advantage over salesmen: they know more about what they're talking about than the clients. Don't underestimate the psychic benefit of being the most knowledgeable one on the phone or at a meeting. A salesperson spends a good part of his day speaking with portfolio managers and buy-side analysts about companies they own or follow, companies that they have reason to know inside and out.

Most important, salesmen generally understand the stock market more thoroughly than analysts. They have a clearer view of the so-called big picture and are less likely to lose the forest for the trees. They are in a better position to recognize that the best company is often not the best stock, that a great story is not always a great value. And this kind of understanding is rarer than you might think.

In fact, just the ability to identify an intelligent idea and get it across coherently is a rare talent. Especially when you're sitting at a long desk with about twenty square feet of your own, with people talking and yelling around you. In this environment, you tend to develop tunnel thinking, somewhat oblivious to the noise and even to the people around you. One time, I accidently lit my wastebasket on fire and had to drown it with my tea. The guy sitting next to me didn't even notice the flames and the smoke. (Unfortunately, the smoke started to spread, creating a minipanic; I took the diplomatic route of acting ignorant. The "source" of the smoke was finally located, an air vent about twelve feet away from me. While the experts fixed this imaginary problem, I just went about my business wearing my best "nobody here but us chickens" look.)

But even with the noise, distractions, and other disadvantages of the trading floor, it did have some good points, the biggest being the traders themselves.

On the equity side, there are several types of trader. The "block traders" execute orders to buy and sell those stocks that are traded on the stock exchanges around the country, the largest by far being the New York Stock Exchange (NYSE). The orders for these "listed" stocks are transmitted from the clients to our trading desk at 60 Broad to the floor of the stock exchange, and each is executed by the specialist for that particular stock. Specialists are responsible for maintaining "orderly markets" in their stocks, putting together buyers and sellers, or stepping in as the buyer or seller of last resort.

Once the orders are filled, they are communicated back to the trading floor, and the clients are told what was done and at what prices. Often, the client is the firm itself, buying or selling stocks with its own money for its own account. These decisions are handled by the "position traders."

Unfortunately, position trading is generally a losing proposition for Wall Street. Position traders are usually in the business of helping clients and losing money. For example, if a large institutional investor wants to sell 300,000 shares of General Motors, and there are only buyers in the market for 200,000 shares, the client might ask the firm to buy the remaining 100,000 shares for its own account.

This is normally an unwelcomed request, for a simple reason. The firm ends up with 100,000 shares that it now wants to get rid of, but there are no buyers left. Supply and demand being what they are, the price is likely to go down, unless someone new steps up to buy in size or some unexpected good news comes to the rescue.

To make matters worse, the firm doesn't make much on the two hundred thousand GM shares that it was able to find a buyer for, known as "agency trading." Let's say that the equity desk negotiated a commission of eight cents per share; the firm gets $16,000 for the two hundred thousand shares it sold to others and $8,000 for the one hundred thousand shares it was stuck with. If the price declines by one-half—less than 1 percent—the loss on that one hundred thousand–share position is $50,000, or twice what it received in total commissions.

Grim business.

The "over-the-counter traders" are similar to the position traders; they buy and sell shares for their own account, in their case, shares of companies not listed on any exchange. A stock traded over the counter (OTC) is usually assigned two or three "market makers" at different firms; these traders are responsible, as you might guess, for making markets in the OTC names. This involves giving bids to customers who want to sell and making offers to those who want to buy. Their business is generally profitable, more like specialists than position traders.

Drexel traders prided themselves on being regular guys—most had worked their way onto the desk from clerical jobs in the back office. College degrees were rare, MBAs were distrusted, and bullshit was held to a minimum.

There was also an underlying machismo that had survived the 1970s and 1980s. Alan Alda would've felt uncomfortable on the desk, and Richard Simmons would've been pummeled. In fact, Wall Street at all levels liked the tough-guy image; even Fred Joseph, a polite, refined man, hunted deer with bow and arrow, and was once overheard telling his investment bankers at a high-yield bond conference: "If you can't write a ton of business in this place, it's like not being able to get laid in a whorehouse."

On the trading floor, bad taste was always in style. A salesman recalled one of I. W. Burnham's visits to the ninth floor: "[An OTC trader] yelled, 'Hey, Stubby!' Mr. Burnham, being the aristocratic gentleman that he is, replied, 'I beg your pardon.' The trader yelled back, 'Hey, Stubby, you run this joint? I got to tell you a few things I don't like about this place.'"

Once, a stripper showed up for a trader's birthday, paralyzing the whole floor and costing the firm thousands of dollars in lost business. (The guys on the Coast tried the same routine for Milken's fortieth birthday—Michael never left his phone, and his eyes never left his desk. And the stripper never returned.)

The trading floor was always in motion, to use a tired cliché. But it was also on the move, literally. During the 1980s, to accommodate the increase in trading personnel, the various departments moved from the east side of the ninth floor to the west side and then back again. With each move, miles of wiring connected beneath the elevated floor had to be reconfigured and rerouted.

In later years, my desk was located near the absolute corner of the trading floor, which occupied a space about the size of a football field. To my left and in front were the other institutional salespeople of my department, occupying three rows. Beyond them were the block and position traders spread out around the semblance of a large, X-shaped desk—it was the East Coast's version of Milken's layout. Next to them, in one long row, were the "options traders." Farther down were the OTC traders and those who traded international stocks (until they were fired in April 1989).

If you looked across the floor, you could see a tremendous diversity of people: WASPs, Jews, Catholics, Italians, Irishmen, you name it. Blacks were certainly underrepresented, particularly in positions of authority. Whether this reflected direct prejudice—and I'm speaking of all brokerage firms now—or some perception that clients would be uncomfortable is unknown and, in the final analysis, irrelevant. The same walls that Jewish bankers faced a century ago are facing blacks now, and they've got their work cut out for them.

Women traders had it tough—they just weren't entirely accepted. But saleswomen and female analysts faced a mixed bag. Some were the victims of male chauvinism; others benefited from a form of reverse discrimination. Those who played up to the egos and the insecurities of male managers and clients often received favored treatment. It wasn't that either party acted or reacted consciously. It wasn't that Wall Street was necessarily any different from anywhere else. It just was.

Another fact of life for salesmen, analysts, and traders was T&E: travel and entertainment. Fortunately, most of my clients were in the northeast, so few trips lasted more than a day. They normally involved escorting an analyst to various meetings with various clients.

The overwhelming majority of these business trips were very much as you would guess: routine, productive, and dull. Occasionally, with bad planning and bad luck—missed trains, delayed flights, late clients—even a day trip could last a lifetime.

Once on a trip to Pennsylvania, the analyst and I got so lost we had to ask for directions at a gas station. Off we went, and promptly got lost again. After another thirty minutes of driving around, we stopped again for directions, only to find ourselves back at the same gas station as before.

My favorite fiasco was a 1987 visit to New Jersey with our chemical analysts. These two analysts had just joined the firm from Dean Witter and were considered heavy hitters. I had invited along a friend of mine to drive, to reduce the chances that we'd end up wrapped around a tree. At breakfast, we realized that the handouts were still in the car, but we didn't know where the car and its driver were.

Once I had found the handouts, we faced the next problem: the handouts themselves. Some of the figures were so small that they were virtually impossible to read, especially at eight in the morning. Then the check arrived, and my credit card was rejected, although fortunately, not in front of the analysts. (The clients were friends and wouldn't have been surprised.)

We began the next appointment by locking the keys—and of course, the handouts—in the car with the engine running. I sat through the meeting, picturing my friend trying to break into the car with a coat hanger on the other side of the conference room wall some forty feet away.

Our one o'clock lunch meeting in Newark didn't involve lunch, so by the time we arrived at our three o'clock meeting we were desperate. I only had enough change for two candy bars, which the analysts didn't think to share. And to round things out, my sales manager gave me grief for taking this high-priced talent to New Jersey before they had even met with the major New York accounts. He even threatened to fire me if it happened again, a strangely hollow ultimatum that added the perfect finishing touch to the trip.

At times like this, it was absurd to tell myself that I had a great job, but even such mixups didn't change the basic fact that I was fortunate to be where I was. As an institutional salesman, I was given a desk, a phone, analysts to tap for ideas and information, accounts to cover, and a good deal of freedom to say what I wanted when I wanted. I didn't have to risk my own money, and I was paid more than the average guy working as hard, or harder.

There were also fancy lunches to remind us all how lucky we were to be a part of the Street. At these lunches, analysts or invited guests would speak, and there would often be a sense in the room that we all belonged to a special club. Occasionally, these lunches were worth the three hours out of your day; more often, they were a waste of time and money.

If nothing else, Wall Street did more than its share to support the witty and the wise, the expert speakers who shot up on the Metroliner from the nation's capital, entertained and enlightened for about an hour (for about $10,000), and returned home a little better off for the experience.

The most impressive was Barber Conable, currently the president of the World Bank, articulate and humorous, who told us in 1984 not to underestimate Walter Mondale because "his choice of vice-president was certainly better than Jimmy Carter's." The most irritating if witty speaker was Mark Shields, political pundit and raconteur, who predicted in 1988 that Dukakis would win, took his fee, and returned to his happy place on a weekly TV show, from which he could righteously criticize Drexel.

In addition to lunches, there were shows and other events to enjoy with clients. And there were boondoggles in places like Puerto Rico and Captiva Island and Vail, opportunities for clients to spend time with managers, and salesmen with clients. Which raised a difficult question: At what point does the valid process of entertaining clients—after all, people prefer to do business with people they know and trust—slip into the invalid?

For one of our lesser competitors, the question was easily answered: it—or more precisely, its salesman—had long ago blitzkrieged through the invalid into the embarrassing and illegal. As one Drexel salesman recalled, "I met with the director of research from this midwestern account, a distinguished-looking guy puffing on his pipe, and he said to me, 'I think you do an excellent job, and I like your research, but what I really like is ———. With them, I get into the back of a limo, and there's a girl in there, and she takes down my pants, and pulls my pud.' "

In comparison to those guys, my department was in Mr. Rogers's neighborhood. Money was spent ethically, if sometimes extravagantly. Perhaps the greatest waste was an annual ritual known as the megaclub, in which the salespeople who had reached a certain level of commissions would get a free long weekend at some resort. If the question earlier was where to draw the line, the question here was practical: Why do it at all?

The motivation argument was a weak one, because these people were paid a percentage of their commissions and, therefore, already had a reason to maximize business. The argument that it was important to develop relationships with clients didn't even exist, because no clients were invited.

Perhaps the biggest drawback was that this freebie went to those whose success may have been as much a reflection of their accounts as of their abilities. Total commissions are not always the best measure of a salesperson's success. Because institutional accounts split up their commission business among the various Wall Street firms, market share is often the better guide. Ask yourself: Who's the better salesman, the one with $150,000 in commissions—15 percent of the business from an account that pays Wall Street $1 million a year in total commissions—or the one with $200,000—2 percent market share from an account that generates $10 million in annual commissions?

The major reason for the megaclub was probably the worst one: It allowed the managers and the major producers of the department to enjoy a free one on the house. It was a ritual repeated throughout Wall Street, a tradition that preceded and continued through the glory days of rising markets and rising profits.

These glory days, the bull markets in stocks and bonds, fattened the profit margins of the brokerage houses in three ways: gains on the securities held by the firms, more trading by the clients, and a greater volume of new offerings of stocks and bonds.

New offerings are usually a bull market phenomenon, especially in the stock market. Rising prices encourage companies to sell stock, because they get more money for each share—this is common sense. Rising prices also encourage investors to buy shares, since people have a dangerous habit of assuming that the good times will continue—this is greed.

The first wave of new issues in the 1980s was in 1983, when speculators developed a seemingly insatiable appetite for small companies, particularly small technology names. These types of stock had been rising sharply since the bear market of 1974, and almost a decade later, had become the darlings of the market.

The wave peaked out in the second half of 1983. One expert argued that the actual turning point was a new issue called Muhammed Ali Arcades, an unusual concept whose original investors evidently didn't include the champ himself. This particular deal defined that moment in time when a crowd stops and subconsciously asks itself: What's wrong with this picture?

Plenty, as it turned out. The shares of these small new issues plummeted in price, as the reality of poorly conceived business plans intruded on the blind hopes of speculators. Sadly, and predictably, the players who were hurt the worst were small retail customers, people unfamiliar with investing and reliant on sometimes unscrupulous outside advice.

Drexel Burnham had little participation in the 1983 boom, because it didn't have a strong reputation in small technology stocks. Companies prefer to sell their shares through a firm that is well known in their industries. Drexel's relative absence from the boom, and subsequent bust, was a blessing. The firm didn't accumulate the bad will that accrued to those who underwrote these small-cap tragedies.

In the 1984–1986 period, by contrast, Drexel was a major player in stock offerings, in large part because of Michael Milken. He had established the firm's reputation among middle-size companies, and in some cases, had already sold bonds for them. He had made it possible for managers and raiders to "take companies private," buying up all the public stock with monies raised from junk bonds; later, these same companies were going public again, seeking buyers for their shares. Milken had also contributed mightily to the environment of success that had attracted a corps of aggressive and talented investment bankers.

These bankers arranged stock offerings for some of the more famous companies of the 1980s. This underwriting process included presentations to potential investors, known as "road shows," at 60 Broad Street and throughout the Drexel system. As an institutional equity salesman for the firm, I had the opportunity to meet several of the decade's top financial celebrities.

There was Carl Lindner, the billionaire investor/raider/Baptist who leaned over and politely introduced himself in a quiet, gentle voice, evidently unaware that I, and everyone else in the room, knew exactly who he was.

There was Saul Steinberg, the enfant terrible of the 1960s, who had prospered after his takeover attempt of Chemical Bank had been crushed; when his private insurance company, Reliance, went public, he asked potential investors to be his partners, although his squeeky voice and not-so-squeeky reputation didn't help his case. Almost four years later, the shares of his company have fallen by 50 percent from the offering price, while the stock market has risen by 50 percent.

There was Bill Farley, the corporate builder who was considering a bid for public office (the presidency, no less) and who already had a politician's talent for giving me the willies. His company, Fruit of the Loom, took three years to earn what it was supposed to earn in one, but it eventually became a success story, benefiting from the popularity of its new products and the skills of its managers.

There was Frank Lorenzo, with a quiet, some say ruthless, intensity, who structured a huge airline, and made his name synonymous with union busting. His wife once described him as "just a simple guy who likes to buy companies," while organized labor viewed him as evil incarnate. As a newscaster might say, he reaped the wind when he voluntarily put Continental into bankruptcy to cut wages, and sowed the whirlwind when he was forced to put Eastern into bankruptcy to pay creditors.

There was Rupert Murdoch, the urbane, impressive media baron from Australia, who was building a newspaper and television empire on three continents. His $1.1 billion purchase of six Metromedia TV stations formed the basis for an increasingly viable fourth network.

There was Ted Turner, the folksy, less impressive media baron from Atlanta, who had tried to buy CBS and had once suggested that if Drexel would raise the money, he'd buy Russia. But if Turner himself seemed offbeat, his track record was clearly on the money. "He's inately a genius," commented media analyst John Reidy. "He's worth a billion-five, and he's the major factor in cable."

There was Richard Bernstein, the recent owner of Golden Books and its stable of titles like *The Poky Little Puppy;* he smoked cigarettes with such ferocity that it seemed he would suck out the filter. After the price of his company's shares plummeted due to disappointing results soon after the offering, Bernstein returned to speak to the Drexel sales force with a claim of naïveté that came across as contrived and cynical.

There was Bob Pittman, only twenty-seven at that time, who had created Music Television (MTV) and could have easily sold shares of stock in himself. There was the management team of McCaw Cellular Communications, which raised billions of dollars from stock and bond offerings, even though they were so young that a man sitting near me commented, "They seem like nice boys."

There were great Drexel deals, such as an offering of Telex stock in 1981 to skeptical investors at less than $5 per share, which would rise almost twentyfold at its peak. There were awful deals, none worse than the sale of stock with warrants for Flight Transportation, a company that was accused of fraud and whose chief exec unwittingly taught me a memorable lesson: Never invest with anyone who wears sunglasses indoors. (Drexel reimbursed its clients for almost all losses caused by this fiasco, at a cost of $7 million.)

There were public partnerships, primarily sold by other firms, that were designed for small unsophisticated investors, to their regret. "Wall Street in general has done a lousy job of selecting and selling limited partnerships," acknowledged Howard L. Clark to *The Wall Street Journal.* (Clark had replaced Peter Cohen in January 1990 as the chief executive officer of brokerage giant Shearson Lehman Hutton.) Some $85 billion of these public limited partnerships were sold in the 1980s—this figure does not include the totals for *private* investment partnerships that were sold to supposedly sophisticated individuals during the decade.

All in all, there was no aspect of this business that put salesmen in a more difficult position than the selling of deals. New offerings are approximately *ten times* more profitable to Wall Street firms and their salesmen than normal trades. Managers want the deals done, and "selling the calendar" is always a top priority; salespeople want the commissions, and the praise that leads to new accounts and to greater commissions in the future.

But a salesman must not only look after the interests of his firm; he must also look after those of his clients. In theory, there isn't any conflict: Wall Street wants to give the best advice possible, and clients want to get the best advice. With deals, however, theory can take a beating because new issues are usually not great buys. The shares of new issues are rarely underloved and undervalued and, historically, they are below-average performers in the market.

Should a salesman sell a deal that the firm wants sold, even if there are better ideas available? There is a case to be made that a salesman's first priority is to his firm, and that new offerings are the lifeblood of an otherwise unprofitable business. There is a better case to be made, however, that the clients' interests should be paramount and that good advice is in the firm's best long-term interest—credibility is a hard-won asset that can pay off handsomely, even if it never seems to.

Warren Buffett, the chairman of Berkshire Hathaway and this country's premier investor, recently wrote about one of his companies, the *Buffalo News,* and the trade-offs between profits now and profits later. His discussion could have easily applied to Wall Street itself. Both the *News* and the Street provide a valuable service that relies on the unique expertise of its people. And both face a balancing act between short-run and long-run profits.

In the case of the *News,* the emphasis has been on long-term profits, focusing on more news and less advertising. This has hurt its immediate profitability, but has created a better product that will benefit future profitability.

In the case of the Street, the emphasis has been on short-term profits, focusing on ideas that produce the greatest commissions and fees, but not necessarily the best results. This has helped its profitability in any given year, but has hurt its reputation with its customers. The selling of deals, in short, creates a problem.

Different institutional salesmen dealt with this problem in different ways. A few avoided deals, although this approach didn't do wonders for their current or future incomes. Many tried to focus on the occasional pearls; the problem here was that everyone wanted these likely winners, and the demand for them dwarfed the supply—in these "hot" deals, a client might request 50,000 shares, and receive 1,000.

Many salespeople sold the deals as best they could, out of loyalty to their firm and to themselves. They weren't being malicious; almost certainly, they cared about their clients. They just let themselves believe in the deals they sold, because they wanted to believe and because it was easy to believe.

The investment bankers, whose loyalties were to the companies they represented, would come to them with enticing stories of the future prospects for a growing industry, for a great new product, for a dramatic earnings turnaround. They provided projections that justified the prices that were being asked, forecasts that were detailed and well reasoned.

And when those forecasts proved optimistic, and the reality fell short of the projections, there were always good explanations. The salespeople could point fingers of blame at the investment bankers who had misled them, and be righteously indignant.

But, over time, this line of reasoning becomes a weak excuse. Good salespeople recognize that an investment banker is under great pressure to get his deal done; more than that, he wants the deal done at close to the lofty price he had predicted when he was bidding for the company's business. Good salespeople recognize that the optimistic forecasts may be more a best-case scenario than a most-likely one. And they treat these great forecasts with great skepticism.

Skepticism was not only the stock in trade of good salesmen, it was also a part of any successful money manager's portfolio. Our clients knew—or should have known—that new issues were more likely to perform poorly and that the projections for the future should be taken with a huge grain of salt.

Those institutional investors who bought deals were smart enough to know the odds. Some of them tried to shift these odds in their favor, by selling their positions in the new issues on the offering day. They took advantage of a fact of life in new offerings: A brokerage firm that underwrites a deal has a responsibility to support the price of the shares for several days.

Therefore, a client can play a "heads I win, tails I break even" game. If the stock price rises after an offering, the client can "flip" his shares for a quick profit; if demand in the aftermarket is weak and the broker has to support the price, the client can usually sell his shares back at no loss.

From the viewpoint of the broker, however, a flipper is a pain in the ass, a client who isn't interested in owning the shares he buys. There were two ways to deal with this problem. One was to use the miracle of computerized trading, and track down which accounts were selling shares after the offering. Then the firm could take back the large commissions that flowed to the salesmen on these accounts; after all, a salesman shouldn't profit at the expense of his firm, and it's reasonable to assume that most salesmen knew which of their accounts were legitimate buyers and which were flippers.

Another approach was pioneered, it seems, by none other than Milken, although no one ever owned up to it. This approach was simple and effective: Support the price of a new issue at a level below the offering price. That way, if clients wanted to flip their shares, they took a loss.

Although flipping was an unpleasant reality, the blame here lies primarily with the salesmen, not the clients. Institutional investors couldn't be expected to pass up the opportunity for an easy profit, faced as they were by tremendous, and unfair, pressures to outperform the market. Their performance was measured every three months, a time frame that precludes investing in any real sense of the word.

In any three-month period, stocks will rise or fall for many reasons, only one of which involves valuation. In that short time period, stocks will sell for what the crowd is willing to pay for them, and the driving factors may be fear and greed, not logic. As the great author and investor Benjamin Graham once noted: In the short run, the stock market is a voting machine, a reflection of popularity; in the long run, it is a weighing machine, a reflection of reality.

Some of the best minds in the country, therefore, were forced to become speculators, trying to make educated guesses on which stocks would rise or fall in the near future. Rather than buying cheap and selling dear, they were under pressure to outguess what everyone else would be buying or selling. It's as if they found themselves in a car race in which all the drivers watched each other instead of the track.

Naturally, institutional investors have wills of their own, and there was no law that required a short-term mentality. But those who ignored the focus on quarterly performance were at risk of losing their clients, primarily pension funds. The treasurers of pension funds are not experts on the market and are susceptible to the foolish hope of great results every quarter of every year.

This problem is exacerbated by the advisers to pension funds, who would look fairly useless if they simply counseled patience, even though this is often the best advice. In addition, the impressive qualities of money managers in general—knowledgeable, articulate, persuasive—encourage pension funds to believe that beating the market in the short term is less of a challenge than it actually is.

The result was a strange but carefully balanced world of misplaced priorities, in which both Wall Street and its clients found themselves trying to make money quickly and letting the long term take care of itself. Which, unfortunately, it did.

The Street's priorities led to a boom in profitability when the deals—with their enticing commissions and not-so-enticing fundamentals—were plentiful. These same priorities led to a decline, even disappearance of profits, as the deals soured, leaving clients with the bitter taste of hard-earned money wasted.

These priorities contributed to the rise and fall of Wall Street in the eyes of its customers, a loss of esteem not easily regained.

CHAPTER EIGHT

THE CITY ON
THE EDGE OF FOREVER

"Jim, do you realize what you've done?"

—DR. McCoy, CHIEF MEDICAL OFFICER,
STARSHIP *Enterprise*

The last chapter was description; this one is dialogue: a fictional conversation with a favorite client, a portfolio manager with some $60 million in stocks. The events are based on facts—some past, some future—telescoped into one morning's call . . .

—This is Walt.
　　Hi, Walt. Dan.

—How are you?
　　Fine, how you doing?

—Okay, I guess.
　　Where were you yesterday?

—I had a board meeting. Took the whole morning.
　　How'd it go?

—It's the same old b.s. I try to explain what we're doing, but they don't understand.
　　Well, I don't envy you trying.

—Yeah, it's pretty frustrating.

  How was your weekend?

—Good. The boys are starting baseball now that the basketball season is over.

  You still playing basketball on Sundays?

—No, that ended last week. How was your weekend?

  I went to some black-tie function the other night, Friday, a big thing for the Air/Space Museum. You'd think of all the charities to support—of course, they got to use the ship, which probably wasn't a coincidence.

—What ship is that?

  Oh, it's a World War Two aircraft carrier that's been put to bed, turned into a museum.

—How was the party?

  All right, I guess. Kind of, I don't know—all those yuppies crammed together. Can you imagine what one U-boat could've done.

—I think it could have done a lot of good.

  Yeah, maybe. You ever notice how the preppy types have such . . . great hair?

—Isn't that your group?

  No, but I'm jealous. That must be some gene pool up in Connecticut. Anyway, what are you buying?

—Nothing. The main fund is seventeen percent in cash, and we may go up to twenty percent. I don't like the market here. But it's not easy [sitting on cash when the market's rising]. We underperformed the averages by two point two percent in the first quarter, and we're trailing by another one point eight percent for the first six weeks of this quarter.

  Ignore all that short-term stuff—just worry about investing.

—I wish I could. But I had to explain to the board why I'm lagging this year, and it's not a lot of fun.

  If you're thinking about raising cash, what would you sell?

—I'm not sure. We may lighten up on the cyclicals, since I think the economy is heading for trouble.

  Any names in particular?

—Some of the steels, and maybe a little GM.

Well, Rand is negative on GM, and he's a great stock picker. You know, I was going through an old article from 1975, and it talked about some bright young analyst who had been right on the auto stocks, and it was him—over a decade ago.

—Yeah, he's one of the best.

What price were you looking to sell the GM?

—I'm not sure, maybe seventy-two.

Do you want me to put in a seventy-two limit [sell at a price of $72 per share, or better] for you?

—No, I'll have Leonard [his trader] call Joe [our trader].

I'll let Joey know.

—Okay.

Anyway, you didn't miss much yesterday. Our economist talked again about the unemployment numbers that came out on Friday—said the same basic things: payroll numbers weaker than expected . . . still looking for the strong bond market near term, then heading down as the economy picks up in the second half. Nothing new there. He was in again this morning to talk about the updated numbers on the first quarter's GNP [gross national product]; they came out about a half hour ago. Did you see them?

—Sure. They seemed to be in line.

Yeah, they were. Consumption a little stronger than expected. Inventories a bit weaker than he thought, which is a good sign for a second half pickup in the economy [as companies rebuild their supplies]. The bond market just opened a little weaker on the news, down about twenty ticks [twenty–thirty-seconds or about two-thirds of 1 percent].

There was some stuff on investment strategy as well. We're still positive on the market, no change there. Did you read the last strategy piece?

—I glanced at it. Did you get Salvigsen's latest piece? [Stan Salvigsen is a top-notch investment strategist, who writes about the economy and the markets with his partner, Mike Aronstein.]

No, I don't get his stuff until you send it to me.

—I'll send you a copy. It was a good one; it's called "The Briar Patch Effect."

　　What did it say?

—He still thinks we're in big trouble with the debt.

　　Is he as negative as before?

—More than ever. He thinks we're facing possible deflation [and depression] at some point. He talks about the dangers from all the government guarantees—like the S&Ls—that have only made things worse [by encouraging bad lending and, accordingly, bad debts].

　　So he's still buying T-bonds [treasury bonds]?

—Sure.

　　Send it along. Anyway, we've got a few interesting ideas today. No new recommendations, which is kind of surprising for a Tuesday. Jerry talked about the Cippalone [tobacco liability] trial, which should be decided any time now—it's gone to jury. I think Philip Morris [the number one tobacco company] is a good buy. I mean, I wouldn't want these guys as friends, but the company does throw off a ton of cash.

　　They've never lost a [product liability] case, but that's not the real issue. Jerry [our tobacco analyst] was saying that they could afford to lose one case a week at one million dollars a shot, and still pay all their legal costs for the year by January third.

　　The important thing is that a class action suit against them isn't going to happen, and without that, the litigation question isn't really a factor. Plus, think about it, if you sue tobacco companies for selling cigarettes, why not sue liquor companies? What's the difference? Or why not sue cereal companies for selling sugar to kids? Where do you draw the line?

　　Anyway, the numbers are great. The company earned almost eight dollars [per share] last year, and it should earn over nine dollars this year. And the free cash flow [the money earned over and above the company's needs] should be an additional eight or nine a share. That's pretty damn impressive for a stock selling close to eighty.

　　One of my smarter clients made the point that if you looked at [Philip] Morris's financials and covered up the name, it would look like a screaming buy. Also, Peter Lynch [the former manager of the top-rated Magellan Fund] has pointed out that, over time, the stock price of a company tends to track its earnings, and earnings here should grow fifteen to twenty percent for the foreseeable future.

—You like the analyst, don't you?

Yeah, he's good at what he does. Works hard, thinks it through. Nice guy, too.

As for Morris, he thinks it's cheap long term. Of course, they could go out and overpay for another acquisition like they did in '85 with General Foods. They probably will at some point: Buying General Foods was not too bright, but once they did that, it makes some sense to buy another food company and get the economies of scale with distribution and SG&A [selling, general, and administrative costs]. The shareholders would be a lot better off if they just took all that cash and bought back stock, but even if they don't, the second acquisition wouldn't be as bad as the first.

So it's a good idea: great business—you know how many Marlboro cigarettes alone are sold every year?

—I don't have the slightest idea.

One hundred and twenty *billion.* Twenty percent of all the cigarettes smoked are Marlboros.

And if Congress bans advertising, it would help Philip Morris since they're already the best known. Remember the ban on TV advertising back in the seventies? That helped the tobacco companies. They're all better off if nobody advertises.

Anyway, they have the business, the numbers are powerful, and you have an issue with the trials that is scaring investors, but which isn't really a big long-term negative.

—We already have a pretty full position. We're not going to sell any. Maybe we'll buy more, at some point.

I'll let you know what happens with the trial when the decision comes through.

Scott [our airline analyst] reemphasized his recommendation on UAL and AMR [United and American Airlines]. He puts the breakup value on UAL at a hundred and fifty or more, stock's around a hundred; American's worth about seventy. He makes a good case for them: no new airports, value of the gate slots, a few airlines controlling most of the air traffic. Now that the wars are about over, the survivors can start raising prices. You have any interest in these?

—Not really.

Yeah, I don't like 'em either. I've been so wrong on the airlines for so long, but I can't see changing now. It just seems like a lousy business, needing to spend all that money on new planes. Not much left over for the shareholders.

As someone was saying, it's been a tough group for stockholders to make money in for a helluva long time. Maybe it's going to change now, but if it does, it'll do it without me. [Which is exactly what happened, for a while.]

He also likes Texas Air as a speculative trade—he puts the value of Eastern, net of debt, at sixteen dollars per share or more, and the stock's about twelve. So you're getting Continental Airlines for less than nothing. You ever fly Continental?

—A few times. They don't fly much out of here, and if I go from Chicago, I usually take someone else.

One of our aerospace analysts was in Denver once. He's afraid of flying to begin with, will only go in a [Boeing] seven sixty-seven, and only a new one—he even checks the serial numbers on the plane. Well, his airline—American, I think—canceled the flight because a storm was heading in. So he asks the agent what to do, and she says that she can put him on a Continental flight leaving in a few minutes. So he says, "But I thought you said there was a storm coming." "Yeah," she says, "but they think they can make it."

Harlan was in this morning pushing Penn Central. He's a great analyst, as you know—one of the few that I'd give my money to manage, if I had any.

—Oh, come on. You guys on Wall Street make a fortune.

Mine's pretty well tied up—I still live like a college student.

—I have no sympathy for you guys. None at all.

It *can* get kind of crazy sometimes. We had one analyst who was making maybe thirty thousand a year as a professor. Then he joins us for about a hundred grand. Then he gets hired away for something like three hundred grand. His income went up tenfold in a year.

But someone who's been around for a while made an interesting point. He basically said that people may look like they're getting overpaid now, but this is a feast or famine business, and when things get bad, they get really bad. You and I have seen mostly good times, but there were fifteen lousy years before the party started.

—I still have no sympathy for you guys.

Fair enough, I don't have much either. Hell, a friend of mine in Drexel's training program told me that some guy there expects to be making half a million two years from now—and this clown doesn't even have a job yet.

—I'd like to know where that fellow ends up.

[At another firm.]

Fair enough. Anyway, Harlan's case on Penn Central is simple: the stock's selling for twenty-two, the company has about twenty dollars per share in cash or cash equivalents, and the rest of the businesses are worth maybe fifteen dollars. [Carl] Lindner's one of the smarter guys out there, and he was trying to buy shares at twenty-four. This idea isn't a home run, but there's not much risk, and it makes sense.

Stimpson was in this morning, also. You missed a beauty. He said, "Here's an opportunity for us to do some business," and he suggested swapping out of Federated [Department Stores] and into May [Department Stores]. I have a client that owns a lot of Federated, but I told him that he probably shouldn't listen. There's a bid on the table for Federated [from Campeau Corporation], and in this day and age, deals usually get done. Plus, I didn't like that attitude of trying to get people to do things just to do things. He's a nice guy, and maybe that's not what he meant, but still . . .

—What was the name of your last retail analyst?

You mean Edith Kessler?

—Yeah, where did she end up?

She went over to ——— about a year ago—I'm pretty sure she's still there. You should've seen her make a presentation waving those red fingernails around. Even James, who's the best businessman I know, was mesmerized. I think most of us in this business had a tough adolescence. You were lucky, Walt, getting married when you were, what, sixteen?

—No, I was twenty-two. I'm from Indiana, not India.

Oh, sorry.

—Hey, it's better than New York.

I don't know about that. If you ignore the danger and the dirt . . . and the expense . . . and the generally crummy lifestyle, this a nice place to live.

—Why don't you move out to the real country?

I'm what my friend calls a classic New Yorker: unhappy in the city and miserable everywhere else. So when are you coming to visit?

—I might be there for a conference in July.

That's a good time of year—no humidity. Let me know once you have it set up. We'll see a show or something.

—Fine, I'll know soon.

I'll take you to a Crazy Eddie store—you can tell everyone you meet how you were smart enough to avoid that gem.

—I'm sure glad I did.

What a fiasco. The analyst, you remember him, came in the morning after the company announced that it was getting into home shopping, a big thing back then. He said, and I remember his words, "We should be putting our clients into the stock right here." It opened at twenty-one and something, a new high, and then went down to just about zero. He recommended it all the way down until it hit about five, and then dropped coverage. It's not often that you see a stock lose almost a hundred percent of its value.

If you're interested, Walt, Carrigan's on the hoot-and-holler talking about the insurance stocks. I can get the details and call you back.

—No, the group doesn't show up too well on our momentum work [a type of analysis that focuses on past stock movements to predict future ones].

Well, if the bond market does well these guys should benefit, but as for pricing in the industry, I don't think we're going to tell you first when it improves. By the way, do you remember the insurance analyst we had when you and I first started talking?

—No, I don't think I do.

Once, a long way back—I was pretty new here—this guy was boasting to me about being right on some earnings projection, and I asked him if he wanted to speak on the system. He turned to me and said, "Who the fuck do you think you are, telling me what to do?"

—He sounds like a fun guy to work with.

He was a wild man. I heard that one of the salesmen almost got into a fist fight with him. He was a bright, bright guy, but man, was he arrogant—made some remark about his seven-figure income once. He took in a ton doing corporate finance work [acting as an investment banker advising companies on restructurings, mergers, and acquisitions].

—What's he doing now?

I heard he quit Wall Street for spiritual reasons—he's running a used car dealership in Tibet.

—I sure don't doubt it.

Anyway, on the deal front, it's pretty quiet. The one you should look at is Circus Circus. They're doing a secondary [offering]; the two head guys are selling some of their holdings. That's usually a bad sign [if management is selling, why should you be buying?], but these guys have been selling some of their shares every so often ever since they went public at seven and a half in 1983, and the stock is at thirty-eight now. And, even after the offering, the two of them will still own some sixty percent of the stock.

The casino business is a license to steal, and nobody runs their business better than this company. They're breaking ground on a new casino in Las Vegas, the largest in the world. It's unlikely that they'll be going into Atlantic City any time soon. They don't like the politics and the economics. It's funny: When they came public back in '83, part of the attraction was that they would probably enter Atlantic City; now, part of the attraction is that they won't.

My biggest concern is that we get a nasty recession, especially on the consumer side, and discretionary spending goes down the tubes. But even this might not hurt them as bad as others, since they focus on the small spender. Plus, people might shift their vacations from real places to Vegas.

I've liked this stock since we did the first offering, and the management has treated its shareholders right.

—I'll take a look.

I'll have Sherry send you the red herring [the prospectus].

We also filed one million three hundred and fifty thousand shares of Metcalf & Eddy, involved in water supply and waste-water treatment . . . also handles hazardous and solid waste. It's a great industry, given the mess out there. It's an IPO [initial public offering] and the price range puts the shares at about sixteen times latest twelve months' earnings. Allen [& Company] has the books [they're the lead manager on the deal], and Kidder [Peabody] is a comanager. Corporate finance will be in to talk to us this afternoon, and I'll let you know if it sounds interesting.

—Okay.

As for the others, we've already talked about them.

—Is that it?

Yeah, that's about all. You've been quiet.

—Yeah, I guess so.

Something bothering you?

—It's just the same old stuff.

Like what?

—The other day, we had a problem with one of our holdings: Abbott Labs. This is a classic, just an absolute classic. The stock is down from 48 to 44 in about a week. Nestlè announced that they were entering the baby formula market, and five or six analysts pulled their recommendations. They're afraid that Nestlè's advertising is going to take business from Abbott. But it's not going to happen. I've got two kids and I'll tell you: You feed your baby what your doctor tells you to. And that's where Abbott is strong—with the doctors. We own a position in the stock, and we're probably going to add to it. Down four points in a week and now people pull the recommendations—it really makes me mad. We're just going to have to do our own work, that's all.

Well, you know, we've talked about this before—why don't you just rely on the three or four really great stock pickers at each firm you deal with, the few who consistently outperform the market? If you do that with five or six shops, you'll have about twenty analysts you can rely on.

—It's just the whole business that annoys me. You guys recommend a stock, and then when something goes wrong, you pull it off the list and we get stuck.

First of all, it wasn't us. Second, you're a big boy, and you know by now that these things happen, so you should expect them and avoid them. Analysts are under pressure to be on the winners and off the losers. And clients want ideas that are going to outperform in the next quarter or two, which is ludicrous, but that's what they want.

—I'm just tired of all the whores on Wall Street.

Oh, hell, we have this "whores" discussion every three months, Walter. But like I said, you know the way things are, so why don't you deal with—You know what annoys me? I've talked with you just about every morning for over six years, and some other salesman can call up every now and then, and push the deals and make as much or more.

—Yeah, I know, but we've been cutting back on deals. We do the ones that look good on our work.

I don't want to beat this to death, but I probably will, anyway. People make a living selling stocks, but a killing selling deals.

Some guy from some firm pushes some deal and sends you the internal sales memo [a confidential memo from a firm's investment bankers to its sales force]—which he isn't allowed to do if you haven't noticed—and you do fifty thousand shares on the offering, and you give that firm twenty-five thousand dollars, and you put five grand in his pocket.

And you do fifty thousand shares with us, on some regular stock that seems to make sense, and we make a fraction of that. So do me a favor and don't stick us with everyone else. We've given you some pretty lousy ideas, for sure: that American you-know-what deal in '81 was a lemon, and I really screwed up with the Alloy [Computer offering]—I let myself get caught up in a story I didn't really understand, but you did get out whole. Be angry if you want, but be fair. You've done all right by us.

—No, I'm just fed up with the whole thing. If the deal is hot, we get zip; if it's a dog, we get all the stock we ask for.

Then don't ask for any. Just worry about putting your own kids through college.

—Don't remind me.

Listen, I'll be out till next Tuesday. I'll be finishing up in Omaha for the Berkshire Hathaway annual meeting.

—How much stock do you own?

One share.

—That's it?

Hell, the shares are about forty-five hundred dollars each.

—Yeah, I know.

I just own one share so I can go to the annual meeting and hear Warren Buffett.

—Well, when you see Buffett, ask him about that deal he did with Salomon Brothers.

[The deal was one of the most interesting I saw during eight years on Wall Street, with lessons that went beyond the particulars of this story. As for those particulars: In the middle of 1987, Minerals & Resources, a company controlled by South Africa's Harry Oppenheimer, decided to sell its 14 percent position in Salomon Inc., the parent company of Salomon Brothers. There was little interest in its twenty-one million share stake, but eventually, a potential buyer emerged. That buyer was none other than Ron Perelman, the corporate raider who had built a huge conglomerate through acquisition, the crown jewel being Revlon. The cosmetics company had been taken over, with Drexel's financing and advice, following a bruising battle with the company's management, which was attempting a leveraged takeover of its own.

[The possibility that Perelman would become Solly's largest shareholder had to be a nightmare for Salomon chief exec John Gutfreund. Here was Perelman, a guy who had spent the last decade accumulating companies, and it wasn't likely that he'd be happy with an ownership stake of only 14 percent, regardless of his assurances. And if Perelman decided to bid for control of Salomon, the firm that would probably raise the money for him would be Drexel, Gutfreund's least favorite company on the planet.

[Also, if Perelman went after Salomon, Gutfreund almost certainly couldn't count on the shareholders to support him against Perelman. The stock price of Salomon had already collapsed from over $55 per share to $35 per share in just over a year, a casualty both of a poor market for brokerage stocks and of poor decisions by Solly's management. Stockholders were unlikely to reject a bid of perhaps $50 per share for their shares.

[Gutfreund had a problem. The solution, as he saw it, was for Salomon to repurchase the Minerals & Resources stake at $38 per share and sell a special issue of convertible preferred stock to Buffett. By placing a large issue of preferred stock with Buffet, an issue that could be converted into a significant piece of the common stock, Gutfreund would make a takeover considerably more difficult. There was no agreement from Buffett that he would support Gutfreund in the face of a takeover bid from Perelman, but frankly, there didn't need to be. Buffett's reputation was of a man who stood firmly behind the managements of the companies in which he invested—he would not vote his shares in favor of a takeover.

[But now there was another problem: the numbers didn't make sense. The cost to Salomon would be $809 million to buy back 14 percent of its stock. Then the company would turn around and sell a 12 percent ownership stake to Buffett for $700 million. So far, so good. Solly was buying twenty one million shares at $38, and selling eighteen million at $38—same price at both ends.

[The problem was that the company's costs would increase by about $50 million a year! Buffett would own preferred shares paying $63 million a year in dividends, rather than common shares paying $12 million in annual dividends.

[It was a fiasco. Perelman offered to buy a convertible preferred on more favorable terms to Salomon than it was giving Buffett, but of course, his kind offer was refused. He walked away, and within two months, was probably thanking his lucky stars, as the price of Solly's shares plummeted to seventeen; almost three years later, the stock languishes at twenty-five.]

What would you like me to ask Buffett about the Solly deal, Walter?

—Ask him if the deal was his idea originally, or was it John Gut-freund's.

He's not going to answer that. In fact, I doubt he's going to answer much of anything about that deal. He was offered a great bargain, and he took it; he did right by his shareholders.

—Do you think Michael Milken had anything to do with Perel-man's interest in Salomon Brothers?

It's a damn good question, and I don't know. It's no secret that Solly and Drexel hate each other. Maybe this was going to be the Milkman's ultimate "in your face" shot. It also would've been a smart move to finance a takeover of Solly—new manage-ment, new relationship. A good investment. And when it comes to investing, there are very few people in his league.

He's actually got a lot in common with Buffett—disciplined, motivated. Both are geniuses, which sure as hell doesn't hurt. Common sense. Confidence. Not much interest in following the crowd. Not much interest in this conversation, either.

—What do you mean?

I can tell I'm boring you.

—Not really. When is the Buffett meeting?

Next Monday. I'm just going for the day.

—But you're out for the week.

Taking some vacation.

—You can't do that. Remember what happened the last time you did?

CHAPTER NINE

THE MISSILES
OF OCTOBER

This is the end of capitalism as we know it.

—A STOCK TRADER, OCTOBER 20, 1987

Walking off the plane, I was in for a rude awakening: The headline read: "Stock Prices Fall on a Broad Front; Volume is Record." It was Saturday, October 17, 1987, and I was returning from a vacation in Ireland, a week during which I had been oblivious to the growing chaos on Wall Street. *The New York Times* brought me back to reality in a hurry. "Dow Drops 108.36." In five trading days, the Dow Jones Industrial Average had fallen by 235 points, almost 5 percent of its total value.

The scary part of the equation was not how far the market had fallen in a day or a week, but rather how far it might fall when it opened again on Monday. Friday's big loss was the first 100-point decline, and more than half of it came in the last hour and a half. This was a recipe for national fear, the kind of fear that puts institutions and individuals on the phone with their brokers, each giving a variation on the same theme: "Just get me out!"

This kind of fear had been absent during the market's 17.5 percent tumble from its August 25 peak, and seemed to be missing in the decline of Friday, October 16. Saturday's *Times* reflected this lack of serious concern, at least among the pros. "Several experts predicted that the market's recent drop was just a pause before a healthy climb," noted one article.

The question on that Saturday was whether the sentiment of individual stockholders and institutional investors would now be jarred into panic, with everyone heading for the exit at the same time. Was the great bull market of the 1980s over and a bear market now in its place? Within three days, a new question would emerge: Was the financial system itself facing a meltdown?

The bull market in stocks, which had celebrated its fifth anniversary only two months earlier, had been peculiarly unsatisfying for many investors. The market had more than tripled, certainly, but it only seemed easy to make money in retrospect. The "logical" decisions at each point in time had a nasty habit of leading investors down the wrong paths.

Consider August 1982. The country was deep in the worst economic decline since the Great Depression; interest rates were in double digits; and Mexico was on the brink of defaulting on its loans, a default that might trigger a chain reaction of bankruptcies among Third World countries. Meanwhile, the stock market had fallen by 20 percent in a year and languished not far above the level of two decades earlier.

The mood among investors and experts varied between pessimism and catatonia. Those in the market were hurting, and those on the sidelines had little interest in joining the massacre. There didn't seem to be any good reasons to buy stocks, but in fact, there were a few great ones.

The Federal Reserve, which controls the supply of money, began leaning on the spigot in a big way, flooding the financial markets with dollars. The battle against inflation, which it had been fighting since October 1979, had turned in its favor. The economy was in the tank, and the potential catastrophe in Mexico provided yet another reason to get money into the system. Accordingly, the cost of money— interest rates—went down, and bond prices went up.

This lay the foundation for the glorious bull market. Stocks were cheap and the outlook was improving. The market rose by 50 percent within a year, and the pessimism of 1982 was replaced by the optimism of 1983. This optimism approached euphoria when it came to small technology names, and as discussed earlier, the demand was more than satisfied with a crop of new issues.

In the same way that the pessimists of 1982 missed the rally, the optimists of 1983 rode the decline. Stock prices fell by some 20 percent by mid-1984, as interest rates rose sharply in response to our supercharged economy. These high rates succeeded in slowing the country's growth, and rates began falling again in May. In late July, the consensus of pessimism was once again disappointed, as stocks rose quickly and sharply.

Both the stock market and the bond market rose fitfully into April 1986. At that point, bonds peaked (and interest rates bottomed). Stocks went into a yo-yo pattern, rising in June, falling in July, rising in August, falling in September. Those investors who tried to jump in and out of the market once a "trend" was established were whipsawed; everyone else was just knocked off balance.

A sharp two-day decline in September, followed by the Republicans' loss of the Senate and the Boesky scandal, contributed to a level of pessimism not seen since 1982. But instead of fulfilling expectations, the market once again fooled the crowd. Stocks rose by 50 percent between November 1986 and August 1987.

They rose in spite of rising interest rates, which had climbed by two percentage points since the spring. Because bonds compete with stocks as investments, the higher rates made stocks an increasingly unattractive place to invest. But no matter—the market was riding the wave of the Greater Fool Theory, the expectation that someone somewhere would have the cash and the desire to pay more for stocks in the future. The most likely prospects, Wall Street prophesized, were the Japanese, with their yen to spend and their yen to spend it here.

On August 24 and 25, the market rose sharply to new all-time highs, and then quietly worked lower over the next six weeks. Investors were unconcerned. Even a ninety-point decline in the Dow on October 6 was treated with apathy by the vast majority of experts. After all, hadn't every decline in the last five years proven a buying opportunity?

But this time was different. Investors, having spent years reluctantly absorbing one lesson, were about to learn another: Overvalued stocks decline, and often with a vengeance. Valuation may take a while to assert itself, but it always does.

The catalyst for the decline might be invisible as it was in August, or apparent for all to see as it was in October. The week preceding Monday, October 19 provided two such catalysts that were body blows to the market. Both originated from Washington. Congressman Dan Rostenkowski, the head of the powerful House Ways and Means Committee, proposed an idea designed to raise the cost of takeovers. Because takeovers were the bread and butter of the market's spectacular and speculative recent runup—"Every stock was in play," recalled a NYSE floor trader—any measure to slow them down was flirting with disaster.

The other blow was delivered on Sunday as *The New York Times* headlined "an abrupt policy shift" from the Reagan administration, which would now allow the dollar to fall in value. Normally, a falling dollar is beneficial for stocks to the extent it's inflationary, and stocks rise with inflation.

The concern, however, was that our economic relationship with a major trading partner, West Germany, was moving from cooperative to confrontational. Treasury Secretary James Baker in particular was upset with the actions of the West German central bank, which on Wednesday had raised its benchmark interest rate for the fourth time in several months.

How instrumental either of these events was in creating the crash is unknown and perhaps irrelevant. What mattered was that stocks were selling for more than they were worth, and the greed that had sustained their prices for a time had now been displaced by fear. And because fear is the stronger emotion, the decline would likely be swifter than the advance.

"By the end of the week, everybody was long and wrong," according to a trader, meaning that investors owned stocks and were better off if they hadn't. Arriving at 60 Broad early on the morning of Monday the nineteenth, I was expecting bad news, and the early reports were certainly grim. The foreign markets, which had opened before ours, were getting battered. "Everybody in Europe and Japan was trying to unload American stocks," the trader remembered. This heavy selling overseas assured that the U.S. market's opening was going to be ugly.

More than that, it was a nightmare. The first indication of just how bad things might be came within a minute of the opening bell, when the futures market opened in Chicago. The S&P futures market is a proxy for the stock market, and its opening price implied an *immediate* decline of over 4 percent! Already, the market was down by the same amount as it had fallen on Friday.

One institutional fixed income salesman recalled walking over to our OTC trading desk around 10:00 A.M. "Look over here," an OTC trader said, showing him a stack of tickets a foot and a half thick, three to four hundred orders waiting to be executed. Individual investors, which own the bulk of OTC stocks, wanted out.

While the stock market was in panic, the bond market was in disarray. In the government bond market, a trade of treasury bonds is easily done: A bid for the bonds is made by a bond trader, and if the client accepts it, the trade is over. But that is on a normal day, and October 19 was not a normal day.

A major client called up his Drexel fixed income salesman that morning, and asked for a bid on $13 million T-bonds, not a large order for this market. The salesman called up the trading desk and was told, "We can't give you a bid—we don't know where the market is. We can take an order (to sell the bonds once we find out a fair price]."

The salesman relayed the news to the client. "You know I never give an order in the government bond market," replied the client. "I can get (these trades) executed anywhere."

"Not today."

Soon afterward, the client called back: "Take an order."

Back at the stock market, the situation had slipped from hopeless to impossible. By 11:00 A.M., only one and a half hours into the trading day, the average stock was 8 percent below its Friday closing price. A powerful rally followed, cutting the decline in half. At this point, Drexel's head trader made a fateful decision.

Believing that the worst was behind the market, he announced that the trading desk was going to make a big bet on an upside move—the desk bought stock index futures. His gamble would cost the firm $25 million.

"There was a sense on the floor that (the rally) was bullshit," recalled one of the NYSE traders, who didn't share the optimism of Drexel's head trader. "Right or wrong, you had to get some liquidity. The momentary lift was just a gift from the gods. The first rally always fails; the only ones who didn't sell were morons."

Around 1:00, Richard Phelan, the president of the NYSE, suggested that the exchange might close before the end of normal trading hours, creating a feeling of panic that the exits, however narrow, might be shut entirely. The market fell another 4 percent in an hour. At 2:15, it was down by 13 percent on the day. Already the scapegoats were being lined up; according to *Time,* a man climbed on a car, yelling, "Down with Reagan. Down with MBA's. Down with yuppies."

The last hour was bizarre—the market just sank, minute by minute. "It wasn't as wild as people would think," remembered a senior trader on our desk. "It was busy, very busy. Everyone was thinking, 'It'll stop here . . . it'll bounce here . . . can you believe this?' "

In the institutional sales department, I sat quietly like many others, and watched as the prices on my Quotron machine fell, and then fell further. People didn't call and people didn't seem to make calls. What was there to say? History might have been happening, but at the time, there was a sense of unreality, as if those numbers on the Quotron screen had become unhinged from the actual world. As if we were all watching a plane suddenly lose its ability to fly and slowly, unbelievably but inevitably, tumble out of the sky.

On the floor of the exchange, there were no buyers—none. As for the sellers, their orders reflected an edge of desperation: "Sell one hundred thousand McDonalds . . . if you can't, sell one hundred thousand Reynolds . . . if you can't, sell one hundred thousand Coke."

The big names got mauled, not because they were inferior stocks, but because at least they could get sold at some price. In the over-the-counter market, some trading desks refused to answer their phones. Because a market maker in an OTC stock is required to make a bid, many simply hid from their clients. To the credit of Drexel's OTC traders, they answered the phones, even though it meant losses.

Black Monday suffered from a series of factors that fed on the decline and contributed to it, that forced investors and speculators to sell stocks regardless of their underlying values.

The biggest factor was the feeding frenzy of portfolio insurance and program trading. Portfolio insurance was designed to protect an institution against a significant decline in the market. The idea was simple: If the market fell by a certain amount, a computer would automatically sell stock index futures, thereby protecting the current value of the portfolio.

Unfortunately, portfolio insurance, some $60 billion of it at the time of the crash, had a difficult time dealing with the real world. The initial declines in the market triggered the selling of futures, which quickly made the futures cheaper than the actual stocks they represented. The program traders then stepped in to take advantage of this discrepancy. They bought the cheap futures and sold the relatively more expensive stocks, locking in a risk-free profit.

But the decline in stock prices that resulted from this program trading triggered additional selling of futures by portfolio insurers. Unless investors step in at some point, the computers can create something of a downward spiral. But average investors—individual and professional—were unwilling to buy stocks until they stopped falling; if anything, they wanted to get whatever they had in the market out.

Some of them had to get out, like it or not. Individuals who had bought stocks with borrowed money received "margin calls," forcing them to sell unless they put up more money.

Mutual funds needed to raise cash to pay their clients—individual investors who had decided that the market wasn't for them, after all. Also, these funds needed liquidity to meet the anticipated, if unpredictable, redemptions of investors who would be calling once they heard of Monday's massacre on the evening news.

Some specialists on the floor of the New York Stock Exchange and the American Stock Exchange were facing the possibility of bankruptcy. The stocks they had accumulated as part of their obligation as buyer of last resort were in a near free-fall that Monday afternoon, and their capital was being rapidly depleted. They were forced to sell what they could when they could.

By the time the bell rang at four o'clock, the market was down 22.8 percent. This was almost twice the decline in the Crash of 1929. In dollar terms, the stock market had lost $500 billion in one day, and $1 trillion in two months.

President Reagan reacted to the debacle by trying to reassure the public. "I don't think anyone should panic, because all the economic indicators are solid," he said, which perhaps was true if you ignored the budget deficit, the trade deficit, and the debt situation. More to the point, his choice of words sounded vaguely similar to Herbert Hoover's six decades earlier, a similarity that wasn't going to reassure anyone.

The chairman of the Federal Reserve, Alan Greenspan, received the news that the Dow Jones Industrial Average had closed down 508 points when he stepped off a plane in Houston. He had left Washington around noon, when the market was rallying sharply. His reaction to the number was relief: He thought the decline was 5.08 points.

Only one week earlier, he had been on the cover of *Fortune* magazine, his picture below the heading, "Why Greenspan is Bullish." Although the article focused on his positive view of the economy, the implication from the title was that he was favorable on the stock market, as well. The reporter, Sylvia Nasar, noted that "the stock market's speculative fever, a longtime Greenspan worry, has cooled a bit." That is, until it plummeted 30 percent in one week.

If the *Fortune* article raised some doubts about the new Fed chairman, his actions following the crash earned him nothing but respect. He had already commissioned a report from his staffers on how to deal with a financial crisis, although it's unlikely that he had any idea of just how bad things could get in one day.

That evening I watched "Adam Smith's Money World," which, of course, focused on the crash. Among the guests were Tom Wolfe, author of the then best-selling *Bonfire of the Vanities*, and Jimmy Rogers, a successful private investor and a well-known bear on the market. Wolfe observed that once the dust had settled, you would find it impossible to find anyone who would admit to having owned stocks on Monday morning. Somehow, everyone would've been smart enough, by their own admission, to have sold before the debacle. It was a good comment, astute and funny.

Less humorous was Rogers's comparison of Black Monday, not with the Crash of 1929, but with the Panic of 1907. Rogers was still negative on the market, and his comparison was clever for two reasons. First, it talked about an event that almost nobody knew anything about and, second, it introduced a terrifying word to millions of nervous investors: *Panic*—with a capital *P*.

Greenspan of the Fed was determined not to let this happen. Financial panics are based on fear, he knew, and the best way to stop them was to restore some confidence—specifically, some confidence that there would be money available for those who needed it. In the 1907 panic, there was none. In the Depression, there wasn't enough. In October 1987, there would be plenty.

Monetary policy was turned on a dime. The tight policy of the summer, designed to slow an overheating economy, was immediately replaced by one of ease. On Tuesday morning, banks were called and told that they shouldn't hesitate to lend, because the Fed's window would be open if they needed funds. Greenspan also approved the following announcement, released before the market's opening: "The Federal Reserve, consistent with its responsibility as the nation's central bank, affirmed today its readiness to serve as a source of liquidity to support the economic and financial system."

The world seemed a much friendlier place early that Tuesday. Overnight, the bond market had enjoyed its sharpest rally in history; the interest rate on government bonds had fallen by more than one percentage point. Stocks were still overvalued relative to bonds, but the gap had narrowed significantly in twenty-four hours.

There were some comments at the morning meeting that we were still positive on the market—just white noise as far as I was concerned. The real issue was that bond market rally and its favorable implications for the stock market—for the short term, at least. I left the meeting in high spirits.

The market responded as hoped, rising over 10 percent in the first hour of trading! Then it began to sink. As *The Wall Street Journal* later reported, the specialists on the NYSE had already lost two-thirds of their $3 billion in capital, and were in danger of losing the rest. They owned stocks that were dropping in value, and they weren't interested in buying more.

The brokerage firms were hurting, as well. They were long stocks and were having difficulty getting credit from their banks. As for individuals and institutional investors, once the market started falling, their interest in buying disappeared.

The shares of the most famous names in American business stopped trading. Hundreds, perhaps thousands, of smaller stocks were frozen. The financial markets began to shut down.

A little after noon, the Chicago Mercantile Exchange closed down its stock index futures market. Leo Malamed, chairman of the Merc, had been told that the NYSE was considering a halt in trading, and he was afraid that his market, already battered by Monday's losses, would be overwhelmed with sell orders. Other futures and options markets soon followed.

By 12:30 P.M., the stock market had given back all its gain and more, and the NYSE, the most important stock exchange in the world, was debating whether to close its doors. Several brokerage firms, including Salomon Brothers and Goldman Sachs, reportedly told government officials that they were in favor of a shutdown.

There was an eerie feeling, on our trading floor and throughout Wall Street, a feeling described by a trader on the NYSE as, "Holy shit, the system's not working." At this point, anything could've happened, and something unbelievable did. A small futures contract on the Chicago Board of Trade, the only stock market–related contract still trading, started rising rapidly. In a matter of minutes, it was up by 20 percent!

This extraordinary rally gave a boost of confidence to shell-shocked specialists and investors. It was just what the market needed, and not a moment too soon. An interesting question would later surface: Had at least one brokerage firm manipulated this futures contract? The matter was never really pursued and for good reason: When the cavalry comes to the rescue, you thank it, you don't investigate it.

Another positive came into the picture around the same time: Various companies, with the encouragement of the government, began announcing share repurchases—General Motors, Citicorp, GAF, Shearson Lehman, and U.S. Steel among them. These buy-back proposals told investors that someone—and someone knowledge-able—was willing and able to buy stocks. Although these announcements didn't require companies to buy anything immediately or at current prices, they did remind investors that maybe the world wasn't ending, after all.

Meanwhile, back at 60 Broad, I was trying to get clients to buy Kellogg, on the macabre but simple concept that, even if the economy did go into a depression, people weren't going to cut back on corn-flakes. At $38 a share, investors were paying less than ten times earnings for one of the strongest companies in America.

If I'd been smarter, I would've also pushed another idea that was just about a sure thing. One salesman, who I'd run into that morning outside the men's room, had mentioned that Dreyfus was selling for $16 per share, even though it was sitting on $13 per share in cash. Their whole business, net of cash, was being offered for almost noth-ing. Unfortunately for my clients, I was less struck by his idea than by him: this salesman, a long-time veteran and one of the best, was confused and flustered, the first and last time I ever saw his that way.

By noon on Tuesday, the entire Street was feeling pretty much the same. An hour later, everyone started feeling a whole lot better. The market was rising. Stock prices climbed from their lows of the day, and never returned. "Institutions, in classic fashion, put in bids at the old lows, thereby confirming the lows," a trader said, referring to investors' natural inclination to hope for prices that wouldn't be seen again.

By the 4:00 P.M. bell, the Dow Jones Industrial Average was up over 100 points to 1,850. The next day, it rose almost 200 points more. The crisis was over, at least for now. The market would remain volatile for weeks, and the volume of trading would remain heavy, but the sense of panic was gone.

On Wall Street, the results were bad but not fatal. The specialists lost a reported $750 million on Friday and Monday, but still managed to earn a terrific profit for the year. The brokerage firms, which might have gone under if the market had continued to tank and the banks had cut off their credit, survived.

At Drexel, the biggest loss was on the equity trading desk, which cost the firm $25 million and the head trader his job. "He was out of his element," one trader commented. "He was an intelligent guy; he knew the business, but he didn't handle pressure. When those [phones] start to ring, you've got to perform." Later in our conversation, this trader noted, "A smart guy plays the percentages. You can't just throw caution to the wind."

Almost every investor was hurt by the crash, and a few were hurt badly. The one hurt worst was actually one of the smartest and most successful investors in history: George Soros. He had bet that the overvalued market would continue to rise, feeding on its own optimism and speculation.

After Black Monday, he decided that the Greater Fool Theory was no longer valid, and sold his stock index futures contracts. Unfortunately for him, the execution of his trades was disastrously handled, adding to his problems. The net result was an $800 million loss in two weeks (although he still showed a significant profit for the year). If there was a lesson to be learned, it was that even the greatest investors can get massacred trying to trade the market.

The most tragic result of the crash was the killing of a Merrill Lynch branch manager by an irate and deranged investor named Arthur Kane. In response, according to *Time,* several Merrill employees in Queens starting wearing buttons that said, "I am not the branch manager."

If the sense of panic among investors was gone, the sense of fear was not. Some investors dealt with this fear by walking away from the market, for good—or at least, for now. The market is just a casino, they thought, a place to gamble and eventually lose.

As logical as this might have seemed, and still seems, to many, it's simply not true. The market was and is a place to invest in the future of companies, and all its dramatic ups and downs don't change a thing. If anything, a volatile market helps investors, giving them that many more chances to buy low and sell high.

While some investors left the market, most stayed. For many of them, however, the lesson learned was not to look harder for good ideas, but rather to look for new experts to give them easy answers. This is too much to expect of anyone, and dangerous to rely on. One top guru to emerge from the crash, a strategist for a major Wall Street firm, almost immediately tripped up by incorrectly trying to predict the market's direction in the week following the crash.

Investors in general did share a common concern: Did the stock market debacle of 1987, so similar to that of 1929, mean that another savage bear market was on its way? The 1920s pattern of declining inflation, continuing economic growth, rising stock prices, growing speculation, and eventual collapse had been repeated in the 1980s. Would the 1929–1932 decline, a fall of almost 90 percent from top to bottom, be repeated as well?

More important, people wondered if the crash of 1987 would be followed by a depression. Nobody knew, of course, but it sure as hell was worth wondering about (and, considering the debt crisis, it still is). Part of the problem was that almost nobody understood exactly what had happened in the twenties and thirties, but everybody knew that they didn't want it to happen again.

The 1920s were good years for the general public, especially for the investing public—much like the 1980s. But the economy and the stock market were fundamentally different back then, and direct comparisons between the two eras could be misleading.

The stock exchange wasn't regulated by the government, and the public had little protection. The NYSE was run like a private club for the benefit of its members—brokers, floor traders, and specialists. Its higher purpose, that of allowing corporations to raise money and people to invest in the future of these corporations, was easily lost in the shuffle.

The biggest problem was that companies weren't required to tell their owners much about what was going on, and their managers were free to trade on inside information. The average investor was flying blind.

Pools were formed to manipulate stocks, buying and selling the shares among themselves and creating a rising price. Eventually, small investors would jump on the bandwagon of this "winner," allowing the pools to unload their own positions.

In other schemes, operators, sometimes illegally in league with the specialists on the floor, relentlessly knocked down the prices of stocks, short selling the shares until small investors wanted out or were forced out by margin calls. Then the boys in the game could then buy back their shares at bargain-basement prices.

"There were no short selling rules," recalled one veteran who began as an $8-a-week runner on the NYSE in 1927. "They would bang the bids, and stocks kept coming in—they made a lot of money. It was legitimate in those days."

Things were a mess. Still, the public didn't really understand what was being done to them, and the bull market obscured the thievery under a wave of easy profits.

But business as usual was about to be replaced with business by regulation. The Crash of 1929 and the horrible, grinding bear market of June 1930 to July 1932 transformed the huge gains of the 1920s into devastating losses. Then, in early 1933, the Senate Banking and Currency Committee, with its young counsel, Ferdinand Pecora, exposed Wall Street's shady practices.

The public rightfully felt raped, and the Great Depression only fueled the anger. The crash didn't cause the Depression—the buildup of debt, the shaky structure of the banking system, and the Smoot-Hawley Tariff Bill get primary blame for that—but the Street's greed and the economy's collapse were easily associated.

The result was the Securities and Exchange Acts of 1933 and 1934, which created the SEC and laid down laws to prevent fraud in the markets. The laws were vague, certainly. At the time, their vagueness was seen as a minor victory for Wall Street, which had opposed any regulation at all.

But there was an irony to it. "The law as it stands forbids and requires so little that we may truthfully say there is no body of laws as yet governing the securities markets until the commission considers, adopts and promulgates them," was journalist John T. Flynn's reaction, as noted in John Brooks's *Once in Golconda*. Brooks then comments: "But the point—and for Wall Street's whole future, a crucial point—was that the commission existed, and had broad powers to do just that. An historic moment had passed almost unrecognized. The cops were on Wall Street's corner, and they were well armed."

More than fifty years later, Drexel Burnham would find out just how well armed they were.

CHAPTER TEN

STATE OF SIEGE

The future ain't what it used to be.
—POGO

The laws that were written in the distant wake of the Crash of 1929 became the basis for the government's investigation of Drexel Burnham, the most intensive in the history of the Street. By the time of the second crash, in October 1987, the firm had been the focus of prosecutors from the Securities and Exchange Commission and the U.S. attorney's office for almost a year. During that time, the outlook for both Drexel and Wall Street had changed significantly, and for the worse.

In a sentence, what a difference a year makes. In November 1986, Wall Street was riding a wave of prosperity, and no firm more successfully than Drexel. The most profitable end of the business—mergers and acquisitions—was on a tear, junk bonds were the catalyst, and my firm dominated that market. For the year, it would earn $545 million.

By November 1987, the end of Wall Street's glory days was in sight. Although the brokerage firms had averted a crisis—a possible collapse of the industry, in fact—brought on by October's crash, the high profitability they had enjoyed was a thing of the past. The stock market would eventually recover to new highs, but Wall Street's bottom line would not.

The bond market, which had been declining since April 1986, was marginally profitable in most of its segments. Municipal and government bonds had become too competitive, as banks and foreign firms vied for the business. The mortgage-backed securities (MBS) market, where thousands of home mortgages were pooled together and sold as bonds, had produced huge profits for a few firms in the early 1980s; by 1987, however, the MBS market had become a low-margin business as well, under the onslaught of new competition. For Merrill Lynch, it became an intensely negative-margin business in April 1987, when one trader lost $400 million on one security.

High-grade corporate bonds, never very profitable, stayed that way. In addition to low margins, the firms that traded these bonds faced "event risk." This was the risk that something bad would happen to the underlying company—a leveraged takeover, for example—that would cause a downgrading of the bond's safety rating and, accordingly, a fall in its price. As Steve Joseph noted—and thousands on Wall Street and Main Street had learned—"One long and wrong would kill you."

The high-yield market had held together during 1987, producing generous profits for brokerage firms and modest profits for bondholders. An ominous trend was developing, however, as deals fell in quality and buyers showed less appetite for junk bonds in general—this gathering storm would have devasting consequences to Wall Street, especially to the firm that had pioneered this market.

The stock market had obviously been the one most impacted in the year. Ten months of rising prices were wiped out in two months; more important to the Street's future profits, the public's enthusiasm for stocks, particularly new issues, was shot to hell in twenty-four hours. And potential buyers of companies no longer envisioned a future in which anything they bought could eventually be sold for more. Takeover fever was cooling.

By late 1987, Wall Street was a very different place to work from just a year earlier. And no firm faced challenges greater than those at Drexel Burnham. It had suffered the changing fortunes of Wall Street along with its competitors. Unlike other firms, however, Drexel was deep in the midst of an investigation that threatened its future, even its survival.

If the crash of October 1987 was a watershed event for my department—and for every equity department on Wall Street—the revelations of November 1986 had been a cataclysm for my firm. While the Street had seen the world change, Drexel had seen the world turned on its head.

There was no warning—it had just happened. On Friday, November 14, 1986 at 4:40 P.M., Ivan Boesky's guilty plea was announced—one felony and a fine of $100 million. On Monday the seventeenth, the unbelievable became a reality for ten thousand employees: Their firm was under investigation by the SEC.

Subpoenas had been delivered at the time of the Boesky announcement, requesting information on transactions that involved Drexel Burnham and its star, Michael Milken; Carl Icahn, the raider and Drexel client; Victor Posner, whose takeover of Fischbach would later emerge as the subject of Boesky's guilty plea; and Boyd Jeffries, the head of a Los Angeles–based brokerage firm that specialized in buying and selling shares in the "third market"—the legal but uncommon practice of trading shares when the stock exchanges are closed.

The mood that Monday morning at 60 Broad was one of shock, as if the tests from a routine checkup had just come back, and there was something . . . something, well, seriously not right. We wanted answers, but at this stage, there were none. Someone told me that the West Coast operation wasn't taking calls. There was a sense of dread on the trading floor that day, a fear that people pushed just to the side.

Meanwhile, the stock market was heading south on the rumors that the major force behind the takeover boom might be in deep trouble. The Dow Jones sold off fifteen points that first day, a relatively big move at that time; the following day, it plummeted an additional 43 to a level of 1,817.21. The hardest hit was Gillette, which had been considered vulnerable to a Drexel-financed takeover—its shares fell by 11 percent in one day.

In corporate finance, one investment banker described the impact of Boesky's allegations as "an immediate barometric change. We went from invulnerable to vulnerable . . . from a powerful group of investment bankers to villians." Said another, "There was a certain amount of distrust"—after all, no one knew what the government wanted, or how many were under suspicion.

In the high-yield department, one executive recalled: "When it hit, it was pretty devastating to everyone." According to a West Coast investment banker, "There was a definite, anxious feeling . . . an air of impending doom," although not a sense of certainty.

"All the people who worked for Michael Milken believed him to be honest," he said, adding that "they may think that the laws are wrong." His comments reveal two important factors in understanding the actions and attitudes of many employees during the investigation: A strong faith in Milken and an underlying belief in his integrity, if not necessarily in the rules that are supposed to define that integrity.

The initial word from management was a memo on that first Monday to all officers from Robert Linton, the chairman of Drexel's board, and Fred Joseph, our chief executive officer, stating, "We have been cooperating. And we intend to continue cooperating." These comments could be interpreted either positively or negatively.

On Tuesday, *The Wall Street Journal* reported that "the Securities and Exchange Commission has issued a formal order of investigation targeting Drexel Burnham Lambert Inc. in an intensifying probe focusing on Drexel's high-yield 'junk bond' operations and its ties to Ivan F. Boesky." The paper also identified eleven transactions that were under investigation; the companies involved in these transactions were Fischbach, Occidental Petroleum, Diamond Shamrock, Harris Graphics, Pacific Lumber, Lorimar, Telepictures, Unocal, Wickes, Phillips Petroleum, and MGM/UA. Most of these names would remain the focus of the investigation for over two years.

The following day, Wednesday the nineteenth, the *Journal* noted that Drexel was also under investigation by the U.S. attorney's office: ". . . a grand jury has issued subpoenas as part of a related criminal probe." That same day, Fred spoke to employees in the first of many conference calls; his tone was encouraging. He told us that the firm hadn't "uncovered any wrongdoing internally," that "we have absolutely no indication that any individual at DBL has done anything to violate securities laws," that a grand jury had been in place since May and Drexel was *not* a target of that investigation, that "the U.S. attorney may make a statement saying that no firm is the target," and that "there is no reason to believe that the firm will be faced with criminal proceedings."

He also noted that Drexel's 1986 revenues would exceed $4 billion, and that the firm had $700–800 million in excess net capital—cash above and beyond what the regulators required—which sounded reassuring even if we didn't exactly know what that meant.

The investigation provided a bitter irony with the *Journal*'s revelation on Thursday, November 20 that Boesky had been allowed to sell at least $440 million in stocks prior to the announcement of his plea bargain. In effect, he was permitted to trade on a significant piece of inside information—that Wall Street's major arbitrageur was about to accuse the most influential force on the Street of massive fraud. In doing so, he saved his investors and himself tens of millions of dollars.

Around this time, the head of my department spoke to us, first to the senior salesmen, then to the juniors—as with most managers, he loved a hierarchy. He predicted, based on what he had been told by his superiors, that we were in for a two-year process, which turned out to be one hell of a prediction. There was a sense in that small office, or at least in my imagination, that we were ready for anything that was thrown at us—already, there was an us-vs.-them attitude that would both help and hurt our cause.

On November 26, Fred was back on the system, telling us that he didn't have much to report, but he wanted to keep open the lines of communication. "The firm is going to be tough as nails on any violators of securities laws," he said. There was "no firm grip on where they think they're going . . . the direction seems to be on aggressive hostile takeovers." If so, fine—he felt good about this area.

He added that no senior officers were at risk, in management's view, which was very good news if that applied to Milken, as well. He later commented that the firm "will become more aggressive with the press," which had the impression that we were stonewalling, an impression that it had almost certainly gotten from the government.

Drexel's relations with the press were never warm. The firm was the target of a massive investigation, which put it in a difficult position. Drexel didn't know which transactions to focus on beyond what it read in the press, and it didn't know what Boesky had told the government.

Regardless, the firm's own investigation, conducted primarily by its in-house legal staff and lawyers from Cahill Gordon, was hamstrung—unknown to most, the principal target of the allegations, Mike Milken, would only deal with Drexel's investigation through his attorneys. Whatever the truth, the shortest path to it was unlikely to be between two sets of lawyers.

And even if the firm had all the facts, the best place to defend itself was in the courts, not in the press. For those making the accusations and investigating them, the priorities were different. Those in Boesky's camp and in the government wanted the allegations to seem as overwhelming as possible; perhaps others would step forward to cut a deal with the prosecutors, reducing their possible sentences by pleading guilty to lesser charges and implicating others. The more individuals who came forward, the stronger would be the case against those that didn't, and their firm.

If there were those who were willing to illegally leak confidential information, the press was willing to print it (which is its right and, to some extent, its responsibility). Reporters and their editors were obviously not interested in sitting by, waiting until the financial story of the decade reached the public record.

For the first several weeks of the investigation, the morning papers were the low point of my day. I would grab them early when I arrived at the train station and quickly glance at the *Journal*'s headlines in the near dark as I walked to the 6:38 Valhalla Express. Inevitably, there would be an ominous article to help get the blood flowing.

On December 5, the *Journal* carried a front-page article: "Deals in Boesky Probe Show Increasing Links With Drexel Burnham." There was no doubt: We were the focus of the government's investigation, and were likely to stay that way.

The article outlined the main transactions under suspicion, most of which had been identified on November 18. There were nine deals, each involving an actual or attempted takeover, each involving purchases of stock by Boesky in advance of public knowledge of these deals, and each involving Drexel as an adviser to one or both companies in every transaction:

- Pennsylvania Engineering's takeover of Fischbach Corporation.
- AM International's acquisition of Harris Graphics.
- Lorimar's merger with Telepictures.
- Occidental's aborted takeover of Diamond Shamrock.
- Maxxam's acquisition of Pacific Lumber.
- Carl Icahn's attempted takeover of Phillips Petroleum.
- Trans World's purchase of shares from Golden Nuggett.
- Mesa Petroleum's attempted takeover of Unocal.
- Wickes's purchase of a division from Gulf + Western.

The principal allegation against the firm, not surprisingly, was insider trading, a serious crime that had evolved from the Securities and Exchange Act of 1934. The core of the act was Section 10-b, which made it unlawful to buy or sell any security using "any manipulative or deceptive device or contrivance in contravention of such rules and regulations as the Commission may prescribe as necessary or appropriate in the public interest or for the protection of investors."

Which is to say, the SEC was given the authority to prohibit whatever it felt needed to be prohibited. Insider trading was high on that list. The commission believed it unfair for a company's managers and advisers, who have access to information that its shareholders and potential shareholders do not, to be allowed to profit by trading on this information. Certainly, in the 1920s, these insiders had lined their pockets by doing just that.

In time, the SEC expanded Section 10-b to include 10-b-5: "Anyone in possession of material inside information must disclose it to the investing public or abstain from trading." And, as William Hancock noted in *Executive's Guide to Business Law,* "The category of persons owing a duty under rule 10(b)(5) is virtually unlimited." Investment bankers and other advisers are, according to the courts, clearly within that category.

As for what constitutes *material* information: "The courts hold that . . . insider trading activity itself is highly pertinent evidence of materiality." This means that by simply trading on the basis of any information, you are implying that the information is material, whether or not you thought it was. So there.

The December 5 article also raised the possibility that another law had been broken in at least one of the nine deals under suspicion. This was the law, also created by Section 10-b, that prohibited one party from buying a stock for the benefit of another, thereby disguising who actually owns the shares. This type of deception can be as insignificant as holding shares for someone until they raise the necessary cash, or as significant as assisting the takeover of a company by allowing someone to control a large position in violation of rules requiring disclosure of that fact.

The common term is "parking," and apparently, it was not uncommon on Wall Street. People on the Street viewed this crime more like parking on a sidewalk than parking on a pedestrian, but until the takeover boom of the 1980s, the violations had probably involved the insignificant situations of one person doing a favor for another. Regardless, it was against the law, and Drexel was under suspicion for playing a role in breaking that law.

The firm's official reaction, delivered through someone identified only as "a spokesman," to the allegations—trial by media, actually—was included in the article: "It is hardly news that Drexel Burnham had an investment banking relationship with the particular companies you have chosen to focus on. It's all well understood that Mr. Boesky took positions in most large merger transactions, and that some of these were Drexel clients would not be surprising. Apart from Dennis Levine, who stole information and sold it to Mr. Boesky, we know of no one at Drexel Burnham who provided inside information to Mr. Boesky. We in no way would condone any violation of the securities laws."

The position that the firm staked out in the first weeks was the position it would hold to for the next two years: It knew of no wrongdoing by anyone, and the accusations were made by a convicted felon hoping to reduce his sentence by implicating others.

After the initial shock and the subsequent wave of bad publicity, the trading floor fell back to normal, a different kind of normal, but a routine, nevertheless. Life in the trenches wasn't dramatically changed; people did what they had always done—their jobs. Our product was the same, and our clients were almost entirely supportive. The cloud hanging over the firm's head was a major concern, but not a daily one.

In the high-yield department—the focus of the investigation—the concerns were more immediate. The government wanted information from the employees of the department and from their boss. Junk bonds would continue being sold—$1 billion was raised for Safeway Stores in mid-December, an extraordinary accomplishment considering the environment—but the key person behind this department and this market would progressively fade from the scene during the next eighteen months.

The firm as a whole found itself on a long road to oblivion, a step-by-step process that would last over three years. Jesse Livermore, the legendary stock trader, argued six decades earlier that all surprises follow the direction of the major trend, and for Drexel, that trend was down.

The year 1986 ended with a letter from Fred Joseph announcing that we had hired our ten thousandth employee in December, up from some fifteen hundred in 1974, when he had joined the firm. The number of employees who owned stock in the firm was about two thousand and our excess capital was more than $800 million. Business was strong: Since the Boesky announcement only six weeks earlier, $6.6 billion in high-yield debt had been raised in fifty different issues. What didn't need to be said was that the firm was completing the most successful year since it opened its doors in 1935; at the same time, its future was never as uncertain.

If misery loves company, and it does, Drexel got some in February 1987. The heads of risk arbitrage at Goldman Sachs and Kidder Peabody, Robert Freeman and Richard Wigton, were arrested, along with a former Kidder associate, Timothy Tabor. The charge was insider trading.

The accusator was Martin Siegel, a "bright, articulate, charming" investment banker, who had left a $2.5 million a year job at Kidder to join Drexel in 1986. Although his office was next to Dennis Levine's, and both had dealt illegally with Ivan Boesky during their careers, neither knew of the other's crimes. The circle was completed when Levine fingered Boesky, who then fingered Siegel. During 1983 and 1984, Siegel had received $700,000 in cash, some of it in a suitcase, in exchange for passing along inside information.

Dennis Levine and Marty Siegel had another distant connection, in spirit only. Levine's picture had appeared in Drexel's 1985 annual report, published in the spring of '86. Following his arrest on May 12, I was told at the time, Levine's picture was replaced—with Siegel's. For the firm, it was a bizarre reminder that everything that could go wrong would go wrong.

As for Siegel, once implicated, he cooperated with the government, pleading guilty to one count of insider fraud and accusing in turn Freeman, Wigton, and Tabor, among others. Interestingly, Siegel had not engaged in any insider crimes since joining Drexel, indicating as one senior exec noted, "He wanted to go to DBL as a whole new person." Regardless, he was caught, and now he was trying to cut his losses.

On a human level, the arrests of the three arbs was sad, especially in the case of Wigton, who was handcuffed and led off his trading floor. As for the outcomes of these highly publicized arrests . . . well, they were more than sad, they were disturbing. It's a story for a later chapter.

However unfortunate on a personal level, it was a relief to see other brokerage houses dragged into the unhappy family of government suspects. In the *Journal*'s article of two months earlier, there had been some foreshadowing: "The SEC is also known to be investigating other transactions that haven't yet been identified and could involve firms other than Drexel." Now the possibility was a reality.

The two firms involved dealt with the crisis in very different ways. Goldman Sachs, the last of the great Wall Street partnerships, stood behind its partner, Freeman. He was innocent until proven guilty, the firm believed, and he would be treated accordingly. On the Street, whatever opinion each person had of Goldman, their opinion was now that much higher.

Kidder Peabody, a prestigious investment bank with a roster of blue-chip clients, took a different tack. It suspended Wigton until the resolution of his indictment and negotiated a $25.3 million settlement with the government within four months. Kidder was a subsidiary of General Electric, recently acquired. The boss of GE, Jack Welch, was said to have been infuriated by the accusations, believing that he had been misled by the former partners of Kidder who had sold him the firm.

In advance of its settlement with the government, General Electric replaced Kidder's senior management. The top spot went to Silas Cathcart, formerly the chairman of Illinois Tool Works Inc., prompting one officer to tell *The Journal:* "I was thinking just the other day that what we need in here is a good tool and die man."

Kidder's settlement had some encouraging implications for Drexel. There were multiple allegations involved, as with the investigation of my firm, and the cost of the settlement was not significant by Wall Street standards. Because the core of the government's case against Drexel was a $5.3 million payment by Boesky to the high-yield department, hardly a big-ticket item, perhaps a reasonable fine could be agreed on.

Even Boesky's payment of $100 million as part of his guilty plea, the highest in history, would be affordable. After all, the firm had over $1 billion in equity, it had earned over $500 million in the previous year alone, and it had already begun putting aside money for a settlement. Drexel also had a diverse portfolio of "merchant banking" positions—ownership stakes in various companies that it had financed over the years. These equity holdings were worth a great deal more than their stated values, we thought, further boosting the true value of the firm.

What this line of reasoning ignored, however, was that the government was almost certainly not interested in letting Drexel off the hook for less than its punishment against Boesky. He had been given a favorable deal *because* he had implicated the top guns on Wall Street—Milken and his firm. Drexel couldn't expect better treatment.

Also, that $5.3 million payment did not involve a single transaction. According to Boesky, the payment was the net result of many illegal transactions, some for which he owed Drexel, and others for which he was owed. The firm's position, from beginning to end, was that the $5.3 million was a payment for legitimate investment banking services, specifically research that the Coast had done for Boesky's arbitrage company. The government, not surprisingly, was more comfortable with Boesky's explanation than with Drexel's.

By mid-1987, the investigation had been expanded. In addition to the demand for documents from Drexel, the government had subpoenaed information, reported *The New York Times,* "from more than a dozen financial institutions that were among the largest 'junk bond' clients of Drexel Burnham Lambert, Inc., a number of sources with knowledge of the investigation said yesterday." According to that same late-February article, the SEC was also investigating the activities of Carl Icahn, who had been involved in several takeover battles, in most cases with Drexel's support.

Meanwhile, the firm went on a public relations offensive, hoping to shore up morale, and to counteract the image that the allegations were creating with the public and with potential corporate clients. In February, Drexel took out huge advertisements in major publications with the slogan: "Ten Thousand Strong." Beneath the heading was a list of all the employees by name.

There was also an effective ad headed "It's Time to Fight Back," listing "seven myths about Drexel Burnham and our business that are frequently heard these days. They appear with something you rarely hear at all—the facts."

Another advertisement stated that "95% of the Companies in America are Considered Junk," pointing out "that of the 23,000 corporations in the United States with sales greater than $25 million, fewer than 800 are considered investment grade." In a similar vein, another ad was headlined, "Junk Bonds. Who Needs Them?" with subheadings that included, "Workers Need Them" and "Rising Stars Need Them." The ad also included a list of ninety-three companies, drawn from a pool of over one thousand, that had raised money in the high-yield market.

Television spots, created by Chiat/Day, appeared presenting specific cases in which Drexel's high-yield financings had helped out communities, and highlighting its new slogan, "Helping People Manage Change." The TV ads, according to one well-placed officer, generated a strong and favorable response on Main Street.

Personally, I found the ads dull and downbeat. Someone recently made an interesting point about these spots—he said that they reminded him of political advertising. They certainly did have an unsettling, even eerie quality to them, with their stark landscapes and threatening themes. There was, for example, a spot that showed an empty playground with a ghostly swing rocking back and forth. We learn of a municipal insurance crisis that might have closed playgrounds such as this, and that thanks to Drexel Burnham, the necessary money was raised—children fade into the scene. Unfortunately for the firm, one ad actually caused negative publicity with reports that it hadn't been filmed in the town it was referring to, a somewhat irrelevant if correct criticism.

While trying to win the hearts and minds of the general public, Drexel was also trying to influence the generals. A strong lobbying effort was focused on Washington, which had to be the least enviable job at the firm. For one thing, it's smart politics to steer clear of potential scandal, unless you're on the offensive. For another, politicians weren't terribly fond of takeovers, and of the folks who financed those takeovers. Although hostile takeovers represented less than 5 percent of junk-bond financings, it was these that made the front pages and brought pressure from the target companies, and their employees.

The word from Washington was rarely good, but on April 1 of 1987, it was just annoying. One of our senior executives in the capital was quoted talking of the youngsters on Wall Street who didn't have the experience to "absorb the ethical standards of the industry." Scapegoating the so-called greedy kids of the Street might play well on Capitol Hill, but it didn't say much for the man.

Later that month, the news from Washington was bad—predictable but still bad. Senator William Proxmire, chairman of the banking committee, was told by Gary Lynch, director of enforcement at the SEC, that "major cases" were upcoming. Lynch had joined the SEC out of Duke Law School and had succeeded John Fedders as head of the Enforcement Division in 1985, at age thirty-five. Low-key but intense, extremely knowledgeable, terse in speech, Lynch was clearly the type that you would rather have on your side of the table. Drexel, of course, never had that choice.

Back in New York, Fred Joseph was on the system a few days later, on Friday, April 24, predicting that "most likely, investigations will go on for quite some time." He reassured the rank and file that there was "nothing in the subpoenaed documents that we're concerned with," emphasized that the firm still hadn't found anything wrong, and noted that the first quarter had been "spectacular." It was difficult not to come away from his talks feeling better about things.

The following Tuesday, he was on the system again. Charles Thurnher, a senior vice-president in charge of administrative matters on the West Coast, had been advised by his lawyer to cooperate with the government, according to Fred. Whether he would or not was unknown (the previous day's *New York Times* had indicated that Thurnher had already agreed to cooperate). Regardless, it had an ominous ring to it, suggesting that he had something to hide and something to tell. Fred pointed out that immunity from prosecution didn't necessarily imply guilt—on Thurnher's part or anyone else's.

Still, it raised questions of why the government would offer him immunity, and why his lawyer would want him to take it. There was certainly a logical explanation: The investigators wanted more information so why not give immunity to a small but centrally located player; from Thurnher's point of view, why shouldn't anyone accept immunity if offered, regardless of what they knew?

But, then again, maybe he knew a great deal that would hurt Milken and the firm. He certainly knew a great deal more than all but a handful of the employees, and if there was incriminating evidence, it seemed likely he would be aware of it.

There was also the feeling, however simplistic that it was wrong for one member of Drexel to incriminate another. (What's the highest paying job at Drexel?—was a question asked at the time. Answer: Charlie Thurnher's food taster.) If this was a firm known for its intensity, it was also known for its intense loyalty, whether to I. W. Burnham, Michael Milken, fellow employees, or to the concept of the firm itself.

Fred tried to put the various concerns to rest, arguing again that Drexel knew of "no wrongdoing by anyone at the firm," and that if anything illegal was found, the guilty party would be gone. He also noted that the government now seemed more interested in the behavior of individuals than of the firm as a whole, which was comforting because it implied that the risk to Drexel, and its stockholders, was diminishing.

A similar point was made to me about a week later by a senior analyst with excellent connections within the firm. During our out-of-town trip to meet with clients, he predicted that the firm wouldn't be indicted, although he thought that Milken and others would be. "They've been hoping for us to fess up," he said, "but we're not going to, because there's nothing to fess up to." Now, *that* was encouraging to hear.

More good news came with a mid-May review of business for 1987's first half. Revenues were well over $1.5 billion in less than five months, down from 1986's extraordinary pace, but still excellent by any other measure. Profits after deducting taxes (and reserves for a potential settlement) were $122 million, excess capital now exceeded $1.1 billion, our market share was holding, and the backlog of investment banking business waiting to be done was described happily as "almost too strong."

Meanwhile, all was relatively quiet on the legal front with the U.S. attorney's office. At the SEC, interviews with various members of the firm had been scheduled for the next several months, and it was suggested that the investigators were "sort of flopping around," with one senior officer noting that he was "not overwhelmed by their preparation or knowledge."

Life was definitely looking brighter, especially if you were young, ignorant, and on the East Coast. I worried too little about the future of my firm, and too much about most everything else. The stock market was booming, of course, offering everyone on the ninth floor, and on trading floors throughout Wall Street, an unusual opportunity to make a good deal of money—an opportunity that was soon to end. Stocks were rising, volume was heavy, and new issues were popular.

By late September, the market was within 10 percent of its all-time high, and the crash was still a month away. Business at the firm was very strong, as Fred Joseph explained on Monday the twenty-first. Revenues were estimated at $3.6 billion for the year, the firm had been profitable in every month, and the value of the stock—which, as mentioned before, was primarily owned by two thousand of the employees—was comfortably above $1 billion.

The SEC, Fred told us that Monday, was conducting an "active, major investigation into . . . anything." The U.S. attorney's office was much less active, waiting, he thought, for the SEC to conclude. "Very important from our point of view," Fred noted, "we have not found any evidence of wrongdoing by anyone at the firm."

The upcoming major case against Drexel that had been implied in April had not arrived yet; if anything, its resolution seemed a distant problem. Perhaps there wasn't really a case against the firm at all; no charges had been brought after ten months of intensive investigation, and management continued to argue our innocence. Wishful thinking, perhaps, but there were reasons to be hopeful.

The attack against the firm faded further into the background as 1987 wound down, and remained there until the following April. "The first year, we all felt we lived in a police state," recalled a senior officer from the high-yield department. There was hope that 1988 would bring better news but, of course, it didn't.

If the focus in Washington during April 1987 was on the investigation, in April 1988 it was on the limited partnerships at Drexel. These limited partnerships, as you might remember, were available to selected members of the high-yield and corporate finance departments. The implied promise was that the participants could invest alongside Mike Milken. "I asked Fred Joseph how these partnerships would be screened," recalled one senior investment banker. "He said, 'Basically, Michael will be making the decisions.' "

By 1988, there was a mind-boggling assortment of different partnerships—only sixty-eight known to the public at the time—primarily involving Drexel officers, but with a few well-known outsiders: in one group, RWLC Partners, three of the eight partners were Lionel Richie; Steve Wynn, chairman of Golden Nuggett; and Kenny Rogers, whose most popular song offered some good advice about knowing when to hold 'em and when to fold 'em.

On April 28, the House of Representatives' Subcommittee on Oversight and Investigations, chaired by John Dingell of Michigan, considered a set of disturbing allegations: that the partnerships engaged in self-dealing, allocating themselves portions of junk-bond deals, at the expense of clients. Another question raised was whether the high-yield department treated these partnerships more favorably than clients in the *after market,* where these newly issued bonds traded publicly.

The hearings began a little after 10:00 A.M., with an introductory speech by Representative Dingell, who one Wall Street executive described as "the most powerful man in the country," referring to Dingell's authority over the SEC and the financial community. Following the chairman's introduction were initial comments from Representatives Ron Wyden of Oregon, Norman Lent of New York, Jim Slattery of Kansas, Michael Bilirakis of Florida, and Gerry Sikorski of Minnesota. The overture had a definitely congressional tone: "I want to commend you, Mr. Chairman, for undertaking this inquiry and say that I believe you've shown great concern for procedural fairness in this matter and I think that is something that this member very much appreciates. . . . Mr. Chairman, I too, commend you for holding this follow-up hearing. I quite often ask at the outset that we be open-minded and objective, and since these are information-gathering sessions, the only way we can actually gather information in an objective manner, is to be open-minded. . . . Mr. Chairman, thank you. I too, add my midwestern and flat tenor or bass voice to the chorus of commendations to you and the staff for this ongoing effort to examine our securities markets."

Fred Joseph received his first surprise of the day when, contrary to what he thought was an understanding with committee staffers, his lawyer, Irwin Schneiderman of Cahill, Gordon & Reindel, was not permitted to testify without waiving attorney-client privilege. Because Schneiderman obviously wasn't willing to reveal confidential discussions with his client, he chose not to be sworn in as a witness. He retained his role as a counsel to Joseph, which meant that Fred would have to provide answers for the record on all questions, including those of securities law.

The major law in question was Section 10-b-6 of the Securities and Exchange Act of 1934. You might recall that 10-b-5 dealt with insider trading; this one focused on fraud in the distribution of new issues. As Representative Dennis Eckart explained at the hearing: " 'The overall purpose,' the SEC says, 'is to assure a public distribution of securities for which there is a public demand, to make certain that NASD members do not restrict the supply of the offering by withholding shares, thereby forcing [your customers] who want to purchase the securities to acquire them in the market at a higher price.' "

Simply put, until every client's order is filled, nobody connected with the firm is entitled to any portion of a deal.

The committee focused on two high-yield offerings: Texstryene and Beatrice. In the Texstryene deal, 25 percent of the bonds went to the limited partnerships, even though at least two clients didn't receive their requested allotments. Lutheran Life ordered $2 million worth of bonds and received $500,000; Vanguard Mutual Fund asked for $5 million and was allocated $750,000, fully 85 percent less than its request.

As for the Beatrice deal, to quote Representative Slattery: "BCI Holdings Co., Inc., of course, is the corporation that was set up to acquire the Beatrice Companies in a leveraged buyout in 1986. The Beatrice leveraged buyout was the largest, up to that time, at least, involving $2.5 billion in high yield bonds issued by Drexel.

"The bonds were sold on April 10, 1986 and divided into four issues. One issue was for $950 million at 12.75 percent, and there were other issues adding up to the total of $2.5 billion.

"Now, the subcommittee's investigation has identified at least twenty-four insider accounts which purchased over $235 million of BCI notes. Now, the insider transactions ranged from a $40 million purchase by Western Capital, which was owned by Lowell and Michael Milken, to a $170,000 purchase by Lowell Milken IRA [individual retirement account].

"The BCI bonds went up in value almost immediately, and by June 30, the insider accounts had resold $61,385,000 of the notes to Drexel for a $2,804,000 profit.

"The subcommittee staff has also learned that while Drexel insider accounts were purchasing over $115 million of the 12.75 percent notes, Drexel's public clients were denied BCI notes they wished to purchase."

Fred Joseph responded that the rule against selling new issues to insiders applied to the offerings of stocks, not of high-yield bonds. He pointed out that the use of the word *shares* indicated that the intention was to regulate equity deals. Fred also argued that, unlike stocks, the junk bonds of one company are essentially the same as the junk bonds of another company with the same rating; therefore, one is interchangeable with the other, and "there is no opportunity to harm someone by holding a bond out of the market by not allowing them to participate in the issue."

Legally, this argument has not been settled, even to this date. A 1983 SEC ruling suggests that high-yield securities are covered by Section 10-b-6, contrary to Drexel's point of view. The ruling allowed two new exceptions, neither of which were junk bonds, the logical implication being that they were still under its umbrella. But as a senior Drexel official noted, the SEC doesn't seem eager to settle this question in the courts.

As a practical matter, however, junk bonds are very similar to stocks. And there were times when junk-bond deals generated more demand than supply, and the price of those bonds did rise in value immediately. Clients who weren't allowed to participate did get hurt by being denied the profits from this increase.

More important, basic fairness dictates that professional responsibility supercedes personal greed, that insiders stand behind their clients, not ahead of them. And unless I have completely misread Fred Joseph for the past nine years, he believes exactly the same.

The second set of allegations against the high-yield department and the partnerships involved self-dealing in the after market. Specifically, the subcommittee examined the Texstryene deal again. The debt was offered on February 11, 1986 at $987.50 per bond. Between February 12 and February 19, the department repurchased 6,950 bonds from clients at no more than $1,000 per bond.

On Friday, February twentieth, 200 bonds were purchased from two clients, in both cases for $1,005 per bond. On the same day, 3,400 of the same bonds were bought from a limited partnership for $1,040 per bond. On Thursday the twenty-seventh, 1,000 Texstryene bonds were bought from a client for $1,030 per bond. The following day, three partnerships sold 9,000 bonds for $1,065 per bond.

Something was wrong, something that couldn't be explained away by market fluctuations. The partnerships were given better prices than clients—sweetheart deals—and the decisions were made by those who personally benefited from them. The congressmen may have been concerned that clients were being mistreated, but in reality, it was Drexel Burnham's employees that were being cheated by a few of their peers. The bonds in the partnerships were bought back at unfairly high prices, effectively taking some $400,000 from the stockholders of the firm on this one deal alone.

Fred Joseph's performance at this hearing was generally criticized, but let's be realistic. He testified for seven hours in lousy health, under oath to a committee that hadn't convened to congratulate his firm for its contributions to society. He was forced to address questions of securities law that he had expected his lawyer to handle. Ask yourself how carefully you'd choose your answers if you were constantly under threat of perjury, and how you'd feel on the receiving end of a discussion such as the following:

MR. DINGELL: You believe, or you know?

MR. JOSEPH: I believe so.

MR. DINGELL: See, I believe in the Almighty—

MR. JOSEPH: I think so, if that's helpful.

MR. DINGELL: —but I never met him and I never shook his hand, and I've never seen him, but I've got a strong belief. So, you are functioning on belief, as opposed to knowledge?

MR. JOSEPH: I'm saying I think so. I'm not absolutely positive.

Or consider his widely ridiculed statement: "I think I'm confused." It was one sentence in response to a legal question, one comment at a hearing that generated one hundred pages of questions and answers. If anything, it shows clearly why you can lead a full life without ever testifying before a congressional committee.

The most important problem Fred Joseph had was that he sat down at the table with a very weak hand. The allegations that the limited partnerships had taken advantage of clients and fellow employees were very serious and almost certainly true. Fred was forced to bob and weave in defense of an indefensible situation, one that was a minuscule part of Drexel Burnham, but one that had hurt its stockholders and its customers.

As the chief exec of the firm, he was nominally responsible for these partnerships, even though his own participation in them was insignificant (he invested in two partnerships during the 1987–88 period.) In fact, only three members of the firm's executive committee, less than one in five, chose to join up for the easy profits.

The reports of these questionable profits for the chosen few, carried in the following morning's papers, were bad for morale at Drexel and bad for the image of the firm. The partnerships told a story of greed— but more than that, of abuse.

Perhaps there was a lesson to be drawn from these surprising and depressing revelations, a lesson that what had happened on a small scale probably happened on a larger one as well. Or perhaps these abuses were isolated mistakes made by a few without Milken's knowledge.

An answer here would have gone a long way in addressing the real question: Was Mike Milken guilty? This had been the focus of the battle between the government and the firm; in the following year, the two sides would finally resolve the battle, if not the doubts.

CHAPTER ELEVEN

MOTHER OF MERCY

"You threaten like a dockyard bully."
"How should I threaten?"
"Like a minister of state, with justice."
—A MAN FOR ALL SEASONS

Charges were filed on September 7, 1988. The Securities and Exchange Commission alleged that "Drexel Burnham Lambert, Michael Milken, and others devised and carried out a fraudulent scheme involving insider trading, stock manipulation, fraud on Drexel's own clients, failure to disclose beneficial ownership of securities as required, and numerous other violations of the securities laws."

The transactions, and the alleged crimes, as cited in the SEC civil complaint were

- Pennsylvania Engineering's 1984 purchase of Fischbach (stock parking)
- AM International's 1986 acquisition of Harris Graphics (stock parking)
- Lorimar's 1985 merger with Telepictures (insider trading)
- Boesky's 1986 short sales of Lorimar shares (stock parking)
- Maxxam Group's 1985 takeover of Pacific Lumber (fraud)
- Golden Nugget's sale of MCA shares (stock parking)

- Turner Broadcasting's 1985 acquisition of MGM/UA (stock parking)
- Occidental Petroleum's proposed 1985 merger with Diamond Shamrock (insider trading)
- Drexel's 1985 purchase of Phillips Petroleum shares (stock parking)
- Stone Container's 1986 convertible bond offering (stock manipulation)
- Kohlberg Kravis's 1985 takeover of Storer Communications (insider trading)
- Trades between Boesky and Drexel in 1985 to create tax losses (tax evasion)
- Viacom's 1986 leveraged buyout (insider trading)
- Wickes's 1986 takeover of National Gypsum (fraud)
- Wickes's 1985 convertible preferred offering (stock manipulation)
- Boesky's 1985 short sales of Wickes shares (stock parking)
- Boesky's 1986 payment of $5.3 million to Drexel (repayment of illegal profits)

Representative Edward Markey (D–Mass.) commented on these charges by stating, "Wall Street con artists like Ivan Boesky were mere puppets controlled by one of the most successful Wall Street firms of the 1980s." What he forgot, or forgot to mention, was that these were *alleged* crimes; nothing had been proven. This may seem a technicality to many, but, of course, it's not—it's the basis of our legal system.

If the firm was unhappy that it was facing these charges, it certainly wasn't surprised. In February 1988, the SEC staff had recommended taking action against Drexel. In May, the staff had prepared a confidential memo to the commissioners of the SEC. This memo, which was leaked to *The Washington Post* in August of the following year and quoted in part there, outlined the staff's case; among the allegations:

- In 1985, Milken directed a Boesky employee to buy and sell bonds, some at nonmarket prices, which provided Boesky with quick profits at Drexel's expense.
- In 1986, Milken indirectly encouraged the destruction of documents involving transactions with Boesky

- Also in 1986, Milken and Boesky discussed a cover-up of the allegedly fraudulent $5.3 million payment.

The SEC commissioners voted unanimously in June to give their go-ahead for the staff to file civil charges against Drexel.

The firm had made its case before the vote—"We stated that we were convinced that they were wrong," Fred Joseph explained in a memo to employees—but its point of view didn't carry the day. Fred's memo also raised for the first time "the possibility of a settlement to put this behind us."

That same month, management considered another possibility: slashing the size of the firm from almost ten thousand employees to only two thousand. The idea was rejected as impractical, and as you might guess, was never mentioned to the rank and file.

For three months, we waited for this shoe to drop and, when it came, the sense of the employees was an acceptance of the inevitable. As for the clients, there was little backlash. We had informed every one of them of the likelihood of civil charges at the time of the SEC green light, and almost none of them deserted us when these charges became a reality.

If the SEC filing wasn't a surprise, somewhat puzzling was its delay until September. As a *Wall Street Journal* editorial noted in July, "There's a heavy air of expectation in the canyons of Wall Street and along the palm drives of Beverly Hills that someone is finally going to officially charge Drexel Burnham Lambert with something. Leaks and innuendo have kept the investment bank in the headlines for two years, but now Drexel is girding for a full-scale legal fight."

Well, now the fight was on. Twenty-one SEC attorneys, after twenty months of investigation, had produced the official complaint, 184 pages in length, dealing with eighteen transactions. Seventeen of those involved the firm—four of its employees, actually: Mike Milken, his brother Lowell, and two traders, Cary Maultasch and Pamela Monzert. All but two of these transactions involved Ivan Boesky as cohort and principle witness.

"The evidence was overwhelming," argued Gary Lynch, the SEC enforcement chief at the time, currently a partner at Davis, Polk & Wardwell. "There were always multiple witnesses on every allegation. There was substantial corroboration for all allegations from inside and outside the Boesky organization."

Needless to say, Drexel's view of the case was different. In a letter to clients on the day of the filing, the firm said, in part:

> A thorough examination of the SEC complaint shows that the charges rely almost entirely on accusations by convicted felon Ivan Boesky. The most telling aspect of this action is that, after an almost two-year investigation which we understand to be the most exhaustive in SEC history, the SEC essentially has charged nothing beyond what Boesky alleged in 1986 when he was bargaining for leniency.

To be exact, eight of the nine allegations raised in the *Journal* article of December 1986, almost two years earlier, were included in the SEC complaint; the remaining nine hadn't been mentioned at the time, and two of the transactions—the 1985 Lorimar/Telepictures merger and the 1986 Viacom leveraged buyout—didn't involve Boesky.

The following day, September 8, I. W. Burnham sent a memo to the members of his firm:

> I am writing to you now as one of the many thousands of employees of the firm that I founded on April 1, 1935. I am obviously the employee with the longest length of service, but not yet the oldest employee. I have been Honorary Chairman of the Board of Directors since May 1984.

> The waiting period for the charges by the SEC is now over and I would like to tell you that I think we should all support completely the leadership the firm has had from our Chief Executive Officer, Fred Joseph, and from our Chairman of the Board, Robert Linton. They and many others of our Executive Staff and, in addition, all kinds of specialists and advisors have done a wonderful job in leading this firm through the past two years of accusations, innuendo and false rumors. From the very beginning we have been told by our attorneys that they felt that our firm and its employees are innocent of the charges that might eventually be unleashed against us and them. We have to believe that.

Burnham had always thought the world of his employees, and by September 1988, his opinion had been justified in one important respect: their loyalty. The accusations and rumors that he referred to had been lousy for current business and threatening to future prospects. And still, almost nobody had left.

In my department, not one person had chosen to leave since the Boesky scandal broke. On the entire trading floor, I only knew of one trader who had left because of the threat to the firm, and he returned before the SEC charges were filed. In the research department, I can remember only one analyst who left for another firm, and he went over as part of a team with a group of investment bankers. In corporate finance, "virtually everybody stayed," as well, recalled a New York–based investment banker. And if loyalty to the firm was strong on the East Coast, loyalty to Milken was fierce on the West Coast.

"It was almost an obsession," remembered a senior equity trader in New York. "I wouldn't even talk to people [regarding other jobs]. There was no way I could move out and leave those people behind." He said it best not because that was the feeling in everyone, or even in most people, but because that was the feeling in the best people. And Drexel had more than its share.

His comments reminded me of those in *Goodbye, Darkness,* an autobiographical account of the Pacific War by William Manchester. Although slightly wounded, Manchester had left the field hospital to rejoin his Marine company rather than return to the States, and to safety, alone. Whatever was going to happen, he wanted to share it with them. And he was very nearly killed.

For Drexel, the SEC charges were just the first part of the shooting war. The SEC is permitted to file only a civil complaint; criminal charges are the province of the U.S. attorney's office. This would be the real battle, and a nasty one. But it was a mismatch—the prosecutors had a new and awesome weapon and a willingness to use it. Drexel's best defense was an appeal to fairness, which as history has repeatedly shown, is one poor excuse for a defense.

The key figure on the other side of the table was Rudolph Giuliani, the U.S. attorney for the Southern District of New York. To one former assistant U.S. attorney, he was "fair, energetic, problem oriented, funny . . . [with] a can-do, creative approach." To the folks at Drexel Burnham, he was the anti-Christ.

In a 1987 *Vanity Fair* article, Gail Sheehy provided a vivid description of Giuliani, that of a "bloodless white face with dark steady eyes"—"Just look at his eyes," said a senior Drexel official—"and goofy haircomb . . . [with] his monk's face and his altar-boy lisp."

His upbringing, in fact, was strongly Catholic; he even considered entering the priesthood. Instead, he attended New York University Law School, graduating with honors in 1968. After serving as a law clerk for two years, he became an assistant U.S. attorney for the Southern District. The high point of his five years as a prosecutor there was reached during the 1974 bribery trial of Brooklyn congressman Bertram Podell. His cross-examination was reportedly so intimidating and effective that the defendant asked for a recess, and pleaded guilty.

In 1975, Giuliani went to Washington, becoming an assistant to the deputy attorney general in the Ford administration. "Previously a liberal Democrat," *Current Biography* noted, "Giuliani switched to the Republican party during that period after concluding that the Democratic party's view of global politics was, in his words, 'dangerous.'"

When Carter came in, he went out. After four years in private practice as a partner at New York–based Patterson, Belknap, he returned to Washington in the wake of Reagan's victory, to take the number three position at the Justice Department—associate attorney general. Interestingly, he downplayed the previous administration's focus on white-collar crime, concentrating instead on the fight against drugs.

In 1983, Giuliani returned to the Southern District of New York, this time as the boss. In his first full year as U.S. attorney, the number of indictments rose by more than 20 percent. His office secured convictions in several major organized crime cases, and he personally prosecuted Stanley Friedman, the head of the Bronx Democratic party, who received a twelve-year sentence for bribery.

The focus shifted to the securities business when Ivan Boesky, realizing his days were numbered following Dennis Levine's decision to cooperate with prosecutors, chose to cut a deal with the government in the second half of 1986. The primary responsibility for the ensuing criminal investigation fell to the securities fraud unit, headed initially by Charles Carberry; in August 1987, he was succeeded by Bruce Baird.

Baird, who projects a sense of calm that you wouldn't expect in a high-level prosecutor and who possesses a sense of purpose that you would, was a seven-year veteran of the Southern District by that time. He had been the head of the narcotics unit, and before that, had served in the organized crime unit. Working under him were two young assistant U.S. attorneys, John Carroll and Jess Fardella, formerly of the narcotics unit.

But the main man was Rudy Giuliani. His style was hands-on, and those with problems found that the best way to resolve them was to speak with him directly. "You could always go in and talk," recalled a former assistant U.S. attorney. On Giuliani's door was a sign that read "This is an open door," although it was said to be always closed. Behind it was a scene described as similar to "a floating crap game," with Rudy usually surrounded by his prosecutors, in wide-ranging discussions.

The tone of the office was set by the boss, and in the case of white-collar crimes, that tone was, in Giuliani's own words in a 1987 *Washington Post* interview, "If you can present people with the distinct possibility, even if not the probability, that they could be caught and that they can be held up to public shame, ridicule and possible prison sentences, you're going to be able to affect their behavior."

He also had the weapon that would certainly affect their behavior once caught, a law that made it much riskier to face trial and possible conviction, a law that for better or worse encouraged defendants to plea-bargain rather than to fight in court. This law had sat on the books for more than a decade, a sleeping giant, until Giuliani pioneered its use. It was one part, Title IX, of the Organized Crime Control Act of 1970. Officially, it was called the Racketeer Influenced Corrupt Organizations Act, better known as RICO. (The common wisdom is that this acronym was inspired by the gangster Rico, portrayed by Edward G. Robinson in the 1930 film "Little Ceasar.")

RICO is perhaps the most powerful and least understood statute in this country, an extraordinary law with extraordinary possibilities. To get a handle on RICO, consider first the state of mind when the act was written. Two decades ago, the Republicans had recaptured the White House, partly on a law-and-order pledge. In particular, people were fed up with the government's inability to deal with mobsters, and with their success both in expanding illegal ventures—drugs in particular—and in infiltrating and corrupting legitimate businesses.

Congress met fire with fire, approving the act in 1970. An excerpt from the introduction explains what the government had in mind:

The Congress finds that (1) organized crime in the United States is a highly sophisticated, diversified, and widespread activity that annually drains billions of dollars from America's economy by unlawful conduct and the illegal use of force, fraud, and corruption; (2) organized crime derives a major portion of its power through money obtained from such illegal endeavors as syndicated gambling, loan sharking, the theft and fencing of property, the importation and distribution of narcotics and other dangerous drugs, and other forms of social exploitation; (3) this money and power are increasingly used to infiltrate and corrupt legitimate business.

That explanation is fairly straightforward; certainly, it is broad enough to cast its net around virtually every member of organized crime. In the case of Title IX, RICO, the net potentially covers the entire sea. Its definition of what constitutes a racketeer is someone who commits at least *two* listed crimes within a ten-year period. The list of crimes ranges from murder, kidnapping, arson, extortion, and the sexual exploitation of children to mail fraud and wire fraud, which means that a law was broken using a letter or a telephone.

The potential penalties under RICO are severe: up to twenty years in prison for each violation and damages amounting to three times the ill-gotten gains. It was a prosecutor's dream, and Giuliani made that dream a reality. RICO paved the way for stiff sentences in the Southern District's successful prosecutions in the mid-1980s of organized crime and of politician Stanley Friedman.

In September 1988, the employees of Drexel didn't know much about RICO, but we sure knew that we didn't want it anywhere near our firm. At that time, the outlook was cloudy. "Based on recent actions, it is obvious that the Government will consider racketeering charges in any case involving a series of actions," a memo from Corporate Communications noted. "We know that the normal meaning of racketeering is not applicable to the firm or its people."

Soon after, Fred Joseph, in a meeting with my department, announced the encouraging news that our lawyers believed that the firm wouldn't be "RICO'd"—the odds were less than one in five. He mentioned, however, the story of a friend of his in the firm who had suffered a heart attack, but was given an excellent chance of survival; when your life is on the line, Fred pointed out, even a one in ten chance seems awfully high.

But who were we kidding? The number was a hell of a lot higher than 10 or 20 percent; if we had thought about it realistically, rather than hiding in the comfort of a lawyer's blind guess, we would have realized that the chances of being RICO'd were closer to 100 percent. Giuliani had already extended RICO into the area of securities law, to the case of Princeton/Newport, an arbitrage firm that had been fingered by Boesky.

On December 17, 1987, the government had raided the offices of Princeton/Newport, confiscating 336 tapes in search of incriminating conversations. At the time, the raid was reminiscent of the Feds crashing a numbers racket or busting up a speakeasy in prohibition Chicago. The raid produced evidence of tax evasion, which led to the August 1988 indictments of six people, five from Princeton/Newport.

The sixth, Bruce Newberg, was a trader in Drexel's junk-bond department. Bright and high-strung, Bruce had spent most of his career working for Michael Milken, who regarded him highly. It would have been a coup for the prosecutors, who had indicated that Newberg would also be indicted in the cases against Drexel and Milken, to secure him as a cooperating witness against his former boss. Even facing the possibility of more than twenty years in jail, however, the young trader refused.

The prosecutors' ultimate target was becoming increasingly obvious. "We have no real interest in Princeton," attorney Jack Arseneault recalls being told by Bruce Baird. "We have no real interest in Berkman [his client]. However, we believe that Berkman can help us with Regan [another defendant], and Regan can help us with Drexel Burnham and others. If you cooperate with us, fine. If you don't, we'll roll right over you." Baird claims that these comments were "not accurate."

Two things seemed clear: Drexel was the target, and the prosecutors had no problem with playing hardball. In an August 4 memo responding to a *Wall Street Journal* article, we were told, "Our lawyers concur with the observations in the story that prosecutorial pressure tactics have been a driving force in many aspects of the Princeton/Newport case."

In the words of Paul Grand, the attorney for Charles Zarzecki, "it was a prosecution that was, I think, carefully and specifically designed to destroy Princeton/Newport as an ongoing business because the people refused to give up their right to a trial and to give evidence against others."

However justified or unjustified the tactics were, the result was that

Princeton/Newport went out of business in December 1988. Structured as an investment partnership rather than as a corporation, its limited partners were allowed to withdraw some or all of their money once a year. For Princeton/Newport, that date was November 19.

The partnership was told that additional charges would be filed against it. As Diane Parker, who worked with one of the attorneys on the case, explained to *Barron's* magazine: "Well, the government missed one deadline and then another, and then changed it to December 5. So Princeton/Newport changed the redemption date to December 10" to allow its partners an opportunity to see the new indictment before deciding what to do with their money.

"But the prosecutors kept putting it off and putting it off, and then finally they said that they weren't going to do anything until January." According to Bruce Baird, "The superseding indictment was delayed in the normal course of business."

Realizing that the limited partners would withdraw their money in the face of threatened but unknown charges, Princeton/Newport ended its partnership and closed its doors on December 8, 1988.

There was another aspect of the Princeton/Newport case that was ominous for Drexel. RICO provided for the pretrial freezing of assets. Freezing assets in advance of a trial simply assures the government that if it wins its case, there is something left to win. (Organized crime has a nasty habit of bleeding dry the assets of indicted companies under their control—cash disappears, inventories of products vanish. By the time the trial is over, the corporation is just a shell, with no assets to pay any settlement to the government.)

Princeton/Newport had been required to post a bond of $24 million, later reduced to $14 million, even though the alleged illegal profits were only $446,000. The questions that Drexel faced were: If indicted under RICO, how much would it be required to put up before trial? More serious, how much more would it be required to post in the future when the government returned with superseding charges? And the real question: Would the firm survive to see its day in court?

A financial institution is held together by confidence—the confidence of its employees, its clients, and its lenders. The company must have a reputation for integrity and the potential for a bright future to attract and retain the type of people who can ensure that integrity and future. The two-year investigation against Drexel had certainly questioned its integrity—in several specific instances, at least—and clouded its future. Still, the firm itself remarkably had held together.

As for the clients, their confidence is crucial. They must believe in the quality of a firm's products, which in Wall Street's case, are ideas. When the products are as amorphous as this, credibility is an important part of the equation. The seller must have an image of integrity to maintain the confidence of the buyers.

On another level, there must be an aura of respectability about the firm that *allows* the clients, who have a fiduciary responsibility to protect the savings and pensions that they invest, to listen to its ideas. This responsibility, broad and ill-defined, might involve avoiding a firm that is under indictment, even if nothing has been proven. The clients don't know for sure, and often, the easiest approach is to steer clear of any potential trouble.

The risk to Drexel's relationships with its clients if indicted was unknown, but there would be damage. Especially if there was a RICO indictment. Aside from the possible penalties in the future, there was the certain and immediate stigma that this particular law created. RICO accuses its victims of being racketeers, members of criminal organizations.

The bizarre thing about it is that, if you are in fact a member of organized crime, the stigma doesn't matter. Your friends won't mind if they read that you are a suspected racketeer; in fact, they probably don't even read. And being called a racketeer won't hurt your reputation among business partners that have nicknames like "Slippery Nick" and "The Weasel."

As for clients, they are not likely to turn their backs on you, since your relationship with them is based on a different kind of trust—the understanding that, for a generous fee, you won't burn their companies to the ground. Essentially, the racketeering label does its real damage to those who don't consider themselves racketeers, but who will be tried and convicted in the court of public opinion long before they ever hear a verdict.

If the confidence of employees is important and that of clients is crucial, the confidence of lenders is mandatory. Almost all of a financial institution's money comes from lenders, not stockholders. In Drexel's case, more than $28 billion of its $30 billion in assets were borrowed—fully 96 percent of its capital was in loans of one form or another. This type of leverage is common in banks, savings and loans, and brokerage firms.

Most of the assets that these firms hold are fairly liquid; they can be converted into cash quickly. The great danger is that some of the current lenders might decide that they want their money back just when no other lenders are willing to step in with new money. This can cause a sense of panic among the remaining lenders, who might also try to take out their money, and immediately. The result is a variation on the Depression-era nightmare: a run on the bank. Money is withdrawn faster than the assets can be liquidated at fair value, and the financial institution collapses.

A run-on-the-bank scenario can affect institutions as diverse as the dubious Vernon Savings & Loan and the extraordinary Bedford Falls Building & Loan. All you need is a loss of confidence, valid or not. To maintain this confidence, the government decided in the 1930s (after the Crash) to guarantee people's deposits.

And because confidence is such a fragile commodity, Congress even made it illegal "to defame a financial institution," according to one Drexel officer. And yet, he argued, the prosecutors had spent two years casting a dark shadow of doubt over Drexel, a financial institution whose survival depended on the confidence of its lenders.

To this point, the confidence had been maintained—when loans had come due, there had always been lenders willing to roll those loans over, to provide the firm with a steady flow of cash to run its business. The big question was: Would the cash flow dry up and the lenders disappear if Drexel were indicted, particularly under RICO? The management believed that the firm could survive if indicted under the Securities and Exchange Act of 1934, but not if the racketeering statute was used.

The reasoning was simple: Under RICO, Drexel would have to post a bond in advance of trial, to avoid a freezing of its assets. The bond, it was believed, could amount to as much as $1 *billion*. This potential debt to the government would take precedence over all debts that the firm incurred subsequently. Because most of a brokerage firm's loans are short term in nature, it wouldn't take long before all of its lenders would be forced to take junior positions—similar to a second mortgage on your home—to the government's claim.

To make matters worse, this claim would approach the total value of the shareholders' equity. If the claim ever had to be paid, the stockholders would lose most of their money; if there were other legal or operating losses as well, the firm's equity might be more than wiped out, and the firm's debts would then exceed its assets. For those who like equations, $D > A = B^2$ (D, debt; A, assets; B, bye).

Lenders like equations—their lives are ruled by them. What they don't like is lending their money to companies that have equations like the one above. And if that didn't scare them off, the likelihood of a superseding indictment, and an additional unknown bond, might.

What was known in December 1988 was that an indictment was coming, and soon. After twenty-five months of investigation, during which Drexel had spent $140 million in legal and other fees, during which the firm had lost untold hundreds of millions of dollars in potential profits on deals that didn't get done or that wary clients took elsewhere, during which one and a half million documents were examined . . . after twenty-five months during which Drexel stuck to its original claim that it was innocent, Giuliani decided that the firm would be prosecuted under the RICO statute.

"Peter Fleming [one of Drexel's top attorneys] said of Rudy that he's a reasonable man," recalled Burt Siegel, the head of the equity operation and a member of the board of directors. "He can be reasoned with, even if the people who work for him are tough." This was a miscalculation, he noted later.

Siegel, who one salesman praised as a "smooth-elbowed man in a sharp-elbowed world," pointed out another miscalculation: the hope that, even if Giuliani wouldn't listen to reason on the use of RICO, the Justice Department itself would. The hope was that the department, which was required to approve each RICO case, wouldn't give the go-ahead regardless of Giuliani's wishes. This was a naive hope, however, given both the strength of his relationship with Washington—he had worked in prominent positions at the Justice Department for almost five years—and the generally poor perception of Drexel throughout the government.

If Giuliani's choice of weapon was considered unfair at 60 Broad Street, it was viewed as entirely appropriate at One St. Andrews Plaza, the home of the U.S. attorney's office. "The high-yield bond department was a criminal organization," said Bruce Baird, later noting that "the basic Justice Department rule is that you bring the most serious charge that fits the facts."

The evidence behind those facts, in Drexel's view, was primarily based on the testimony of Ivan Boesky. Unknown to the firm at that time, the government claimed that "at least six former employees of the Boesky organization have corroborated pieces of the Boesky story." The government's hand was further strengthened in the late fall when three important employees of the high-yield bond department became witnesses.

Jim Dahl, Milken's top salesman (other than himself), was required to testify under an arrangement used in Mafia cases in which the witness is given immunity, like it or not. Accordingly, Dahl couldn't refuse to answer questions under the Fifth Amendment, because he was now guaranteed against incriminating himself with his specific responses. He could, however, be indicted for perjury if he answered those questions untruthfully. Following his grand jury testimony, Dahl evidently became a cooperating witness in exchange for complete immunity.

Cary Maultasch, a second witness, worked out of New York, about a hundred feet from me on the trading floor, handling equity transactions for Milken's department and clients. Like Jim Dahl, Maultasch had been told by prosecutors in September that he would likely be indicted along with Drexel and Milken. Unlike Dahl, he wasn't offered immunity; eventually, he agreed to cooperate with the government in return for a deferral of its decision on whether or not to prosecute him.

Terren Peizer, an aggressive and successful young trader who had been hired from First Boston, also agreed to cooperate. Given that he was offered immunity and that he sat next to Milken at the X-shaped desk, the implication was that he had something interesting to say. Neither Peizer nor Dahl found themselves very welcome back in the high-yield department. "They were not allowed on the floor," recalled a trader in this intense and close-knit department. "No one would talk to them."

"The whole thing changed with Dahl and Peizer and Maultasch," said Burt Siegel, adding that the board of directors "had no idea what they said."

There was also a lingering doubt regarding the Princeton/Newport allegations. That indictment concerned the parking of stock to generate tax losses, an accusation that had also been raised against Drexel and Boesky in the SEC complaint. Among the tapes that had been confiscated was a conversation in which Drexel's Bruce Newberg called his counterpart at Princeton/Newport, Charles Zarzecki, "a sleaze bag." Zarzecki responded, "You taught me, man." Newberg: "Welcome to the world of sleaze."

The picture painted was one of crummy morals, if not criminality.

One question raised was whether Milken knew of Newberg's actions, and whether the firm was liable for those actions. Another obvious question was the familiar one of whether Newberg's attitude was unusual, or whether it reflected a general way of doing business in that department.

The government's most compelling piece of written evidence was a collection of notes by Boesky's accountant, Setrag Mooradian. These notes allegedly dealt with the much-discussed $5.3 million payment from Boesky to Drexel. Lowell Milken had contended in a 1986 letter that the payment was for perfectly legal research, and the firm, after its own investigation, had agreed that it was for "legitimate investment banking services." The government, on the other hand, believed that the $5.3 million was the amount that Boesky owed Milken's department for its share of illegal profits.

The Mooradian notes purportedly showed, on a several-page ledger, the profits and losses from various transactions that influenced the $5.3 million figure. Among these transactions were the Maxxam/ Pacific Lumber, Turner Broadcasting/MGM/UA, AM International/Harris Graphics, and Kohlberg Kravis/Storer Broadcasting deals.

One possible problem with Mooradian's notes, however, was that they might have been reconstructed by the accountant from memory or from fantasy. At the time of Dennis Levine's arrest, certain documents at the Boesky organization were said to have been destroyed. The original notes, if they existed at all, might have been part of that group—after all, if they were what they were supposed to be, they were certainly incriminating.

Fred Joseph faced two difficult questions: did Mooradian ever take notes regarding an allegedly illegal payment to the firm and, if so, were these the actual notes, or were they reconstructed? More specifically, were these profits and losses recorded at the time of the actual deals during 1985, at the time of the $5.3 million payment in March 1986, or after Boesky's decision to cooperate with the government in late summer 1986?

One lawyer representing Drexel believed that the Mooradian notes were reconstructed in the late summer; another agreed with the prosecutors that they were "contemporaneous," written in March 1986. There was no way to know for Drexel to know for sure. One senior official familiar with the negotiations pointed out that Fred

Joseph was permitted to view the notes for only about a minute. According to this official, Fred's best guess was that the Mooradian notes were originals.

More important to the board of directors than Drexel's chances in court were Drexel's chances of getting to court. Senior management thought that in the event of a RICO indictment the firm could not avoid bankruptcy. Even with a settlement, Drexel's survival was far from certain, but a critical wound has great advantages over death.

In negotiations with Giuliani, Fred's greatest leverage, oddly enough, was that threat of death. Many in the firm were willing to take a RICO indictment, whatever the consequences, rather than accede to what they considered was a grossly unfair settlement. Rudy wanted a settlement—no rational man is eager to put nine thousand people out of work for the alleged crimes of a handful. It was also common knowledge at the time that Giuliani would likely run for mayor of New York. The thought of putting thousands of people out of work, people with family and friends, would have been political suicide.

And even if Drexel did survive a RICO indictment—which the prosecutors believed it could—the case against the firm would be a challenge for the U.S. attorney's office, dealing with technical issues and relying heavily on circumstantial evidence. A settlement was the best of either world for Rudy.

It was a classic case of brinksmanship. Giuliani was holding most of the cards, but if he insisted on anything too unreasonable, he would end up holding a corpse. And a corpse that big is difficult to bury, if it can be buried at all. Joseph, on the other hand, wanted to protect his firm and his employees. Cutting off Drexel's future to spite its prosecutor might provide a great psychic dividend, but that sense of moral superiority would likely wear off long before thousands of good people found new jobs.

Joseph proposed a settlement offer of $100 million; Giuliani asked for $750 million. On Monday, December 19, negotiations fell through for reasons that had to do with much more than money. The government insisted on a number of points that the board of directors found "objectionable on every ground," according to a board member. Among the provisions was one that was extraordinary, perhaps even unprecedented: The firm must waive its attorney-client privilege, allowing the government to examine discussions between Drexel personnel and its lawyers, conversations that had been conducted in confidence.

Another of the unacceptable points allowed the government, at any time in the future, to "arbitrarily decide that we had abrogated the agreement," according to a senior executive familiar with the negotiations. Because, in his opinion, "the prosecutors had lied to us in many ways," giving them carte blanche to terminate the settlement at their discretion would keep the firm and its employees at the mercy of people he didn't trust.

The board voted twenty-two to zero against the government's proposal.

That afternoon, Fred told the employees, "At the present time, discussions may be winding down. We could be indicted at any time, beginning tomorrow. . . . It's very clear that the firm didn't do anything wrong, and couldn't really know." This was the first time in memory that Fred had spoken of the firm's innocence and not of the individual employees.

At the time, I was glad to hear that we would fight, rather than settle. I was aware that there was a real chance of bankruptcy, but it took another eighteen months to realize how disastrous that might have been. Besides, I felt that if we believed what we were saying then fighting the charges according to the law was the right thing to do. Pleading guilty as an accommodation, as the lesser of two evils, arranged and signed by a few people behind closed doors, was not what this system was all about.

If my reaction to the breakdown of negotiations was one of grim satisfaction, that of the investment bankers was of outright joy. When Fred made an appearance that evening at the corporate finance department's annual Christmas party, he was cheered. The battle was on.

Within forty-eight hours, the battle was off. The U.S. attorney's office responded to Drexel's defiance by dropping all but two of the conditions that the board had objected to. The remaining two applied directly to Milken: He must be fired and his bonus for 1988 must be withheld. "They were really paranoid about Michael running the company," recalled Burt Siegel. He noted that the main prosecutors on the case all had worked in the narcotics unit, the implication being that these men were used to drug kingpins who held onto control of their operations in fact if not in appearance.

The board considered the new terms. There were three other important factors—two old, one new. The prosecutors still refused to indicate how large a bond Drexel would be requested to post when it was indicted. Clearly, uncertainty worked in their favor; better to let the firm imagine the worst. They weren't eager to make it any easier for Drexel to decide in favor of fighting the charges.

Another logical consideration for the firm was that its relationship with the judge on its case, Milton Pollack, couldn't be much worse. The blame for that was squarely on Drexel. The firm had asked Judge Pollack, who was presiding on all Boesky-related matters, to remove himself from the case based on a supposed conflict of interest. The conflict was a stretch at best: A company owned by Pollack's wife was being bought out, and Drexel was involved in the financing.

The firm's argument was insignificant, bordering on insulting. The more likely reason that Drexel wanted a different judge was that, if its case should come to trial, Pollack had a reputation for being tough on white-collar defendants. In the St. Joe Mineral case, his threat of a $50,000 per day fine encouraged an Italian bank in Switzerland to "persuade" the defendant, Guisseppe Tome, to face a U.S. court. Instead, Tome pleaded guilty. This novel approach to the problem of extradition came to be known as "Pollack's Law."

Not surprisingly, Pollack, an eighty-one-year-old judge who had served on the bench since his appointment by LBJ, refused to excuse himself from the Drexel case. The firm appealed his decision to a higher court, but lost. The firm's strategy on this one was the public relations equivalent of the Little Big Horn or Gallipoli.

The problem with Pollack was small potatoes compared with one that had materialized in recent months. In November 1988, for a reason unrelated to the investigation, senior management was told of a partnership that it had been unaware of: the MacPherson Partners. This partnership had benefited from some shenanigans on an offering of high-yield securities for Storer Broadcasting.

The offering included equity warrants; most of these sweeteners ended up in the high-yield partnerships. The bulk of the remainder were sold to one client in particular. This client then resold the warrants back to Milken's group, which in turn sold them to the MacPherson Partnership. Among the beneficiaries were individual money managers, raising the question of whether this scheme was a payoff to favored individuals for doing business with the department.

This partnership, which the firm reported to the U.S.

attorney's office, seriously hurt Mike Milken's credibility with the board. According to Steve Joseph, management had heard allegations that "individuals were receiving warrants directly" and had questioned Milken. "Michael had said that it never had happened."

On Wednesday, December 21, assistant U.S. Attorney John Carroll called Tom Curnin, Drexel's lead outside counsel, to say that, unless the firm settled the case, a RICO indictment would be filed that evening. The firm's lawyers were said to have checked their sources in Washington and confirmed that all the necessary papers had been filed with the Justice Department. It was decision time.

"There was not a lot of acrimony in the discussions," remembered Siegel, even though the board was highly politicized. "The Belgian investors very much wanted to settle," he added, referring to the six seats controlled by Groupe Bruxelles Lambert, which had owned over 20 percent of Drexel since 1976.

"The biggest block, the Frogs, was into the firm for nothing," was one West Coast officer's view of the Belgians. His comment, an insult to the wrong country, did make one interesting point: Groupe Lambert's stake in the firm, although worth a great deal on paper, was mostly profit; its initial investment was only a small fraction. As for the others on the board, "the older people had a high percentage of their net worth in the firm," this officer noted—they didn't want to risk bankruptcy. "So they voted their pocketbooks," he concluded. "That was a business decision, and that was done."

The settlement terms were six felonies and $650 million. Take it or leave it. The board had been told to decide by 4:00 P.M., when the grand jury was scheduled to leave. As the deadline neared, one of the senior executives went "bat shit," according to a participant. Fred Joseph assured him that the grand jury would wait. Around 4:05, the final vote was taken. The result: sixteen to six in favor.

"There was a school of thought among those who voted against, that the firm couldn't survive that kind of settlement, and if the firm goes down, let it be the fault of the government," was Siegel's analysis of the decision. "The majority opinion, and I was among them, was that we absolutely could not survive a RICO indictment. But there was a chance that we could settle, and run the business."

Another Drexel director who voted in favor also argued that the firm needed a settlement. According to him, the firm knew from the banks that a RICO indictment would cost it its credit rating and, accordingly, its lenders. Although, in his opinion, there had been "no real improvement in the settlement terms" from those that had been unanimously rejected only two days earlier, he had accepted the proposal.

The six directors who found the terms unacceptable, regardless of the risks, were Leon Black, cohead of mergers and acquisitions; Herb Bachelor, overall head of corporate finance; John Kissick, in charge of the West Coast's corporate finance department; Alan Sher, head of the retail system; Howard Brenner, a senior vice-president of trading; and Fred Joseph.

Fred made a tactical error by voting against the settlement that he had negotiated. He had hoped that his protest vote would be a signal to the employees, especially those loyal to Milken, that he opposed the settlement in principle. Instead, he just invited criticism.

"I didn't think we were guilty," explained Howard Brenner, one of the remaining five who voted against the proposal, later noting: "I didn't like the fact that we hadn't settled with the SEC." That settlement would still have to be negotiated and approved before the firm could try to put the scandal behind it.

In his opinion, the prosecutors made "criminal law out of administrative offenses." And, repeating the most common objection, he argued that "RICO was being used unjustly."

He also argued an uncommon point: "I don't think they would have RICO'd the firm if it had refused to settle." In this high-stakes poker game, he believed that Giuliani was bluffing. Drexel had three hundred and fifty thousand retail accounts throughout the country; although these accounts were insured by the Securities Investor Protection Corporation (SIPC), there is never any foolproof insurance against fear. If the firm went bankrupt, its individual clients might have panicked at the thought of losing their savings, instigating a loss of confidence in all brokerage firms, healthy or not.

The director who explained these various reasons for opposing the settlement also raised a pragmatic objection: Even if the firm was guilty, a $650 million penalty was unfair. "The fine was a hideous amount of money," was one salesman's description. "It had no relation to anything in reality."

According to Siegel the firm had added up the actual damages, assuming it was guilty of every charge—the total was $150 to 200 million. Analyzing each count in the SEC complaint, I estimated a number closer to $73 million:

Fischbach/Boesky financings	$33,000,000
Harris Graphics	7,000,000
Lorimar	2,000,000
Lorimar short sales	—
Maxxam/Pacific Lumber	3,000,000
MCA	—
MGM/UA	3,000,000
Occidental Petroleum/Diamond Shamrock	—
Phillips Petroleum	—
Stone Container	8,000,000
Storer Communications	1,000,000
Tax loss trades	1,000,000
Viacom	2,000,000
Wickes/National Gypsum	7,000,000
Wickes convertible preferred stock	2,300,000
Wickes short sales	4,000,000
TOTAL	$73,300,000

Note that the total includes $30 million in fees for three financings of Boesky-controlled companies. The $73 million total doesn't include the $66 million fee Drexel received for arranging the MGM deal with Turner Broadcasting, which almost certainly would've happened without the alleged insider trading; if you disagree, add in the fee to the total.

Regardless, the settlement as approved called for a payment of $650 million over three years, $500 million upon approval by Judge Pollack. Of the total, $300 million was assessed as a fine; the remaining $350 million was to be set aside to pay civil claims against the firm. If all those claims ended up costing more than $350 million, the additional amount would come out of Drexel's pocket; if the claims came in at less than $350 million, whatever was left over went to the government.

The financial impact on the firm was "not horrible," according to Fred Joseph, who was naturally trying to make the best of a difficult situation that day, Wednesday the twenty-first. Based on his explanation to us, it seemed that Drexel had already set aside about $400 million for the possibility of a settlement, now a certainty.

If the financial part of the agreement appeared manageable, the legal side was unknown. We were accepting six felony counts. Although the firm wasn't actually pleading guilty—the wording was that we "can't dispute the allegations"—almost no one would note the difference. To the world, Drexel was now an admitted felon.

The firm was allowed to choose its crimes from among Boesky's allegations, with the exception of the Fischbach deal—the government insisted on that one. Boesky had pleaded guilty to one felony—conspiring to file a false statement—regarding Fischbach, and with Drexel's plea to stock parking, the prosecutors' case against Milken on this transaction would be considerably strengthened.

The firm's remaining five choices reflected a desire to minimize its potential liability to the inevitable civil lawsuits. It effectively pleaded guilty to two transactions involving stock manipulation—Stone Container and C.O.M.B. (not part of the SEC complaint)—and three transactions involving stock parking—Phillips Petroleum, Harris Graphics, and MCA.

The reaction to the settlement was mixed, as expected. Representative John Dingell said in a statement: "Pickpockets get several years in the slammer for stealing small amounts of money, and deservedly so. Now we have executives apparently admitting to receiving hundreds of millions which they may have stolen." In response to a question from *The Wall Street Journal* on the settlement's deterrence value, he quoted from Gilbert and Sullivan's "The Mikado": "My object all sublime / I shall achieve in time— / To make the punishment fit the crime."

The *Journal* itself had a somewhat different point of view:

After much waiting, the government's extraordinary case against Drexel Burnham Lambert has ended in a rather ordinary way. Drexel pleaded guilty to six felony counts and agreed to a $650 million fine. There will now be no trial, and while the guilty plea sends a message, it must be said that the rest of the securities market is left to wonder what precisely the message is.

CHAPTER TWELVE

HAS THE JURY
REACHED ITS VERDICT?

> Son, you're on your own.
> —*Blazing Saddles*

If the settlement with the government took the employees of Drexel from the fire into the frying pan, it put its most famous employee on a skillet of his own. Michael Milken, as required in the settlement, would be fired once he was formally indicted. His fate would be separated from that of his firm's.

More than that, his firm would cooperate with the prosecutors in the continuing investigation of his activities in the mid-1980s. Although Drexel had officially been cooperating since Boesky's initial allegations more than two years earlier, there is cooperation and then there is cooperation. According to both Gary Lynch of the SEC and Bruce Baird of the U.S. attorney's office, Drexel hadn't exactly set the standard.

"There was a pattern of delay in response to document requests," said Lynch. "They certainly weren't cooperative," was Baird's comment, who noted that if you feel you have "a decent chance" of winning the case, this isn't a bad strategy. And Drexel did feel that it had a strong case.

Now the firm had a settlement, one that required its cooperation. And it no longer had the threat of prosecution hanging over its head.

For Milken, that threat was a certainty—it was only a matter of time. On March 29, 1989, a grand jury handed down a ninety-eight-count indictment against him, with seventeen counts against his brother and twenty-two counts against Bruce Newberg. The indictment dealt with twenty transactions, most of which were familiar from the SEC complaint six months earlier. (Almost every transaction involved multiple counts against the defendants, the most common being mail fraud and wire fraud.)

Milken potentially faced up to 520 years in jail—175 with a lenient parole board. He was also liable for the vast majority of a potential forfeiture that, according to government calculations, was $1,845,404,494—an almost inconceivable amount of money. The lion's share of this, some 60 percent, comprised the *entire* amount in salaries and bonuses that the three men had received between 1984 and 1987—even though the transactions identified by the prosecutors provided only a small fraction of that income.

The indictment contained several trades in which, according to the 1988 SEC complaint, Cary Maultasch was involved. Maultasch was not actually named in the government's indictment. He would probably have been called as a corroborating witness. Jim Dahl and Terren Peizer, the other two junk-bond employees who had received immunity in late 1988, did not appear to figure in these charges; their testimony would probably be used in a superseding indictment.

"The three-year investigation has uncovered substantial fraud in a very significant segment of the American financial community," announced Benito Romano, the acting U.S. attorney since Giuliani's retirement on January 31. "A serious criminal problem has infected Wall Street." Milken's statement offered a different perspective: "In America, an indictment marks the beginning of the legal process, not the end. After almost two and a half years of leaks and distortions, I am now eager to present all the facts in an open and unbiased forum."

Well, this forum is hardly open or unbiased, but nevertheless, let's consider the indictment as a jury might, because to tell you what you might already know, a jury never did. To keep you reading, you've been chosen as the foreman. In fact, yours is the only vote that matters—everyone else in the Southern District of New York was able to find a valid reason to be excused from jury duty.

So the verdict is in your hands. I'll try to give you both sides of the case as best I can—no hidden agenda. You make your own decision here; I'll give you mine in the last chapter.

Now let's review the charges against Michael Milken in the 110-page indictment, in the order in which they're presented. This indictment, along with the SEC May 1988 memo, the September 1988 complaint, and the October–November 1990 sentencing hearing—and with some educated guesses—are most of the evidence we have. You have your work cut out for you: no witnesses; no give and take between the prosecution and the defense; no chance of your verdict holding up on appeal. But what the hell.

The first two counts of the indictment are the big ones: RICO charges. Specifically, Milken was accused of racketeering conspiracy and participation in a racketeering enterprise. That is, he arranged and took part in a pattern of illegal activities.

The following fifty-four counts involved mail fraud and wire fraud. Whenever a trade is completed, a written confirmation of that trade is generated and sent to both parties; in an illegal trade, the sending of the "confirm" is mail fraud. Similarly, if a telephone is used to place an illegal order, wire fraud is committed.

Counts fifty-eight through ninety-one dealt with securities fraud; ninety-two through ninety-seven concerned false filings of who owned what; count ninety-eight involved assisting in the preparation of a false tax return. Ninety-eight counts in all—an overwhelming number of charges against anyone. And if only one of them were found to be true, Milken would face up to five years in prison. If two or more were found to be true, then he could be convicted of racketeering and could face an additional twenty years for each of the two RICO charges.

The average person, at some level, must wonder: How can this guy not be guilty? If not, why would the government bring a huge and frivolous case and why would a grand jury approve an indictment based on these charges? And not just two charges or even three, but ninety-eight!

The guilt or innocence of an individual, however, is not determined by the sheer force of numbers, or even by a grand jury. The decision belongs to a group of people who get to hear both sides of the argument and who are decent enough to give the defendant the benefit of the doubt. Here, the burden of fairness is on you, the reader-jury.

The Takeover of Fischbach (main allegation: stock parking). This one is a bit convoluted. According to the prosecutors, Milken and Boesky "commenced a secret arrangement involving a series of unlawful securities transactions" by mid-1984. (All quotes in this chapter are from the indictment unless otherwise noted.) This alleged arrangement was central to fourteen of the twenty transactions under suspicion.

The first on the list was the takeover of Fischbach Corporation, a construction company. In the government's view, Milken and Boesky illegally assisted Pennsylvania Engineering (PenEn), controlled by Victor Posner, in taking control of Fischbach.

PenEn had agreed in 1980 that it wouldn't attempt to acquire Fischbach unless another company purchased more than 10 percent of Fischbach's stock. Allegedly, Milken had Boesky, who was promised indemnification against loss, purchase more than 10 percent of Fischbach, and the standstill agreement was off. PenEn raised $56 million through high-yield bonds in February 1985 and used the proceeds to buy a majority position in Fischbach.

One disturbing piece of evidence found among the Boesky files was a May 1984 memorandum regarding Fischbach, written by Boesky employee Nancy Hollander. The memo concludes with: "I will communicate the situation to Mike Milken. He just wanted to let the situation stand as it was today." Which raises the question: Why should Milken have any say in this "situation"?

If the allegations are true, Milken, by promising to indemnify Boesky, would have been guilty of stock parking. True or not, Milken earned some $3 million in commissions for his department and about a third of that for himself. Bear in mind, though, if he indemnified Boesky, he stood to give back some or all of the profits in the event that Boesky lost money, which in fact, Boesky did.

Another consideration: If Boesky (or anyone else) had bought the 10 percent position by his own choice or on Milken's recommendation—provided that Milken didn't promise to pay any of Boesky's losses and wasn't acting on inside information of PenEn's intentions—then there were no laws broken. Assuming this were the case, what then would have been Boesky's motive to buy 10 percent of Fischbach? Perhaps he hoped that by freeing PenEn from its stand-still agreement his shares would rise in value if and when PenEn came into the market.

After reading the details of this first transaction, you probably now realize that any review of alleged financial fraud ranges between the dull and the confusing. Transactions such as these are difficult to understand—it is a problem faced by lawyers, prosecutors, judges, and juries. But it is important to look at the details and the allegations for yourself and to draw your own conclusions.

Golden Nugget's Sale of MCA Stock (stock parking). By July 27, 1984, Golden Nugget (GNG), a gaming company, had bought 2.4 million shares of MCA, with the thought of possibly acquiring the whole company. Deciding against a tender offer, GNG sold 1.1 million shares to Milken's department. These shares were then sold to Boesky, supposedly with the understanding that Drexel would cover his losses—if true, Drexel would remain the real owner of the shares, and the "sale" to Boesky would constitute illegal parking of stock.

The question here is, what purpose did Boesky serve in this alleged scheme? What difference did it make if Drexel sold to Boesky who then sold the shares in the market, or if Drexel just sold the shares directly? Either way, the market was going to have to absorb the shares, and the price of those shares was likely to go down.

(A GNG representative evidently tried to cushion this blow, according to the indictment, by stating publicly in October that GNG held just under 5 percent of MCA and that "for now" it planned to maintain its current position. Meanwhile, GNG was in the process of selling almost half its position, which it *didn't* state publicly. Isn't something wrong here?)

The sale of the MCA stock to Boesky raises another question: Why would Milken accept responsibility for any losses? Unless he was interested in doing GNG a multimillion-dollar favor, the motive behind this one is weak. And if he did want to do this favor, why not just sell the shares himself and take the loss directly? Why break the law by secretly arranging to reimburse Boesky's company for this same loss? It doesn't make much sense.

The Diamond Shamrock (DIA)/Occidental Petroleum (OXY) Merger Talks (insider trading). On January 4, 1985, Drexel was hired as an adviser to Occidental Petroleum, which had agreed on the previous day to merge with Diamond Shamrock. That same day, the two companies publicly announced that a merger was possible. Also on the fourth, Boesky bought 3.6 million shares of DIA, allegedly "with the understanding that the Drexel Enterprise and the Boesky Organization would split profits and losses."

On January 7, DIA and OXY publicly announced the details of the proposed deal, and Boesky bought an additional 150,000 DIA shares. He also sold short 260,000 OXY shares, in the hope that they would decline in value. After the close of the market on the seventh, the two companies announced that the merger had fallen through, causing sizable losses for Boesky.

This allegation accuses Milken of directly or indirectly passing along inside information to Boesky, which is a serious crime. The facts, however, are far from conclusive. It appears that Boesky began purchasing Diamond stock *after* the public announcement on January 4, when the whole world was told that a merger was in the works. Perhaps Boesky was doing what risk arbitrageurs do, buying shares in a possible deal in the hope of making a small but quick profit if the deal went through.

Even if he was given inside information, that information became public with the announcement that January 4 morning. Taking things one step further, even if Boesky *was* somehow trading on inside information, it doesn't necessarily mean that he had received that information from Michael Milken or from one of Milken's associates. Although Drexel would be a prime suspect, there were several other companies who had access to the same inside information, and a number of people within those companies who could have passed it along.

The most damaging piece of evidence is an entry on a three-page ledger allegedly found in Boesky's files, an entry which strongly suggests that Boesky was splitting his losses on the Diamond/Occidental deal with someone—that someone almost certainly was Drexel, if the ledger is to be believed. This ledger is an integral part of another allegation—concerning the $5.3 million payment—and is explained in more detail below.

Repayment Trades (reimbursement for illegal transactions). In late November 1984, Boesky allegedly sent ledger sheets to Milken, detailing $10 million in losses from the Fischbach and MCA transactions and additional losses from other trades. From January to mid-March, "the defendants Michael R. Milken and Lowell J. Milken conducted a series of sham and bogus trades at artificial prices . . . to repay the Boesky Organization for its losses on trades made on behalf of the Drexel Enterprise."

According to a letter from Boesky to Milken dated November 28, 1984 and released by Assistant U.S. Attorney John Carroll, Boesky told Milken that "it will be appropriate to resolve all of the enclosed." The enclosed was evidently a three-page ledger, which listed the profits and losses from ten stocks and one bond, but which in no place refers to Milken or Drexel.

The ledger, said to have come from Boesky's files, includes the two names mentioned above: Fischbach and MCA. But it also mentions eight other stocks, none of which figures in the indictment. The question here is, if this ledger is in fact evidence of an illegal arrangement between Milken and Boesky, why wasn't Milken charged on all ten names? Perhaps the prosecution wanted to focus on those transactions that it felt had the best chance in court. Perhaps the other eight figured in the repayment trades. Or perhaps none of these transactions were illegal.

As for the alleged repayment trades, if they took place, they must exist on some computer—it would be important to see whether or not Boesky was in fact given unfair prices.

A reference to these trades was included in the SEC's May 1988 internal memo, which alleged that Milken himself suggested bond trades for the Boesky organization, resulting in quick profits for it. "Some of these trades were at prices significantly different from market prices," says the memo, "but many were at or near prevailing market prices."

The person who claims to have taken these orders from Milken is Michael Davidoff, Boesky's top trader, who pleaded guilty to one count of securities fraud and is cooperating with the government. Indeed, at Milken's sentencing hearing in October–November 1990, Davidoff did briefly acknowledge that these trades had occurred; his testimony, however, did not touch on the issue of whether the trades were bogus or legitimate.

Another factor in your decision here must be whether or not you believe that the underlying transactions—Fischbach and MCA—were illegal. If not, then there were no illegal profits and losses to reconcile. From the other perspective, if in your opinion there is enough evidence to determine whether the reconciling trades were bogus, then you'd have a much clearer idea on the legality or illegality of the underlying transactions.

Tax Loss Trades (tax evasion). In late February and early March 1985, according to the indictment, a Boesky employee asked Milken and others to help Boesky's company evade taxes. To do this, Drexel sold Cigna and OXY stock to Boesky in early March. Both stocks were about to pay a dividend; after the record date, the shares fell in price as expected. (The record date is the day that determines who is entitled to a dividend payment. If you are the owner of record on that day, you will receive the dividends on your shares; if you are the owner on the following day, you won't. Therefore, a stock will fall in price by the amount of its dividend.)

After the record date, Boesky then repurchased the shares from Milken's department at a lower price, establishing a loss for tax purposes. The dividends that he was entitled to were not actually paid until April, after the end of his March tax year.

Accordingly, he was able to take a write-off in one year and not have to pay taxes on the dividend until the following year. He still had to pay the same amount of taxes, but not for a year; in effect, he finagled an interest-free loan from the government.

This type of tax loss trade is not illegal. The allegation is that Milken's group had an understanding with Boesky that it would reimburse him if the stocks fell by more than the amount of the dividend. In the case of the three trades, that difference was about $3 million.

Why would Milken or anyone else guarantee Boesky's losses on these trades? Even if you assume away ethics, there was no possible profit on this deal for the person offering the guarantee. The best explanation, if you believe the allegation here is true, would be that these trades were just one part of an ongoing illegal relationship.

In a trial, Milken's attorneys would highlight Michael Davidoff's testimony that he was told by his Drexel contact, Cary Maultasch, that nothing could be done regarding the losses incurred on these tax trades—the implication being that there was no illicit understanding between Milken's department and Boesky's firm on these trades. This testimony would not necessarily exonerate Milken, however, since the losses here may have later become part of such an understanding.

Purchase of Phillips Petroleum Stock (stock parking). On March 5, 1985, Phillips announced a recapitalization plan that involved a buyback of 55 percent of its stock. Boesky owned over four million shares, but his capital was less than required by the SEC. The allegation is that Boesky sold his shares to Drexel, with the understanding that he would be responsible for any losses and would be entitled to half of any profits. In effect, Milken's group would park the stock for him, in return for 50 percent of any profits.

In a complicated series of transactions, Boesky's company sold 4.1 millin shares on March 7 and 11 to Drexel, which then resold the shares to three clients and six employee partnerships. After the Phillips recap was completed, and 55 percent of its shares had been respurchased, the three sold their remaining shares to Drexel, which then resold them to seven partnerships.

Between April 12 and 19, Boesky bought 1.75 million shares—this figure is almost 45 percent of what it had sold Drexel only a month before, which coincidentally or not, is about the number of shares it would have been left with if it had tendered its 4.1 million shares of Phillips. Between April 19 and June 3, Boesky sold the 1.75 million shares he had just repurchased from Drexel.

The circumstantial evidence here is fairly compelling. Boesky had a capital problem, and the series of transactions that followed fit the pattern you would expect if Milken's group was in fact parking stock for Boesky until his capital position improved.

The fact that ten different employee partnerships controlled by Milken bought and sold two million shares in one month doesn't add to the credibility of these transactions. On the other hand, the partnerships took a loss on the trades, which would seem unusual if there was a sweetheart deal between Boesky and Milken. As I indicated earlier, analyzing financial transactions can be frustrating.

Reconciling the Books (repayment of illegal profits). By May 1985, according to the indictment, ". . . the Drexel Enterprise owed the Boesky Organization for profits on the unlawful Phillips Petroleum trading. In or about mid-May 1985, a Drexel Enterprise member and a Boesky Organization employee attempted to reconcile the outstanding balance on the Boesky Arrangement." It is unclear whether or not the balance was reconciled, or if so, what exactly was done about it.

The Takeover of Storer Communications (insider trading). This one is confusing. In early April 1985, Drexel was hired by Kohlberg Kravis Roberts & Co. (KKR), the best known of the firms that arrange buyouts. On May 3, KKR announced an agreement to buy Storer.

By July 1, Comcast Corp., another media company, was considering a competing bid for Storer. KKR considered raising its bid if Comcast made an offer.

On July 8, Milken allegedly "caused" Boesky to buy 124,300 shares of Storer, with the understanding that all profits and losses were Drexel's.

On July 16, Comcast did make a higher bid for Storer.

On July 22 and 23, Boesky sold thirty-eight thousand shares, allegedly on Drexel's behalf.

On July 29, Comcast increased its first offer. Eventually, KKR—Milken's client—increased its bid and won the company. Drexel's fee was $49,550,000. Drexel's alleged profit from Boesky was $1,066,000.

The allegations here are very serious: The abuse of inside information. Among the questions that should be asked: Why did Milken, who was involved with KKR since early April, wait until July—two months after KKR's public announcement—before having Boesky illegally buy shares for Drexel's benefit? Why did he have Boesky sell thirty-eight thousand shares two weeks later? He certainly knew that KKR was considering a higher bid, and in fact, it did raise its proposed price.

Why would Milken do something so illegal and dangerous? His personal share of the "illegal profit" was no more than $150,000; his share of the entirely legal fee from KKR was more than $6 million. From another angle, why would he be involved in a corrupt scheme that produced $150,000 in income over five months, at a time when his legitimate income exceeded $500,000 a day?

Perhaps he thought that KKR would lose to Comcast, and he wanted to make an easy profit, legal or not. Perhaps both his sense of ethics and perspective were absolutely shot. Perhaps he didn't do anything wrong.

The Takeover of Pacific Lumber (insider trading). Since the spring of 1984, Drexel had been an adviser to Maxxam, a real estate company, regarding a possible acquisition. On September 30, 1985, Maxxam made an offer to buy the shares of Pacific Lumber at $36 per share. Two days later, the company raised its bid to $38.50 per share.

> From on or about October 1, 1985, to on or about November 8, 1985, the defendant Michael R. Milken and another Drexel Enterprise member caused the Boesky Organization to buy approximately 1,843,000 shares of Pacific Lumber common stock, at prices that were often above Maxxam's then publicly announced offering price, and to sell approximately 769,000 of those shares. . . . The defendant Michael R. Milken secretly agreed with the Boesky Organization that any profits or losses on these shares would belong to the Drexel Enterprise.

On October 28, 1985, Maxxam raised its offer to $40 per share, and completed the takeover in December. Drexel's fee was $20.5 million and two hundred and fifty thousand Maxxam warrants. The alleged illegal profits from trading on inside information was $1,025,000, less than $1 per share.

This allegation is similar to the previous one, and the questions raised there would apply here as well. In addition, there is specific testimony regarding this transaction, that of Cary Maultasch. At Michael Milken's sentencing hearing, Maultasch spoke of asking Milken's opinion on the deal at Michael Davidoff's request. At times, Milken gave his opinion reluctantly, according to Maultasch; on other occasions, he offered none.

Interestingly, the SEC's allegation that Milken wanted to drive up Maxxam's acquisition price because of a disagreement over Drexel's fee—a very serious and bizarre charge—is not included in the U.S. attorney's indictment.

The Acquisition of Harris Graphics (stock parking). In April 1983, Harris did a financing through Drexel; as part of that financing, 3.2 million shares were sold at $1 per share. The firm purchased 300,000 of these shares. By October 1984, partnerships composed of both selected Drexel employees and selected clients had purchased 1.2 million shares (11.8 percent). At that time, an initial public offering of 3,000,000 Harris shares was completed.

From May to September 1985, Boesky bought 853,800 shares of Harris, allgedly with the understanding that Drexel would cover all losses and divide any profits. Also as part of the understanding, Boesky was to speak with Harris's management privately and offer to buy the company at $17 per share, a 10 to 20 percent premium to the stock's price at the time. In September 1985, Boesky filed a Schedule 13-D form with the SEC; this form is required of anyone who purchases more than 5 percent of a company.

Since May 1985, members of Milken's department had been trying to find a buyer for the company. On May 9, 1986, AM International agreed to buy Harris for $22 per share. Drexel raised $100 million for AM to assist in its acquisition; the fee was $4 million. In addition, Drexel earned a $6.3 million profit on its three hundred thousand shares.

Boesky's profit was $5.6 million and Milken's was $6.5 million. The partnerships made an additional $19.4 million.

The allegation here is that Milken and Boesky had an arrangement in which Boesky bought stock for Drexel's benefit. The logic is that Milken wanted to put Harris "in play," creating the impression in its management and in potential acquirors that a buyout was inevitable. The activity in Harris's stock, the public filing of a Schedule 13-D, and the various overtures to management by Boesky and others regarding a takeover would all be consistent with such a strategy. More specific is Maultasch's testimony that Milken referred to various Drexel holdings of Harris as "yours" and "ours," which suggests a parking arrangement.

There is also a question that is not raised because it doesn't involve the law: How did individual employees, through the partnerships, end up with four times as many shares—bought at the bargain price of $1 each—as did their firm?

The MGM/UA/Turner Broadcasting Deal (insider trading). In early July 1985, MGM/UA told Drexel that Turner Broadcasting (TBS) was interested in buying the MGM Film Library. On the sixteenth, MGM/UA publicly announced that it had approached Drexel regarding the sale of the film library. On August 7, MGM/UA and TBS publicly announced an agreement in which TBS would buy MGM/UA, and then resell UA—United Artists—back to Kirk Kekorian, MGM/UA's largest shareholder and one of the more astute financiers in the country.

On the same day as the announcement, Boesky began buying shares of MGM/UA, allegedly with the understanding that all profits and losses were to be split between the company and Drexel. From August 7 through November 8, 1985, Boesky purchased 2.7 million shares and 169,000 warrants.

Drexel eventually raised $1.4 billion for TBS and received a fee of $67 million. Boesky's profit was $3.6 million.

Based on what we know, this aspect of the case against Milken seems to be weak. If Milken was willing to pass along inside information to Boesky for personal profit, why didn't he do it in July, when the world hadn't already been told about the deal? Boesky didn't begin buying shares until the day of the announcement, along with every legitimate risk arbitrageur in America.

And again, there is that mismatch between Milken's legitimate income from this deal—over $7 million—and his share of the alleged profit from Boesky—about $220,000. If Milken cheated on this one, he is every psychiatrist's dream patient.

The $5.3 Million Check (repayment of illegal profits). Maybe he is that patient. If there is a smoking gun, this would be it. According to the September 1988 SEC complaint:

> During 1985 and the first three months of 1986, [Charles] Thurnher, at Milken's direction, systematically kept track of the profits and losses on securities transactions that were part of the Arrangement. Thurnher kept Milken apprised of the results of these tracking activities. [Cary] Maultasch provided Thurnher with information about securities that were subject to the Arrangement [with Boesky] and instructed him not to store the trading information in a computer.

The May 1988 SEC memorandum adds an ironic twist to the story. According to the memo: "Thurnher did not trust Mooradian, believing that he sometimes claimed Boesky had purchased amounts of Fischbach stock in excess of reported daily volume or at prices beyond reported daily high and low prices. Thurnher thought Mooradian's calculations of Boesky's losses from Fischbach to be inflated. He has admitted that he, in turn, fabricated a loss figure for a position in Unocal common stock that Boesky had asked Milken to take for him."

As for the allegation in the indictment: Boesky's company owed

Milken's department for its share of illegal profits, and on March 21, 1986, the two conducted a series of trades at artificial prices to reduce Boesky's debt; the remainder, $5.3 million, was paid by check to Drexel.

At this time, Boesky was in the process of raising money for a new limited partnership. His auditors insisted on an explanation, in writing, for the payment. After some debate, the following explanation was drafted:

> There was an oral understanding with Ivan F. Boesky of The Ivan F. Boesky Corporation that Drexel Burnham Lambert Incorporated would provide consulting services. There were no formal records maintained for the time devoted to such consulting services. There were no prior agreements as to the specific value of such consulting services to be performed. There was no prior determination of the specific value for such consulting services until March 21, 1986, which amounted to $5,300,000.00 due to Drexel Burnham Lambert Incorporated. Such amount was mutually agreed upon.

The agreement was signed by Ivan Boesky and Lowell Milken.

Drexel raised $660 million in high-yield debt for Boesky's new arbitrage partnership; the financing fee was $26.6 million.

The potential smoking gun in this allegation is the set of notes—a several-page ledger, actually—that was said to be kept by Boesky's bookkeeper, Setrag Mooradian. As mentioned in the last chapter, there was a good deal of uncertainty as to whether the Mooradian notes were the real McCoy.

It appears that they were. The original notes allegedly kept track of numerous transactions by Boesky in 1985 and 1986, and were destroyed after Dennis Levine's arrest in May 1986 but prior to Boesky's decision to plead guilty and cooperate some four months later.

Copies of these notes were found, again allegedly by the government, in Boesky's files about a year later, and were publicly released by Assistant U.S. Attorney Carroll in June 1989. In his words, the notes were "one of the contemporaneously created 'scoresheets' comparing the Boesky Organization's tallying of the arrangement with the defendants' tallying of the arrangement."

The notes from early 1986 begin with the following comments, written by hand on ledger paper:

"Ivan,

the new items on Page 2 haven't been analyzed yet. Charlie is calling me Tuesday with details on these trades & other questions such as Phillips & Unocal. On Page 1, I've made some comments on some of our differences.

Set"

Logically, the three people referred to in this memo are Ivan Boesky, Charles Thurnher from Milken's department, and Setrag Mooradian.

The notes list forty-nine different securities—stocks, bonds, and warrants. On page 1, there is a comparison between "Seemala P&L & Interest" [profits and losses, with interest, for one of Boesky's companies] and "Their P&L & Interest" for twenty-eight securities, including those of MCA, Fischbach, Diamond Shamrock and Occidental Petroleum. (Diamond and Occidental, which were not included on the ledgers mentioned earlier, are listed as "DIA 50%" and "OXY 50%" which would be consistent with Boesky's allegation that any profits or losses on these two transactions were meant to be split evenly.)

Page 2 of the ledger lists sixteen securities, valued as of December 31, 1985. Each listing ends with the comment "we owe" or "they owe us" and an amount under the heading "Drexel." Page 3 records five securities, their "Cost or Proceeds with interest," their market value as of January 31, 1986, and what is evidently their profits or losses at that time. Among the five is MGM, which is part of the indictment; the MGM entry, however, doesn't indicate a 50-50 split, as alleged by Boesky.

The evidence in the Mooradian notes is compelling, but not conclusive. For example, if the figures in these notes are a record of an illegal arrangement, why are only eleven of forty-nine transactions discussed in the indictment? And why is MGM listed as a $3.2 million *loss* to Boesky in the ledger, but as $3.6 million *profit* in the indictment? More generally, could Boesky have felt that he was entitled to reimbursement for ideas that didn't work out, while Milken felt differently?

If the Mooradian notes were thought to be a smoking gun lying in Boesky's files, there was no such gun in Drexel's files; in fact, there was no gun at all. Charles Thurnher told prosecutors that he had discarded Boesky-related documents in April 1986, after Milken had said that he didn't want to be kept informed of transactions with Boesky. According to Thurnher, as quoted in the May 1988 SEC memo: "He told me to forget it—that it was all a bunch of [expletive] anyway and he didn't care."

According to the SEC enforcement division: "The staff doubts that Thurnher spontaneously destroyed documents based on such a casual remark and without direction from Milken. . . . The staff believes it more likely that the records were destroyed after the commission's case against Dennis Levine was filed on May 12, 1986."

The difference of opinion and timing is significant. Thurnher's statement indicates that Milken didn't ask for documents to be destroyed, and that he had lost interest in his department's transactions with Boesky *before* Levine's arrest, which was the first public announcement of an insider trading investigation. In short, no cover-up. The SEC staff, by contrast, implied that Milken probably took a more direct role in the destruction of the documents, and that these documents may have been destroyed after the possibility of investigation and prosecution had become public.

The SEC memo also includes a related allegation that wasn't part of the indictment, but would likely become part of the trial: that Milken and Boesky discussed a cover-up of the $5.3 million check. "Boesky and Milken met in July 1986 to discuss how they could substantiate the 'consulting services' gloss which they had used to conceal the true nature of the $5.3 million payment," said the SEC staff. "In this meeting, Milken cautioned Boesky that they needed to be more careful because of the 'new environment,' which Boesky understood to be a reference to the Levine case and its progeny."

The allegations in the memo provide some additional considerations in your decision, but bear in mind, they present the SEC's point of view, not Milken's.

Purchase of Wickes Shares (stock manipulation). In April 1985, Wickes Companies, a low-tech conglomerate, sold eight million shares of convertible preferred stock through Drexel. One of the terms of the deal allowed Wickes to redeem—repurchase the shares at a stated price—the preferred if the underlying common stock traded above $6.08 per share for twenty of thirty days.

By April 23 of the following year, Wickes common had sold above $6.08 per share for nineteen of twenty-seven days.

On or about April 23, 1986, the defendant Michael R. Milken and other Drexel Enterprise members caused the Boesky Organization to purchase approximately 1,900,000 shares of Wickes common stock in order to manipulate the price above $6.08 per share. On that day, Wickes common stock closed at $6.125. As a result, Wickes was able to force the redemption of the $2.50 Preferred.

Drexel's fee for handling the redemption was $2.3 million.

The logic behind this allegation is compelling. Milken's client wanted to redeem the preferred; the common shares were near but below the required price; Boesky stepped in at a crucial moment, buying 1.9 million shares in a single afternoon; the stock closed above the required price.

In Milken's defense, the standard of proof is "beyond a reasonable doubt." The issue of manipulation is not in dispute—Milken's lawyers have acknowledged that Wickes was manipulated, but have argued that their client had nothing to do with it. This allegation was a focus of Milken's sentencing hearing in October 1990.

Purchase of Stone Container Shares (stock manipulation). On March 27, 1986, Stone Container, a packaging company, filed an offering to sell $100 million of convertible bonds and $100 million of convertible preferred stock. Both issues were to be underwritten by Drexel.

The company allegedly told the high-yield bond department that it didn't want the deal done unless its stock price was higher. (This is perfectly legal—a company has every right to decide on a minimum price at which it's willing to sell, just as any investor does.)

On April 14, Boesky bought 29,100 shares—37 percent of the total number of shares traded that day—and the stock rose above $46 per share, closing at 46¾, up 1¾ points. Seventy-eight thousand shares traded that day, two to three times the stock's normal volume.

On April 15, Boesky bought an additional eighty-five hundred shares, and Stone closed at $46.375 per share. That same day, the high-yield bond department completed the $200 million offering of debt and preferred stock; Drexel's fee was $5.9 million.

On May 1, Boesky sold his shares to Drexel at a loss, less than three weeks after buying them.

The allegation here is that Boesky bought Stone's shares for the benefit of Drexel, with the understanding that he would be reimbursed for any losses. In a trial, the defense would probably agree that a manipulation had occurred, but again, that Milken was not involved.

Sale of C.O.M.B. Shares (stock manipulation). C.O.M.B., a discount retailer, filed an offering to sell $25 million of convertible bonds through Drexel. Bruce Newberg of Drexel's high-yield group allegedly conspired with Charles Zarzecki of Princeton/Newport to reduce C.O.M.B.'s stock price in advance of the offering: "On or about April 11, 1985, the defendant Bruce L. Newberg, in a recorded telephone conversation with coconspirator Zarzecki, told Zarzecki of the impending public offering of the convertible debt and instructed him to sell C.O.M.B. common stock. The defendant Bruce L. Newberg agreed with Zarzecki that Drexel would cover any loss Princeton/Newport suffered on such sales. In that recorded conversation, Bruce L. Newberg told Zarzecki:

The stock is sixteen bid, up from fifteen and three eighths.

I don't want this thing to be sixteen bid.

I want, y——, y——, you know, to get rid of it, y——, ah, you know. I want, I want it down to at least fifteen and three quarters and hopefully lower. Umm . . . , I wouldn't mind you selling a little bit first. And um . . . , you're indemnified, uh, you know, my—, it's, y——, you know what I'm saying."

On that day, according to the indictment, Princeton/Newport sold short forty thousand shares of C.O.M.B., and the stock closed at fifteen and seven-eighths. That same day, April 11, C.O.M.B. decided to postpone its offering until April 16.

On April 15, Princeton/Newport allegedly sold short seventy-five hundred shares of C.O.M.B., and the share price again ended the day at fifteen and seven-eighths.

The evidence in this case is more compelling than in the previous one because of the tape. Bear in mind, however, that the person on that tape is Newberg, not Milken. And Newberg isn't testifying against Milken; in fact, he is pleading not guilty himself. Where, then, is the evidence that implicates Milken?

Sale of U.S. Home Shares (stock manipulation). U.S. Home, a home builder, filed an offering on March 28, 1985 to sell bonds and warrants. On April 10, two days before the expected offering date, Newberg allegedly told Princeton/Newport to sell short fifty thousand or more U.S. Home shares. "Thereafter, in a recorded telephone conversation, a Princeton/Newport co-conspirator said to Zarzecki, 'Okay it's bad for Drexel to be doing this shit because . . . they're stepping on the stock basically, right?' "

On April 11, Princeton/Newport sold short nine thousand shares.

The allegation here is similar to that in the C.O.M.B. transactions, that Newberg arranged for Princeton/Newport to knock down the price of a corporate client's stock. The indictment, however, doesn't include any conversations between Newberg and Princeton/Newport regarding the U.S. Home deal. And what is the case against Milken?

Games with Mattel (stock parking). This one is a bit convoluted (for a change). According to the government, on April 24, 1984, Drexel agreed to purchase, with the option to resell, $172 million of debt and equity securities as part of Mattel's recapitalization. On June 4, Mattel filed a proxy seeking approval from its shareholders for this recap; the proxy failed to disclose, as required, that Drexel owned 6.9 percent of Mattel's convertible preferred stock because Lowell Milken and another high-yield employee hadn't told the company of this position.

In July, Drexel's ownership of the preferred had risen to 7.8 percent, and this position was hedged by a short position in the common stock—that is, when the short position in the common was netted out against the long position in the convertible preferred, Drexel had no stake in the company. On July 12, Bruce Newberg allegedly "caused the Drexel Enterprise to transfer its hedged Series A Preferred position to Princeton/Newport with the secret understanding that the Drexel Enterprise retained ownership of and the economic risk on these securities."

Between August 23 and September 6, Princeton/Newport bought an additional 55,000 shares of the preferred and shorted additional shares of the common, again as part of an alleged parking scheme.

From January to March 1985, Princeton/Newport sold a chunk of the preferred shares that it had bought, and on April 8, sold what it still owned to Drexel.

These allegations are difficult to get a handle on. First of all, there doesn't seem to be any possible illegality with Drexel's purchase of the $172 million position, unless you believe that the failure to disclose Drexel's preferred ownership on the proxy taints the whole transaction.

As for that preferred stake, it seemed to be hedged by a short position, implying that Drexel's actual ownership stake in the company was somewhere between little and nothing. More important, why would Lowell Milken and his associate want to hide Drexel's hedged position from Mattel? What is the motive, and where is the criminal intent?

And what is the evidence? According to an October 15, 1990, business law article in the *New York Times*, Mattel was aware, from at least two sources, of Drexel's holdings in the company.

The parking allegation is an unusual one. Logically, a person parks stock with others to retain his equity stake in a company without the public's knowledge. Why would anyone want to park a hedged position, which has no equity stake? What did Newberg expect to gain from such a scheme, and why was it necessary to begin with? And if Princeton/Newport was parking this hedged position, why did it sell "a substantial portion" in the open market, and not to the firm for which it was supposedly holding the shares?

And again, where is the evidence against Michael Milken?

Tax Loss Trades (tax evasion). From November 1984 to February 1986, Princeton/Newport sold and repurchased securities to create short-term capital losses and long-term capital gains, a legal strategy to reduce taxes. Allegedly, these transactions were done with the understanding that Princeton/Newport would be responsible for any gains or losses in the security prices between the sale date and the repurchase date—such an understanding would have made these trades illegal.

Two specific 1985 trades are cited, and one tape is referred to: "The defendant Bruce L. Newberg and an employee of Princeton/Newport, in a recorded telephone conversation, discussed the repurchase price of the Lear Petroleum securities and a sham transaction in Trinity convertible bonds."

Unless that tape is incriminating—and if so, why wasn't the specific dialogue quoted as in earlier cases?—these allegations against Newberg aren't nearly as strong.

And what is the case against Milken? That he conspired with Newberg, who isn't testifying against him? There must be more than that.

The Merger of Lorimar and Telepictures (insider trading). On September 10, 1985, Lorimar and Telepictures, both involved in movie/television production, met to discuss a possible merger of the two entertainment companies. That same day, both companies contacted Milken for his advice.

The following day, according to the government, Lorimar shares were purchased for the High-Yield Bond Department's account. Additional shares were bought on September 17 and 19, bringing the total purchases for the three days to 30,000 shares.

On September 30, according to the earlier SEC complaint, Cary Maultasch, who worked for Milken, purchased 106,900 Lorimar shares for the high-yield convertible bond account at the firm—this purchase accounted for 85 percent of Lorimar's total volume that day. On October 2, Maultasch placed an order with Drexel's trading desk to purchase an additional 110,000 shares at a price of $30 per share or less; 53,000 shares were purchased, almost half of that day's volume.

Negotiations continued on the merger until October 3, and the final agreement was announced on October 7.

The trading profit on the 159,900 shares purchased for the high-yield convert account is estimated at $1.2 million (I don't know how the prosecutors arrived at the $4.3 million figure stated in the indictment). Drexel's fee for advising on the merger was $2.1 million.

The circumstantial evidence here is devastating. Because of Maultasch's alleged involvement, a real jury would likely have the opportunity to hear his view of events. The SEC complaint stated: "During this period, Milken communicated this [merger] information either directly or indirectly to Maultasch for the purpose, among others, of purchasing Lorimar common stock for Drexel's benefit." It would be interesting to hear what exactly that meant.

If Maultasch were to testify, the indications are that he would deny receiving instructions to buy Lorimar stock directly from Milken. Therefore the evidence of insider trading is far from overwhelming. As it is, however, it's disturbing.

The Viacom Leveraged Buyout (insider trading). On September 10, 1986, Viacom, an entertainment company, contacted Milken regarding a proposed buyout of the company by its management. Viacom's managers wanted Drexel to finance the deal for them.

On that same day, the high-yield bond department bought 296,576 shares of Viacom stock, accounting for 21 percent of the volume. Also on the tenth, the department sold $10,500,000 of Viacom convertible bonds and purchased $500,000 of a different Viacom convert.

The Viacom leveraged buyout proposal was publicly announced on September 16; on completion of the deal, Drexel received a fee of $8.4 million. According to the government, the trading profits from the September 10 transactions was $1.8 million.

Here again, the circumstantial evidence seems devastating—certainly, there is the appearance of insider trading for large profits. But the facts of this case are more bizarre than conclusive.

The reason is that the prosecutors made an unlikely mistake. They thought that the $10,500,000 convertible bond sold on September 10 represented the equivalent of 26,355 shares—not a very significant sale in the face of a 296,576-share purchase that same day. In reality, however, that convertible bond sale represented the equivalent of 263,550 shares; they were off by a factor of ten.

Accordingly, the trading done on the tenth increased the department's ownership of Viacom shares by 51,000, not 272,000. This is still a lot of stock, especially when it is bought on the same day that Milken was told of an impending acquisition of the company. But why would someone trading on this inside information sell this huge convertible bond position? It is a puzzlement.

Another factor to consider is that, according to the defense, the trader involved here denies receiving instructions from Milken. This trader, Peter Gardiner, would later become a key witness in Milken's sentencing hearing, during which his credibility would be severely questioned. Which raises an additional question: How much weight should be put on his denial that Milken, and he, traded on inside information?

A final consideration is the date. This allegation is the only one of the twenty that occurred after Dennis Levine's arrest in May 1986. Once it became apparent that Levine was cooperating with the government, Milken might have suspected that Boesky was in trouble, since Levine couldn't cut a deal unless he had something to offer in return. If Milken thought that Boesky's days were numbered, he would have realized the risk to himself, the fact that his name might pop up in conversation when Boesky was hauled in by the prosecutors.

Therefore, if Milken was cheating with Boesky, he might have realized that every transaction he had done, *or would do,* could fall under intense scrutiny. (On the other hand, if Milken *didn't* have an illegal arrangement with Boesky, the date of this allegation doesn't matter. But under that assumption, all the Boesky-related allegations against Milken, fourteen in all, are out the window.)

Assuming that Milken *was* part of a scheme with Boesky, trading on inside information in September 1986 for a $500,000 illegal profit on a deal that would generate a legitimate $8.4 million fee doesn't seem like a smart bet for a smart man. Perhaps this ignores ego and greed, but that's for you to determine—you're still the foreman.

And now it's time for your verdict.

CHAPTER THIRTEEN

THE LAST MILE

"How, from where we started, did we
ever reach this Christmas?"

"Step by step."

—The Lion in Winter

The indictment of Milken was followed, two weeks later, by a settlement between Drexel and the SEC. With this settlement, in April 1989, the firm found itself at a crossroads. Within a year, the firm would find itself in bankruptcy.

The SEC settlement had been expected soon after the firm's agreement with the U.S. attorney in December; instead, negotiations had dragged on for more than three months. "If you want to put us out of business, let us know," Fred Joseph told Gary Lynch. The SEC did not want the firm closed down; it did, however, insist that careful safeguards be set in place to monitor Drexel's activities. Perhaps, as one officer suggested, it was also under pressure from Congress, pressure to further punish a firm that hadn't developed much goodwill on Capitol Hill even in the best of times.

The provisions of the SEC agreement tightened up the firm's oversight procedures and seemed reasonable, at least from my perspective. The major sticking point—whether the high-yield department should remain in Beverly Hills—was resolved in Drexel's favor. Concurrent with the agreement, the firm announced that John Shad would join us as our new chairman. He replaced the somewhat invisible Bobby Linton, whose resignation, we were told, "was not required or requested by the SEC." Shad had been the chairman of the SEC during the 1981–1987 period, before becoming the U.S. ambassador to the Netherlands. At sixty-six, Shad was returning to the private sector, where more than two decades earlier, as an executive for E. F. Hutton, he had hired a young Harvard graduate named Fred Joseph.

Given the past relationship between the two, it was logical to assume that Shad was chosen primarily for appearances. He certainly looked and sounded the part of the Wall Street executive: tall and heavy jowled, with a deep voice and a sterling résumé to match. Shad was now the nominal head of Drexel Burnham, but the power was expected to remain with his former protégé.

I doubt many employees viewed Shad's appointment as anything more than necessary. Having suffered for twenty-nine months under seige, the employees couldn't be expected to welcome an outsider to the top ranks of the firm. It didn't help that this outsider was rumored to be receiving a multimillion-dollar salary for showing up. What most people didn't realize was that Shad didn't care about the money—he added it to an earlier $20 million donation to Harvard Business School; he took the job out of a sense of obligation, a sense that he *was* necessary.

Along with Shad, the firm hired two others to serve on its board of directors: Roderick Hills, a former chairman of the SEC as well, and Ralph Saul, a former president of the American Stock Exchange. These three "outside directors" also served as the Oversight Committee, with primary responsibility to catch anyone, who in spite of everything that had happened, might still be interested in playing the dark keys.

Drexel also brought in a new lawyer, Saul Cohen, who was promised more than $2 million a year. In Cohen's case, the money wasn't donated to anyone, and with no apologies. His philosophy on the subject was simple, as explained to *The Wall Street Journal:* "You're not taken seriously [among investment bankers] unless you make lots of money. I was the most expensive . . . general counsel in the universe, and they knew it." To his credit, he earned his income. He faced a difficult challenge, one that touched on a more significant issue at the firm, and he did one hell of a job.

His challenge was to negotiate an "appropriate" fine with each of the fifty states—after all, Drexel had admitted guilt to six felonies, and every state would feel obligated to mete out some punishment before it would allow business as usual. Negotiating these fines would be particularly important if the firm wanted to remain a retail brokerage firm, dealing with individual investors.

And that was part of the larger question: Did Drexel want to stay in retail? Did it want to remain a full-service broker or, now that it had settled both the criminal and civil investigations, did it want to become a smaller, more focused firm?

The top officers of the firm met on the weekend immediately following the April 13 settlement to analyze Drexel's strengths and weaknesses and to consider its future. Under pressure from representatives of the high-yield bond department, the decision was made to jettison the retail sales department and to cut back in several other East Coast operations. Total layoffs: four thousand employees.

It was a fateful choice, more than anyone likely realized at the time. The numbers supported the decision. Retail had been unprofitable in fourteen of the previous fifteen years, losing, by one executive's measure, about $50 million a year. (Determining how much a retail system actually loses is difficult, because it helps to move the merchandise that makes other departments more profitable. For example, corporate finance's success is dependent in part on retail's ability to sell the deals. The actual losses from Drexel's retail system are in dispute as well—according to one former executive, Smith Barney was solidly profitable with the sixteen retail branches that it picked up as a result of Drexel's decision to exit the business.)

More than the retail system's unprofitability was the fact that its sales force had been shrinking, implying that the best people were heading in the wrong direction. "The good ones were being picked off; the poor ones stayed," argued one observer in the firm.

But there were other factors involved. Loyalty was one. "Hang in there, hang in there, then you cut them," was how an equity trader described the April announcement, although he did feel it was the correct business decision. He added, "They stressed for two years through all the bullshit, 'Be loyal, be loyal,' then they dropped the hatchet."

Another consideration was insurance—specifically, insurance against the collapse of the firm. "Retail was the face of the firm in forty cities," said a former exec—Drexel was the broker for three hundred and fifty thousand individual accounts, representing perhaps a million Americans who sure as hell wouldn't want to see their broker go bankrupt. And because of that, the government would have a strong vested interest in helping the firm in a crisis. Once retail was gone, Drexel had, in the words of a senior investment banker, "no widows and orphans."

"They underestimated the impact of retail," another banker argued. "I asked them, 'How do you propose to sell equity deals?' They said, 'Oh, we'll go back to the way it was ten years ago; we'll syndicate deals.' " The problem with this, he pointed out, was that things had changed, and Drexel was the major reason. We had led the way in outdating the old style of placing a deal and in angering our competitors. The West Coast had opposed the idea of sharing commissions by syndicating pieces of its bond deals to other Wall Street firms; for years in the highly profitable junk-bond market, a Drexel syndicate was a contradiction in terms. At this point, the Street wasn't likely to help us out.

Of course, there was the institutional equity group—my department—which could try to place the stock deals that our corporate finance department put together. But the chances that we could sell everything on the deal calendar were slim. For one thing, the new offerings that had been sold in recent years had, on balance, done poorly, and portfolio managers were understandably skeptical. Once burned, twice shy—just like everyone else.

The larger problem was that deals throughout the Street are generally overpriced, as mentioned earlier, and institutional investors are smart enough to be selective. Sadly, the overvalued is more easily sold to the relatively unsophisticated retail investor.

If the environment for "working the calendar" was poor, the environment for working in general was worse. Morale on the trading floor had bumped along the bottom since the December settlement four months earlier. The letdown was similar to running a marathon, and being forced to quit with a mile to go. This letdown wasn't discussed or even consciously felt, it was just there.

The circled wagons were gone, the logic that we're innocent until proven guilty was now irrelevant. We could look anyone in the eye and say that we had been forced into a settlement, but still, we had pleaded guilty. It was an odd and uncomfortable position to be in.

There was also a sense that we had played into Giuliani's hand that day in late December, that we had given the mayor-aspirant a big, fat gift, one that he had received as a result, as the British would say, of bad sportsmanship. He was now a hero, a latter-day Thomas Dewey, having taught those crooks on Wall Street—us—a well-deserved lesson.

It hardly seemed fair. Fairness dictated that if the firm had broken the law, let that fact be proven in court. And if, because of RICO, the firm never saw its day in court, let there be no doubt as to why.

But this didn't happen, and life went on. We explained the settlement to our clients and friends; we told them again of RICO and coercion. And we did our jobs as best we could.

In early February, the equity department spent a Friday evening and Saturday at the Vista Hotel in lower Manhattan to consider the outlook. "The one message I want everyone to walk away with tomorrow is that we are going to achieve growth with profitability in 1989," said the senior vice-president at the podium. "And the only way we are going to achieve this is contained in a paraphrase of the old Gillette jingle from the boxing matches. We've got to 'look smart, act smart, and be smart.'"

The smart bet, as you might guess, was to take all the money spent by the department on this lost weekend and apply that money against our losses. Large group meetings are the classic example of the reach exceeding the grasp—very little gets accomplished. It is a familiar pattern. The group tries to address its major grievances, inevitably locking in on some irritating but essentially irrelevant problem. Everyone instinctively feels safe attacking this paper tiger, and discussion flares. Of course, little if anything is ever subsequently done, but then again, who cares?

On Saturday, the various equity departments—sales, trading, and research—were grouped in separate rooms, and each department head spent the morning talking with each group. In one meeting, the head of the international equity effort was asked if the firm was planning to expand its coverage of international stocks. The question was perfectly valid because we were only following about ten foreign stocks. In response, the head man proceeded to list most of these stocks, effectively avoiding the real issue. His answer, however, did highlight another basic fact of meetings: People easily become defensive.

The upshot of the 1989 equity conference was not a surge in

motivation. What did wake up the equity group was the decision, ten weeks later, to drop the retail system, eliminate the international equity department, and severely cut back on the trading of over-the-counter stocks. Now, people had something more fundamental to worry about: their jobs. Was there another shoe to drop? Further cutbacks? Further layoffs? A jolt of fear cleared away the malaise that had settled in during the previous four months.

As management steered away from its "weaknesses," it continued to focus on its strengths—or more specifically, on those areas that had been its strengths in the past. Obviously, the core of our profitability for years had been the high-yield bond department. Tied in with this department was the investment banking effort on both coasts, which generated the deals that the junk-bond group sold to its clients.

But there was trouble in paradise. The high-yield bond department was particularly angry at the treatment of Milken, who was essentially fired by his firm. More important, the main man was gone and the market that he had pioneered was about to go to hell in a handbasket.

The collapse of junk bonds was far from apparent at the beginning of 1989. Fred Joseph was more concerned about the consequences if his high-yield employees and investment bankers left for greener pastures following the settlement than about the consequences if they stayed.

In corporate finance, "there were a bunch of people putting tremendous pressure on Fred for compensation," recalled one investment banker. "We can go anywhere," was the attitude, according to another. Fred guaranteed the bankers that the bonus pool for 1989 would be at least three-quarters of the 1988 pool—this wasn't an exorbitant offer because Drexel's corporate finance income in the first few months of the year was likely to be enormous.

In the high-yield bond department, individual agreements were negotiated with the top employees, fixing minimum and maximum levels. Ironically, the firm was forced by the government to make multimillion-dollar deals with both Jim Dahl and Terren Peizer, two employees who had agreed to testify against Milken and the firm, and who weren't welcome in their own department.

In that department, there was an "underdog mentality," according to one West Coast officer, a desire to show the world that the junk-bond group could still sell the deals. The first half of 1989 was notable for one deal that had been negotiated in the previous year: the $25 billion takeover of RJR Nabisco by the leveraged buyout firm of Kohlberg Kravis Roberts & Co. The deal was a boon for Drexel—$227 million in fees—and the financing was a masterpiece. There would be almost $13 billion in senior debt lent by banks. At the other end of the financial structure, KKR would invest $1.5 billion for the stock in the new company and purchase $500 million in debt that for several years would pay interest in the form of more bonds rather than in cash, known as payment in kind (PIK).

Drexel had already sold $5 billion in high-yield bonds. The $5 billion in bonds were divided into two debt issues: $1.25 billion of first subordinated increasing rate notes and $3.75 billion of second subordinated increasing rate notes—the interest rate on these issues would rise every three months. In the event of bankruptcy, these bonds would only have a claim on RJR assets after the banks had been paid in full; on the brighter side, their claim would come ahead of the new stockholders. And not surprisingly, the "first" notes would get paid before the "second" notes.

In the spring of 1989, Drexel was the lead manager on the sale of $4 billion in bonds, the proceeds of which were to redeem most of the increasing-rate notes described above. Drexel sold $3 billion of 12-year subordinated bonds—$1 billion of PIK; $2 billion sold at a significant discount from face value. With Merrill Lynch as co-manager, Drexel also placed $525 million of 12-year subordinated bonds (interest paid in cash), $225 million of bonds with a reset feature (the interest rate could be raised in the future), and $250 million of 10-year floating rates notes (interest rate would rise and fall with market rates).

The old stockholders of RJR received a terrific price for their shares, more than a double in less than a year, but only three-quarters of that price was paid in cash. The other quarter was in the form of two esoteric securities: a senior converting debenture—a zero-coupon bond that in four years could be converted into shares of stock if the holder chose (but then they wouldn't receive any interest payments)—and a cumulative exchangeable preferred stock—a preferred that pays its dividends in cash *or* in additional stock and is exchangeable into debt.

The purpose of this incredible collection was to allow the new company to take on a tremendous amount of debt and still have a reasonable chance of paying it; that's why several of the securities don't pay out cash for several years. All this debt made the equity extremely risky, but the new stockholders, KKR, were willing to take on that risk for the opportunity to make an enormous profit.

From the other side of the coin, these securities had to be designed to attract investors with different risk/reward profiles to a company with more debt than most countries. Making this deal work for both borrower and lender was quite an achievement, whether or not you believe deals like this should be done in the first place.

The RJR Nabisco deal, an unqualified success for the firm, also highlighted a concern. When Fred Joseph had thanked Henry Kravis of KKR for hiring Drexel as its adviser and financier, Kravis replied, "Fred, don't thank me. I'm using Drexel because you're the only ones that can get it done. As long as you are, I'm going to use you." The problem was how to maintain that top ranking, and at what cost?

The top deal makers remained with the firm, comforted by compensation guarantees and probably secure in the knowledge that they couldn't do any better anywhere else. Unfortunately, two crucial ingredients for continued success were missing. Milken was gone and the market was changing for the worse.

Without Milken, the high-yield bond group was a shadow of its former self. He ran a department of nearly three hundred people without relying on a chain of command; he was the difference between the ultimate entrepreneurial organization and organized chaos. As he slowly disappeared from the scene to focus on his defense, there was no one willing or able to replace him.

Eventually, John Kissick, the head of West Coast corporate finance, was given responsibility for the entire high-yield group. "The reins were thrust upon Kissick," said a West Coast bond trader, who viewed him as much better suited for his previous job: "He was not a people person . . . he didn't want to be in the public eye." With Kissick often off the trading floor and the head trader, Warren Trepp, "doing his own thing," according to the same source, the decision-making process appears to have taken a beating.

How badly the junk-bond market suffered from the loss of Milken is unclear, but one thing is certain: It did suffer. He had given the market a sense of confidence in its ability to price these new securities correctly and to trade them efficiently. One investment banker recalled a comment from a colleague in April 1989: " 'This place is in trouble. Nobody knows how to make a market in this shit.' " "In the last year," the banker argued, "no one wanted to admit that without Milken, the high-yield market wasn't mature enough to survive the bumps."

The problems that would emerge ranged from the subtle to the obvious. By 1989, the junk-bond market was a victim of its own success and that of the stock market. Stock prices had tripled during the 1980s, creating two significant dangers. First, takeovers were more expensive and the bonds sold to finance them were, therefore, more likely to fail. In 1984, takeover prices were six times a company's cash flow, on average; in 1989, the ratio was up to nine. Looked at from a different perspective, whereas cash flow had averaged one and a half times interest payments in 1984, the coverage ratio had declined to only one in 1989. In a nutshell, the chances of bankruptcy had risen dramatically.

Second, the buyouts of the past seemed brilliant in retrospect because rising prices had allowed the buyers to sell off part or all of their acquisitions at higher and higher prices. But rising prices in the future were hardly guaranteed—logically, the more prices have risen in the recent past, the *less* likely they'll rise in the near future.

More important to the high-yield market than the raising of money to pay for takeovers was the raising of money to finance the ongoing operations of existing companies. Unfortunately, companies in general had a good deal more debt on their books than a decade earlier—taking on more debt would naturally create more risk for both the sellers and the buyers.

Meanwhile, the enthusiasm of these buyers was fading fast. By April 1989, Milken was officially gone. That same month, a study was released by Professor Paul Asquith of Harvard that sent a shudder through the financial community. The study analyzed the frequency of high-yield bond defaults; the media interpreted the results to mean that junk bonds missed interest payments significantly more often than had previously been thought. This conclusion was inaccurate, but it did raise a valid question: Just how risky are these bonds?

Over the next year, Drexel would find out the hard way. The firm was determined to focus on its previous strength: selling lucrative junk-bond offerings to its vast network of buyers. But looking forward, this strategy involved underwriting high-risk deals in a market that was facing a crisis of confidence. What made these deals particularly high risk was that they put the firm in the dangerous position of buyer of last resort. In a solid market, it's a calculated bet; in an uncertain market, it's an invitation to disaster.

A brokerage firm borrows most of the money it uses, and most of that debt is borrowed short term. It must be very careful about picking up assets that can't be easily sold, because its liabilities must be paid every few weeks or months. Normally, these debts can be paid by selling new short-term loans; if not, they must be paid out of the firm's cash. And, as you probably know from dealing with debts of your own, the less cash you have, the less likely your lenders will accept new loans. In fact, if you have trouble paying one lender, they'll all want cash.

For a broker, business is a balancing act. It must maintain a strong financial position to keep its lenders happy, but it must also be active in the markets it serves. It must be willing to buy the securities that its clients want to sell; otherwise, these clients won't want to deal with the firm in the future. This applies to new offerings as well. The corporate client wants its bonds sold to the public; if the brokerage firm can't find buyers for all these new bonds, it will find itself under pressure to buy the remainder for itself—in the hope that it will scare up, perhaps literally, some more buyers in the future.

If the broker places all the bonds, it banks a nice fee from a happy seller; if a chunk of these bonds ends up in its inventory, it takes in a nice fee and a potential time bomb. Can the bonds be sold? At what price? When will the firm need the cash that's tied up in those bonds?

Drexel's management realized the potential dangers, although it certainly underestimated them. There were other considerations as well. It wanted to retain its number one ranking in the junk-bond market: "To maintain our position, the firm is prepared to commit whatever resources are necessary, whether it is capital or personnel," Fred Joseph reportedly told those attending the 1989 high-yield bond conference on April 5.

Drexel also wanted to prove to its present and future corporate clients that it could still do the deals, and it wanted to maintain the flow of fees that these offerings provided. "The firm needed to show it could close deals with Milken gone in the face of bad markets," argued an East Coast investment banker.

There was perhaps no single deal that highlighted these motives, and their consequences, more clearly than the West Point-Pepperel financing. Bill Farley, a health and leverage fanatic, had been a corporate finance client since July 1984, when Drexel raised $75 million toward his purchase of Condec, a defense contractor. The following month, the high-yield department sold $150 million more in bonds for the parent company, Farley Metals.

In 1985, Drexel raised $500 million for Farley's $1.4 billion buyout of Northwest Industries, a collection of companies, the crown jewel being Fruit of the Loom. Next was West Point-Pepperell, a Georgia textile company. After a bitter battle, Farley's $1.6 billion bid was accepted in February 1989. And that's when the story really begins.

The West Point financing involved a relatively new approach for Drexel: a bridge loan. This is a loan made directly from a brokerage firm to a borrower, one who needs cash in a hurry to pay for a takeover. Ironically, the bridge loan had been designed by other Wall Street firms to compete with Drexel, specifically with Milken's "highly confident" letter—his promise to raise whatever money was necessary, and quickly. Because they couldn't match his ability, they chose the high-risk approach of lending their own money. In theory, once the takeover was completed, they could sell junk bonds for the new company, which would repay their loan with the proceeds.

The great danger, of course, is that the brokers won't be able to sell those junk bonds, and the temporary bridge loan becomes a permanent nightmare—in this case, Drexel's nightmare.

A key factor in the successful completion of the West Point-Pepperell acquisition, and the repayment of the bridge loan to Drexel, was the sale of a major West Point subsidiary, Cluett Peabody. Cluett boasted a collection of well-known apparel companies, and was originally expected to sell for $800 to 900 million. A buyer was located—Bidermann Industries U.S.A., a subsidiary of Paris-based Bidermann Group; the price, however, had fallen by almost 20 percent.

The "due diligence" was set in motion, with Bidermann's investment banker, the Lodestar Group, preparing estimates for Cluett's profits, and comparing these estimates with the projections prepared by Farley's investment banker, Drexel. Unfortunately, Lodestar's estimates for the second half of 1989 were some 40 percent *below* those of Drexel, the primary reason being the worsening climate for retail companies. Further complicating the negotiation process for Farley Industries was that its desire to sell Cluett Peabody was a great deal stronger than Bidermann's desire to buy Cluett.

As you can imagine, the selling price took a beating. When the smoke finally cleared months later, substantially all of Cluett—Arrow shirts, Gold Toe socks, and Schoeneman menswear—was sold for $410 million—$350 million in cash and $60 million in debt of discounted value—effectively one half of the original expectations for these three divisions.

There was also a human side to this fiasco. Milken had always argued that the prime consideration in the financing decision should be the qualities of the managers. "In the long run, people are what determine the credit-worthiness of a company," he told interviewers at *New Perspectives Quarterly* in the fall of 1989. Decades earlier, J. P. Morgan had offered much the same point of view. The West Point deal raised some serious doubt on this score.

From Drexel's perspective, "it was a deal that was done without much of an eye on the consequences," according to an East Coast investment banker, who noted how unusual such an attitude was—normally, he argued, investment bankers are able to convince themselves that their deals will turn out favorably.

When all was said and done, Drexel apparently ended up with some $180 million of its cash tied up in a bridge loan to West Point-Pepperell.

The West Point deal was not the only bridge disaster of 1989. The firm also sank $43 million into a loan to Paramount Petroleum, a refinery that slid into bankruptcy within six months of cashing the firm's check.

The man who brought this deal to the firm was Peter Ackerman, the mastermind behind the RJR Nabisco financing. A brilliant, creative strategist, he had worked with Milken for years, arranging how deals should be structured. It was challenging work and the pay was pretty good: Ackerman would earn more than $100 million in the 1988–1989 period, in large part due to RJR.

Unfortunately, the RJR deal was one of the few bright spots for the firm in 1989. Two others were deals in which Drexel benefited by refusing to participate: the proposed acquisition of Prime Computer by longtime Drexel client Ben LeBow and the takeover of Ohio Mattress, known on Wall Street as "The Burning Bed," which left First Boston holding a $450 million bridge loan.

But if Drexel dodged a few bullets, it caught several others. One was the refinancing of JPS Textile's debt. JPS was created in May 1988 with the acquisition of J. P. Stevens, a South Carolina textile company, by Odyssey Partners, a leveraged buyout firm. The new company was now selling almost $400 million in junk bonds to repay the original debt, which required interest payments that rose over time. Incredibly, Drexel was unable to sell more than half of the offering and ended up buying some $200 million of this unwanted debt for itself.

There were also the Edgcomb Metals and Memorex deals, which saddled the firm with $100 million in bonds that were essentially wallflowers; and the Resorts International debt, which only made a single interest payment.

Integrated Resources, a long-time client, found itself on the road to bankruptcy, which proved costly to Drexel. A former packager of tax shelters, Integrated's "costs were just out of sight," according to one investment banker. "You can defer a lot of costs," he added, "but sooner or later. . . ."

In June, the company, which was rechristened "Disintegrated Resources" by one high-yield bond analyst, was unable to meet a payment on its short-term paper. Drexel, following the precedent set by Goldman Sachs in the Penn Central bankruptcy, decided to guarantee its customers' investments in the company—the price tag of Drexel's guarantee could eventually reach $100 million.

Far more disturbing than this was the subsequent decision by Drexel's board of directors to indemnify against loss the private partnerships that involved selected members of the firm. These secretive partnerships, once so attractive, which had operated in a separate but unequal status, were now in danger of being used for possible illegalities in the purchase and sale of junk bonds. And the partners were concerned. The partners were also senior investment bankers and important high-yield personnel.

But not to worry. If the partnerships, which had benefited at the expense of the firm and perhaps at the expense of the law, end up devastated by lawsuits, the firm will pay the losses. Or more specifically, the stockholders of the firm will pay. It's reminiscent of the scene in the film *Brazil,* where a fellow is brutally arrested in his living room, while his wife, stupid with shock, is politely asked to sign the necessary forms requiring her to pay for his interrogation.

The expected price tag for guaranteeing the partnerships is unknown.

If Drexel's financing choices were within its control, there were several crucial events in the second half of 1989 that were not and that soon haunted the firm's earlier decisions. The first of these events was the savings and loan bailout bill passed in August. This long-overdue legislation, Congress's first attempt to resolve a several-hundred-billion-dollar crisis at least partly of its own making, included a body blow to the junk-bond market: savings and loans were required to sell their high-yield bonds by 1994.

This provision was significant for two reasons. First, the market was told that $14 billion of junk bonds, 7 percent of the total, were going to be sold. Second, these bonds would probably be dumped sooner rather than later, because there was no reason to wait. S&Ls were no longer permitted to carry these bonds on their books at face value; if they had been, they probably would have held onto the bonds for a few more years to avoid recognizing any losses in their values.

(This quirk of accounting—carrying bonds at par—was still permitted for other types of bonds. In fact, to go back a few years, if all financial institutions had been forced to account for bonds at market value instead of face value during the 1980s, a large chunk of the insurance industry would have gone bankrupt, because their bond holdings were worth significantly less than their stated value. The losses incurred in "marking to market" these bonds would have wiped out their equity.)

Not only was the high-yield market faced with the near-term prospect of $14 billion in bonds coming down the pike, it also had to deal with the reality that S&Ls would not be buyers of these bonds in the future. Supply up, demand down—a bad combination.

That's not to say it was a bad move on Congress's part. The whole concept of allowing S&L's to invest in any risky asset with taxpayer-guaranteed money is a bizarre experiment in "free-market" socialism. And although high-yield bonds were an excellent investment up until the time of the bail-out bill, their future performance would have been suspect, for reasons outlined later.

In addition, the concentration of junk-bond holdings in the thrift industry—half of *all* holdings among 3,000 thrifts were in the hands of only five of them—was a danger sign, a signal that a few players were making some enormous bets with federally insured deposits. In fact, each of the top five owners of junk bonds is now insolvent, and all of these thrifts have been seized by the government.

All in all, junk bonds didn't cause the savings & loan crisis, but they will add to its eventual cost. Still, to keep things in perspective, the junk-bond holdings of thrifts will add less than one percent to the total losses that taxpayers face.

The month following the S&L bill was the calm before the storm. A minor reorganization of senior management was announced on August 30—the main winner seemed to be Arthur Kirsch, the director of our equity research department, who would now become the head of sales and trading as well, reporting directly to Fred Joseph. Fred also reassured employees that the firm wasn't planning any further eliminations of stock market–related departments. "We must be in equities, however difficult," he said. Our institutional equity department was highly regarded on the Street and was needed to sell new offerings of stock.

As for business, August had been a lousy month, we were told. Still, the firm had earned some money for the year, the backlog of investment banking deals yet to come was described as strong, and our fixed costs had been reduced to $750 million from $1.1 billion. To the average employee, who had no idea of the bridge loans and bonds accumulating dust in our basement, the outlook for the firm seemed encouraging.

Fred also mentioned that the settlement with the government, signed eight months earlier, was nearing its final stage. Two weeks later, the agreement was finalized following the prosecutors' decision to drop their insistence that Drexel withold Milken's bonus for 1988—a year in which no crimes were alleged to have been committed (this bonus, estimated at no more than $50 million by Drexel, was never paid). On September 11, the settlement was approved by Judge Milton Pollack and the firm's carefully worded guilty plea was formally entered: "Based on the information available to us, we are not in a position to dispute the allegations."

In addition, as part of the settlement, $500 million was given to the government. "How do you replace $500 million in cash," asked Burt Siegel. "Nobody was willing to put new money in." His conclusion: "You pray for a good market. When the market runs against you, there's no place to hide."

Unfortunately, that would be the story for October, as the stock and bond markets went down with a passion. On Friday the thirteenth, stocks fell more than 7 percent, suffering their worst decline since the crash two years earlier. The financing for the proposed $6.8

billion acquisition of United Airlines fell through, creating a crisis of confidence that spread through the stock market. The hardest hit was United itself, which fell 57 points to $223 per share. Drexel lost $25 million on its large position in these shares alone.

In the junk-bond market, the only way things could have been worse was if it rained. The refinancing of Ohio Mattress fell through, turning First Boston's temporary bridge loan into something considerably more permanent. More significant, Campeau Corporation, the Canadian retail giant that had paid $6.6 billion for Federated Department Stores in 1988, defaulted on its bonds. According to a First Boston officer familiar with the negotiations, Chairman Robert Campeau was offered a deal by its lead banker, Citibank, which would have allowed him to meet his interest payments. Evidently, Campeau refused the offer; by the time he was forced to reconsider, it had been pulled.

Drexel had no part in the Campeau and Ohio Mattress fiascoes, but as the largest player in the junk-bond market, it also suffered the consequences. Although the firm's inventory of high-yield bonds was only half what it had been in 1986, its holdings still approached $2 billion. And those positions were all affected by the weakness in the market.

The month of October 1989 ended with an $86 million loss for Drexel. To add insult to injury, someone among the small group of executives who were aware of these losses leaked this information to *The Boston Globe*. The public disclosure of these private problems undoubtedly caught the attention of the bond rating agencies, as well as of the firm's lenders.

In late November, Drexel was dealt a serious blow: The safety rating on its short-term debt was reduced. "We didn't expect the downgrade," said an accounting officer. "For once, the rating agencies were proactive." Still, the agencies must have been aware of the front-page problems in the junk-bond market, and they had been clued into the firm's miserable October results.

Drexel's commercial paper rating was cut from A-2 to A-3. This may not seem like a big deal, but as one Wall Street exec told *The New York Times*, "There is no A-3 market to speak of—it trades by appointment only. When you go from A-2 to A-3, you're essentially out of the market."

Specifically, the problem was with the firm's commercial paper, its short-term IOUs that aren't backed by any specific assets. Drexel had $700 million in commercial paper outstanding, which had to be continuously reborrowed, usually every thirty to sixty days. And if it couldn't be reborrowed, it had to be repaid.

The firm was now in danger of being squeezed out of business—it was losing money, and cash, and there was the ongoing risk that its lenders would take their money and run. During December alone, $420 million of Drexel's commercial paper was redeemed by lenders, according to the SEC.

Unlike most of the other major firms on the Street, which were subsidiaries of huge corporate parents, the firm didn't have a Big Daddy to bail it out if worst came to worst. As for Groupe Bruxelles Lambert, which owned 26 percent of Drexel's stock, "relations were pretty poor," according to Drexel's Burt Siegel—during the glory days, Lambert had been treated less like a rich uncle than an unwanted aunt.

The Lambert Group did lend the firm some cash at year-end, backed by specific assets, but it declined to make an equity investment. On that subject, the bottom line given to Fred Joseph was to improve the bottom line: start showing profits, and Lambert would consider making a further investment after the end of the first quarter, in April 1990.

Drexel ended 1989 with a $40 million loss and decidedly mixed prospects for the new year. "I really believed we had a good chance of getting there," recalled Fred Joseph at a meeting for Drexel debt holders. "Every department expected to break even at worst."

One officer on the West Coast who was involved with Drexel's efforts to maintain its borrowings from the banks, however, was a great deal less optimistic. Given his position, he had access to excellent information from both the auditors and the rumor mill. "I knew it was going badly," he said. "The banks could pull their lines [of credit] at any time." Many in his department took their cash and securities out of their personal accounts at the firm, to avoid the risk that these assets might be frozen if Drexel went bankrupt.

This officer also mentioned the bonus payments. The bonuses, many of which had been guaranteed in early 1989, amounted to $150 million in December and an additional $110 million in January 1990. What concerned him was that Drexel paid $64 million of these bonuses, not in cash, but in a PIK preferred stock. "We all know why people issue PIK preferreds," he noted. "And it's not because you're healthy."

By the end of January 1990, the firm's health was considerably worse. In addition to the nearly $200 million cash outflow from the bonuses, Drexel lost $52 million from its operations. Fees from investment banking transactions were less than $10 million in the month, although these fees were expected to reach $120 million in the subsequent two months.

These large investment banking fees, as well as the operating improvements from the firm's other departments, never had the opportunity to be realized, however. In February, Drexel's financial structure collapsed. For months, more cash had been going out the door than coming in, and the firm finally ran out of sources to replace it.

Drexel's best source toward the end, interestingly, was itself. As loans came due and lenders demanded their money, Drexel Burnham Lambert *Group,* a holding company that was responsible for the debts, borrowed cash from its subsidiary, Drexel Burnham Lambert *Inc.,* which was the brokerage firm that you think of when you hear the name Drexel.

This holding company structure, which is common on Wall Street, became a nightmare for the firm and its regulators. DBL Group was borrowing the money from DBL Inc., because it was desperately short of cash, and DBL Inc. had more than it needed. DBL Inc.'s excess cash was the amount of money that it held above and beyond the amount that the regulators required. This extra cash was the famous "excess net capital" that Fred Joseph had been referring to for three years, which had reassured employees that the firm was in terrific financial shape even if we didn't really know what the term meant.

Now Drexel, specifically the Group, needed that money to pay its debts. It borrowed $220 million from DBL Inc. over several months, reducing the broker's excess capital to $330 million. The firm didn't inform the SEC, which is responsible for regulating DBL Inc., because it was only borrowing *excess* cash, which by definition, was money that wasn't required in the first place.

The SEC found out on February 7. The following day, it told Drexel to stop upstreaming cash from DBL Inc. to DBL Group. This cash might be excess capital, but the regulators had the right to keep it where it was, and that's exactly what they did. Their concern was that DBL Group would borrow too much from DBL Inc., thereby threatening the broker's survival by replacing its cash with IOUs from the Group.

The SEC's job was to keep the broker solvent, and they were taking no chances. Its actions made it likely that the Group would default on its loans, which in turn, would probably create a chain of circumstances that would throw the broker into bankruptcy as well. But its concern at this point was that DBL Inc. maintain as strong a financial position as possible.

In the SEC's mind, allowing DBL Group to borrow the remaining $300 million in excess capital from DBL Inc. would only have postponed the firm's default by one or two days. Although the commercial paper outstanding had been reduced to $150 million by early February, Drexel had other short-term loans that were maturing in that month and next, in total about $700 million according to the SEC.

The firm believed, however, that these lenders would roll over their loans when they came due rather than demanding repayment. It proposed a plan to the SEC, the NYSE, and the New York Federal Reserve Bank on Friday, February 9 that involved reducing its operations and selling major portions of its bond and stock holdings. The result, it hoped, would be a leaner firm with enough cash to run its businesses effectively. But the SEC didn't buy this argument.

Another source of cash for DBL Group had been a different subsidiary, DBL Trading Corp., which specialized in commodity and foreign-exchange transactions. Allegedly, Trading Corp. had leased gold from various foreign governments, then sold the gold and purchased future contracts for an equivalent amount. Since futures contracts require only a small up-front payment, usually less than 10 percent of the total value, Trading Corp. was left with the vast majority in cash, some of which it lent to DBL Group. (Whether or not Trading Corp. had the right, legally or ethically, to lend this money is in dispute.)

According to one senior executive, a major bank pulled DBL Trading Corp.'s line of credit, and $200 million was subsequently transferred from DBL Group to Trading Corp. in two transactions. Evidently, this left Trading Corp. with approximately $600 million in loans, many of them the result of gold-leasing agreements. Among the lenders were several Eastern European countries, which were soon to receive a painful introduction to capitalism.*

*In a July 9, 1991, decision, a Federal District Court judge reportedly permitted a lawsuit from the Central Bank of Yugoslavia against Drexel and four of its officers—Fred Joseph, Dirk Wright, Leon Plack and John Kissick—to proceed.

By Monday the twelfth, Drexel was running out of room fast. On the trading floor, one salesman described the scene as "eery, complete quiet, no phones ringing, no nothing." Another salesman advised him, "Don't talk to anyone. Don't call your wife, don't call clients and don't tell anybody anything. Everything is being taped." (Which was not true, according to an official at Drexel.)

The rating on its remaining commercial paper was reduced further that day; although only $150 million were left, this downgrade would certainly send an ominous message to the firm's other lenders.

Drexel turned to its bankers, hoping for a temporary $350 million loan. As collateral, the firm offered a package of assets, most of which were its remaining junk bonds. The market value of this package was estimated at $800 million, more than twice the requested loan, but the banks refused. "The banks were petrified," said a senior Drexel officer. "They had already lent us $1.05 billion" from an ongoing credit line and were unwilling to take on more risk.

Among foreign companies, there was evidently no interest in acquiring the firm. No Japanese or European broker was eager to take on the responsibility of Drexel's contingent liabilities—the unknown sums that the firm might owe in the future if lawsuit settlements exceeded the amounts already set aside.

At 1:00 on the morning of Tuesday, February 13, Fred Joseph spoke with Richard Breeden, chairman of the SEC, and Gerald Corrigan, president of the New York Federal Reserve Bank. Their advice: Put yourself in bankruptcy. At 11:00 A.M., the firm announced that it had defaulted on $100 million in loans. Before the end of the day, the news was official: After fifty-five years on Wall Street, Drexel Burnham was finished.

The end for Michael Milken came two months later. A bit after noon on April 24, 1990, he entered Room 110 at the Southern District Courthouse to plead guilty to six felonies. He looked composed—not relaxed, but in control of himself. His wife and his mother sat in the front. Around them in the standing-room-only crowd were reporters from, as best as I could tell, every newspaper with a circulation of more than ten.

Judge Kimba Wood, the most recent—and, at forty-six, the youngest—appointee to this federal district court, entered soon after Milken, and the proceedings began. It was a ritual of questions asked and answered, almost by script. If you go to trial, do you understand that you will have a presumption of innocence? Yes, your honor. Do you understand your right to change your plea? I do. Do you understand that you have to acknowledge guilt? Yes. Are you seeing a doctor or psychiatrist? No. Is your mind clear? (Pause) Yes, your honor.

And so on.

Arthur Liman, Milken's principal attorney, clarified that the prosecutors had agreed not to recommend a specific sentence; John Carroll, the assistant U.S. attorney on the case since its inception, concurred, pointing out that this was consistent with general practice. Judge Wood noted that the settlement of the criminal case included a $200 million fine to the government, and that the settlement of the SEC's civil case required an additional $400 million payment to a fund for shareholders who had been hurt by the crimes that Milken was now acknowledging.

Those crimes carried a maximum penalty of twenty-eight years in jail. The judge told Milken that she might order that he serve his sentence consecutively or concurrently—if concurrently, the maximum penalty would be five years. She also warned against attempting to predict her final decision, which would be announced some five months later.

Interestingly, by agreement, Milken's cooperation in the government's ongoing investigation would not begin until after that final decision. Liman argued that his client had an obligation to cooperate "fully, accurately, and truthfully," but clearly, the prosecutor's leverage over Milken would drop significantly once sentenced. Carroll acknowledged as much: When asked by Judge Wood if the defendant's cooperation would be as complete after her decision, the prosecutor replied, "We certainly hope so."

As part of the plea process, Milken read an intriguing statement, known as an allocution, admitting his crimes. It's lengthy, but because of the carefully chosen wording of his admissions, it's worth seeing in full.

I was the founder and head of the High Yield and Convertible Securities Department at Drexel. In pioneering the creation of new instruments for the financing of companies, most of which did not have access to the capital markets because they did not have investment-grade ratings, and in making markets in such securities, we operated under unique, highly demanding, and intensely competitive conditions.

But I do not cite these conditions as an excuse for not conforming to all of the laws that governed our highly regulated business. I am here today because in connection with some transactions, I transgressed certain of the laws and regulations that govern our industry. I was wrong in doing so and knew that at the time and I am pleading guilty to these offenses.

One of the accounts we did business with was the Boesky organization, which also did business with many other firms. Drexel did some financings for and trading with the Boesky firm, but Drexel's business with the Boesky organization never approached 1 percent of the business of our department.

He traded in stocks; I traded primarily in bonds, or their equivalent. But because he was a major factor in the securities markets, he had the potential to become a more significant account. We were not social friends and had little in common. His philosophy of business was different from mine.

The relationship started as an arm's length and correct one. Unfortunately, however, certain of our transactions involved reciprocal accommodations, some of which violated the law, including those that are referred to in this allocution.

In 1984, our department had purchased some securities of Fischbach, a company in which Victor Posner had an interest. Drexel had provided financing to several other companies which Mr. Posner had an interest in.

In early 1984, Mr. Posner publicly announced that he intended to acquire Fischbach. Boesky was familiar with the Fischbach situation and wanted to purchase Fischbach securities. I encouraged him to do so. I do not remember exactly what I told him almost six years ago, but I indicated to him that he would not lose money.

The Boesky organization began buying Fischbach securities and eventually bought over 10 percent of Fischbach including securities that had been owned by Drexel. Over the next months, he called me incessantly to complain that the price of the stock was dropping, that Drexel was responsible for his losses, that my comments to him were guarantees against loss and that he expected us to make good.

I assured him that Drexel would make good on his losses. These assurances were not recorded on the books of Drexel and I did not expect that they would be reflected in any Schedule 13-D's filed by the Boesky organization, and, in fact they were not. Thus, I assisted in the failure to file an accurate 13-D. This was wrong and I accept responsibility for it. This is the basis for Count 2 and is one of the overt acts in Count 1 [conspiracy].

As for Count 3 and the second overt act of the conspiracy count, in the fall of 1984, a client of Drexel, Golden Nugget, wanted to sell a substantial amount of MCA stock. I wanted the shares to hit the market in a way that would not identify our client as the seller and adversely affect the price that it might receive.

So I turned to Boesky, whose business it was to buy and sell large amounts of stock and who I knew had an interest in entertainment company stocks, including MCA. I told a Drexel employee to ask him to buy the blocks of MCA shares as they became available from Drexel's client.

I did not tell the client how I was disposing of the stock. Drexel crossed the blocks between its client and the Boesky organization which subsequently resold most of these shares into the market. When Boesky complained that he had lost money on his initial purchases of MCA, I promised that we would make up any losses the Boesky organization suffered on its purchases and sales and thereafter it bought more MCA stock from Drexel acting on behalf of our client.

This promise was not recorded on Drexel's books nor made public, and it was wrong not to do so. It was my intent that the block sales would enable our client to receive a better price than it might have obtained if I had not agreed that Drexel would make up the Boesky organization's losses on the MCA stock.

In July 1985, the Boesky organization asked Drexel to purchase approximately one million shares of stock in Helmerich & Payne. The Boesky organization agreed that it would repurchase this stock in the future and promised that it would make up any losses Drexel incurred while holding this stock.

Although I was not involved in the purchase of these securities, I later learned of this understanding. I approved this understanding. I also gave instructions to sell the stock back.

The understanding that the Boesky organization would make up any losses was an oral one and the stock while held by Drexel was not, therefore, charged to the Boesky organization's net capital as required by the securities laws and rules. This is the basis for Count 4 and the third overt act.

As I stated earlier, there were other accommodations of a similar nature between the Boesky organization and Drexel, some of which were wrong. After Boesky complained about his losses and insisted that we make them up, I asked a Drexel employee in early 1985 to check the amount of the losses that the Boesky organization had incurred.

In order to make up these losses, I caused Drexel to execute certain bond trades which resulted in profits to the Boesky organization. Thereafter, a Drexel employee tried to keep track of how the Boesky organization stood, in terms of profits and losses, on these and certain other transactions, though so far as I know this score-keeping was never exact.

Counts 5 and 6 and the remaining overt acts relate to transactions between Drexel and David Solomon. Mr. Solomon was a portfolio manager who specialized in high-yield securities. His company, Solomon Asset Management Company Inc., was a large customer of Drexel, as well as of other firms.

Among the institutions for which Mr. Solomon managed a high-yield portfolio was the Finsbury Fund, an offshore fund that had been underwritten by a Drexel affiliate. Drexel paid an annual 1 percent commission to its salesmen for selling this fund abroad and charged this commission to the High Yield Department because the Finsbury Fund traded in high-yield securities.

Sometime in 1985, I agreed with Solomon and officials of Drexel that the High Yield Department would recoup the commission for Drexel. To attempt to do so, we charged Solomon a fraction of a point more on certain purchases he made for his clients or a fraction of a point less on certain sales he made for his clients to help recoup the 1 percent commission paid to Drexel salesmen.

All adjustments were to be within the bid/ask range for the particular security at the time of the transaction. To the best of my information, this was done on a number of trades and the adjustments totaled several hundred thousand dollars.

These adjustments were not disclosed by Drexel or me to the shareholders of Finsbury or to Solomon's other clients. The confirmations for Solomon's purchase of securities were mailed by Drexel and did not disclose the adjustments or that they were made to reimburse Drexel for the selling expenses of the Finsbury Fund. This failure to disclose was wrong and is the basis of Count 5.

In December 1985, Mr. Solomon asked whether Drexel could engage in securities transactions with him on which he could generate short-term losses for his personal income tax purposes.

In light of the customer relationship between Mr. Solomon and Drexel, I assisted him in purchasing from Drexel certain securities, set forth in the information, which traded at a significant spread between the bid and the ask price. Drexel thereafter repurchased these securities at a substantially lower price, thus generating a loss for him and a profit for Drexel.

I either told him that we would provide him with an investment opportunity or opportunities in the following year to make up his loss to him, or that was implicit in the conversation. In fact, in the following year, we did provide him an investment opportunity which turned out to be profitable and ultimately more than made up the losses he suffered. I thus assisted Mr. Solomon in taking a tax loss to which he was not entitled, and this is the basis of Count 6 and the fifth overt act.

So there it was: Milken admitted that he had broken the law and knew it at the time. The felony counts involved conspiracy, stock parking, fraud, and the filing of a false document. Two of the five specific transactions cited—Fischbach (false filing) and MCA (stock parking) were part of the original indictment; the following three—Helmerich & Payne (stock parking), Finsbury Fund (fraud), and David Solomon (stock parking)—would have been part of the superseding indictment that had been threatened.

"Because of the tremendous amount of publicity that has surrounded this case," Milken said summing up his statement. "I wish to make clear that my plea is an acceptance of personal responsibility for my own failings and actions, and not a reflection on the underlying soundness and integrity of the segment of the capital markets in which we specialized and which provided capital that enabled hundreds of companies to survive, expand and flourish.

"Our business was in no way dependent on these practices. Nor did they comprise a fundamental part of our business and I regret them very much."

The most dramatic, and human, moments came within seconds of the end. "This investigation and proceeding are now in their fourth year," Milken concluded. "This long period has been extremely painful and difficult for my family and friends as well as myself.

"I realize that by my acts I have hurt those who are closest to me . . ." He broke down. It was as if the magnitude of what he was admitting, of what had been suffered and what would be suffered, had sunk in.

He struggled to complete his statement, fighting back the tears, as Liman offered emotional support by placing his arm on Milken's back: "I am truly sorry. I thank the court for permitting me to add this apology and for its fairness in handling this complex case."

Judge Wood responded immediately: "Thank you, Mr. Milken." In time, she asked him another question. His voice cracked as he began to answer.

Within half an hour, Milken would leave the courthouse, again in control—his wife with him—nodding and then smiling to his supporters. It would be that smile, and not the earlier pain, that the photographers would capture and the newspapers would print the next day.

If most people have a smile that reassures, Milken does not. His comes across more that of the cat who got the canary or of the fellow who beat the system. It wouldn't be surprising if people, looking into that smile over breakfast or on their commute to work, said to themselves, "That bastard thinks he bought himself a great deal, doesn't he?"

But he didn't. The smile was meant to tell the world that he hadn't been beaten, at least not completely. It was a show of bravado.

"As the wolves of Wall Street go, he wasn't too bad," proclaimed one syndicated columnist on the courthouse steps. Later, I realized what Drexel had no doubt already learned for itself: Milken was now an easy target for the backhanded compliments and clever criticisms of the serenely self-righteous, as well as for the justifiable skepticism and anger of the average person on the street.

Someone who has known Milken for years drew a crude but effective analogy, one that he associated with Drexel's decision to settle, but which he recognized applied to Milken's decision as well. This analogy, which I've cleaned up considerably, involves a fellow "with a gun to his head, maybe a real gun, maybe a water pistol," forced to strip naked and run through the streets. "And the picture is shown throughout the country.

"This guy can say, 'I never [did this] before; I thought it was a real gun. But the reality is that you're a [fool], and your kids will know."

Then why settle? If Milken genuinely believed in his innocence, why would he, of all people, put himself in that picture? Because it was the lesser of two "terrible, terrible choices," argued his friend: To fight the charges—the ones we considered in the last chapter *and* those in the superseding indictment that the prosecutors were ready to file—to fight all these charges would involve another year before a trial even began and at least six months of sitting in court each day, both Milken and his wife. And then, when all that was done, Milken would still face the possibility of a RICO conviction. On the other hand, to settle the case would make Milken an admitted felon and would place him at the prosecutors' beck and call in their ongoing investigation.

In trying to explain Milken's decision, this friend mentioned the story of two professors who were captured in the jungle by natives and put in a cage. The chief gives the first professor a choice: death or ru-ru. "I'll take ru-ru," the professor says. The natives drag him out of the cage, beat him, then toss him into a pit with tigers, and then throw the bloody carcass on the ground in front of the cage.

"Death or ru-ru!" says the native chief to the second professor.

"I think I'll take death," the professor replies.

"Okay," says the chief. "But first, a little ru-ru."

CHAPTER FOURTEEN

FORTUNE AND
MEN'S EYES

Death, humiliation, and pain—
are you ready for that, Dundee?

—*Best of Times*

The history of Drexel Burnham was one of surprises—surprises that in retrospect seem to have had a malicious inevitability about them. If you thought up this story yourself, no one would believe it; like a badly contrived tragedy, the mighty are brought down by a chain of tragic flaws and unlikely events. An honorable second-tier firm rises to the top on the back of an extraordinary individual, but in the process, the seeds are sown for the destruction of both the individual and the firm.

The unconventional success of Drexel Burnham was, oddly enough, the result of its desire to achieve conventional success. In 1973, Burnham & Co., a retail-oriented broker, acquired Drexel Firestone, an old-line investment banking firm, with the hope of improving its position in the syndicates that dominated Wall Street's clubby atmosphere.

In the bargain, Burnham & Co. also picked up a "nuclear power-cell," a twenty-six-year-old trader who would propell the firm to the first rank not by joining the club, but by beating it. He would focus on a market that Wall Street had ignored and ignore the etiquette that the Street had relied on. He would make a fortune for himself and an absurd amount of money for his associates. Primarily because of him, his firm would become the most profitable on Wall Street, but also one of the riskiest.

In 1986, at the absolute height of Milken's power and that of his firm, both would be forced onto a slow, improbable path to disgrace and ruin. Dennis Levine, a successful investment banker, would be implicated for insider trading, the victim of naked greed and of an anonymous letter from Venezuela that put the authorities on his trail. His arrest and cooperation, although not a threat to Drexel, would scare Ivan Boesky into cutting a deal with the government, his chief bargaining chip being the allegations against the most influential man on Wall Street.

The SEC had already initiated four investigations "in which Michael Milken was named as a witness, officer and/or principal between 1981 and 1985.

Name	Open	Closed
Leasco Corp.	08-14-79	10-21-81
Certain Issuers	01-26-82	03-29-84
Drexel Burnham Lambert, Inc.	03-19-84	09-30-86
Centrust Savings Bank	04-19-85	pending"

By late 1986, none of these investigations had turned up sufficient evidence for prosecution. But now the government had a witness. And with that witness, came a weapon: the ability to force others at Boesky's firm to cooperate rather than face prosecution. This cooperation meant that certain allegations could be corroborated and that other people—members of Milken's department—could be implicated. In a widening web around the main target, these people would themselves choose to cooperate in return for leniency or immunity.

As the walls around Milken were slowly being chipped apart, his firm, which had chosen to support him completely, became aware of another weapon—this one unexpected—that was being rolled onto the battlefield: RICO. The U.S. attorney on Drexel's case, Rudolph Giuliani, happened to be the man who had pioneered the use of this powerful statute against individuals—mobsters mainly—and was now extending its sights to financial firms.

Princeton/Newport was hit first, and was destroyed before it ever went to trial. Drexel Burnham, as a corporation rather than a partnership, stood a better chance of surviving, but no one knew how much better. Under the weight of both the RICO threat and the evidence, within an hour of indictment the firm acquiesed to a draconian guilty plea after twenty-five months of arguing its innocence.

Six felonies and a $650-million fine, inconceivable only a year earlier, were devastating but not fatal. It was the decisions and events of the following year that drove a weakened firm into bankruptcy.

The loss of Milken did not destroy the firm's belief that it could continue to dominate and prosper in the junk-bond market—*his* market. Because of this belief, bridge loans were offered and new offerings were accepted, loans and deals that he might not have done or that he might have gotten done.

Along with this focus on its previous strengths, Drexel also "restructured" its areas of weakness. Retail was the primary casualty; its elimination saved the firm tens of millions in annual losses, but cost the firm its direct contact with the average person on the street.

Events spiraled out of Drexel's control in the second half of 1989 with the passage of the S&L bill, the collapse of the junk-bond market, and the mini stock market crash. These unpleasant surprises led directly to a shocking one: The firm's commercial paper was downgraded, thereby rendering it too risky for money-market funds, its chief customers. Drexel's risky financial structure—the most highly leveraged among the major firms—which had seemed acceptable only five months earlier, was now in danger of collapse.

The last and worst of the surprises came in February 1990 when management realized that the firm would not be able to survive without outside help and that nobody—not the regulators, the banks, the foreigners, or the Street—was going to provide that help.

Of course, the real surprise here was that Drexel put itself in a position to need such support. Throughout its glory days, the firm had managed to alienate the powers that be among competitors, regulators, and corporate America. Hostile takeovers and hardball tactics invited retaliation, whether or not these takeovers and tactics were justified.

"We understood the implications of getting into the financing of large acquisitions before we did it," Fred Joseph noted in a May 1986 interview for *Manhattan, inc.* "And we succeeded beyond our expectations, and the heat was greater than we expected." But, in retrospect, hostile takeovers probably generated more heat than the firm ever anticipated. "They didn't think about it or about the concerted effort against them," one West Coast officer said about his colleagues. "There was a certain naïveté."

But there was also a tremendous arrogance among the rainmakers. "A crummy neighbor" was how one East Coaster described the firm's image. "If it ain't illegal, we can do it."

When it came to Drexel, the other neighbors got mad. And eventually they were given a chance to get even—the top people at Drexel, in trying to change the comfortable status quo, left their firm vulnerable to the establishment that despised them.

Bear in mind, however, that if the firm's unpopularity was due to the actions of hundreds, its vulnerability was due to the actions of a dozen. Four people were investigated and cut deals, four are still under investigation, and four were indicted. The net result: three convictions and ten thousand people out of their jobs.

When one thinks about such a mismatch, or that a firm with $800 million in equity went down the tubes seemingly overnight, one knows that some serious mistakes were made. Now that I've stated the obvious, let's consider some specifics, naturally with the benefit of twenty/twenty hindsight.

1. The Partners vs. the Shareholders. The partnerships—numbering in the hundreds—that Michael Milken created beginning in the late 1970s caused a series of problems for the firm. Even though these partnerships were ripe for abuse, Drexel's top management allowed them. "I thought it was sensible," one senior executive said of the idea. "It would keep people from being distracted," spending time worrying about their personal investments.

But the partnerships also gave selected officers a terrific alternative to investing their money in the shares of their firm. More, this alternative investment was in competition with their firm. Although in theory the partnerships were only entitled to those bonds, stocks, and warrants that Drexel refused for its stockholders, in practice the lines could not have been so clearly drawn.

The members of the partnerships—representing only some 2 percent of the firm's employees—were the rainmakers, the big boys. And management wanted to keep them happy. If not, it wouldn't have allowed the partnerships in the first place. If not, why would the partners end up with four times as many warrants in Harris Graphics, purchased at $1 each and sold three years later at $22 each, as did their firm? If not, why would the partners end up with the lion's share of Beatrice warrants, bought for twenty-five cents each which four years later would be worth *fifty* times that much?

While the partnerships generated huge profits for their participants, they also created a poor image for a firm that found itself very much in the public eye. This image of favoritism, and even self-dealing, particularly affected two important constituencies close to home: the employees and the clients.

Most important, the partnerships encouraged a level of risk taking that endangered the survival of the firm. The partners, with little of their own money in Drexel's stock, didn't need to worry about the bottom line. They were paid based on the *revenues* they generated, *not* the profits. They had a personal incentive to bring in deals, however risky, deals that created huge fees. And they had stood to benefit by encouraging their firm to own large amounts of junk bonds, bonds that kept the high-yield market active and liquid, and profitable.

They made their enormous bonuses, and invested parts of these bonuses in partnerships that had an inside track to the choicest merchandise. It was "heads I win, tails you lose," and it led to a situation in which those who were most important to the firm's future had, proportionally, a minuscule stake in that future.

The final chapter on the Drexel partnerships has yet to be written. The House Oversight and Investigations Subcommittee, which grilled Fred Joseph in April 1988, will be conducting further hearings, perhaps as early as October 1990. The featured witness will be Michael Milken, although his memory may very well become cloudy when answering questions about the abuses and possible illegalities committed by these partnerships.

Meanwhile, the Securities and Exchange Commission is said to be investigating the partnerships, probably with a particular eye on those clients of Milken's who were limited partners. It seems logical that the SEC will want to address the question: To what extent did individual clients benefit personally as a reward for the decisions they made as junk-bond portfolio managers? My guess is that at least a few face a long and discontented winter.

Further in the future, the firm, whose board of directors agreed to use shareholders' money to indemnify the partnerships against loss, may have to make good on that promise. Perhaps those on the board who voted for this proposal—which allegedly includes just about every member of the board—would consider taking the money out of their own pockets instead of out of their employees'. But I wouldn't bet on it.

2. *The Boesky Allegations.* "One of my theories is Don't try to figure out what you will do next when you are in a free-fall," said Fred Joseph over the hoot and holler on November 26, 1986—twelve days after Boesky's arrest. "We ought to take it easy. I have several rules for things like this. The top rule is don't die; and another top one is don't panic."

Actually, panicking would've been a terrific idea. There were several reasons for thinking settlement, fast. "I always want to know my downside," is one smart trader's view of life. But Drexel was flying blind. The firm's response to the subpoenas delivered from the SEC and the allegations leaked to the press was that it knew of no wrong-doing by anyone at the firm. The problem was that it had no way of knowing whether or not laws had been broken—Michael Milken would only address these concerns through his battery of lawyers.

So what, in retrospect, should the firm have done? Milken was under investigation, not indictment. Perhaps if he had been arrested, the firm would have insisted on speaking with him directly, as happened three months later at Goldman Sachs with Robert Freeman (who reportedly also agreed to take a lie detector test). Actually, it's doubtful that Milken would have ever spoken to Drexel's lawyers directly, or that the firm would have demanded it—let's face it, this was no ordinary employee.

But management had other factors to consider. It had almost two thousand shareholders and a legal responsibility to protect their best interests. It also operated in the most regulated industry in the world. As a securities firm, Drexel enjoyed many privileges, the chief one being the protection of the Glass-Steagal Act, a Depression-era law that kept the banks out of the brokerage business. But along with the privileges came the regulations of the SEC. And, as a general rule, you don't take on the folks who interpret and enforce the rules.

This is particularly true when those folks had already conducted four investigations involving Michael Milken, a fact that Drexel's management was aware of, even if the employees and the rest of the world weren't. Under these conditions, fighting "the war," as the government's investigation was known among the firm's top officials, was a high-risk strategy.

On the other hand, settling with the government and effectively cutting off Milken at the knees was a potentially dangerous strategy, as well. He was the reason for the firm's phenomenal success in the 1980s, and he had a nearly fanatical following (by Wall Street standards) among his people and his clients. Nobody on the Street is tied to his job, and a bad deal for Milken might have led to devastating defections in the junk-bond department and in corporate finance.

Another concern: Drexel held nearly $4 billion in high-yield bonds in its inventory, a result of its excessive willingness to back Milken's vision with its own money. At this point, the loss of Milken might have caused a panic in that market, which could have wiped out a major chunk of the firm's equity. In effect, the firm, by its own choices, had made itself a hostage to Milken's future.

Of course, an immediate settlement with the government might have allowed Milken to remain at the firm, but I would guess the odds of that were a thousand to one against. Which raises another question: *Would* the government have settled with Drexel in late 1986, at the beginning of the investigation? One board member offered the opinion that the firm could have settled for $5 million with a three-month suspension for Milken, a ludicrously optimistic hope on his part. Still, as an officer at the firm argued to me in 1987, there is always a settlement offer if you want it.

If Drexel had settled with the government early on, there would have been an uproar within the firm, an anger that I would have shared at the time. Fred Joseph might have been driven out in a popular uprising. Important employees in corporate finance might have moved down the street to Salomon Brothers or uptown to First Boston. These firms might have opened up satellite offices in Beverly Hills to entice the dissatisfied away from Drexel's high-yield bond department. The junk-bond market would certainly have plummeted, at least temporarily, causing huge losses on the bonds that Drexel held.

It would have been a mess, but a decision to settle the case in late 1986 would have been the correct one. Without strong reason to believe that the allegations were false, the firm was forced to recognize the fact that a brokerage firm is too dependent on the rules of regulators and the confidence of lenders, employees, and customers to fight a protracted battle with the SEC and the U.S. attorney's office. Nobody could have fought that battle better than Drexel did—a tribute to the loyalty of its people and its clients—but it was a fight, even without the threat of RICO, that was destined for defeat.

3. COOPERATION Instead of "Cooperation." Once Drexel had decided that it would fight the allegations rather than settle with the government, it should have cooperated fully with the investigation. According to the firm, that's what it did; according to the government, it did not. The government's point of view is more believable on this one.

Part of the problem was that the dominant attitude at Drexel in 1986 was confrontational, because the dominant person at Drexel was confrontational; more than that, he was the focus of the investigation. Another part of the problem was that the firm might have thought that delay would work to its advantage, as it often does in civil and criminal cases.

If the firm thought this, however, it was being naive. This was no ordinary case, and the government prosecutors weren't about to get bored or frustrated and leave for private practice before the investigation was complete. On the contrary, a strategy of delay was more likely to inflame the other side than to wear it down.

This wasn't the Battle of Britain, a total war between the good guys and the bad guys, fighting on the beaches if necessary. This was supposed to be a cooperative effort between a brokerage firm and its regulators, with a common goal: to find out if any laws had been broken.

Initially, Drexel did seem to approach the SEC with that attitude in mind, but was rejected. Following that, I suspect that the firm's management slid into a siege mentality—I know I did—and cooperation became more rhetoric than reality. As a result, Drexel found itself in a war of attrition, without fully understanding or accepting the firepower on the other side.

4. Don't Mess with RICO. The attorneys for Drexel Burnham consistently underestimated the chances that the racketeering law would be used against the firm. "Lawyers are mortal," said Fred Joseph in their defense. "This is beyond their ken of what could happen." But was it?

In late 1986, it is true that RICO was generally unknown. Still, top criminal lawyers—and those are the ones we hired—should have been more conscious of the risk. Rudolph Giuliani had a reputation for aggressiveness, and he had shown his willingness to use RICO against defendants as diverse as Carmine Persico, head of the Colombo crime family, and Stanley Friedman, head of the Bronx Democratic party.

He had also extended RICO's grasp to the financial community in the case of Marc Rich, a commodities trader, whose companies had pleaded guilty to tax fraud and had paid a fine approaching $200 million. And if anyone needed any reminder about RICO's presence or power, there was the twelve-year sentence given Stanley Friedman in November 1986, the same month that Drexel fell under investigation.

There were two conclusions that one feels the lawyers should have reached: RICO could be used against a financial firm such as Drexel and, in the hands of Giuliani, that use was quite possible. Indeed, the indictment of Princeton/Newport in August 1988 made the possibility a near certainty.

By the time Drexel realized it would be indicted under RICO—an indictment it didn't believe it could survive—the firm's bargaining position was almost nonexistent. Except for the argument that RICO would be fatal, an argument the prosecutors didn't accept, Drexel had nothing. The result was an eleventh-hour shotgun settlement.

Of course, the firm wasn't required to settle, RICO or not. Perhaps RICO was a bluff and would have disappeared if Drexel hadn't buckled—after all, there were those three hundred and fifty thousand retail accounts that the firm still had. It's a logical argument, but not necessarily the relevant one, because the government didn't believe that RICO would annihilate the firm. "We asked around," said Assistant U.S. Attorney Bruce Baird, "It was more or less unanimous that it would not cause Drexel's downfall in the short run." Maybe he was right, maybe not—personally, I think RICO would've buried the firm. The problem was that by the time everyone learned the impact of RICO, it would be too late to reverse.

The corollary to the "call the bluff" strategy was the "so what?" strategy. Here again, the firm would refuse to settle, and if RICO kicked Drexel into bankruptcy, so be it. Liquidate the firm—sell off the assets, pay off the debts—and give the remainder to the stockhold-ers. At least there would be no doubt of the cause. Unfortunately, martyrdom makes more sense for revolutionaries than for ten thou-sand employees with bills to pay. As for the two thousand stockhold-ers among those employees, the fire sale of assets that would occur might wipe out their stake by wiping out the firm's equity. Not much of a strategy there.

Also suggested was the "thanks, but no thanks" approach: Take the settlement and then refuse it after Rudy Giuliani's resignation in late January 1990. The firm had a valid excuse to renounce the settlement—as of February, it still hadn't come to terms with the SEC, which was one of the requirements of a final settlement.

The logic behind the strategy of tearing up the deal was that al-though Benito Romano, who had succeeded Giuliani as U.S. attorney for the Southern District of New York, would have indicted Drexel, he might have not RICO'd the firm. And even had he supported the idea of dropping the bomb, Richard Thornburgh, the new U.S. attorney general and the man who had the final say on the use of RICO, might have just said no. Indict Drexel under the securities laws if you want, but not under a racketeering statute.

As clever as this idea sounds, however, I doubt it would have worked for one simple reason: It's too clever. The new prosecutors would have realized Drexel's game and, because of that, would have refused to give the firm what it wanted even if they felt in their heart of hearts that RICO was unfair.

5. *Life without Mike:* Everybody knew that Milken was the best, but very few realized just how much better he was. "You're playing on the Lakers," was the analogy drawn by one West Coast officer, "and you think you're hot shit, but if you don't have Magic Johnson feeding you the ball . . . you're [just] shit." According to an East Coast investment banker: "A couple of guys thought they were the smartest that ever walked the hallowed halls of Wall Street." "They surrounded Milken with the best and brightest," said another banker, "but they couldn't clone him."

With the loss of Mike Milken, who had faded from the day-to-day scene by April 1988 and had officially left the firm a year later, Drexel pretty much became just another firm. In high-yield bonds, it had a tremendous head start, but it had lost its edge. "We were as much at risk from a bad street crossing as we were from the SEC," noted one officer in explaining the importance of Milken to his firm and his market.

Drexel, however, chose to focus on the strengths it had enjoyed under Milken, even though it no longer had his analytical skills, his salesmanship, and his influence. The firm had depended on his knowledge and insight, on his ability to understand what the stuff was really worth. Drexel had also relied on his ability to move the junk-bond merchandise—one West Coast officer recalled that it had never been easy to sell the junk-bond deals, even in the glory days of the mid-1980s. Milken had made all the difference.

Without him, the confidence that had helped this market grow to $200 billion in a decade was replaced with doubt. The clients weren't as eager to buy, the bonds weren't as carefully tailored to what these clients wanted, and the deals weren't as successful. It was a very different ball game.

What hadn't changed was that a young, volatile market like the high-yield bond market offered both tremendous profits and extraordinary risks. When Milken ran the show, he was able to find the profits and, if not avoid, at least defer the dangers. When he left, the risk-to-reward ratio shifted.

Rather than catering to the implicit threats of the rainmakers, the firm would have been better served if Fred Joseph had told them, in the words of one officer, "Look, guys, there's a three-part enemy. One part is our past. One part is public opinion. And one part is you."

Rather than offering the so-called superstars guaranteed incomes, Fred could have leveraged the one piece of good fortune that had come his way: the financing of the RJR/Nabisco buyout. The RJR deal, which mitigated the impact of Milken's departure, provided $227 million in fees, and many of the big boys in corporate finance and on the Coast had a claim to a slice of the largest pie in Wall Street's history. Fred, as chief exec, had the major say in the allocation of the slices, which would be part of the 1989 bonuses. These bonuses were almost a year away, and it is not likely that the folks with a claim were going to leave the firm and give up *their* leverage—out of sight, out of luck.

Most important, rather than holding to a strategy that had been made obsolete by events, Drexel should have steered clear of those deals that weren't being sold. "We didn't need to portray ourselves as the junk-bond powers that we had been under Michael," said a two-decade veteran of the firm. Some fees would have been sacrificed, some clients would have been angered, and some investment bankers would have screamed bloody murder, but the firm wouldn't have stuck itself with the unwanted debt of West Point-Pepperell, Paramount Petroleum, WPS Textile, and others.

Our competitors may have ended up with *relatively* more bridge loans and unwanted bonds than we did, as one senior exec argued, but they were in better financial shape. The other major firms on Wall Street had wealthy parents and deep pockets that could absorb this illiquid junk debt. What for them were expensive learning experiences was for us a banzai charge.

6. The Face of the Firm. If the decision to focus on the high-yield bond market was half of Drexel's 1989 strategy, the decision to eliminate the retail system was the other. The first decision was easy—nobody lost, until almost everybody lost; the second decision was extremely difficult and still controversial over a year later.

Perhaps the firm couldn't have afforded to subsidize the retail operation, or perhaps it couldn't have afforded *not* to. The retail sales department might have continued to shrink, eventually bleeding the firm dry. But it would have provided the firm with an army of retail customers—a million investors and their families, easily panicked, God bless them—to man the front lines if Drexel needed government help.

"The only way to make money in a highly cyclical business is to be highly diversified," argued one board member in defense of retail. "If you do away with it all that remained would be a high-yield shell that the government didn't like much."

The securities business—so dependent on the confidence of its lenders and its clients—is a risky business under the best of circumstances. For a firm that has pleaded guilty to six felonies and agreed to pay $650 million, the risk of collapse are that much greater.

Drexel would have been better served to keep its retail department and its customer accounts—its insurance policy, its widows and orphans. Should the firm find itself facing the abyss, these customers would have projected just the image—the ghosts of financial crises past and future—that might have forced the government's hand. Loans might have been reluctantly offered from the Fed or from its member banks, or a merger partner might have been arranged at the last minute.

On a less cynical level, a decision to retain retail would have saved the jobs of thousands of employees, which is a pretty good reason all by itself.

7. The Dance of Debt. One bitter irony of Drexel's fall is that the firm that came to represent the leveraging of American business put itself out of business when it couldn't pay its own debts. In effect, the experts on leverage building did a poor job on their own house.

On Wall Street, firms employ *double leverage,* with both their holding companies and their subsidiaries borrowing money. Drexel was reportedly the most aggressive, using more double leverage than its seven major competitors. Viewed from another perspective, again according to Standard & Poor's, Drexel had the most short-term debt relative to its equity as of September 30, 1989.

Without a secure fallback position, this is a formula for disaster. And Drexel had no strong back-up plan. It didn't have an American Express or a Credit Suisse to write a check if worst came to worst. It didn't even have written commitments from its banks to provide it a line of credit in a pinch. (Even written commitments would have been suspect; however, Integrated Resources had such commitments, but it still didn't get its money when needed.)

Drexel was in a cash business and found itself running out of that cash, with fewer sources as time went on. One possible source was the payment of bonuses in December 1989 and in the following month. Of the $260 million paid, $196 million was paid in cash, the rest in preferred stock. If the firm had decided to pay all bonuses above $100,000 in stock, it probably would have saved over $100 million in cash.

Another source was the excess net regulatory capital, which the firm did tap into until the SEC closed down the pipeline in early February 1990. The SEC, however, cannot require a firm to put up excess capital, it can only require a firm to leave that money there. Accordingly, Drexel should have tried to remove the excess before its crisis occurred. By August 1989, when the S&L Bill passed and the Ohio Mattress deal failed, the firm should have realized that serious problems were possible.

By December, with the downgrading of its commercial paper,

those problems were inevitable; by mid-February, its problems were terminal. Drexel Burnham made the one mistake it could not afford to make: It gave up control of its own destiny.

The demise of Drexel raised serious questions about the junk-bond market. Was this market more speculative than investors ever realized? Was it in fact a pseudomarket levitated by Milken the Magician, a confidence game based on smoke and mirrors?

"Drexel junk was never anything but a boiler-room scam," Benjamin Stein wrote in *Barron's* April 1990. "The junk-bond effort was probably the single biggest private financial scandal of the century." Buyout specialist Theodore Forstmann offered a less overheated, but still negative, point of view to *The New York Times* in June 1990: "Now that there is no more of that phony money around, we're getting back to the real money people." Money manager David Schultz, in putting together a fund to invest in companies devastated by too much debt, told *The Wall Street Journal,* "It's the flip side of the Milken Revolution."

Not surprisingly, there were other interpretations of the revolution. "All that stuff about financing America—it really was true," said one Drexel officer, who argued that his firm did not "simply follow the gaggle of investment banking firms trying to chase the *Fortune* 100. . . . The things we were doing made a difference—they certainly made a difference to the clients." "All firms said they were interested in small- to medium-sized companies," said a manager on my trading floor, "but very few of them did much about it." In the words of another officer: "I'm hard pressed to find negative results on the economy from funding high-yield companies." These companies ranged from American Motors to Cablevision to Fox Television to Hasbro to MCI Communications to Pier One to Zayre.

What were the facts? First and most important, junk bonds are not inherently evil—they're just bonds that pay a higher yield and involve greater risk. Second, junk bonds are not a new creation. These bonds "existed most of the century, just in different forms at different times," said a high-yield specialist at First Boston.

As for the statistics, 95 percent of U.S. companies with sales *above* $35 million a year would be junk-bond companies if they tried to raise money. Of these twenty thousand companies, some eight hundred have sold bonds, raising $200 billion in the public market and an additional $100 to 150 billion in private placements. Less than 5 percent of this money was used to finance hostile takeovers.

How risky are junk bonds? The answer to this one would resolve a great deal of the controversy; unfortunately, the answer is we don't know. Historically, these bonds have been good investments. Over the decades, the return from junk bonds, including the impact of all defaults, was better than the return from U.S. Treasury bonds.

The junk bonds that floated around during most of the twentieth century, however, were very different from the junk bonds sold in the last decade or so. The first group were primarily those of companies that were once considered high quality, and that later fell on hard times. The more recent group were the bonds of companies that were too young or small to receive an investment-grade rating at *any* time. One group wasn't necessarily a better investment than the other—they were just apples and oranges, not comparable.

Nevertheless, you might say, the new group of junk bonds—the original-issue high-yield bonds—have now been around for more than a decade. Shouldn't we be able to judge their risk from their performance?

Not quite, and here's why: The junk-bond market has grown so rapidly that the popular measure of risk, the default rate, is irrelevant. The default rate is the number of bonds that miss an interest payment in a given year relative to the total number of bonds outstanding. For example, if $3 billion worth of junk bonds default and there are $100 billion worth in the market, the default rate is 3 percent.

The problem is that newly issued bonds tend not to default for at least a few years for the simple reason that their companies have plenty of cash on hand for a while; after all, these companies raised a ton of cash when the bonds were sold to the public. In a growing market, where the supply of newer bonds dwarfs the supply of older ones, results get confused. Which means that the default rates for junk bonds were fairly meaningless, because the high-yield bond market was unquestionably a growing market. (According to First Boston, junk bonds grew from $8 billion to $200 billion in a decade.)

Another approach to gauge the risk of junk bonds is to look at *cumulative* default rates—the percentage of bonds that miss an interest payment at some point in their lives. The Asquith study, mentioned in the previous chapter, concluded that 34 percent of all junk bonds issued in 1977 and 1978 defaulted by the end of 1988—more than one out of three. Compare this figure with the current wisdom at the time that the *annual* default rate was only about 3 percent. What's interesting is that these two figures are the same—an annual default rate of about 3 percent will result in a cumulative default rate over eleven or twelve years of 34 percent.

Still, neither of these figures tells us what we need to know: How risky are the junk bonds issued more recently, the $100 billion worth sold in the last three years alone? It's difficult to be optimistic. Success leads to excess, and the safety that was built into the earlier junk bonds, the margin of error that made them salable to skeptical investors, faded with that skepticism. "We created such a demand for our product that, over time, the quality dropped," said one East Coast investment banker. According to a West Coast officer, "The market was killed due to truth."

Perhaps the greater truth was that the high-yield bond market served—and continues to serve—a valid purpose. Junk bonds give thousands of companies an alternative that they didn't have fifteen years ago. And while they are currently viewed as the financial equivalent of asbestos, it's good to remember that you can't judge a market simply by its players or by the short-run impact of fear and greed, ignorance and hubris.

The impact of 1989's junk-bond debacle was felt in varying degrees by Drexel's competitors. In March 1990, First Boston sold the majority of its $450 million Ohio Mattress loan to its Swiss-based parent company, leaving it with $700 million in bridge loans, almost 40 percent of those to the bankrupt Campeau Corporation. The following month, Kidder Peabody announced that it would sell all its high-yield, illiquid inventory to its parent, General Electric, taking a $25 million loss.

Also in April, Shearson Lehman Hutton decided to sell its $480 million junk-bond portfolio, only accumulated in the previous fifteen months, at an expected loss of $115 million. Merrill Lynch, reportedly with $540 million in bridge loans and $350 million in junk bonds, replaced its top high-yield specialists, Ray Minella and Jeffrey Berenson, in June 1990.

The mess in the high-yield market was the most visible disaster on Wall Street in recent years, but it certainly wasn't the only one. In response to bad markets and bad decisions, retrenchment has now become the major strategy on the Street, replacing the expansionist visions of the early 1980s, which were heralded by the acquisitions of Bache by Prudential Insurance, Shearson by American Express, and Dean Witter by Sears.

Although the brokers needed—and in time, many could not survive without—the deep pockets of their new owners, there was little in common between these firms and their parents. This cultural clash was highlighted by a dignified advertisement that appeared in a parody of *The Wall Street Journal*: "The Investment Banking Firm of Dean Witter Reynolds is Proud to Announce a Sale on Socks at Sears."

The price tag for this ill-advised expansion was highest at American Express, which had followed its acquisition of Shearson in 1981 with those of Lehman Brothers in 1984 and E. F. Hutton in 1988. In the first quarter of 1990, these firms reported a staggering loss of $917 million, leading to the infusion of $1.35 billion by American Express into its brokerage subsidiary.

The chairman of the parent company, James Robinson, announced that "Howard Clark [the head of the subsidiary] and his team have our full support as they move to reduce Shearson's risk profile and get back to basics by focusing on the things they do best." What made this statement striking was that the shareholders of American Express would have been better served if Robinson had taken his own advice when he took the helm in 1978. By my estimates, the market value of American Express would have risen to almost $20 billion if it hadn't diversified into the brokerage business; with that diversification, the market value rose to $10.4 billion. The difference: roughly $9 billion.

The shareholders who suffered because of the bad times in the financial markets, however, deserve a great deal less sympathy than the investors who suffered during the "good" times that preceded them. From the penny-stock bucket shops that cheated people out of an estimated $2 billion a year to the august Wall Street firms that sold unattractive deals through an army of often unqualified, unprincipled retail brokers, the average investor was abused by those who were supposed to protect his financial security.

Yet, no firm on Wall Street was ever meaningfully held to account for giving ill-conceived, self-serving advice to an unsophisticated family man investing for his kid's education or to an elderly woman concerned about the quality of her retirement. And that is a crime as great as anything that any firm was convicted of in the 1980s.

The SEC, Congress, and Wall Street should require every retail broker, from the boiler room to the private office, to provide a complete account of his or her advice to every prospective customer. It's possible in this age of computerized trading—all purchases and sales are recorded. The aggregate results for the clients of every broker can be tabulated and provided. To pay for the costs involved, the brokerage firms could charge the customers one cent more on each share they buy or sell, which would raise over $100 million a year. This approach would give both the brokers and their customers the same goals—that's what this business is all about, isn't it?

If the judgment and tactics of Wall Street deserve to be questioned on some points, so also do those of its prosecutors. And I think it's fair to say that certain aspects of the Drexel investigation reflected bad judgment and perhaps even bad faith.

The use of the RICO statute against a financial firm is a weapon that threatens the basic principle of our jurisprudence that one is innocent until proven guilty. And this principle is surely more important than victory in any given case. Giuliani may not have realized the potential impact of RICO—his prosecutors evidently didn't believe that a racketeering indictment would wipe out the firm—but he didn't need it. He could have indicted Drexel under the Securities Act of 1934, the source of all prosecutions of securities fraud.

That's not to say that using RICO against the firm would have been the incorrect use of the law—it would have been the use of an incorrect law. The passage of RICO reflected the frustration of a country in which the criminals were thought to hold the legal cards; with the approval of one section of one act, the balance of power was shifted.

The problem was that RICO was vaguely written, shifting the responsibility and discretion from elected officials to appointed prosecutors. The breadth and reach of our racketeering statute at the time of the Drexel case was unnervingly similar to that of the Soviet "antislander" law, reminding us as Charlton Heston did in the film *Touch of Evil* that "It's only easy to be a policeman in a police state."

"The sorry history of this law and its abuse by ambitious prosecutors is a testament to the indivisibility of rights," wrote Ira Glasser of the ACLU in early 1988. "RICO was passed because a lot of good people were willing to blink at unconstitutional provisions if the intended target was 'organized crime.' "

"Drexel may have broken rules calling for indictments under normal statutes," wrote *New York Times* columnist William Safire almost a year later, "but its junk-bond dealings did not include the kneecapping, kidnapping, murder and pimping that Senator John McClellan had in mind when he put forward what the called "a major new tool in extirpating the baneful influence of organized crime in our economic life."

Still, according to G. Robert Blakey, who as a young lawyer on McClellan's committee wrote the RICO bill, this statute was designed for more than mobsters. "Organized crime was the occasion," he said, "but it didn't define its scope." The Supreme Court agreed, he noted, referring to the June 1989 Northwestern Bell decision.

By a slim five to four majority the Court held: "Neither RICO's language nor its legislative history supports a rule that a defendant's racketeering activities form a pattern only if they are characteristic of organized crime." The minority opinion, however, raised a crucial point: RICO may be unconstitutional. "No constitutional challenge to this law has been raised in the present case, and so that issue is not before us," wrote Justice Antonin Scalia. "That the highest Court in the land has been unable to derive from this statute anything more than today's meager guidance bodes ill for the day when that challenge is presented."

Which is to say that RICO may not be with us for much longer. More important to the Drexel case is whether or not RICO should have been part of the case. Giuliani had the authority under law to use it, but did he have the responsibility according to fairness *not* to use it?

"The high-yield bond department was a criminal organization," said Bruce Baird. But the alleged crimes, even if true, constituted an insignificant part of Drexel's business, or of its revenues and profits.

At the time of the negotiations with the government, Milken's department was accused of some twenty illegal transactions over the course of three years. The firm as a whole, however, had completed about ten *million* transactions during that same time period.

If every transaction alleged to be illegal was illegal, Drexel earned roughly $73 million in illicit revenues based on the SEC complaint; if one more than doubles that figure to allow for a superseding indictment, one reaches $150 million. During the three years in question, Drexel's total revenues were sixty times as much, exceeding $10 *billion*.

As for profits, $150 million on the top line would have produced about $45 million after bonuses, expenses, and taxes. In the 1984–1986 period, the firm as a whole earned nearly $1 billion.

There is another consideration in the threatened use of RICO against Drexel: If Rudolph Giuliani's decision was intended to coerce the firm into a settlement, this was a violation not just of fairness, but of Justice Department policy. According to L. Gordon Crovitz of *The Wall Street Journal,* there is a 398-page set of guidelines for the use of the racketeering statute; among these guidelines: "Inclusion of a RICO count in an indictment solely or even primarily to create a bargaining tool for later plea negotiations on lesser counts would not be appropriate and would violate the *Principles of Federal Prosecution.*"

Perhaps the most compelling argument against the use of RICO can be made by simply looking at the rewards and the risks from Giuliani's point of view. RICOing the firm doesn't give him much more firepower if he wins the case in court. The onerous twenty-year jail term obviously doesn't apply to a company, and the triple damages provision is for civil cases, not criminal ones.

Of course, a victory in a criminal RICO case would make it easier for aggrieved investors to win a large sum in their civil RICO cases, noted attorney Neil Getnick, who specializes in this area of the law. Still, a victory in a criminal *non*-RICO case would certainly help the plaintiffs in the inevitable civil RICO cases that would follow.

The key point is that, if Giuliani really believed in the concept of innocent until proven guilty, in the absolute right to a trial, why not indict Drexel under the Securities Act of 1934? Even under the worst of assumptions, the firm was not a boiler-room operation based on fraud, or a business infiltrated by organized crime. Drexel may have survived under a RICO indictment, however unlikely, or it may have collapsed with a normal indictment—"Even in the absence of criminal RICO, the Milken matters were life-threatening matters," said Gary Lynch of the SEC—but at least without RICO the firm would have had the chance it felt was necessary for a trial.

Of course, the folks at Princeton/Newport would have liked the same chance, and they certainly didn't get it. In fact, the Princeton/Newport case raised some disturbing questions about prosecutorial tactics. That firm, the first financial one ever RICO'd, was shut down before a trial. The reason, as you might remember, was the superseding indictment that wasn't filed until after the firm had closed its doors.

According to Jack Arseneault, a defense attorney for Paul Berkman of Princeton/Newport, "The superseding indictment did very little to change the earlier indictment," adding that the tactics with the superseder were "vindictive, spiteful, unnecessary." Paul Grand, the attorney for Charles Zarzecki, argued that the new charges had been presented to the grand jury at the time that the old charges had been raised. In his opinion, the prosecutors withheld charges from the original indictment so that they would have the (ultimately fatal) threat of the superseder. In response to a clarifying question on whether there were any new charges that had not been presented to the original grand jury, he replied sharply, "Take it from me, nothing!"

There was also the alleged "roll right over you" threat, mentioned in the previous chapter, and the use of RICO for what was primarily a tax case. Think of that for a moment: If you had cheated on your taxes twice in a ten-year period, you could have faced a RICO indictment and perhaps twenty years in jail—that's no joke.

The threat of RICO in cases that, until the 1980s, had been handled as civil matters gave Giuliani and his prosecutors an incredible weapon to encourage cooperation. Which raises an odd question: Do prosecutors have a responsibility to tell people when they're going to change their methods? Legally no. But what about fairness? How would you feel if speeding on the highway was suddenly prosecuted as reckless endangerment? It's not as absurd or farfetched as it sounds.

On Wall Street, RICO can make all the difference. A person facing the possibility of an indictment, the possibility of a trial before a jury that probably views the Street as a pit of greed, and the possibility of a sentence exceeding twenty years in jail—a person facing these possibilities is a person who is a great deal more likely to plea bargain and cooperate. In the Drexel Burnham case, this category included Dennis Levine, Ivan Boesky, Michael Davidoff, Setrag Mooradian, Gary Maultasch, Jim Dahl, and Michael Milken.

The list of those in the Drexel case who fought RICO in court is not only shorter, it's nonexistent. In a related case, Princeton/Newport, all six defendants including Drexel's Bruce Newberg, went to trial in mid-1989. At that trial, Assistant U.S. Attorney Mark Hansen told the jury, "You don't need a fancy tax law expert because common sense tells you it's fraudulent, it's phony. . . . Doesn't it feel wrong? Doesn't it sound sleazy? If it sounds sleazy it's because it is sleazy. Your common sense tells you that." The jury agreed, finding them guilty on sixty-three out of sixty-four counts.

Their potential sentences exceeded one hundred years each. The judge, obviously unimpressed by the use of RICO in a tax case, sentenced them to terms ranging from three to six *months*. (The defendants are appealing their cases, which may eventually provide the Supreme Court with the opportunity to rule on RICO's constitutionality.)*

It may seem bizarre to say, particularly in view of the guilty verdicts, that the Princeton/Newport defendants showed an unusual sense of honor, in refusing to plea-bargain with the prosecutors. They could have almost certainly received a light sentence, perhaps even complete immunity, in return for testimony against Drexel Burnham and others. Instead, at the risk of spending the rest of their lives in prison, they argued that they were innocent and they demanded a fair trial, rather than use their colleagues and friends as bargaining chips.

In a sad case related to the Princeton/Newport prosecution, a young Drexel employee named Lisa Ann Jones was convicted of perjury. A runaway at fourteen, she had eventually joined Drexel's West Coast office at an initial salary of some $18,000 a year; by the time of the investigation, she was earning $100,000 as an assistant to Bruce Newberg. She was offered immunity in exchange for cooperation, but she refused.

Before the grand jury, Lisa lied on three occasions, motivated by a misguided sense of loyalty to her boss. Among the incriminating evidence was a tape recording from the Princeton/Newport raid that indicates a parking arrangement:

LISA: We bought 295,800—is that an unusual figure?

P/N: We bought them. Bruce wanted us to own them for him for awhile.

The cross-examination of Lisa Jones by Assistant U.S. Attorney Mark Hansen, who also prosecuted the Princeton/Newport case, was said to be brutal. Listening to Hansen's side of the story on television,

---

*On June 29, 1991, the Second Circuit Court of Appeals negated the racketeering and tax convictions that represented the overwhelming majority of the charges; the court reportedly concluded that the defendants were unfairly restricted in showing that the tax transactions were done "in good faith."

one person watching with me blurted out, "I'd like to stick a harpoon in his head."

As for Lisa Jones, she was sentenced to eighteen months, later reduced to ten months, and is currently in prison.

The primary reason the prosecutors wanted cooperation from Lisa Jones and from those involved in the Princeton/Newport case was the Drexel case—but there was another investigation that needed help. Robert Freeman, an arbitrageur at Goldman Sachs, had been arrested in February 1987, along with Richard Wigton of Kidder Peabody and Timothy Tabor of Merrill Lynch.

Within three months, the charges were dropped, although a new indictment was promised "in record time." The new charges never materialized.

The Princeton/Newport case gave prosecutors another opportunity to implicate Freeman, because Jay Regan, a partner at Princeton/Newport, was a friend from college days, and their two firms traded together. Regan, however, argued that his dealings with Goldman Sachs (and with Drexel Burnham) had been legal.

In time, according to allegations reported by *The Wall Street Journal*, the prosecutors did find some evidence of possible illegalities involving Robert Freeman among the Princeton/Newport files, also securing corroboration of some of the original charges against Freeman from one of his employees in Goldman Sachs's arbitrage department. On August 17, 1989, Freeman announced that he would plead guilty to one count of mail fraud; on April 17, 1990, he was sentenced to four months in jail and fined $1 million.

As for Richard Wigton and Timothy Tabor, the investigation against them was dropped in August 1989, two and a half years after Wigton had been handcuffed on his trading floor and Tabor had been forced to spend a night in a holding cell.

In commenting on the tactics against Wall Street defendants, Bruce Baird told *The New York Times*, "Every poor kid who goes through the Manhattan criminal courts in an average day gets a fraction of the due process given to the average white-collar defendant with the best of defense counsel." And he's probably right.

A poor kid from the street has an advantage over a defendant from Wall Street in at least one regard—his vulnerability to leaks of confidential information to the media. Drexel Burnham and other defendants, so dependent on public respect, were particularly vulnerable to trial by media. "Constant, unbelievable leaks," was the comment of Gerald Lefcourt, Bruce Newberg's attorney; "I've never worked on a case where I've seen so many leaks," said another attorney.

It appears the sources of these disclosures included unknown officials within the government. If true, these officials, who are responsible for upholding our standards and our laws, used unethical *and* illegal tactics.

"This constant stream of innuendo, for almost two years before the filing of a civil complaint, created public antagonism against Drexel and cost Drexel valuable reputation and business," wrote Dean Henry Manne and Professor Larry Ribstein, both of George Mason Law School. "All of this made the SEC's case seem stronger than it was, and may have undermined Drexel's right to a fair trial."

The staff of the SEC's enforcement division, for its part, denied in a May 1988 memorandum that it had disclosed confidential information; this memo, which was leaked to *The Washington Post* in August 1989, stated, "The staff has not been the source of any information which has appeared in the press and has strong suspicions that Drexel itself or persons representing their interests have been providing information to the press for the purpose of being able to make accusations against and discredit the [SEC] staff as well as to isolate and discredit cooperating witnesses."

This discussion of leaks raises another issue: accountability. Consider the situation at the SEC, one of several government offices which handled confidential and damaging information. Even if some of the alleged leaks did originate there, it's important to recognize that the head of the SEC's enforcement division, Gary Lynch, was never accused, publicly or privately, of leaking information or of condoning those leaks. ("Gary's a straight guy," was Fred Joseph's comment.) But Lynch had 21 attorneys working on the Drexel Burnham case, any one of whom could have walked to a pay phone and called *The Washington Post* or *The Wall Street Journal*.

Could the SEC have prevented anonymous leaks? Should it have been held liable for the actions of those employees who were allegedly breaking the law? Criminally liable? Should it have been prosecuted by the Justice Department?

Of course not, and it never was. But Drexel Burnham *was* prosecuted because a dozen of its ten thousand employees were accused of breaking the law. It was faced with a RICO indictment that it genuinely believed would destroy the firm, and it agreed to a harsh settlement to avoid that possibility.

Which raises two crucial questions. First, did the board of directors or anyone in senior management know about these allegedly illegal transactions? The answer, I believe, is no.

Second, could they have known? In most cases, no. How do you prevent someone from making secret deals with a client? How do you discover a scheme by a small group operating within a huge firm and involving the exchange of unwritten favors?

Review the allegations in the Milken indictment. Of the eighteen, I doubt that any internal compliance system could have caught thirteen of those: MGM/UA, Fischbach, Harris Graphics, Phillips Petroleum, Diamond Shamrock, Storer Broadcasting, Maxxam, MCA, Mattel, C.O.M.B., U.S. Home, the tax loss trades in 1985 and 1986, and the $5.3 million payment.

The allegedly bogus trades between Boesky and Drexel in the first half of 1985 and on March 21, 1986 could have been flagged by an ideal system, one that could detect discrepancies in prices on trades with different customers on the same day, and on trades with the same customer on different days. The Stone Container and Wickes transactions could have been identified only by a system programmed to notice unusual volume in the shares of a corporate client—a long shot at that time.

As for the final two allegations, the Lorimar merger and the Viacom buyout, at least one of these was said to be questioned by Drexel's compliance people, who evidently were satisfied with the answers they got, rightly or wrongly.

In effect, there was little opportunity for Drexel, or for the government, to suspect most of these transactions until Ivan Boesky became a cooperating witness. The prosecutors indirectly acknowledged the difficulty of identifying the secret schemes of a few employees: They never even raised the threat of indicting or sanctioning Drexel's senior management. Yet, the firm itself was forced to plead guilty to six felonies and pay $650 million.

As this unfortunate story becomes just a bad memory for most, it's natural to wonder what's happened to the key players. Among the prosecutors in the U.S. attorney's office, John Carroll and Jess Fardella, the two assistant U.S. attorneys on the Drexel case since its inception, have remained. Mark Hansen, who tried the Princeton/ Newport and Lisa Jones cases was hired by the law firm of Weil, Gotshal & Manges.

Charles Carberry, the head of the securities fraud unit at the time of Boesky's arrest, joined the private sector on October 1, 1987. Bruce Baird, who succeeded Carberry and who provoked extraordinary criticism from various combatants, was hired by the Washington-based law firm of Covington & Burling in the summer of 1989.

Rudolph Giuliani resigned as U.S. attorney for the Southern District on January 31, 1989, and became a partner at White & Case and later at Anderson Kill, both New York law firms. To no one's surprise, he ran for mayor of New York, easily winning the Republican primary against Ronald Lauder. In the general election, Giuliani lost to David Dinkins, but his showing was better than expected, boding well for his political future.

Currently, the smart money is betting that Giuliani will run for the U.S. Senate in 1992 against Alphonse D'Amato, the Republican incumbent who has boosted the concept of "politics as usual." But if, as some claim, he is an easy target for Giuliani, he won't be an easy opponent—D'Amato has a reputation as a tough fighter and there is little love lost between the two.

John Shad, the head of the SEC, became the head of Drexel Burnham in April 1989, a post that he resigned in August 1990. Gary Lynch, the head of the enforcement division, joined the New York law firm of Davis, Polk & Wardwell.

On Wall Street, Dennis Levine received a two-year sentence and currently heads a New York–based advisory firm called Adasar. As for the two men he implicated, his friend Robert Wilkis was sentenced to a year and a day in jail, while Ivan Boesky served approximately two years of his three-year term.

Among the major figures that Boesky fingered, Marty Siegel bought a multi–million–dollar house in Florida after pleading guilty to two insider trading charges and was eventually sentenced to two months in prison. Siegel, as part of his cooperation with prosecutors, implicated Robert Freeman, Richard Wigton, and Timothy Tabor of trading on inside information provided by him.

Freeman left Goldman Sachs in August 1989, at the time of his decision to plead guilty; his firm has not been penalized by either the U.S.

attorney's office or the SEC. Wigton has remained on Kidder Peabody's payroll since May 1987 when the prosecutors dropped the original charges against him, while Tabor left Merrill Lynch following his arrest.

Boyd Jeffries, also fingered by Boesky, pleaded guilty to two felonies and was sentenced to five years probation—he is teaching golf to kids in Aspen, Colorado (seriously). Jeffries, in turn, implicated Salim Lewis and James Sherwin. Lewis, an arbitrageur pleaded guilty to three felonies for manipulating the stock price of American Express in May 1986, and was sentenced to three years of community service. Sherwin, vice-chairman of GAF Corporation, was convicted of stock manipulation after two mistrials. Sherwin's boss, Sam Heyman, was identified as an unindicted co-conspirator, which is theoretically self-explanatory.

Ivan Boesky also implicated John Mulheren, the head of Jaime Securities and the godfather of one of his children. Mulheren, the only person accused by the former arbitrageur who chose to face trial, was convicted on one count of conspiracy and three counts of parking; the jury deadlocked on the remaining twenty-six charges. On November 14, 1990, he was sentenced to one year in prison.*

As for Michael Milken, after three and a half years of arguing his innocence, Milken pleaded guilty to six felonies and paid $600 million, a settlement very similar to that of his firm. One week after the Mulheren sentence, Milken received his: the harshest given any Wall Street defendant.

What if Milken had instead fought his case in court, and won? He could "probably create the most powerful bank in the world," one investment banker speculated a few weeks before the plea bargain. "He could raise $10 billion in equity in a week." I don't doubt it. And with $10 billion in equity, "The Bank of Milken" would control $200 billion in assets. Just imagine.

But when the imagining is done, there is the reality that Michael Milken's chances in court would have been slim. To begin with, this is the wrong time to be a Wall Street defendant, especially if you're the defendant who, in many people's eyes, represents everything that went wrong with Wall Street. Especially if you're the defendant who made $550 million in one year.

The average panel of jurors, each of whom earns less in a year than Milken earned in an hour, would find it hard to comprehend that anyone could earn that much legally. And whether they're right or wrong, they're still the jury.

*This sentence was later overturned; per the *New York Times*, the Second Circuit Court of Appeals concluded that the jury had "engaged in false surmise and rank speculation."

Then there is the evidence. The prosecution would have played to the jury's suspicions of greed by highlighting the partnerships, particularly MacPherson Partners. It was a partnership with all the elements—a prosecutor's dream, and for good reason. (In fact, MacPherson was to become a key issue in Milken's presentencing hearing.)

Once the prosecutors had finished with MacPherson, and the other several hundred partnerships, they would have moved on to the charges in the first indictment, which were considered in an earlier chapter. The lead witness would have been Ivan Boesky who would have repeated the allegations he had made in 1986.

Michael Davidoff, Boesky's chief trader, would have been called to the stand to discuss the 1985 trades he conducted, allegedly on Milken's instructions.

Setrag Mooradian would have testified about the ledgers he kept that recorded the profits and losses on transactions said to be related to Drexel. He would have explained to the jury what the various categories and figures signified, what he meant by cryptic entries such as: "they owe us (4627000-)," implying a loss of \$4,627,000.

Charles Thurnher, Milken's administrative head, and Cary Maultasch, who handled equity trades for Milken, would have been asked to corroborate details of the various allegations.

For color, the prosecutor could have entered into evidence such documents as a December 18, 1984 memorandum from Lance Lessman to his boss, Ivan Boesky. It reads in part:

> I received a call from a guy named Alan B—— at the relevant firm. He refused to discuss face value numbers with me indicating that he felt that these things were better discussed by his king and my king.

The jury would also have been asked to consider charges that were not in the original indictment, including Milken's involvement with David Solomon. The key witnesses here would have been Solomon himself and Drexel's Terren Peizer, who reportedly alerted investigators in late 1988 to alleged schemes that supposedly would help Solomon avoid taxes and that allowed Milken's department to take advantage of some of Solomon's clients. Evidently, Peizer also provided the government with a notebook page that included figures on the suspect tax trades.

The prosecutors might also have accused Milken of an alleged tax evasion scheme with Columbia Savings & Loan, by far the largest junk-bond owner among the nation's three thousand thrifts. This allegation was made by Drexel's Jim Dahl, who received immunity.

Milken's defense attorneys, some of the best in the country, would naturally have attempted to discredit the witnesses, virtually all of whom had plea-bargained their testimony for favorable treatment by the prosecutors. As for the written evidence, they would try to dismiss it as irrelevant or inconclusive.

And they almost certainly would have lost, buried under the tremendous wealth of their client, the apparent logic underlying the allegations against him, the testimony of customers and key employees, the ledger sheets regarding transactions with Boesky and Solomon, and the weight of more than one hundred charges.

So Milken settled. But his agreement with the government, reached after forty-one months, raised several questions: At what point does the public have the right to learn the truth, to hear both sides of a story that had dominated the financial world? At what point do the prosecutors have a *responsibility* to take their case to court?

And where is the line that separates a settlement from an injustice? At least in one aspect of Michael Milken's case, that line was crossed: The seventeen-count indictment against his brother was dropped as part of the settlement.

The government should never allow a man's brother to be a bargaining chip, a hostage to a deceptive higher purpose. If the prosecutors truly believed the allegations against Lowell Milken, they should have pursued those allegations; if not, they should never have brought the charges in the first place. This is a simple standard of justice.

Here's another question that may seem absurd in view of Michael Milken's settlement: Was he guilty? There are those who no doubt believe that Milken never broke the law, that he was forced to plead guilty with a gun at his head, a shotgun with a RICO indictment in one barrel and a poisoned public opinion in the other.

Once his sentence—unknown at this writing—is served, his public relations people will probably intensify their image-building campaign. Mike Milken will be presented as the gifted entrepreneur who shook up the status quo, and was, in effect, railroaded into jail. The accusations against him will be dismissed as overblown or untrue, as petty allegations that in any event were irrelevant to his extraordinary success or as schemes that he was too intelligent to risk his career for.

Some of these arguments may well be valid, but as brilliant and as motivated as Milken is, as unnecessary as these alleged crimes were, the evidence seems convincing.

The bitter irony is that, of all the powerful enemies in the wings, perhaps the only one who could have destroyed Milken was Milken himself. If the prosecutors did indeed hold a gun to his head, the bullets were provided by him. When the SEC investigated him during the early 1980s, he didn't recognize the implications. He didn't raise his department above suspicion; instead, the record says, he took part in illegal schemes.

"Am I a good man or a bad man?" is a question asked by Anthony Hopkins in the film *The Elephant Man*—it is a question that people try to apply to Mike Milken even though they couldn't answer it about themselves. Milken is as complex as the average person, and then some. He is brilliant, naive, ruthless, compassionate, selfish, and generous. He is a man who appears to be motivated by extraordinary greed who spent almost nothing on himself and who contributed almost $200 million to charity in 1987 alone.

He was, in the words of a friend, "a great screamer, a great belittler," but he was also a boss who was concerned about his people as people. He worked eighteen hours a day, yet he cared deeply about his family. "He was one of those guys who focused on different parts of the financial services industry, and became the absolute best at them—trader, salesman, corporate finance, M&A," said a West Coast investment banker, who added, "He's probably the best lawyer in the country today." But when it came to his own case, he refused to accept the inevitable.

"Mike Milken was a decent man," said one of his traders, "but the world and history will view him as the plague." "He was always fair, always challenging, always asked about your family," said another member of the fourth floor. "He had it right."

But, of course, in some important respects he did not. His obsession with success colored his judgment, and his sense of invincibility colored it further. He took great risks, and when those risks threatened to ruin him, he invoked the loyalty of ten thousand employees. He learned from history how much one man can accomplish, but he ignored or was oblivious of the antagonism one man can provoke and the damage one man can cause his followers.

Milken began the process that ended with the firm's collapse, but it was senior management, particularly Fred Joseph, that must accept the responsibility for the decisions of the final years. Perhaps the top executives could not have known of illegalities in Milken's department. Certainly, they should have known enough about the dark side of Milken's tactics to be concerned in the wake of Boesky's arrest, and to be eager to settle with the government. But they also didn't want to lose the golden goose, and when it was lost, they didn't want to adjust to a new reality. Their mistakes were honest ones, but those employees who lost their jobs and their savings might not care about that distinction.

It's easy to question decisions after the fact, but one thing that few people would question was whether Fred Joseph cared about his firm. He may have had, in the words of one corporate finance officer, "a magical belief that he could charm, talk, work his way out of anything, a feeling of manifest destiny that he could prevail." Or perhaps in his dealings with the rainmakers, he was, as one salesman argued, "never able to say no—he couldn't see through a good line of bullshit."

But he also represented Drexel with tremendous grace under pressure and his priorities were clear. And although he was wrong about the firm's chances in January 1990, he wasn't deceitful: he took his entire bonus in preferred stock, and exercised options to buy common stock as did four other members on the board of directors. One month later, the value of that stock was decimated by Drexel's bankruptcy.

For all the criticism that Fred Joseph has received over the last year and a half, if Mike Milken had Fred's stricter view of the law, Drexel Burnham would currently be the premier firm on Wall Street. There would have been no investigation, no *reason* for an investigation. By the end of this year, the firm's profits might have reached $1 billion, and its influence would have been immeasurable. Rather than fighting the Establishment, the firm probably would have reconfigured it, and joined it.

Instead Drexel Burnham and Michael Milken are finished. And even now, it's hard to believe, and hard not to believe in him. We all realized that Milken was a once-in-a-lifetime phenomenon, an aggressive visionary who we felt would never be so self-destructive as to do what he evidently did.

As one Drexel executive noted, if every allegation against Michael Milken were true, he still *legally* earned $530 million of his $550 million bonus for 1986.

The firm I joined in June 1981 was very different from the firm I left in September 1989, but one thing hadn't changed: it was a good place to work. More than that, it was a *better* place to work, better than any other on Wall Street.

And when Drexel collapsed, the Street was quick to hire the majority of our investment bankers and traders and salesmen and analysts. But the world wasn't such a friendly place for those in the back office, the men and women who key-punched the trades or sent out the dividend checks or delivered the securities or made sure that each trade balanced at the end of the day. Such administrative jobs were already filled throughout the Street.

And worse, the investments that all the employees had in their firm, the shares of stock that they had earned in Drexel's profit-sharing plan or bought each year with their savings, were destroyed. "There were rapacious people who just raped the place," said one salesman, "but there were also secretaries and clerks and other folks whose nest eggs went up in smoke." And while The Great Acquisitor received more in his January 1990 bonus than the average family will earn in one hundred years, thousands of regular people took overnight losses that totaled in the hundreds of millions. Said one trader to his colleague, "I will never have the financial security that I had two years ago."

The final words belong to I. W. Burnham, who founded the firm on April 1, 1935. "The securities business has always been people and capital," he wrote in September 1988. "This firm has always had both, and today we have more wonderful people and more capital than ever before in the past. We will certainly be able to withstand the storm and come out with flying colors."

And so we should have.

EPILOGUE

MR. SMITH GOES TO JAIL

"And one day, . . . that lack of moderation
will be his downfall."

—*Tinker, Tailor, Soldier, Spy*

Legend tells of a not-so-great king with a magic mirror and an unhealthy competitive streak. Each Thanksgiving, he would ask his mirror to name the meanest one of all and, given his law and order policies, he would usually get the nod. Occasionally, the mirror would name another, and the king would burst in on his court spewing a list of orders designed to regain the title. This past year, however, as the court stood frozen in fear, the king simply walked by, muttering, "Who the hell is Kimba Wood?"

If the king didn't know, most everyone else on that Thanksgiving Day of 1990 did. Kimba Wood was the judge who had sentenced Michael Milken the day before, seven months after he had pleaded guilty to six felonies, four years after the first subpoenas had arrived at his desk.

Judge Wood's decision was the harshest in the history of Wall Street, sentencing Milken to more jail time than Boesky, Levine, Siegel, and the six Princeton/Newport defendants *combined*. The symbol of the 1980s was finished, as was the culture he represented—at least in the eyes of the media. It made good copy, with drama and intrigue, a grand sweep, a clear and clean ending.

The Age of Greed stepped aside for the New World Order; Michael Milken, having filled the lead role in a cautionary tale, quickly became irrelevant, even nostalgic, a bit like Nixon in the mid-1970s. After forty months of fighting government allegations of widespread fraud, Milken had decided to plead guilty to six charges, most of them insignificant but all of them felonies. There would be no trial, after all—just the sentencing. Or so it seemed.

As part of the agreement, the U.S. Attorney's Office was permitted the opportunity to state why it felt that Milken had committed numerous crimes beyond the six to which he had pleaded: "Specifically, this Office may bring to the Court's attention conduct that is not alleged in Information SS 89 Cr. 41 (KMW), or acknowledged by Michael R. Milken in his allocution." Milken, for his part, retained the right to explain why he hadn't committed any crimes other than those he had admitted.

Both sides filed their sentencing memos, as well as their replies to the other side's arguments. But over the course of more than four hundred pages, they seemed to agree on only one point: that the defendant was, in fact, Michael Milken. Other than that, the defense and the prosecution might have been talking about two different people in parallel universes: one good, one evil.

The defense focused on Milken's personal qualities, as highlighted in more than one hundred letters from friends, peers, and charities. Concerning his admitted crimes, the defense argued: "Michael, as he told the Court, knew that what he did was wrong, but he justified his actions by believing both that they did not affect his core business and that they did not injure any third party."

But to the prosecution, "Milken's criminal conduct was calculated and systematic, rather than gratuitous and aberrational, and Milken's criminal activity was a significant and necessary component of the growth of his power in the high-yield market."

Defense: "Michael Milken's acceptance of responsibility and contrition for what he has done are not matters of form; they are genuine and heart-felt."

Prosecution: "Milken's decision reflects surrender, not contrition."

Prosecution would quote from defense: "With regard to the Helmerich & Payne transaction, Milken pronounces that he 'erred in failing to recognize that fidelity to the securities laws must be placed above service to his client.' His piety rings false."

Defense: "Unlike so many others, Michael could never accept success that was not real or legitimately earned."

Prosecution: "Carefully examined, Milken's complaint that he recovered the Finsbury fee from [name withheld] because [] was doing too much business away from Drexel is a brazen admission of the arrogance and corruption at the heart of Milken's business ethos."

The differences of opinion between the defense and the prosecution extended far beyond Milken's role in the six crimes to which he pleaded. The two sides were also completely at odds on whether Milken had broken the law on eighteen other transactions, involving allegations of insider trading, bribery, manipulation, obstruction of justice, and assorted fraud. These charges were dropped as part of the guilty plea, but the prosecutors wanted Judge Wood to consider them in determining Milken's sentence.

The defense attorneys' point of view was simple: Michael Milken had committed no crimes other than those in his plea. Further, to prove this fact would require a lengthy hearing, little different from an actual trial, a trial which the defendant had sought to avoid by pleading guilty to the six lesser charges.

Their argument was supported by a decision earlier that year in a similar case, that of Robert Freeman, formerly the head arbitrageur at Goldman Sachs, who had pleaded guilty to one count of insider trading rather than face trial on twenty others. The judge on that case, Pierre Leval, had rejected the government's attempt to introduce its evidence on the unadmitted allegations. "The Court, of necessity, must sentence the defendant on the transaction to which he pleaded guilty," he stated in his ruling, "and cannot enlarge this sentencing proceeding to include trial of twenty alleged other crimes."

But in a session with both sets of lawyers, held only four days before Milken's scheduled sentencing date of October 1, Judge Wood dropped the first of several bombshells on the defense. Noting that unadmitted crimes can be considered when deciding a sentence, she pointed out an obvious but terrifying fact to the defense: due process would only be violated by a jail term that exceeded the maximum allowed.

In Milken's case, the six felonies that he had already admitted carried a maximum term of twenty-eight years, a potential sentence so absurd that it might as well have been twenty-eight hundred years. Even as a passing reference, the defense team didn't want the judge to mention the possible existence of a maximum sentence.

The defense's most practical argument against a hearing—that it could take up to a year to contest each of the allegations—went by the boards a few minutes later. Judge Wood ordered that she would limit such a hearing to forty hours, forcing each side to choose only those transactions that would best support their point of view.

She deflected aside various attempts to postpone the hearing (prosecution) or to reconsider her decision entirely (defense), establishing a tone that would carry through the shooting match to come: unassuming, well reasoned, and tough.

The purpose of the proceedings would not be to find guilt, but to get a "sense of character," in order to fit "the punishment not only to the crime, but to the offender." The proceedings were officially known as a Fatico hearing, named after the case of Daniel and Carmine Fatico: the two brothers had pleaded guilty to a single hijacking charge, but, as part of the sentencing decision, the government was permitted to introduce evidence that they were members of organized crime.

Since a Fatico hearing focuses on character more than crimes, the defendant does not have the same rights as in a trial. There is no jury, and the allegations need only be proven by the "preponderance of the evidence," not "beyond a reasonable doubt." This distinction might seem subtle to the layman, but in Milken's case, it would become crucial.

The prosecution chose to present three transactions, concerning Wickes Cos., Storer Broadcasting, and Caesars World; the allegations involved were manipulation, bribery, and insider trading, respectively. Testimony in these cases would also attempt to highlight obstruction of justice and naked greed.

The hearing began on October 10, 1990. Milken, in court for the first time since his April guilty plea, sat to Arthur Liman's left; on his other side was Martin Flumembaum, another attorney from Paul Weiss. The jury box was allocated to influential members of the press, a slight irony since if ever there was a case of trial by media, the entire Drexel fiasco was it.

Behind Milken sat his friend and family attorney, Richard Sandler. Among the guests were members of Milken's family. His three children, however, were spared the experience of facing curious onlookers in the courtroom and a twice-daily gauntlet of photographers outside on the courthouse steps.

Milken arrived each morning with his wife and disappeared each lunch hour to an adjacent room where the entire Paul Weiss legal team congregated. He watched the hearing, as columnist Murray Kempton noted, with the frustration of an active man forced to sit quietly, writing notes with a speed that suggested he'd rather be doing almost anything than sitting quietly.

The proceedings were a far cry from television courtroom dramas; there were few dramatic moments. Evidence was presented piecemeal—the purpose of direct examination, cross-examination, redirect, recross, etc. is not to tell a coherent story, but for each side to bring out only those points that support its case. Bear in mind that this was a securities fraud hearing, which is like watching paint dry for high stakes.

And the stakes were huge, given the controversy surrounding both the defendant's character and the prosecution's tactics. Here, after four years, was the best opportunity to measure Michael Milken as master criminal or scapegoat.

The first allegation was that Milken had arranged for the manipulation of Wickes stock. The circumstantial evidence of manipulation was compelling: the stock needed to close at more than $6/share for twenty out of thirty days before the company could get rid of its preferred stock, as it wanted to. By April 23, 1986, the stock had closed above $6/share for nineteen of twenty-eight days; that day, Boesky bought 1.9 million shares, more than half of all the shares traded. Further, most of his purchases were within twenty minutes of the stock market's close.

As a result, Wickes closed above $6/share. Within two days of his purchases, oddly enough, Boesky begins selling his shares, eventually losing $400,000.

In the view of Assistant U.S. Attorney John Carroll, the stock had been manipulated and "that Michael Milken was behind that manipulation."

Arthur Liman, Milken's lead attorney, quickly deflated one of the government's best weapons in this allegation: he agreed that there *was* manipulation, and that Drexel was involved—but not his client.

Carroll called his first witness: Michael Davidoff, formerly the head trader for Ivan Boesky, and an employee of Boesky's for thirteen years. Davidoff would set in motion the chain of events that would presumably link Milken to the manipulation of Wickes stock on April 23.

Davidoff, speaking unpretentiously and with an occasional stammer, recalled a phone call on the afternoon of the 23rd from Cary Maultasch, a Drexel stock trader who, though located in New York, worked for Milken's department. According to Davidoff, Maultasch asked him to buy Wickes *for Boesky's account*. Since Davidoff had been authorized by Boesky some time earlier to accept trading instructions from Maultasch, Davidoff executed the order. Other orders followed, designed to close the stock that day at a price of 6⅛. Davidoff also testified that he had informed Boesky of the trading.

The next day, Maultasch called again. "He indicated that he did not want to continue to buy Wickes," said Davidoff. "As a matter of fact, he would like to start to sell out the stock that he had bought."

On cross-examination, Martin Flumembaum clarified that Michael Milken had not spoken with Davidoff, nor had Milken's name even come up in Maultasch's conversations about Wickes.

Next on the stand was Cary Maultasch himself, who, like Davidoff, was a cooperating witness. His criminal charges had been dropped in return for that cooperation. Maultasch had worked for Milken from June 1983 to January 1989, and prior to that for Salomon Brothers. Concerning the April 23, 1986, conversation with Davidoff: "I told him that I needed a favor . . ." Specifically, to buy Wickes stock.

And who gave Maultasch the order?

Peter Gardiner.

Gardiner, a trader in Milken's department between June 1985 and February 1988, was the lead witness the following Monday morning. He spoke quickly, with a smooth manner although he was obviously and understandably nervous. Here, finally, was the guy who seemingly would link Milken with the manipulation that both sides agreed had occurred.

But Gardiner, who was able to clearly recall some conversations from that afternoon four and a half years ago, was unable to recall whether or not he had even spoken with Cary Maultasch before the close of trading.

Among the conversations Gardiner did recollect were several incriminating to Milken, though rarely to himself. He claimed that Milken had asked his people to find buyers for Wickes, which might have been illegal given Drexel's investment banking relationship with the company at that time. (An employee on the trading floor that afternoon would soon after take the stand to dispute this claim.)

Gardiner also testified that, after the close of trading, Milken asked him "to call Cary and find out how many Wickes we had bought," which he did (and did remember). This recollection implied that Milken both knew of the Wickes manipulation and of the stock-parking arrangement with Boesky.

The defense, not surprisingly, tried to destroy Gardiner's credibility. He had perjured himself before the grand jury two years earlier, for which he was not prosecuted as part of his cooperation agreement with prosecutors, a copy of which he had received only that morning. Liman began his cross-examination on this point:

"Mr. Gardiner, in your direct examination, you used a phrase that you were 'economic with the truth' when you appeared before the grand jury. Do you remember that?"

"Yes."

"In fact, you lied through your teeth when you testified before the grand jury, didn't you?"

"Yes, I did."

Gardiner attributed his perjury to "a state of denial that extended from my first days at Drexel," later testifying that it was "one of the greatest regrets of my life, yes."

Liman brought out that, although Gardiner claimed to be troubled by conscience, he had waited over a year to cooperate with the government:

"Didn't you tell David Mills [a friend] that your greatest nightmare was that Michael Milken would plead guilty and cooperate with the government?" (Thereby implicating Gardiner.)

"It's possible that I said that. I have no recollection of it. . . ."

When pressed on the question of whether he had called Maultasch to arrange the manipulation, he replied, looking at the judge, "Your Honor, I can't answer yes or no. I just don't know." And soon after: "Let's get something straight about my recollection with regard to Cary's participation. I don't recall calling Cary to place the orders through Boesky, period. I recall calling him at Mike's direction after the fact."

Following Gardiner's testimony, the prosecution rested its case. Judge Wood then asked John Carroll to summarize why the prosecution had reason to believe that Milken had participated in the manipulation of Wickes stock. Carroll, caught off guard, argued that the manipulation of Wickes was initiated by Drexel, that Milken was an active participant, and was "the only person there who was in a position to, in essence, authorize these transactions to make good on the Boesky organization's losses . . ."

The prosecution, in arguing that Milken was the missing link in the Wickes manipulation, was asking for a leap of faith, even if a logical one. Its answer to the question of who ordered the manipulation was, in effect, another question: Who else but Milken?

Liman, in response to Carroll's summary, went on the attack, concluding with an attempt to convince the judge to reconsider continuing the hearing: "This is polarizing, and I am emotional, and I am emotional because I feel it, but I would urge your Honor—because we are breaking new ground and your Honor is trying to reach one of the more difficult judgments that any judge has to make about an individual, not because it's Michael Milken but because it's a sentence—to think whether this kind of proceeding is filling the need that your Honor saw."

It would have been a dream come true for the defense if the judge had agreed, in view of the evidence yet to come. But it was a dream that vanished with a sentence: "Let me say," replied Judge Wood, "that so far the hearings have been very helpful to the Court."

The next transaction was the most damaging to Milken. Since the purpose of the hearing was to develop a clearer picture of Milken's character, greed and lousy ethics were fair game. And these were at the heart of the prosecution's allegations in the Storer Broadcasting transaction.

As summarized in the government's post-Fatico hearing memorandum: Storer Broadcasting was acquired by the buy-out firm of Kohlberg, Kravis, & Roberts (KKR) in 1985. Drexel agreed to raise $1.5 billion: $1.2 billion in high-yield debt, $260 million in preferred stock. In order to make the offering more attractive to potential investors, KKR included 68 million warrants entitling the holders to purchase 32 percent of Storer's equity. The cost of the warrants, originally set at $.14 each, was reduced by 50 percent at Milken's specific request (he initially asked that the price be reduced to zero).

Ninety-eight percent of these warrants ended up in partnerships set up by Michael and Lowell Milken, in a dizzying and disturbing series of transactions. The two Milken families became the owners of nearly 60 percent of the warrants, which in less than three years would be worth more than $150 million; other beneficiaries included important clients of the High-Yield Bond Department.

The process was convoluted, beginning prior to the November 1985 public offering of the Storer deal. "To the best of my recollection, Michael said that there would have to be some commitment in connection with the preferred stock," Fred Joseph, Drexel's former chief exec, testified. "It was a $250 million issue and was the firm prepared to make that commitment. For some reason, I thought I recollected a $150 million number. In any case, I told him the firm was not prepared to make a commitment of that size, and he said, 'Would it be okay if we did?' I took 'we' to mean the High-Yield Department, principals of Milken, maybe their families, maybe the partnerships. I said from the firm's point of view that was fine, that was good, and he then said that, you know, equity goes with the preferred or will go with the preferred, and I said I understood that."

Eventually, by the prosecution's account, five partnerships committed to purchase $154 million of the $261 million preferred issue. By the time payment was due, the partnerships had managed to sell all but $66 million of their commitment. In the next four days, the balance was sold; the partnerships, by this time the owners of no preferreds, did however keep 82 percent of the warrants.

As for the remaining 18 percent, one high-yield client had been allocated 16 percent at the time of the deal. This account, Atlantic Capital, whose portfolio manager had formerly worked for Milken, had received the warrants in conjunction with its purchase of $30.5 million in Storer preferred. (Atlantic was the only account among the buyers of preferred stock that was allocated warrants.)

Within a week of paying for the preferreds and the warrants, however, Atlantic resold both to Milken's department at the price it had just paid for them—in the case of the warrants, $.07 each. Although Drexel was stuck with a large chunk of Storer preferred, the firm never received the warrants. Unbeknownst to senior management, the warrants were placed a month later in another partnership, MacPherson Partners.

The price of these warrants was set at $.088 each, which Lowell Milken had considered a fair price, even though *that same day*, the High-Yield Department had repurchased the remaining 2 percent of the warrants from another client for $.80 each, a price almost ten times greater.

The existence of the MacPherson Partnership was to come as a nasty surprise to Drexel's Board of Directors, though it wouldn't find out until Storer was resold almost two years later. What made MacPherson so disturbing was the list of its partners. This list included several important high-yield clients, decision-makers at institutions, some of which had purchased the Storer preferreds but which had not received warrants. One of the individuals who benefited *personally* from MacPherson, which would turn a $50 million profit on a $950,000 investment, was Richard Grassgreen, who with Perry Mendel ran a public company, a child day-care chain called Kindercare, later renamed Enstar.

Grassgreen, in an eleventh hour deal with prosecutors, decided to plead guilty to two felonies and cooperate against Milken. His agreement was announced on October 22, and he was on the stand the following afternoon.

The core of his testimony involved a telephone conversation with Milken about the Storer preferreds. "Eventually, Michael picked up the phone, said hello, said to me at that time, the Storer deal is a great deal, you ought to do as much as you can. I said, I have.

"He then advised me, he said, there are warrants for you in the Storer deal. I asked him if he meant it was for Kindercare. He said, no it was for you and Perry. I said, could Kindercare get some? He said, it's for you and Perry."

The final transaction, Michael Milken's purchase of Caesars World bonds, was chosen to highlight the prosecution's allegation of insider trading. It was an odd choice since this transaction, which dates back to 1983, had been investigated by the Securities and Exchange Commission in the mid-1980s, long before Boesky's arrest and cooperation. The SEC had concluded that there were insufficient grounds to charge Milken; in addition, the Caesars allegation was not part of the U.S. Attorney's criminal indictment against him in 1989.

The case as presented by the prosecution were simple, if inconclusive. Milken was informed on June 27 of an upcoming meeting with Caesars management on June 29 to discuss various financing options. Among these options was a debt-for-equity swap, whereby the company would repurchase bonds, to the benefit of the debtholders.

The meeting, which Milken attended, took place at 4:00 P.M. West Coast time and lasted two hours. Either that day or the next, Milken purchased $3.2 million worth of Caesars World bonds for Drexel from a high-yield client.

The prosecution continued that on July 1, John Kissick, head of Drexel's corporate finance on the West Coast, was called by Peter Ackerman, who also worked for Milken. Ackerman told Kissick that Caesars was interested in the debt-for-equity idea.

Also on July 1, Milken bought $3.2 million of the Caesars bonds from Drexel for his personal account.

Two weeks later, Caesars' decision to do a debt-for-equity swap was publicly announced. Milken then resold his bonds to the firm within two weeks for a $550,000 profit.

What is known about this transaction is rivaled by what isn't. The prosecutors claimed that Milken purchased the bonds from his client, First Investors, after the June 29 meeting with Caesars. They noted that the tickets recording the trade by each side were written on June 30. The defense responded that at both Drexel and First Investors, the trade tickets, though written on the 30th, were marked "as of" June 29, indicating that the trade had occurred on the 29th with the paperwork completed the following day.

The prosecution pointed out that, although First Investors was trying to sell Caesars bonds for weeks, Milken was not a buyer until the time of the meeting. The defense responded that Milken only bought about half of the bonds that the client was selling; if he was trading on inside information, why wouldn't he buy the whole lot?

One possible answer, although the government doesn't offer it, is that he might not have wanted to be too conspicuous; perhaps he wanted to retain a certain "plausible deniability," to use a popular term among politicians. But most everything about this transaction is conjecture. It's not clear whether or not Milken was told of Caesars' July 1 decision to pursue a debt-for-equity offering, or when (or if) he received approval to buy the bonds for his own account, or why his purchase was executed on July 1.

Still, the circumstantial evidence raises serious doubts. Even if Milken had bought the bonds from First Investors on June 29, it might have been on the evening of the 29th—after the meeting with Caesars. And even if the trade was executed before the meeting, the bonds were certainly bought after Milken knew that there was going to be a meeting.

Two minor points: the portfolio manager who did the trade with Milken was out of town on a business trip. This suggests a sense of urgency to the trade, even though the bonds had been for sale for weeks. Second, the explanation that Milken's personal purchase of the bonds was delayed until the 1st because his boss was in the Far East is odd, since the guy was there from June 26 to July 7.

Nevertheless, the evidence was not conclusive, in this transaction or in the previous two. After eight days of testimony and sixteen witnesses, there was reasonable doubt on most of the legal issues, which is the goal of a defendant in a criminal trial.

But this defendant was facing a different standard, one of character more than law. Whether or not Michael Milken had won the legal battles, he had lost the war.

Perhaps the prosecutors had been unable to prove with certainty that Milken was behind the manipulation of Wickes stock, that the evidence was "crystal clear," as they claimed. Still, the testimony of Davidoff, Maultasch, and Gardiner had drawn the image of a department—Milken's department—that was willing to break the law without question.

Perhaps the prosecutors had also been unable to provide the evidence that "conclusively demonstrates that Milken bought securities of Caesars World ('CW') in June and July 1983 based on material, non-public information misappropriated from CW," as again they claimed. Yet, the timing of Milken's purchases—bonds that were destined for his own account—left him open to accusations of greed and deception.

These accusations were at the heart of the Storer/MacPherson transaction, as well. And here the government was able to paint a disturbing portrait. Milken may very well have beaten the charges if they were fought in a trial. Insider trading, which was alleged by the prosecutors, wasn't even raised in the testimony, let alone proved. And the evidence of bribery and deception was mostly circumstantial, leaving room for reasonable doubt.

But this wasn't a jury trial, and the Storer testimony left a sour taste of misplaced priorities and lousy ethics. Kohlberg Kravis, a valued client, was misled. It provided valuable warrants to make its offering more attractive to institutional buyers, and these warrants were skimmed by the partnerships.

The defense questioned the then-current value of these sweeteners, but its argument was specious and fundamentally irrelevant. According to the testimony of Ben Bayse, a fund manager who participated in MacPherson, Milken himself had argued in 1985 that the equity in Storer was worth twenty to thirty times its cost. More important, even if the warrants were worth a penny, that wouldn't justify deception.

The deception was not only on Kohlberg Kravis but on Drexel itself. The firm, which didn't want to buy Storer preferreds in the first place, ended up with a $27 million chunk after the partnerships quickly resold their shares to the firm within days. Drexel became the owner of more than 10 percent of the preferreds, without being offered any of the warrants.

As for the bribery allegation, common sense is more compelling than legal definitions. If you offer fund managers sweetheart deals for their personal accounts, you are going to influence their decisions, regardless of what they say. When they profit personally because of their fiduciary control over billions of dollars, something is wrong. The obligation might not be requested or reminded, but it's there.

The impressions left by the Wickes, Caesars World, and Storer transactions were made more credible and damaging by the testimony on other issues involving Michael Milken.

There was Jim Dahl, a former top salesman for Milken and now a cooperating witness for the government, alleging a stock-parking arrangement—in which he participated—with Columbia Savings & Loan. "From whom did you learn that," asked John Carroll. "Michael," replied Dahl.

There was Peter Gardiner, who though unclear on certain events was unequivocal on others. "I parked securities routinely with Milken's knowledge," he alleged.

There was Cary Maultasch, the primary contact with Boesky's firm, whose testimony that Milken referred to various holdings of Harris stock as "yours" and "ours" implied a parking arrangement with that stock.

There was Fred Joseph, former head of Drexel, who was appearing voluntarily and without immunity. He testified to speaking with Milken in the spring of 1988, more than two years after MacPherson was formed. "Then I had a conversation with Mike Milken where I asked him—I relayed that conversation to him probably quite briefly, and asked him if any fund managers were in any partnerships. He said, to the best of his recollection, no."

There was Prescott Crocker, a fund manager and a rarity at the hearing: an unassailable witness. He recalled a conversation that suggested a willingness by Milken to engage in sham trades to solve a problem with a trade involving Caesars World bonds. Reference to this conversation was also made in a memo that Crocker had written at the time of the trade: "3:15 P.M., 7/18/83 Mike Milkin [sic] came to the phone and stated flatly that there was no inside information involved, that my timing as a seller was unfortunate, that Drexel had acted as agent and that his buyer would not cancel the trade. Tough luck! However, he did offer to compensate CRYS for its 'losses' (to be negotiated) by shorting bonds to us and buying back at higher levels."

Beyond the allegations against Michael Milken's business code prior to Ivan Boesky's arrest were those concerning his actions in its wake. By this time the focus of a massive government investigation, Milken, in the eyes of prosecutors, had conspired to obstruct justice.

There are few nonviolent crimes that the courts take more seriously than this, and for good reason. Obstruction undercuts the system of justice more effectively than most crimes, is easily accomplished, and is awfully tempting—particularly in a securities fraud case where the alleged felonies are subtle and complex, and their proof heavily dependent on witnesses.

In support of the obstruction of justice charge, the prosecution relied on its four cooperating witnesses from Drexel. Gardiner testified that, following Ivan Boesky's arrest, a senior West Coast officer suggested a fall clearance: "Yes, he said, 'Clean out your desks. Get rid of anything that isn't nailed down,' I think he said, 'and don't throw it in the company garbage. . . .' He said by way of reassurance, 'Listen, I talked to Mike, you know. Let's get rid of the stuff.' "

Maultasch, who flew out to the West Coast office after Boesky's arrest on Friday, November 14, 1986, spoke of a comment from Milken: "To the best of my recollection, at some point on the Saturday following my subpoena, he said, I assume there are no records."

There was also a private meeting early one morning in which Milken allegedly wrote down questions on a small yellow pad, showed them to Maultasch, and then erased them. "To the best of my recollection," Maultasch testified, "he was asking me what I recalled about the securities that were mentioned in my subpoena."

Dahl offered the damning picture of Milken leaning over a running faucet in the men's room and saying, "There haven't been any subpoenas issued." (There had been, two days earlier.) "Whatever you have to do, do it."

According to Peizer, who was only in his midtwenties at the time,

Milken approached him on the Monday following Boesky's arrest, asking if he had the blue ledger book recording the Solomon dealings. Milken then suggested that Peizer give the book to Lorraine Spurge, a close associate of Milken's.

Peizer spoke of handing over the ledger book near the kitchenette, after turning on the faucet, presumably in fear of electronic surveillance. "It just seemed like everyone was talking and running faucets, or whatever," Peizer added.

Later in the course of the investigation, Peizer himself received subpoenas to produce documents. He alleged that, while clearing out his desk, Milken said, "If you don't have them, you can't provide them," and then opened his own desk drawers. How did Milken say this? asked Judge Wood. "He said it kind of, you know, glibly, if you will," Peizer replied. What was his expression? "Kind of, like, you know, a smile. I don't really recall."

"The aroma that pervaded that courtroom," said one attorney, "was an aroma of obstruction."

Arthur Liman and the defense team tried to diminish the impact of the testimony throughout by raising questions on the credibility of cooperating witnesses and by raising doubts on the allegations of all prosecution witnesses.

The cooperating witnesses offered the most damaging testimony, but they were also the most vulnerable. There is a potential conflict of interest in the testimony of someone who trades the freedom of others for his own. The value of his testimony, and his bargaining power, is dependent on the severity of the allegations. When that testimony is based on conversations that only the defendant and he were privy to, the danger is apparent: Who's lying?

"You people think if you tell a lie and don't get caught, it's the same as telling the truth," said Robert Redford in *Three Days of the Condor*, a comment much at home in the courtroom of a criminal case.

In Milken's case, the cooperating witnesses did have some credibility problems. Gardiner had already perjured himself in his grand jury testimony two years earlier. Peizer had initially withheld an incriminating document from prosecutors, a document which Liman suggested Peizer had saved as a possible bargaining chip if things got too hot for him.

The defense raised almost every possible difference of fact or interpretation with every prosecution witness. Some differences were valid and well considered, others were creative and counterproductive.

In the Wickes transaction, for example, Arthur Liman pointed out that no evidence tied Milken directly to the manipulation, which was absolutely true. As for Storer/MacPherson, however, his arguments that the disclosure of the partnerships' holdings of the warrants was Drexel's responsibility, not Milken's, and that the law "does not prohibit brokers from providing investment opportunities to money managers on the same terms that the opportunities are provided to others" were both a bit of a stretch.

On one point the defense team was particularly adamant: Michael Milken was never an inside trader. But if insider trading was never conclusively proven by the prosecution, there was testimony that did raise questions about Milken on this score. Cary Maultasch alleged that on three deals—MGM, Pacific Lumber, and Harris Graphics—he had asked and occasionally had received Milken's opinion on behalf of Michael Davidoff, Boesky's trader.

In addition, Davidoff testified that he was told by Boesky that "we were going to be buying stock in MGM, we will be buying stock for Drexel Burnham" and that some of the orders were called in by Milken himself. Davidoff, however, could not remember whether or not Milken's calls were in 1985 or 1986, let alone whether they were at the time of the MGM deal.

The evidence also showed that although Milken met with MGM on July 15, 1985, and with the acquiror, Turner Broadcasting, on July 28, Boesky's first purchases under the alleged scheme didn't immediately follow either meeting. The question here was why, if Milken was interested in trading on inside information, would he wait until *after* the first public announcement of the deal?

Also favorable for the defense was Maultasch's statement that he didn't consider Milken's comments inside information. This statement reflected, at least in part, the conflicting loyalties of the cooperating witnesses. Although they had cut deals in return for incriminating testimony, they shared a bond with their former boss.

For one thing, they were all co-defendants with Milken in the avalanche of civil suits, as noted by *The Wall Street Journal*: everyone who felt that they had lost money as a consequence of Milken's crimes, both admitted and alleged, was trying to recoup their losses, with treble damages.

Any testimony that helped the civil litigants was likely to hurt the cooperating witnesses financially. Perhaps this explains their faulty (selective?) memories, their ability to recall more clearly the conversations that hurt Milken alone, such as those related to obstruction of justice.

On a more human level, the cooperating witnesses were also faced with the reality of whom they were burying: the man whom they had worked with for years, who they respected, and who had made them wealthier than they ever had a right to expect. How much impact this fact had on each of them is anyone's guess, but whatever loyalty remained seemed greatest with Maultasch and Peizer.

Cary Maultasch had been left with the worst options from day one. With Boesky and several of his employees as government witnesses, Maultasch was a dead man. "So he made his peace," said an attorney familiar with the case.

At the Fatico hearing, his testimony included some points that reflected well on Milken: that Milken complained frequently about Boesky, implying that their relationship was not a warm one, and that, in Maultasch's opinion, Milken had not tried to obstruct justice.

When asked if he believed that Peter Gardiner was a liar, Maultasch agreed, assisting the defense in impugning Gardiner's credibility. He also was quick to agree that Milken had frequently told him, in Liman's words, "The edge that he had on competitors was that he worked harder."

Terren Peizer was helpful as well, at one point by only stating the obvious: "And is it a fact," asked Liman, "that Michael Milken was a very effective person in presenting the facts of a transaction to his clients?"

"The best," Peizer replied.

"Did he believe in what he was selling?" he was asked soon after. "Yes, he did."

And these cooperating witnesses believed in him. But if they were willing to take orders from him, they sure as hell weren't willing to take the fall for him.

The most favorable view of Michael Milken during the hearing came from Tom Connors, a former employee who was not appearing under a cooperation agreement (he had never been under investigation). Connors was called as a witness for the prosecution to provide some background on the Storer offering. Under cross-examination by Liman, he offered his opinion of Milken: "Michael was a great salesman. He was very thorough, extremely thorough and intelligent. He was a brilliant analyst. . . . He also, from a narrower scope, could tear apart a company's balance sheet, income statements. He was as good as there ever was in the business in that area."

(If the most flattering comment on Milken's skills came from a prosecution witness, the least came from a witness for the defense. Joe Harch, a former investment banker at Drexel, seemed far from eager to agree with prosecutor John Carroll on anything; asked a leading, and seemingly obvious, question—whether he had high regard for Milken as a trader—Harch replied, "No.")

Another piece of testimony that presented Milken more as solid businessman than wheeler-dealer was provided by fund manager Ben Bayse, a prosecution witness. Milken, in encouraging Bayse to buy Storer preferred stock, spoke of cash flows, deregulation, and rising cable values—a first-rate and, as time would prove, correct analysis of the industry. And at no time did Milken mention the possibility that Bayse could get warrants for his personal account.

The defense also found some support from Drexel's Fred Joseph. Under cross-examination by Liman, Joseph related a conversation with Henry Kravis, head of Kohlberg Kravis, indicating that he wasn't upset about the Storer warrants. "He said to me some people think he should be troubled by Drexel's affiliates' purchase of so many warrants," Joseph testified, "but he thought it was baloney."

Unfortunately for Michael Milken, however, the image emerging from the Fatico hearing was not one of a solid businessman, nor could the allegations be dismissed as baloney. Throughout, Arthur Liman and his team tried to reduce, redefine, and replace that emerging image with a divide-and-conquer strategy: each allegation, each piece of evidence, each damaging comment was broken down into small components, and each component was questioned, muddled, or explained away.

The defense strategy was extremely well prepared and well executed, and the Paul Weiss team was no doubt one of the best that money can buy. But those who cynically think of high-priced lawyers as the best *justice* that money can buy underestimate the power of evidence and testimony in a Fatico hearing, in the court of a qualified judge.

Michael Milken, for all his wealth, was in the worst of all worlds. The prosecution may have had, in the view of some experts, a weak legal case, but Milken had already pleaded guilty to six felonies; he couldn't afford to win on narrow points of law.

His lawyers, it seemed (to this non-lawyer), were fighting the wrong war. Their best hope was to avoid the courtroom altogether by insisting, as a condition of the plea agreement, that there be no Fatico hearing. Given the precedent set in the Robert Freeman insider trading case, where the judge had refused to permit such a hearing, the prosecution may well have relented on this point in order to secure a guilty plea.

Instead, Milken found himself in court, but not on trial. He didn't have the luxury of a jury, all of whom would have to be convinced beyond a reasonable doubt. He was being tried on his character before one judge.

And the character that was put on display by the testimony was one that the judge didn't seem to think much of. Prior to the Fatico hearing, Milken's personal values had been the focus of more than one hundred letters from supporters, all favorable, some touching. During the hearing, Milken's professional values became the focus, and the testimony was damaging.

Even if the credibility of each cooperating witness could be questioned, the sheer weight and the general consistency of their allegations were difficult to ignore. And, if their testimony is to be believed, then the most damning witness against Milken was Milken himself.

The testimony regarding the obstruction of justice charge showed a man who chose his words very carefully, who knew how to get across a message without incriminating himself. Who, if worse came to worst, could step into a courtroom and claim reasonable doubt.

But if plausible deniability works with a jury of twelve, a difficult standard of proof, and good lawyers, it backfires with a single judge who is able to master the intricacies of securities law and is bright enough to read between the lines. Milken, in effect, was too clever for his own good.

It would have been interesting to hear another version of these events from the only other person in a position to offer one, but Michael Milken never took the stand. The defense wanted immunity, but the prosecutors weren't about to give him that, their concern being that immunized testimony might limit the upcoming prosecutions in state courts.

One concern that Arthur Liman raised was that his client wasn't protected from further criminal prosecution until after the sentencing.

One possible concern that Liman didn't raise was the fear that the judge would punish Milken severely if she felt he was lying: in two recent securities cases, those of Paul Bilzerian and Jay Regan, the presiding judges had added to their sentences specifically because they had suspected perjury.

Judge Wood, who clearly wanted to hear Milken, tried to reassure the defense that she would handle the prosecution's cross-examination on a question by question basis. As for Liman's concern that the government might tear up Milken's plea agreement and use his testimony against him, Wood responded, "We are in a never-never land, but I am trying to give you the latitude to be in whatever world you want to be in. I have a very hard time conceiving of a situation in which the government breaches the agreement and I don't have the power to force them to hew to their agreement."

But the defense wasn't budging. As great as the risks of not taking the stand, those of testifying were potentially even greater. The prosecutors, according to one attorney, might have followed Milken with two new witnesses to rebut his testimony: Ivan Boesky and David Solomon. Neither had testified, but both might have helped the prosecution to allege perjury.

Rather than put Milken on the stand without immunity, Liman chose to discuss the Fifth Amendment, the fact that it was designed to protect the innocent, not the guilty. His point was correct, although he probably delivered it to the wrong person. It's unlikely that any judge wants to hear a minilecture on the Bill of Rights, and this judge wasn't showing much sympathy for the defense at this point, anyway.

Judge Wood had grown increasingly testy to Arthur Liman as the hearing had progressed. During the cross-examination of Peizer on October 19, she had said to Liman, "I don't know whether you are asking the information of the witness or arguing at this point. I heard the testimony that is favorable to your client." On the 22nd, with another prosecution witness on the stand: "Mr. Liman, I have let you ask leading questions up to now, but I am satisfied at this point that this witness is not hostile to your client." Later, she chided him, "Mr. Liman, if you want me to take the testimony into account, it would be better to elicit it other than by leading questions."

During Fred Joseph's testimony the following day, she ordered Liman to put his objections in writing, which was unusual to say the least. And in a sidebar to both counsels, she told him, "[Y]ou often have a long way of telling me something that I already know is in your mind. . . ."

Guessing what was in *her* mind narrowed down to two choices. The first was that she was grandstanding to show the world that, however new to the bench, she wasn't intimidated by this famous defense attorney. Accordingly, if she gave Michael Milken a light sentence, she wouldn't be open to nasty insinuations.

The other choice was that she was genuinely annoyed with the defense and probably with its client as well.

On the morning of November 21, 1990, she answered this question and several others. "We're here today for the sentencing of Michael Milken," she announced, then turned the floor over to the defense for its final statements.

Arthur Liman's comments were addressed to the judge, but were probably directed more to the media, a large part of the standing-room-only crowd. Liman, with his New York accent and occasionally overdramatic style, will rarely be confused with Gregory Peck in *To Kill a Mockingbird*, but he does have a commanding courtroom presence. More important, after a two-week hearing that focused almost exclusively on Milken's faults, Liman had an opportunity to balance the scales, and he was impressive.

He spoke of Milken's crimes as "deviations of an otherwise admirable life"—that his client "is not cut from the same cloth as Ivan Boesky." But beyond saying what Milken was not as a businessman, he highlighted what he was as a person.

He read a letter from a Milken family friend whose daughter was brain damaged in an accident. "Stacy was very vulnerable to all sorts of dangers," it read in part. "She was a small girl in a grown woman's body. On one of many occasions she left the house for a walk and did not return home. I am not capable of describing the fears that seized me at those times. Michael would drive up and down the streets looking for her. We would be up all night looking and worrying about her."

Milken, who had been unemotional throughout the Fatico hearing, sat silently in tears. Later, when Liman spoke of Milken's friendship with an abused child, he was again unable to fight back the emotion, his fingers pressed between his eyes. He was also deeply affected by a letter, which according to Liman had been provided by Lori Milken without her husband's knowledge. The letter, from the McLaren Hall for abused children, began: "Dear Mike, Hi. How are you doing?"

Following Liman, Assistant U.S. Attorney Jess Fardella offered a brief and effective summation of the government's view. He noted that Milken had asked to be treated fairly on facts, not myths, and that the prosecution was asking the same. He also acknowledged Milken's energy, intelligence, and talents, in arguing that these gifts made his crimes "all the more inexcusable," crimes that were "not isolated, technical, or aberrational."

Finally, Judge Wood read her opinion. She made reference to the avalanche of letters—some favorable to Milken, others not—concluding, "I note that these letters also reflect a legitimate public concern that everyone, no matter how rich or powerful, obey the law as alluded to by Mr. Fardella, and that our financial markets in which so many people who are not rich invest their savings be free of secret manipulation. This is a concern fairly to be considered by the Court."

Another consideration to fairness that she emphasized was the Court's responsibility to treat the defendant as a person rather than as a symbol, to sentence Michael Milken for his conduct alone and not for that of a decade he might represent.

"To the extent that your crimes benefited your clients," she said of Milken's conduct, "that is, of course, no excuse for violating the law. In addition, there is no escaping the fact that your crimes also benefited you, not necessarily by lining your pockets directly and immediately, but by increasing your clients' loyalty to you . . ."

"It was suggested," Judge Wood noted later, "that if you were truly disposed to criminal conduct, you could have made much more money by committing more blatant crimes such as repeatedly misusing insider information.

"These arguments fail to take into account the fact that you may have committed only subtle crimes not because you were not disposed to any criminal behavior but because you were willing to commit only crimes that were unlikely to be detected. . . .

"Your crimes show a pattern of skirting the law, stepping just over to the wrong side of the law in an apparent effort to get some of the benefits from violating the law without running a substantial risk of being caught. . . .

"You also committed crimes that are hard to detect, and crimes that are hard to detect warrant greater punishment in order to be effective in deterring others from committing them."

The bottom line was: ten years.

The logic behind Judge Wood's decision can be easily rationalized when compared to the Boesky case. Ivan Boesky pleaded guilty to one felony, cooperated extensively, and was sentenced to three years; Michael Milken pleaded guilty to six felonies and had not cooperated at all. Once the judge seemed to conclude that Milken had a criminal mentality, a willingness to break the law if he could get away with it, he was in trouble.

Among the reactions to the decision was one by a man congratulating the judge on her courage. Yet, a lengthy sentence for this particular defendant, far from courageous, was a popular decision: for even if Judge Wood didn't view Milken as the symbol of what went wrong in the 1980s, most everyone else did.

Interesting in view of her harsh sentence, the judge rejected most of the allegations against Milken raised at the Fatico hearing. She did, however, believe he had obstructed justice, based on the testimony of Terren Peizer and Jim Dahl (in her findings, she stated she did not consider Peter Gardiner's testimony credible). Also, she believed Milken had misled Kohlberg Kravis on the destination of the Storer warrants.

But the purpose of the Fatico hearing was to offer a sense of character, and here it seems that Michael Milken lost badly in her eyes. One suspects that, to Judge Wood, whose former law practice had been business related, Milken wasn't the kind of guy with whom she would have liked to deal.

The judge's decision, initially as subtle as a firing squad, took on some nuance with the question of parole. Assuming good behavior, Milken must serve between one-third and two-thirds of his sentence. In a February 19, 1991, meeting with the prosecution and defense, Judge Wood offered her recommendation: "Specifically, the court believed that a period of thirty-six to forty months' incarceration fit the crimes and the offender. . . ."

But the decision is not hers at this point. "He's prey to the whims of the Parole Commission," said an attorney familiar with the case, describing it as "notoriously independent." He added: "Given the notoriety of the case, I fear that the Parole Commission is going to slam him."

"The judge has more faith in the system than the system deserves," was the view of Paul Grand, an attorney for one of the Princeton/Newport defendants.

But Judge Wood can influence the commission's decision, if she so chooses. The defense, as part of its appeal, will file a Rule 35 motion, asking for a reduction of sentence. If she defers her decision until after the Parole Commission announces what percentage of Milken's sentence should be served, she can then adjust the sentence accordingly.

Well before Judge Wood made her decision, one major question hung over this case, a rhetorical one once Milken received a ten-year sentence: Should he have stuck with a not-guilty plea and fought his case in court? Although there is something to be said for the underlying philosophy of *Shannon's Deal* that "only suckers go to trial," could Milken have done any worse?

If this had been a trial, the prosecution's strategy would have been adjusted accordingly. Evidence and testimony would have been presented on twenty or thirty transactions, not just three. Also, Ivan Boesky and David Solomon would almost certainly have taken the stand, focusing their testimony on the most damning allegations—namely, those to which Milken had pleaded guilty.

Boesky's value as a witness has been criticized based on his testimony at the trial of John Mulheren, where he was evasive under cross-examination, certainly. Not surprisingly: considering the incongruity between his alleged insider trading profits and his claim of poverty to those who are suing him, he is the absolute dream contestant for *I've Got a Secret*.

But on the stand, Boesky did carry himself with an arrogant authority that fit the cliché of a Wall Street crook. If a jury might not like him or trust him, it might very well believe him. Particularly if his central allegations were supported by circumstantial evidence and by the testimony of peripheral players.

The defense would, of course, attack Boesky's credibility in disputing each allegation. As for the Mooradian notes, which showed the profits and losses of an alleged parking scheme, the attorneys would argue that keeping track was "the nature of the business"—that these figures were not from illegal parking, but rather were the result of legitimate recommendations, some of which had worked out well, some of which hadn't.

Also, without admitting that Milken was involved in any stock parking, they would point out to the jury that this offense had never been criminally prosecuted until the mid-1980s.

In addition, the defense would have vigorously fought the insider trading charges, which a jury is likely to view far more seriously than parking. Even if nobody can clearly define insider trading, everyone knows it is wrong. (Unless, of course, the trading is in the real estate or commodities markets, where inside information is treated like an early Christmas present.)

Most of all, the defense team would have cast doubt over everything. But, bear in mind, the jury might be in no mood to give Milken the benefit of the doubt. Main Street is sick of Wall Street, and with reason. The mind-numbing complexity of a financial fraud trial might work to the defendant's disadvantage, regardless of the "beyond a reasonable doubt" concept.*

Based on less than forty hours of Fatico testimony, it's difficult to imagine how a jury would handle an actual trial. Six months in a sensory deprivation tank might be the nearest thing to sitting through an estimated one thousand hours of testimony, and the jury's final decision on many of the charges might have less to do with the evidence than with its gut feeling about the defendant.

The greatest risk to Milken would be a jury that found him guilty of several charges on the merits, and then assumed he was guilty of the rest. And even if he were convicted on only 10 percent of the counts, this would still add up to some twenty felonies. If that happened, any sentence would be possible, from the three months given most of the Princeton/Newport defendants to the thirty years given Woody Lemons, former head of bankrupt Vernon Savings & Loan.

Michael Milken, in deciding to plead guilty, chose the devil he knew over the one he didn't, probably in the belief that he would avoid the courtroom. Instead, the Fatico hearing put him on trial under a set of rules for which he was least prepared, presenting him in the worst possible light.

He was shown to be greedy and devious in the business dealings highlighted by the prosecutors. In fairness, these dealings accounted for a small fraction of a month's work, let alone that of a decade. All things considered, he worked harder and smarter than perhaps anyone else in this country, yet he cut corners in a manner that wasn't only wrong, it was stupid. He was willing to break the law for hundreds of thousands of dollars at the same time he was earning hundreds of millions.

His values allowed for the unethical and the illegal, but these same values also included extraordinary decency, generosity, and humility. His concern for those less fortunate was more than genuine, his

---

*The July 10, 1991, reversal of John Mulheren's sentence would offer a compelling argument in the event of a guilty verdict, however, in that case, the appeals court reportedly ruled that the jury based its conviction on ambiguous and insufficient evidence.

idealism never more apparent than in the simple efforts that separate those who really care from those who merely go through the motions.

"He thinks he's Jimmy Stewart," suggested someone who knew Michael Milken better than most. And in his own way, certainly in his own mind, Milken has more in common with Jefferson Smith and George Bailey than with Senator Paine or Henry Potter.

For all he's been accused of, there is the strong possibility that Milken views himself as the victim, not the villain. Though he's admitted to crimes, it's unlikely he considers himself a criminal. In this regard, he would be little different from the tens of millions of people who cheat on their taxes each year, knowingly and, at times, even proudly.

Securities fraud is one of the easier crimes to rationalize, since the victims are invisible, and the line that separates black from white unclear. What in retrospect are insidious crimes might at the time seem more like obstacles. What surely looks like naked greed might have seemed justified under a perverted sense of fairness, a variation of the Panama Canal "we stole it fair and square" defense: it might not be ours by law but it's ours by right.

Securities fraud is also one of the more tempting crimes, since, in addition to the illusion that nobody gets hurt, there is the sense that "everybody's doing it," an untrue and untenable excuse. But still, the perception of familiarity does breed contempt.

Whatever drove Michael Milken's contempt for the rules, his lack of moderation buried him. For even if he felt that his actions were justified, he could have refrained for no more complex or honorable a reason than that they weren't worth it. With Ivan Boesky and David Solomon, he could have added up his possible gains from cheating and said, so what? With every crime he committed, he could have steered clear simply by saying, so what? And then, when industry rivals criticized his hardball tactics or prosecutors investigated those tactics, he could have said to them, so what?

Instead, they got to say to him, so long. His crimes, however helpful, weren't necessary for his success, but he committed them nevertheless, and he was destroyed for them.

When the smoke cleared, Michael Milken faced another in the series of ironies that ran through the Drexel story. In order to get his sentence reduced, Milken was required to cooperate, which he had agreed in principle to do. The irony, as noted by *The New York Times*, was this: if Milken was in fact the person he claimed, his crimes were limited to those he had already admitted; if so, he had nothing to offer the prosecutors and no chance of a cut in his sentence.

If, on the other hand, Milken was a liar and a master criminal, then he was in great shape, legally. He would have immunity against further criminal prosecution, and his cooperation against his cohorts would give him a strong argument for a lesser prison term.

Indications are that Milken has told the prosecutors little, for reasons that could range from the genuine to the honorable to the cynical. Perhaps he actually had done what he'd said he'd done, and no more—as he has claimed.

Perhaps he doesn't believe in trading other people's freedom for his own. Although the courts frown on that attitude, it is an honorable one. When Arthur Liman argued that Michael Milken is no Ivan Boesky, he was talking in terms of crimes, but the contrast might also apply to them as people.

From a cynical point of view, Milken's motivation to cooperate was slight. Assuming he did have other crimes to confess, doing so would hurt his defense in the upcoming civil lawsuits that are trying to separate him from every dollar he has. Also, his cooperation might be of limited value because of the statute of limitations; the prosecution has already complained that Milken "has effectively conferred immunity upon many other associates." And regardless of his cooperation, the prosecutors are under no obligation to ask the judge for a reduction in his sentence.

Certainly, Milken's sentence provided the strongest motivation to "cooperate fully." Ten years is an eternity, and even if he only serves a third of that, it's still one-third of an eternity. His sentence is longer than the combined sentences of ten Wall Streeters, none of whom became cooperating witnesses: Paul Bilzerian (convicted: 9 felonies), John Mulheren (convicted: 4 felonies), Robert Freeman (pleaded: one felony), Lisa Jones (convicted: one felony), and the six Princeton/Newport defendants (convicted: 63 felonies each, almost entirely tax related).*

Everyone is entitled to an opinion of what punishment Michael Milken deserved, though only one person's carries any weight. Judge Wood felt that a ten-year prison sentence with an additional three

---

*The securities fraud case against Mulheren and the tax and racketeering convictions against the Princeton/Newport defendants were both thrown out on appeal.

years of community service was justified; in my opinion, Milken deserved the opposite.

Milken broke the law, and once caught he probably did try a cover-up. But his crimes—at least, those crimes in which the evidence was compelling—seem motivated more by disdain for obstacles and by petty greed. These crimes weren't a major factor in his success nor were they even a minor percentage of his business over the years. Further, the majority of the convincing evidence points to stock parking, a felony for which, at that time, no one had *ever* been criminally prosecuted.

There were also sham trades to settle accounts with Ivan Boesky and, almost pathetically, to kick back a few hundred thousand dollars from David Solomon. Milken played fast and loose with the partnerships as well, primarily at the expense of his firm—for which, remember, he was making a fortune.

As for insider trading, Milken himself seemed to view this crime differently from others. Although he had access to an extraordinary amount of inside information, the allegations here are few and far from conclusive. The most interesting is the MGM transaction, where the evidence indicates a sharing arrangement with Boesky; if true, Milken would have been trading on inside information for his own benefit.

The timing of the MGM trades, however, has more in common with risk arbitrage than with insider trading. The same can be said of the Diamond Shamrock and Pacific Lumber transactions, which resulted in a loss of millions. It's as if Milken drew the line at blatant insider trading.

This might seem like a subtle distinction when talking about felonies, but they are worth considering when talking about Michael Milken. Perhaps the explanation is no more complicated than the one suggested by Judge Wood: Milken only wanted to commit crimes not easily detected, motivated by practicality rather than morality. At odds with that explanation, however, is Milken's lack of concern in involving minor, and unnecessary, players in the schemes—not the actions of someone paranoid about detection.

For these reasons, among others, a reasonable argument can be made that justice would have been better served by a prison sentence comparable to Boesky's, plus ten years working where Milken could do some good. From helping disadvantaged kids, for which there are few people evidently more gifted, to minimizing the damage from the savings & loan mess, for which there is no one more qualified, this country should have taken fuller advantage of him, out of fairness and selfishness.

Wherever he is eventually assigned for community service, one place he will never be permitted to work is back in the financial community. Which is a pity, because the junk-bond market could use him. High-yield bonds did more for small companies in the 1980s than they did for corporate raiders; these companies were made less dependent on a banking system that lent for the future with its eyes fixed on the past. And now, with companies more in need than ever, the spigot is all but off: according to Salomon Brothers, new high-yield offerings fell by 95 percent last year.

Meanwhile, those junk bonds already on the market have plummeted in price. Among the largest losers from the junk-bond debacle were a handful of savings & loans, which speculated wildly with taxpayer-guaranteed money. In response, the regulators have sued both Milken and Drexel for over $10 billion, figures that make better headlines than sense.

It is true that federally insured S&Ls shouldn't have been allowed to buy junk bonds or to speculate in commercial real estate (which caused losses many times greater) or to finance their shenanigans with brokered deposits. But that's exactly what the regulators and the politicians went out of their way to allow.

What they weren't smart enough to realize was that these speculative investments were destined to hurt the thrifts, even without the legion of crooks that entered the industry. Junk bonds, for example, had never been tested in a serious downturn, which Milken *was* smart enough to realize. And with all the debt that had accumulated in the system, a serious downturn was inevitable.

Debt is wonderful when it's borrowed—the problem is that it has to be repaid. The same debt that had financed economic growth in the '80s was destined to hurt that growth in the '90s, as the loans came due. It is no different for a nation than it is for an individual. The contrast between the two decades is captured in a comment by Will Rogers: "I'm less concerned about the return on my principal than the return *of* my principal."

Michael Milken and his firm contributed to the debt explosion of the 1980s, but their role was fairly minor. Drexel underwrote some $200 billion in junk bonds during a decade in which debt rose by more than $5 trillion. The Great Debt Peddler wasn't the guy in

Beverly Hills, it was the guy in Washington. Ronald Reagan was the one who, as George Will observed, asked the nation to be brave enough to accept a tax cut, to which the nation replied, "What a great communicator!"

Another factor to consider is that not all debt is created equal. Debt that finances purchases from foreign companies is different from debt that finances growth for those in the United States. In one decade, our country went from being the world's greatest creditor to being its largest debtor, and junk bonds weren't the reason.

Junk bonds did, however, play an important role in hostile takeovers, for which they deserve both credit and blame. The takeover boom did make managements more accountable to their shareholders, but it also preyed on the myopia of both managers and stockholders. As with most ideas, the boom made sense in moderation.

Unfortunately, moderation doesn't drive the financial markets, because fear and greed drive people, and people *are* the financial markets. It may seem tempting to regulate motivation, but the result is just a variation of the workers' paradise, with its impressive rhetoric and its accompanying economic coma.

In our system, there will always be imbalances and inequities. Success breeds excess, and if the Age of Greed is over, it is because the opportunity for greed is over, not because its symbolic leader was buried.

To make Michael Milken a symbol of what went wrong in the 1980s is to ignore a complex and contradictory man who had more impact, both negative and positive, than all but a few. To dismiss Drexel Burnham as an upstart firm that got what it deserved is to miss the reality for the reputation. Beyond the dozen who did the damage were the thousands who did their best, who demonstrated unusual loyalty in good times and bad, who were proud to be part of a creative, entrepreneurial company.

"You say to people, are you an entrepreneur?" said a senior officer. "They say, yeah, I'm an entrepreneur." Most people don't know what it means. But Drexel did and, for that, it deserves credit.

Six years ago, on April 1, 1985, Drexel Burnham celebrated its fiftieth anniversary. The Ballroom of the Waldorf Astoria was packed with over six hundred stockholders—all of them officers of the firm—and their guests, there to enjoy Drexel's accomplishments and its potential.

In the nearly four years since I had joined the firm, it had earned some $400 million, its net worth had quintupled, and it had already made a controversial mark on corporate America. As bright as Drexel's immediate future seemed at that time, imagination was still no match for reality—in the following year it would earn more than any other firm on Wall Street before or since.

This month would have marked Drexel Burnham's fifty-sixth year in business. Instead, the firm is in bankruptcy and Michael Milken is in jail.

INDEX